Joseph Ratzinger in Dialogue with Philosophical Traditions

Joseph Ratzinger in Dialogue with Philosophical Traditions

From Plato to Vattimo

Edited by Alejandro Sada
Tracey Rowland
Rudy Albino de Assunção

t&tclark
LONDON • NEW YORK • OXFORD • NEW DELHI • SYDNEY

T&T CLARK
Bloomsbury Publishing Plc
50 Bedford Square, London, WC1B 3DP, UK
1385 Broadway, New York, NY 10018, USA
29 Earlsfort Terrace, Dublin 2, Ireland

BLOOMSBURY, T&T CLARK and the T&T Clark logo are trademarks
of Bloomsbury Publishing Plc

First published in Great Britain 2024

Copyright © Alejandro Sada, Tracey Rowland, and Rudy Albino de Assunção, 2024

Alejandro Sada, Tracey Rowland, Rudy Albino de Assunção, and Contributors
have asserted their right under the Copyright, Designs and Patents Act, 1988,
to be identified as Authors of this work.

Cover image: Joseph Cardinal Ratzinger, Munich, Germany,
1985 © IMAGO/Wolfgang Maria Weber

All rights reserved. No part of this publication may be reproduced or transmitted
in any form or by any means, electronic or mechanical, including photocopying,
recording, or any information storage or retrieval system, without
prior permission in writing from the publishers.

Bloomsbury Publishing Plc does not have any control over, or responsibility for, any
third-party websites referred to or in this book. All internet addresses given in this
book were correct at the time of going to press. The author and publisher regret
any inconvenience caused if addresses have changed or sites have ceased
to exist, but can accept no responsibility for any such changes.

A catalogue record for this book is available from the British Library.

Library of Congress Cataloging-in-Publication Data
Names: Sada, Alejandro, editor. | Rowland, Tracey, 1963-, editor. |
Assunção, Rudy Albino de, editor.
Title: Joseph Ratzinger in dialogue with philosophical traditions : from Plato to Vattimo /
edited by Alejandro Sada, Tracey Rowland, Rudy Albino de Assunção.
Description: New York : T&T Clark, 2024. | Includes bibliographical references and index.
Identifiers: LCCN 2023029561 (print) | LCCN 2023029562 (ebook) | ISBN 9780567706850
(paperback) | ISBN 9780567706867 (hardback) | ISBN 9780567706874 (epub) |
ISBN 9780567706881 (pdf)
Subjects: LCSH: Benedict XVI, Pope, 1927-2022–Knowledge–Philosophy. |
Catholic Church and philosophy. | Philosophy–History.
Classification: LCC BX1378.6 .J6697 2024 (print) | LCC BX1378.6 (ebook) |
DDC 282.092–dc23/eng/20231012
LC record available at https://lccn.loc.gov/2023029561
LC ebook record available at https://lccn.loc.gov/2023029562

ISBN: HB: 978-0-5677-0686-7
PB: 978-0-5677-0685-0
ePDF: 978-0-5677-0688-1
eBook: 978-0-5677-0687-4

Typeset by Integra Software Services Pvt. Ltd.
Printed and bound in Great Britain

To find out more about our authors and books visit www.bloomsbury.com
and sign up for our newsletters.

CONTENTS

Abbreviations (J. Ratzinger Collected Works) viii
Foreword x

Introduction 1

Introductory Study: Gottlieb Söhngen's Understanding of Theology and Philosophy 4
Christian Poncelet

1 Plato: God, Conscience, and Truth 13
   Manuel Schlögl

2 Augustine of Hippo: The Reciprocal Dependence of Faith and World 22
   Emery de Gaál

3 Bonaventure of Bagnoregio: The Metaphysics of History 42
   David González Ginocchio

4 Thomas Aquinas: How We Know God 66
   Pablo Blanco-Sarto

5 Immanuel Kant: Distinguishing *Verum* and *Ens* 78
   Jacob Phillips

6 Georg Wilhelm Friedrich Hegel: Reason, Historicity, and Community 94
   Eduardo Charpenel

7 Auguste Comte: Science, Reason, and Religion 118
   Euclides Eslava

8 Karl Marx and Marxism: The Problem of the Priority of *Praxis* 133
   Tracey Rowland

9 Friedrich Nietzsche: Eros, Morality, and the Death of God 148
   Owen Vyner

10 Martin Buber: Personalism and Relationality 163
   Mariusz Biliniewicz

11 Hans Kelsen, Richard Rorty, and John Rawls: Philosophical Relativism and Religious Traditions of Wisdom 179
   Rudy Albino de Assunção

12 Romano Guardini: Liturgy, Christian Existence, Truth, and Ethics 207
   Marcela Jiménez Unquiles

13 Ludwig Wittgenstein: The Scope of Reason 221
   Tracey Rowland

14 Martin Heidegger: Being and Time 232
   Conor Sweeney

15 Edith Stein: The Reasonableness of Faith 247
   Mary Frances McKenna

16 Karl Popper: Fideism, Rationalism, and
    Rationality 272
    Eduardo Echeverría

17 Josef Pieper: Philosophy, Philology, and
    Theology 287
    Hanna-Barbara Gerl-Falkovitz

18 Jean-Paul Sartre: Truth, Freedom, and Responsibility 299
    Alejandro Sada

19 Albert Camus: The Meaning of Life 315
    Alejandro Sada

20 Robert Spaemann: Person, Ethics, and Politics 325
    Christian Schaller

21 Jürgen Habermas: Democracy and Religion
    in Pluralistic Societies 332
    Mary Frances McKenna

22 Gianni Vattimo: Nihilism and Truth 358
    Thomas G. Guarino

Bibliography 371
Contributors 404
Name Index 406
Subject Index 409

ABBREVIATIONS

(J. Ratzinger Collected Works)

Joseph Ratzinger Gesammelte Schriften (JRGS)

JRGS 1   *Gesammelte Schriften. Volk und Haus Gottes in Augustins Lehre von der Kirche. Die Dissertation und weitere Studien zu Augustinus und zur Theologie der Kirchenväter*, Band 1 (Freiburg: Herder, 2011).

JRGS 2   *Gesammelte Schriften. Offenbarungsverständnis und Geschichtstheologie Bonaventuras. Habilitationsschrift und Bonaventura-Studien*, Band 2 (Freiburg: Herder, 2009).

JRGS 3/1   *Gesammelte Schriften. Der Gott des Glaubens und der Gott der Philosophen. Philosophische Vernunft—Kultur—Europa—Gesellschaft*, Band 3/1 (Freiburg: Herder, 2020).

JRGS 3/2   *Gesammelte Schriften. Der Gott des Glaubens und der Gott der Philosophen. Philosophische Vernunft—Kultur—Europa—Gesellschaft*, Band 3/2 (Freiburg: Herder, 2020).

JRGS 4   *Gesammelte Schriften. Einführung in das Christentum. Bekenntnis—Taufe—Nachfolge,* Band 4 (Freiburg: Herder, 2014).

JRGS 5   *Gesammelte Schriften. Herkunft und Bestimmung. Schöpfung—Anthropologie—Mariologie,* Band 5 (Freiburg: Herder, 2021).

JRGS 6/1   *Gesammelte Schriften. Jesus von Nazareth. Beiträge zur Christologie*, Band 6/1 (Freiburg: Herder, 2014).

JRGS 6/2   *Gesammelte Schriften. Jesus von Nazareth. Beiträge zur Christologie*, Band 6/2 (Freiburg: Herder, 2014).

JRGS 7/1   *Gesammelte Schriften. Zur Lehre des Zweiten Vatikanischen Konzils. Formulierung—Vermittlung—Deutung*, Band 7/1 (Freiburg: Herder, 2012).

JRGS 8/1   *Gesammelte Schriften. Kirche—Zeichen unter den Völkern. Schriften zur Ekklesiologie und Ökumene*, Band 8/1 (Freiburg: Herder, 2010).

JRGS 8/2	*Gesammelte Schriften. Kirche—Zeichen unter den Völkern. Schriften zur Ekklesiologie und Ökumene*, Band 8/2 (Freiburg: Herder, 2010).
JRGS 9/1	*Gesammelte Schriften. Glaube in Schrift und Tradition. Zur Theologischen Prinzipienlehre*, Band 9/1 (Freiburg: Herder, 2016).
JRGS 9/2	*Gesammelte Schriften. Glaube in Schrift und Tradition. Zur Theologischen Prinzipienlehre*, Band 9/2 (Freiburg: Herder, 2016).
JRGS 10	*Gesammelte Schriften. Auferstehung und ewiges Leben. Beiträge zur Eschatologie und zur Theologie der Hoffnung*, Band 10 (Freiburg: Herder, 2012).
JRGS 11	*Gesammelte Schriften. Theologie der Liturgie. Die sakramentale Begründung christlicher Existenz*, Band 11 (Freiburg: Herder, 2008, 2014⁴).
JRGS 13/1	*Gesammelte Schriften. Im Gespräch mit der Zeit. Interviews—Stellungnahmen—Einsprüche*, Band 13/1 (Freiburg: Herder, 2016).

Joseph Ratzinger Obras Completas

JROC IV	*Introducción al cristianismo*. Obras completas IV (Madrid: Biblioteca de Autores Cristianos, 2018).
JROC VI/2	*Jesús de Nazaret. Escritos de cristología*. Obras completas VI/2 (Madrid: Biblioteca de Autores Cristianos, 2021).
JROC VII/1	*Sobre la enseñanza del concilio Vaticano II*. Obras completas VII/2 (Madrid: Biblioteca de Autores Cristianos, 2014).
JROC VIII/2	*Iglesia. Signo entre los pueblos*. Obras completas VIII/2 (Madrid: Biblioteca de Autores Cristianos, 2020).

Joseph Ratzinger Collected Works

JRCW 11	*Collected Works. Theology of the Liturgy. The Sacramental Foundation of Christian Existence* 11 (San Francisco: Ignatius, 2014).

FOREWORD

Professor Gottlieb Söhngen, Joseph Ratzinger's academic teacher and doctoral supervisor, was convinced that one could not sufficiently prepare for theology without philosophy: "No matter how long the path via philosophy is, it is never a detour to theology; rather one can embark on actual theological work too early rather than too late." Similarly, Joseph Ratzinger/Benedict XVI defends the idea of a strong philosophy as the inner framework of theology. A weak philosophy does not correspond to a strong theology. Both theology and philosophy are holistic sciences, which, admittedly with different sources of knowledge, look for answers to the ultimate questions of existence. They develop together. They ask questions about the nature of the human person and the perfected human person with the help of reason and in the light of faith.

For Ratzinger/Benedict XVI the legacy of Greece, along with the legal tradition of Rome and the biblical tradition of Jerusalem, are the foundation of the West. "Hellenization" in the sense of an option for rationality and communicability is a positive characteristic of Christian theology from its beginnings (cf. the Regensburg Speech). The translation of God's name in the Septuagint with "*ego eimi ho on*" makes the biblical message audible in the god-seeking world of Greece. "Christ called himself the truth, not the custom" is one of Ratzinger/Benedict XVI's favorite quotations from Tertullian. Biblical scholars who are not sufficiently enlightened about their own deistic-philosophical preliminary decisions can bring the necessary and important historical exploration of biblical sources into disrepute.[1]

The process of Hellenization in the sense of an option for rationality was simultaneously a process of de-Hellenization in the sense of offering correctives to Greek philosophy in the areas of theology and anthropology. In light of the revelation of the Trinitarian nature of God, the accident of relation, which was insignificant for Greek ontology, takes on the rank of substance and makes an understanding of "God as love from all eternity" conceivable[2]. The holistic biblical view of human nature, which sees the body and the soul as a unity, cannot do without the concept of the soul. It transforms the wholeness of the body and soul into the principle of the

---

[1] Cf. Ratzinger's 1988 Erasmus Lecture, published in 1989.
[2] Cf. The reception of the concept of the person and more dialogical philosophical approaches.

identity of earthly life and the transfigured corporeality at the resurrection of the dead (according to the ground-breaking study from Ratzinger/Benedict XVI in the field of eschatology). It [the Christian corrective to Greek philosophy] offers what Ratzinger called the concept of a dialogical soul.

Since the Enlightenment, philosophy has shackled itself with its denial of human reason's ability to transcend the merely empirical in the pursuit of truth. Hence, the call of Pope Benedict to "unleash" reason. "The courage to engage the whole breadth of reason, and not the denial of its grandeur—that is the program with which a theology grounded in biblical faith enters the debates of our times."[3]

Conversation and dialogue with classical and contemporary philosophers is one of the outstanding characteristics of the theologian pope's thought. A compilation of his most important interlocutors and an overview of the related topics, as provided in this book, closes a gap in Ratzinger literature. I heartily thank the editors and wish them a wide readership.

Regensburg on the Feast of Saint Athanasius, May 2, 2022
Rudolf Voderholzer
Bishop of Regensburg and Director of the Pope Benedict
XVI Institute of Regensburg, Germany

Translation from German by Tracey Rowland

---

[3] Benedict XVI, *Faith, Reason and the University: Memories and Reflections. Lecture in the Meeting with the Representatives of Science*, Apostolic Journey to München, Altötting and Regensburg (September 9–14, 2006), Regensburg, September 12, 2006.

Introduction

At the origin of this book is the convergence of some of our common concerns as researchers of Joseph Ratzinger/Benedict XVI's thought. Somehow, the object of this book (philosophy and many philosophers, in particular) imposed itself on us for two reasons: the omnipresence of the philosophical theme in Ratzinger and the flagrant absence of more complete and systematic research on the German author's contributions to this very relevant field. The meeting of our intellectual and interior concerns occurred because although each one of us followed a particular path, each one explored an angle of Ratzinger's work within the same hermeneutic horizon.

Alejandro Sada (Mexico) did his doctoral thesis at the University of Navarra (Spain) on the nature of philosophy in J. Ratzinger's thought and, during that period, he was impressed by the Bavarian theologian's capacity for dialogue, not only with fellow professors and students, but above all with the great philosophical traditions. He then began to dream of a book devoted to this subject.

Meanwhile, Professor Tracey Rowland, the 2020 Ratzinger Prize winner, has focused her work in recent years on the relationship between faith and culture, history and ontology. For example, in her thesis at Cambridge University, she sought to integrate Alasdair MacIntyre's philosophy of culture with the theology of culture found in J. Ratzinger and Henri de Lubac. Rowland also has an interest in the history and philosophy of Central Europe and is thus versed in the tradition of Marxism.

For his part, Rudy Albino de Assunção, in his research on the relationship between the Church and modernity from the perspective of the German theologian and pope—which originated with his doctoral thesis at the Federal University of Santa Catarina (Brazil)—saw that the Ratzingerian reading of the genealogy of modernity, and the historical relationship of the Church with it, must be framed within analysis of the broader (historical) interlocution between Christianity and philosophy.

We all realized that we were in the presence of an author who truly puts into action all the energies of faith and reason to try to find solutions to concrete problems. Who is the human being? Why is the world the way it is? How should we orient our lives, both individually and socially? What is the crisis of the modern world? How do we face the challenges that the future holds for us? Joseph Ratzinger not only develops in his work a theory of how faith and reason should collaborate, but actually makes them work together in the face of the most difficult questions, for both theology and philosophy.

Thus, our conversations resulted in the idea to produce a collective work in which we wanted to bring together the intellectual dialogue that Ratzinger has established over decades of theological activity with diverse philosophical traditions, from antiquity to the present day. We began by profiling a list of the great names in philosophy, including Plato, Augustine, Bonaventure, Kant, Hegel, Camus, Sartre, Heidegger, Wittgenstein, Nietzsche, and so on. With it, the book *Joseph Ratzinger in Dialogue with Philosophical Traditions* emerged.

This is a collective work because such an effort demands gathering researchers from different parts of the world who are experts both in the philosopher with whom Ratzinger had some kind of dialogue, or intellectual confrontation and in the German theologian himself. The result has exceeded our expectations and now is available to the interested public as one more fruit of the work started by Ratzinger at the end of the 1950s. At that time, the young professor from Bonn was teaching classes on the philosophy of religion and on fundamental theology, and, in dialogue with Protestantism, wrote about the God of faith and the God of philosophers.

Finally, after two years of hard work, we are pleased to present this collection of essays that seeks to bring to light all the dialogical creativity of Joseph Ratzinger's thought and his formidable ability to make philosophy and theology collaborate in an authentic search for truth. Following the beautiful foreword by Rudolf Voderholzer, Bishop of Regensburg, this book offers an introductory study by Christian Poncelet. Poncelet's essay is not focused on the works of Joseph Ratzinger, but on the way in which his teacher Gottlieb Söhngen understood the relationship between philosophy and theology. On several occasions, Ratzinger confessed his closeness to Söhngen's vision; thus, we can regard it as a kind of intellectual inheritance and a point of reference for Ratzinger's articulation of the relationship between philosophical and theological thought. Subsequently, nineteen authors from ten different countries offer twenty-two chapters exploring the way in which Ratzinger approaches the thought of the great philosophers of the Western tradition: from Plato to Gianni Vattimo.[1] The result is a

---

[1] The philosophers appear in chronological order (date of birth). In the case of articles with more than one philosopher studied, the birth date of the oldest philosopher prevails. Another important note: in general, magisterial or pontifical texts are taken from the Holy See's website (www.vatican.va), except in specific cases where the author has used a particular publication, which will always appear in the bibliography. In addition, all citations made from texts not published in the English language have been translated by the authors of each chapter.

road map that makes visible the breadth of Joseph Ratzinger's mind. We are confident that the reader will discover in these pages a door that opens onto the reason to which the German theologian so urgently summoned us, and will find inspiration and clarity when facing the intellectual challenges that keep the contemporary world immersed in a climate of perplexity and confusion.

The original chapters were written in different languages: English, Spanish, and German. A team of translators has ensured that each text is available in all three languages, so that, after this first English edition, the book will be published in Spanish and German. We would like to sincerely thank the professionals who worked on the translations and took up the hard work of editing and layout, especially David González Ginocchio, Christa Byker, Stefan Münzing, and Aurora Fosado Gómez. We are truly grateful to each of the authors who participated in the creation of this book. We would also like to express our gratitude to the Panamerican University (Mexico), which offered the support needed to make this project possible, especially through its research fund called *Fondo de Fomento a la Investigación* (Research Promotion Fund).

Alejandro Sada, Tracey Rowland, and Rudy Albino de Assunção

Introductory Study: Gottlieb Söhngen's Understanding of Theology and Philosophy

Christian Poncelet

Triplex Usus—The "Inner Plan" in Gottlieb Söhngen's Thinking

Gottlieb Söhngen was a "figure who had a decisive influence on Joseph Ratzinger."[1] Therefore, the question of the relationship between theology and philosophy in his thinking can also contribute to a deeper understanding of Benedict XVI.

If one reads the writings of the theologian from Cologne, one can recognize a structure that underlies Söhngen's thinking. In the foreword to the collection of essays *The Unity of Theology*, Gottlieb Söhngen says that looking back at his efforts to solve the problem of theology, it becomes clear to him that he "had for two decades created and written according to an inner plan."[2] He then refers to the table of contents of the work, wherein his purely philosophical essays are not included.[3] Using this overview of contents, a dichotomy can be drawn in that, first, the problem of the unity of theology is dealt with (natural and supernatural, historical and

---

[1] P. Pfister (ed.), *Joseph Ratzinger und das Erzbistum München und Freising* (Regensburg: Schnell und Steiner, 2006), p. 119.
[2] G. Söhngen, "Vorwort," in *Die Einheit in der Theologie* (München: Zink, 1952), p. iv.
[3] Cf. *ibid*.

systematic theology), then the unity of "the peculiarly Christian and the universally human" is addressed.[4] If one supplements this division with the philosophical writings, a threefold classification results. The "inner plan" that lies behind this classification into pure philosophy, theological unity, and human-Christian unity is encountered in a brief form in Söhngen's "The Wisdom of Theology through the Path of Science," which appears in the first volume of *Mysterium Salutis*.[5] In it the author presents his understanding of theology, in which both aspects, scientific and [divine] wisdom, human reason and being moved by the mystery of God, are brought together into a unity, as is shown by his adoption of St. Bonaventure's formulation in another publication: "Theology as a science of faith is the cooperation of the supernatural eye and the light of divine faith with the double natural vision of the historical and philosophical sciences and methods."[6] Theology "happens through an addition."[7] By this, Söhngen means that the mystery of divine wisdom, including the revelation of God and its biblical testimony is assigned as an "addition to the scientific consideration of this mystery, first through scientific philosophy, insofar as this makes claim to the whole of knowledge and of being,"[8] and then through theology.

This tripartite division is conceptually found in Söhngen as "*triplex usus philosophiae*"[9] (*usus philosophicus*, *usus theologicus*, and *usus cosmicus*).[10] He himself never addresses or explicates upon this triple use of philosophy, but this tripartite division allows us to define the relationship between philosophy and theology systematically. The first case is about "philosophizing for the sake of philosophy."[11] The theological use of philosophy as the second area means a service of rational science for the talk of God. Finally, with the *usus cosmicus* of philosophy in third place, Söhngen goes beyond the scientific realm, in order to relate reason to wisdom, which

---

[4] Cf. *ibid.*, p. xii.
[5] *Id.*, "Die Weisheit der Theologie durch den Weg der Wissenschaft," in J. Feiner and M. Löhrer (eds.), *Mysterium Salutis. Grundriss heilsgeschichtlicher Dogmatik* 1 (Einsiedeln, Zürich, Köln: Benziger, 1978), pp. 907–80.
[6] *Id.*, *Philosophische Einübung in die Theologie: Erkennen, Wissen, Glauben* (Freiburg, München: Karl Alber, 1955), p. 1.
[7] *Ibid.*, p. 128.
[8] G. Söhngen, "Die Weisheit der Theologie durch den Weg der Wissenschaft," p. 942.
[9] *Ibid.*, p. 943.
[10] Cf. *ibid.*, p. 945. "Söhngen's student Joseph Ratzinger in his office as Pope provides a reference to Bonaventure in 2011 in a speech on the occasion of the awarding of the Ratzinger Prize to three professors." Cf. Benedict XVI, *Address on the Conferral of the First "Ratzinger Prize,"* June 20, 2022.
[11] G. Söhngen, "Die Weisheit der Theologie durch den Weg der Wissenschaft," p. 945.

he describes as the "natural disposition of man as a citizen of the world,"[12] i.e., meaning a lifeworld use of reason.

It is true that Söhngen himself based his talk of *usus* on the formula of the "*triplex usus legis*"[13] originating in Protestantism. Nonetheless, forerunners in Bonaventure's theology can be recognized where a threefold structure in the understanding of truth can be established.[14]

The distinction between *veritas rerum*, *veritas vocum/sermonum*, and *veritas morum* could be viewed analogously to the threefold division of the *triplex usus philosophiae* into *usus philosophicus*, *usus theologicus*, and *usus cosmicus*. Since the pure, philosophical use of reason corresponds to Bonaventure's *veritas rerum*, which is geared toward *cognitio naturalis*, the *usus theologicus* can be understood analogously to *veritas vocum*, since it is about the object area of knowledge—in this case God. The *veritas morum*, which concerns the practical orientation in life, could be seen parallel to the *usus cosmicus*. This coincides with Söhngen's own categorization within the themes of philosophy: "The order of all things is threefold: things are as real beings, they are true as objects of thought, and they are good as ends of aspiration."[15]

Söhngen's borrowing from the Protestant *usus legis* can be found in his monograph on the unity of "law and gospel."[16] This approach is original and characteristic of Söhngen's understanding of philosophy. If theology takes the side of grace or the gospel, this seems plausible, after all it is a science, "of which we ... here below alone know by the divine faith."[17] To think of philosophy as analogous to the law certainly does not carry the same degree of plausibility. However, he explicitly connects both great concepts in the form of the question: " ... isn't philosophy taken as a piece, also a form of law for the theologian?"[18] According to Söhngen, law is not primarily to be seen as written law, whereby philosophy would be a static set of rules similar to a collection of regulations. Rather, in his theological usage, law appears as part of the gospel, i.e., God's promise, the "word of grace revealed in Jesus Christ"[19]: "The gospel, however, embraces and contains its opposite, the law."[20]

---

[12] *Ibid.*
[13] Cf. *ibid.*
[14] Cf. Bonaventura, *Collationes in Hexaemeron* 4, 2 (V 349 ab); Bonaventura, *De reductione artium ad theologiam* 4 (V 320 b); A. Speer, *Triplex veritas: Wahrheitsverständnis und philosophische Denkform Bonaventuras* (Werl, Westfalen: Coelde, 1987), pp. 48–52.
[15] G. Söhngen, "Philosophie," *Lexikon für Theologie und Kirche* 8 (1936), p. 244.
[16] Cf. *id.*, *Gesetz und Evangelium. Ihre analoge Einheit. Theologisch, philosophisch, staatsbürgerlich* (Freiburg, München: Karl Alber, 1957), pp. 5–6; *id.*, "Gesetz und Evangelium," *Lexikon für Theologie und Kirche* 4 (1960), p. 832.
[17] *Id.*, *Philosophische Einübung*, p. 119.
[18] *Id.*, "Die Weisheit der Theologie durch den Weg der Wissenschaft," 945.
[19] *Id.*, *Gesetz und Evangelium*, p. 28.
[20] *Ibid.*, p. 27.

In the passage in *Mysterium Salutis* he seems to be using "law" in an analogous sense, since elsewhere he contrasts philosophy with the attempt to find insight with law:

> Probably the philosophically most important analogue from pre-Christian times can be found in Plato towards the end of his dialogue about the statesman ... and reads in the original Greek 'law and insight', *nomos* and *phronesis* ... The law must remain a living word, a living saying in constant living interpretation, assertion and realization from the spirit of discernment of the discerning man.[21]

It is thus clear that Söhngen, in saying that philosophy is the law for the theologian, is sticking to a dynamic understanding of reason's search for truth. Although viewed historically, Greek philosophy provided the very foundations of Christian theology,[22] Söhngen does not mean that theology is committed to a specific philosophy, a specific system.[23] As far as the scientific definition and formation of concepts from which a system of thought is composed are concerned, Söhngen explains:

> It goes without saying that when it comes to the metaphysical we are not primarily thinking of science, but rather, to use Kant's language, of the metaphysics that is inherent in the deeply hidden nature of man, of the metaphysical interests of mankind as they express themselves in language, or rather in languages; as these world-viewing and life-viewing interests of mankind, in concepts and images, but probably originally in images and picture words and then only when they fell on fertile soil in concepts and conceptual language.[24]

In a later publication, Söhngen explains *nomos* as "that which belongs to the essence, the essence of a thing."[25] From this it can be concluded that philosophy does not confront theology as something alien, but as its *lex/nomos*, which helps it in its pursuit of its own concerns and saves them from missing their target.[26]

---

[21] *Ibid.*, pp. 109–10.
[22] Cf. *id.*, "Die Weisheit der Theologie durch den Weg der Wissenschaft," p. 944.
[23] Cf. *id.*, *Der Weg der abendländischen Theologie: Grundgedanken zu einer Theologie der Weges* (München: Anton Pustet, 1959), p. 27.
[24] *Id.*, *Analogie und Metaphor Kleine Philosophie und Theologie der Sprache* (Freiburg: Karl Alber, 1962), p. 88.
[25] *Id.*, *Grundfragen einer Rechtstheologie* (München: Anton Pustet, 1962), p. 27.
[26] Cf. *ibid.*, p. 29. The Greek goddess Dike "reminds every being: to remain what it is according to its essence, and prevents it from slipping into unbeing."

Philosophical Use of Reason

The *usus philosophicus* summarizes "philosophizing for the sake of philosophy"[27] in the sense of the rational striving for knowledge after truth, initially without reference to revelation.[28] Söhngen does not regard philosophy for its own sake as useless for theology even if it undertakes reflections that are not explicitly of a theological nature. This is made clear by Söhngen's statement about his own career: "I believe ... : No matter how long a path via philosophy is taken, it is never a detour to theology; rather one can embark on the actual theological work too early than too late."[29] However, Söhngen does not deny that philosophy can come into conflict with revealed truths. He traces this back to an "ideologically over-interpreted and overwhelmed"[30] philosophy.

Within this first space, Söhngen's work *Being and Object* is of central importance, since it can be understood as a fundamental clarification of the capacities of reason. Based on the scholastic axiom *ens et verum convertuntur*, Söhngen studies the relationship between thinking and being, including epistemological problems, such as that of the irrationality of beings,[31] and how these can be fruitfully processed for theology. The subject matter and orientation of the work are due to the intellectual-historical context, i.e., neo-Kantianism, realism, phenomenology, neo-Scholasticism, but above all through the rediscovery of ontology, especially through the philosophy of Nicolai Hartmann, who exerted great influence on Söhngen.[32] The relationship between cognition and being is ontologically anchored in Söhngen's conception, in the sense that "the knowing subject is the world of being open to knowledge: the more thought-bearing the being, the more being-bearing it is, the more it is in truth being."[33] The knowing subject is part of the world of being and is therefore not alien to being. Conversely, the world of being is open to knowledge.[34] On the one hand, the ontological anchoring of recognition is emphasized, without, on the other hand, the structure of being based on cognition, which itself comes from the reason of a Creator God, being neglected.[35]

---

[27] Id., "Die Weisheit der Theologie durch den Weg der Wissenschaft," 945.
[28] Id., *Philosophische Einübung*, p. 122; "Die Weisheit der Theologie durch den Weg der Wissenschaft," p. 941.
[29] Id., *Die Einheit in der Theologie*, p. vii.
[30] Id., *Philosophische Einübung*, p. 123.
[31] Cf. id., *Sein und Gegenstand: Das scholastische Axiom ens et verum convertuntur als Fundament metaphysischer und theologischer Spekulation* (Münster: Aschendorff, 1930), p. 70; G. Söhngen, "Irrational," in *Lexikon für Theologie und Kirche 5* (Freiburg: Herder, 1933) pp. 603–4.
[32] Cf. W. Röd, *Der Weg der Philosophie von den Anfängen bis ins 20. Jahrhundert* 2 (München: Beck, 1996), pp. 439–40; G. Söhngen, *Die Einheit in der Theologie*, p. vii.
[33] Id., *Sein und Gegenstand*, p. 251.
[34] Ibid., p. 307.
[35] Cf. *ibid.*, p. 334.

Theological Use of Reason

In second position is the theological use of philosophy, i.e., the service of rational science to talk about God. Under this sign, the relationship between theology and philosophy can be explored internally within theology[36] and *ad extra* as a conversation between revealed theology and autonomous philosophy. In this context, Söhngen's explanations of the problem of analogy, which are based on Bonaventure, appear to be of particular importance. Natural theology as *analogia creaturae*[37] or *analogia e naturali cognitione*[38] is affirmed as a possibility—even after Revelation,[39] but under the conditions of salvation history it is in danger of "overthinking" God.[40] This is where Söhngen's formula of the *analogia entis* comes into play in *analogia fidei* as the lynchpin, whereby it is not primarily a matter of knowing the human being, but further and more fundamentally of its ontological quality, its concrete existence, its situation in the history of salvation.[41] Reason healed by faith is the starting point for responsible philosophical and theological science. However, "faith" in this context does not mean a superordination of faith-based knowledge over rational knowledge.[42] Theology is "not the legislator of philosophy and the world sciences."[43] It means here faith as the personal surrender to God, as a new being in Christ. A thinking shaped by this existential turning point forms the framework of responsible philosophical as well as theological science.

As far as the language form of theology is concerned, the *kerygma*, which can be qualified as metaphorical, remains for Söhngen the decisive point of reference for theological thinking and speaking despite its "translation" into the conceptual.[44] Both the primacy of the testimony of revelation and the justification for the application of pure reason in the area of revealed theology remain in balance.[45] The limits of this

---

[36] Cf. *id.*, *Philosophische Einübung*, p. 131.
[37] *Id.*, "Bonaventura als Klassiker der analogia fidei," *Wissenschaft und Weisheit* 2 (1935), p. 104.
[38] *Id.*, "Die Weisheit der Theologie durch den Weg der Wissenschaft," p. 923.
[39] Cf. *id.*, *Grundfragen einer Rechtsthoelogie*, p. 38. Here the author emphasizes the greatness of the ancient natural theology, which also holds against the background of Christianity and its theology. See then: *Die Einheit in der Theologie*, p. 245.
[40] Cf. *id.*, *Die Einheit in der Theologie*, p. 243; *Philosophische Einübung*, pp. 34, 74; "Bonaventura als Klassiker," pp. 102, 109.
[41] Cf. *id.*, "Analogia Fidei, II: Die Einheit in der Glaubenswissenschaft," *Catholica* 3 (1934), pp. 176–208, at p. 192; *Analogia entis in analogia fidei*, pp. 201–7.
[42] Cf. *id.*, *Philosophische Einübung*, pp. 121, 116–17.
[43] *Ibid.*, *Philosophische Einübung*, p. 122.
[44] Cf. *ibid.*, pp. 127–8; "Analogia Fidei," p. 196; *Analogie und Metaphor*, pp. 83–7.
[45] This can be illustrated, for example, by Söhngen's evaluation of the *conclusio theologica*: cf. C. Poncelet, *Dreifacher Gebrauch der Vernunft* (Regensburg: Friedrich Pustet, 2017), pp. 162–8, 180–2.

pure reason are scripture and tradition as witnesses to revelation.[46] This demarcation goes hand in hand with the assertion of the category of historicity, without which the Christ event degenerates into a pure idea, which is in danger of forming ideologies within the framework of an absolutized reason, which in practice can have fatal consequences, as Söhngen illustrates with the attempts to found a natural, unhistorical religion and with the violence in the course of the terror in the course of the French Revolution.[47]

Lifeworld Use of Reason

Concerning the *usus cosmicus*, Söhngen goes beyond the scientific realm to relate reason to wisdom, which he describes as "man's natural disposition as a citizen of the world,"[48] a formulation that plays with Kant's distinction between the "scholastic concept" and the "concept of the world."[49]

In this sense, philosophy enters into a relationship with the Christian faith through both reference to man's everyday life in the world and to building a worldview,[50] insofar as the quest for wisdom is interpreted as a quest for salvation. Although Söhngen acknowledges the plurality of minds and languages, he assumes that there is a single truth and that all people and peoples have sought it in a common scientific effort.[51] Söhngen presents the tension between *humanitas* and *humanitas christiana* with reference to the dimensions of wisdom, love, and a hopeful orientation toward the future. Among other things, he encourages the discovery of forgotten truths and values that have been buried in the Christian life or thinking of an epoch outside the church.[52]

Above all, the tense relationship between *fides* and *ratio* becomes clear in the positioning of the cross of Christ. Following the Pauline theology of the cross (above all 1 Corinthians), the striving for worldly wisdom and the

---

[46] Cf. G. Söhngen, *Symbol und Wirklichkeit im Kultmysterium* (Bonn: Hanstein, 1940), pp. 49–50.
[47] Cf. id., *Einheit in der Theologie*, pp. 249–351; *Analogia Fidei*, p. 192.
[48] Id., "Die Weisheit der Theologie durch den Weg der Wissenschaft," p. 945.
[49] Cf. I. Kant, *Kritik der reinen Vernunft* 2, W. Weinschedel (ed.) (Frankfurt, Main: Suhrkamp, 1974), pp. 866–7.
[50] For example, also, K. Wenzel, "Theologische Implikationen säkularer Philosophie? Vom 'Kampf um Anerkennung' zur Anerkennung unbedingten Anerkanntseins," *Theologie und Philosophie* 86 (2011), pp. 182–200. At p. 186 underlines that the "decision about the relationship of theology to philosophy... can have symptomatic significance for the determination of the relationship of (ecclesiastically constituted) Christianity to the secular world as such ...".
[51] Cf. Söhngen, *Der Weg der abendländischen Theologie*, p. 36; also: *Einheit in der Theologie*, pp. 390, 404.
[52] Cf. *ibid.*, p. 382.

wisdom of God must be distinguished from one another,[53] but the cross as a judgment on a sinful world is also a call for the "Christian penetration and shaping of the world."[54] Since this cross as a mystery is permanently present in the cult of the people of God,[55] living within the church can be considered an anthropological precondition of theology. The crisis of the cross as the place of judgment over the wrongness of the world and as an incentive to act out of love remains present in the form of the church. In this way, the category of historicity that is effective in the *usus theologicus* is grasped in the *usus cosmicus* in the concrete presence of the cross of Christ in the history of the people of God. At the same time, the philosopher remains part of history as a human being and needs this concrete, existential point of reference, without which any terminology would become empty.

Mutual Reference of Theology and Philosophy

If we proceed in the order from *usus philosophicus* via *usus theologicus* to *usus cosmicus*, we are following the path of the order of knowledge. For Söhngen, however, factual truth, i.e., the general and everyday meaning of faith, takes precedence over rational truth. Reflected experience contributes to the building of knowledge and the attainment of wisdom, for "the mind has experience; and with experience comes understanding. Understanding without experience turns into fables and ravings, it loses the ground under your feet; and experience without understanding becomes blind and mindless feeling."[56]

As a central aspect, it must be emphasized that for Söhngen theology and philosophy are separate paths that are, and must be, open to one another if they do not want to unhealthily slip into erroneous forms.[57] A self-contained philosophy, which denies the possibility of a revelation of God *a priori*, tends to become an ideology out of an overestimation of human reason,

---

[53] Cf. *id.*, *Humanität und Christentum* (Essen: Augustin Wibbelt, 1946), pp. 59, 61; *Der Wesensaufbau des Mysteriums*, p. 91.
[54] *Id.*, "Zur Frage eines christlichen Sozialismus: Soziale Struktur und soziales Ethos," *Politische Studien* 5/54 (1954), pp. 6–20, at p. 17.
[55] Cf. *id.*, *Der Wesensaufbau des Mysteriums* (Bonn: Hanstein, 1938), p. 25.
[56] *Id.*, *Philosophische Einübung*, p. 88.
[57] This openness and impartiality of theology toward philosophy do not always seem to be self-evident, if one follows the judgment of Wenzel (cf. "Theologische Implikationen säkularer Philosophie," p. 185). The fact that Christian theology addresses secular philosophy with a non-apologetic intention is no longer a matter of course, even in the Catholic milieu of thought. Rather, mutually exclusive tendencies seem to be very attractive at the moment: on the one hand, the gradual transformation of theology into cultural studies, as is also happening under the label of Religious Studies, on the other hand, the conception of systematic theology, in particular, as biblical theology. In contrast, compare Martin Wendte's more optimistic balance sheet: "Von Göttern, Engeln und Idealisten: Philosophie und Theologie in neuem Gespräch über alte Fragen," *Philosophische Rundschau* 57 (2010), pp. 228–53.

just as faith unrelated to natural knowledge becomes an ideological system, whereby both tendencies—rationalism and fideism—meet as a vanishing point in this ideological deformation.

The fact that reason is open to revelation and thus capable of a rationally responsible act of faith lies in the openness of the spirit to the world as a whole, which Söhngen assumed. The power of cognition is structurally applied to the whole of being, because being itself is spiritually and rationally structured. And conversely, according to Söhngen, knowledge is anchored in the being of the world. This basic idea, as we encounter it in *Being and Object*, appears as the great supporting foundation for the relationship between theology and philosophy.

Translation from German by Tracey Rowland

1

Plato: God, Conscience, and Truth

Manuel Schlögl

Introduction

Joseph Ratzinger has described himself as a "Platonist"—at least in a certain "sense"[1] and "a bit of."[2] Thus, the amicable relationship between Ratzinger's theology and Plato's philosophy is undeniable. But controversy remains regarding just how far this affinity extends and whether its impact on Ratzinger's theology is more positive or negative. Critics accuse Ratzinger of idealism or spiritualism,[3] a pessimistic devaluation of history, and, therefore, of maintaining considerable distance from the modern world and its problems[4]—all of which they see as Platonism's effect on his thinking. The theologian Heiko Nüllmann accuses Ratzinger of a lack of "humanity" because, like Plato, he accepts a transhistorian truth even in terms of morality and fails to recognize the intersubjective

---

[1] Cf. J. Ratzinger, "Glaube, Geschichte und Philosophie: Zum Echo auf meine 'Einführung in das Christentum'," *JRGS* 4 (2014), pp. 323–39, at p. 329.
[2] *Id.*, "Salz der Erde," *JRGS* 13/1 (2016), pp. 205–458, at p. 246.
[3] Cf. W. Kasper, "Das Wesen des Christlichen. Rezension zu Joseph Ratzinger, 'Einführung in das Christentum'," *Theologische Revue* 65 (1969), at pp. 182–8.
[4] Cf. A. Jall, *Erfahrung von Offenbarung: Grundlagen, Quellen und Anwendungen der Erkenntnislehre Joseph Ratzingers* (Regensburg: Pustet, 2019), pp. 456–7.

dependency of moral actions.⁵ Opposed to this, theologians like Michael Schneider⁶ and Ralph Weimann⁷ interpret Ratzinger's "option for the Greek,"⁸ especially Platonic philosophy, as one of his greatest achievements because it led him to rediscover the connection between biblical revelation and natural reason, between the question of God and the question of truth.

To gain greater clarity on the relationship between Ratzinger and Plato, I will first outline all of the historical development in his work, before discussing the most important points that elucidate the inspiring effect of the Greek philosopher on the German theologian.

Ratzinger and Plato: The History of an Encounter

Ratzinger first encountered Plato's philosophy through references found in the Church Fathers' writings and in his study of medieval theology; later on, he went back to Plato's works. In his first academic research on Augustin and Bonaventure, he speaks nearly exclusively of (neo-)Platonism, but hardly about Plato himself.

For Augustine, neo-Platonistic dualism seems to be "the great breakthrough experience"⁹ that made him abandon Manichaeism and helped him find a more positive reception of reality. Despite this positive influence, Ratzinger notes that neo-Platonism is not yet Christianity because it undervalues sensuality, bodily and worldly reality, in favor of the *mundus intelligibilis*. Augustine had to convert from this "nearly pure metaphysical theology ... to a more and more historical understanding of Christianity"—and this "concrete historical figure" of faith is "nothing else but the Church."¹⁰ In Bonaventure, Ratzinger finds a plea against Aristotelism and for Platonism and, moreover, for a "philosophy" that is able "to get in line with the ordered structure of Christian wisdom."¹¹

---

⁵ Cf. H. Nüllmann, *Logos Gottes und Logos des Menschen. Der Vernunftbegriff Joseph Ratzingers und seine Implikationen für Glaubensverantwortung, Moralbegründung und Interreligiösen Dialog* 52 (Würzburg: Echter, Bonner Dogmatische Studien, 2012), p. 378.

⁶ Cf. M. Schneider, *Einführung in die Theologie Joseph Ratzingers* (Köln: Patristisches Zentrum Koinonia-Oriens, 2008), pp. 29–31.

⁷ Cf. R. Weiman, *Kontinuität. Ein Zugang zum Dogmenverständnis in der Theologie Joseph Ratzingers* (Doctoral Thesis, Pontifical Athenaeum Regina Apostolorum, 2010), pp. 95–153.

⁸ *Id.*, *Kontinuität*, p. 112.

⁹ Cf. J. Ratzinger, "Volk und Haus Gottes in Augustins Lehre von der Kirche," *JRGS* 1 (2010), pp. 41–418, at p. 75.

¹⁰ *Ibid.*, pp. 76–7. As interpretation see A. Nichols, *The Thought of Pope Benedict XVI: An Introduction to the Theology of Joseph Ratzinger* (London: Burns&Oates, 2007), pp. 22–3.

¹¹ J. Ratzinger, "Die Geschichtstheologie des heiligen Bonaventura," *JRGS* 2 (2012), pp. 419–659, at p. 633.

From these intellectual footmarks, Ratzinger began to develop his own theological synthesis in the 1960s. It can be found in his most successful book, *Introduction to Christianity*, which explicitly refers to Plato's "Symposium" and "Politeia."[12] Above all, Ratzinger closely follows the belief of the Fathers that Platonic philosophy is the perfect conversation partner for rationally accessing biblical faith and proclaiming it to the world.

"The decision of the early church for philosophy,"[13] Christianity's secret alliance with the philosophical enlightenment and its criticism of myths and gods, was first of all a decision in favor of *Plato's* philosophy. This appropriation of Platonic thought also meant a crucial "transformation of the god of the philosophers,"[14] insofar as the Christian faith is based on the Incarnation of God in Jesus Christ. The question of truth is bound to a historical person, and the answer can only be found in dialogue with him.

The famous theologian and later Cardinal Walter Kasper accused Ratzinger's *Introduction* of having an "extreme Platonic approach,"[15] i.e., transhistorian idealism. To answer his critic, Ratzinger confessed that if Platonism "means that you say yes to a truth that simply *is* and which I simply accept and which transforms me by receiving it," then "in this sense ... indeed I am a 'Platonist' and will be one."[16] This emotional debate must be contextualized with the attraction of Marxism at the time with its primacy of the collective and practice. Ratzinger, however, points to the inaccessible objectivity and existential relevance of the truth known by faith, and he sees his position as supported by Plato's understanding of truth.

In later publications, Ratzinger stays true to this position. He defends, for example, Plato's importance "for the foundation of each philosophy" against Karl Rahner's position.[17] He also emphasizes—with the authority of a Prefect of the Congregation of Faith—the topic of Christianity and religions, pointing to the inner connection between Christian belief and philosophical enlightenment,[18] the easy recognizability of truth,[19] and the humanity and defenselessness of those who bind themselves to the truth.[20] Up to his last lectures before his election as Pope, Ratzinger underlines Plato

---

[12] Cf. *id.*, "Einführung in das Christentum," *JRGS* 4 (2014), pp. 54–322, at p. 102 (*Symposium*, 191d), p. 267 (*Politeia*, 361e-2a).
[13] *Id.*, "Einführung," pp. 136–41.
[14] *Id.*, "Einführung," pp. 141–5.
[15] W. Kasper, "Das Wesen des Christlichen," p. 184.
[16] J. Ratzinger, "Glaube, Geschichte und Philosophie," p. 329.
[17] *Id.*, "Vom Verstehen des Glaubens. Anmerkungen zu Karl Rahner, 'Grundkurs des Glaubens'," *JRGS* 9/1 (2016), pp. 296–312, at p. 299.
[18] Cf. *id.*, "Das Christentum—die wahre Religion?," *JRGS* 3/1 (2020), pp. 439–56.
[19] Cf. *id.*, "Glaube und Bildung," *JRGS* 9/2 (2016), pp. 916–28, at pp. 925–6.
[20] *Id.*, "Der Dialog der Religionen und das jüdisch-christliche Verhältnis," *JRGS* 8/2 (2010), pp. 1120–36, at p. 1133.

as the real "discoverer of spirit in the West"[21] and accentuates his enduring importance for Europe.[22]

Seen as a whole, Plato's influence on Ratzinger's work increased over time. Starting from a primarily historical and apologetical interest, the theologian comes to see an actual interlocutor in Plato,[23] who helps by securing the spiritual foundations of Western culture against the "dictatorship of relativism"[24] and by making a plea for universal truth.

Discussion

[A] Plato *Christianus*? Faith and Philosophy among the Church Fathers

Ratzinger's theology consciously connects to the synthesis of faith and reason in the first centuries *post Christum natum*.[25] He judges modern times critically insofar as the understanding of reality therein is characterized by human feasibility and fades out the dimension of faith.[26] But his recourse to the Church Fathers is by no means naive. As clearly as few other theologians of his time, Ratzinger differentiates where the Fathers were able to legitimately develop the faith of the church using Plato's philosophy and where they had to resist the temptation of Hellenizing Christianity.[27]

Plato *christianus*, i.e., the Christian acceptance and integration of Platonic criticism of the pagan gods and its decided monotheism,[28] the idea of the union of humanity[29] or emphasis of conscience,[30] stands side by side

---

[21] *Id.*, "Theologische Probleme der Kirchenmusik," *JRGS* 11 (2008), pp. 571–85, at p. 579.
[22] Cf. *id.*, "Europa—verpflichtendes Erbe für die Christen," in *JRGS* 3/2 (2020), pp. 701–16, at pp. 708–9, 713.
[23] Cf. H. Nüllmann, *Logos Gottes*, pp. 310–12.
[24] Cf. M. Gruber (ed.), *Diktatur des Relativismus. Der Kampf um die absolute Wahrheit für die Zukunft Europas* (Heiligenkreuz: Be&Be, 2014)
[25] Cf. J. Ratzinger, "Die Bedeutung der Väter im Aufbau des Glaubens," *JRGS* 9/1 (2016), pp. 498–521. As interpretation see M. C. Hastetter, *Vergegenwärtigung der Vätertheologie. Joseph Ratzingers/Papst Benedikts XVI. Beitrag in der patristisch-ökumenischen Theologie im Nachgang zu Georg Florowskis Neo-Patristischer Synthese* 1 (St. Ottilien: EOS, 2019).
[26] Cf. J. Ratzinger, "Einführung," pp. 70–9. As interpretation see P. Sottopietra, *Wissen aus der Taufe. Die Aporien der neuzeitlichen Vernunft und der christliche Weg im Werk von Joseph Ratzinger* (Regensburg: Anton Pustet, 2003); H. Nüllmann, *Logos Gottes*, pp. 186–246.
[27] M. Schlögl, "Chresis. Zum Verhältnis von Glaube und Kultur in der Religionstheologie Joseph Ratzingers," in *Mitteilungen des Instituts Papst Benedikt XVI* 8 (Regensburg: Schnell & Steiner, 2015), pp. 82–9; *id.*, "'Um möglichst viele zu gewinnen' (1 Kor 9,19). Zur Transformation der jüdisch-hellenistischen Antike durch das Christentum," *Internationale katholische Zeitschrift Communio* 50/4 (2021), pp. 422–30.
[28] Cf. J. Ratzinger, "Variationen zum Thema Glaube, Religion und Kultur," in *JRGS* 3/1, pp. 365–89, at p. 375.
[29] Cf. *id.*, "Volk und Haus Gottes," p. 101.
[30] Cf. *id.*, "Gewissen und Wahrheit," in *JRGS* 4, pp. 696–717.

with Plato *anti-christianus*,[31] i.e., certain Platonic tendencies that are in no way connectable with Christian theology, and had to be discarded or at least completely transformed.[32]

First, there is the concept of God, which Plato gives a certain personal imprint to by naming it "Father" and "Lord," but, seen as a whole, Plato's God does not actually have the personality, responsiveness, and willingness to relate that are characteristic of the biblical God and make him believable.[33] The same applies to the event of the Incarnation, which led to a much deeper relationship between God and the world than Plato could have anticipated, and gave equal dignity to body and spirit.[34] It also meant that the idea of the soul's ascension and union with God ("theosis") as the highest goal of human desire became central in the spirituality of the Fathers. Here too, the Christian theology of creation and christology allow for a clearer view of this union, which cannot be a dissolution of finiteness, and cannot signify man's perishing in God. Union with the God Jesus Christ retains the independence of creation even in its completion because it is a "union of love."[35]

[B] The Rehabilitation of the Soul in the "Eschatology"

Ratzinger's most detailed statement on Plato can be found in his 1977 book *Eschatology*, which he called in retrospect his "most elaborated work."[36] Already in the foreword, an inner change to his point of view is detected. While Ratzinger initially joined the general reserve against Plato's dualism and body hostility and planned for a "de-Platonized eschatology,"[37] he discovered in his years of exploration on the subject that such "antitheses"[38] could not really be true. Instead, in this case, he saw quite a few things in common between Plato's metaphysical doctrine of the soul and the Christian doctrine of the soul's immortality. Ratzinger's significant project to rehabilitate non-dualistic, relational-dialogical discourse on the immortal

---

[31] Cf. *id.*, "Variationen," p. 370. See also E. von Ivánka, *Plato christianus. Übernahme und Umgestaltung des Platonismus durch die Väter* (Einsiedeln: Johannes, 1990).
[32] Cf. *id.*, "Glaube-Wahrheit-Toleranz," in *JRGS* 3/1, pp. 483–500, at p. 495.
[33] Cf. *id.*, "Die christliche Brüderichkeit," in *JRGS* 8/1, pp. 37–101, at pp. 67–9.
[34] Cf. *id.*, *Zur theologischen Grundlegung der Kirchenmusik*, p. 511. Therefore, J. Ratzinger, "Der Geist der Liturgie," *JRGS* 11 (2008), pp. 29–194, at p. 114 demands a "Platonism, transformed by the Incarnation."
[35] *Id.*, "Theologie der Liturgie," in *JRGS* 11, pp. 639–56, at p. 650.
[36] *Id.*, *Aus meinem Leben. Erinnerungen (1927–1977)* (München: DVA, 1998), p. 175.
[37] *Id.*, "Eschatologie," in *JRGS* 10, pp. 29–276, at p. 36. As interpretation see T. Marschler, "'Seele'—Joseph Ratzingers Stellungnahmen zu einem eschatologischen Zentralbegriff und ihre Relevanz für die aktuelle Diskussion," in *Hoffnung auf Vollendung. Zur Eschatologie von Joseph Ratzinger*, G. Nachtwei (ed.) (Regensburg: Anton Pustet, 2015), pp. 97–124.
[38] *Id.*, "Eschatologie," p. 36.

human soul uses Platonism without accepting it uncritically.[39] Reflecting on the death of Socrates, Plato made the important insight "that the immortality [of man] is grounded in his relation to the truth."[40] Only a longing for and focus on the truth gives him the hope that death does not have the last word in this life, and the courage to use his life for the good and, if it should be required, to give it up.

Thus, Ratzinger recognizes "an inner parallel"[41] between the death of Socrates and the death of the early Jewish martyrs in the Maccabees period—and, at the same time, significant difference between them. While Socrates asked Asklepios to sacrifice a rooster because death would free him from the "disease" of earthly material existence, according to Christian belief, the biological body disintegrates in death, but the soul retains a certain form of corporeality in relation to the resurrection of the body of Jesus Christ and will be clothed with a new, immortal body in eschatological perfection.

At this point, Ratzinger recognizes Thomas Aquinas' decisive, further development of the doctrine of immortality.[42] By distinguishing body and corporeality, and by declaring the soul to be the *forma corporis,* i.e., the creative and supporting power of the human body, the medieval thinker is able to appreciate materia as God's good creation and, at the same time, to keep the spirit as a principle and an independent force of human existence, which continues in communion with God even after biological death. Against that, Plato "would ... never admit that the 'immortal soul' is so closely connected to the body, belonging to it and one with it, that it must be called its 'form' and cannot exist otherwise than in the most intimate relationship to it."[43]

Plato, in Ratzinger's view, could not solve the "dilemma between spiritualism and naturalism on his own."[44] Thomas Aquinas was the first to achieve an ingenious "synthesis" by going back to Aristotle, but, above all, to the biblical theology of creation, which must be "reexecuted" and appropriated under the presuppositions of modern thought.[45]

[C] The Question of Conscience and the Truth

The support Ratzinger seeks from Plato when it comes to the question of the human capacity for truth is, in a certain respect, even more pressing and topical than the arguments found in his *Eschatology,* a book that remains in the domain of academic theology.

---

[39] Cf. *ibid.*, pp. 95–102, 154–6.
[40] *Ibid.*, p. 275.
[41] *Ibid.*, p. 111.
[42] Cf. *ibid.*, pp. 159–68, 184–7.
[43] *Ibid.*, p. 384.
[44] *Ibid.*, p. 184.
[45] Cf. *ibid.*, p. 187.

In an important 1992 lecture on "Conscience and Truth," the Cardinal states that, in the Modern Age, "subjectivity" has increasingly emancipated itself from "authority."[46] Conscience is now the highest norm, even when it goes against religious or political authority. This development resulted in boundless individualism and conformism, which increasingly obscures the human ability to perceive what is true and good.[47]

Ratzinger counters this with the witness of the truth, which recognizes in conscience an objectivity of the good that must be obeyed. Along with Cardinal John Henry Newman, he names Socrates and Plato's dispute with the sophists. In Plato's time, the fifth and fourth centuries before Christ, Athenian democracy went through a deep crisis in which Ratzinger sees an "intellectual-historical parallel [to] today's dispute about ethics."[48] Then and now, there is a "crucial decision between two basic attitudes ... : confidence in the human capacity for truth, on the one hand, and a world view, on the other hand, in which humans alone create their own standards."[49]

If the latter is true, human actions are determined by "ability" rather than by the notion of "should."[50] Being right is assigned to whomever has knowledge and power on his side; in communication, it is no longer the content that counts, which is replaced by rhetoric and formal labeling (like "new," "progressive," and so on). Anyone who still asks after the truth is considered "outdated" or "conservative," or will be silenced like Socrates. Thus, in Ratzinger's eyes, Plato's dispute about truth with the sophists is a warning for our time, for the media age and its understanding of factuality and interpretation.

Not satisfied with the description or criticism, he offers a solution for which he draws on Plato in a daring way, adapting the Platonic doctrine of anamnesis under a Christian sign.[51] Plato, like his teacher Socrates, was convinced that all knowledge is based on the memory of original knowledge that the soul possesses before entering the world, but forgets at birth and then must slowly rediscover it. Ratzinger also assumes that humans have a "primal memory of what is good and true."[52] However, this conviction is not based on belief in the pre-existence of the soul, as with Plato, but is interpreted first in the light of Gen 1:26-27 as knowledge of being created in the image of God and then combined with Rom 2:14-15 as an expression of the natural law that God has "written on the hearts" of all people.[53] This memory, which is anchored in the order of creation, involves the order

---

[46] Cf. *id.*, "Gewissen und Wahrheit," p. 705.
[47] Cf. *ibid.*, pp. 698–704.
[48] *Ibid.*, p. 708. See also *id.*, "Die Gabe der Weisheit," in *JRGS* 5, pp. 257–69, at pp. 262–6.
[49] *Id.*, "Gewissen und Wahrheit," p. 708.
[50] Cf. *ibid.*, p. 709.
[51] Cf. *ibid.*, pp. 709–13.
[52] *Ibid.*, p. 711.
[53] Cf. *ibid.*, pp. 710–11.

of salvation. In so doing, Ratzinger refers in particular to the Johannine writings, and speaks of "the new anamnesis of faith," which happens in the insertion of the individual in the "new We" of the church through faith and baptism.[54] Through a living connection with the risen Jesus Christ and other Christians as "one body in Christ" (1 Cor 12:27), every believer has access to knowledge of God and human salvation. This helps him to recognize the true and good in every situation and to stand up for it.

In Plato's doctrine of anamnesis, Ratzinger sees a "vessel for Christian *Logos*" because both are about "liberation through truth and to truth."[55] With his findings, the philosopher prepared a development that Christianity later realized, namely that "human capacity of truth," experienced in conscience, must be regarded "as the limit of all power and as a guarantee of [man's] likeness to God."[56]

Plato's Legacy in Ratzinger's Theology

How is Plato's legacy in Ratzinger's theology to be judged? From what we have seen, his own statement that he is "a bit of a Platonist" certainly seems true.[57] The theologian has recognizable sympathy for the philosopher from Athens. He cites Platonic dialogues partly in the original, partly from secondary sources. Some Platonist mediators and interpreters particularly important to Ratzinger include Romano Guardini (1885–1968), Helmut Kuhn (1899–1991), Josef Pieper (1904–97), and Robert Spaemann (1927–2018). He especially likes to take up Platonic commentary from his colleague and friend Pieper.[58]

Ratzinger never claims to undertake a scientific interpretation of Plato; rather, he incorporates related concepts and terms into his own train of thought. He is a far too independent and creative spirit to simply and uncritically adopt Plato's philosophy. As Aidan Nichols notes, Ratzinger "holds that the Church has much to do in order to 'correct and purify' Plato's intention."[59] The frequent and uncritical accusation of Platonism against Ratzinger is, therefore, incorrect, and rather rests on critics' inaccurate readings. Ratzinger's reception of Plato is akin to the *chresis* of the Church Fathers:[60] He always superimposes onto the philosopher's

---

[54] Cf. *ibid.*, p. 713.
[55] *Ibid.*, p. 708.
[56] *Ibid.*, p. 709.
[57] Cf. *id.*, "Salz der Erde," p. 246.
[58] Cf. M. Schlögl, "Der Glaube braucht den Mut der Vernunft zu sich selbst," in T. Möllenbeck and B. Wald (eds.), *"Die Wahrheit bekennen." Josef Pieper im Dialog* (München: Pneuma, 2017), pp. 275–93.
[59] A. Nichols, *The Thought of Pope Benedict XVI*, p. 120.
[60] Cf. C. Gnilka, *Chresis I: Der Begriff des rechten Gebrauchs* (Basel: Schwane. 2012); *Chresis II: Kultur und Conversion* (Basel: Schwabe, 1993); M. Schlögl, "Chresis."

texts the scale of revelation, the Holy Scripture, and the faith of the Church. And he only relies on what serves the Christian faith, and testifies to its rationality and universality; meanwhile, he tacitly ignores other topics (like the pre-existence of the soul).

Conclusion

For Ratzinger, Plato is more than a historical reference point for understanding the history of Christianity; rather, he is a relevant interlocutor with the potential to shape the future of Europe. Plato, experienced in the political crises of his time, combined questions of truth, ethics of conscience, and theory of state. The universal good that man can recognize in his conscience should form the basis of political action. Such a state does not develop by itself; it must be consciously chosen and designed by individuals and social groups willing to subordinate their own interests to the good and truth that apply to everyone.

In a lecture given shortly after the fall of communism, Cardinal Ratzinger invoked Plato's legacy as the spiritual basis of a future Europe.[61] He spoke of the "priority of ethics over politics"[62] and the "indispensability of the idea of God for ethics."[63] Europe owes the world "the knowledge of the *Logos* as the basis of things, the look at the truth, which is also the standard of the good."[64]

This "knowledge" remains Plato's legacy in Ratzinger's theology, and beyond.

---

[61] Cf. J. Ratzinger, "Europa—Hoffnungen und Gefahren," *JRGS* 3/2 (2020), pp. 646–66.
[62] *Ibid.*, pp. 662–3.
[63] *Ibid.*, pp. 663–5.
[64] *Ibid.*, p. 665.

2

Augustine of Hippo: The Reciprocal Dependence of Faith and World

Emery de Gaál

Introduction

In 2007 Pope Benedict XVI[1] undertook a pilgrimage to Pavia "to venerate the mortal remains of this Father of the Church ... By doing so, I wished to express to him also ... my personal devotion and gratitude in regard to

---

[1]The Augustine bibliography of Ratzinger is found to a large extent in *Joseph Ratzinger Gesammelte Schriften. Volk und Haus Gottes in Augustins Lehre von der Kirche*, henceforth abbreviated *JRGS* 1 (Freiburg: Herder, 2011). This is rightfully the first volume of Pope Benedict's collected works. It encompasses *c.* 90 percent of his studies on Augustine's theology. The first section covers his dissertation (pp. 43–418), followed by diverse texts, including homilies, dictionary entries, book reviews, and introductions. In total this volume is 792 pages long. Cf. also Pope Benedict XVI, *Great Christian Thinkers: From the Early Church through the Middle Ages* (Minneapolis: Fortress Press, 2011). J. Ratzinger, *The Unity of the Nations: A Vision of the Church Fathers* (Washington, DC: Catholic University of America Press, 2015). Pope Benedict XVI, *General Audience*, January 9, 2008. Valuable: Benedikt XVI, *Leidenschaft für die Wahrheit. Augustinus* (Augsburg: Sankt Ulrich, 2009). The secondary literature includes J. L. Cong Quy, "Der Einfluss des Augustinus auf die Theologie des Papstes Benedikt XVI," *Augustiniana* 56 3/4 (2006), pp. 411–32. L. G. Müller, "'Augustinus ist mir immer ein großer Freund und Lehrer geblieben', Präsentation von *JRGS* 1 an der Deutschen Botschaft am Heiligen Stuhl am 14. März 2012," in *Mitteilungen Institut Papst Benedikt XVI* 5/2012 (Regensburg: Steiner & Schnell, 2013); P. Fletcher, *Resurrection Realism: Ratzinger the Augustinian* (Eugene: Cascade, 2014). D. E. Burns, "Ratzinger on the Augustinian Understanding of Religious Freedom," *Communio* 44 (2017), pp. 296–328. M. van Ittersum, *Baptism in the Tradition of Augustine? The Theology of Joseph Ratzinger with Respect to Baptism* (Enschede: Ipskamp, 2018).

a figure to whom I feel very linked for the role he has played in my life as a theologian, priest, and pastor."[2] Asked which two books he would take with him to a deserted island, he famously responded the Bible and Augustine's *Confessions*.[3] In a general audience in 2008 the pope observed:

> This is his most famous work; and rightly so, since it is precisely Augustine's *Confessions*, with their focus on interiority and psychology, that constitute a unique model in Western (and not only Western) literature—including non-religious literature—up to modern times. This attention to the spiritual life, to the mystery of the "I," to the mystery of God who is concealed in the "I," is something quite extraordinary, without precedent, and remains for ever, as it were, a spiritual "peak."[4]

Benedict XVI donated a significant amount from his private funds for the restoration of the Basilica of St. Augustine (354–430) located in present-day Annaba, Algeria, the former Roman harbor city of Hippo Regius, Augustine's birthplace.[5] Indeed, in order to understand the mind of Joseph Ratzinger/Benedict XVI it is indispensable to familiarize oneself with his first work, his award-winning doctoral dissertation on Augustine's ecclesiology: *Volk und Haus Gottes in Augustins Lehre von der Kirche* (People and House of God in Augustine's Teaching on the Church), directed by Gottlieb Söhngen (1892–1971) and convincingly defended in 1951. First published in 1954, it was republished in 1992, followed by a reprint in 1998, and fittingly stands since 2011 at the beginning of his collected writings. Alas, this seminal text still awaits translation into English. Indeed, the majority of his writings on Augustine remain untranslated. In addition to the dissertation and patristic studies, the first volume of the collected *Joseph Ratzinger Gesammelte Schriften* contains i.a. the North African theologian's understanding of politics, *confessio,* ecclesiology, pneumatology, and six book reviews, a foreword to an Italian study on Augustine, and six homilies on Augustine.

In an interview with the Italian politician Giulio Andreotti (1919–2013), then Cardinal Ratzinger observed that Augustine is not a distant personality speaking from a wholly foreign context to us. Though the issues may have changed: ever again in every age human beings gain their center in a supernatural, Christological sensibility that is one of charity.[6] On this point Augustine is an important and abiding point of reference for human culture and the self-understanding of the human person, Ratzinger continued.

---

[2] Benedict XVI, *Great Christian Thinkers, From the Early Church through the Middle Ages,* p. 115.
[3] Cf. T. George, "Benedict XVI, the Great Augustinian," *First Things,* February 19, 2013.
[4] Benedict XVI, *General Audience,* January 9, 2008.
[5] Cf. T. George, "Benedict XVI, the Great Augustinian," p. 1.
[6] Cf. J. Ratzinger, "The Power and the Grace," Interview with G. Andreotti, *30 Giorni,* May, 2005.

Probably no single theologian—including even the *Doctor Angelicus*, Thomas Aquinas (*c.* 1215–74)—influenced occidental intellectual life from antiquity to the present more than Augustine. Aurelius Augustinus probes both the nature of the human person and that of the Church. At the same time the *Doctor Gratiae* (Doctor of Grace) centers faith on "a loving and petitioning meditation on God by the human being and the salvation gifted him in Jesus Christ. Arising from grace, man is capable to gain insight into faith, not as a theoretic construct, but as an encounter with the living God in the heart of every human being."[7]

In the introduction to the first volume of his collected texts, Benedict XVI writes concerning his dissertation that it "not only opened a life-long friendship with St. Augustine, but guided me on the track of Eucharistic ecclesiology and so granted me an appreciation for the reality of the Church that corresponds to the profoundest intentions of the Second Vatican Council and leads at the same time to the spiritual center of Christian existence."[8]

The *Ouverture*: The Dissertation on Augustine's Ecclesiology

It took Ratzinger only from July of 1950 until March of 1951 to compose his substantial dissertation *Volk und Haus Gottes in Augustins Lehre von der Kirche*. In 1940, the Dominican theologian Mannes Dominikus Koster (1901–81) had boldly "announced" in his study *Ekklesiologie im Werden* (Evolving Ecclesiology) that the future central category for ecclesiology would be "people of God, not mystical body of Christ."[9] Inspired by this study, Gottlieb Söhngen had speculated that the term "people of God" is more germane to Augustine than "body of Christ." Ratzinger's dissertation could not confirm Söhngen's hypothesis. Ratzinger had read Henri de Lubac's (1896–1991) pioneering *Corpus Mysticum* (1939). The title of his book notwithstanding, De Lubac's studies revealed that Augustine does not use the adjective "*mysticum*" for the Church, but very much "*corpus Christi*." To the mind of the African Church Father "Body of Christ" captures *the* fundamental ecclesial reality. The term "*corpus Christi*" (Body of Christ) both denotes continuity with the Old Testament's understanding of Israel as "the people of God" and demarcates a quantum leap into a new reality grounded in Christ's enduring Eucharistic presence (cf. 1 Cor 10:16).

---

[7] G. L. Müller, "Augustinus ist mir immer ein großer Freund und Lehrer geblieben, Präsentation von *JRGS* 1 an der Deutschen Botschaft am Heiligen Stuhl am 14. März 2012," p. 45.
[8] J. Ratzinger, *JRGS* 1, p. 9. This and subsequent quotations from the *JRGS* are the author's translations.
[9] M. D. Koster, *Ekklesiologie im Werden* (Paderborn: Bonifacius, 1940), p. 4.

This insight contributed to the Second Vatican Council (re-)discovering the concept "*communio*" as the basic feature of being Church.[10] The two terms, *communio* and "People of God," overcome a one-sided juridical and institutional understanding of the Catholic Church, understandably prevalent after the Council of Trent (1545–63).[11] Though rooted in the Old Testament, the term "People of God" needs to be seen afresh as an ecclesial community gathered by Christ and the Holy Spirit from the Lord's Eucharistic real presence. "My result was thus, briefly stated: the two load-bearing elements of Augustine's vision of the Church are a Christological relecture of the Old Testament and the sacramental life with its center in the Eucharist."[12] This grants Ratzinger a deeper insight into Augustine's understanding of the *Civitas Dei* not merely as the "City or State of God," but including the dimension *Bürgerschaft Gottes* ("citizenship of God," nota bene not exclusively "city").[13] The primary reality of the Church is neither empirical nor Idealistic—as the nineteenth and twentieth centuries may imply, but sacramental. This enradication of all ecclesial reality in Christ and the Holy Spirit the most recent council underscored in the documents *Lumen gentium* (dogmatic constitution on the Church) and *Ad Gentes* (decree on missionary activity).[14] As Benedict remarks in his 1992 introduction, the subsequent more popular "sociological reflection" on the term "people of God" does not do justice to the ecclesial reality of faith.[15]

In his dissertation Benedict first presents the pagan Augustine's understanding of the Church until 391. Overcoming vainglorious skepticism, the humility of Christian faith accesses for the baptized Augustine the Church as mother and *salus populi* (salvation of the people). His discovery of charity in turn brings him to apprehend the new Temple of God in the interiority of man. Amid pagan, Gnostic, Manichaean, and Donatist contestations and misunderstandings of what Christian faith and Church are, Augustine uncovers an underlying *ecclesia*-defining tradition in the concept "people of God."

The Christian people bear the image of God. It lives a *disciplina* that encompasses not merely moral and legal aspects of life, but apprehends an interior, sacramental core, from which, among others, i.e., as secondary

---

[10] Cf. "Really partaking of the body of the Lord in the breaking of the Eucharistic bread, we are taken up into communion with Him and with one another. 'Because the bread is one, we though many, are one body, all of us who partake of the one bread'" (Vatican Council II, *Dogmatic Constitution on the Church* Lumen gentium, November 21, 1964, §7). The term "communio" occurs thirty-five times in *Lumen gentium (LG)*.
[11] Cf. *JRGS* 1, p. 48. For a brief summary cf. van Ittersum, *Baptism in the Tradition of Augustine? The Theology of Joseph Ratzinger with Respect to Baptism*, pp. 55–68.
[12] *JRGS* 1, p. 53.
[13] Cf. *ibid.*
[14] Notably *LG* §33: " ... People of God and make up the Body of Christ under one head" and *AG* §7: "one people of God and be built up into one temple of the Holy Spirit ...."
[15] Cf, *JRGS* 1, p. 57.

moments, also moral and legal dimensions issue forth. The fellow North African, Tertullian (c. 155–c. 220), aided Augustine in discovering over and against Gnosticism "the right of the flesh."[16]

Ratzinger concludes: "One of Augustine's greatest accomplishments is ... his teaching of the double pledge of our salvation. Not only is the *pneuma* lowered into us from above, vouching for our salvation, but likewise the *sarx* from our lower, as the body of Christ, now in the interior of God, entered his above. Human flesh in God—never will such a reality once reached, completely suffer shipwreck. Thus, Tertullian can formulate the daring antithesis to the Apostle's word 'flesh and blood will not inherit the kingdom': 'Be now of good cheer, flesh and blood: you have taken possession of heaven and of the Kingdom of God in Christ!'."[17]

This insight is grounded in a then developing, grand Christological synthesis that will find fuller articulation after Augustine's death at the Council of Chalcedon in 451. The first sentence of the above quotation frames Ratzinger's eschatology as expressed in the 1970s.[18]

While *in* history, the Church is singular in history as "people of God" *from* (in the sense of enabled by) "the pneumatic Christ."[19] Faithful to Tertullian, to Augustine's mind the Church does not claim a particular "*Ort*" (location) in history as she " ... consists in a constant movement to that, what is beyond all history, which is her end and her beyond—the new world after Christ's return."[20] Tertullian and in his wake Augustine "set our sight on the future life, after the return of Christ, which we own now only as 'spe, non in re' ... only the fulfilled Christ will be the true Church."[21]

Ratzinger shows how Cyprian of Carthage (c. 210–58) expands on Tertullian. While there is no gainsaying that there is a juridical component to the *corpus Christi* (body of Christ), its primary reality is first and foremost sacramental. It is "the pneumatic people of the faithful" replacing the old covenantal "people of God" of the Israelites. This view is anchored constitutively in the Eucharist. For Augustine it is of abiding significance that for both Tertullian and Cyprian the Church is grounded in the "*communicatio corporis Christi*," i.e., the sharing and living in the one body of Christ.[22] To Cyprian, whoever addresses God as Father need comprehend himself, the Christian believer, as son in the body of Christ, superseding membership in the natural family or the abstract body politic. Ratzinger concludes that the Church emerges in this context as "the We of the Sons

---

[16] *Ibid.*, p. 141.
[17] *Ibid.*
[18] *Id.*, *Eschatology. Death and Eternal Life* (Washington, DC: Catholic University of America, 1988), pp. 182ff.
[19] *JRGS* 1, p. 149.
[20] *Ibid.*
[21] *Ibid.*, pp. 149–50.
[22] Cf. *ibid.*, p. 165.

of God."²³ The unity of the exalted Christ with Christians gains contours. From within such an understanding of many formed to one body of Christ for Cyprian, a religious demand arises that compels Christians to ransom captured fellow Christians from the hands of pagan barbarians, Ratzinger underscores. Based on the liturgy, Cyprian apprehends in Christians a unique "*Geistigkeit und Innerlichkeit*" (spirituality and interiority) grounded in their singular relationship with God.²⁴ This dimension is wholly unknown and inaccessible to their pagan contemporaries.

Optatus of Milevis (died 397) sees revealed truth as the "divine seed of life" which "effects an overarching faith vouching for salvation also outside the limited confines of the communicative community of the Church" according to Ratzinger.²⁵

At the conclusion of the first section Ratzinger reflects on the thoughts of North African theologians regarding the relationship of Church and state, since this will influence Augustine's claim of the *duae civitates*, the two citizenships. While Christians are called to pray for the state, the *Imperium Romanum* (Roman Empire) is in the final analysis part of the evil powers to Tertullian. This is positively nuanced by Cyprian: the Church is found somehow within the state as an organ. He critiques the schismatic Donatus Magnus (died c. 355) for asking provocatively "Quid est imperatori cum ecclesia?" (what do emperor and Church have in common?).²⁶ Does one not find virtues, such as holy priesthood, chastity, and virginity, held in esteem by Christians and Romans alike, but not amongst barbarians, Cyprian counters? The real danger at that juncture in history was, in Ratzinger's judgment, that the Christian religion faced the prospect of being subsumed under an essentially still pagan Roman state. This was not a local African dispute, but one of preserving "the Christianness of the whole Church of Christ. To this hour of decision the great Bishop of Hippo was sent—the saint Augustine."²⁷

In the second section, Ratzinger turns to Augustine's understanding of the Church as people and house of God. He gains an appreciation for the universal *ecclesia catholica* (the catholic Church), consisting of all peoples as "*eine Ablösung und Fortsetzung der Sichtbarkeit Jesu Christi*" (a dialectical replacement and continuation of Jesus Christ's visibility) in the world.²⁸ The ecclesial and pneumatic Christ is present as "the inner unity in the Lord" within "the Church of the peoples as the one people from Abraham's seed, which is Christ."²⁹ As with the preceding African theologians, Augustine views the

---

²³ *Ibid.*, p. 166.
²⁴ Cf. *ibid.*, p. 169.
²⁵ Cf. *ibid.*, p. 185.
²⁶ Cf. *ibid.*, p. 192.
²⁷ *Ibid.*, p. 194.
²⁸ Cf. *ibid.*, p. 229.
²⁹ *Ibid.*

Christ mystery also as a physical reality. In the strength of the sacramentality of the Eucharist, there exists a true participation in Christ's "Eucharistic *pax*." And precisely in his tangible, real presence, a spiritualization sets in. Between the external ecclesial *pax* (peace) and genuine *caritas* (charity) between *sacramentum* (sacrament) and *res sacramenti* (the matter of the sacrament, Christ) within the one Church a qualitative difference must be noted, i.e., between the *signum* (sign) and the *res significata* (the matter signified) there is an abiding contrasting asymmetry but also enabling tension. This results in a "*Doppelbegriff von populus Dei*" (double term of the people of God), i.e., of the visible and invisible Church.[30]

The new House of God is the result of the self-immolation of Jesus Christ, in which Christians join. The preceding intellectual currents, i.e., 1. antignostic Christian *soma* (body) understanding and 2. the anti-Arian exegesis of Athanasius (c. 298–373), aided Augustine in crystallizing his thoughts. From the realist appreciation of the Eucharist, as articulated by Tertullian, Hilary of Poitiers (315–68) and John Chrysostom (347–407), results a sacramental ethics for Augustine. This distinguishes the body of Christ from the pagan state of deities. Thus, Augustine achieves a remarkable "synthesis of the metaphysical term body ... As with the anti-Donatist controversy also here the cohering key term is called caritas."[31]

On this background the young Ratzinger investigates Augustine's discussions of the concepts "tent of God," "cult," and the growth of "God's temple," which in their Christian transformations all possess Christ as their constitutive foundation. This yields the insight into Christ as the ecclesial *caput* (head) and *angularis* (cornerstone). By itself the *domus* (house) term is a lower form of community vis-à-vis *civitas* (city, citizenship). Nevertheless, as house of God, it denotes a pneumatic, supernatural, and celestial edifice. Jesus Christ's temple is both "*Wohnstätte und lebendiges Opfer für Gott*" (*abode* and living *sacrifice* for God).[32] This edifice is the supernatural "*Einheit im Glauben und* in der Liebe" (unity in faith *and* in charity).[33] While forcefully enunciated, unambiguously formulated, and adding original accents, Ratzinger stresses that Augustine's ecclesiology is in no way idiosyncratic, but the organic outgrowth of his engagement with Scripture and Christian thinkers.

Augustine sees the enduring polarity inherent to the figure of the two cities and citizenships expressed in the Old Testament by the images of the cities of Jerusalem and Babylon. It prefigures the polarity he encountered in the confrontation of the Church versus the city and state of Rome. Rome is but a metaphorical *chiffre* or figure for the transitory nature of the world, dramatically underscored by Alaric's pillage of putatively eternal Rome in

---

[30] Cf. *ibid.*, p. 231.
[31] *Ibid.*, p. 296.
[32] Cf. *ibid.*, p. 336, including n. 46. Emphases in the original.
[33] *Ibid.*, p. 337. Emphasis in the original.

410.³⁴ Amid the travails of the world, the *populus Dei* living the sacraments, the Church, owns a dignity unperturbed, as inherently uncontestable in her essential nature by the vicissitudes of history. This comes about through and in the "Opfer des lebendigen Gottes zu sein durch die caritas im Leibe Jesu Christi" (to be the sacrifice of the living God by virtue of being charity in the body of Jesus Christ).³⁵ The Old Testament image of "people of God" anticipates the Christian Church as the definitive people of God, and yet, "*aber ihr empirisches Volk gleichfalls nur Bild ist für das wahre Volk*" (but its empirical people is mere image for the true people).³⁶

Most deliberately, Augustine resists from deriving his understanding of the Church as "house of God" from a theological reflection on a physical church building. Therein one can detect, according to Ratzinger, "a conscious antithesis" to the Old Testament's preliminary and (partially still) pagan, and therefore necessarily superficial understanding of cult centered around the Temple. For this reason Ratzinger interprets Augustine skipping over the House of God concept to "the *living* people of God, of the *ecclesia sive congregatio*" (church or assembly) inchoately hinted at by the physical house of God. In the body of Christ both the adoration and *inhabitatio* (the indwelling) of God occur.³⁷

Ratzinger discovers in his study that Augustine uses terms like *fundamentum, petra, aedificare,* and *compages caritatis* (foundation, rock, to build, and incorporation into charity) to describe the tangible and sacramental reality called the Church. Using such images, he defines the essence of the Church as being grounded in a community of faith and charity in Christ. Little wonder, in the ecclesiology of Augustine the term "house of God" is merely an interpretative tool, but wholly deficient in conveying the essence of the Christian Church. She is the one *catholica* (universal reality) uniting *omnes gentes* (all peoples) to *una gens* (one people). Grounded ontologically in God, she is the *civitas* endowed with the Holy Spirit as "the pilgrim colony on earth."³⁸ The intersection of cult and sacrament generates the body of Christ. This Latin term *corpus Christi* is neither mythical nor blurry, but eminently concrete as the "unus panis—unum corpus sumus multi" (one bread—as one body we are many) as Ratzinger quotes Augustine's memorable line.³⁹

While the terms "people of God" and "city of God" have pre-Christian origins, "the notion of corpus Christi rests on the reality of the sacrificing Church."⁴⁰ In the conclusion to his dissertation, Ratzinger points to the

---

³⁴ Cf. *ibid.*, pp. 346.
³⁵ *Ibid.*, p. 382.
³⁶ *Ibid.*, p. 397.
³⁷ Cf. *ibid.*, p. 412. Emphases in the original.
³⁸ *Ibid.*, p. 414.
³⁹ Cf. *ibid.*, p. 415.
⁴⁰ *Ibid.*, p. 417.

Doctor Gratiae seeing the angels included in the Church. People of God and Body of Christ are not mutually excluding entities. Rather, *Corpus Christi* expresses "the inner reality," which is imperfectly circumscribed by the secular terms *civitas* and *populus*.[41]

Ratzinger concludes with the following observations:

> The Church is the state of the people of God, prefigured in the state of the Hebrew people, through Christ established and led out of the demons' bondage to freedom on the foundation of faith—from ages accessible to the elect in faith—to the unity in charity in his body, built as sacrifice of the one true God, in the war against demons awaiting through him, in the strength and wisdom of God and awaiting in hope the definitive purification and unification in the offering of peace on the seventh day ... Such is the yearning echoing throughout the writings of Augustine: the yearning for eternal peace. He, the one journeying restlessly throughout his life, though restless only for the sake of the final rest, which remained for him in this life constantly his secret restlessness ... However, that he found this rest in no other manner than in charity and in the peace (pax!) of Jesus Christ evidences how truly Christian he has become. Comprehending the one truth of Jesus Christ from within the center of the vitality of his actually lived presence. And thereby of course Augustine stands for all ages.[42]

Thereby Augustine alerts every generation again of the kairotic quality inherent to every moment of human history.

The Augustinian Meaning of *Confessio*

Based on his dissertation but expanding beyond its scope, Ratzinger, while teaching at Freising Seminary in 1957, pens an article for *Revue des Études Augustiennes* on Augustine's understanding of *confessio*: "Originality and Handing Down in Augustine's Term of *confessio*."[43] At first he explores the question whether the term and the meaning of *confessio* are original to Augustine. In the extra-Christian use, i.e., in classical Latin, it simply meant admitting one's criminal offenses at court. This he discovers by comparing the term's usage in the writings of Quintilian (c. 35–100), Livy (c. 64 BC–c. AD 17), and Cicero (106–43). A more positive use of the word is found with Seneca. Mainly, however, this Latin word has a forensic

---

[41] Cf. *ibid*.

[42] *Ibid.*, pp. 317–18. Especially here the attempt was made to stay as close as possible to the style and ductus of the original German text.

[43] J. Ratzinger, "Originalität und Überlieferung in Augustins Begriff der *confessio*," in *JRGS* 1, pp. 457–79.

flavor. Often it is the counter-term to *defensio*. It carries the meaning of "admitting something." An exception to this use Ratzinger notes is found in an anonymous panegyric on Constantine, the son of Constantius in the fourth century, the time when Christian concepts were allowed to enter public discourse. There *confessio* means "*lobpreisen*" (to laud or praise).[44] It comes as no surprise, Ratzinger remarks, that "the bishop Augustine must repeatedly explain to his listeners, that *confiteri* not merely means 'to admit transgressions', but equally 'to praise'."[45] Also the Christian thinkers Jerome (*c.* 347–420), Prosper of Aquitaine (*c.* 390–*c.* 450), Eucherius of Lyon (380–449), and Hilary of Poitiers use the word in its laudatory meaning. Ratzinger concludes that this meaning of the word is "part of an 'old-Christian special use of language'."[46]

Such use is the result of a Christian theology of martyrdom. Over and against pagan conventions in Christ "a revalorization of values" occurs. The true saints are those worshiping the Christian God, who are now considered enemies of the state, atheists, and criminals. Perplexingly to the surrounding pagan imagination, "the confessio turpis ugly admission of guilt becomes the confessio gloriosa glorious witness."[47] The basis for this most ironic shift in meaning is Christian Scripture: "Everyone therefore who acknowledges me before others, I also will acknowledge before my Father in heaven; ... " (Matt 10:32). On this background *confessio* becomes "one of the Lord's most precious words."[48] It emerges also as a counter term to the deniers of the Christian God. And yet, in the spirit of Christian humility one also encounters its original Latin meaning of admitting one's sin in the context of the sacrament of reconciliation. This dual understanding begins with late Judaism and is carried over into Christianity (cf. Tertullian[49]) to Augustine's days.

The Latin term *confessio* is a narrower equivalent to the Greek word *homologia* as found in the Septuagint version of Psalms 47 and 49–51. Redeemed from an existential hardship, the saved believer praises God. Already in the original Hebrew the words *jada,* or *hoda* carry the dual meaning "to praise and profess" Ratzinger remarks. Augustine points out that Origen is mindful of this double meaning when arguing that *eucaristein* (to give thanks) and *exomologeisai* (the penitential rite with public confession of sins that was practiced by early Christians) essentially convey the same in the Eucharist. To these meanings, Ratzinger argues, Augustine brings "a speculative, deeper" meaning (*Vertiefung*) to bear.[50]

---

[44] Cf. *ibid.*, p. 461, n. 14.
[45] *Ibid.*, p. 462.
[46] *Ibid.*
[47] *Ibid.*, p. 464.
[48] "der teuersten Worte des Herrn" in *ibid.*
[49] Tertullian, *Adversus Marcionem* IV, 28, 4.
[50] Cf. *JRGS* 1, p. 469.

Examining *Confessions* X, 1–4, Ratzinger discovers that *confessio*, beyond the Latin lexical meaning, denotes both "doing truth" and "sacrifice" in Augustine's usage. "Let me know thee, O my Knower; let me know thee even as I am known. O Strength of my soul, enter it and prepare it for thyself that thou mayest have and hold it, without 'spot or blemish'."[51] This stands in apparent conflict with John 3: 19f: "This is the verdict: Light has come into the world, but people loved darkness instead of light because their deeds were evil. Everyone who does evil hates the light, and will not come into the light for fear that their deeds will be exposed." Ratzinger sees Augustine resolving the arrest to a state of distance to God by way of the term the redemptive word *confessio*. The universality of grace is in prominent evidence: the human being loves light, overcomes sin by believing God is good, and enters supernatural light by "doing the true." Thereby *confessio* becomes for Augustine a key term in his theology of grace. The human being admits his nullity and recognizes that only to God honor is due.

In this engraced process, confessing sins to God and praising God become one single moment, an "indivisible unit."[52] In the Augustinian synthesis, *confessio* now emerges as an inner event between God and the human soul. "Zu-sich-selbst-Kommen und so ein Hinkommen zu dem Gott" (coming to oneself and coming to God) occur in one word'[53]. As Augustine succinctly formulates: " ... we lay bare our feelings before thee, that, through our confessing to thee our plight and thy mercies toward us, thou mayest go on to free us altogether, as thou hast already begun; and that we may cease to be wretched in ourselves and blessed in thee ...."[54]

There is inherent to the word *confessio* a more realist dynamism than the Roman mind could imagine prior to the advent of Christianity. Augustine repeatedly reminds his Latin-speaking congregation of this latent dual meaning. "The celebrated motto of the *Confessiones* 'inquietum est cor nostrum donec requiescat in te' is unveiled as the description of the *confessio*, having as content the stepping out of the restlessness of this world into the rest of God,"[55] as Ratzinger succinctly observes. Leaving behind the egoistic self also entails a sacrifice that then in turn prepares one for the Eucharist as *logikē thusia*, i.e., as a *Logos*-filled sacrifice. Sacrifice describes for the Church Father unification of man with God. In the form of reconciliation with and return to God, it becomes sacrifice in the strength of the preceding sacrifice Christ had performed—*nota bene* in the strength of Christ, as only Christ stands in perfect union with God the Father. In this sense *Confessio* incorporates the dimension of coming to

---

[51] Augustine, *Confessions* X, 1, 1.
[52] *JRGS* 1, p. 473.
[53] *Ibid.*, p. 474.
[54] Augustine, *Confessions* X, quoted in Latin, *JRGS* 1, pp. 474–5, n. 49.
[55] *JRGS* 1, p. 475.

light in divine effulgence: a "venire ad lucem." Some Hebrew Psalms permit him, the trained Roman orator, to see even the painful process of confessing sins as part of a praise of God.[56]

Knowledge of God

In a 1970 *Festschrift* honoring the Patristic scholar Johannes Quasten (1900–87), Ratzinger describes Augustine's epistemology as regards God.[57] *Pace* Max Scheler (1874–1928), by way of introduction, Ratzinger does not see such great opposition between Augustine's approach to knowledge of God and the more metaphysical approach Aquinas chooses.[58] Famously, for Augustine, insight into matters divine is preceded, but also accompanied by an existential change, by *metanoia*, or conversion. No "*Sinnendinge*" (things of the senses) can contain lasting truth. "As an independent and higher realm of insight the interiority of the spirit stands ... vis-à-vis exterior insight."[59]

Ratzinger cites *Tractatus in Ioannem* 1, 19 to illustrate the point. While even a blind person is aware of the sun when standing in sunlight, there is also a blindness of heart. Playing on the phonetic similarity and yet material dissimilarity of *corpus* and *cor*, it is *corde*, by way of the heart, that the interior of man discovers within himself God. Ratzinger sees Augustine echoing "Blessed are the pure in heart, for they will see God" (Matt 5:8). As the heart of man is never pure, a purgation of the heart must occur. Thereby knowledge of God comes about. A simple logical demonstration will not suffice. Grace somehow acts on ethical efforts on part of the human being. While there does exist a neo-Platonic *ascensus-reditus* (ascent-return) component to Augustine, the ancient Greek exhortation "recognize yourself" is but a first step. This philosophical call, Ratzinger points out, permits Augustine to see Christians overcoming the Jewish cultic understanding of purity, for " ... in cleansing their hearts by faith he has made no distinction between them and us" (Acts 15:9).[60]

And yet, oftentimes a characteristic of philosophy stands in the way: *superbia*, pride. It is overcome by way of deliberate asceticism. While Porphyry (*c*. 234–*c*. 305) values philosophy and *intellectus* as offering provisional purification from magic and cults, Ratzinger finds that Augustine apprehends Christ as the *Logos* (Word) become flesh offering the highest form of purgation. *Fides* is not simply a mental process, but one accompanied by divine grace. While for Platonists there existed an

---

[56] Cf. *ibid.*, pp. 478–9. No Psalms are cited.
[57] Cf. *ibid.*, pp. 511–29.
[58] Cf. This remark remains unsubstantiated. *Ibid.*, pp. 511–12.
[59] *Ibid.*, p. 513: "The interiority of the spirit stands therefore as an independent and higher realm of knowledge as opposed to the external cognition."
[60] *Ibid.*, p. 517.

unbridgeable difference between *soma* (body) and *sema* (sign), martyrs illustrate the dignity of the body, by loving and sacrificing their bodies for Christ.[61] Overcoming this ancient irreconcilable disjuncture between body and soul means for Augustine overcoming all vainglory and actuating the incarnate charity of Christ, which leads to ever greater knowledge of God. Such interiority grounded "in solitude with God" leads then to concrete availability for fellow human beings. Interhuman *caritas* becomes an elongation of the faith path.[62] The intellect needs to become seeing in faith. This Ratzinger summarizes nicely in Augustinian terms: the *reversio in interiorem hominem* (turning to the interior man) results in an *aversio ab exteriore hominem* (a turning away from the exterior man). This is called *metanoia* or conversion. This multi-dimensional process results in *pistis,* or faith expressed in *humilitas* (humility) and *oboedientia* (obedience) which in turn require lived *caritas* or *agape* (charity) to find expression. Ratzinger summarizes: "In the execution of these three steps of purifying conversion man becomes able to behold God."[63] Using Scripture as the basis, for Augustine, the human organ for such "seeing" is the heart.

As God is not merely an objective, impersonal, intellectual reality, but volition and person, an exclusively abstract or intellectual knowledge of God is insufficient. "God's freedom must by necessity correspond to humility and obedience capable of listening on part of the human being."[64] Ratzinger readily admits that even in his late works the African Church Father remains a Platonist of sorts as Augustine does not deny the philosopher who overcomes pride can understand the Blessed Trinity. And yet argues: "Determining the path of religious insight, purgation is ultimately nothing else than an unfolding of charity towards its true form. It is, as made clear in the *Civitas Dei*, in its innermost a handing over to the eternal charity by becoming free of a false love of the world."[65]

The Holy Spirit as *Communio*

Shortly after his essay on knowledge of God in Augustine, Ratzinger offers in 1974 a presentation of Augustine's understanding of the third person of the Blessed Trinity. "The Holy Spirit is recognizable in the way in which he forms human life. A life formed from faith is in turn a sign of the Holy Spirit."[66] The Spirit draws us into the mystery of Christ. The essence of the

---

[61] Cf. *ibid.*, p. 519.
[62] Cf. *ibid.*, pp. 523–4.
[63] *Ibid.*, p. 525.
[64] Cf. *ibid.*, p. 526.
[65] *Ibid.*, p. 529.
[66] *Ibid.*, p. 530. Cf. J. Ratzinger, "The Holy Spirit as *Communio*: Concerning the Relationship of Pneumatology and Spirituality in Augustine," *Communio* 25 (1998), p. 324.

Holy Spirit can only be approximated by way of entry into his holiness. Augustine struggles to objectify this highly subjective process. Using traditional names for the third Person of the Blessed Trinity he attempts approximations:

> As already stated, Augustine attempts to grasp the particular physiognomy of the Holy Spirit by investigating his traditional names, first, the designation "Holy Spirit." But this presents him with an aporia. While the names "Father" and "Son" bring to light what is characteristic of the first and second Persons of the Trinity, the name "Holy Spirit" does not support the presentation of the particularity of the third Person as giving and receiving, i.e. being as gift and being as reception, as word and response—characteristics which are so completely one that unity, not subordination arises within them. On the contrary, each of the two other Persons of the Trinity could be named in this way. Above all, God himself and as such could be named this way since John 4:24 also states: "God is spirit." Being spirit and being holy is the essential description of God. That is what identifies him as God.[67]

For Augustine the Holy Spirit represents both the commonality of God and his unity. "The general name 'Holy Spirit' is the most appropriate way to express him in the paradox characteristic of him—mutuality itself,"[68] What appears as abstract, ontological consubstantiality is actually interpersonal *communio*. In the process of gaining this insight Augustine succeeds in revising our understanding of the divine Spirit. At first he confirms John's statement that "God is spirit" (John 4:24). Yet, Spirit is more than mere opposition to matter:

> as ancient metaphysics had taught. In case of the Holy Spirit it is radical alterity on the basis of the dynamics between Father and Son. *Communio* thereby becomes an essential element of the notion of the Spirit, thus truly giving its content and thoroughly personalizing it. Only one who is familiar with the 'Holy Spirit', can know what spirit means. And only one who begins to know what God is, can know what the Holy Spirit is. Furthermore, only one who begins to have an idea of what the Holy Spirit is, can begin to know who God is.[69]

Such a personalist view is the basis for designating the Spirit as gift and charity. Key to such an understanding is 1 John 4:7-12 plus 16b including verse 13: "Verse 12: If we love one another, God abides in us ... Verse

---

[67] Cf. *ibid.*, p. 532. Cf. *id.*, "The Holy Spirit as *Communio*," p. 326.
[68] *Ibid.*, p. 533. Cf. *id.*, "The Holy Spirit as *Communio*," p. 326.
[69] *JRGS* 1, p. 533. Cf. *id.*, "The Holy Spirit as *Communio*," p. 327.

16b: God is love, and he who abides in love, God abides in him. Verse 13: We recognize that we abide in him and he in us because he has given us of his spirit"[70] as Ratzinger sums up. Combining this with Rom 5:5, the believer discovers that "the love of God is poured out through the Holy Spirit who is given to us."[71] Such charity is the *opus proprium* the defining task of the Holy Spirit. Whence does he come, Augustine asks? Augustine detects via John 4 and 7 in the Spirit not the one born of the Father, but rather the one coming into being as "given" or better gifted: "non quomodo natus, sed quomodo datus" (not insofar as he was born, but under the consideration of his being given)—as gift.[72] This movement of being gifted as gift is the specific charism of the Holy Spirit.

This permits Ratzinger to read Augustine interpreting the immanent Trinity as one completely open to its economic dimensions. In the human petitions of the "Our Father," the Father—in cooperation with the Spirit—lends an ear to human concerns. Paraphrasing *De Trinitate* V 14, 15, Ratzinger summarizes as follows: "He is 'our bread', ours as one who is not ours, as something completely given. 'Our' spirit is not our spirit,"[73] thereby evidencing the Spirit as charity and gift *ad extram* (vis-à-vis the outside). Divine charity's dynamism unfolds itself in salvation history. Ratzinger concludes: "Without love, Augustine says, faith can 'exist but not save', esse non prodesse, in the inimitable Latin of the bishop of Hippo."[74] In the Donatist controversies, Augustine demonstrates that being Christian entails intending the whole, both of the world and of the Church in their respective integrities. Being a Christian sect betrays the Spirit's charity. Unmistakably and succinctly Ratzinger concludes: "The activity of the Spirit is 'the house', the granting of the home, of unity. Because the Spirit is love."[75]

This Augustinian insight into the nature and mission of the Holy Spirit dovetails well with an entry, "Fraternité" (Brotherhood), which Ratzinger had written in French for *Dictionnaire de Spiritualité* in 1964.[76] Divine charity manifests itself as fraternity amongst Christians. However, Augustine cautions that on the basis of divine predestination those outside the Church may actually be within her fold and vice versa. Fraternal embrace must be extended to Donatists and false brethren for the sake of peace and the inner unity of the Church. Ratzinger cites *Enarratio in Psalmo* 48, 8 "Whoever

---

[70] *JRGS* 1, p. 535. Cf. *id.*, "The Holy Spirit as *Communio*," p. 328.

[71] *JRGS* 1, p. 535; italicized in the original German. Cf. *id.*, "The Holy Spirit as *Communio*," p. 328.

[72] Cf. *JRGS* 1, p. 538; italicized in the original German. Cf. *id.*, "The Holy Spirit as *Communio*," p. 330. Ratzinger writes "Geschenkter," correctly rendered into English as "the one gifted as gift," ergo interpreting the Spirit in the double meaning of *donum* and *datum*.

[73] *JRGS* 1, p. 539. Cf. *id.*, "The Holy Spirit as *Communio*," p. 331.

[74] *JRGS* 1, pp. 540–1. Cf. *id.*, "The Holy Spirit as *Communio*," p. 332.

[75] *JRGS* 1, p. 547. Cf. *id.*, "The Holy Spirit as *Communio*," p. 337.

[76] Cf. *id.*, "Fraternité," in M. Viller et al. (eds.), *Dictionnaire de Spiritualité ascétique et mystique* 5 (Paris: Beauchesne, 1964), pp. 1141–67. Translated into German in *JRGS* 1, pp. 608–48.

says to God our Father, says to Christ brother." This Ratzinger connects immediately with *Sermo* 59, 2: reciting "the Our Father prayer unanimously unites Emperor and beggar, servant and master."[77]

Augustine and the Church Once More

In an essay honoring the noted patristic scholar Hugo Rahner (1900–68), Ratzinger visits Augustine's ecclesiology again at the eve of Vatican II in 1961, ten years after his dissertation on the same topic.[78] He notes that Augustine entered at baptism a reality he had little knowledge of. But preaching later "Quantum quisque amat ecclesiam Christi, tantum habet spiritum sanctum" (to the degree one loves Christ's Church, to that degree one possesses the Holy Spirit) indicates the growth of his ecclesiality.[79] As Ratzinger states, this insight is gained later ever again by never surrendering his yearning for solitude and interiorization. The comparison between Martha and Mary in Luke 10:38-42 leads Augustine in *Sermo* 103, 104, 179, and 255 to prioritize contemplative life. The Platonic opposition of the multitude versus the one leads him to apprehend the one God as the proper perspective to appreciate the multifarious and the Church. The amorphous and shapeless *hen* (One) of Plotinus he leaves behind as a Christian and values the vivacity of the Blessed Trinity. Over and against the Donatists, he praises "the love of unity"[80] and hence the Church as "*communio*." In the two women of Luke 10 he sees the tension of two types of life exemplified: that of present labor and the one of future bliss. Yet, he sees the two materially allied in Christian service while on earth as an anticipation of the joys of celestial beatitude. In Mary Augustine perceives a representative of hope pining for the eschatological character of the *unum*. As Ratzinger summarizes the African church father,[81] while on earth the fate of the Christian is exemplified by Martha. This is nothing short of an inversion of Platonic mysticism, Ratzinger remarks, and a turn to an ecclesial piety.[82] "There is even a mode of activity that is the direct result of meditation, namely proclamation and teaching."[83] Such Augustinian unity of active and contemplative life contradicts the interpretations Origen (*c*. 184–*c*. 253) and Jerome had supplied, who valued Mary over Martha.

---

[77] *JRGS* 1, p. 629.
[78] Cf. *ibid*., pp. 480–510. First published as J. Ratzinger, "Die Kirche in der Frömmigkeit des heiligen Augustinus," in J. Daniélou and H. Vorgrimler (eds.), *Sentire cum ecclesiam. Das Bewusstsein der Kirche als gestaltende Kraft der Frömmigkeit. Festschrift für Hugo Rahner zum 60. Geburtstag* (Freiburg: Herder, 1961), pp. 152–75. Reprinted in J. Ratzinger, *Das neue Volk Gottes. Entwürfe zur Ekklesiologie* (Düsseldorf: Patmos, 1969, reprint 1970), pp. 24–48.
[79] *JRGS* 1, p. 480.
[80] *Ibid*., p. 483.
[81] Cf. *ibid*., p. 486.
[82] Cf. *ibid*., p. 487.
[83] *Ibid*., p. 489.

Isidore of Seville (c. 560–636) and Gregory the Great (c. 540–604) follow Origen's interpretation, Ratzinger notes.[84]

Reflecting on *Sermo* 122 and *Enarratio psalmum* 119, 2, Ratzinger registers that Augustine has more success in convincing Gregory the Great and Isidore of the ecclesial meaning of Jacob's Ladder (Gen 28:12), i.e., the angels ascend as well as descend. The story teaches of Christ mercifully turning to his body on earth, the people of God. Until and including Ambrose an exclusively ascending interpretation, i.e., a Christological interpretation, had been dominant: ascending on the stair to the cross of Christ.

This dialectics of ascent and descent one finds prefigured in the early Augustine of the *Confessions* IV 12, 18, when treating the washing of the feet. Christ knocks at the door of his beloved, the Church. Since 391 Augustine finds himself repeatedly torn from contemplative life to serve lovingly his brethren in the body of Christ, though he never ceased to cherish Mary's part. As the scholar Ratzinger observes: "he ever deeper learned to understand and to affirm, that the Christian in this aeon is commissioned for something else; in place of the neo-Platonic mysticism of ascent, which he was able to savor in the vision at Ostia, steps a mysticism of service, which one may define as the actual basic disposition of the Bishop Augustine, as Augustinian spirituality."[85]

Here Ratzinger quotes Augustine again, who captured ecclesial existence in the formula: "Quantum quisque amat ecclesiam Christi, tantum habet spiritum sanctum" (to the degree one loves the Church of Christ, to that degree one possesses the Holy Spirit).[86] Evidencing the presence of the Holy Spirit, the love of Christ and that of his Church, Augustine's brethren are congenial; much as *Corpus Christi* and *Mater Ecclesia* (Mother Church) are. This Augustine is able to appreciate, argues Ratzinger, because he apprehends his brethren, the Church, sacramentally shaped as one from the Eucharistic altar.

At this point Ratzinger refers to one of his great theological inspirations, Henri de Lubac and his seminal study *Corpus Mysticum* (1944). There De Lubac portrays Augustine as viewing the Church through an eminently Eucharistic lens.[87] This perspective was seconded by the one honored in this *Festschrift*, Hugo Rahner SJ (1900–68), who had contributed the pioneering studies *Mater Ecclesia* and *Maria und die Kirche*.[88] There Hugo Rahner

---

[84] Cf. *ibid.*, pp. 490–3.
[85] *Ibid.*, pp. 502–3.
[86] *Ibid.*, p. 504. Cf. Augustine, *Tractatus in Ioannem* 32, 8.
[87] Cf. *JRGS* 1, p. 508. Cf. there n. 93.
[88] Cf. H. Rahner, *Mater Ecclesia: Lobpreis aus dem ersten Jahrtausend christlicher Literatur* (Köln: Benzinger, 1944); *Id.*, *Mary and the Church* (London: Darton, Longman and Todd, 1961); originally printed in 1951. Hugo Rahner's first title has never been translated into English. The *Festschrift* is: J. Daniélou and H. Vorgrimler (eds.), *Sentire Ecclesiam—Das Bewußtsein von der Kirche als gestaltende Kraft der Frömmigkeit. Festschrift zum 60. Geburtstag von H. Rahner* (Freiburg, Basel, Wien: Herder, 1961).

had demonstrated that in the first millennium Christians had understood the Church represented in the sublime *Theotokos* (Mother of God). As Ratzinger summarizes: "Christian piety is according to Augustine piety from the cross, and as such it encompasses the longitudinal and traverse beams, the dimension of length and breadth: it runs to the Father only in unity with the Mother, the holy Church of Jesus Christ."[89]

Civitas Dei in Augustine

The *Civitas Dei* concept is of decisive import for Augustine's thinking. Yet, Ratzinger had given it only passing attention—a mere three pages in his dissertation.[90] This he compensates for when reacting in 1954 to Wilhelm Kamlah's (1905–76) interpretation of Augustine's teaching on *Civitas Dei* with a paper delivered at a conference on Augustine convened in Paris. A Protestant theologian-turned philosopher, Kamlah had anticipated Bultmann's thesis of demythologization and regarded Christianity as having undergone a profound alteration when encountering Greek culture.[91]

Ratzinger notes with surprise that Kamlah also sees *Civitas Dei* denoting *Bürgerschaft Gottes* (God's citizenship), just as Ratzinger had done in his dissertation. However, Kamlah uses Augustine's term *Civitas Dei* to designate merely a (Lutheran) *Gemeinde*, i.e., a parish.[92] Ratzinger takes exception with such an "ideological construction,"[93] which contradicts both scriptural and patristic evidence. Kamlah's claim that *Civitas Dei* stands for a Christian parish is contradicted early on in Christianity by Clement, Tertullian, Origen, and Ambrose (*c.* 340–97). In addition, Ambrose refers to the celestial Jerusalem as the City of God.[94] Kamlah lacks appreciation for the concreteness of the New Testament term *ekklesia* and the allegorical phrase "city of God" as utilized in the Old Testament. Sensitized by the pillage of Rome in 410, Augustine embraces now *a fortiori* the allegorical use of the concept "City of God"; namely, "as an apology against the idolatrous civitas deorum" (i.e., Rome, the city of deities).[95]

Ratzinger elaborates that the *civitas Romanorum* (the state of the Romans) relates to the *civitas Dei* as letter relates to spirit. Rome is but another historic manifestation of the *civitas confusionis* (city of confusion),

---

[89] *JRGS* 1, p. 510.
[90] Cf. *ibid.*, pp. 338–40.
[91] Cf. *ibid.*, pp. 338–9.
[92] Cf. J. Ratzinger, "Herkunft und Sinn der Civitas Dei-Lehre Augustins. Begegnung und Auseinandersetzung mit Wilhelm Kamlah," in *Augustinus Magister II* (Paris: Beauchesne, 1954), pp. 965–79, reprinted in *JRGS* 1, pp. 420–39.
[93] *JRGS* 1, p. 423.
[94] Cf. *ibid.*, p. 425.
[95] *Ibid.*, p. 31.

symbolized in the Old Testament by Babylon. However, the Church as city is *secundum spiritum*, according to the Holy Spirit and thereby owns an eschatological perspective wholly alien to ancient Rome. Ratzinger faults Kamlah for not apprehending the unity of the four interrelated dimensions: empirical, eschatological, sacramental, and personal holiness. Such ecclesial unity is empirical and yet in the *sursum corda* (lift up your hearts) of the Eucharist the faithful express heaven as their actual home, when joining in Christ's sacrifice. Paraphrasing *Confessions* XIV 28, Ratzinger writes, "The center of the city, the point from which it unfolds is her love. The earthly city is marked by a self-love that verges on contempt of God; the city of God is being edified through a love of God verging on contempt of self."[96] Kamlah's categories of empirical, theocratic, and idealistic are ultimately not helpful. The Church is both pneumatic and sacramental. The city of God is the Church as the community of members of the body of Christ. She is "the pneumatic polis of God"[97] on earth within a state. She feels alien and awaits the world to come.

Conclusion

In a restrained way Ratzinger's language is often poetic when turning to Augustine. This is an indication of his inner congeniality with the North African church father.

The Danish philosopher Søren Kierkegaard (1813–55) preached the radical irreconcilability of the world and the gospel.[98] Despite sympathy for Kierkegaard's timely reminder of the necessity of unconditional discipleship, Ratzinger sides with Augustine on this matter and affirms a Christian turn to the world as of defining necessity for authentic Christian discipleship. With Augustine and Kierkegaard, Ratzinger is highly mindful of the non-domesticability of Christian faith and of the Church. Yet, along with Augustine, Ratzinger also knows of the reciprocal dependence of faith and world. Suffering with and for the world is entry into the mercy of Christ, of crucified love.

Pope Benedict XVI presents Augustine as "the first modern human being."[99] Not so much in proving the superior intelligibility of the Christian

---

[96] "The center of the *civitas*, the point from which it unfolds, is its love. The *civitas terrena* is characterized by the *amor sui usque ad contemptum Dei* [the love of self to the contempt of God], the *civitas Dei* is built up by the *amor Dei usque ad contemptum sui* [the love of God to the point of self-contempt]" (*Ibid.*, p. 437).

[97] *Ibid.*, p. 438.

[98] Cf. J. Ratzinger, *Introduction to Christianity* (San Francisco: Ignatius, 2004), p. 39. Cf. *JRGS* 4, pp. 54–5.

[99] *Id.*, "'Unruhig ist unser Herz, bis es ruhet, o Gott, in dir.' Augustinus der erste moderne Mensch. Am Fest des heiligen Augustinus," in *JRGS* 1, pp. 697–703, at p. 697. Homily delivered on the feastday of St. Augustine, published first in 1965.

statement, but in the turn to the interior presence of Christ lies the key to New Evangelization. In a monastic community the *Doctor Gratiae* wished to savor the Word of God, His truth and beauty, for listening to the Word of God is both the content and purpose of human life. In the relative quiet of scholarly pursuits Ratzinger had intended to spend his life savoring the Word of God, and yet was called to serve as archbishop, prefect, and finally as pontiff. In this sense also his rare public statements as pope emeritus from relative monastic seclusion in the Vatican need be understood. "'*Aperi mihi et praedica me!*—Open to me and preach me!' And for Christ's sake, who comes to us in human beings, in their need, in their ordinariness and in their banality, waits for us, in them Christ knocks at our doors."[100]

---

[100] J. Ratzinger, "'Unruhig ist unser Herz, bis es ruhet, o Gott, in dir'," in *JRGS* 1, p. 703.

3

Bonaventure of Bagnoregio: The Metaphysics of History

David González Ginocchio

Introduction

Over the years, Pope Benedict XVI expressed continued appreciation for Giovanni di Fidanza, Bonaventure of Bagnoreggio (1221–74). This admiration was most recently notable in his weekly teachings, as Pope, of the great Fathers and Doctors of the Church, wherein he devoted three consecutive lectures to the Franciscan.[1] Bonaventure is of course an appreciated figure in the Church: he was General of the Franciscan order, was declared Doctor in 1588 by Pope Sixtus V, addressed by fellow Scholastics as the *Doctor seraficus*, and considered by his contemporaries as a representative of the Augustinian-Aristotelian school associated with other Franciscans such as his master Alexander of Hales, Jean de La Rochelle, and to some extent Duns Scotus.

There are many facets of Bonaventure and the Franciscan tradition worth exploring. For example, Keith Douglass Warner[2] has written on the Franciscan spirit with regards to contemporary ecological issues, noting that "Bonaventure's influence on Ratzinger was less in terms of content and

---

[1] Cf. Benedict XVI, *General Audience*, March 3.10.17, 2010.
[2] Cf. K. D. Warner, "Bonaventure in Benedict: Franciscan Wisdom for Human Ecology," in J. Schaefer and T. Winright (eds.), *Environmental Justice and Climate Change: Assessing Pope Benedict XVI's Ecological Vision for the Catholic Church in the United States* (Lanham: Lexington, 2013), pp. 3–18.

more through his thought structure," in the form of a relational metaphysics of the good that permeates creation and history. I believe this is correct, and extends, of course, to Bonaventure's philosophy of history and history of salvation, which Ratzinger studied in depth. So Ratzinger was not only interested in his pastoral labor or his preaching, but also in the implications of his thought: while some may think of him mostly as the Franciscan general or a mystic theologian, Bonaventure was a Master of theology at the University of Paris and undertook nuanced discussions regarding epistemology and metaphysics. I will hence focus on his *Habilitationsschrift* (which was not published in full until the recent edition of the *Gesammelte Schriften* in 2009). Ratzinger narrates in *Milestones*[3] that Michael Schmaus was contrary to some points of view and remarks in Ratzinger's work, mostly in what is now the first section, that dealt with Bonaventure's Scholastic-period thinking on revelation (§§1–7) and salvation history (§§8–11).[4] Ratzinger withdrew these first paragraphs and presented only the second section on Bonaventure's theology of history. The *Collected Works* have now made the complete study available (*JRGS* Bd. 2), curated by Prof. Marianne Schlosser, a Bonaventure scholar.[5]

A reader of Ratzinger may well be glad that we are now able to read this first section: indeed, reading the young professor's *Habilitationsschrift* on Bonaventure's notion of revelation and salvation history is quite an enlightening experience, no less because we are able to get a glimpse of his young, analytic mind at work, as well as experience his methods in action.

---

[3] J. Ratzinger, *Milestones: Memoirs, 1927–1977* (San Francisco: Ignatius, 1998), pp. 106–7.
[4] "Ratzinger gives a sober and respectful explanation of the most pertinent of Schmaus' motives for his rejection: the latter's concern that in the work the young *wissenschaftlicher Forscher* advocated (and projected onto Bonaventure) a 'dangerous modernism that had to lead to the subjectivization of the concept of revelation.' This alleged 'subjectivization,' Ratzinger surmises, must have stemmed, in Schmaus' mind, from the subversion of the older, neo-Scholastic view of revelation as propositional, mere information deposited into the mind of the recipient. So prominent was this older view that, according to Ratzinger, it was at that time commonplace to refer even to sacred scripture in the vernacular simply and directly as 'revelation.' Against this view, 'Ratzinger discerns in his research on Bonaventure a notion of revelation as God's action in the history of redemption (*Heilsgeschichte*), always already grasped by a recipient and interpreted by the receiving subject of the church,'" M. Boulter, *Repetition and Mythos: Ratzinger's Bonaventure and the Meaning of History* (Doctoral Thesis, Maynooth University, 2020), p. 54. In a way, Ratzinger felt somewhat vindicated "from the fact that Vatican Council II did not link its debate on salvation to the already existing patristic term *dispositio* but rather coined for itself, as a borrowing from the German, the expression *historia salutis*," J. Ratzinger, *Principles of Catholic Theology* (San Francisco: Ignatius, 1987), p. 172. We should also acknowledge that although Ratzinger's eschatology falls outside the aims of this chapter, an interpretation of history is ultimately incomplete without it.
[5] J. Ratzinger, *The Theology of History in St. Bonaventure* (Chicago: Franciscan Herald Press, 1989). As the first paragraphs are not available in English, I offer my own translations from the Spanish edition of Ratzinger's Collected Works, quoted henceforth as "*Hab.*" with page numbers corresponding to the Spanish edition; German page numbers appear as *JRGS* 2.

The first paragraph (§1), a general introduction to his dissertation, contains several methodological considerations that may be considered central to his particular way of thinking: the problem of Revelation entails a historical conception, insofar as problems are never *only* "past" or "present." The whole history of thought constitutes a particularly long conversation involving humanity itself. In the particular case of the Church, past doctrines may be considered within their historical context or may be read as part of a greater conversation, thus achieving greater lucidity. It also involves an ecumenical dialogue, a hermeneutical approach, and a contemporary interpretation.[6]

This seems to me a very early example of Ratzinger's "method": he states a problem and embarks on a multifold analysis, by setting up first the *contemporary* understanding of the problem, and then its history, from the first way in which the problem was formulated and the questions it raised, to the various forms of understanding such a problem or cluster of questions through time and the different ways in which religious and philosophical approaches have attempted to deal with it. It is only then that he offers his own "metaphysical" understanding of the question, i.e., how the problem occupies a topological space in Christian thought and practice, and then suggests a way to acknowledge these in contemporary Church practice and discourse. This allows Ratzinger to engage problems as a systematic theologian while also playing into his knowledge of phenomenology, hermeneutics, etc. It also highlights the usefulness of incorporating history, biblical philology, and metaphysics into theology. Without these, a true understanding of the problem would be incomplete; and yet, a merely theoretical approach is insufficient: spiritual practice and the life of saints is where the view of a theologian should ultimately be directed.

In the present paper, however, I will focus mostly on what we may loosely call the "metaphysics of history," that is, the way in which we may say there is a *meaning* in history. This is a true touchstone of Christian thought, as it forces a reflection on its own faith. It is also a point of contention for analogous but different reasons in Bonaventure's times and in the twentieth century, which means Ratzinger found certain inspiration for himself in Bonaventure, in both practical and theological terms. I will divide this chapter in three sections: in the section "Bonaventure and the Sense of History" I will engage with Bonaventure's qualified reappropriation of Joachim of Fiore, his idea of history, and Ratzinger's own reading. The section "Faith and Philosophy" will further highlight in what sense this idea of history goes against "Aristotle" or rather, in a broader sense, against naturalism, implying Ratzinger's idea of the mutual purification(s) of faith and reason. Finally, the section "Metaphysics, History, and Human Nature" will turn back to the way in which Bonaventure's theology of history entails a limit on mankind's ability for *self-realization*, a conviction that would serve Ratzinger when arguing in contemporary settings.

---

[6]Cf. *Hab.*, pp. 17–18; *JRGS* 2, pp. 70–1.

Bonaventure and the Sense of History

History is a nuclear dimension of the Christian faith. Certainly no one can *believe* Christianity's claims are "true" in a meaningful sense if they are not accompanied by a view of human *history* as the theater of actual salvation.[7] It is a fundamental problem because

> the antithesis that exists between salvation—historical and metaphysical theology is not a question of the concepts and constructions of the theology of history but of a basic principle of methodology: of the link between history and faith, of the link between faith and the *factum historicum* of the saving act of God in Jesus Christ and in the whole history of God's covenant with man.[8]

Bonaventure's interest in the theology of history emerges gradually: in a sense, he evolved from the early systematic theological synthesis of his *Commentary on the Sentences*[9] toward the historical-symbolical perspective of his *Collationes in Hexaëmeron*,[10] wherein he aimed to offer a holistic view of the *understanding* of Christian faith.[11] He was not the first one to employ such an approach. Hugh of Saint-Victor's (1096–1141) influence is notable here. "Hugh's thought is far removed from the static approach of Peter Lombard. For him, Christianity is essentially history; the journey, not of a single soul, but of humanity which, issuing from the living God through Christ and in Christ, returns to God for the life of eternity."[12]

Perhaps this endeared him to Ratzinger, who found Scholasticism, in general, an arid method of thought.[13] Before Bonaventure, Ratzinger had

---

[7] Cf. 1 Cor 15:12-17.
[8] J. Ratzinger, *Principles of Catholic Theology*, p. 172.
[9] In I Sent, procem. q. 2, concl.
[10] Bonaventure, "Collationes in Hexaëmeron," *Opera Omnia* 5 (1891), pp. 327–55. See B. McGinn, "The Significance of Bonaventure's Theology of History," *The Journal of Religion* 58 Supplement (1978), pp. 64–81.
[11] Though in In I Sent, procem. q. 3, concl. he notes that theology, as a science, improves our intellect not just *in se*, but also *prout extendit ad affectum* and *ad opus*. In the first regard, theology can be called a speculative science; but with regards to what it produces, it is a practical science. As extensive to affections, moreover, it becomes wisdom.
[12] J. G. Bougerol, *Introduction to the Works of St. Bonaventure* (Paterson: St. Anthony Guil, 1964), p. 38.
[13] J. Ratzinger, *Milestones*, p. 44. Though it should be noted that in *Milestones* he admits that his "difficulties in penetrating the thought of Thomas Aquinas" and his "crystal-clear logic," which was for him "too impersonal," "may also have had something to do with the fact that Arnold Wilmsen, the philosopher who taught us Thomas, presented us with a rigid, neo-Scholastic Thomism that was simply too far afield from my own questions." It should also be said that Ratzinger admired Bonaventure's skills as the General of the Franciscans, an experience he perhaps appreciated more fully after becoming a bishop and

already studied Augustine's view of the Church, which naturally implied a certain conception of man and God's action in time, an unavoidable aspect of Augustine's conversion. "Christ's intervention in time had demonstrated (and Augustine came to realize this more and more) that the road to eternal union with God lay not in flight from temporality, as the neo-Platonists had it, but in the actualization of human temporality in the process of conversion."[14] Augustine contemplated this action through a division of human history in seven ages: five before Christ and one after, awaiting his Second Coming and the eternal seventh age.[15]

Augustine based his division on religious events: from Adam to Noah, from Noah to Abraham, etc. He had no intention of drawing parallels between his age (the last age of history) and a synchronic reading of the Old and New Testaments.[16] Bonaventure will go beyond Augustine, keeping the Christocentric interpretation of history while incorporating the cultural currents of his time. In this, he follows, to an extent, Joachim of Fiore's theory of the *concordia* of significant events between history and the biblical Testaments: through the relation between the Old and New Testaments, Joachim intended to infer correspondences in the historical future and Bonaventure warmly engages in such an exercise. By doing this, he was in a way embracing Joachim while also subtly restraining him, as many Franciscans, the "Spiritualists," had come to believe that with St. Francis, the third age of the Spirit announced by Joachimism had begun.[17]

Pope himself: "Ratzinger noted in his foreword that the 'bitter controversies of the 1260s and 1270s' were 'similar to the post-Conciliar mood which we are experiencing' in the late 1960s. As for methodology, Ratzinger finds Bonaventure evenhandedly discoursing with unruly elements under his care in an effort 'to preserve the unity of the Order'. For Ratzinger, Bonaventure becomes a model for the pastoral use of sound theology to successfully—that is, with charity—resolve threats from unorthodox members of his community," W. L. Patenaude, *Loving in the Present: The Theological and Pastoral Influences of St. Bonaventure's Critical Retrieval of Joachim of Fiore on Joseph Ratzinger/Benedict XVI* (Theology Graduate Thesis, Providence College, 2013), p. 3.

[14] B. McGinn, "The Significance of Bonaventure's Theology of History," p. 74.

[15] Cf. Bonaventure, *Hexaëmeron* 15.

[16] Ratzinger also does not attempt this, which does not mean that the Bible has no import on our understanding of history: "Thus salvation-historical theology in this first phase of the debate is to be defined as a theology that knows itself bound to Scripture as to the witness of the historical acts of God that are man's salvation. In other words, two concepts are combined here that will later be separated: the link to Scripture is essentially also a link to the events it records and to the historical character of these actions, which are the bearers of salvation and, consequently, truly 'salvation history'," *Principles of Catholic Theology*, p. 174.

[17] Franciscan *spirituales*, *Fraticelli* or Zelanti, opposed the "Relaxed" or Conventual Franciscans in their ardent defense of poverty and literal following of St. Francis' rule. Their zeal called into question the idea of possession, and eventually led into the extended discussion of the difference between *usus* (*pauper*), *dominion* and the division of the Order. See G. Castillo, "Dominio y uso en la noción de pobreza de San Buenaventura en la Apología pauperum," *Cauriensia* 11 (2016), pp. 141–55; N. Şenocak, "The Making of Franciscan Poverty," *Revue Mabillon* 24 (2013), pp. 5–26.

Bonaventure reads history in light of the Scripture, which (following Augustine), presents a "supernatural vision" of the ages of the world, "from its origin to its fulfilment."[18] Already in the *Breviloquium*, composed in 1257 (shortly after being appointed General of the Franciscans), he moves from the standard style of doctrinal compendia in Scholasticism to a "brief summary of true theology" with a historical perspective, beginning with the Trinity, and dealing with creation, the Fall, the Incarnation, Grace, and the Final Judgment. Bonaventure would only expand this view throughout his career. The *Collationes in Hexaëmeron*, for example, read *Genesis* in an Augustinian fashion, linking the symbolic creation of the world in six days and the ages of history,[19] with Christ acting as the Exemplar of creation and, through his Incarnation, the principle of redemption of the material world.

Ratzinger found this symbolic-historic interpretation of history and dogma fascinating: a living example of the individual richness of Scholastic thought in an age seemingly absorbed by standardized exegesis.[20] According to Bonaventure, we are living through *both* the sixth historical age from Adam and the seventh age of the repose of souls in Christ, awaiting the eight

---

[18] J. G. Bougerol, *Introduction to the Works of St. Bonaventure*, p. 92.

[19] Bonaventure, *Hexaëmeron* 3, §24.

[20] But see also Heidegger's view in the conclusion to his own *Habilitationsschrift* on Scotus: "Thus, what also is found throughout the whole of the medieval worldview—just because it is so radical in its conscious teleological orientation—is a whole world of multifarious differentiations of value. *The possibilities of experience and the fullness of experience resulting from this for subjectivity are accordingly conditioned by that dimension of spiritual life that stretches into the transcendent and not like today by the breadth of its fleeting content.* In this attitude of life running its course broadly on the surface of things, the possibilities of mounting uncertainty and complete disorientation are much greater and almost limitless, whereas in contrast the basic development of the form of life of medieval man from the outset did not in any way lose itself in the breadth of content of sensible reality and anchor itself there. Rather, it subordinated this very sensible reality—as something in need of being anchored—to the necessity of a transcendent goal. What is opened up in the concept of living spirit and its relation to the metaphysical 'origin' is an insight into its basic metaphysical structure in which the uniqueness, the individuality, of its acts is joined together in a living unity with the universal validity, the subsisting-in-itself, of sense. Looking at this from the side of the objects involved, what stands before us is the problem of the relation between time and eternity, change and absolute validity, world and God, a problem that in terms of theory of science finds itself reflected in history (formation of values) and philosophy (validity of values). *If we keep in mind the deeper essence of philosophy as worldview, then even the conception of the Christian philosophy of the Middle Ages as a Scholasticism that stood in conflict with the mysticism of this period must be exposed as a fundamental error. Scholasticism and mysticism belong together essentially in the medieval worldview. The two pairs of 'opposites'—rationalism-irrationalism and Scholasticism-mysticism—do not coincide with one another. And when one attempts to equate them, such an attempt is based on an extreme rationalization of philosophy. Philosophy as a rationalistic construction detached from life is powerless—mysticism as irrational experience is without a goal,*" M. Heidegger, *Supplements: From the Earliest Essays to Being and Time and Beyond* (Albany: State University of New York Press, 2002), p. 68; emphasis mine.

age of eternity.²¹ From a historical perspective, this sixth age can better be known by comparing the Old and New Testaments in diverse ways.²²

As noted by McGinn, the sixteenth *collation* incorporates a Joachite scheme in which three ages "mutually *both succeed and correspond* to each other,"²³ namely the seven days of creation and the seven ages of both Testaments. While Bonaventure retains a historical perspective (*tempus originalia*), his schemes also integrate an allegorical (*figuralia*) and salvific dimension,²⁴ so we find a triple reading of every age. The fourth age, for example, is that of Light, the establishment of the Law, the conversion of Gallia, Britannia, Germania, etc.²⁵ Hence his conviction that the seventh day was that of peace after God's creation and of Christ's birth and should correspond to a peaceful time for the Church, but only after times of strife: as in creation there was light, followed by darkness and then light again, Bonaventure draws the comparison between the Old Testament at the time of the prophets and captivity, and the current age of the Church at the time of Henry IV and Frederick II.

All in all, Bonaventure's reading is theological, and it attempts to incorporate human history into a theological scheme and not the other way around. That is why it is such an encompassing, complex view that nevertheless retains Christ as its focus.²⁶ This is why he ultimately rejects the

> Joachite conception of the abolition of the Gospel—the coming Third Age of the Holy Spirit—a view that had been advanced by the Franciscan Herard of Borgo San Donnino. As he said in *Collation* 16.21: "After the New Testament there will not be another nor can any sacrament of the New Law be abrogated, because it is the Eternal Testament". Even a

---

²¹ Cf. Bonaventure, *Hexaëmeron* 15, §§17–18.

²² "In each case, it is only in the first comparison, that in terms of unity, where the usual relation of the Old Testament to the New Testament as that of letter to spirit is maintained. The others are forms of historical comparisons based upon a letter-to-letter connection. [...] Anyone familiar with the history of medieval exegesis cannot fail to catch the accents of Joachim of Fiore in these views," B. McGinn, "The Significance of Bonaventure's Theology of History," p. 68. The first comparison hinges on its *spirit* (Bonaventure, *Hexaëmeron* 15, §23): from *timorem-litteram-figuram* to *amorem-spiritum-veritatem*; the second distinction is according to *dualitatis*: the Old Testament has *tempus ante legem* and *sub lege* while the New Testament has a *tempus vocationis gentium* and a *tempus vocationis Iudaeorum* (Bonaventure *Hexaëmeron* 15, §24) etc.

²³ B. McGinn, "The Significance of Bonaventure's Theology of History," p. 68.

²⁴ Cf. *Temporal gratiosa*; Bonaventure, *Hexaëmeron* 16, §11.

²⁵ Cf. *ibid.*, 16, §§13 and 24.

²⁶ "In true Bonaventuran fashion we can summarize his theology of history under seven headings. The vision is scriptural in basis and historicizing in tendency. It is cosmic in import (i.e., the formation of the cosmos is the image of history) and organic in its view of the relation of one age to another. Apocalyptic in its expectation of the approach of a new age, it is optimistic in its hope for a better time to come before the end of the world," McGinn, "The Significance of Bonaventure's Theology of History," p. 72.

cursory reading of the *Collationes in Hexaëmeron* indicates that Christ is the center of all history and the source of all knowledge, historical, philosophical, or theological.[27]

While it is simply not precise to regard Ratzinger as a *disciple* of Bonaventure, he is evidently a thankful reader that finds many personal insights echoed or even anticipated in him, and it is remarkable indeed how Ratzinger and Bonaventure's intellectual paths resemble each other in some respects.[28]

Faith and Philosophy

Even if we do not find Bonaventure's historical insights compelling, what a contemporary reader may appreciate is his overall aim to reconcile faith and reason, or theoretical and empirical thought. In a broader sense, the issue is not just whether Scripture or prophecy allows for an allegorical reading of history, but whether history *itself* allows for the kind of articulation that could derive *meaning* from it. To understand what it is that Bonaventure was trying to do, we must turn not only to Joachim, but to the increasing presence of Aristotle and the long secularizing process of European universities, in which science seemed to gradually deconstruct and limit the purview of theology.[29] At this time, Aristotle was being universally adopted by the faculties of Arts, giving way to the development of "Latin Averroism," which held that theology and philosophy have distinct methods and ways of knowing. While this in itself could be read in a positive, collaborative sense, the perceived danger was in the belief that while philosophy could certainly not deduct revealed truth, perhaps revealed truth was in the end something rather different from the kind of rational discourse espoused by philosophy. In other words, perhaps philosophy dealt with actual rational proof, while theology was the domain of dogma, requiring a different, non-scientific kind of reasoning. Three main doctrines were hard to reconcile with Aristotle,

---

[27] *Ibid.*, pp. 72–3.
[28] Ratzinger himself had acknowledged the parallels between the post-Vatican II Church and that of Bonaventure's times in his *Theology of History* (pp. xiii–xiv), and he openly admires Bonaventure's pastoral abilities. While he "may not agree with every detail of Bonaventure's correction of unorthodox elements under his care, the pastoral and theological methodology employed by the Franciscan General helped shape Ratzinger's understanding of eschatology, ecclesiology, and the commandment to sacrificially love God and one's neighbor here, now and radically," W. L. Patenaude, *Loving in the Present: The Theological and Pastoral Influences of St. Bonaventure's Critical Retrieval of Joachim of Fiore on Joseph Ratzinger/Benedict XVI* (Theology Graduate Thesis, Providence College, 2013), pp. 3–4.
[29] Cf. R. Pasnau, "The Latin Aristotle," in C. Shields (ed.), *The Oxford Handbook of Aristotle* (New York: Oxford University Press, 2012), pp. 665–90; D. A. Callus, "Introduction of Aristotelian Learning to Oxford," *Proceedings of the British Academy* 29 (1943), pp. 229–81.

the *"philosophorum princeps"*: the immortality of the soul, the created character of the world, and the question of the ultimate happiness of man.[30]

Bonaventure certainly tries to make faith and reason compatible: the latter should be able to interpret the signs in Scripture, to take the appropriate schemata from the relation between the tale of creation and the unfolding of God's action in the Old and New Testaments, but a theologian should only do so by placing Christ as the central reading key of the whole exegesis. Reason's participation is essential in this project, but its proper place can only be fully appreciated when considered as a search for *sapientia*, knowledge aided by faith.[31] When this role is usurped by a rationalization of faith, and not as the relevant concourse of the mind in order to shape a theological system of thought, but as if the knowledge of faith was just a milestone in the historical development *of reason*, then an immanent futurology trades places with theology. Bonaventure would face extreme forms of this endeavor, from both the Aristotelian rationalists and the Spiritual Franciscans who anticipated an immanent *eschaton*.[32]

Both the separation of faith and philosophy and the dialectical consideration of history as a process that will culminate in a definitive immanent age imply the substitution of supernatural hope for the optimism of progress. Bonaventure himself was both not an optimist in this sense *and* he was an Aristotelian, if not a "pure" one like the Latin Averroists.[33]

---

[30] Cf. S. Ebbesen, "Averroism," in *The Routledge Encyclopedia of Philosophy* (Taylor and Francis, 1998), https://www.rep.routledge.com/articles/thematic/averroism/v-1

[31] For Bonaventure, *sapientia involves* "both theology and philosophy, the relationship between these two disciplines, and finally the foundational unity of all knowledge," C. M. Cullen, *Bonaventure* (Oxford: Oxford University Press, 2006), p. 24. Thus, while *communiter* it means the general knowledge of all things, it is *proprie* the cognition of God unto the union of our minds with God (*stricte*). Reason is certainly not excluded from this search, because wisdom and truth are metaphysically united.

[32] As I intend to show below, both rationalism and Joachimism are not as far apart in this regard as they may seem. Some contemporary authors have actually postulated that Joachim's theories served as an inspiration for modernity: "The common background idea for scholars like Karl Löwith, Eric Voegelin, Norman Cohn, and Jacob Taubes was that Joachim of Fiore with his Three Ages theory stating the supremacy of the kingdom of Holy Spirit imbued with spirit of love and justice started a process in which Christian eschatology was 'immanentized' (Voegelin) or 'secularized' (Löwith), or it was even declared that 'immanence directs itself polemically against theological transcendence' (Carl Schmitt). The four authors recognized the transformation of Christian eschatology into ideologies of inner-worldly progress as the decisive formative power of modernity," I. Leitane, "Transcendence and Immanence," in A. L. C. Runehov and L. Oviedo (eds.), *Encyclopedia of Sciences and Religions* (Dordrecht: Springer, 2013), p. 2279.

[33] Cf. the words of Longpré: his "system" was "neither a corrected form of Aristotelianism nor the thought of Avicenna or Avicebron more or less purified, but the authentic philosophical and theological teaching of Augustine, translated by the most ardent of all Franciscan souls, and entirely aimed toward the peace of that contemplation whose model is Saint Francis stigmatized on Mount Alverno," *Saint Augustin et la pensée franciscaine*, quoted in J. G. Bougerol, *Introduction to the Works of St. Bonaventure*, p. 31.

His *Collationes* (including the *Collationes de decem praeceptis* of 1267 and the *Collationes de septem donis* the next year) can be read as part of a larger program against rationalism. Nevertheless, he recognized Aristotle's authority as a master of natural philosophy,[34] and realized the need to study and comment on his metaphysics, even if he was certain that some doctrines are knowledgeable by faith and thus the rationalistic errors were repugnant to reason (e.g., the eternity of the world). It is worth noting that Bonaventure argues extensively against the eternity of the world, but in Aristotelian terms he is able only to provide approximate or hypothetical arguments and not a straight refutation: the arguments themselves are taken from Aristotle's idea that the existence of an actual infinity is impossible.[35] Notably, Scotus holds a similar opinion:[36] as many properties of a substance can only be known through *propter quid* demonstrations after the knowledge of the subject, and many subjects are not *naturaliter cognoscibilia* for us, we are prone to error. For Bonaventure, ancient philosophers could only look at truth *quasi per umbram et de longinquo*.[37]

Bonaventure himself was not wholly opposed to Aristotle and after reading Aristotle on the eternity of the material universe, sought to understand his argument. Ratzinger actually speaks of two lines of opposition to Aristotle in Bonaventure: an "objective-metaphysical opposition" shown here against the eternity of the world, and a "prophetic-eschatological line." While the first line has to do with natural philosophy, Ratzinger conceives the second one against the rationalistic understanding of history, "an eschatological

---

[34] Cf. *Hab.*, p. 569 (*JRGS* 2, p. 641).

[35] See F. J. Kovach, "The Question of the Eternity of the World in St. Bonaventure and St. Thomas—A Critical Analysis," *The Southwestern Journal of Philosophy* 5 (1974), pp. 141–72. Aquinas holds an analogous position in his *De aeternitate mundi*: he does not claim that the world was not created, but that it *seems* to be possible to hold both that the world is created and that has no temporal beginning: "Thus, it is clear that there is no contradiction in saying that something made by God has always existed. Indeed, if there were some contradiction, it would be amazing that Augustine failed to see it, for exposing such a contradiction would be a most effective way of proving that the world is not eternal, and although Augustine offers many arguments against the eternity of the world in XI and XII *De Civitate Dei*, he never argues that his opponents' view is contradictory." He also considers the argument by Bonaventure and others that this would imply the existence of an infinite number of souls: "if the world had always existed, these people argue, there would necessarily be an infinite number of souls. But this argument is not to the point, for God could have made the world without making men or creatures with souls, or he could have made men when in fact he did make them, even if he had made the rest of the world from eternity. In either case, an infinite number of souls would not remain after the bodies had passed away. Furthermore, it has not yet been demonstrated that God cannot cause an infinite number of things to exist simultaneously," T. Aquinas, *On the Eternity of the World* (1997).

[36] Cf. Duns Scotus, *Ordinatio* prol. 1ª pars, q. un., 41. Scotus enumerates some of these errors: the knowledge of the Trinity, of the free creation of the universe, on the number of separated substances according to cosmological movements etc.

[37] In I Sent, d. III, 1ª pars, cap. I, concl.

phenomenon in Aristotle, or in heretical Aristotelianism. Here was the Beast that was to rise from the abyss."[38]

It is understandable, then, that the three sets of *collationes* argue against Averroism, or in other words, rationalism.[39] Bonaventure criticizes the views of an eternal material world, the unity of intellect, as well as a deterministic Ethics. His arguments adopt a theological perspective, taking the Commandments as a starting point to argue for the closeness of the soul to God, as well as taking God's gifts as a source of intellectual and practical orientation. This does not mean that theology makes away with philosophy; rather the opposite: theology needs philosophy even if philosophy by itself is not enough to guide the mind in its journey to God. In other words, both reason and faith have an important role in keeping each other clear of their particular wrongful inclinations, either blind fideism or an über-rational systematization that renders faith superfluous. This, of course, can be understood in line with Ratzinger's view, as he noted in his dialogue with Habermas:

> there exist *pathologies in religion* that are extremely dangerous and that make it necessary to see the divine light of reason as a "controlling organ." Religion must continually allow itself to be purified and structured by reason; and this was the view of the Church Fathers, too. However, we have also seen in the course of our reflections that there are also *pathologies of reason*, although mankind in general is not as conscious of this fact today. [...] It is important that both great components of the Western culture learn to *listen* and to accept a genuine relatedness to these other cultures, too. It is important to include the other cultures in the attempt at a polyphonic relatedness, in which they themselves are receptive to the essential complementarity of reason and faith, so that a universal process of purifications (in the plural!) can proceed.[40]

The method of Bonaventure's writings seems like an attempt at these mutual purifications: he employs faith as the guide and starting point to a similar process of purification in which reason is not set up against revelation

---

[38] J. Ratzinger, *The Theology of History in St. Bonaventure*, pp. 148–9.

[39] "The historico-theological anti-Aristotelianism which develops after 1267 must be clearly distinguished from this objective anti-Aristotelianism. This second development is directed not primarily against the historical Aristotle but against the contemporary form of Aristotelianism. It is a battle against a self-sufficient philosophy standing over against the faith. Thus, his anti-Aristotelian ism develops here into a general anti-philosophical attitude. In this case, the rejection of Aristotle is the rejection of a self-sufficient philosophy. This does not, however, exclude the recognition of philosophy and of Aristotle in their proper place. Philosophy must be integrated into the truth coming from Revelation," *ibid.*, pp. 159–60; *Hab.*, pp. 569–70; *JRGS* 2, p. 641.

[40] J. Habermas and J. Ratzinger, *Dialectics of Secularization: On Reason and Religion* (San Francisco: Ignatius, 2006), pp. 77 and 79.

but rather brings its own methods to help ascertain a clearer understanding. From this perspective, Latin Averroism becomes a wholly rational account, inimical to the understanding of faith.

> Nothing could be more obvious than that this sign of the crisis of the sixth age was borne in upon the mind of the Franciscan by the conflict over radical Aristotelianism that broke out at the University of Paris in the 1260s and raged into the 1270s. As Ratzinger has shown, however, this polemic is based upon a fundamental difference regarding the concept of time which had separated Bonaventure from Aristotle at the very beginning of his teaching career.[41]

Turning, then, to the central question of the meaning of history, we must assume that Aristotle is right in pointing out that history, *by itself*, has no clear and distinct *logos*, in the sense of an overarching meaning. According to Aristotle, while we may speak of *teloi* in natural processes, history, understood as the continued whole of human actions, is *kata symbebekós*.[42] The integration of a stream of actions into a complete whole (the *plot, mythos*) is a *synthesis ton pragmaton*.[43] From within, history is built upon free actions, not by necessity; there is no logical, necessary connection between my actions and the actions of others. Indeed, while some events naturally flow from others, discrete actions are not preceded by necessity.[44] My actions have an effect on the physical world, which will undoubtedly affect the way others can inhabit it; in this sense, my actions influence others, but this influence cannot mean that what I do determines others' freedom. History stems from character. Free will is an essential attribute of mankind's actions, turning history as a whole into something too big for us to grasp.[45] In a way, this signals to the Augustinian mystery of the two cities that will only achieve a final *catastrophe* through supernatural intervention. By itself, history fails to provide the basic building blocks of science: a chain of necessarily caused events that can be logically construed into necessary, causal explanations (*kathólou*). This is why Aristotle finds poetry more "philosophic" than history: because a poet can actually *build* up the meaning of a particular (enclosed) set of actions, which in themselves

---

[41] B. McGinn, "The Significance of Bonaventure's Theology of History," p. 70.
[42] "*Poiêsis* is more philosophic and of more stature than history. For poetry speaks rather of the general things while history speaks of the particular things. The general, that it falls to a certain sort of man to say or do certain sorts of thing according to the likely or the necessary, is what poetry aims at in attaching names.But the particular is what Alcibiades did or what he suffered," Aristotle, *Poetics*, D. W. Lucas (ed.) (Oxford: Clarendon Press, 1968), 1451b1–11.
[43] Cf. Aristotle, *Poetics* 1450a 4–5.
[44] Cf. *ibid.*, 1450b 29–30.
[45] Hence why Homer selected only a fragment of the war in his *Iliad*; a full consideration of the events in Troy would exceed our capacity to view them in a dramatic fashion, "in a single view" (cf. *ibid.*, 1459a 30–7).

are only particular (*kath' ekaston*). To say that there is no immanent *mythos* means that human actions are not necessarily built from the beginning so that they form by themselves an overarching plot: human history has to do with particulars, and for Aristotle there is no theoretical science of the particulars, which can occur in one way or another. Human action can be studied, however, in the way of *practical* sciences, as a way of discerning "with reason," *meta logou*[46] what is beneficial and detrimental for men, in line with their proper good. But this is all open to freedom, while a determinate set of actions as the poet narrates them is not.

Bonaventure's objection to the idea of history as lacking meaning does not refer specifically to the distinction between theoretical and practical sciences, but rather to the general "rationalistic" view that there is *no* rational approach to history *at all*. Such an approach would certainly not be philosophical as philosophy was then understood, but then reason is not only philosophy, and as theologian Bonaventure is right to call for a deeper and wider sense of reason:

> [I]n the case of the later Bonaventure, practically nothing has changed as regards the inner understanding of the philosophical and theological problems. In as far as he philosophizes and theologizes, he does so with the same materials and the same methods as he had used earlier. But there is a new element involved which may be called extraphilosophical, or extra-theological if we understand theology in the restricted sense of speculative-Scholastic, systematic theology.[47]

Poetry is more philosophic than history, according to Aristotle, because it speaks of general things, or *types*, thus framing what is free (that is to say, not necessary or incidental), human action, as if it had a *reason* for being, as if it was itself *meta logou*. Aristotle cannot of course fathom a way for bending the whole of human history while preserving the actual freedom of human beings, but Bonaventure can, by accounting for a higher recapitulation of freedom. This is why in his *Hexaëmeron* the whole of history is measured by *Christus medium*: a *medium* by essence, nature, distance, doctrine, moderation, justice, and concord.[48] This is the differential thesis brought by Christianity, one which Ratzinger knows well by studying both Augustine and Bonaventure's salvation history: the whole of human history, according to Christianity, can be read as the ultimate story, and Bonaventure claims we already have a key to access this standpoint, as it has been made accessible to us by looking into the correspondences between both Testaments and

---

[46] Cf. Aristotle, *Nicomachean Ethics*, C. Rowe (ed.) (Oxford: Oxford University Press, 2002), 1140b22.
[47] J. Ratzinger, *The Theology of History in St. Bonaventure*, p. 161; *Hab.*, 571; *JRGS* 2, 643.
[48] Cf. Bonaventure, *Hexaëmeron* 1, §10.

human events, read in the light of the creation *myhos* of *Genesis* and the fulfillment of its promises in Christ's *Pascha*.

Bonaventure's own view of history is built upon grace, which descends upon man "through the Incarnate Word, principle of our re-creation; through the Crucified Word, principle of our resurrection; through the Inspired Word, principle of our sanctification."[49] These are received as *habits* in our mind, e.g., as a gift of knowledge that allows us to consider the truth of a thing (philosophy), the truth of faith (theology), the truth of our love (contemplation), and finally the preternatural light of revealed glory in heaven (a subject on which Bonaventure planned to expand in the *Hexaëmeron*). Bonaventure's psychology makes thus no attempt to surgically separate natural and supernatural knowledge.

The gift of understanding (*dono intellectus*) helps us fathom the spiritual sense of things. It is the gift of faith as applied to temper rationalistic errors, as Bonaventure makes clear by enumerating, again, Averroes' mistakes. These mistakes have three roots: one against the cause of being, the second against the *ratio* of understanding, and the third against the order of life.

> The error against the cause of being is the eternity of the world, that is to say, to affirm the world is eternal. The error against the *ratio* of understanding is that of fatal necessity, as to say that everything that happens does so out of necessity. The third is the unity of the human intellect, as when saying that there is the one intellect in all. These errors are signified in the *Apocalypse* by the number of the beast, which is there said to have a name and whose number is six hundred and sixty six, a cyclical number.[50]

Bonaventure's reasoning here is noteworthy: the nature of the number of the beast (a cyclical number with three circles)[51] refers to an incorrect assumption of natural philosophy, namely, the eternal circularity of movement and time (first error), of the motion of the heavens (second error), and of intellection (third error). These theses are false because they deny free will and banalize any difference between merit and gift, *si una est anima*. It is after showing how the three errors contradict faith that Bonaventure provides a detailed rational argument against them (showing how the purifying of faith and reason may be performed). To the first error he answers that God has to be the total cause of beings, and this can only

---

[49] J. G. Bougerol, *Introduction to the Works of St. Bonaventure*, p. 129.
[50] Bonaventure, *Collationes de septem donis* 8 (1891), §16.
[51] The Quaracchi editors refer here to Rupert of Deutz and Richard of St. Victor, whose commentaries on the Apocalypse show that the cyclical number can be seen as that of the Antichrist because it doubles and then multiplies the number of the Trinity referring also to the sixth day, that of the creation of man.

mean creation *ex nihilo*.⁵² To the second, that man's path in life cannot be determined by the stars, which are created and ordered by God, "as it would follow that God would be the origin of evil."⁵³ And finally, the unity of intellect goes against individuality and the principle of distinction, and "while some say that one intellect irradiates over all, this is impossible, for no creature can do this. Only God."⁵⁴

The *Collationes in Hexaëmeron* continues this historical, systematical exposition of Christian doctrine. As a whole, it is a very dynamic text, in which different approaches are founded upon grace and lead the soul to a growing ascension and understanding in the road to the gift of wisdom (a journey detailed in his *Itinerarium*). In the *Hexaëmeron* he begins with the light or vision of intelligence or natural reason,⁵⁵ then its continuation by faith,⁵⁶ and Scripture.⁵⁷ In *Hex*,⁵⁸ Bonaventure warns against the use of "Aristotle," meaning here the abuse of philosophy ("he is not simply rejecting—as is clear from a cursory reading of any of his early, middle, or late works—either the discipline of Aristotelian *epistêmê* or the thirteenth-century Christian equivalent of the same. Rather, he is protesting the use of Aristotelian *epistêmai* in an autonomous manner").⁵⁹ Theology, read through the Bible and the Fathers, should occupy the first place. This opens the way for the last visions: that of intelligence illuminated by contemplation,⁶⁰ prophecy, rapture, and glory (Bonaventure did not have the opportunity to lecture on the latter three). The dynamic nature of natural understanding, ascending with the help of Scripture and faith to the contemplation of God, materializes the way in which reason is effectively expanded so as to make use of God's aid while engaging in its own search.

Metaphysics, History, and Human Nature

Just as Bonaventure's commentaries⁶¹ should be read in light of the historical presence of Averroism in the University of Paris, they are also a meditation on God's free action in history. Ratzinger faced a similar problem when dealing broadly with a materialist comprehension of history and his engagement of Marxism and liberation theology. Both had to contend with a false

---

⁵²Cf. Bonaventure, *De septem donis* 8, §17.
⁵³*Ibid.*, §18.
⁵⁴*Ibid.*, §19.
⁵⁵*Id.*, *Hexaëmeron* 1, §§4–7.
⁵⁶*Ibid.*, §§8–12.
⁵⁷*Ibid.*, §§13–18.
⁵⁸*Ibid.*, §19.
⁵⁹Cf. M. Boulter, *Repetition and Mythos*, p. 58.
⁶⁰Cf. Bonaventure, *Hexaëmeron* 1, §§20–3.
⁶¹*Id.*, *Commentaria in Quatuor Libros Sententiarum Magistri Petri Lombardi* 1 (1882).

sense of historicity, or the *telos* of history, which we may, in lieu of a better term, call "false spiritualism." The main point of my reading here is that both the liberation theology criticized by Ratzinger and the form of Joachimism opposed by Bonaventure suggest that history is a closed, immanent situation that can only be resolved from within, so that an ultimate intervention in history can only adopt the form of an "utopian hereafter."

William Patenaude made the argument that Bonaventure provided Ratzinger with the resources to proclaim Christian action "in the present," as opposed to "a retreat into a privatized form of religious individualism or sectarianism that minimizes or excludes charity toward other humans and the world generally; or a godless eschatology rooted in the hope that human suffering can be eliminated through rational politics and technological power."[62] If Joachimism and a certain strand of liberation theology can be read as a false spiritualism, it is precisely because they appeal to an immanent comprehension of history in which it is man, and not God, who performs the *synthesis ton pragmaton*, the unity of all actions and processes into a culminating age of peace. In this way, history becomes the *theathrón* of man and not God's action.[63]

As we have mentioned, Bonaventure maintains Christ at the center, but in a new way, since "for Augustine, as for all early Christian thinkers, Christ is the beginning of the end of time, whereas for Bonaventure in dependence on Joachim he is the middle of time."[64] Hence, Augustine fixes his gaze on the inner history of the soul, while Bonaventure aims to link this inner view with a comprehensive understanding of all of human history. "Bonaventure is apocalyptic and optimistic in the hope that he holds out for the imminent seventh age; Augustine was notably antiapocalyptic and pessimistic in his view of the future."[65] At any rate, they conceive the end of history as an event originating from the outside of history. "Thus, the alluring ideas of millennium and Sabbath Age were placed outside the range of visionary speculation on a climax to history. For the medieval disciples of St. Augustine that climax was already past. The space between the First and

---

[62] W. L. Patenaude, "Loving in the Present," p. 2.

[63] "Thus, it almost seems, at the moment, as though the idea of salvation history, which has only recently made its appearance in Catholic theology, will soon be extinguished. In fact, it was not really pursued in the form in which Cullmann understood it but was converted almost at once into the new guise of a theology of hope, which, in turn, quickly assumed concrete form as political theology, theology of liberation, theology of revolution. Bultmann's existential formalism was, in fact, abandoned, but, though itself unable to survive because of its total contentual hollowness, it had prepared the way for the new concept by its relativization of past history and, ipso facto, of its Christian content. With political 'theologies,' theology as theology has been abandoned, the self-destruction of theology has been accomplished," J. Ratzinger, *Principles of Catholic Theology*, p. 180.

[64] B. McGinn, "The Significance of Bonaventure's Theology of History," p. 75.

[65] *Ibid.*

Second Advents was one of waiting, a period in which nothing significant happens except the garnering of souls."[66]

For the Spiritualist Franciscans, following Joachite doctrines, the second age of the Son was past, and St. Francis announces the beginning of the third age of the Spirit. In a third age, Christ, his Cross and Gospel would be replaced with the Holy Spirit and a utopian historic development, implying the end of all institutions and structures and signaling a time of eternal peace. Joachim himself seems to suggest this is just a manner of speaking, as the whole of history "pertains simultaneously to the Father, Son, and Spirit."[67] We must then consider not only what Joachim himself taught—still a matter of debate—but the way his teachings were received. There is certain debate in whether a new spiritual Church would replace or renew the old. For the matter at hand, "the crucial point here is that—however mystically conceived—it is still a new stage of *history* which he envisages,"[68] a seventh day that precedes the eight day of eternity and encapsulates the internal necessity of history.

Bonaventure is inspired by Joachim but is not a Joachite himself;[69] he does not believe in the third age of the Spirit, and he does not conceive a new Gospel that can abolish the former. Still, there are important similarities: the immanent hope for a coming age of contemplation, the view of Scripture as the deciphering code with which to read the signs of the times, and the opposition to a rationalistic philosophy that had no room for Christ. Indeed, "Joachim's view of history is not fundamentally Christocentric. This is not to say that Christ does not play an important role in the abbot's thought; but significant as that role is, it does not dominate the total structure of understanding of history as it does in Augustine and Bonaventure."[70]

My argument here is that Ratzinger recovers the fundamental insights of Bonaventure and develops them on his own when he opposes the idea of history as dominated by an internal sense of progress owing to mankind's inherent ingenuity. This is an important theme in order to read his commentaries on earthly power and scientific development. Ratzinger is not, of course, against progress and even has lauded the Enlightenment and scientific revolutions. But it is true that he is wary of human progress.

---

[66] M. Reeves, "The Originality and Influence of Joachim of Fiore," *Traditio* 36 (1980), p. 273.
[67] *Ibid.*, p. 292.
[68] *Ibid.*, p. 293.
[69] For a detailed account of Joachim of Fiore and his doctrines, see M. Riedl (ed.), *A Companion to Joachim of Fiore* (Leiden: Brill, 2017). Riedl's contribution "Longing for the Third Age: Revolutionary Joachism, Communism, and National Socialism" (pp. 267–318) may be of particular interest for the topics of this chapter; here he notes that Karl Löwith "recognized [Joachim's] work as the historical link between biblical lore and modern ideology" (p. 269). I have also found M. Reeves, *The Influence of Prophecy in the Later Middle Ages: A Study in Joachimism* (Notre Dame: University of Notre Dame Press, 1994), recommended by Patenaude, very informative.
[70] B. McGinn, "The Significance of Bonaventure's Theology of History," p. 77.

In a homily on the Solemnity of Pentecost,[71] he explains that Babel "is the description of a kingdom in which men had concentrated so much power that they thought they no longer needed to rely on a distant God and that they were powerful enough to be able to build a way to heaven by themselves in order to open its gates and usurp God's place." He further adds that our times seem to tell a similar tale, as "The progress of science and technology have enabled us to dominate the forces of nature, to manipulate the elements and to reproduce living beings, almost to the point of manufacturing the very human being. In this situation praying to God seems obsolete or pointless, because we ourselves can construct and achieve whatever we like."

I believe James Corkery goes perhaps a bit too far when he affirms (quoting *Introduction to Christianity*), that Ratzinger

> was always uncomfortable with an emphasis, typical of the "age of progress" (the 1960s) in which he lived as a young theologian, on the idea that we—sinners in need of God's mercy at every moment—could do anything without the help of God. If we were to make any progress at all, such progress would be a gift, not a product of the "making" capacities of the over-confident, arrogant "man of the future."[72]

I do not believe that Ratzinger denies the idea of human progress;[73] certainly, progress is, in a way, a form in which the creation of man can manifest the greatness of his Creator.[74] Rather, I believe, Ratzinger is

---

[71] Benedict XVI, *Papal Mass on the Solemnity of Pentecost*, May 27, 2013.

[72] J. Corkery, "Reflection on the Theology of Joseph Ratzinger (Pope Benedict XVI)," *Acta Theologica* 32 (2012), p. 19. Cf. J. Ratzinger, *Introduction to Christianity (Revised Edition)* (San Francisco: Ignatius, 2004), pp. 63–6; *id.*, *Faith and the Future* (San Francisco: Ignatius, 2009), pp. 92–3.

[73] He actually notes that "reaction and resentment against technology, which is already noticeable in Rousseau, has long since become a resentment against humans, who are seen as the disease of nature. This being that emerges out of nature's exact objectivity and straightforwardness is responsible for disturbing the beautiful balance of nature. Humans are diseased by their mind and its consequence, freedom. Mind and freedom are the sickness of nature. Human beings, the world, should be delivered from them if there is to be redemption. To restore the balance, humans must be healed of being human," J. Ratzinger, *"In the Beginning ..." A Catholic Understanding of the Story of Creation and the Fall* (Grand Rapids: Eerdmans, 1985), pp. 93–4. Technology by itself is not the problem but rather "the theological concealment of the concept of creation" (*ibid.*).

[74] Patenaude expresses a similar idea in a different way: "The second strand involves human history itself, which, given its interplay with revelation, must be viewed as more than a progression of isolated events to be studied scientifically or solely within historical-critical (or scholastic) methodologies. For Ratzinger (and, in his own age and way, for Bonaventure), doing so would deny the unchanging nature of the human person. Indeed, a proper anthropology must remain independent of the social or technological advances of the ages upon ages. And so Ratzinger/Benedict XVI will maintain the human person's intrinsic capacity and desire to be in relation with others—to love and receive love, divine and human, no matter what the obstacles or temptations to do otherwise. Thus, history must be viewed hermeneutically as the telling of an organic, unified drama (indeed, a love story) about a community in time that

continuously warning against the idea that human progress is a form of disposition, by humanity, of itself: the idea that history is entirely of our own making, in the sense that we can model and mold our very essence. For Ratzinger, history cannot change from within, by a temporal event, but must be wholly redeemed.[75]

What Ratzinger wishes to prevent us from, I believe, is a technological conception *of the human essence*, i.e., the mistaken conception of humanity as a "technological device" which can be intrinsically improved upon. At its core, this mistake involves an erroneous conception of freedom, which in turn projects human action not as taking place *in* history but as *possessing* history.

> Man, precisely as man, remains the same both in primitive and technologically developed situations. He does not stand on a higher level merely because he has learned to use more highly developed tools. Mankind begins anew in every single individual. This is why it is not possible for the new, ideal society to exist—the society built on progress, which not only was the hope of the great ideologies, but increasingly became the general object of human hope once hope in a life after death had been dismantled.[76]

It is not surprising that in this regard he quotes Heidegger in a sympathetic fashion, as Heidegger denounced the coming of the age of technology.[77] In his *Introduction to Christianity*, Ratzinger recuperates this thought: "the Freiburg philosopher has a good deal of justification for expressing the fear that in an age in which calculating thought is celebrating the most amazing triumphs man is nevertheless threatened, perhaps more than ever before, by thoughtlessness, by the flight from thought."[78] *Calculating thought* is

---

finds full meaning only in recognizing its movement toward a Christological completion—that is, an ideal state that gives meaning to the present but remains always beyond the grasp of any individual or group," "Loving in the Present," p. 4. I believe this wording is far closer to Ratzinger's thought: human nature is a gift, and our journey through history consists in disposing of our current situation according to this gift. Human nature is not something that we can ourselves modify or subject to our own constructive whims.

[75] "For [the Franciscan Spiritualists], the idea that such an Age of the Holy Spirit would occur within human history—as did the Age of God the Father and the Age of the Son—resonated with their own conviction of a renewal brought to the Church, in history, by Francis. But an eschaton within time was at odds with long-existing understandings of history's place in theology and ecclesiology," Cf. W. L. Patenaude, "Loving in the Present," p. 9.

[76] J. Ratzinger, *Values in a Time of Upheaval* (San Francisco: Ignatius, 2006), p. 25.

[77] In his own way, Heidegger also conceives the technological interpretation or "enframing" of the world as problematic and contrary to the very human way of being: "the rule of enframing threatens man with the possibility that it could be denied to him to enter into a more original revealing and hence to experience the call of a more primal truth," *The Question Concerning Technology and Other Essays* (New York, London: Garland, 1977), p. 287.

[78] J. Ratzinger, *Introduction to Christianity*, p. 71.

at the root of the problem: it confuses theological hope with technological expectations, and turns the Kingdom into an earthly utopia, against which Ratzinger continuously warned in his engagement with liberation theology.[79]

Ratzinger sets forth this argument in different places. For example, in his set of homilies "*In the Beginning ...,* " he affirms:

> To go straight to the point: the foundations of modernity are the reason for the disappearance of "creation" from the horizons of historically influential thought. [...] The Christian idea of the world's dependence on this something else seems to deprive the world of its power. The world has to be protected against this threat: it is self-grounding; it is itself the divine. The contingency of individual things is indisputable, but the contingency of the world as a whole is not accepted.[80]

And he goes on to criticize the modern limitation of reason, which views humanity in the same line as the objectification of the world brought about by science. It is only through Christianity's idea of transcendence that we can fully grasp the richness of man:

> The idea of creation is on a different level altogether. Reality as a whole is a question pointing beyond itself. If we are to grasp the concept of creation, we must expose the limitations of the subject/ object schema, the limitations of "exact" thought, and we must show that only when the humanum has been freed of these limitations will the truth about humankind and the real world come into view. And yet we must not try to overstep the limitations by denying God, because that would also be the denial of humankind—with all its grave consequences. In fact, the question at stake here is: "Do human beings really exist?" The fact of human beings is an obstacle and irritation for "science," because they are not something science can exactly "objectify." Ultimately, science does center on humankind—but in order to do so, it has to go further and focus on God.[81]

---

[79] And also with the historical-critical method of biblical exegesis: "On the other extreme, the historical-critical method of the 19th and 20th centuries takes itself not at all to be constituted by mythos but regards itself as 'pure *Wissenschaft*' or science. In this regard, HCM regards itself as tantamount to Aristotle's ideal for *epistêmê*. The temporality in view here is 'chronotic time.' The purported output of this work is the establishment of bare particulars, or brute facts: 'this or that happened; this or that existed.' For example, that Jesus of Nazareth actually lived (or did not actually live) during the reign of Caesar Augustus or that Alcibiades performed (or did not perform) this or that action in this or that year or that Abraham begat (or did not beget) Isaac. The bare particulars are regarded as wholly non-kairotic, according to the methodological assumptions of HCM, and in this nonkairoticism they are at one with HCM's method," M. Boulter, *Repetition and Mythos*, p. 108.
[80] J. Ratzinger, "*In the Beginning ...,*" pp. 82–3.
[81] *Id.*, "*In the Beginning ...,*" p. 86.

There is a longer and, in my mind, clearer argument in his *Principles of Catholic Theology*. Here Ratzinger reprints two papers, "*Heil und Geschichte*" (1970) and "*Heilsgeschichte, Metaphysik und Eschatologie*" (1967), which in a way condense his thoughts from the *Habilitationsschrift* to the *Eschatologie*. From the first article, we can construe the following argument:

   a. History is the realm of man and thus also the realm of religious experience. This realm is by itself unproblematic until it "begins to contradict the fundamental experiences of his life, when, instead of sheltering him, it begins to divide and rend him, when, instead of offering a way, it increases almost beyond endurance the dilemma of existence, when its own structure begins to topple, when it becomes unquestionable in itself—only then does such history become a problem."[82] At that moment we experience the problem (or the need) of salvation.

   b. According to Ratzinger, Christianity itself appeared at a time of historical turmoil, and its message became the "foundation of a new history, which, paradoxically, is experienced as the end of all history and, for that reason, affects all mankind."[83]

   c. "The beginning and end of this new history is the Person of Jesus of Nazareth, who is recognized as the last man (the second Adam), that is, as the long-awaited manifestation of what is truly human and the definitive revelation to man of his hidden nature; for this very reason, it is oriented toward the whole human race and presumes the abrogation of all partial histories, whose partial salvation is looked upon as essentially an absence of salvation. By offering temporary salvation, all these histories cut man off from his last end, from his very humanness, which they concealed and kept from him by lulling him with what was provisional."[84]

The last point is the key: the Christological understanding of Christianity means that it presents itself as the key to the definitive understanding of human nature, which binds all humans across history while at the same time remaining open to the newness of Christ. Hence, for Ratzinger, the "first and primordial statement is the good tidings that the power of death, the one constant of history, has, in a single instance, been broken by the power of God and that history has thus been imbued with an entirely new hope."[85] That is why Christ stands above and at the end of history, and why mankind

---

[82] Id., *Principles of Catholic Theology*, p. 154.
[83] Ibid., p. 156.
[84] Ibid.
[85] Ibid., p. 185.

cannot *existentially* progress in any meaningful way without finding its own truth in Christ. The problem with false spiritualisms—which Ratzinger will call Gnosticism—is that they substitute Christ for "humankind," and the history of salvation for a history of human progress, in which man becomes God. Ratzinger links this process to modernity, and ultimately to the cult of praxis: "Redemption is now construed strictly as the 'praxis' of man, as the denial of creation, indeed as the total antithesis to faith in creation."[86] He also notes two distinct features of this development: the individual is subsumed unto the species, and creation is rejected as a dependence *ab alio* in favor of the ideal of absolute emancipation. If humankind takes the place of Christ, then it becomes the only true subject of history and particular human beings are little more than "avatars" of its worldly development. The negation of a radical sense of salvation thus becomes, for Ratzinger, an ultimate denial of the human essence. Christianity, on the contrary, defends a radical innovation, signaled by the Resurrection as the true form of the eschatological:

> the Evangelists, and especially Matthew, described Christ's Cross and Resurrection as the final hour; they wanted to make it plain that this was not just any resurrection, such as an Elias or some other miracle-worker might have brought about, but a resurrection of a kind never before known, after which death would be no more. That means also, then, that in this awakening the realm of history has been transcended, that he who arose from the dead did not return, as anyone else might have done, to a this-worldly history but stands above it, though by no means without relationship to it.[87]

And so, we return to our original theses: according to Ratzinger, Bonaventure is not wholly opposed to Aristotle, but rather to the excision of faith from rationality. Faith and reason go hand in hand in interpreting the universe and man's place in it, a *locus* that itself has not been given to man by man himself but by God. Both our interior landscape and human history as such are open to real *action* and freedom in a way that technology, which is preordained and programmed, could never be. To this extent, Bonaventure's interpretation of history should be upheld, even if its historical accuracy owes too much to Joachite presuppositions or a medieval (limited) perspective. History is open-ended because human freedom is, and yet history and the human heart remain themselves open to mankind's eternal destiny. This idea, that metaphysics is related to human history, is what motivated Ratzinger's initial study.[88] It allows him to read the relation between nature, faith, and

---

[86] *Id.*, "In the Beginning ...," p. 105.
[87] *Id.*, *Principles of Catholic Theology*, p. 186.
[88] Cf. *id.*, *The Theology of History in St. Bonaventure*, p. xi.

history according to two different models: the Gnostic and the Christian. In Gnosticism, "the mystery of suffering, of love, of substitutionary redemption, is rejected in favor of a control of the world and of life through knowledge."[89] Creation is dependence and God the origin of dependence. The Gnostic seeks to take control of nature and history and become its own *ersatz* creator. The Christian model accepts humanity as dependence and our existence as a gift, open to be fulfilled by another. In this way, the question of history becomes not only a problem of "the relationship of history and ontology, of the mediation of history in the realm of ontology," but also "a more revolutionary kind of questioning"[90] regarding history and theology that allows us "to comprehend history as mediation in such a way that even the future can be hope only because it promises the freedom to be."[91] Ratzinger argues here against conceiving Christianity as just another name to call the fulfillment of the human essence, in a way that "adds nothing to the universal but merely makes it known,"[92] precisely because it would "amount to man's self-affirmation."

> In other words, this liberation is not very far-reaching. One who escapes into the pure rationality of the human will have either to reestablish the particularity of the Christian claim or to acknowledge the emptiness of the universal rationalism that leaves man without a way yet challenges him again and again to seek for a concrete—for a particular—option.[93]

Ratzinger's answer, like Bonaventure, is to leave open the question of history. The *logos* of history cannot be deduced by mankind because its final meaning is not the universalization of our own aspirations. "A synthesis that combines being and history in a single, compelling login of the understanding becomes, by the universality of its claim, a philosophy of necessity, even though this necessity is then explained as a process of freedom. By its very nature, insistence on freedom involves the rejection of a closed system."[94] It is freedom in the sense of openness and dependence, looking "in the direction of a spirituality of conversion, of ec-stasy"[95] toward the person of Christ as "the Event of the new and unexpected."[96]

Ratzinger's studies on Bonaventure, then, may not be the center of his theology. There is certainly a lot in the haphazard elements of Bonaventure's theology that Ratzinger did not follow after his *Habilitationsschrift* nor can

---

[89] Id., "In the Beginning ...," p. 96.
[90] Id., Principles of Catholic Theology, pp. 158-9.
[91] Ibid., p. 162.
[92] Ibid., p. 166.
[93] Ibid., p. 167.
[94] Ibid., p. 170.
[95] Ibid., p. 169.
[96] Ibid., p. 170.

they easily be readopted in contemporary theology. What *can* be found in his thought, after this thesis, is the radical conviction that Christianity is a reality that is living in history, both within and without the inner self, a personal path of following and testimony, but also a way of living that runs through Christendom across civilizations and reflects upon the universe. History has a meaning, there is an economic engagement with history that can be called "salvation history," but it is only through faith that we can elevate our understanding toward it. Likewise, it is faith that can purify reason toward acknowledging that human progress is not the final word in history.

4

Thomas Aquinas: How We Know God

Pablo Blanco-Sarto

Introduction

Along with the diversity of sources found in Joseph Ratzinger's theology, we can appreciate that love, truth, and beauty are in turn linked to the concepts of person and existence, as can also be found in the best classical theology formulated by the Fathers of the Church and the medieval masters. This is a constant in Ratzinger's thought. In his formative years in Freising, he did a lot of reading, including the novels of Dostoevsky and Gertrude von Le Fort, and French literature of the time represented by Claudel and Bernanos, while also maintaining avid interest in the scientific theories of Einstein and Heisenberg, to name just a few examples. Moreover, "in the domain of theology and philosophy, the voices that moved us most directly were those of Romano Guardini, Josef Pieper, [or the later Catholics] Theodor Häcker, and Peter Wust."[1] He also approached other philosophers of the time, apart from the "philosophy of dialogue" found in Ferdinand Ebner and Martin Buber. He remarked:

> Heidegger and Jaspers interested me a great deal, along with personalism as a whole. Steinbüchel wrote a book entitled *The Revolution of Thought* [*Der Umbruch des Denkens*], in which he recounted with great verve the revolutionary shift from the dominance

---

[1] J. Ratzinger, *Milestones: Memoirs (1927–1977)* (San Francisco: Ignatius, 1998), pp. 42–3.

of neo-Kantianism to the personalistic phase. That was a key book for me. But then from teh beginning Saint Augustine interested me very much – precisely also insofar as he was, so to speak, a counterweight to Thomas Aquinas.[2]

These interests were pursued without renouncing the importance of the nihilism of Nietzsche, the spiritualism of Bergson or the thought of many other philosophers.[3] As a theologian, the fruits of this broad erudition, formed in art, science, and philosophy, have always remained a source of inspiration for Ratzinger.

The Problem of the Supernatural

Joseph Ratzinger's theology will always be a theology in continuous dialogue with the faith of the Church and with other authors, both classical and modern. His formative years—and beyond, as can be seen in his extensive work—were especially marked by the thinkers who his teacher Gottlieb Söhngen (1892–1971) called the "three great masters," namely Augustine of Hippo, Thomas Aquinas, and Bonaventure. Söhngen's motto was "with St. Thomas, beyond St. Thomas; with Augustine, beyond Augustine."[4] In an interview during his pontificate, when asked how he prayed, Pope Benedict responded by alluding to these three masters: "I am friends with Augustine, with Bonaventure, with Thomas Aquinas. Those saints are asked: 'Help me!'."[5] However, with respect to Aquinas, as pointed out elsewhere, he initially found his scholasticism difficult: "'I had difficulties in penetrating the thought of Thomas Aquinas'—Ratzinger continued recalling his seminary years—, 'whose crystal-clear logic seemed to me to be too closed in on itself, too impersonal and ready-made'."[6] According to Rossi, Ratzinger's theology has "a harmonious architecture of simple lines that, when traced

---

[2] *Id., Salt of the Earth: The Church at the End of the Millennium* (San Francisco: Ignatius, 1997), p. 60.
[3] Cf. *ibid.*, pp. 28–51. On this topic, see Läpple's article entitled "Theologie als Krisis und Wagnis des Theologen," *Die Besinnung* 1-2 (1947), pp. 52–60, in A. Läpple, *Benedikt XVI. und seine Wurzeln*, pp. 28–41.
[4] Cf. J. Ratzinger, *Convocados en el camino de la fe* (Madrid: Cristiandad, 2004), p. 27; G. Valente, *El profesor Ratzinger (1946–1977). Los años dedicados al estudio y a la docencia en el recuerdo de sus compañeros y alumnos* (Madrid: San Pablo, 2011), p. 46.
[5] Benedicto XVI and Peter Seewald, *Luz del mundo. El papa, la Iglesia y el signo de los tiempos* (Barcelona: Herder, 2010), p. 30.
[6] J. Ratzinger, *Milestones*, p. 44; cf. *id., La sal de la tierra*, p. 67; T. P. Rausch, *Pope Benedict XVI: An Introduction to His Theological Vision* (New York, Mahwah: Paulist Press, 2009), pp. 47–9.

with conceptual rigor, composed a rather complicated design, but clear in its luminosity."[7]

It can be said to have something of the simple nobility of Gothic cathedrals. He missed, however, the personal and intimate depth that he saw in the writings of St. Augustine. But, in spite of a translation of the treatise on love in the Angelic Doctor that left a deep impression on him, Ratzinger was unable to find this depth in his writings.[8] Distance between St. Thomas and Bonaventure constituted a starting point in the thought of the young Bavarian scholar.

His initial reservations toward scholasticism are also well known, when he referred to his teacher, Arnold Wilmsen, who taught "a rigid, neo-scholastic Thomism that was simply far afield from my own questions."[9] Thus, Ratzinger is usually considered a follower of the Augustinian-Bonaventurian line; while true, we can also trace Thomas Aquinas' noticeable influence on him. As we will try to show in this chapter, this is clear in his texts, especially regarding the unity between reflection, spirituality, and pastoral purpose.[10] We will address the apparent affinity between Ratzinger and St. Thomas by examining three major themes found in his writings, namely a) the problem of the supernatural, b) the knowledge of God, and c) the method of theological science. A genetic and chronological methodology will also serve to trace this possible influence.

That Scholasticism seemed to Ratzinger to be a too cosified and impersonal approach is clear. However, alluding to *Surnaturel* from De Lubac, he affirmed, "I admired a new interpretation of St. Thomas Aquinas, very different from the neo-scholastic philosophy that we had studied up to that moment." On the other hand, when referring to his *Doktorvater* (his director of his doctoral and habilitation work), Söhngen, he noted, "He belonged to that dynamic current in Thomism that took from Thomas the passion for truth and the habit of asking unrelenting questions about the foundation and the goal of the real; but all of this he consciously placed in relation to the questions that philosophy asks today."[11] In fact, the German theologian finds points of inspiration in the thought of Aquinas. Dorothea Kaes states, "Ratzinger finds confirmation of his position in Thomas insofar as he has emphasized the reference of theology to the faith experience of the saints, without the former losing its relation to reality. In particular, Augustine's and Bonaventure's exposition

---

[7] M. Rossi, T. Rossi and T. F. Rossi, *L'anima tomista di Benedetto XVI. L'impronta di san Tommaso nei temi chiave di Papa Ratzinger: un'eredità per la chiesa del futuro* (Roma: Angelicum University Press, 2013), p. 239.
[8] Cf. A. Läpple, *Benedikt XVI. und seine Wurzeln*, p. 55; E. Gaál, *The Theology of Benedict XVI: The Christocentric Shift* (New York: Palgrave McMillan, 2010), p. 31.
[9] J. Ratzinger, *Milestones*, p. 56.
[10] Cf. M. Rossi, T. Rossi and T. F. Rossi, *L'anima tomista di Benedetto XVI*, pp. 12–13.
[11] J. Ratzinger, *Milestones*, p. 55.

of the simple seems to him to be related to Thomas' affirmation that love is the eye that lets man see."[12] He thus combines both perspectives. Tracey Rowland, winner of the 2020 Ratzinger Prize and a connoisseur of twentieth-century neo-Scholasticism, sees that "throughout his work he refers to the position of St. Thomas: whenever he finds in it a valuable intuition."[13]

His doctoral thesis on Augustinian ecclesiology includes four mentions of the *Summa theologiae*. There, he lays out a different relationship between the natural and supernatural, as well as what refers to the proofs of the existence of God. While Augustine proposed an interior route to access God, Aquinas proposed one through the sensible things, using the concept of causality in a purely metaphysical sense.[14] Thus, Ratzinger points out that, between the two, there is a different conception of being and knowledge, although he does not accept the dichotomy proposed by Max Scheler between Augustinian-religious knowledge and Thomistic-metaphysical knowledge. For Augustine, in reality, the two are intimately united.[15] As a point of confluence between the two authors, Thomas Aquinas "sees *the res sacramenti* of the Eucharist in the *unitas corporis mystici*,"[16] the fruit of the sacrament of sacraments.

In addition, in his writings on St. Bonaventure, Ratzinger proposed other approaches to the thought of St. Thomas. Here the differences are reflected in their respective gnoseologies, which give rise to Thomism's ontological orientation and Bonaventurianism's historical-salvific orientation, respectively. Thus, differences appear regarding the doctrine on revelation, theological anthropology, and the doctrine of grace, which are the three main themes for which Ratzinger relies on Thomas Aquinas, according to

---

[12] D. Kaes, *Theologie im Anspruch von Geschichte und Wahrheit* (St. Ottilien: Dissertationen Theologishe Reihe, 1997), pp. 187–8; cf. Le Redaction, "Le futur Benoît XVI et Henri de Lubac," *Bulletin de la Associtiation Internationale Cardenal Henri de Lubac* 7 (2005), p. 8.

[13] T. Rowland, *La fe de Ratzinger. La teología del papa Benedicto XVI* (Granada: Nuevo Inicio, 2008), p. 24. See also G. Bachanek, "Šv. Tomas Akvinietis Josepho Ratzingerio (Benedikto XVI) apmąstymuose," *Logos* 65 (2010), pp. 29–40; and especially M. Á. Correas Mazuecos, "Los 'pensadores de la fe' de Joseph Ratzinger. Tradición y diálogos teológicos," *Excerpta e dissertationibus in sacra theologia. Cuadernos doctorales de la facultad de teología* 67 (2018), pp. 159–217.

[14] Cf. P. C. Sicouly, "Fe y razón en la lectura del pensamiento patrístico y medieval de Joseph Ratzinger/Benedicto XVI: una mirada a sus primeras obras (1951–1962)," *Ciencia Tomista* 138 (2011), p. 127.

[15] Cf. *JRGS*1, pp. 552–60; Aquinas, *De veritate*, q. 10 a. 6; A. Bellandi, *Fede cristiana come stare e comprendere. La giustificazione dei fondamenti della fede in Joseph Ratzinger* (Roma: Pontificia Università Gregoriana, 1996), p. 138, n. 11.

[16] *JRGS 1*, p. 293, n. 88; cf. STh III, q. 80 a. 4c; q. 60 s.c.; Also Seen In J. Ratzinger, *El nuevo pueblo de Dios. Esquemas para una eclesiología* (Barcelona: Herder, 1972), pp. 99–100; P. Martuccelli, *Origine e natura della chiesa: la prospettiva storico-dogmatica di Joseph Ratzinger* (Frankfurt am Main: Peter Lang, 2001), p. 254.

Schenk.[17] In turn, throughout his 1955 habilitation thesis, he insists that both perspectives are complementary, since neither of them exhausts the richness of Christian truth. Bonaventure also synthesized the Augustinian theory of interior illumination and that of Aristotle's abstraction, while, on the contrary, Aquinas opted unilaterally for the Aristotelian one: "According to him, one can only speak of divine illumination because that light proper to human reason has been created by God and, in that sense, is a participation in the light of God" (1 Cor 2:1).[18] Therefore, for St. Thomas as well, there is no internal revelation, because "like all knowledge, revelation also comes from outside: it is a complete fact, concluded once and for all." He also notes the paradox that "he has granted to the historical event the rank of positive origin in the salvific event." For Thomas Aquinas, the meaning of *revelatio* is not subjective, but rather objective; he thus relies on an objectivization of the relational act of revelation, although he clearly distinguishes between faith and revelation, unlike the Seraphic Doctor.[19]

Thus, the Thomistic concept of *supernaturalis* prevailed in Catholic theology. Ratzinger relates it to the Bonaventurian concept of *desiderium naturalis*, which was contrary to thought at the time. He thus places Bonaventure "in the line of spiritual evolution that had logically led to Thomas Aquinas."[20] However, he insists that the Thomistic concept of *supernaturalis* carries the danger of overlooking the creature's immediate openness to the Creator. In contrast, the Bonaventurian concept of *supernaturalis* better reflects the relational character of grace.[21] Similarly, Thomas and Bonaventure do not understand the person seen as *imago Dei* in the same way, according to their respective "dynamic-actual" and "static-substantial" conceptions. While Bonaventure addresses the question in the knowledge of God, Aquinas deals with it in anthropology. According to Ratzinger, Thomas Aquinas was more concerned with the spiritual nature of the person than with *actualitas*; thus, "in Thomas

---

[17] Cf. M. Rossi, T. Rossi and T. F. Rossi, *L'anima tomista di Benedetto XVI*, pp. 152–8; R. Schenk, "Bonaventura als Klassiker der analogia fidei. Zur Rezeption der theologischen Programmatik Gottlieb Söhngens im Frühwerk Joseph Ratzingers," in M. Schlosser and F. X. Heibl (eds.), *Gegenwart der Offenbarung*, Ratzinger Studien 2 (Regensburg: Friedrich Pustet, 2011), pp. 37–44.
[18] In *JRGS* 2, p. 728; cf. R. Voderholzer, "Offenbarung und Kirche. Ein Grundegedanke von Joseph Ratzingers Habilitationsprojekt (1955/2009) und seine theologische Tragweite," in M. Schlosser and F. X. Heibl (eds.), *Gegenwart der Offenbarung*, p. 59.
[19] Cf. *JRGS* 2, pp. 141, 108; cf. pp. 111, 221, there is mentioned STh I q. 1; H. Verweyen, *Ein unbekannter Ratzinger. Die Habilitationsschrift von 1955 als Schlüssel zu seiner Theologie* (Regensburg: Friedrich Pustet, 2010), p. 46. In "History of the salvation, metaphysics and eschatology" (1967) Ratzinger will note the Copernican shift from allegorical interpretation to literal interpretation, cf. J. Ratzinger, *Teoría de los principios teológicos. Materiales para una teología fundamental* (Barcelona: Herder, 1985), p. 215.
[20] *JRGS* 2, p. 304; H. Verweyen, *Ein unbekannter Ratzinger*, pp. 66–72.
[21] Cf. *JRGS* 2, p. 312.

everything shifts: the question of the act and the object becomes, for the first time, separable."[22] The Angelic Doctor bases the doctrine of grace on his concept of the supernatural, in order to make it comprehensible to Aristotelian ontology. This was his great achievement, but, in theology, Aristotelianism had already been replaced by other philosophical systems at the beginning of the twentieth century, making a new theological synthesis necessary.[23] St. Thomas spoke of supernature as elevated, transformed, and divinized nature; he placed special emphasis on the axiom *gratia praesupponit naturam*. At the same time, however, "he was relegating to the background the historical-salvific distinctions," Ratzinger argued.[24]

Knowledge of God

This leads us to rethink the relationship between philosophy and theology. For Ratzinger, St. Thomas represents the line of theology understood as *philosophia supernaturalis*, proper to the objective-metaphysical approach, while Bonaventure sees it as a practical science nearer to a historical-concrete perspective. The Angelic Doctor grounded theology in scientific knowledge and "precisely in this activity by which the intellect draws conclusions [from the articles of faith,] the true essence of theological science is seen."[25] This is understood above all as thought faith, as *fides quaerens intellectum*. Against the thirteenth-century theory of the double truth proposed by Siger of Brabant (1240–80), Aquinas suggested a subtle formula of reconciliation between faith and reason that is much more elaborate than that of Bonaventure. The problem consisted in understanding the unity and difference between philosophy and theology, without separating the two disciplines. From 1267 onward, the Seraphic Doctor elaborated an anti-Aristotelianism that was not "anti-Thomistic."[26] For his part, Ratzinger always denied—with Thomas—the cosified or essentialist character of theology. In a later conference in 1979, he affirmed that "if I am not mistaken, it was Thomas who was the first to reach, without hesitation, the consequence of the concept of theology: the object of this science—Thomas Aquinas even speaks of

---

[22] *Ibid.*, pp. 340, 326, 329.
[23] Cf. *ibid.* pp. 339–40.
[24] Cf. *ibid.*, pp. 278, 304; cf. Valente, *El profesor Ratzinger*, p. 236. All these considerations were explained and deepened in specific seminars on Thomas in the first half of 1956 in Munich and on Bonaventure in Bonn in the first half of 1962.
[25] *JRGS* 2, p. 204; cf. p. 384.
[26] Cf. *ibid.*, pp. 263–4, 614–15, 801–2; P. Hofmann, "Offenbarung und Geschichte. Joseph Ratzingers Kommentar zu Gaudium et spes als angewandte Bonaventura-Rezeption," in M. Schlosser and F. X. Heibl (eds.), *Gegenwart der Offenbarung* (Regensburg: Friedrich Pustet, 2011), p. 88.

'subject'—is God." And he concluded with the following words: "theology deals with God, but it interrogates in the manner of philosophy."[27]

There is, however, an old text that appeared in 1960, dated on the feast of St. Thomas the previous year and dedicated to his father, who had recently passed away. It was one of Ratzinger's first publications. The inaugural lecture on the occasion of his taking up the chair of fundamental theology at the University of Bonn, it is entitled *The God of Faith and the God of the Philosophers*.[28] He stated there that the problem is as old as "faith and philosophy being side by side,"[29] and then recalled the famous Memorial of Blaise Pascal, sewn into the lining of his jacket and discovered on the night of November 23–4, 1654, at the death of the French scientist and thinker: "Fire. God of Abraham, God of Isaac, God of Jacob, not the God of philosophers and wise men." In this regard, the young theologian affirmed: "The mathematician and philosopher Pascal had experienced the living God, the God of faith, and in such a living encounter with the you of God, he understood– with manifestly joyful and startled amazement – how different was the irruption of the reality of God in comparison with what mathematical philosophy (of a Descartes, for example) knew how to say about God." If the philosophy of that time – of Descartes, especially – was a philosophy from the *esprit de la géometrie*, Pascal's *Pensées* sought to be a philosophy developed from the *esprit de la finesse*, from the understanding of the whole of reality, which penetrates it more honestly than mathematical abstraction.[30] It consisted, therefore, in overcoming mere mathematical reason in search of an "open reason," as our theologian later repeated time and again.[31]

To address this controversial question, Ratzinger developed a historical comparison of Thomas Aquinas and the Swiss evangelical theologian Emil Brunner (1884–1976), an early companion of Karl Barth (1886–1968). He summarized the thought of Aquinas as follows: "for Thomas, the God of religion and the God of the philosophers are perfectly compatible

---

[27] J. Ratzinger, *Teoría de los rincípios teológicos*, pp. 381, 385.

[28] It will nevertheless be an important text, as it will be included in the anthology prepared by his disciples in 1997: cf. *id.*,"Der Gott des Glaubens und der Gott der Philosophen. Ein Beitrag zum Problem der Theologia Naturalis," in S. Otto Horn (ed.), *Vom Wiederauffinden der Mitte: Grundorientierungen. Texte aus vier Jahrzehnten* (Freiburg, Basel, Wien: Herder, 1997), pp. 40–59. There, Pfnür affirms as such when highlighting the two antagonistic visions presented and studied there (cf. V. Pfnür, in *ibid*, pp. 19–20; the Ratzinger quotation is from page 10 in the original text). However, we have not found reviews and commentaries in German-language theological journals of the time on this work of his youth: cf. P. Blanco-Sarto, *Joseph Ratzinger: razón y cristianismo. La victoria de la inteligencia en el mundo de las religiones* (Madrid: Rialp, 2005), pp. 58–64.

[29] J. Ratzinger, *El Dios de la fe y el Dios de los filósofos* (Madrid: Taurus, 1962), p. 11.

[30] Cf. *ibid.*, p. 12; here quoted: R. Guardini, *Christliches Bewusstein. Versuche über Pascal* (München: Kösel, 1950 [1935]).

[31] On this topic, see P. Blanco-Sarto, *Joseph Ratzinger: razón y cristianismo*, passim.

with each other; on the contrary, the God of faith and the God of philosophy are partially distinguished: the God of faith surpasses the God of the philosophers, adds something to him." This position goes directly against the Basel theologian's rejection of the *analogia entis*, considering philosophy as lesser. Indeed, "outside of Christian faith, philosophy is – according to Thomas – the highest possibility of the human spirit in general."[32] Philosophy thus becomes the queen of the human sciences because of the breadth of its knowledge, although it is true that faith "seeks to give a new image of God, higher than philosophical could ever set and think."

For this reason, faith does not contradict the philosophical doctrine of God either and, in order to illuminate their relationship, the formula *gratia non destruit, sed elevat et perficit naturam* should be applied and with full meaning. Christian faith in God accepts in itself the philosophical doctrine of God and consummates it. "In short: the God of Aristotle and the God of Jesus Christ are one and the same. Aristotle has known the true God, which we can know more deeply and profoundly thanks to faith, just as in the vision of God in the hereafter we will know the divine essence more closely and with greater intimacy." And so he concludes, "These are three degrees of the same path."[33] Philosophical knowledge, knowledge by faith, and a direct vision of God in eternal beatitude are different phases of the same itinerary, which contain and imply one another, as Aquinas also states.[34]

In light of Brunner's harsh and categorical criticism, Ratzinger then tries to get to the heart of the matter, to the basic issues at stake: "Here is becomes a question about the essence of Christianity in general; a question about the legitimacy of the concrete synthesis between Greek and biblical thought that gives form to Christianity." He thus points to the question of the legitimacy of the coexistence of faith and philosophy, and of the validity of the *analogia entis* as a positive relationship between knowledge by reason and knowledge by faith, between natural and supernatural being. In short, he puts us in the position of "deciding between the Catholic and the Protestant understanding of Christianity." Here then is the heart of the matter, namely whether, in short, there is *analogia entis* and the possibility

---

[32] J. Ratzinger, *El Dios de la fe y el Dios de los filósofos*, pp. 17–18; here quoted is S.Th. I, q.1, a.1., where speaking about the differences between philosophy and theology, Natural and Christian theology; cf. STh I q.1 a.1 s.c.; STh I q.1 a.1 ad 2. On the Swiss theologian, see P. Blanco-Sarto, "Analogia entis, analogia fidei. Karl Barth dialoga con teólogos católicos," *Scripta theologica* 51/1 (2019), pp. 67–95.
[33] J. Ratzinger, *El Dios de la fe y el Dios de los filósofos*, pp. 18–19; the quotation is from STh q.2, a.2, ad 1.
[34] Cf. *ibid.*, pp. 19–20; he refers, above all, to "Die christliche Lehre von Gott" in the first volume of the E. Brunner, *Dogmatik* 1 (Zollikon, Zürich: Evangelischer, 1953).

of a meeting (or, on the contrary, an abyss) between faith and reason, the natural and the supernatural, God and man.[35]

Therefore, the abyss between faith and philosophy may not be as deep as some had suggested. Even though it might sound like a provocation in the theological environment alluded to earlier, Ratzinger attempts a solution, offering the following: "The appropriation of philosophy, as carried out by the apologists, was nothing other than the necessary interior function that complements the external process of the missionary preaching of the gospel to the peoples of the world." If the Christian message is characterized by not being an esoteric and secret doctrine addressed exclusively to a small group of initiates, and by being a message from God to all, then Christianity must be interpreted outwardly, within the general language of human reason. "The true requirement of the Christian faith cannot become visible in its magnitude and seriousness except through this link of union with what man has grasped—in some way already beforehand—as absolute."[36] If Christianity rejects Gnosticism and Hermetic thought, then it clearly opts for reason and universality, just as the Angelic Doctor suggested in his time.

In this way, faith and philosophy choose the path of ultimate harmony, despite their evident differences and divergences; here, Ratzinger recalls the harmony between the two that Thomas Aquinas had proposed. "For it is clear: if faith grasps the philosophical concept of God and says: 'the Absolute- of which you knew something in some way - is the Absolute of which Jesus Christ speaks (who is the "Word") and to whom it is possible to speak', nevertheless this does not simply abolish the difference between faith and philosophy, much less transform into faith what was hitherto philosophy." Rather, philosophy remains something else, with its own entity, to which faith refers "in order to express itself in it as that other thing and thus to be able to make itself comprehensible."[37] Difference and harmony between the two, therefore, coexist. The God of Abraham, Isaac, and Jacob is a God to whom one can appeal, at the same time that he can be accessed—perhaps in a more distant but real way—through reason and knowledge. There is thus no abyss, but a bridge (perhaps quite long and somewhat risky to cross, but a bridge nonetheless). The divine *Logos* wants to reckon with the human *logos*. However, Ratzinger, then a young professor from Bonn, also proceeded with a timid approach to Brunner's position: "In any case, it can and must be said here: although the appropriation of the philosophical concept of God by the apologists and the Fathers was

---

[35] Cf. J. Ratzinger, *El Dios de la fe y el Dios de los filósofos*, p. 26; there is a reference to Ratzinger's master, G. Söhngen, *Die Einheit in der Theologie* (München: Zink, 1952). On this, see also G. L. Prestige, *Dios en el pensamiento de los Padres* (Salamanca: Sígueme, 1975), pp. 18–19.

[36] J. Ratzinger, *El Dios de la fe y el Dios de los filósofos*, p. 39; new references to Pannenberg's aforementioned article.

[37] *Ibid.*, p. 40.

undoubtedly legitimate (indeed, essentially necessary), it should also not be argued that this appropriation has not always been carried out with sufficient criticism."[38]

This critique therefore moves with personalist notions since "the knowledge that God is person—a self that goes out to meet a you—demands a revision of philosophical statements, a rethinking of them in a way that has not yet been conveniently realized. In this task of appropriating a deeper concept of God, Catholic and Protestant theology—coming from different places—can meet again."[39] He then proposes considering the Augustinian principle of *quaerite faciem eius semper*,[40] which is perfectly compatible with the aforementioned *crede ut intelligas, intellige ut credas*.[41] "The task of theology remains unfinished at this precise moment in the world. It consists in always asking for the face of God 'until He comes' and He Himself is the answer to every question."[42] Scholars like Tura, Krieg, and Bellandi[43] have pointed out the personalist tone of Ratzinger's theology and, in fact, Ratzinger further attempts to realize this philosophical synthesis between personalism and metaphysical thought.

Faith and Theology

In addition to the themes of truth and creation, Ratzinger also turned to St. Thomas to address theological methodology. In a 1993 text delivered at a conference in Rome on the teachings of the then Blessed Josemaría Escrivá (1902–75), Ratzinger recalled the scientific and sapiential character of theology: "Theology, science in the full sense of the word, is in fact the exercise of scientific reason." However, it was also opportune to speak of the "reality of heaven"; indeed, it is necessary, for only in this way can theology be understood. "Thomas Aquinas repeated it in a famous and widely repeated formula: theology is the science subordinate to the science of God and the blessed." The theologian must be a man of science, but also—as

---

[38] *Ibid.*, p. 41; cf. M. Rossi, T. Rossi, and T. F. Rossi, *L'anima tomista di Benedetto XVI*, pp. 27, 207–12, 241, which relates to the *tertia pars* of the *Summa Theologiae*.
[39] J. Ratzinger, *El Dios de la fe y el Dios de los filósofos*, p. 42.
[40] *Enarrationes in psalmos* 104, 3: *Corpus christianorum* 40, 1537.
[41] *Sermones* XLIII, 9: PL 38, 257–8.
[42] J. Ratzinger, *El Dios de la fe y el Dios de los filósofos*, pp. 42–3.
[43] On the importance of phenomenological and personalist thought in Ratzinger, Krieg recalls "die vorgefaßte Meinung vom Begriff der Person und von Jesus als der vollkommenen Person," R. A. Krieg, "Kardinal Ratzinger, Max Scheler und eine Grundfrage der Christologie," *Theologische Quartalschrift* 160 (1980), p. 111. According to Bellandi, this personalism comes from the doctrine of incarnation (cf. A. Bellandi, *Fede cristiana come stare e comprendere*, p. 188). The dual nature of Christ as God and man, *Logos* and flesh, finds its correlate in the Christian concept of person. This can also be seen in R. Tura, "La teologia di J. Ratzinger. Saggio introduttivo," *Studia Patavina* (1974), pp. 154, 158–61.

a theologian—a "man of prayer"; he must be attentive to the succession of history and the progress of science, but also—and even more so—to the testimony of those who, having traveled the path of prayer to the end, "have reached—already on earth—the high summits of divine intimacy; the testimony, in short, of those whom we are accustomed to call saints."[44]

This is a methodological requirement rather than a pious recommendation; after a long and arduous journey, science culminates in seeing God and reality, namely as a gift received directly from God. Wisdom and holiness are thus at the very heart of theology, which is conceived of as a science subordinate to the wisdom of God and to that of the saints. This "also implies a reference to the vital union with God," which is possible on earth for those who, opening themselves in faith to the divine word, embrace it not only with their intelligence, but also with their whole heart. "For God is at once and inseparably truth, goodness and beauty, and the unitive power of love leads not only to allowing oneself to be transfixed by his goodness, but also to a deepening of his truth."[45]

Similarly, in 2000, when receiving an honorary doctorate from the University of Wroclaw/Breslau in present-day Poland, the theologian-prefect offered a new approach to the question of faith as rational knowledge that could well serve as a summary of the present section. He started from everyday language, pointing out that, when one says, for example, "I believe that the weather will be fine tomorrow," or, "I believe that this or that news is not telling the truth," where the word "believe" is equivalent to think, to give an opinion, "it expresses an imperfect form of knowledge." We speak here of faith in that it has not attained the status of certain and rigorous knowledge. In fact, "many people think that this meaning of faith is also valid in the religious sphere and that, therefore, the contents of Christian faith are a prior [and] imperfect level of knowledge."[46] However, this is not the normal meaning of the main word we repeat in the creed: "In reality, for Christian believers, the expression 'I believe' indicates an absolutely peculiar certainty, in some respects greater than that of science; but, of course, it also carries within itself a moment of 'shadow and image', a moment of 'not yet'."[47]

It amounts, as Aquinas maintained, to simultaneous and duly integrated thought and assent, intelligence and will, knowledge and freedom. "Assent is caused by the will, not by the direct understanding of the understanding: in this consists the particular form of free will in the decision by faith.

---

[44] J. Ratzinger, "Messaggio inaugurale," in M. Belda, J. Escudero, J. L. Illanes and P. O'Callaghan (eds.), *Santità e mondo. Atti del Convegno teologico di studio sugli insegnamenti del beato Josemaría Escrivá (Roma, 12–14 ottobre 1993)* (Roma: Editrice Vaticana, 1994), pp. 19–20.

[45] *Ibid.*, p. 21. See also P. Blanco-Sarto, *Joseph Ratzinger: razón y cristianismo*, pp. 95–7.

[46] J. Ratzinger, *Convocados en el camino de la fe*, p. 18.

[47] *Ibid.*; cf. pp. 22–3; Aquinas, *De veritate*, q. 14, a. 1, co. On this topic, see M. Rossi, T. Rossi and T. F. Rossi, *L'anima tomista di Benedetto XVI*, pp. 53–7, 96–9, 105–18.

Cetera potest homo nolens, credere non nisi volens, St. Thomas quotes St. Augustine for this: everything else man can do without willing it, [but] faith can only attain it voluntarily." This statement reveals the particular spiritual structure of faith, which is not only an act of the intellect, but also involves the convergence of all the spiritual powers. "Moreover: man carries out faith in his own self, and never outside of it; it has a dialogical character by nature," thus emphasizing the relational character of the act of faith. The whole structure of spiritual powers is set in motion and converges in the "yes" of faith only because the foundation of the soul, the heart, is touched by God. "When the heart comes into contact with the *Logos* of God, with the incarnate Word, it touches that intimate point of its existence." Ratzinger's theology of the *Logos* appears once again. Knowledge by faith thus proceeds from the prior trust that one places in the one who can make him worthy of a higher knowledge. That is, a relationship that increases knowledge wherein if one accepts and trusts in the *Logos*, one's own *logos* will be profoundly enriched.[48]

The practical repercussions of these affirmations for theology are significant. Theology deals with God, but interrogates in the manner of philosophy, as noted. "In this metaphysical (ontological) commitment of theology there is not—contrary to what we have been fearing for a long time- a betrayal of salvation history"; quite the contrary: if theology wants to be faithful to its historical starting point (to the salvific event of Christ witnessed in the Bible) it must go beyond history and dedicate itself, in the last analysis, to God. If it wants to prove its fidelity to the practical content of the Gospel—the salvation of man—it must first of all be *scientia speculativa* rather than directly *scientia practica*. "It must postulate the primacy of truth, of a truth that rests on itself and for whose very being it must first ask itself, before [even] assessing its practical usefulness for human endeavors."[49] Theology must recover the primacy of *logos* over *ethos*, of orthodoxy over orthopraxis; this position, Ratzinger concludes, is found in Thomas Aquinas as well as in Bonaventure. In this regard, the Dominican Aidan Nichols pronounces as follows: "Ratzinger's sympathy for Bonaventure and the Franciscan school should not be regarded as anti-Thomistic. Indeed, Ratzinger has expressed himself on the subject of Thomas with a good deal more warmth than a formal ceremony requires."[50]

---

[48] Cf. J. Ratzinger, *Convocados en el camino de la fe*, p. 25; the quotation remains from *De veritate*, q. 14 a.1 co., that makes reference to 2 Cor 10:5; P. Blanco-Sarto, "*Logos*. Joseph Ratzinger y la historia de una palabra," *Límite* 14/1 (2006), pp. 57–86.
[49] J. Ratzinger, *Teoría de los principios teológicos*, p. 385.
[50] A. Nichols, *The Theology of Joseph Ratzinger: An Introductory Study* (Edimburgh: T&T Clark, 1988), p. 62. Cf. J. Ratzinger, *Teoría de los principios teológicos*, pp. 385–87.

5

Immanuel Kant: Distinguishing *Verum* and *Ens*

Jacob Phillips

Introduction

It would seem a natural assumption to consider Joseph Ratzinger an anti-Kantian theologian. After all, as far back as his 1954/5 course on Fundamental Theology, he calls Immanuel Kant (1724–1804) "the Aristotle of Protestantism" with Friedrich Schleiermacher being "its Thomas."[1] During his 1959 Inaugural Lecture at the University of Bonn, he held "the disintegration of speculative metaphysics by Kant" responsible for a modern situation whereby "the gap between metaphysics and religion [is] unbridgeable." It is thanks to Kant, then, that "theoretical reason" has "no access to God" and "religion has no seat in the room of ratio."[2] Ratzinger's later writings show no sign of softening his frustrations. In *The Nature and Mission of Theology* from 1993, for example, Kant is presented as the beginning of the "progressive replacement of metaphysics by history."[3] In the Regensburg Address of 2006, Kant is said to have

---

[1] All quotes from Ratzinger's Course in Fundamental Theology are quoted by E. de Gaál, *O Lord I Seek Your Countenance: Explorations and Discoveries in Pope Benedict XVI's Theology* (Steubenville: Emmaus Academic, 2018), p. 84.
[2] Quoted by M. A. Agbaw-Ebai, *Light of Reason, Light of Faith—Joseph Ratzinger and the German Enlightenment* (South Bend: St. Augustine's Press, 2021), p. 73.
[3] J. Ratzinger, *The Nature and Mission of Theology: Essays to Orient Theology in Today's Debates* (San Francisco: Ignatius, 1995 [1993 is the date of the German edition]), p. 21.

"anchored faith exclusively in practical reason, denying it access to reality as a whole."[4]

The volume and spread of statements like these show that it is quite right for commentators like Tracey Rowland and Emery de Gaál to hold that Ratzinger and Kant are opposed thinkers, not least due to the apparently hostile tenor of the former's mentions of the latter. Rowland glosses Ratzinger's oft-repeated statement that "reason has a wax nose" as meaning its "shape is determined by theological convictions and 'pure reason' á la Immanuel Kant simply does not exist."[5] De Gaál is even clearer, saying that the 2005 encyclical *Deus caritas est* shows it "is useless for Benedict to demonstrate the absurdity of Kant's transcendental aesthetics."[6]

So Ratzinger cannot be called a Kantian theologian, unlike some of his contemporaries.[7] At the same time however, the impact of Kant's influence on the history of Western thought, not to mention the volume, complexity, and breadth of his work, means that the epithet "anti-Kantian" needs careful consideration, on at least two fronts. First, Kant is one of the most important and influential philosophers in history, and inextricable from the intellectual "revolution" that was the Age of Reason.[8] Ratzinger is not only a theologian whose intellectual *raison d'être* is to bring philosophy and faith into critically constructive conversation, he does so with a markedly accommodating attitude to intellectual developments which depend to some extent on Enlightenment thought. As put by Maurice Agbaw-Ebai, "Ratzinger is not interested in rolling back the objectively good gains of the *Aufklärung*" such as emphasizing "the value of human rationality in moral discernment" or "paying attention to the historical dimension of truth claims."[9] If Kant is centrally important for the Enlightenment, and Ratzinger refuses to sweep the philosophical insights of the Enlightenment away *tout court*, then it seems unlikely his attitude to Kant should be considered exclusively hostile.

---

[4] Benedict XVI, *Faith, Reason and the University: Memories and Reflections. Lecture in the Meeting with the Representatives of Science*, Apostolic Journey to München, Altötting and Regensburg (September 9–14, 2006), Regensburg, September 12, 2006.
[5] T. Rowland, *Ratzinger's Faith: The Theology of Pope Benedict XVI* (London: Bloomsbury, 2008), p. 5.
[6] E. de Gaál, *O Lord I Seek Your Countenance*, p. 12.
[7] The most obvious examples of explicitly Kantian theologians would be the Transcendental Thomists, see A. M. Matteo, "Marechal's Dialogue with Kant: The Roots of Transcendental Thomism and the Search for Ultimate Reality and Meaning," *Ultimate Reality and Meaning* 22/4 (1999), pp. 264–75.
[8] Revolution is of course Kant's own word, referring to his first Critique as offering a "Copernican Revolution," I. Kant, *The Critique of Pure Reason*, P. Guyer and A. W. Wood (eds.) (Cambridge: Cambridge University Press, 1999).
[9] M. A. Agbaw-Ebai, *Light of Reason, Light of Faith*, p. 2. Please note Agbaw-Ebai means the German Enlightenment specifically.

Second, because Kant himself is of course an incredibly complex thinker, with a large written corpus, he is unlikely to fit into any simplistic characterization. As many an undergraduate philosophy student will testify, "[t]here are few philosophical texts so confusing and so perplexing as Kant's works"[10], and, moreover, these works cover a period of fifty years of active publication. If someone is marking himself or herself out against Kant, then, the key thing to be established is which element from Kant is being critiqued. This is not only because a full-scale refutation of Kantian philosophy would be more than a lifetime's work, but also because Kant's own thought develops and changes. Indeed, in Kant's own lifetime, he battled what he saw as misappropriations of his thought, most famously with his revision of the *Critique of Pure Reason* published in 1787, six years after the original, first edition of 1781.

This leads us into the complex and contentious territory of Kant reception. Indeed, some of those considering themselves Kantian, such as the neo-Kantians, are dismissed by others as mere "anti-Kantianism."[11] In the English-speaking world, embattled interpretation endures to this day. Paul D. Janz highlights one reason for this being a flawed translation of the *Critique of Pure Reason*, by Norman Kemp-Smith. In the 1960s, P. F. Strawson put forward a reading of Kant which was highly influential in its day, but which is "at fundamental points ... obviously at odds with what Kant actually says." This reading is held by Janz to reflect Strawson's uncritical acceptance of the Kemp-Smith translation.[12] More recently, John Milbank has been criticized for wrongly depicting Kant's critical philosophy as the "attitude of pure reason itself," rather than an attempt to set limits on "pure reason," and for thereby presenting Kant as "the culmination" of the "continental rationalism" which he seeks to critique and delimit.[13] Therefore, epithets like "Kantian" and "anti-Kantian" are unlikely ever to be straightforward and must always be tethered both to particular elements of his writings and to a sufficient awareness of the manifold complexities of his reception.

This chapter works from the tension between the plentiful dismissive remarks about Kant's work in Ratzinger's writings on the one hand, and Ratzinger's accommodating, but not uncritical, attitude to Enlightenment philosophies on the other. It does so by bearing in mind that this tension is heightened by the sheer volume and complexity of Kant's writings, and their contentious reception. The task of this chapter is therefore to explore the

---

[10] T. K. Seung, *Kant: A Guide for the Perplexed* (London: Continuum, 2007), p. vii. Paul Guyer begins his survey of Kant's writings in 1755, showing how large the corpus is beyond the three Critiques, in *Kant* (London: Routledge, 2006), p. 21.
[11] Cf. F. Kaufmann quoted by S. Fisher, *Revelatory Positivism?* (Oxford: Oxford University Press, 1988), p. 21.
[12] Cf. P. D. Janz, *God the Mind's Desire* (Cambridge: Cambridge University Press, 2004), p. 130.
[13] Cf. *ibid.*, p. 131.

relationship between Ratzinger and Kant by mapping out some of the shades of grey both within Ratzinger's own comments about Kant, and drawing attention to certain implicitly Kantian characteristics of Ratzinger's writings. The first step to this end is to focus on the primary works of Kant at play in Ratzinger's thought in the section "The *Critique of Pure Reason* and *Religion within the Bounds of Reason Alone*," before discussing Ratzinger's references to Kant in the section "Ratzinger's References to Kant," and more implicit tendencies in the section "Implicitly Kantian Tendencies." The ground will then be clear for me to offer a more nuanced position on Ratzinger and Kant than that suggested from a first glance at Ratzinger's works.

The *Critique of Pure Reason* and *Religion within the Bounds of Reason Alone*

The *Critique of Pure Reason*

One of the many problems that attend attitudes to Kant in theological discourse is a tendency for only one of Kant's works to receive considerable attention on reading lists and syllabi in philosophy of religion and philosophical theology: *Religion within the Boundaries of Mere Reason* (1792). I will turn to this book shortly, but first I want to concentrate on what is surely the most important and influential of Kant's works, the *Critique of Pure Reason* (1781 and 1787). Kant's works are notoriously difficult, as we have seen, and this certainly true of the *Critique*, a fact compounded by the differences between the afore mentioned first and second editions. For the purposes of this chapter, however, a very basic overview of the primary aim of the work, and a similarly concise summary of its outcomes, will suffice to provide the elements necessary for addressing Ratzinger's positions.

In terms of the book's primary aims, and contrary to many misinterpretations, Kant is seeking to *critique*—as in establish the limits and boundaries of—"pure reason."[14] Pure reason means the ratiocinative faculty undertaking noetic analysis, such as in mathematics or deductive logic. The knowledge that results from this is differentiated from employing the faculty of reason to understand worldly experience, which depends ultimately on sensory perception. Kant wants to steer a path between two prevalent philosophical outlooks of his milieu: "dogmatism" and "skepticism." Dogmatism is pure reason writ large, an overstepping of the bounds within which pure reason should function, seen particularly in Spinoza and Leibniz. These two are criticized by Kant for an unwarranted

---

[14]Much of the analysis in subsection I.A is taken from J. Phillips, *Human Subjectivity in Christ in Dietrich Bonhoeffer's Theology: Integrating Simplicity and Wisdom* (London: T&T Clark, 2019).

application of "pure reason without an antecedent critique of its own capacity."[15] This book is, then, precisely the "antecedent critique" to which he refers: establishing not only what pure reason can achieve, but also what it cannot. "Dogmatism" is rebuked for arrogating to itself "the proud name of an ontology," which means allowing reason to make claims to domains in which it cannot rationally demonstrate any legitimate jurisdiction, the mistaking of noetic truths as genuinely descriptive of ontology or metaphysics.[16]

However, the title of the book does not capture a second domain of knowledge which Kant also critiques. In 1771 he mentions an early working title for the *Critique of Pure Reason* which better describes his twofold concern, for he says he is working on a book to be called *The Bounds of Sensibility and of Reason*.[17] His evaluation of "skepticism," then, seeks to delimit not the bounds of pure reason, but of knowledge gained via sensory perception. Kant's main protagonist of a skeptical outlook is David Hume (1711–76).[18] Hume is seen as guilty of downplaying the demands of conceptual, rational cognition with an empirical, experience-oriented philosophy. This of course led Hume to question the fundamental tenets of traditional metaphysics, such as the law that "every event has some cause," because Hume extrapolated that a law encountered in experience cannot be said to apply universally and necessarily, i.e., apart from the "finite range of prior cases" which are the full available data of any and all experiential knowledge.[19]

From here, one can turn directly to one of the primary outcomes of the *Critique*, hoping readers can forgive my skipping the vast amount of philosophical reflection which space will not permit me to cover. Kant concludes with three "antinomies of pure reason." The antinomies arise from not heeding the boundaries of either pure reason or sensibility, from "either using the ideas of pure reason without respect to the limits of sensibility or taking the limits of sensibility to be the limits of all conceivable reality."[20] More exactly, Kant argues that what has traditionally been held to be knowledge of God, the world, and the soul, are actually mere antinomies. He writes that philosophers have often mistaken the conclusions of pure reason in a "dogmatic" fashion, ascribing that pure reason must apply to ontological reality. To give a (vastly abridged) example from his discussion of the self (and thereby the soul), Kant describes the necessary deduction that "I, as a thinking being, am the absolute subject of all my possible judgements" (A348). This is an outcome of pure reason focused on self-awareness. That

---

[15] P. D. Janz, *God the Mind's Desire*, p. 128.
[16] Cf. I. Kant, *The Critique of Pure Reason*, p. 358.
[17] Cf. P. Guyer, "Introduction," in P. Guyer (ed.), *The Cambridge Companion to Kant's Critique of Pure Reason* (Cambridge: Cambridge University Press, 2010), p. 3.
[18] Kant also has Cartesian and Pyrrhonian skepticism in mind, cf. P. Guyer, *Kant*, 11f.
[19] Cf. *ibid.*, pp. 12–13.
[20] *Ibid.*, p. 153.

means one's awareness of being the same self in all one's judgments can be deduced to be a necessary condition of self-awareness. In his own words, we are conscious "of the thoroughgoing identity of ourselves with regard to all representations that can ever belong to our consciousness" (A116).[21] If we were not conscious of this thoroughgoing identity, then we could not be self-aware, and there would be no way of knowing with certainty (necessarily) that one's experiences genuinely pertain to the same subject of experience. This would surrender to David Hume's "bundle theory" of the self as "nothing but a bundle or collection of different perceptions, which succeed each other with an inconceivable rapidity, and are in a perpetual flux and movement."[22] However, Kant shows that the necessary condition of self-awareness, deduced by pure reason, is wrongly inferred to posit the existence of an immortal soul, the self as "substance," or a metaphysical entity that is traditionally held therefore to endure after physical death. Otherwise dogmatism has again "arrogated to itself the proud name of an ontology."

Now, the key point is that Kant is not denying the existence of the immortal soul (nor the world, nor God, in the other two antinomies). Rather, Kant has shown that the soul is not knowable by sensible perception, agreeing with Hume, yet nor is it properly known by pure reason. The soul as traditionally conceived is therefore not something proper to philosophical reflection; its existence cannot be established *a posteriori* or *a priori*. This example serves aptly to bring in one of the most oft-quoted of Kant's statements from the *Critique*, where he writes that he wants "to deny knowledge *in order to make room for faith*" (Bxxx; my italics).[23]

Leaving aside the counter-arguments to Kant's findings from classical philosophy, it is a fair question here to ask whether some things are indeed better known in faith than grounded exclusively in reason and/or experience. This basic question needs to be asked of almost every elementary student of theology at some juncture. Even the most argumentatively tight argument for God's existence will arrive at something that falls far short of the God of Scripture and Dogma, i.e., the God of revelation, who is known in his fullness only by faith.

Of course, the properly Catholic response to this is to question any intractable rupture between faith and reason, citing *Dei filius*' comment that "between faith and reason no true dissension can ever exist."[24] The challenge for anyone wanting to interpret Kant sympathetically from a Catholic perspective on points like this, then, is to scrutinize the boundary set on pure reason and inquire as to whether "dissension" or complementarity applies in Kant's denial of knowledge of the soul by reason/experience, for

---

[21] I. Kant, *The Critique of Pure Reason*, p. 237.
[22] D. Hume, *A Treatise of Human Nature* (Oxford: Clarendon Press, 2007), p. 165.
[23] I. Kant, *The Critique of Pure Reason*.
[24] Vatican Council I, *Dogmatic Constitution* Dei filius, April 24, 1870, §4.

example, and the understanding of the soul provided by faith. Responding to this question would take us far beyond the remit of this chapter, but the fact is that it is, at least in principle, permissible from a Catholic perspective to acknowledge the perpetual threat of rational reductionism in religious matters. That is, the danger of overly confidently ascribing truths of reason to metaphysical realities. Then it is a short step to agreeing with Kant that there are circumstances whereby an overreaching "knowledge" needs to be denied to make room for the fullness of knowledge that comes through faith. This requires a two-sided caveat: this faith-filled knowledge cannot be understood as working against reason, but it does have the upper hand. To quote *Dei filius*, again, "faith is above reason."[25] Bearing in mind the trajectory of Enlightenment philosophy, and the rationalist shadows of Descartes, Spinoza, Leibniz et al., this Kantian endeavor could even prove something worth celebrating, if it is put to work to protect fundamental truths about God and the soul from being reduced to a grounding in reason alone. It is perhaps therefore a deficit that popular conceptions of Kant so often lump him in with the rationalists he sought to counter.

Religion within the Boundaries of Mere Reason

Readers would be forgiven for thinking the presentation of Kant offered in the previous section runs counter to that they have received previously, for he is often presented as the philosopher who argued that God and the soul are untenable notions unless their existence can be proved by pure reason. The reasons for this include the fact that elements of the *Critique* like that discussed above are not usually taught under the heading "Kant's philosophy of religion." But it is also because Kant's only book dedicated to religion does itself threaten to come close to exactly this position. Appearing mere five years after the second edition of the *Critique*, *Religion within the Boundaries of Mere Reason* (hereafter: *Religion*) was immediately received in precisely the way one might expect if Kant is indeed one of the great enemies of orthodox Christian faith. It was published with the imprimatur of Kant's own Königsberg philosophy faculty, but not the theology faculty, and even caused Frederick Wilhelm II to issue a royal rescript prohibiting Kant from publishing any further criticisms of religion.[26]

The reasons for this problematic reception can be clearly discerned from a very brief comment on the book's contents. Its overarching aim is roughly analogous to the twofold aim of the *Critique*, in that Kant seeks to inquire into an apparent gulf between "historical faith" meaning the doctrines of Christianity itself (an experiential knowledge, insofar as believers encounter the historical faith in experience), and "a pure rational religion," which

---

[25] Ibid.
[26] cf. P. Guyer, *Kant*, p. 38.

works only with what can be known by pure reason according to the *Critique of Pure Reason*, and the second critique: the *Critique of Practical Reason* (1788). The prefaces to the book therefore claim that it seeks first to "provide an inquiry into the scope of overlap" between these two, but then also to use "pure rational religion" "as a guide for distinguishing between which elements of the former are matters of 'genuine religion' rather than 'cult'."[27]

There is thus a significant shift here. While the first *Critique* sought "to deny knowledge to make room for faith," *Religion* inquired into what a Christianity construed only by the knowledge of pure reason would involve. Kant interrogates Original Sin, Christology, Ecclesiology, and various other things. Taking Christology as an example, thinking of a "Messiah," "Son of God" language, notions of divine "nature," not to mention the Resurrection, obviously cannot be subscribed to within the domain of "pure rational religion," and we are left with Christ as moral exemplar.

In summary, this section gives just one example of how the phrase "Kant's philosophy" can mean different things to different people, due not least to the apparent variances within Kant's own endeavors. In the first *Critique* he sets out "to deny knowledge to make room for faith," which is not in and of itself necessarily antithetical to *Dei filius*, in principle. In *Religion,* however, crucial elements of faith are pushed aside for the sake of pure reason, in a way which seems to invert *Dei filius'* qualification that "faith is above reason."

Ratzinger's References to Kant

Problems with Kant

Turning now to Ratzinger's own comments about Kant, the primary problem he detects is the rupture between reason and metaphysics bequeathed to us from the *Critique of Pure Reason*. In his Inaugural Lecture, Ratzinger begins with Blaise Pascal's mention of the "'God of Abraham, God of Isaac, God of Jacob' not of the philosophers and scholars," for with this, Pascal "discovers something philosophy is unable to reach on its own."[28] Against this background, he claims, Kant's denying of knowledge (of the God of the philosophers and scholars) to make room for faith (in the God of Abraham)

---

[27] L. Pasternack and C. Fugate, "Kant's Philosophy of Religion," in E. N. Zalta (ed.), *The Stanford Encyclopedia of Philosophy*, Summer 2022 Edition, https://plato.stanford.edu/archives/sum2022/entries/kant-religion/ quotation from Pasternak and Fugate's translation of Königlichen Preußischen (later Deutschen) Akademie der Wissenschaften (ed.), 1900–, *Kants gesammelte Schriften*, vol. 6 (Berlin: Georg Reimer [later Walter De Gruyter]), pp. 12–13.

[28] Quote from Pascal's 1654 Memorial, quoted in E. de Gaál, *O Lord I Seek Your Countenance*, p. 72.

brought about "a radical aggravation of the problem." There is thus a deepening of Pascal's fissure caused by Kant's "dismantling of speculative metaphysics."[29]

This last point can be explained further by turning to the *Introduction to Christianity*, where Ratzinger charts an architectonic scheme of the development of Western thought, working from the "magic" stage, then onto the "metaphysical" and the "scientific." Unsurprisingly, the move from the "metaphysical" to "scientific" stage is particularly salient for present purposes. Ratzinger describes our modern, scientific attitude in terms inextricable from the first *Critique*: "[w]e have given up seeking the 'in-itselfness' of things and sounding the nature of being itself," he writes, "we have come to regard the depths of being as in the last analysis unfathomable." Needless to say, this uses precisely Kant's language for the ontological reality that lurks beyond the limits of pure reason, the "thing-in-itself." Moreover, Ratzinger considers the first stage of the takeover of the scientific attitude to be the "birth of the historical approach" which he says was "prepared by Descartes and attained its full development" in Kant and Giambattista Vico (1668–1744). Prior to this, we read, the Middle Ages worked from the principle that "*Verum est ens*," truth *is* being, meaning reason by definition accords with ontological reality. This was "because God, pure intellect, made it, and he made it by thinking it." Then "all being is meaningful, '*logos*,' 'truth,'" and "human thinking is the re-thinking of being itself."[30]

Leaping forward to Ratzinger's later writings, *The Nature and Mission of Theology* also charts an architectonic scheme for understanding the relationship of philosophy to theology. Here, Ratzinger observes that St Thomas Aquinas drew a "line of demarcation" between the two domains. Philosophical knowledge is, for Thomas, "that sort of knowledge which reason as such can gain by itself, without the guidance of revelation." Theology, however, does not "discover its contents by itself but rather receives them from revelation."[31] These distinctions are described as "still inchoate in St Thomas" works', until they "reached their full rigour in the modern period." It seems natural to suggest a key proponent of this "full rigor" is Kant himself, who is mentioned shortly afterward in relation to a situation whereby the "process of separation is complete." Ratzinger then turns to Martin Luther and Karl Barth, as primary examples of those who accept the separation as integral to properly theologizing. Hence, Barth's infamous rebukes to the *analogia entis*, which Ratzinger glosses as "a term for the ontological option of Catholic theology, for its synthesis of the philosophical idea of being and the biblical conception of God."[32] In other

---

[29] Quoted in E. de Gaál, *O Lord I Seek Your Countenance* and in M. A. Agbaw-Ebai, *Light of Reason, Light of Faith*, p. 73.
[30] J. Ratzinger, *Introduction to Christianity* (San Francisco: Ignatius, 2005), pp. 30–1.
[31] *Id.*, *The Nature and Mission of Theology*, p. 16.
[32] *Ibid.*, pp. 17 and 19.

words, the term *analogia entis* serves for Barth as a way of denying the *verum est ens* principle, insofar as *verum* could be construed as the God of Scripture (cf. John 14.6). Interestingly, Ratzinger points out that the Barthian antipathy is not toward "philosophy as such," but "rather metaphysics," specifically.[33] Here Kant enters the scene, as the figure ultimately responsible for this antipathy. Ratzinger thus roots the proponents of a separation between *verum* and *ens* "in the progressive replacement of metaphysics by history which has taken place in philosophy since Kant."[34]

In the Regensburg Address, Kant is again put at the center of the rupture between *verum* and *ens,* and again as feeding directly into Protestant theologies thereby. The program of "dehellenization" is singled out as supremely emblematic of the fundamental problem. This refers to a pattern of thinking prevalent in nineteenth-century Liberal Protestantism, most often linked with the church historian Adolf von Harnack. The program works from the supposition that the earliest sources of the faith, or what are held by historical criticism to be the earliest sources (such as "Q"), provide the most authentic and authoritative knowledge about Jesus. This means that other sources traditionally considered pinnacles of authenticity and authority, like the Chalcedonian Definition and the Nicene Creed, are questionable because their concepts and mode of expression are so very different, thus seeming to be artificial and unwarranted accretions or even depletions of the original *kerygma*. The concepts of Greek philosophy are then problematized, terms like *ousia* or *hypostasis*, and hence, "dehellenization." Ratzinger goes as far as to argue that Kant cleared the way for dehellenization because he showed that the grounding conviction of terms like *ousia* or *hypostasis* was intellectually unsustainable. That is, he denied that reason could confidently know ontology. He writes, "[w]hen Kant stated that he needed to set thinking aside in order to make room for faith, he carried his programme forward with a radicalism that the Reformers could never have foreseen."[35]

Ratzinger admonishes the separation of *verum* and *ens*, reason and metaphysics, philosophy and theology. Indeed, as he states in *Milestones*, this was one of the exciting possibilities afoot in the academic scene during his seminary days: "we could detect a return to metaphysics, which had become inaccessible since Kant."[36] Here, mention needs to be made of a passing comment by Ratzinger which is particularly important. The book *Religion* is summarized above not only because it helps explain the profound antipathy toward Kant among many theologians. Ratzinger himself actually connects the "denying" of metaphysics in the *Critique* with the reductionism

---

[33] Cf. *ibid.*, p. 20.
[34] *Ibid.*, pp. 20–1.
[35] Benedict XVI, *Faith, Reason and the University: Memories and Reflections. Lecture in the Meeting with the representatives of science*, Apostolic Journey to München, Altötting and Regensburg (September 9–14, 2006), Regensburg, September 12, 2006.
[36] J. Ratzinger, *Milestones: Memoirs 1927–1977* (San Francisco: Ignatius, 1998), pp. 43–4.

of *Religion*. In the Regensburg Address he argues that Kant's setting "thinking aside to make room for faith" meant that he went on to deny faith any room whatsoever. The "radicalism" evinced by the *Critique* meant he "*thus* anchored faith exclusively in practical reason, denying it access to reality as a whole."[37] As it stands, then, Ratzinger's attitude to Kant seems exclusively negative.

Kant's "Breakthrough"

Were this chapter to end here, it might seem that Ratzinger does indeed want thinking to go back, somehow, to the premodern era. Yet, we know that Ratzinger is a remarkably accommodating thinker when it comes to modernity, so it is natural to ask if that supposition adequately captures his position toward Kant's antinomies. He does indeed speak of "return" in *Milestones*, but he also says "we wanted not only to do theology in the narrow sense but to listen to the voices of man today," to carry "the baggage of the challenges, difficulties, joys, and hopes of the world" with him. These challenges and difficulties include Kant's legacy in Western thought. A more exact approach to the Ratzingerian task is shown in his struggles with the challenges of developing a post-critical mode of biblical exegesis. On this front, he argues that there cannot be "a retreat" to a "framework founded on the principle that the history of thought seriously began only with Kant," yet nor can there be a return "to the mediaeval or patristic frameworks alone."[38] Ratzinger thus neither accepts the separation of *verum* and *ens*, nor does he want to return to the understanding of *verum est ens* that predates Kant. There are good grounds, therefore, to revisit the examples given above to try and deduce if Kant is really just someone Ratzinger wishes to sweep aside, or someone with a certain legitimacy.

Beginning with the Inaugural Lecture again, then, Ratzinger brings Kant into the discussion after having outlined two ways by which the "God of faith" and the "God of philosophers" are classically interrelated in theological discussion. On one hand is a dialectical theologian of high profile in the 1920s, Emil Brunner, who presents "an irreconcilable contradiction" between the two.[39] While we know enough now to accept that this contradiction is, to Ratzinger's mind, an outworking of Kant, it is surprising that the example of an opposing position is Aquinas. Ratzinger argues that boundaries between faith and reason which he describes as "inchoate" some decades later, as quoted above, are now presented as decidedly murky. Indeed, he suggests there is confusion between the two in Thomas: "bringing the God of religion and that of philosophy precariously close to

---

[37] Benedict XVI, *Faith, Reason and the University: Memories and Reflections* (my emphasis).
[38] Quoted by T. Rowland, *Ratzinger's Faith*, pp. 56–7.
[39] Cf. E. de Gaál, *O Lord I Seek Your Countenance*, p. 74.

coinciding." Against this background, the clear differentiation of Pascal's formula is a helpful step in moving beyond a too close conflation. Ratzinger even states that it is with Kant that "Pascal's thoughts" are brought "to a breakthrough."[40] This breakthrough is the distinction of faith from reason, which does not necessarily entail the caesuras that eventually followed in thinkers like Brunner. Ratzinger states it is "only now," presumably meaning the 1920s, that Kant's distinction has "led to a radical aggravation of the problem," implying the questions the dialecticians raise are necessary to ask. If correct, this position is differently nuanced to the Regensburg Address he gave forty-six years later. There, the distinction between reason and metaphysics in the first *Critique* led directly into the reductionism of *Religion*. As put in *Fides et ratio*, "St Albert the Great and St Thomas were the first to recognize the autonomy which philosophy and the sciences needed if they were to perform well in their respective fields." But, from "the late mediaeval period onwards," the "legitimate distinction between the two forms of learning became more and more a fateful separation."[41] Ratzinger's earlier connecting of this "legitimate distinction" with Kant as a "breakthrough" would suggest that the *Critique of Pure Reason* need not inevitably lead into the missteps of *Religion*. It might therefore have elements distinct from the illegitimate separations that followed.

This same point is perhaps even more apparent in Ratzinger's even earlier lectures on Fundamental Theology. While Ratzinger here states that "Kant became the Aristotle of Protestantism" and "Schleiermacher became its Thomas," he again positions Thomas ambivalently in his scheme. This scheme distinguishes between "systems of identity, duality, and of conformity" between faith and reason. Both identity and duality are problematic, and it is implied that a twentieth-century rediscovery of *verum est ens* will therefore need to seek *conformity* between the two. Aquinas is placed among those with a system of identity. Yet identity is deeply problematic when pushed to the point that "religious and metaphysical insights" are completely identical, for this is, says Ratzinger, tantamount to Gnosticism. The issue here is that philosophical knowledge (or better, *gnosis*) then subsumes salvific authority. It is therefore necessary that tendencies toward identity move toward duality, insofar as this move evinces *Fides et ratio*'s "legitimate distinction." The proponents of duality are said by Ratzinger to be philosophers of "the Enlightenment, and especially Kant." Again, there is a legitimacy at play, albeit only insofar as it does not lead into a breach or separation.

In *The Nature and Mission of Theology*, the interplay of legitimate differentiation and illegitimate separation is described in terms of "distinction" and "opposition." Here, Ratzinger is more sympathetic to

---

[40] Quoted by M. A. Agbaw-Ebai, *Light of Reason, Light of Faith*, p. 73.
[41] John Paul II, *Encyclical Letter: Fides et ratio on the Relationship between Faith and Reason*, September 14, 1998, §45.

Thomas. One might ask if his 1950s comments were indicative of an animus common among some of those reacting against neo-Scholasticism while being hugely excited by the newer currents emerging on the intellectual scene. Thomas is now presented as the exemplar of "distinction," in whom there is a clear "line of demarcation" between the two domains of knowledge. But, Ratzinger still holds that the distinction "reached" its "full rigour only in the modern period." Interestingly, however, there is also what seems to be an acknowledgment of certain neo-Scholastic tendencies as themselves reflecting modern "oppositions": people "read" such oppositions "back in St Thomas," we read, "thus imposing on him an interpretation which severs him more radically from the preceding tradition than is warranted by the texts alone."[42]

Taking all these examples together, it seems that Ratzinger's mentions of Kant use him as more than just a motif of separation or opposition between faith and reason, theology and philosophy, metaphysics and God. That is, Kant might well also be one in whom there is articulation of the legitimate distinction between the two sides to knowledge. Put differently, Ratzinger detects manifold problems with systems of metaphysical religion or sheer "identity," and it is therefore necessary and right that such systems move toward distinction. Distinction itself goes on to present manifold problems when it comes to separation, but the point is that achieving conformity—harking back to *verum est ens*—will be done in a way which maintains "the objectively good gains of the *Aufklärung*."[43] That is, there are times when a denial of philosophical knowledge is necessary to make room for faith, insofar as such denials do not trespass over *Dei filius*, the principle that "between faith and reason no true dissension can ever exist."[44] One might go so far as to suggest that, working in a broadly post-Kantian framework, Ratzinger is arguing that *verum* isn't *ens* as such, yet neither is *verum* opposed to *ens*. Rather, he seeks to show that *verum* conforms to *ens*, and this means he frames the motivating task of his intellectual *oeuvre* in a decidedly post-Kantian way.

Implicitly Kantian Tendencies

Ratzinger's direct mentions of Kant are indeed two-sided and require the application of significant nuance to be properly understood. But there are also some moments in the Ratzinger corpus where the Kantian legacy goes further than a tacit acceptance of the inevitability of modernity, of the unavoidable fact that "identity" had to move to "opposition" before contemporary theology can establish "conformity." For reasons of space

---

[42] J. Ratzinger, *The Nature and Mission of Theology*, pp. 16–17.
[43] M. A. Agbaw-Ebai, *Light of Reason*, p. 2.
[44] Vatican Council I, *Dei filius*, §4.

I will give just one example, from Pope Benedict XVI's lectures on the European project given at Subiaco in 2005. This discussion takes us beyond fundamental theology, and into public theology.[45]

In these lectures, Ratzinger notes that, by the time of the Enlightenment, people could live as if God doesn't exist, *etsi Deus non daretur*. He suggests that the deleterious consequences of the European crisis of faith could be mitigated by rephrasing the classical *etsi*-formulation. Now, he says, we must encourage people to live *etsi veluti si Deus daretur: as if* God *does* exist. His hope is that both people with and without faith can participate in this commitment. Agnostics and atheists would thereby accept that belief in God provides a moral base for civic life, without needing necessarily to have faith themselves.

Ratzinger reminds us that Enlightenment philosophers sought to establish moral orientations by means of the human *logos*, so their evidential grounds and rationales are perceptible to all, thus applicable to those living *etsi Deus non daretur*. This well-known phrase is emblematic of the Enlightenment but actually originates earlier in the writings of Hugo Grotius.[46] The most emblematic example of this way of thinking, however, is surely Kant's *Critique of Practical Reason*, which purports to show—on purely philosophical grounds—why it is necessary to postulate the existence of God in order to account for the intrinsically ethical character of some human action. Note that it is necessary only to *postulate* God's existence, for the verification of whether God actually exists is not for Kant under the preserve of reason, but only of faith. In Ratzinger's words, Kant "denied that God could be known within the sphere of pure reason" but "at the same time" presented God as a postulate of practical reason "without which he saw no coherent possibility of acting in a moral manner."[47] Ratzinger acknowledges many unfortunate consequences some centuries later, however. This search for a "kind of reassuring certainty" that "could go unchallenged despite all the disagreements, has not succeeded."[48] So he asks, "I wonder if the situation of today's world might not make us return to the idea that Kant was right?"[49] By this he asks if the motivating quandary for Kant's *Critique* is correct: there is no "coherent possibility of acting in a moral manner" if we live *etsi Deus non daretur*.

Turning from Ratzinger's diagnosis to his solution, he presents this as an inversion of the original *etsi*-formulation, saying it is necessary to "reverse

---

[45] For a fuller discussion of this element of the Subiaco lectures, see J. Phillips, "After etsi veluti si Deus daretur: Joseph Ratzinger and Robert Cardinal Sarah," in M. A. Agbaw-Ebai and M. Levering (eds.), *Joseph Ratzinger and the Future of African Theology* (Eugene: Pickwick, 2022).
[46] Cf. H. Grotius, *De iure belli ac pacis libri tres*, prolegomena, §11, 31 (Indianapolis: Liberty Fund, 2005).
[47] J. Ratzinger, *Christianity and the Crisis of Cultures*, p. 51.
[48] *Ibid.*
[49] *Ibid.*

the axiom of the Enlightenment." He borrows the phrasing for this from Pascal, who advised his own associates who did not have faith that they could live well if they lived *"etsi veluti si Deus daretur."* People without faith in God can thus accept the roots of their moral norms in the Christian dispensation that gave birth to the Enlightenment, and therefore avoid the serious moral confusion resulting from the detachment and estrangement of Enlightenment philosophy from itself. As Ratzinger puts it, "[e]ven the one who does not succeed in finding the road to accepting the existence of God ought nevertheless to try to live and to direct his life *veluti Si Deus daretur."*[50] Marcello Pera fleshes this out with more detail, saying that while for a person "inside the Church" moral norms are rooted in the Christian God, for someone "outside the Church" they are rooted in "the God of his conscience."[51]

Here, it is striking how measured Ratzinger is in his criticisms of the Enlightenment project. The issues he highlights result from its long-term consequences, its forsaking of its Christian roots. This obviously aligns with Ratzinger/Benedict XVI's overarching desire for people to rediscover "a necessary correlation between reason and faith" as things "called to purify and lead one another."[52] Yet it should be pointed out that Ratzinger's *etsi-*reformulation cannot be considered a reversal of the Enlightenment *per se*, he only reverses the meaning of the *etsi-*phrase. If anything, Ratzinger is highlighting that the original Enlightenment conundrum is unsolved, and intensifying the problem. He admits Kant was right in his understanding of this problem, and even seems to think Kant was right to postulate God's existence as a way of rendering broadly Christian moral norms as applicable to all. Ratzinger's position is not therefore a critique of the Enlightenment in any straightforward sense, but actually close to a restating of the Kantian quandary in a more optimistic mode, now hopeful of a new rapprochement, of a new conformity between faith and reason.

Conclusion

It is relatively self-evident that Ratzinger himself was not particularly interested in Kant interpretation. There is nothing to suggest he had reason to undergo a painstaking reading of the *Critiques*, and Kant is usually mentioned briefly as emblematic or exemplary of a juncture on the cusp of modernity, as is indeed common and correct. But we can conclude that the Ratzinger-Kant relationship is complex, and that, contrary to appearances,

---

[50] *Ibid*.
[51] Marcello Pera in the introduction to J. Ratzinger, *Christianity and the Crisis of Cultures*, p. 20.
[52] J. Ratzinger, *Values in a Time of Upheaval*, p. 43.

simply to accept a one-sided characterization of Ratzinger as "anti-Kantian" would be inaccurate.

The intellectual legacy of Kant endures in Ratzinger's theology, yet the foregoing analysis perhaps raises more questions than it does answers. We are left wanting to interrogate Kant further to ask if Ratzinger is right that the rebuttal of traditional metaphysics in the *Critique* inevitably leads to the rebuttal of Christian faith in *Religion*. We are left wanting to interrogate Ratzinger's work further to establish exactly how the distinction between *verum* and *ens* can be maintained without lapsing into opposition or separation, and then establishing the degree to which Kant's "denying of knowledge to make room for faith" might be deemed legitimate within a Ratzingerian purview. We are led to ask whether Kant needs to be understood as just the "Aristotle of Protestantism" or whether he also impacts on movements like neo-Scholasticism. We might even be led to ask how sustainable Ratzinger's cautious acceptance of much Enlightenment philosophy truly is, given his broader intention to think through how *verum* conforms to *ens*.

Nonetheless, the fact remains that in Kant himself we do see something of what Ratzinger argued philosophy needs to do if it is to remain genuine philosophy, indicative of a genuine love of wisdom or knowledge. In *Truth and Tolerance* we read that "a philosophy that no longer asks who we are, what we are here for, whether there is a God and eternal life, has abdicated its role as a philosophy."[53] Such cannot be said of Kant. The questions of who we are and of God are important for the *Critique of Pure Reason*, and the question of "what we are here for" is central to the *Critique of Practical Reason*. Yet, we must always be orientated by the fact that, for Ratzinger, it can never be enough to say it is "the starry heavens above me and the moral law within me" that "fill the mind with ever new and increasing admiration and awe, the more often and steadily we reflect upon them."[54] Rather, our ultimate admiration and awe are always apportioned first to the Triune God, as revealed in the person of Jesus Christ.

---

[53] Quoted by M. A. Agbaw-Ebai, p. 2, n. 14.
[54] Immanuel Kant, *Critique of Practical Reason*, 33–6.

6

Georg Wilhelm Friedrich Hegel: Reason, Historicity, and Community

Eduardo Charpenel

Introduction

As is well known, Hegel is and has been a philosopher of difficult assimilation. The complex philosophical system he produced—expressed in an intricate and arduous language which has never been easy to elucidate—has been, from his own time onward, the subject of heated disputes and debates. Since then, much has been at stake as to what position one should take with regard to his ideas and theories. In general, the stances that have been taken toward the Hegelian philosophical system have been radical. More often than not, there have been two scenarios: either one has accepted entirely the views of the philosopher of Stuttgart, or one has fiercely criticized what he had to say.

An evident manifestation of this was the split between Hegel's disciples and immediate followers: the so-called right- and left-wing Hegelians. While the former used their master's philosophy to defend traditional views on religion and politics, the latter saw in it a tremendous iconoclastic potential that would serve them to make fierce criticisms of religion (Feuerbach) and of the prevailing economy and political systems (Marx and Engels). It is no exaggeration to say that all philosophy that came after him was defined in relation to his figure: very few sought to continue his legacy in an orthodox manner, others—in particular, the left-wing Hegelians and Kierkegaard—

sought, at the end of the day, to *use* Hegel *against* Hegel, and others ended up explicitly developing thoughts or proposals that departed radically from the thought of the philosopher of Stuttgart (neo-Kantians, positivists, phenomenologists, early analytical philosophers, etcetera). Although, in this convulsive context, Hegel never lost the status of being a prominent figure—at least as an object of distant reverence in the pantheon of the history of ideas—it is easy to understand why he was never well regarded in circles such as that of Catholic philosophical-theological thought in the twentieth century.

In this sense, Joseph Ratzinger was perhaps no exception. This can be noticed, on the one hand, in the fact that Ratzinger never mentions Hegel as one of his influences or intellectual references, and, on the other hand, in the explicit critical judgments and opinions that appear in his writings in relation to the crowning figure of German idealism.

One could tell the story so far, and hereafter list a whole series of errors that separate Hegel from Catholic orthodoxy, especially from Ratzinger's perspective.[1] But I think that things are and should not be so simple, at least when it comes to assessing the relationship of one of the central figures of the philosophical canon with the strong tradition of Christian faith and religion from which Hegel himself, as a Protestant, never abjured. In favor of this speaks not only that, in recent decades, Catholic thinkers and scholars such as Charles Taylor, René Girard, Quentin Lauren, S.J., and Daniel Jamros, S.J. have approached Hegel with great intellectual profit.[2] Rather, the fact that an attentive look at Hegel's writings can shed light on decisive aspects of the Christian tradition should, in my view, invite a reappraisal that is both reflective and constructive.

---

[1] To mention just one example: in his *Introduction to Christianity*, Ratzinger criticizes the Trinitarian conception held by Hegel, accusing it of being "monarchist": a theological error according to which God is understood as one indivisible being in direct contrast to Trinitarism: "The subsequent history of Monarchianism in modern thinking has only confirmed this once again. Hegel and Schelling, in their efforts to interpret Christianity philosophically and to rethink philosophy from Christian premises, went back to this early Christian attempt at a philosophy of Christianity and hoped by starting from here to make the doctrine of the Trinity intelligible and useful, to elevate it in its allegedly pure philosophical sense into the true key to all understanding of Being," J. Ratzinger, *Introduction to Christianity* (San Francisco: Ignatius, 2004), p. 134. However, it is a disputed question, in this particular case, whether Hegel held in fact such a view, as shown persuasively by P. Trawny, *Die Zeit der Dreinigkeit* (Würzburg: Königshausen & Neumann, 2002), pp. 54ff.; and K. von Stosch, *Trinität* (UTB: Tübingen, 2017), p. 83ff. Since there are contested issues in the interpretations, I want to avoid the path of taking Ratzinger's reading of Hegel as correct and criticize the latter. On the contrary, I think that developing a discussion by attending to Hegel's own theses and arguments can be a much more fruitful intellectual exercise. In this way, the real distance that exists between the authors can be established with more accuracy.

[2] In this regard, one should also not forget Hans Küng's important Habilitationschirft entitled *The Incarnation of God: An Introduction to Hegel's Theological Thought as Prolegomena to a Future Christology* (Crossroad: New York, 1989; published originally in German in 1970). By

In order to develop the coordinates of what I would like to call "a possible dialogue," I will explore three topics where, in my opinion, *at least initially*, a rather short distance exists between Ratzinger and Hegel: 1) the encounter between Greek thought and the Christian religion, 2) the historical development of Christianity as a faith that evolves (without losing its characteristic and distinctive essence) over time, gaining in each moment of its development a new understanding of itself, and 3) the strong sense of community and church to which Christianity invites. I say "at least initially" because, undoubtedly, also, Hegel and Ratzinger more often than not arrive at very different positions in spite of having points of contact in their thought.

To be sure, I believe there are substantial differences that separate Hegel's and Ratzinger's appreciations of Christianity. Thus, I entirely want to avoid the temptation of conflating Hegel with Ratzinger or vice versa. These important differences will be brought up in the concluding section of the present essay. But, as I mentioned before, I believe that highlighting certain crucial similarities will contribute to reassessing the proximity of these two decisive figures in the history of theology and philosophy. If it is possible to transcend, to some extent, the radical interpretations that separate or unite such influential authors and find instead some common grounds, it will therefore be equally possible to appreciate the complex relationships that mediate between such important thinkers. This exercise will be reserved for the final part where I will contrast the thinking of both figures. But first let us review some core ideas of the proposals of each of them.

Athens and Jerusalem: The Rise and Fate of Christianity

Christianity, for Hegel, is unthinkable without the mediation of Greek thought and philosophy. In the history of Christianity, one cannot regard as a mere accident the fact that the word of Jesus was communicated and transmitted in Greek, with all the philosophical nuances and connotations this implied, to the new believers of this faith. Although we of course know that Jesus did not deliver his teachings originally in this manner, the fact that they were indeed spread and diffused through the Gospels and the letters of

---

Küng's own account in a late foreword to the work, what he sought to do there was not simply to oppose the "God of faith" to the "God of philosophers"—a strategy that he, for many systematic reasons, dismissed. Rather, what he was looking for were points of convergence between the German thinker and the cores of the Catholic faith as such. Given the complex and sometimes polemical intellectual relationship between Küng and Ratzinger, it is possible to think that a book written on Hegel by the former was a reason that did not encourage the latter to approach the sage of Stuttgart.

Paul in the language of Plato and Aristotle would forever mark the way in which this message would be received and interpreted. Hence, for example, Hegel opposes a Protestant theological intention of trying to find a kind of Christianity that was not mediated by such a filter.³ Hegel does not deny that such an archaeological and philological finding could be possible. But he does question whether such a discovery would tell us anything essentially different or new from what we have already learned through Revelation. In essence, the Christian theses are unique and unrepeatable. Let us review some of them. For Hegel what is decisive in this new religion is, in the first place, that, unlike what was held in ancient philosophy (in neo-Platonism, for instance), the absolute is understood here as spirit. Anticipating what will be Schelling's criticism, Hegel already states in his *Lectures on the History of Philosophy* that for him God must be something more than a mere thought or conceived entity.⁴ Moreover, even if a philosophy such as neo-Platonism claims that the One has a relationship with itself, this relationship is never thought from the subjective and particular sphere. For this reason, Hegel does not hesitate to affirm in regard to neo-Platonists the following: "To them spirit is thus not individual spirit; and this deficiency is made good through Christianity, in which spirit is found as actual, present spirit, immediately existent in the world here and now, and the absolute spirit is known in the immediate present as man."⁵ The relationship of the human being with these contents is unique, since they are there for him, so to speak, in order to be recognized and incorporated radically into his own existence. This could not be done in a religion where the distance between the divine and the human is unbridgeable. As we know from the discussion of the *Phenomenology of Spirit*, all attempts to grasp divinity by equating the latter with forces of nature such as light or darkness (Zoroastrianism), animals or anthropomorphic animals (Hinduism and Egyptian religion), or even as extraordinary human beings (Greek religion) prove insufficient and unsatisfactory. It is only when God renounces his abstract identity and becomes man that an accomplished religion comes into being: a movement which, in the eyes of Hegel, goes not from men to God but from God to men. A religion where, we could say, the Hegelian dictum "bei sich selbst sein in einem Anderen" (being with oneself in another) acquires a concrete and specific meaning. For God is no longer understood as a hidden or irrational force operating behind the scenes on the cosmic stage. In Hegel's words: "The Christian life signifies that the culminating point of subjectivity is made familiar with this conception, the individual himself is laid claim to, is made worthy of attaining on his own account to this unity, which is to

---

³Cf. G. W. F. Hegel, *Lectures on the History of Philosophy: The Lectures of 1825–1826, Volume III: Medieval and Modern Philosophy* (Berkeley: University of California Press, 1990), p. 28.
⁴*Id., Lectures on the History of Philosophy: Medieval and Modern Philosophy* 3 (Lincoln: University of Nebraska Press, 1995), p. 1.
⁵*Ibid.*, p. 2.

make himself worthy of the Spirit of God—Grace, as it is called—dwelling in him."[6] It is in the very possibility of receiving this spirit that the human being, transcending his immediacy (his barbarism, his proclivity to evil, etc.), can actualize his full nature.

Since this must occur for Hegel not by mere subjective feeling but by reason, the fact that the Greek world had paved the way for this new conception is particularly favorable to the interests of mankind. In general terms, it is possible to say that Christianity is, for Hegel, a true religion since one is able to rationally grasp its content.[7] This is explained, on the one hand, by the fact that in Christianity it is revealed that the human being shares a common nature with God, and, on the other hand, by the nature of Christian doctrines themselves, which are expressed in terms and concepts close to those of philosophy. A characteristic example of this is the notion of *logos*, which is central to the entire Hegelian understanding of Christianity:

> Thus man reaches this truth, because for him it becomes a sure intuition that in Christ the *logos* has become Flesh. We thus first have man through this process attaining to spirituality, and in the second place we have man as Christ, in whom this original identity of both natures is known. Now since man really is this process of being the negation of the immediate, and from this negation attaining to himself—to a unity with God—he must consequently renounce his natural will, knowledge, and existence. This giving up of his natural existence is witnessed in Christ's sufferings and death, and in His resurrection and elevation to the right hand of the Father. Christ became a perfect man, endured the lot of all men, death; as man He suffered, sacrificed Himself, gave up His natural existence, and thereby elevated Himself above it.[8]

Thus, it can be seen that, for Hegel, Christianity implies a call to follow the way of Christ. This means for Hegel that man, as a natural being, must break with his natural constraints and limitations and rationally understand his role in the world, for only in this way can good triumph over evil in his existence. In the face of this task, the Christian benefits greatly from the legacy of Greek thought, since thanks to this background he is able to link his intelligence with the premises of the Christian faith.

Turning now to Ratzinger, we can see that there are many points of coincidence in suggesting the necessity and crucial character of what we could call the "Greek mediation." Curiously, one can see for instance that he is also taking a stand against those who look for some sort of "dehellenization" of

---

[6] *Ibid.*, p. 3.
[7] In this respect, Hegel's assertion that the philosophy of the Middle Ages was valuable because philosophy and theology were inseparable is quite illustrative. See *ibid.*, pp. 45–60.
[8] *Ibid.*, pp. 4–5.

Christianity.⁹ The reason why this has sometimes been suggested is because it is thought that the God of the Jewish tradition cannot be homologated without further ado with the conception of God or the divine held in the Greek world. While Ratzinger certainly emphasizes different aspects of the novelty and radicality of the God of the Bible, it is no less certain that he values the Greek and philosophical legacy that accompanied the interpretation, the reception, and the spread of Christianity. Thus, Ratzinger affirms: "The New Testament was written in Greek and bears the imprint of the Greek spirit, which had already come to maturity as the Old Testament developed."¹⁰

A clear example of this can be observed in the Preface to the Gospel of John, a text which was written in Greek and which uses Hellenic concepts and ideas, but which at the same time refers to Jewish culture. In relation to it, Ratzinger affirms that "modifying the first verse of the Book of Genesis, the first verse of the whole Bible, John began the Prologue of his Gospel with the words: 'In the beginning was the λόγος'. This is the very word used by the emperor: God acts, σὺν λόγω, with *logos*."¹¹ The interpretation that Ratzinger provides of the importance of the notion of *logos* is very suggestive: this term, which means word and thought in Greek, helped to understand better the Semitic notion of Messiah, thus moving from the Jewish conception of a "Son of man" and at the same time Messiah, to a "divine person" or a "God-man" that was closer to the Hellenic culture, offering thereby an image of Jesus Christ which was easier for others to assimilate.

The bond between Athens and Jerusalem, so to speak, becomes indissoluble. Hence, it is possible to affirm that "the encounter between the Biblical message and Greek thought did not happen by chance. [...]. This vision can be interpreted as a 'distillation' of the intrinsic necessity of a rapprochement between Biblical faith and Greek inquiry."¹² In this way, Greek culture and thought helped to shed light upon fundamental aspects of Christianity itself, such as the rational deepening of the mysteries of faith and the possibility of harmoniously uniting faith with a human way of searching for truth. Furthermore, when John uses the concept of *logos* to refer to Jesus, he not only uses what it means in itself in Greek culture, but also mixes there the Jewish notion that had been given to that word when it was translated into the Septuagint, and that synthesis serves as a basis in Christianity. In short, for John, "*logos* does not mean simply the idea of

---

⁹ Cf. J. Ratzinger, *Principles of Catholic Theology: Building Stones for a Fundamental Theology* (San Francisco: Ignatius, 1987), p. 158.
¹⁰ Benedict XVI, *Faith, Reason and the University: Memories and Reflections. Lecture in the Meeting with the Representatives of Science*, Apostolic Journey to München, Altötting and Regensburg (September 9–14, 2006), Regensburg, September 12, 2006.
¹¹ *Ibid.*
¹² *Ibid.*

the eternal rationality of being, as it did essentially in Greek thought. By its application to Jesus of Nazareth, the concept of *logos* acquires a new dimension."[13]

In fact, this is only one of many cases that Ratzinger deals with throughout his oeuvre. By delving into discussions about the translation of the Septuagint into Greek and the formation of core theological concepts in the Greek patristic, Ratzinger explores and affirms the synthesis between "the Greek and the biblical image of God."[14] The encounter of Greek culture with Judeo-Christian roots served as a solid foundation for faith. Despite the differences, both horizons shared the idea that beliefs could be clarified by reason.[15] The radical nature of this encounter resulted, however, in the God of the philosophers being purified and henceforth in being conceived as a person. Thus,

> this God who had been understood as pure Being or pure thought, circling around forever closed in upon himself without reaching over to man and his little world; this God of the philosophers, whose pure eternity and unchangeability had excluded any relation with the changeable and transitory, now appeared to the eye of faith as the God of men, who is not only thought of all thoughts, the eternal mathematics of the universe, but also *agape*, the power of creative love.[16]

For Ratzinger, then, the God of faith is intimately united with the God of the philosophers; so much so that even the Fathers of the Church themselves believed that, through the Greek mediation, they could find the true relationship between philosophy and faith, thus uniting Plato and Moses.[17] For the same reason, the Christian must realize that "there can be many different approaches to the one God,"[18] and that trying to separate the God of faith from the God of the philosophers is to deprive faith of its objectivity.[19] The Fathers of the Church themselves like Justin Martyr, who had studied philosophy, recognized in their conversion to Christianity that this was in fact the *vera philosophia*, so they did not put aside their

---

[13] J. Ratzinger, *Introduction to Christianity*, p. 134.
[14] *Id.*, *Der Gott des Glaubens und der Gott der Philosophen* (Leutesdorf: Johannes, 2005), p. 20. Translations from titles referred in German are my own, unless otherwise indicated.
[15] Cf. *id.*, *Introduction to Christianity*, p. 51.
[16] *Ibid.*, p. 101.
[17] Cf. *ibid.*, p. 83.
[18] *Id.*, *Principles of Catholic Theology*, p. 73.
[19] It is in this same sense that Ratzinger radically claims that "the God of Aristotle and the God of Jesus Christ is one and the same" (cf. *id.*, *Der Gott des Glaubens und der Gott der Philosophen*, p. 16). Whereas Aristotle knew the truth of God, the Christian can apprehend that truth through faith; they are different degrees of the same path that leads to the truth of God (cf. *ibid.*). In short: "the biblical name for God is here identified with the philosophical concept of God" (*id.*, *Introduction to Christianity*, p. 84).

philosophical studies, but saw Christianity as the completion of philosophy. And this position was not only assumed in the Patristics but was adopted until the fourteenth century.

As I have pointed out, one can find various points of intellectual coincidence and convergence between Hegel and Ratzinger, at least concerning certain fundamental theses or principles. To be sure, as pointed out, this does not guarantee that from such common grounds they reach the same conclusions. This will be discussed further in our concluding remarks. For the time being, however, it is worth reviewing other thematic axes where, at the outset, the closeness between our authors is at least plausible.

Preservation and Transformation of Christianity through History

For Hegel, Christianity can be conceived as a "consummate religion" (*vollendete Religion*).[20] In describing his innovations and contributions, Hegel highlights the following decisive point: "It was Christianity, by the doctrine of the incarnation of God and the presence of the Holy Spirit in the community of believers, that first gave to human consciousness a perfectly free relation to the infinite and thereby made possible the conceptual knowledge of mind in its absolute infinity."[21] The Christian religion has therefore, for him, an enormous speculative value that cannot be equated with that of any other religion. For not only from a theoretical level is the Christian religion capable of vindicating people but also from a practical point of view *as individuals*: "This Idea came into the world through Christianity, according to which the individual *as such* has an *infinite* value since it is the object and aim of God's love, destined to stand in its absolute relationship with God as spirit, and to have this spirit dwelling *in himself*, i.e. man in himself destined to supreme freedom."[22] Thus, from a Hegelian perspective Christianity has been a landmark not only because of the enormous cultural, historical, and social influence to which it has given rise, but also for its enormous intellectual and speculative legacy. For one crucial thesis cannot be overlooked: for Hegel art, religion and philosophy

---

[20] A useful depiction of what Hegel means by this is provided by Hodgson: "Because the concept of religion entails the *unity* of subjective consciousness and its object, namely God as absolute essence or spirit, when the concept of religion becomes objective to itself, this unity of finite and infinite consciousness comes fully to expression. For this reason, Christianity is the 'consummate' or 'absolute' religion—terms Hegel tends to use synonymously in this section, although elsewhere he favors the former," P. C. Hodgson, "Introduction," in G. W. F. Hegel, *Lectures on the Philosophy of Religion: Volume III. The Consumate Religion* (Oxford: Oxford University Press, 2007), p. 163.
[21] G.W. F. Hegel, *Philosophy of Mind* (Oxford: Oxford University Press, 2010), p. 3.
[22] *Ibid.*, p. 215.

share the same themes and concerns. It is only in the manner of approaching their objects that these three manifestations of the absolute spirit differ. For Hegel, among art, religion, and philosophy, philosophy ranks the highest since it does not deal with affects or representations but, ultimately, with concepts.

Despite the above, however, one must certainly avoid believing that Christianity has remained intact from its emergence to the present day. Rather, what we see according to the Hegelian account is that Christianity, in order to become what it is, has had to undergo various processes and transformations. This can be seen in Hegel's *Lectures in the History of Philosophy III,* where he describes the development by which Christianity, through the first fathers of the Church, has been shaped into what it is:

> We know that the church fathers were very cultivated men philosophically and that they introduced philosophy, in particular Neoplatonic philosophy, into the church. They conformed the Christian principle to the philosophical idea and built the philosophical idea into it, and in doing that they developed a Christian system of doctrine. In that endeavor they went beyond the mode in which Christianity first appeared in the world, for the doctrinal system as the church fathers developed it philosophically was not present in the initial appearance of Christianity. They dealt with all the questions concerning the nature of God (as what subsists in and for itself), questions concerning human freedom and the relationship of humanity to God (who is what is objective), questions concerning the origin of evil, and so on. They introduced and adopted into Christian doctrine what thought determined for them about these matters.[23]

As is well known, Hegel is the philosopher of historicity and the topic of religion is not kept out of his general approach. In a certain sense, of course, both the content and message of Christianity can be considered as eternal. But Christianity does not exist apart from its own development and its own history:

> The Christian religion can be grasped, then, with respect to its beginnings, and in this way it is a relic from the past. But Christianity is likewise living, contemporary spirit that has fathomed itself from that time onward, that has brought itself to a more profound consciousness. So the fact that God is triune is not a matter of whether it says so explicitly in the Bible. That is literalism. The spirit of the community, of the church, the spirit as existent there, is effective spirit, is actual spirit. Christ wills to be in his community and to teach it; "the spirit will lead the way into all truth," but not by referring to the letter of the text. And so what stands in the Bible

---

[23] Id., *Lectures on the History of Philosophy: The Lectures of 1825–1826, Volume III: Medieval and Modern Philosophy,* pp. 27–8.

is, as known previously, not yet what is true. The church, the community, is what recognizes truth, is what has received this consciousness, the spirit of truth that, from out of itself, has brought itself to determinate consciousness. This is the foundation of the Christian religion, of reason and of the speculative idea.[24]

The two passages just quoted point, in my opinion, in the same direction: namely, to the fact that Christianity, as a manifestation occurring in space and time, must submit to cultural, social, political, and philosophical developments. Or to put it in another Hegelian way: Christianity itself is a cultural, social, political, and philosophical phenomenon. For its doctrinal cores, its dogmas, its rites, and of course also its theological-philosophical notions are products whose maturity has only been reached through highly significant historical experiences and events. In this sense, it is deeply striking that Hegel reproaches Lutheranism (or, at least, accuses it of a certain *naiveté*) for the intention of returning to a Christianity that was strictly biblical or scriptural. As he puts it: "We all know that Luther defined the purpose of his Reformation as leading the church back to its initial purity, back to the shape of Christianity in the first centuries. But the first centuries themselves already give evidence of this [philosophical] edifice, an extensively developed fabric of doctrine about what God is and the relationship of humanity to God."[25] Paradoxically, one of the virtues that Hegel will find in Lutheranism is precisely that of putting Christianity in tune with the developments and needs of the modern world. Thus, in a way, it can be said that what this critique intends to do is nothing other than to point out directly that Christianity has to be conscious of its own constant unfolding over time.

Before pointing out some additional aspects about the Lutheran Reformation in Hegel's thought, I would like to briefly highlight certain elements that the German philosopher considers crucial, in the framework of universal history, and that favored the consolidation of Christianity as a universal religion. For Hegel, Christianity has indeed an epochal mission inasmuch as it provides a new conception of the human being. In the first place, Hegel emphasizes the fact that human beings, from the Christian standpoint, can no longer be considered as slaves. In eloquent words, it is said in this regard: "Slavery is not something that was done away with by kings; instead, Christianity has ended it. The abolition is worldly, but Christianity is the true humanity."[26] Second, Christianity has profoundly transformed the way in which ethical life is constituted through its conception of the infinite

---

[24] *Id., Philosophy of Mind*, pp. 182–4.
[25] *Id., Lectures on the History of Philosophy: The Lectures of 1825–1826, Volume III: Medieval and Modern Philosophy*, p. 28.
[26] *Id., Lectures on the Philosophy of World History, Volume I: Manuscripts of the Introduction and the Lectures of 1822–3* (Oxford: Oxford University Press, 2011), p. 457.

value of individuality and the person. Thus, says Hegel, after Christianity it becomes unthinkable to return to the beautiful but innocent ethical life of the Greeks, where everything was validated by custom or habit: ethical conduct must now be validated by spirit, and "individuality no longer should be sacrificed in the interest of the collective."[27] Third, a new type of suprasensible State enters into the world; therefore, this State is one that is different both from that State which is a sensible concretion and organization as a church, and also from that State which concentrates on the political and juridical affairs of the community: "thus, there are two kinds of States: one that is eternal within time, and another that embodies worldly purposes."[28] Lastly, and as a consequence of the above, the temporary political state must find a rational constitution that does justice to the specific nature of the human being: "Ethical life and right cannot exist at the behest of external command or decree [...]. The human being is inwardly free; this freedom is to be gained and maintained by one's own efforts, and it cannot be subverted into the mode of external command."[29] Hand in hand with the abolition of slavery comes in Christianity the affirmation of freedom, which implies that human beings are called to determine for themselves the way in which they should live and the way in which they should treat each other. "For that reason also the law and the state must be inherently justified in their purposes, must be independent of private interests and particular opinions."[30]

For Hegel, all of the above has gained particular importance and prominence in the modern world since the Lutheran Reformation. For, in his view, Catholicism would have left, at some point in history, many of these fundamental aspects aside. It is interesting to note that Hegel claims that the Catholic Church, at the time of his writing, no longer exhibits this kind of neglect: "the present-day church is by no means in the same condition, having been inwardly cleansed by the Reformation."[31] However, it is equally true that at that time religious interests seemed to be subordinated to material and worldly interests, which had the effect of distorting the Christian religion.

In this short space it is impossible to develop Hegel's full perspective of the movement initiated by Luther.[32] The crucial aspects that I would like to highlight from Hegel's positive assessment of the Reformation are the following. First, Luther's Reformation played a highly significant role in

---

[27] *Ibid.*
[28] *Ibid.*, p. 458.
[29] *Ibid.*, p. 459.
[30] *Ibid.*
[31] *Ibid.*, p. 503.
[32] For a detailed discussion on the subject see R. Stern, "'This Is the Very Essence of Reformation: Man in His Very Nature Is Destined to Be Free': Hegel, Luther and Freedom," in D. Moyar, K. Padget Walsh and S. Rand (eds.), *Hegel's Philosophy of Right: Critical Perspectives on Freedom and History* (New York: Routledge, 2022), pp. 45–65.

the revaluation of Christian freedom. This movement contributed greatly to revaluing the freedom of the Christian, and consequently, the role of the individual and of one's own conscience. Second, the inwardness of faith is emphasized over practices and rituals. This, in Hegel's view, is not a faith that such and such historical events occurred. On the contrary, "faith is certainty about the eternal, about the truth that subsists in and for itself"[33]—a doctrine which, curiously enough, Hegel characterizes here as "thoroughly catholic,"[34] but which is set aside to the extent that, in their practices, Catholics give more weight to externalities (miracles, phantastic events, etcetera) than to this certainty. Third, this inwardness of faith, however, should not remain purely subjective but should give way to an objective content: "Subjective certainty [...] only becomes authentic when, in relation to this content, particular subjectivity is surrendered; and this happens only by making the objective truth one's own truth. What the subject makes its own is the truth, the Spirit, the Trinity."[35] It is in this manner that, in Hegel's opinion, one goes beyond the pure natural will and one actualizes Christian freedom. Finally, this gives way to the State being determined not by a traditional authority—which was determined by church interests that were disconnected from concrete reality—but by what individuals freely determine. This change in the State is a consequence of the change in the conception of the church itself, so much so that Hegel even goes so far as to affirm that the modern State is based on the reformed church. This is not to say that the state follows religious prescriptions of this or that institution; rather, what is meant is that from this reappraisal of the individual and his freedom these institutions have progressed and, as a consequence, have differentiated themselves for their own benefit.[36]

Let us now turn to Ratzinger's respective views concerning the relationship of Christianity to historicity. This is in fact a central topic in his thought. Ratzinger has spoken at different times about the importance of history and its relationship with different themes of theology and Christianity in general. His reflection on this subject is marked by two equally important aspects. On the one hand, it is true that religion cannot ignore the development of cultural, political, social, and scientific positions and institutions. On the other hand, however, Christianity must keep in mind and spirit Jesus Christ, his life, and salvific action, and make it present every day, eliminating the gap, in a way, between past and present and thus preserving certain things intact throughout the centuries.

Crucial to Ratzinger's entire approach is to affirm that God, who is outside of time, decides to act in history in order to show and make known

---

[33] G. W. F. Hegel, *Lectures on the Philosophy of World History, Volume I: Manuscripts of the Introduction and the Lectures of 1822-3*, p. 504.
[34] *Ibid.*
[35] *Ibid.*, p. 505.
[36] Cf. *ibid.*, p. 506.

his plan of salvation, which lies at the end of time. Inevitably, then, one must recognize that history has a teleological and soteriological dimension. Ratzinger considers the history of Christianity as a real, effective, and salvific history, which is "a path whose direction we call progress and whose attitude we call hope."[37] Thus, history is advancing and evolving in view of salvation, bringing human beings closer and closer to that mystery.

This intention of God has led him to manifest himself in history, to unite himself to it, thus approaching mankind and revealing himself, and later becoming part of it through his Son. In this providential design, different things come to light and developments take place, but they must be interpreted and comprehended under the guidance of faith, which is something that aims at something everlasting, which is eternal life. Thus, Christianity appears in a particular and concrete way in history—linked to a particular place and time, in straight connection and continuity with the promise to the Jewish people, but at the same time transcends those boundaries, aspiring to have a universal and timeless claim.[38]

According to Ratzinger, this guiding thread is decisive, for instance, in our approach to Scripture. The Bible, which was finished many centuries ago and gives account of past events, is not for that reason circumscribed in its message and scope. As Ratzinger says, "the word of historical Revelation is definitive but also inexhaustible, and allows us to continue deepening it."[39] The Holy Spirit continues to act as interpreter of the Scriptures through history, making them contemporary at all times. Like Jesus, the Holy Spirit, as one of the persons of the Divine Trinity, is not in time, and yet is present in all ages, which produces the miracle of introducing time into the space of eternity.[40]

Christianity has this dual nature in its relationship to time: it "appears at a given point in the history of religion,"[41] and yet is also timeless. A paradigmatic subject of this sort within Christianity is the dogma of incarnation. Since incarnation was the moment in which God, who was outside of history, became a temporal and individual man, entering history and thus embracing the human condition. This event was one of the first dogmatic issues faced by the early Church. And it was affirmed that Jesus—a historical man—is God—a timeless being—, and this "is" of the Council of Chalcedon implies the incarnation of God. It was established, then, that Jesus has two natures, and that he is consubstantial with the Father—who is divine and transcendent—but also with humanity. Thus, it is on these

---

[37] J. Ratzinger, *Truth and Tolerance: Christian Belief and World Religions* (San Francisco: Ignatius, 2004), p. 44.
[38] Cf. *id.*, *Principles of Catholic Theology*, p. 159.
[39] *Id.*, *Salz der Erde. Christentum und katholische Kirche an der Jahrtausendwende* (Stuttgart: Deutscher Verlags-Anstalt, 1997), p. 50.
[40] Cf. *id.*, *The Spirit of the Liturgy* (San Francisco: Ignatius, 2000), p. 92.
[41] *Id.*, *Truth and Tolerance*, p. 27.

grounds that Christians believe that Jesus was in the past but continues to make himself present now, and will continue to do so in the future. This means to believe "in the historicity of God's eschatological action."[42] Hence, it is possible to affirm, with regard to the Savior and without contradiction, that "Christ is himself the bridge between time and eternity."[43] The last element here is of crucial importance, since the manifestation of God within history is something that transcends historicity itself.

According to Ratzinger, human history has a teleological and an eschatological dimension. History had a beginning, but it is continually animated by the hope of salvation, and it will end with the full establishment of God's kingdom. In this sense, it is decisive to emphasize that the salvation awaited by the Christian is not alien to history, but is also found within history given that the Word of God became incarnate, died, and resurrected. Therefore, it is possible to speak in his thought on the profound unity of history. In other terms: one should not separate divine history, human history, and the history of salvation. This is the reason why one of the fundamental Christian articles of faith is the belief that Jesus of Nazareth is the Christ, that He rose from the dead, and that there will be a resurrection at the end of time. In sum: Christianity, in Ratzinger's view, cannot detach itself from certain historical events and phenomena. Even if Christianity continues to be transformed over the centuries in some ways, it cannot leave in the past "the choice made by God, who wanted to speak to us, to become man, to die and rise again, in a particular place and at a particular time."[44] This is why the Christian rite implies the diachronic element, the prayer with the Father and with the apostles, which includes, at the same time, a local moment, extending from Jerusalem to Antioch, Rome, Alexandria, and Constantinople.[45]

For all these reasons, it is clear that Christianity cannot be detached from its history. But now let us consider another question, namely: to what extent Christianity, without renouncing to its essence, is also sensitive to the various changes and transformations to which history itself has given rise. To understand this, it is necessary to keep in mind that God's agency within history did not occur once and for all in a single moment, but has been manifesting himself gradually and progressively, establishing the circumstances and the appropriate means to fulfill his salvific promise to mankind. Hence history can acquire a salvific logic thanks to faith.

In this regard, Ratzinger explains, Christianity does not depend only on perennial and essential truths. Since the revelation of God is a historical and progressive process, revelation itself is related to the interpretation of history. This enables human beings to resignify the history of salvation through their

---

[42] Id., *Principles of Catholic Theology*, p. 187.
[43] Id., *The Spirit of the Liturgy*, p. 92.
[44] *Ibid.*, p. 164.
[45] Cf. *ibid.*

powers, experiences, and shared backgrounds. The interpretation of history, in this sense, is also related to the unity of truth, which manifests itself in various forms throughout history. In a word: truth is one, but it discloses itself in multiple ways throughout different times and epochs.

A paradigmatic example of the above is the theory of evolution. Although it might seem to be opposed to divine revelation insofar as the Bible speaks of creation, they are not intrinsically contradictory with each other, since for Ratzinger each explanation takes place on a phenomenological and an ontological basis respectively. For that reason, one should not be tempted to subordinate one to the other: "the theory of evolution and belief in creation belong, with respect to their ultimate fundamental orientation, to entirely different intellectual worlds and have nothing at all directly in common."[46] Rather, the believer must be able to understand now the events of salvation differently in light of new and diverse scientific positions. In this regard, Ratzinger affirms: "the believer must now allow himself to be taught by science that the way in which he had imagined creation was part of a prescientific worldview that has become untenable."[47]

Ratzinger's position is therefore extremely suggestive. Having as direct reference the case of Galileo, Ratzinger is not willing to read the Bible as if it were a document of natural science. Rather, he realizes the need to study the sacred text as one that, in some of its aspects, can be read and interpreted differently, without, of course, compromising the commitment of faith to see the ultimate origin of man's spirituality and transcendence in God. The divine and salvific pedagogy has also led to these changes: ways of reading the Word that, in another time, could have been fully accredited, pass into ways that, without refuting as such the previous ones, do frame them in a broader horizon of understanding, since God's providential agency in history has made it possible to grasp these questions in a different manner. To be sure, it is not possible to speak, in this field, of "progress" without further ado, as if we were speaking of modern technology. As we have emphasized, what is at stake here is a dialectic between the divine and the temporal, which permeates the deepest spheres of faith and reason. And Ratzinger has undoubtedly been one of the most brilliant thinkers in understanding these complex relationships and interactions.

Community and Church

Although one can speak of an intellectual evolution in Hegel through different periods, one of the topics that remain more or less defined throughout his entire itinerary is his conception of Christianity as a religion

---

[46] Id., "Belief in Creation and the Theory of Evolution," in *Dogma and Preaching* (San Francisco: Ignatius, 2011), p. 124.
[47] Ibid., p. 123.

where there is a deep sense of community. For Hegel, Christian experience and religion are unthinkable without a strong sense of bonding between human beings who, on the basis of Christ's teachings, are willing to lead and guide their lives in very specific ways. I would even go so far as to say that, in Hegelian thought, there is no other religion that can presume to achieve something similar. This can be seen in a very exemplary way throughout the entire *Phenomenology of Spirit*, where no religion of nature succeeds in consolidating anything of this kind. And if Hegel deals with the practices and rites of Greek religion, this is only to show the fact that within this religion it only sought to worship the divinity in a partial and biased way, without giving rise to a true brotherhood of human beings. To put it succinctly: it could be said that the Greeks exalted various yet isolated aspects of humanity without having a perfect model of the human, which we find only in Christ. And without this model, as is to be expected, a community of subjects who interpret themselves under a common ideal cannot materialize, as happens in Christianity. In Hegel's words:

> In the disappearance of the immediate existence of what is known as absolute essence, immediacy acquires its negative moment; spirit remains the immediate self of actuality, but as *the universal self-consciousness* of a religious community, a self-consciousness which is motionless in its own substance just as this substance is the universal subject in the universal self-consciousness. Spirit is not the singular individual for himself but the singular individual together with the consciousness of the religious community; and what the singular individual is for this community is the complete whole of spirit.[48]

Certainly, at the beginning of his intellectual itinerary, Hegel in fact questioned the power and scope of this community. Although, as already mentioned, he thought that Jesus had established a new way of thinking about human interaction, this model had ultimately succumbed to the phenomenon of what he called "positivity" in his early theological writings. That is, Christianity for the young Hegel ended up ossifying into rigid rules, dogmas, and patterns that were contrary to the teachings of Jesus. A particularly widespread thesis of the young Hegel is that Jesus became aware of the growing adoration and veneration of his person. For this reason, he realized that the message he came to preach could not be tied to his individuality. This would explain, somewhat rationally, the need for his sacrifice. From the *Phenomenology of Spirit* onward, however, the picture changes quite a bit in his thinking. First of all, the subject of positivity is understood as a necessary dialectical moment of the spirit, which, in its

---

[48] G.W. F. Hegel, *The Phenomenology of Spirit* (Cambridge: Cambridge University Press, 2018), p. 438.

unfolding of learning and self-knowledge throughout history, is forced to have to pass through such a station. But more important than that is the idea that Christ, in reality, resurrects in his community by means of the integration that believers make of the Christian teachings within their own lives. Thus, we read in the *Phenomenology*:

> The *death* of the divine man, as *death*, is *abstract* negativity, the immediate result of the movement which only comes to an end in *natural* universality. In spiritual self-consciousness, death loses this natural significance, or it becomes its already stated concept. Death is transfigured from what it immediately means, i.e., from the *non-being* of *this singular individual*, into the *universality* of spirit which lives in its own religious community, dies there daily, and is daily there resurrected.[49]

Already from this assertion, it is possible to delineate a strong criticism from a more orthodox Christian view, regardless if one is Christian or Protestant. Since, as St. Paul says, "if Christ is not been raised, then our preaching is vain" (1 Cor 15:14), then the perspective that Hegel offers does not do full justice to the salvific message. Certainly, at no time does Hegel explicitly deny the dogma of resurrection. But since he explicitly censures religious language that points to a realm beyond (all of which, to use later Hegelian jargon, are nothing more than forms of a "bad infinitude"), it must therefore be thought that the characterization of the resurrection in these terms is not accidental. This conjecture is confirmed when one observes that, for the German philosopher, religious language remains tied to what he calls *Vorstellung* or representation.

> This *form of representing* constitutes the determinateness in which spirit is conscious of itself in this, its religious community. This form is not yet the self-consciousness of spirit which has advanced to its concept as concept; the mediation is still incomplete. Therefore, in this combination of being and thinking, there is a defect present, that the spiritual essence is still burdened by an unreconciled estrangement into a this-worldliness and an other-worldly beyond. The *content* is the true content, but all of its moments, posited as lying in the element of representational thinking, have the character of not having been conceptually comprehended.[50]

If we take the above into account, then it becomes clear why for Hegel religion is not the supreme form of the absolute spirit but philosophy. Although the Christian religion is the most complete and perfect among religions, it is constrained, so to speak, by the limits of its own expressive

---

[49] *Ibid.*, p. 450.
[50] *Ibid.*, pp. 438–9.

resources. Speaking strictly from Hegel's philosophy, it would not be unreasonable to affirm that the Christian religion hits the mark but does not do so by means that would be the most adequate. For this, it is necessary to make the transition to the concept, to the *Begriff*. With regard to the subject of our interest, it would possibly be necessary to say that the notion of Christian community would have to be revisited from the point of view that speculative philosophy offers, in order to conceive the intrinsic patterns of rationality that give the true foundation to this form of human coexistence and interaction.

Turning to Ratzinger now, one should affirm from the outset that, for him, the community or Church can hardly be separated from faith and the sacraments, since it is through these two elements that the notion of a Christian people of God finds its foundation but also its continuity and consistency.

For Ratzinger, as opposed to, say, Kierkegaard or Schleiermacher, faith is not something that can really be lived on a strictly individual level. He explains in the *Introduction to Christianity* that faith is not the result of individual thoughts and meditation alone, but is the product of dialogue with others, of listening to them and receiving their ideas. Faith depends on something outside of oneself. It requires an exchange "of 'I' and 'You' to the 'We' of those who all believe in the same way."[51] Thus, it is through this "We" as a group of people who dialogue and share faith that the People of God, the community, is generated. The community cannot be done away in the Christian life, since it produces a fullness that could not otherwise be generated. The special community for all that it provides to individuals that, without interaction, they would not be able to obtain. For the same reason, Ratzinger claims that "it is only to one who has entered into the community of faith that the word of faith reveals itself."[52]

From the origins of Christianity, it was fundamental that this type of community could be consolidated before the dogmas acquired their proper form. The members of the community were distinguished by means of a symbol—a term which comes from the Greek word *symballein* which means to unite or fuse. The symbol in question was the baptismal profession of faith. And just as in the ancient rites the different parts of a symbol had to be joined in order to create unity and mutual recognition, so also the Christians were united or joined by means of the symbol that gathered the faith of the believers and united them as a single community.

As Ratzinger puts it: "A *symbolum* is something that points to its complementary other half and thus creates mutual recognition and unity. It is the expression and means of unity."[53] For the same reason, Christianity

---

[51] J. Ratzinger, *Introduction to Christianity*, p. 64.
[52] Id., *Principles of Catholic Theology*, p. 26.
[53] Id., *Introduction to Christianity*, pp. 68–9.

is not something that happens in solitude or isolation, but it is something that occurs in the encounter with the other, where one goes beyond mere individuality. In the community of shared principles and a common way of living, one accepts the others and also the will of God, thereby strengthening the bonds between all of the members. Hence, the personal profession of faith, the word, and the unity is necessary to conform "the fellowship we call Church."[54] In Ratzinger's view, "the Christian belief is not an idea but life,"[55] which becomes present through a committed existence, introducing thereby an intimate relationship between theory and practice, between *logos* and *ethos*. "Christian faith is also an *ethos*,"[56] and this can only be realized in community. The notion of community and Church meets with the sacramental theme, since the sacraments are not a pure liturgical act, but are a change, a process or path, which requires the action of man, his understanding and his will.[57]

In Ratzinger's view, to be Christian is essentially to be communitarian because the Christian God is the opposite of solitude: "God does not exemplify loneliness but ec-stasy, a complete going-out-from himself."[58] He is a Trinitarian God who is the foundation of communion. To grow Trinitarian means to become *communio*, which implies leaving individuality and entering the collectivity.[59] For this very same reason, when one professes the creed, the symbol, the "I" that is professed is not an individual I but a collective I: "the 'I' of the creed embraces the transition from the individual 'I' to the ecclesial 'I'."[60] Consequently, in the form of a subject, the creed already presupposes structurally the self of the church. The self only becomes properly expressed in the ecclesial *communio*: "It is an act of *communio*, through which one allows oneself to be integrated into the *communio* of witnesses, in such a way that, in them and through them, we touch the untouchable, we hear the unheard, we see the invisible."[61]

As can be seen, this community is not only ethical but mystical in nature, since it is the sacrament through which the believer is given faith and membership in the Church. The faith of the believer comes directly from Christ, who transmits it through the Church and its baptism. Hence, faith does not only seek the individual relationship between God and the baptized, but it seeks a relationship with a God who is community and who has communicated with others. In short, faith is not only an "I" and

---

[54] *Ibid.*, p. 71.
[55] *Ibid.*
[56] *Id.*, *Principles of Catholic Theology*, p. 36.
[57] Cf. *ibid.*
[58] *Ibid.*, p. 22.
[59] Cf. *ibid.*, pp. 22–3.
[60] *Ibid.*, p. 23.
[61] *Id.*, "Sources and Transmission of the Faith," *Communio* 10/1 (1983), p. 26.

a "you" but also a "We," a community. For Ratzinger, the sacrament of baptism initiates a new community: the community of believers into which the baptized person enters. Likewise, by being baptized, the person enters immediately into the very existence of the Son and is, in a way, resurrected just like the Son. The new member receives a new existence, and this becomes part of a new and greater community whose purpose is to pray to the Father.[62] This is such a central principle that it is no exaggeration to say that "there is no faith without the Church."[63] Baptism makes it possible to belong to the community, to the Church, whose purpose is to bring everyone united to God himself.

In conclusion, in Ratzinger's thought, one can see that "baptism is the necessary form of entrance into the company of believers if faith is not to be essentially a product of one's own invention and milieu."[64] Therefore, living the faith or walking toward Christ "means always to draw near to all those of whom he wants to make a single body. The ecclesial dimension of baptism is already apparent, then, in the trinitarian formula."[65] That is to say, one must be part of this community of the baptized who share their beliefs in order to be able to put faith into practice. The "People of God" is a category that transcends any ethical or political ideal. It is rather a notion that makes it possible to concretize and embody all that God wants for mankind.

Concluding Remarks and Observations

Having made this review, I believe that we are in a better position to establish some important theses. In the first place, I think it is clear that there are points of agreement where, at least from a general level, there is an important coincidence among the authors. To return to the first case discussed, it seems clear to me that both Hegel and Ratzinger want to emphasize, in their overall interpretation of Christianity, the central influence of Greek thought. For both authors, the definition of fundamental dogmatic and theological premises could not have happened without the Greek mediation. From the providential and teleological point of view of history, it is to be thought that this encounter between Athens and Jerusalem had a profound *raison d'être*. But this is not limited in both authors only to a fortunate cultural expression or formulation. The encounter between Jerusalem and Athens is also an unmistakable sign of the inner rationality of this new faith and this new religion. For its contents are there not only to be felt but also to be thought. The radical nature of the new vision that Christianity offers also lies in the

---

[62] Cf. *ibid.*, p. 30.
[63] *Ibid.*, p. 23.
[64] *Id.*, *Principles of Catholic Theology*, p. 40.
[65] *Ibid.*, p. 33.

fact that this religion invites—on the grounds of its very own nature—to use reason and to cultivate it, as well as to find the right balance between that which our intellect can discover and that which is manifested by God in history and which begins to be transmitted through tradition and worship from the apostles onwards.

And it is precisely on this central point that we find, in my opinion, one of the main disagreements between Hegel and Ratzinger. For while the former, animated by this confidence in reason proposed by Christianity, pretends to give an absolute rational account of religion and faith, the latter considers that this reason must have limits and humility—or in other terms, if reason itself can be expanded—as Ratzinger would grant—, this happens through the support of divine reason which human faith accepts; divine reason cannot be equated without further ado with human reason. In a certain way, then, we can see a certain *hybris* in Hegelian thought, since it claims to account, from the human standpoint, for the totality of the divine. In Ratzinger's thought, on the contrary, what we find is a proposal that opens space for reason itself to be enlightened by faith—a possibility that is totally discarded from the Hegelian speculative horizon—preventing bare human reason from making claims that do not correspond to it. In this sense, a distinctive sign of Ratzinger's proposal is to safeguard a space for the otherness and alterity of the divine. A space that ultimately does not allow itself to be dominated or explained in a totalizing way by human reason itself.[66]

In relation to the second point, we find again, at the beginning, a common starting point: the openness to historical thought on the part of Hegel and Ratzinger. The acute perspective of both thinkers is shown, in fact, in their ability to situate Christianity within the framework of cultural, historical, and social categories. In other words, Christianity, as a mere dictate or prescription of a pure reason, is for them inconceivable. Due to the fact that Christianity is inscribed in history, it becomes necessary to consider that each epoch assimilates and interprets Christianity under coordinates that are not always the same. In this sense, both thinkers see the

---

[66] Another way of presenting this discrepancy is through the idea developed by Alejandro Sada, who adequately characterizes a dimension of reason that is very present in Ratzinger's thought: "At the beginning of all existence there is an infinite mind that is at the same time true reason and creative freedom, and all that originates from it is being-thought and, therefore, also thinkable. Reality is accessible to human reason because it is rational in its innermost structure, since the source from which it springs is Reason itself, the divine *Logos*. In a similar way, the *logos* of man can grasp the rationality of the real because it participates of the creative Reason that stands at the origin of all being," A. Sada, "Reason," in R. A. deAssunção, P. Blanco-Sarto, T. Rowland, and C. Schaller (eds.), *Joseph Ratzinger Dictionary* (San Francisco: Ignatius, forthcoming). I consider that, in any standard reading of Hegel, it would be difficult to find the premise according to which the rational order of the world is seen or interpreted, in its very origin, as a transcendent and radically creative (*schöpferisch*) principle, which can only be tentatively grasped and never possessed in its entirety.

need, on the one hand, to adjust certain practices to the present moment, and, on the other hand, to reinterpret, through historical distance, certain fundamental Christian theses. The latter occurs not to disprove these theses, but to present them in a new light in view of changes and developments in the social, historical and scientific order. Once again, however, this correct Hegelian diagnosis is led ultimately to an excess, since, broadly speaking, nothing in Christianity seems to remain outside the order of immanence and historicity. For this reason, it is difficult to find in Hegel's proposal the more moderate approach that we do find in Ratzinger: namely, a historical order of developments that is subordinated to a transcendent and timeless order. Leaving aside the fact that the salvific character of Christianity may be extremely diluted in Hegelian thought, what is of concern here is the fact that this thought of immanence can argue little in favor of Christianity beyond being a particularly salient cultural phenomenon. In other words, what I mean is that if Christianity has no real safeguard in a supratemporal order, the doors are in principle open to change everything about it, with the prospect of leaving it at the end of the day so altered as to become unrecognizable.

Finally, in relation to the last topic, we find a similar situation. First, we see a fundamental coincidence in the fact that both Hegel and Ratzinger conceive of Christianity as a religion that invites sociality. For them, Christianity is, in its fundamental features, unthinkable from a sphere of isolation or seclusion. The Trinitarian God himself is a God of three persons who promotes interaction and community. This diagnosis is particularly enlightening in the face of appropriations of Christianity that have ignored this fundamental fact. However, once again, we find in the Hegelian case certain problematic elements. First, in his treatment of the Christian community, we find again this aspiration to subsume the elements of transcendence of religious discourse to the logical categories of immanence: hence the need to move from *Vorstellung* to *Begriff*. Leaving aside an analysis from the Christian dogma, this Hegelian theoretical wager seems to do violence both to the sacred texts and to the Christian message itself. Second, as a consequence of the above, Hegel seems to locate the distinctiveness of Christianity in a political and social aspect. That is, in his approach, it would seem that Christian promises can only have a fulfillment in the here and now. But this clearly cannot be the case. Although it is undoubtedly true, for example, that many contemporary ideas about human dignity and human rights derive from Christian thought, it is manifest that to make Christianity solely a salient ethico-political position would be tantamount to caricaturing it. For in reality, if Christianity can be such a thing, it is actually by virtue of the sacramental and faith tradition that lies at the foundation of the Christian community. The commitment and care that each Christian has toward his or her neighbors as children of God cannot be translated into a secular language without some important losses. To be sure, no one can deny that significant progress in matters such as human rights have occurred by means of a process of secularization. But these triumphs should not mislead us into thinking that the entire Christian tradition could be translated without something important being lost in the process. In preserving the sense of a Christian community based on the apostolical and sacramental tradition, the Christian secures a path to a redemption for mankind that cannot be exhausted and will not take place in the sphere of ethics or politics.

With the above arguments, what I have tried to do in this study is to follow a different path from that of interpreters who, based on what Ratzinger explicitly said about Hegel, have tried to evaluate the relationship between these thinkers. Of course, such a study undoubtedly has its merits and its advantages.[67] But I have avoided doing so in the present paper for the following reason: I consider that it would be unfair, with Ratzinger, to ask of him a sophisticated exegetical development such as can be found in the more refined scholarship on the authors of the Western philosophical tradition. The strategy followed here has been somewhat different and has consisted in looking at proposals on the nature of Christianity by both authors and presenting their similarities and differences, in order to judge them from a more systematic point of view. As can be seen, I have not made particular reference to the fact that one author is Catholic and another Protestant. To be sure, from a certain order of analysis this could be extremely important. But from the perspective proposed here, this has not been so relevant, because the developments presented here have been based on a general understanding of the Christian faith from the horizon of the philosophy of religion.[68] And already from this standpoint I believe that at least two things are clear: on the one hand, both authors are brilliant and acute in detecting dimensions of the Christian faith that, from other theoretical fronts, have been rejected or treated in any case in a very marginal way. On the contrary, what I have sought to emphasize is that topics such as the Greek mediation of thought, the historical dimension of Christianity, and the latter's sense of community are fundamental to any right understanding of Christianity as such. But where we have been able to note divergences between the authors has been, principally, in Hegel's interest in avoiding a perspective of transcendence and in encapsulating the Christian faith from the perspective of speculative thought. And in these respects, the proposals advanced by Ratzinger resonate as an important corrective that amends the assertions of reason when they seem to be excessive and when they distort what reason seeks to appropriate. Certainly, with what has been said in the present study

---

[67] For a study of this sort see M. Schulz, "Grenzgänge des Denkens. Ratzinger im Disput mit Hegel," *Internationale Katholische Zeitschrift Communio* 38 (2009), pp. 261–74.

[68] Undoubtedly, other theoretical fronts could be discussed from a purely theological horizon. But that has not been the perspective chosen for the present study, thus avoiding discrediting any position beforehand. I consider that the approach taken here has been more favorable in trying to present initial coincidences between the authors with the aim of then trying to mark the respective and undeniable differences.

I do not claim to have exhausted by far all that could be said about the theoretical and intellectual links between these two enormous thinkers. My wish is only to have laid the foundations for a dialogue that I hope will not only be possible but sustained among those who are engaged in the study of these crucial topics.

7

Auguste Comte: Science, Reason, and Religion

Euclides Eslava

Introduction

Auguste Comte's positivism upheld the advance of the experimental and sociological sciences, which he thought would lead to a new humanity and a new society managed by scientists who would guarantee "order and progress," a slogan the Brazilian flag, under his influence, champions.

However, in our day, we are witness to a series of dramas explained by examining the advance of technological developments that, due to a lack of accompanying ethics, did not end as well as the French philosopher predicted. This includes, among other happenings, recent wars, data manipulation by large companies, the possibilities that biomedical engineering offers, and disproportionate progress in some countries with injustices in many others.

Despite this, Comte's role should not be too harshly judged since his work was only a reflection of his era, of a "progressive estrangement from God operating in the world and, more specifically, a step brought about by radical humanism from the field of philosophy to the sciences, which was characteristic of the cultural milieu during the first decades of the nineteenth century."[1]

This chapter studies Joseph Ratzinger's analysis of Comte's influence on contemporary culture, systematizing the responses that the German

---

[1] J. Sanguineti, *La filosofía de la ciencia según Santo Tomás* (Pamplona: Eunsa, 1977), p. 200.

theologian offers to the French philosopher's challenges, and brings together the proposals for progress that Ratzinger formulated in his pontifical teaching and beyond.

The Law of Three Stages

Starting with his time as a university professor, Joseph Ratzinger has always shown signs of openness and dialogue with the world of the natural sciences. For example, in his memoirs he recalls that, since his youth, he has always believed "that, with the breakthroughs made by Planck, Heisenberg, and Einstein, the sciences were once again on their way to God. The antireligious orientation that had reached its climax with Haeckel had now been broken, and this gave us new hope."[2]

However, in his theological analysis of the contemporary world, he has also lamented the positivism inspired by Auguste Comte (1798–1857) and sees it as at the origin of several contemporary problems. Although he has not directly confronted Comte often, he has made extensive reference to the consequences of his thought, especially the famous law of three stages[3]:

> each of our leading conceptions—each branch of our knowledge—passes successively through three different theoretical conditions: the theological, or fictitious; the metaphysical, or abstract; and the scientific, or positive ... Hence arise three philosophies, or general systems of conceptions on the aggregate of phenomena, each of which excludes the others. The first is the necessary point of departure of the human understanding, and the third is its fixed and definitive state. The second is merely a state of transition.[4]

The theological stage is actually mythological and corresponds to manifestations of humanity's natural religiosity, which seeks supernatural explanations to events whose causes are unknown, as well as the establishment of a personal relationship with the being to whom humanity feels called. According to Ratzinger, this period is the beginning of "a genuine history, to be a path whose direction we call progress and whose attitude we call hope."[5]

---

[2] J. Ratzinger, *Milestones. Memoirs 1927–1977* (San Francisco: Ignatius, 1998), 42–3. Art along with science is the highest gift God has given him.
[3] In several texts on Comte, Ratzinger cites Henry de Lubac's *The Drama of Atheist Humanism* (San Francisco: Ignatius, 1995), pp. 131–267.
[4] G. Lenzer (ed.), *Auguste Comte and Positivism: The Essential Writings* (New York: Harper, 1975), pp. 71–86.
[5] J. Ratzinger, *Truth and Tolerance* (San Francisco: Ignatius, 2004), p. 44.

In addition, in Comte's thought, the scientific or positive stage, which is fixed and definitive, includes social physics or sociology as a more complex, final science; it is responsible for studying society and human behavior and coordinating the development of all knowledge.[6] However, the proposal of a law of history with the consequent myth of human progress was considered problematic from the beginning. Indeed, Durkheim "felt forced to exclude social dynamics from sociology, in order to give it a truly scientific status."[7]

Comte's approach has been criticized for its lack of rigor[8] and oversimplified schematism, pointing to the fact that, over history, these three stages have not occurred in neat successive periods as proposed, but rather have been mixed throughout. Paradoxically, Comte sought to transform science into philosophy (in the "Course in Positive Philosophy") and philosophy into religion (in the "System of Positive Polity").[9]

But the positivist approach bolsters Ratzinger's thesis on the role of Christianity, which evades Comte's criticism by placing itself on a level outside of the law of three stages and its designations. In fact, the German theologian reaffirms that, from early on, philosophy and Christianity were intertwined, as reflected in artistic representations of Christ as the perfect philosopher. Indeed, "as early as the second century, Justin Martyr had characterized Christianity as the true philosophy."[10]

In his work *Introduction to Christianity*, the young professor in Tübingen took on the Comtian law and argued that its view of the Christian faith is a form of positivism.[11] He rightly called this move the "Christian scandal," and when he made a rhetorical statement to suggest that the Christian God's strategy of revealing himself as a human person might have been unnecessary, he traded the temptation that we sometimes experience of asking whether it is time for man to overcome the "naïve years of its childhood and now, grown out of childhood, ought finally to have the courage to awake from sleep, rub its eyes, shake off that beautiful but foolish dream, and take its place unquestioningly in the huge context in which our tiny lives have their proper function, lives that should find new meaning precisely by accepting their diminutiveness."[12]

---

[6] Cf. A. Comte, *The Positive Philosophy of Auguste Comte*, vol. III, H. Martineau (ed.) (Kitchener: Batoche Books, 2000), pp. 6–7. Cf. M. Vitoria, "Auguste Comte," *Philosophica: Enciclopedia filosófica on line*, Francisco Fernández and Juan Mercado (eds.).

[7] M. Bourdeau, "Auguste Comte," *The Stanford Encyclopedia of Philosophy*, on-line, Spring 2022 Edition, Edward Zalta.

[8] Cf. A. Lang, *The Making of the Religion* (London, New York, Bombay, Calcutta: Longmans, Green and Co., 1898), cited by María Vitoria, "Auguste Comte."

[9] Cf. A. Comte, *System of Positive Polity* (London: Longmans, Green and co., 1875–1877); M. Bourdeau, "Auguste Comte."

[10] J. Ratzinger, *The Nature and Mission of Theology: Essays to Orient Theology in Today's Debates* (San Francisco: Ignatius, 1995), p. 14.

[11] Cf. *id.*, *Introduction to Christianity* (San Francisco: Ignatius, 2004), p. 54.

[12] *Ibid.*, pp. 55–6.

The analogy between a naïve childhood dream and the first two stages of Comte's law is easily established.

Ratzinger begins his argument with the history of the Christian creed in the West, which "lingers, so to speak, on the positivistic side of the Christian story."[13] As mentioned, Christianity does not take for granted the theological or fictitious stage that Comte proposes, but, in his approach, Ratzinger goes beyond even the metaphysical or abstract state.

Based on Saint Paul's precept, "Faith cometh by hearing" (Rom 10: 17), the Bavarian theologian explains the origin of the act of faith in dialogue, not in individual reflection. Unlike philosophy, faith is not born from reading or pondering, but from listening, "which consists precisely in being the reception of what cannot be thought out."[14] Thinking about faith "is always a thinking over of something previously heard and received."[15] Another characteristic of the Christian faith's positivism refers to the fact that "the fore-given word takes precedence over the thought, so that it is not the thought that creates its own words but the given word that points the way to the thinking that understands."[16]

To the positivism of faith and the primacy of the word, the social character of faith is added, which points to another difference with the individualistic structure of philosophical thinking because "faith ... is first of all a call to community, to unity of mind through the unity of the word. Indeed, its significance is, a priori, an essentially social one: it aims at establishing unity of mind through the unity of the word."[17]

For the young Ratzinger, Comte's first stage belongs to certain religious manifestations of a mythical nature. The second stage corresponds to the structure of philosophical reasoning. But Christianity fully enters the third stage, and not because it lacks metaphysical rigor since "faith, in its core, from setting the philosophical search for truth in motion again."[18]

Thirty years later, Cardinal Ratzinger delivered a conference in Paris that presents another point of reference for studying his relationship with Comte. There, the prefect of the faith tried to clarify the question of how Christianity, in its origins, thought about its claim to be the true religion in the midst of a cosmos of religions.[19]

---

[13] *Ibid.*, p. 85.
[14] *Ibid.*, p. 92.
[15] *Ibid.*, p. 91.
[16] *Ibid.*, p. 92.
[17] *Ibid.*, p. 93.
[18] *Ibid.*, p. 91. In his famous speech in Regensburg, Benedict XVI would insist on "the profound harmony between what is Greek in the best sense of the word and the biblical understanding of faith in God. [...] The encounter between the Biblical message and Greek thought did not happen by chance" and "the intrinsic necessity of a rapprochement between Biblical faith and Greek inquiry," *Faith, Reason and the University: Memories and Reflections. Lecture in the Meeting with the Representatives of Science*, Apostolic Journey to München, Altötting and Regensburg (September 9–14, 2006), Regensburg, September 12, 2006.
[19] Cf. J. Ratzinger, *Truth and Tolerance*, pp. 162 ss.

To achieve this, he offered the example of Saint Augustine's confrontation with Varro's theses. The latter defined God as the soul of the world sans any kind of worship. In ancient philosophy, "truth and religion, rational perception and cultic prescription, lie on two quite separate planes."[20] The world of religion belonged to custom rather than to the order of reality. The gods did not create the State; instead, the State created them. Religion fulfilled a political role. From these premises, Varro distinguished three kinds of theology, namely (1) mythical or poetic, (2) civil, political or popular, and (3) natural, physical or philosophical theology.

Natural theology was demythologized by the Enlightenment and scientific criticism. Worship (religion) and knowledge were unlinked and juxtaposed as two separate spheres. In this context, "[w]ithout hesitation he [Augustine] indicates that Christianity's place is in the sphere of 'physical theology', in the sphere of philosophical enlightenment."[21]

Like the second-century apologists, Saint Paul in his letter to the Romans, and Saint Augustine in dialogue with Varro, Ratzinger concludes that "Christianity's precedents and its inner groundwork lie in philosophical enlightenment, not in religions."[22] Moreover, Christianity is not based "on mythical images and vague notions,"[23] but is related to rational analysis of reality and what it perceives about the divine.

In light of Paul's speech to the Areopagus, Ratzinger infers that "Christian faith is not based on poetry and politics, the two great sources of religion; it is based on knowledge."[24] The Cardinal's conclusion is clear: "Christianity saw itself as embodying the victory of demythologization, the victory of knowledge, and with that the victory of truth."[25]

In short, Ratzinger is faithful to his methodological principle: "faith does not grow out of resentment and skepticism with respect to rationality, but only out of a fundamental affirmation and a spacious reasonableness."[26] For this reason, he responds to Comte's criticism of the stages saying that Christianity is in the third stage, namely it is both scientific and positive.[27] What is more, the third stage, "the Enlightenment has a Christian origin, and it is not by chance that it was born specifically and exclusively within the sphere of the Christian faith."[28]

---

[20] *Ibid.*, p. 166.
[21] *Ibid.*, p. 169.
[22] *Ibid.*
[23] *Ibid.*
[24] *Ibid.*, p. 170.
[25] *Ibid.*
[26] *Id., A Turning Point for Europe? The Church in the Modern World: Assessment and Forecast* (San Francisco: Ignatius, 1994), p. 105.
[27] Cf. *id., Introduction to Christianity*, p. 54.
[28] *Id., Christianity and the Crisis of Cultures* (San Francisco: Ignatius, 2006), p. 48.

Comte, Modernity, and Freedom

At the beginning of his *Introduction to Christianity*, Ratzinger tranquilly assumes the Comtian law of three stages. However, he clarifies that both magic, metaphysics and the natural sciences have to do with faith: "each of them can help it, and each of them can hinder it."[29] And he proposes a way of overcoming the reduction to appearance that positivism entails: "considering the unconsidered and bringing the human problems it raises before the gaze of consciousness."[30]

To achieve this, he adds two new stages to his history of modern thought: the birth of historicism and the transition to technical thinking. In the first period he highlights Vico (1688–1744), but includes Descartes (1596–1650) and Kant (1724–1804). The key point is Vico's exchange of the scholastic equation "verum est ens" (being is true because it is the work of God, which is understanding par excellence) for the formulation "verum quia factum." For Ratzinger, "this formula denotes the real end of the old metaphysics and the beginning of the specifically modern attitude of mind. Introduction to Christianity."[31]

In antiquity and the Middle Ages, all beings were idea, thought of the absolute spirit, *logos*, reason, truth. "Man can rethink the *logos*, the meaning of being, because his own *logos*, his own reason, is *logos* of the one *logos*, thought of the original thought, of the creative spirit that permeates and governs his being."[32] However, human action was seen as contingent and ephemeral. That is why, until Descartes, it was "Ancient and medieval philosophy took the view that knowledge of human things could only be techne, manual skill, but never real cognition and, hence, never real science."[33] Vico "was to turn the Middle Ages' criterion of truth, redefined once again here in Descartes, on its head, thus giving expression to the fundamental revolution that marks the arrival of the modern spirit. This was the start of the attitude that introduces the 'scientific' age, in which we are still living."[34]

This turn signified that "History, previously despised and regarded as unscientific, now remained, alongside mathematics, the only true science left."[35] In this context, Ratzinger's *Introduction to Christianity* contains just one mention by name of the founder of sociology, as follows: "Through Hegel, and in a different way through Comte, philosophy became a historical question."[36]

---

[29] Id., *Introduction to Christianity*, p. 58.
[30] *Ibid.*
[31] *Ibid.*, p. 59.
[32] *Ibid.*
[33] *Ibid.*, p. 60.
[34] *Ibid.*
[35] *Ibid.*, p. 62.
[36] *Ibid.*

It is worth noting here how Comte summarizes history: "This history can be divided into three great epochs, or stages of civilization ... The first is the theological and military era ... The second is the metaphysical and legalistic era ... ; finally, the third is the scientific and industrial era."[37]

Historicism influenced philosophy through Hegel, theology through Baur, economics through Marx, and the natural sciences through Darwin. On this path, the world lost solidity; it became an evolutionary process that could only be seen as the work of human beings. And man himself became nothing more than a product of evolution. Paradoxically, "when radical anthropocentrism set in and man could know only his own work, he had to learn to accept himself as merely a chance occurrence, just another 'fact'."[38]

Evolutionism generated a perplexing problem, namely "whether the world comes from an irrational source, so that reason would be nothing but a 'by-product' (perhaps even a harmful by-product) of the development of the world, or whether the world comes from reason, so that its criterion and its goal is reason."[39]

To the history of modern thought, Ratzinger adds another period, i.e., passage from the dominance found in Vico's motto, "verum quia factum," to technical thinking, which is marked by the aphorism that sums up Marx's view, "verum quia faciendum." Henceforth, truth is feasibility: "The truth with which man is concerned is neither the truth of being, nor even in the last resort that of his accomplished deeds, but the truth of changing the world, molding the world—a truth centered on future and action."[40]

In this way, Marx offered a new foundation with a philosophy that is not only reflexive, but, above all, geared toward action and transformation of the world: "the truth of man is in what he believes for himself; it is not in the past nor in eternity, which are unavailable. Rather, it is found in the future that man gives to himself, and for which he acts."[41]

Cardinal Ratzinger's last academic speech was delivered on the eve of Saint John Paul II's death, upon receiving the "San Benito" award in Subiaco. In a brief paragraph, the Prefect diagnosed contemporary rationalist culture: "These philosophies are characterized by their positivist—and therefore anti-metaphysical—character (...). They are based on a self-limitation of the positive reason that is adequate in the technological sphere but entails a mutilation of man if it is generalized. The result is that man no longer accepts any moral authority apart from his own calculations. As we have seen, even

---

[37] A. Comte, *Oeuvres d'Auguste Comte* 10 (Paris: Anthropos, 1968–70), p. 112.
[38] J. Ratzinger, *Introduction to Christianity*, p. 63.
[39] *Id.*, *Christianity and the Crisis of Cultures*, p. 49.
[40] *Id.*, *Introduction to Christianity*, p. 63.
[41] *Id.*, *Natura e compito della Teologia*, p. 135. This text doesn't appear in the English edition of *The Nature and Mission of Theology*. Translation is mine. Cf. *id.*, *Introduction to Christianity*, p. 61.

the concept of liberty, which initially seemed capable of expanding without any limits, leads in the end to the self-destruction of liberty itself."[42]

The future pope decries the self-limitation of reason in modern Western thought, which only expresses a part of human reason "this mutilation of reason means that we cannot consider it to be rational at all."[43]

The critique is clear: with a focus on emphasizing empirical findings, i.e., facts that are not free and determined, positivism rejects free reality and assumes that human beings are also "a 'physics of man' in which there exist necessary laws and exact predictions."[44] In this way, "human science on methodological foundations that exclude the *humanum*"[45] emerges.

Thus, the consequences of positivism are not limited to experimental science. The cardinal highlights its ethical derivations and its dangerous implications for freedom. Specifically, he points out that, in the third Comtian stage, "[o]nly quantitative reason, the reason of calculation and experimentation, is considered to be reason at all; everything else is nonrational and must gradually be overcome and likewise brought into the realm of 'exact' knowledge."[46]

This limitation to reason occasions its emancipation and unlimited autonomy: "Reason thereby assumes the form of positive reason, as Auguste Comte understood it, which takes as its only standard what is experimentally verifiable."[47] Consequently, although the entire scope of values belongs to the rational sphere, for positivism, the mechanical forces of nature subject to experimentation are the only thing that binds. This rationalist emancipation "intrinsically contradicts the nature of human reason (which is not divine) and therefore necessarily became unreasonable itself."[48]

In his diagnosis of this problem, Ratzinger points to the "physics of man," "social physics," or sociology that Comte argued for, and with which he signaled an abyss between the world of facts and the subjective world of sentiment, to which morality and religion belong: "Finally even the most complicated and least comprehensible department, the ultimate, longest defended citadel of theology, would be successfully subjected to positivist scientific analysis and exposition. Moral phenomena and man himself—his essential human nature—would become subject matter for the positive sciences."[49]

---

[42] *Id., Christianity and the Crisis of Cultures*, p. 40.
[43] *Ibid.*, p. 43. Cf. E. Eslava, "La razón mutilada. Ciencia, razón y fe en el pensamiento de Joseph Ratzinger," *Scripta Theologica* 39 (2007), pp. 829–51.
[44] *Id., A Turning Point for Europe?*, p. 94.
[45] *Ibid.*
[46] *Id., Church, Ecumenism, and Politics* (San Francisco: Ignatius, 2008), p. 197.
[47] *Ibid.*, p. 213.
[48] *Ibid.*, p. 218.
[49] *Id., Faith and the Future* (San Francisco: Ignatius, 2009), p. 13.

This path leads toward overcoming the question of God, as fulfilled in our time according to Ratzinger's analysis: "Behind such notions is the sense that a great gulf is developing between the world of faith and the world of science, a gulf that seems unbridgeable, so that faith is made very largely impracticable."[50]

Human freedom is also maimed by reducing it to events that psychoanalysis or sociology can quantify. Determinism is an inevitable result of formulating a "physics of man" in which there are only necessary laws and exact forecasts: "An idea of science that is formed on the basis of what is not free is transposed to the realm of what is free, namely, the human realm."[51] Assuming this theory " ... demands by its very nature the exclusion of the factor of freedom."[52]

The key to contemporary nihilism is that, for the sake of scientific progress, reason is limited to its instrumental, calculating, and functional aspect. The possibility that reason can reach "the truth of existence, the truth about us, about creation and about God" is excluded. Indeed, "[t]his false humility abases man, making our action blind and our feeling empty."[53]

Ratzinger adds that freedom, to be truly so, cannot be separated from the good and justice, in relation to other human beings. He further denounces the danger of relativism imposed by the majority: "the modern concept of democracy seems indissolubly linked to that of relativism. It is relativism that appears to be the real guarantee of freedom."[54]

As Prefect, he mentioned two paradigmatic authors who take this position: on the one hand, Rorty and his "banal utopia" whose ideal "is a liberal society in which absolute values and criteria will no longer exist; a sense of well-being will be the only goal worth striving for."[55] On the other hand, Kelsen's legal positivism, since "[t]he strict positivism that is expressed in the absolutization of the majority principle is inevitably transmuted at some point into nihilism."[56]

Ratzinger warns that this implies collapsing the foundations of morality, since it breaks with the moral message of nature, common to all great civilizations: "the most opposite modern views of the world share the same starting point: the denial of the natural ethical law and the reduction of

---

[50] *Ibid.*, p. 15. Cf. Benedict XVI, *Address to Participants in the Plenary Assembly of the Pontifical Council for Culture*, March 8, 2008.
[51] J. Ratzinger, *A Turning Point for Europe?*, p. 93.
[52] *Ibid.*, p. 94.
[53] *Ibid.*, pp. 113–14.
[54] *Id., Values in a Time of Upheaval* (New York, San Francisco: Ignatius, Crossroad, 2006), p. 55.
[55] *Ibid.*, p. 47.
[56] *Ibid*, p. 50.

the world to 'mere' facts."[57] The absence of moral principles constitutes relativism as the philosophical foundation of positivism. In this way, an attempt is made to demystify and unmask all ethical criteria morality is no longer found in being, but in the future, in the society that will be achieved thanks to progress.[58].

This loss of moral foundations entails an additional danger: "For where relativism is consistently thought through and lived (without clinging secretly to an ultimate trust that comes from faith), either it becomes nihilism or else it expands positivism into the power that dominates everything."[59] The new ethical, utilitarian criterion suggests that "'Moral' is what serves to bring about the new society." On this same path, "Thus the moral and the religious have become realistic and 'scientific.'"[60]

But "[s]cience as such cannot give birth to such an ethos. In other words, a renewed ethical consciousness does not come about as the product of academic debates."[61] The problem lies in separating technological capacity from "moral energy." If this ethical force is lacking, if this "know-how does not find its criterion in a moral norm," the power on man "becomes a power for destruction."[62] "The technological mentality confines morality to the subjective sphere. Our need, however, is for a public morality, a morality capable of responding to the threats that impose such a burden on the existence of us all."[63]

Ratzinger's critique of positivism is not a rejection of empirical science: "In affirming this, we are not denying all the positive and important contributions of this philosophy. Rather, we are stating that it needs to be completed, since it is profoundly incomplete."[64] It is rather an analysis of its anthropological consequences and a defense of human freedom, which disappears in the shadow of calculating and instrumental reason: "The spokesmen of the natural sciences tell us that man basically does not possess any liberty."[65]

---

[57] *Id., A Turning Point for Europe?*, p. 40. At a forum with Habermas, he pointed out that, " ... the fundamental transformation of the understanding of the world and of man that has come about thanks to the growth in scientific knowledge has played a major role in the collapse of the old moral certainties," J. Ratzinger, "That Which Holds the World Together: The Pre-Political Moral Foundations of a Free State," in J. Ratzinger and J. Habermas, *Dialectics of Secularization* (San Francisco: Ignatius, 2004), p. 56.
[58] Cf. *id., A Turning Point for Europe?*, p. 135.
[59] *Ibid.*, p. 109.
[60] *Ibid.*, p. 28.
[61] *Id.*, "That Which Holds the World Together: The Pre-Political Moral Foundations of a Free State," p. 56.
[62] *Id., Christianity and the Crisis of Cultures*, p. 42.
[63] *Ibid.*, p. 27.
[64] *Ibid.*, p. 43.
[65] *Ibid.*, p. 42.

Conclusion

Today, unabashed optimism in the face of scientific development is not as common as in Comte's time. On the contrary, postmodernity, in light of the consequences derived from the positivist program, distrusts its larger-than-life tactics. However, Ratzinger does not fail to warn of the risks of the separation between the world of facts and that of morality. In this last section, we will highlight words related to faith and reason that Ratzinger delivered in his time as Pope Benedict XVI.

The Pontiff's key argument is that the human world of freedom and history necessarily transcends all scientific predictions. Freedom cannot be reduced to a deterministic analysis: "Its transcendence vis-à-vis the material world must be acknowledged and respected, since it is a sign of our human dignity."[66] Otherwise, when the "supposed absolute ability of the scientific method to predict and condition the human world"[67] leads to denial of this transcendence and ignoring humanity's singularity and transcendence, humanity is at risk of exploitation.

These are the dangers of positivism without ethics: when man's moral dimension is lost, he becomes a product: "Man has descended into the very wellsprings of power, to the sources of his own existence. The temptation to construct the 'right' man at long last, the temptation to experiment with human beings, the temptation to see them as rubbish to be discarded—all this is no mere fantasy of moralists opposed to 'progress'."[68]

Benedict XVI summarizes the consequences of positivism in a key word, namely secularization, understood as the elimination of the link between temporal realities and the creator. It can even be understood as a kind of arrogance of reason that "closes itself to contemplation and the quest for a superior Truth."[69] This cultural and social process "has not only claimed a just autonomy for science and the organization of society,"[70] but has come "even to the point of neglecting to safeguard the transcendent dignity of

---

[66] Benedict XVI, *Address to the Members of the Pontifical Academy of Sciences*, November 6, 2006.

[67] *Ibid.*

[68] J. Ratzinger, "That Which Holds the World Together: The Pre-Political Moral Foundations of a Free State," p. 65.

[69] Benedict XVI, *Address to Participants in the Plenary Assembly of the Pontifical Council for Culture*, March 8, 2008. In response, one of his first papal addresses contained "the invitation not to see the world that surrounds us solely as raw material with which we can do something, but to try to discover in it 'the Creator's handwriting', the creative reason and the love from which the world was born and of which the universe speaks to us, if we pay attention, if our inner senses awaken and acquire perception of the deepest dimensions of reality," Benedict XVI, *Address to the Roman Curia Offering Them His Christmas Greetings*, December 22, 2005.

[70] *Id.*, *Address to the Participants at the 20th International Conference Organized by the Pontifical Council for Health Pastoral Care on the theme of the Human Genome*, November 19, 2005.

human beings and respect for human life itself."[71] In addition, "secularization does not foster the ultimate goal of science which is at the service of man,"[72] since it "enfeebles the person and hinders him in his innate longing for the whole Truth."[73]

In his diagnosis, he suggests, on the one hand, that the advance of science has led many to consider God's dominion unnecessary in fields that science has developed, but, at the same time, he laments that this fact "has at times been linked to a corresponding 'retreat' of philosophy, of religion, and even of the Christian faith."[74] The sum of these realities has led to "[t]he light of reason, exalted but in fact impoverished by the Enlightenment, has radically replaced the light of faith, the light of God."[75]

Having established the dangers that positivism holds for humanity, we turn to the reasons that Ratzinger offers in defense of freedom and science. First of all, it is important to reiterate that Christianity is compatible with scientific development. Faith helps science by clarifying both its possibilities and its limitations, especially when it comes to satisfying existential and spiritual needs related "to man's most radical questions: questions about the meaning of living and dying, about ultimate values, and about the nature of progress itself."[76]

This reality is not an obstacle, but rather a service, to science, helping to eliminate its possible pathologies in order to "[maintain] vigilance about the sense of responsibility that reason possesses in regards to science, so that it stays on track in its service to the human being."[77] And this is because human beings are defined by freedom and transcendence; indeed, "[m]an is neither the result of chance nor of a bundle of convergences nor of forms of determinism nor physio-chemical interaction; he is a being who enjoys freedom, which, while taking his nature into account, transcends it and symbolizes this mystery of otherness that dwells within him."[78] Although human beings form part of nature, they transcend it "as free subjects who have moral and spiritual values."[79]

---

[71] *Ibid.*
[72] *Ibid.*
[73] *Ibid.*
[74] *Id., Address to the Members of the Pontifical Academy of Sciences*, November 6, 2006.
[75] *Id., Address to Participants in the Plenary Assembly of the Pontifical Council for Culture*, March 8, 2008. Cf. *id., Lecture Prepared for the University of Rome "La Sapienza,"* January 17, 2008.
[76] *Id., Address to the Members of the Pontifical Academy of Sciences*, November 6, 2006.
[77] *Id., Address to Participants in a Congress Held on the Occasion of the 10th Anniversary of the Publication of Pope John Paul II's Encyclical* Fides et ratio, October 16, 2008.
[78] *Id., Address to Participants in an Interacademic Conference on "The Changing Identity of the Individual" Organized by the "Académie des Sciences" of Paris and by the Pontifical Academy of Sciences*, January 28, 2008.
[79] *Id., Address to the Members of the Pontifical Academy of Sciences and the Pontifical Academy of Social Sciences*, November 21, 2005.

Starting with this clarity, philosophy and theology offer the empirical sciences the possibility of interdisciplinary dialogue, for example, with help recognizing "a difference between the mathematical inability to predict certain events and the validity of the principle of causality, or between scientific indeterminism or contingency (randomness) and causality on the philosophical level, or, more radically, between evolution as the origin of a succession in space and time, and creation as the ultimate origin of participated being in essential Being."[80]

Recognizing this metaphysical participation dignifies humanity, opening up unanticipated horizons for human rationality: "the specific natural law itself is a moral law. Creation itself teaches us how we can be human in the right way."[81] Since the practical aspect of reason (and of morality) surpasses experimental reason, "[t]he Christian faith, which helps us to recognize creation as creation, does not paralyze reason; it gives practical reason the life-sphere in which it can unfold."[82]

Morality is not a burden but a stamp of glory and a condition of possibility for the human being, thus,

> Moral obligation is not man's prison, from which he must liberate himself in order finally to be able to do what he wants. It is moral obligation that constitutes his dignity, and he does not become more free if he discards it: on the contrary, he takes a step backward, to the level of a machine, of a mere thing. If there is no longer any obligation to which he can and must respond in freedom, then there is no longer any realm of freedom at all.[83]

Faith "saves reason, precisely because it grasps reason in its whole breadth and depth and protects it from the restrictions of a merely experiential verification."[84] This argument concludes with the idea that the Christian faith is the safeguard of freedom since morality "is not the enslavement of man but his liberation."[85]

In times of spiritual atrophy and emptiness of the heart, recovery of the powerful values that guarantee human happiness is urgent; they include "the dignity of the human person and his or her freedom, equality among all men and women, the meaning of life and death and of what awaits us after the end of our earthly existence."[86]

---

[80] Id., *Address to the Members of the Pontifical Academy of Sciences*, November 6, 2006.
[81] J. Ratzinger, *A Turning Point for Europe?*, p. 44.
[82] *Ibid.*
[83] *Ibid.*, p. 41.
[84] *Ibid.*, p. 112.
[85] *Ibid.*, p. 44.
[86] Benedict XVI, *Address to Participants in the Plenary Assembly of the Pontifical Council for Culture*, March 8, 2008.

This is key for knowledge obtained through calculations and experimentation to transform into wisdom, knowledge that is "capable of directing man in the light of his first beginnings and his final ends."[87] The challenge for contemporary science and faith is to "[enlighten] consciences, in order to ensure that every new scientific discovery will serve the integral good of the person, with constant respect for his or her dignity."[88]

We thus arrive at Ratzinger's proposed strategy for dialogue between faith and reason as a contribution to contemporary society. It involves recalling science and philosophy's responsibility of mutual aid, that religion and reason delimit one another, showing one another their respective limits and helping one another find their way.[89] In this dialogue "faith implies reason and perfection, and reason, enlightened by faith, finds the strength to rise to the knowledge of God and spiritual realities."[90]

"It is the responsibility of philosophy to accompany critically the development of the individual academic disciplines, shedding a critical light on premature conclusions and apparent 'certainties' about what man is, whence he comes, and what the goal of his existence is."[91] And religion has "the task of guiding people's consciences towards goodness, solidarity and peace. Precisely for this reason she feels in duty bound to insist that science's ability to predict and control must never be employed against human life and its dignity, but always placed at its service."[92]

In short, the human sciences help the experimental sciences "sift the non-scientific element out of the scientific results with which it is often entangled, thus keeping open our awareness of the totality and of the broader dimensions of the reality of human existence for science can never show us more than partial aspects of this existence."[93]

---

[87] Id., *Address to Participants in the Colloquium Sponsored by the Vatican Observatory on the Occasion of the International Year of Astronomy*, October 30, 2009.

[88] Id., *Address to the Participants at the 20th International Conference Organized by the Pontifical Council for Health Pastoral Care on the theme of The Human Genome*, November 2019, 2005.

[89] Cf. J. Ratzinger, "That Which Holds the World Together: The Pre-Political Moral Foundations of a Free State," p. 78.

[90] Benedict XVI, *Address to Participants in the Plenary Assembly of the Pontifical Council for Culture*, March 8, 2008.

[91] J. Ratzinger, "That Which Holds the World Together: The Pre-Political Moral Foundations of a Free State," p. 57.

[92] Benedict XVI, *Address to the Members of the Pontifical Academy of Sciences*, November 6, 2006. In another place, he argues, "science, too, must be subject to moral criteria and that its true nature is always lost whenever, instead of serving the dignity of man, it is placed at the disposal of power or of commerce or it takes simple success as its sole criterion," J. Ratzinger, *Europe Today and Tomorrow: Addressing the Fundamental Issues* (San Francisco: Ignatius, 2007), p. 63.

[93] J. Ratzinger, "That Which Holds the World Together: The Pre-Political Moral Foundations of a Free State," p. 57. In his Regensburg speech, Benedict XVI insisted on the importance of expanding reason to avoid the dangers of a mutilated reason, saying, "We will succeed

Science itself then becomes a meeting point for this interdisciplinary dialogue: as a human being, the scientist perceives:

> a constant, a law, a *logos* that he has not created but that he has instead observed: in fact, it leads us to admit the existence of an all-powerful Reason, which is other than that of man, and which sustains the world. This is the meeting point between the natural sciences and religion. As a result, science becomes a place of dialogue, a meeting between man and nature and, potentially, even between man and his Creator.[94]

Translation from Spanish by Christa Byker

---

in doing so only if reason and faith come together in a new way, if we overcome the self-imposed limitation of reason to the empirically falsifiable, and if we once more disclose its vast horizons"; id., *Faith, Reason and the University: Memories and Reflections. Lecture in the Meeting with the Representatives of Science*, Apostolic Journey to München, Altötting and Regensburg (September 9–14, 2006), Regensburg, September 12, 2006.

[94] Benedict XVI, *Address to Participants in the Plenary Session of the Pontifical Academy of Sciences*, October 28, 2010.

8

Karl Marx and Marxism: The Problem of the Priority of *Praxis*

Tracey Rowland

Introduction

In an early lecture delivered in 1958, and later published as *Christian Brotherhood*, Ratzinger cited three works as sources of his understanding of Marxism: *Dialectical Materialism: A Historical and Systematic Survey of Philosophy in the Soviet Union* by G. A. Wetter, published in 1958; J. Lacroix's "Der marxistische Mensch" published in *Dokumente*, 1948, vols 1 and 2; and Karl Löwith's *Weltgeschichte und Heilsgeschehen: Die theologischen Voraussetzungen der Geschichtsphilosophie* (1953).[1] Löwith is famous for his thesis that modern political ideologies are merely secularized versions of Jewish messianism and Christian eschatology.[2] Ratzinger largely agrees with this analysis though he would add to it the rejection of the notion of truth as something divinely given in favor of a notion of truth as a human construction. Indeed, Ratzinger's primary criticism of the thought of Karl Marx (1818–83) is not that it is explicitly atheistic but that it acknowledges no truth whatsoever. As he wrote, for Marx, reality is change, and "man's task is to intervene in this process of change and himself create truth. Far from being the measure of man,

---

[1] J. Ratzinger, *Christian Brotherhood* (London: Sheed and Ward, 1966), p. 18.
[2] The English translation was published as K. Löwith, *Meaning in History: The Theological Implications of the Philosophy of History* (Chicago: University of Chicago Press, 1957).

truth now becomes his creature."[3] Atheism is of course implicit within any system of thought that acknowledges no truth independent of human construction. Ratzinger obviously regards Marx's atheism as problematic. It is however Marx's attitude to truth, rather than his attitude to the God of Christianity who is the source of all truth, that dominates Ratzinger's criticism of Marxist thinking. Ratzinger's general verdict is that while Marxism is the product of Europe, it is, nonetheless, "the most decisive rejection of Europe, in the sense of that inner identity which it has developed over the course of its history."[4] This inner identity is the union of biblical revelation with Greek philosophy.

No Truth without the *Logos*

When Ratzinger criticizes Marx he does not usually refer to particular works of Marx or make distinctions between the young "Romantic" Marx and the mature Marx imbued with the spirit of scientific rationalism. Nonetheless many of his criticisms would appear to flow from statements made by Marx in the "Theses on Feuerbach" and in *The German Ideology* co-authored with Friedrich Engels. It is in the "Theses on Feuerbach" that Marx makes his statement that hitherto philosophy has only sought to interpret the world, whereas he wishes to change it.

Marx's criticism of philosophy in *The German Ideology*[5] for being "mere criticism" or mere "ideology" does not sit well with Ratzinger's high regard for the philosophical achievements of the Greeks. Ratzinger does not merely accept the early Christian adoption of elements of Greek philosophy as something "convenient" or useful for the time, but rather he regards them as something providential and essential for the Christian worldview. As he often remarks, Christianity is the religion of the *Logos*. He points to the passage in the *Acts of the Apostles* (16:6-10) where St. Paul has a vision in a dream of a Macedonian imploring him "Come here and help us." "Here" was Greece. For Ratzinger this passage is scriptural evidence of the providential nature of the union of biblical revelation with Greek philosophy. He believes that the Incarnation occurred at a moment in history when the union of the two was propitious and he has consistently resisted de-Hellenisation movements in Christian theology, including the argument often found in liberation theology, that Greek philosophy is, at best, only of relevance to European Christians.

---

[3] J. Ratzinger, *Faith and the Future* (Chicago: Franciscan Herald Press, 1971), p. 67.
[4] *Id.*, *Church, Ecumenism and Politics: New Endeavours in Ecclesiology* (San Francisco: Ignatius, 2008), p. 214.
[5] K. Marx and F. Engels, *The German Ideology* (Eastford: Martino Fine Books, 2011).

No Freedom without Truth

While Ratzinger regards Marx as the person most responsible for promoting social engineering, rather than the pursuit of truth, he thinks that this orientation goes back to Francis Bacon (1561–1626). In his *Novum Organum* Bacon "disavows the question of truth as the old, outmoded question and transforms it into the question of know-how, the question about power."[6] Ratzinger thinks that this has repercussions not only for truth, but also for freedom. In his reflection on the "Mission of the Catholic Academy" he wrote:

> The question of freedom is inseparably linked to the question of truth. When truth is not a value in itself that merits both active interest and the expenditure of time independently of its results, profit can be the only criterion with which to evaluate knowledge. If this is the case, knowledge has its *raison d'etre* no longer in itself but in the objectives that it serves.[7]

He concluded this paper with the rhetorical question:

> Is truth accessible to man at all? Is the search for it worthwhile? Can we even say that the quest for truth and the knowledge that the truth is the lawful mistress of man are perhaps our only hope of salvation? Or is the final *adieu* to the whole business of truth, which emerges clearly in Francis Bacon's new logic, man's true liberation, which awakens him from his speculative reverie and allows him at last to take in his own hands the dominion over reality, in order to become 'master and lord of nature'?[8]

Ratzinger regards a choice for the "master and lord of nature" option, i.e., the *adieu* to the whole business of truth option, as "a slave's freedom" analogous to that of the *faux* freedom of the prodigal son. Moreover, he regards this *faux* freedom, separated from truth, as embodying two further pathological properties:

a. Marxism makes the assumption that freedom is indivisible, that is, that it only exists as such when it is the freedom of everyone. Freedom is linked to equality: in order for freedom to exist, equality must first be restored. That means that in pursuit of the goal of complete freedom, some renunciation of freedom is required …

b. Associated with that is the assumption that the freedom of the individual is dependent upon the structure of the whole and that

---

[6] J. Ratzinger, *Fundamental Speeches from Five Decades* (San Francisco: Ignatius, 2012), p. 180.
[7] *Ibid.*, p. 185.
[8] *Ibid.*

the struggle for freedom must for the moment be waged, not as a struggle for the rights of the individual, but as the struggle for a changed social structure in the world. As to the question of what this structure would look like and, hence, what the rational means to achieve it would be, Marxism runs out of breadth at this point.[9]

The result is that under "really existing Marxism" of which Soviet Communism is the exemplar, there is neither truth nor freedom.

The Immanentization of the Eschaton

In addition to getting truth wrong and freedom wrong, Ratzinger is also critical of Marx and his disciples for getting eschatology wrong. It is a commonplace observation that Marxist eschatology represents a secularizing immanentization of the eschaton. While this is implicit in classical Marxism it becomes the leitmotif of the works of Ernest Bloch (1880–1959), author of *Geist der Utopie* (1918) and *Das Prinzip Hoffnung* (1938). Leszek Kołakowski, the great historian of Marxism, placed Bloch in the tradition of revolutionary German Anabaptism and Jewish apocalyptic theology. Bloch thought that the task was not to await the *eschaton* but to bring it into being by acts of the human will. Kołakowski summarized Bloch's cosmology in the following paragraph:

> [N]ot only does the universe embody an immanent purpose but, at least in the higher stages of evolution, it requires the participation of human subjectivity to realize its utopian potentialities or actualize its self-anticipations. Man is a product of matter, but since he appeared on the scene he has been, as it were, in charge of its further development: he is the head of creation, as in the theogony of Plotinus and Eriugena or the old neo-Platonist philosophy. That which is "not yet conscious" in us is correlated, in an undefined way, with the "not yet" of nature itself, the subjective "not yet" is to become explicit through our efforts, thus making manifest the essence of the universe.[10]

Bloch was a professor at the University of Tübingen during Ratzinger's brief tenure at that institution (1966–9) and Ratzinger read his *Das Prinzip Hoffnung*. In an essay first published in 1985, Ratzinger remarked that "Hope as described by Bloch is the product of human activity. Its

---

[9] *Id., Truth and Tolerance: Christian Belief and World Religions* (San Francisco: Ignatius, 2003), p. 241.
[10] L. Kołakowski, *Main Currents of Marxism: Volume III* (Oxford: Clarendon, 1978), p. 441.

realization is brought to fulfilment in the human 'laboratory of hope'."[11] Thus, "for Bloch the opposite of what we have heard in Paul is true; the atheist is the only one who hopes and, as long as the Marxist way of transforming the world was unknown, human beings lived in this world without true hope and therefore had to try to be content with an imaginary hope."[12]

Bloch's ideas influenced the development of the political theology of Johann-Baptist Metz (1928–2019) whose work, in turn, influenced the rise of various movements of liberation theology. His reading of Bloch inspired Metz to put eschatology at the center of his theological work and to shift the focus of his theology from dogma to *praxis*. Bloch was also a source of inspiration for Jürgen Möltmann's *Theologie der Hoffnung* (1964) and the affinity of interests between Metz and Möltmann was on show in their co-authored work *Faith and the Future: Essays on Theology, Solidarity and Modernity* (1995), a publication of the *Concilium* series. Together Metz and Möltmann drew concepts like liberation and freedom understood in a political key into the Christian theology of hope. Ratzinger however has been very wary of any blurring of the boundaries between the political and the eschatological. As he writes: "the message of the Kingdom of God is significant for political life not by way of eschatology but by way of political ethics. The issue of a politics that will be genuinely responsible in Christian terms belongs to moral theology, not eschatology."[13] Moreover, in a symposium paper to celebrate Metz's seventieth birthday, Ratzinger wrote:

> The liberal and the Marxist visions of the definitive reconciliation of freedom and natural necessity are riven with contradictions and, above all, they put past time behind them as the mere opening act to that which is definitely valid, a prelude which, in either case, offers no real promise to the living and the dead.[14]

Ratzinger concurs with Josef Pieper's criticism of evolutionary views of history expressed in Pieper's statement that "evolution knows no martyrs."[15] By this Pieper meant that martyrdom makes no sense if history is constantly evolving to some higher level of rationality. One could give one's life for a principle that turns out not to be timeless at all but merely some idea at a low level of evolutionary development.

---

[11] J. Ratzinger, "On Hope," *Communio* 35/2 (2008), pp. 301–15, at 305.
[12] *Ibid.*, p. 302.
[13] *Id.*, *Eschatology: Death and Eternal Life* (Washington, DC: Catholic University of America Press, 1988), p. 59.
[14] *Id.*, "The End of Time? The Provocation of Talking about God," in T. R. Peters and C. Urban (eds.); M. Ashley (trans. and ed.) (New York: Paulist Press, 2004), pp. 23–4.
[15] *Ibid.*, p. 16.

The Problem of the Priority of *Praxis*

While Metz is classified as a proponent of political theology, not liberation theology, his work can be read as a bridge to liberation theology. The major difference is that Metz was writing in the European "death of God" context, while the predominantly Latino liberation theologians are working within a context of sharp social divisions and chronic economic insecurity. The liberation theologians nonetheless share Metz's very political approach to issues in eschatology and Ratzinger has been consistently critical of this orientation. One finds this, for example, in Ratzinger's preface to the 2004 edition of *Introduction to Christianity*. There he notes that liberation theologians often defend their use of Marxist ideas by reference to the argument that they are simply "baptizing" Marx in the manner in which St. Thomas Aquinas "baptized" Aristotle. If in the thirteenth century the philosophy of Aristotle was the representative of "worldly wisdom," so too, the argument goes, is Marx the contemporary representative of worldly wisdom. Ratzinger's primary response to this claim is that Aristotle was actually a philosopher but what Marx offers is a "praxis" that does not "presuppose a 'truth' but creates one."[16] From this it follows for Ratzinger that "anyone who makes Marx the philosopher of theology adopts the primacy of politics and economics, which now become the real powers that can bring about salvation." In theologies that adopt Marx as a partner, the God of Christianity has nothing to do.[17]

Ratzinger has not only been critical of the Marxist substitution of *praxis* for truth, but in the context of the fundamental theology or "building stones" of liberation theology, he has been critical of the idea of reversing the priority of *logos* over *ethos*, a practice that might be described as a specific example of the prioritization of *praxis*. The expression "the priority of *logos* over *ethos*" was used by Romano Guardini and Ratzinger follows in Guardini's footsteps in insisting on the maintenance of this order of priority. Guardini argued that "Truth is a power but only when one does not demand that it have any immediate effect."[18] Ratzinger described this position as a "correct praxeology, a correct statement of the relationship between faith and praxis."[19] In *Principles of Catholic Theology*, Ratzinger wrote:

> If the word "orthopraxis" is pushed to its most radical meaning, it presumes that no truth exists that is antecedent to praxis but rather than truth can be established only on the basis of correct praxis, which has the task of creating meaning out of and in the face of meaninglessness.

---

[16] *Id.*, *Introduction to Christianity* (San Francisco: Ignatius, 2004), p. 14.
[17] Cf. *ibid.*, p. 15.
[18] R. Guardini, *Bericht über mein Leben: Autobiographische Aufzeichnungen* (Düsseldorf: Patmos, 1984), p. 111. Quoted by J. Ratzinger in *A Turning Point for Europe*, p. 72.
[19] *Ibid.*

Theology becomes no more than a guide to action, which, by reflecting on praxis, continually develops new modes of praxis. If not only redemption but truth as well is regarded as "post hoc" then truth becomes the product of man. At the same time, man, who is no longer measured against truth but produces it, becomes himself a product.[20]

Moreover, while the priority of *ethos* over *logos* makes man a product or commodity, this priority also assists the Marxist attack on truth. Here Ratzinger explains that "the concept of the continuity of being in the changeableness of time" (a position that is consistent with giving priority to *logos*) "is now understood as an ideological superstructure conditioned by the interests of those who are favored by things as they are."[21] This becomes a standard form of liberation theology criticism of those who argue that the teaching of the Church cannot change but must forever remain circumscribed by the original deposit of the faith as presented in the scriptures and the tradition of the Church. In particular members of the hierarchy who defend the traditional teachings are often accused of doing so in order to protect their own status and prerogatives. Underlying this criticism is the Marxist epistemological principle that all ideas and truth claims are mere epiphenomena of economic realities, or, as Ratzinger explained, part of an ideological superstructure rooted in economics.

Sections VII and VIII of the Congregation for the Doctrine of the Faith document *Instruction on Certain Aspects of the Theology of Liberation* (1984) promulgated when Ratzinger was Prefect of the Congregation are also entirely devoted to a critique of Marxist social theory. The first argument that is made is that Marxist social theory operates as a closed system. Once one enters into the system at any point other pieces of ideological baggage become collateral influences. The document declares:

> [T]he thought of Marx is such a global vision of reality that all data received from observation and analysis are brought together in a philosophical and ideological structure, which predetermines the significance and importance to be attached to them. The ideological principles come prior to the study of the social reality and are presupposed in it. Thus no separation of the parts of this epistemologically unique complex is possible. If one tries to take only one part, say, the analysis, one ends up having to accept the entire ideology. That is why it is not uncommon for the ideological aspects to be predominant among the things which the "theologians of liberation" borrow from Marxist authors.[22]

---

[20] *Id.*, *Principles of Catholic Theology: Building Stones for a Fundamental Theology* (San Francisco: Ignatius, 1987), p. 318.
[21] *Ibid.*, pp. 16–17.
[22] Congregation for the Doctrine of the Faith, *Instruction on Certain Aspects of the Theology of Liberation* (Rome: Editrice Vaticane 1984), VII §6.

There follows in section VII §10 the Catholic principle that "the ultimate and decisive criterion for truth can only be a criterion which is itself theological." In other words, "it is only in the light of faith, and what faith teaches us about the truth of man and the ultimate meaning of his destiny, that one can judge the validity or degree of validity of what other disciplines propose, often rather conjecturally, as being the truth about man, his history and destiny."[23] This means that the theological presuppositions of social theories need to be examined before any particular social theory could be treated as a worthy intellectual partner for theology, and in Ratzinger's judgment, Marxism fails this test.

Section VIII of the document adds that the law of class struggle is part of the core of Marxist social theory and that this implies an ontology of violence. This represents a reversal of the original peace of the Garden of Eden. Section VIII then returns to Ratzinger's central criticism that there is something wrong with the Marxist notion of truth. Section VIII§7 declares: "The class struggle is presented as an objective, necessary law. Upon entering this process on behalf of the oppressed, one 'makes' truth, one acts 'scientifically'. Consequently, the conception of the truth goes hand in hand with the affirmation of necessary violence, and so, of a political amorality."[24]

Section VIII §9 goes on to argue that "the very nature of ethics is radically called into question because of the borrowing of these theses [about the class struggle] from Marxism. In fact, it is the transcendent character of the distinction between good and evil, the principle of morality, which is implicitly denied in the perspective of the class struggle."[25] In other words, not only is Marxist truth radically subjective, but so too is Marxist ethics. In the earlier work, *Christian Brotherhood*, Ratzinger noted that whereas the philosophies of the eighteenth century fostered the idea of a brotherhood of all men, regardless of social rank, in the Marxist tradition, "humanity is divided into two totally antithetical groups, capitalist and proletariat, and their embattled dialectic is what history is."[26]

The Incarnation as the Centre of History

Underpinning this ontology of violence is the notion that a mere material force is the dynamic of history. It was precisely against this idea that John Paul II directed his attack in his encyclical *Redemptor Hominis* (1979). John Paul II declared that "Jesus Christ, the Redeemer of man, is the center and purpose of human history." This is in direct contradiction to Marx's statement in *The Communist Manifesto* that the history of the world is

---

[23] *Ibid.*, VII §10.
[24] *Ibid.*, VIII §7.
[25] *Ibid.*, VIII §9.
[26] J. Ratzinger, *Christian Brotherhood*, p. 17.

hitherto the history of class conflict. Ratzinger has observed that the essence of modern materialism:

> Consists in the way in which the relationship between matter and spirit is conceived. Here matter is the first and original element; it is matter, not the *Logos*, that stands at the beginning ... If one knows the laws of matter and can manipulate these, then one can also direct the course of the spirit. One changes the spirit by rearranging its material conditions. Thus one can enlarge and remodel history in a mechanical way by enlarging and remodeling structures.[27]

This is the typical Marxist presupposition against which both Wojtyła and Ratzinger have stood opposed. Ratzinger clearly shares his papal predecessor's judgment that the incarnation of Christ, not material forces, is the fulcrum of world history. In a Christmas homily delivered in 1959 he poetically referred to the Incarnation as the "winter solstice of humanity."[28]

The Secularization of Hope

Given this principle of the pivotal significance of the Incarnation, Ratzinger regards all utopian and eschatological visions that expressly exclude hope in Christ as illusory. In *Spe salvi* (2007),[29] his encyclical on the theological virtue of hope, he spent several paragraphs addressing the Marxist secularization of the Christian conception of hope. At §21 he wrote that Marx's "real error is materialism: man, in fact, is not merely the product of economic conditions, and it is not possible to redeem him purely from the outside by creating a favourable economic environment." In §24 *a*) he further declared that "The right state of human affairs, the moral well-being of the world can never be guaranteed simply through structures alone, however good they are. Such structures are not only important, but necessary; yet they cannot and must not marginalize human freedom." People need to desire the good, without this basic orientation of the human person, structures will always be inadequate. Moreover, since the exercise of the human will in the direction of the good cannot ever be guaranteed, not even with all the structures and bureaucratic protocols imaginable, in §24 (*b*) he concluded that "the kingdom of good will never be definitively established in this world." A mere change in social structures can never eradicate original sin or free will. At §35 he explains that the kingdom of God is a gift but nonetheless human persons can open

---

[27] *Id., A Turning Point for Europe*, p. 90.
[28] *Id.*, "The Undefeated Light: Joseph Ratzinger on the True Meaning of Christmas," *London Catholic Herald*, December 19, 2019, pp. 97–100. Original German version is found in *Hochland* (1959/60).
[29] Cf. Benedict XVI, *Spe salvi* (Rome: Editrice Vaticana, 2007).

themselves to "the truth, to love, to what is good" and thereby contribute to the world's salvation as God's "fellow workers" (1 Cor 3:9, 1 Th 3:2). This is a quintessentially Augustinian theology of history. Those who belong to the "City of God" can improve the "City of Man," can be "co-operators of the truth," but it is not for mere humans to bring about the final realm, the New Jerusalem. In the essay "Salvation: More than a Cliché," Ratzinger remarked that Christian faith and the "logically consistent paganism along the lines of Marx and Sartre" have in common "the fact that they revolve around the theme of redemption, but in exactly opposite directions."[30] He suggests that their divergence does not lie, as is commonly assumed, on the point of whether redemption is earthly or heavenly, spiritual or secular, otherworldly or this worldly but rather on the point of whether redemption occurs through "liberation from all dependence, or is its sole path the complete dependence of love, which then would also be true freedom?".[31] In other places he has remarked that "truth and love" are the twin pillars of all reality.[32] It can thus be said that another argument Ratzinger has with the Marxist tradition is its understanding or ignorance of the significance of love and what in contemporary anthropology is called relationality, the way in which human identity is shaped by networks of relationships built upon love. The more a society becomes governed by technology, by material values and interests, the more socially marginalized these networks tend to become.

In this context, in his lecture "What Is Europe?" delivered in 2001, Ratzinger declared that "today we find ourselves in the midst of a second Enlightenment, which has not only left behind the motto *Deus sive natura* but has also unmasked as irrational the Marxist ideology of hope."[33] In its place it promotes a "New World Order" whose "criterion of rationality is drawn exclusively from experiences of technological production on scientific foundations."[34] This project "still shares with Marxism the evolutionary idea of a universe brought forth by an irrational event and formed by its intrinsic rules, which however—unlike the provisions of the ancient idea of nature—cannot contain within themselves any ethical direction."[35] Ratzinger's criticisms here read as echoes of similar concerns voiced by Romano Guardini about "mass man" and his reduction to the status of a cog in a mechanical process.[36] Technological development without reference to goodness and love has a tendency to become oppressively anti-human.

---

[30] J. Ratzinger, *Fundamental Speeches from Five Decades*, p. 35.
[31] *Ibid.*
[32] Cf. *id.*, *Truth and Tolerance*, p. 183.
[33] *Id.*, *Europe: Today and Tomorrow* (San Francisco: Ignatius, 2007), p. 40.
[34] *Ibid.*, pp. 40–1.
[35] *Ibid.*, p. 40.
[36] See, for example, R. Guardini, *The End of the Modern World* (Wilmington: Intercollegiate Studies Institute, 2001).

Integrating Faith and Reason

While Karol Wojtyła/St. John Paul II spent his life fighting the "Old Left" (the kind of Marxist-Leninists who sought to control the peoples of Central Europe who found themselves on the wrong side of the Berlin Wall), Ratzinger/Benedict XVI spent much of his life providing intellectual opposition to the "New Left." These are predominately West European proponents of Eurocommunism and the Critical Theory of the Frankfurt School of Social Research. The ideas of the latter provided the base of the intellectual cocktail favored by the generation of 1968. For many of the leaders of this generation, the idea of a social hierarchy, including a sacerdotal hierarchy as found in the Catholic Church, is a social pathology associated with an authoritarian personality disorder. Nonetheless, in the case of the Frankfurt School's social theory, often summarized as "Critical Theory," Ratzinger acknowledges that there is something right about its critique of German Idealism. To a degree he concurs with the "dialectic of enlightenment" thesis of Max Horkheimer and Theodor Adorno. When Horkheimer and Adorno spoke of the dialectic of enlightenment they were referring to the tendency of reason, understood as pure reason unassisted by the light of faith, to revert "by an inner logic to a justification of the irrational" and to the treatment of reason itself as simply an irrational accident. Ratzinger prefaces his analysis of the dialectic of enlightenment thesis with the statement that "when the Gospel of John names Christ the *Logos* ... it means to say that the very foundation of being is reason, and that reason is not a random by-product of the ocean of irrationality from which everything actually sprang."[37] From this it follows that "the reasonableness of reality must be an essential part of the Christian faith."[38] Conversely, however, Ratzinger asserts:

> As reason sets out on her search, faith commissions her to recognize in the faith the pre-requisite that makes her own operation possible and not to pursue her claim to comprehensiveness to the point of abolishing her own foundation, for that would mean that she was mistaking herself for divine reason and thereby abandoning communication with the divine reason on which life depends.[39]

This, in Ratzinger's view, was the mistake of German Idealism. It was the great Kantian error to abandon communication with divine reason. Ratzinger therefore concludes that Horkheimer and Adorno correctly identified the pathological orientations of Kantian-style "pure" or "absolute" reason but did not take the Christian path out of the cul-de-sac of irrationality by

---

[37] J. Ratzinger, *Church, Ecumenism and Politics*, p. 148.
[38] *Ibid.*, p. 149.
[39] *Ibid.*

illuminating reason with the light of faith. Ratzinger's general assessment is that without the faith of Christianity, the fate of absolute reason is, as Horkheimer and Adorno observed, a dialectical reversion to the irrational. As he writes:

> As a form of materialism, it [Marxism] necessarily rejects the primacy of the *Logos*, in the beginning was not reason, but rather the unreasonable; reason, being a product of the development of the irrational, is itself ultimately something irrational. This means that things, being unreasonable, have no truth; instead, truth is something that only man can determine; it is something man-made, and that means in reality that there is no truth. There are only human constructs, and this necessarily implies the partisan character of reason, which recognizes in advance the compelling force of historical development, runs ahead of it, and thus elevates the compulsion to the status of freedom. Based on these assumptions, positivism can in fact be transcended by humanly imposed meanings that are capable of being depicted as moral because they anticipate the law of historical development; herein lies the fascination of these notions and also the unavoidable inferiority of all bourgeois arguments that remain stuck in positivism. But, according to such a blueprint, what unites the specialized fields and raises them again to the status of a university is the force of partisanship, and with that the university is not reestablished as a place of freedom for enlightenment but, rather, definitively negated.[40]

The Loss of Truth Leads to Political Moralism

What Ratzinger is describing here is the replacement of truth by ideology and morality by political correctness, and political correctness, in turn, negates freedom, the supposed by-product of enlightenment. This has seismic repercussions for the institution of the university, initially founded by Christian monarchs and clerics to pursue a unified vision of reality, the truth, as it were. Once *praxis*-based ideologies and conceptions of political correctness replace truth, the university becomes a mere machine for making and promoting such ideologies.

Rather than using the expression "political correctness" Ratzinger tends to use the expression "political moralism." Thus, he writes that "the political moralism we have experienced, and still witness today, is far from opening the path to a real regeneration: instead, it blocks the way."[41] He is also critical

---

[40] *Ibid.*, p. 152.
[41] *Id., Christianity and the Crisis of Cultures* (San Francisco: Ignatius, 2006), p. 28.

of the tendency of some theologians to "reduce the core of the message of Jesus, that is, the 'kingdom of God', to the 'values of the kingdom', identifying these values with the great slogans of political moralism while at the same time proclaiming that these slogans are the synthesis of the religions."[42] Such projects, he argues, occlude God, even though "it is precisely He who is both the subject and the cause of the kingdom."[43]

Not only did Ratzinger concur with significant elements of the "dialectic of enlightenment" thesis, but in his exchange with Jürgen Habermas, who is also associated with the Frankfurt School, published as *The Dialectics of Secularization: On Reason and Religion* (2006),[44] Ratzinger and Habermas found themselves at some level of agreement. Habermas is an atheist but in his dialogue with Ratzinger he acknowledged the indispensability of at least some elements of the Judeo-Christian framework for the stable operation of any rational and free political system. Foremost among these is the Christian defense of rationality. For his part Ratzinger acknowledged that there can be pathologies of religion as well as pathologies of reason, and thus he concluded that the pair, faith and reason, must work in tandem to purify one another. For Ratzinger the role of the priority of *praxis* principle within the Marxist tradition makes it an enemy of both faith and reason, and thus Marxism ultimately ends up in the wrong place in its understanding of truth, freedom, hope, history, eschatology, ethics, and love. It is not so much a social "science" as a simple political ideology or secularized theology of history as Löwith also concluded.

Ratzinger and Benjamin

Notwithstanding all of these criticisms, David Schütz has observed that there is a convergence of positions between Ratzinger's approach to eschatology and that of Walter Benjamin (1892–1940), author of *The Work of Art in the Age of Mechanical Reproduction* (1935) and *Theses on the Philosophy of History* (1940). Kołakowski described Benjamin's work as an attempt to graft Marx's historical materialism onto his own theory of culture which had nothing to do with Marxism but was rather heavily influenced by Jewish messianism.[45] Hannah Arendt described Benjamin as probably "the most peculiar Marxist ever produced by this movement."[46] Others have used the Latin expression *sui generis* meaning one of a kind.

---

[42] *Ibid.*, p. 29.
[43] *Ibid.*
[44] Cf. J. Ratzinger and J. Habermas, *The Dialectics of Secularization: On Reason and Religion* (San Francisco: Ignatius, 2006).
[45] Cf. L. Kołakowski, *Main Currents of Marxism: Volume III*, pp. 348–50.
[46] H. Arendt, "Introduction," in W. Benjamin *Illuminations: Essays and Reflections*, H. Arendt (ed.) (New York: Schocken Books, 1968), p. 11.

Although Ratzinger does not directly engage with the work of Benjamin (though Metz does), there are some significant affinities between the pair. Schütz summarizes these affinities or convergences in the following three paragraphs:

a. Ratzinger and Benjamin agree on the danger that the ideology of progress represents for the hope of human fulfillment. In particular, they agree that dreams of a future utopia, to be reached through programmatic political, scientific, or economic planning, have the potential to create situations of catastrophic anti-humanity.

b. Both scholars base their opposition to this kind of progressive thinking on a remarkably similar "curved" shape of history, which in both cases is drawn from pre-Kantian religious traditions. The role of the "messianic event" is central to both concepts. Despite the different way each understands this event, it is the mid- or turning-point in an *egressus-regressus* relationship between *der Ursprung* and *das Ziel*.

c. The virtue of hope is central to both Benjamin and Ratzinger. Memory, in particular, ensures that "nothing is lost to history," and the hope of redemption remains open. They both hope in an event whose advent cuts across the "empty, homogenous" timeline of history to "awaken the dead." This event does not only inaugurate a new reality for the present but addresses all past injustice and restores every part of history in its totality.[47]

Conclusion

For Ratzinger, of course, the "event" was the Incarnation, followed by the Paschal Mysteries and the arrival of the whole sacramental economy. His criticisms of the Marxist tradition concur with those of Jean Daniélou who wrote that "our only hope of defeating Marxism depends on our conviction that Christianity is the real marker of history."[48] This position is quintessentially that of Ratzinger. As he wrote in 1958:

> Christian brotherhood, unlike the purely secular brotherhood of Marxism, is above all brotherhood based on the common paternity of God. Unlike the impersonal Stoic idea of God the Father and the vague paternal idea

---

[47] D. Schütz, *The Messianic Shape of History and the Critique of the Ideology of Progress in the Eschatologies of Walter Benjamin and Joseph Ratzinger* (Masters' Thesis, Melbourne: University of Divinity, 2021), pp. 53–4.
[48] J. Daniélou, *The Lord of History* (London: Longmans, 1958), p. 80.

of the Enlightenment, the fatherhood of God is a fatherhood mediated by the Son, and including brotherly union in the Son. If, therefore, Christian brotherhood is to be vitally realized, both a vital knowledge of the fatherhood of God and a vital joining with Jesus Christ in a unity of grace are necessary.[49]

This unity of course is a sacramental unity, not a unity based on class, race, national identity, or shared ideologies.

---

[49] J. Ratzinger, *Christian Brotherhood*, p. 44.

9

Friedrich Nietzsche: Eros, Morality, and the Death of God

Owen Vyner

Introduction

When Pope Benedict XVI promulgated his encyclical, *Deus caritas est*, many expressed surprise that he quoted the strident critic of Christianity, Friedrich Nietzsche. However, those familiar with the *oeuvre* of Joseph Ratzinger prior to his ascendancy to the papacy were familiar with the pontiff's frequent engagement with the German philologist and philosopher.

Ratzinger was introduced to Nietzsche during philosophical studies in his seminary years at Freising when he was nineteen years old.[1] Throughout his academic career, Ratzinger had quoted Nietzsche several times and then later, as pope, he referred to him in encyclicals and homilies. At times, Ratzinger treats Nietzsche as a serious interlocutor, at other times he will quote him approvingly, and still others he boldly disagrees with him.

Nevertheless, despite the frequency of his engagement, one rarely finds an in-depth treatment of Nietzsche. Furthermore, when he does enter more deeply into Nietzsche's writings Ratzinger relies heavily on the insights of

---

[1] Cf. J. Ratzinger, *Milestones: Memoirs 1927–1977* (San Francisco: Ignatius, 1998), p. 43.

Henri de Lubac (1896–1991).² Ratzinger adopts De Lubac's assessment of Nietzsche's thought and its influence.³ De Lubac proposed that no one had attacked the Christian view of the human person with the clarity and vision of Nietzsche. Also, De Lubac believed that Nietzsche's project had ultimately proven successful with the rise of "neopaganism."⁴ It is due to the profound impact that Nietzsche has had on contemporary culture, and his critique of Christian ethics, that Ratzinger considers it essential to converse with this significant opponent.

In the writings of Ratzinger, one will find three areas of substantial dialogue with Nietzsche. First is in the relationship of Christianity and *eros*. Second, and related to this, Ratzinger addresses Nietzsche's characterization of Christianity as a "capital crime against life." The final area of discussion pertains to Nietzsche's well-known claim that God is dead. This chapter will examine these assertions by Nietzsche and present an exposition of the foundations of Ratzinger's response. It will ultimately be argued that while Ratzinger certainly agrees with the essence of De Lubac's assessment, nevertheless, his solution is uniquely Ratzingerian. To this end, it will close with a treatment of Ratzinger's baptismal theology. The themes that will be addressed regarding the Christian view of love and the death of God converge in Ratzinger's understanding of baptism as a sacramental participation in Holy Saturday.

Eros and the Affirmation of the Other

In his homily to the College of Cardinals in 2005, during the Mass for the election of the Roman Pontiff, then-Cardinal Ratzinger spoke of the dynamism of authentic Christian witness. In particular, he referred to the need of the Christian to go forth, bearing an enduring fruit of love and true joy.⁵ As it is known, the very next day he would be elected to the papacy.

The theme of Christian joy as a compelling evangelical witness has been consistent in the writings of Ratzinger. At the same time, he continually raises caution regarding the counter-witness of joyless and faithless Christians. Already in 1958, he published an article in the

---

²Cf. M. Ramage has arrived at a similar conclusion regarding Ratzinger's reliance on De Lubac. See M. J. Ramage, *The Experiment of Faith: Pope Benedict XVI on Living the Theological Virtues in a Secular Age* (Washington, DC: Catholic University of American Press, 2020), p. 2, n. 1.
³Ratzinger mentions the influence of De Lubac on his thought in his memoirs. See J. Ratzinger, *Milestones*, p. 98.
⁴Cf. H. de Lubac, *The Drama of Atheist Humanism* (San Francisco: Ignatius, 1995), pp. 118–19. Originally published as *Le Drame de l'humanisme athée* (Paris: Spes, 1944).
⁵Cf. J. Ratzinger, *Homily at the Mass "Pro Eligendo Romano Pontifice,"* April 18, 2005.

journal *Hochland*, in which he decried the secularization of Christians. He referred to Christians who had become conformed to the world as "pagans" or "heathens."[6] Another example of the thematization of joy is found in *Principles of Catholic Theology* in which he proposes that joy represents the "comprehensive programmatic designation of what Christianity is by nature."[7] Similarly, he immediately warns against the "joylessness and cramped scrupulosity" of Christians today that leads to the understanding that Christianity is opposed to joy.[8] As Benedict XVI, his entire pontificate was directed to expounding Christian joy as an antidote to the challenges of secularism, of which Nietzsche is the ultimate representative.[9]

It is within the above context, that on several occasions throughout his corpus, he quotes Nietzsche's critique of Christianity. For example, in the encyclical *Deus caritas est*, Benedict addresses Nietzsche's statement that Christianity poisoned *eros*.[10] Benedict writes: " ... [D]oesn't the Church, with all her commandments and prohibitions, turn to bitterness the most precious thing in life? Doesn't she blow the whistle just when the joy which is the Creator's gift offers us a happiness which is itself a certain foretaste of the Divine?"[11] Later, in the same encyclical Benedict frames his discussion on Christian love within the context of the Nietzschean criticism employing it as representative of contemporary views on Christian teaching. Benedict expresses it thus: "I am thinking of Nietzsche but also of so many others—that Christianity is an option opposed to life. With the Cross, with all the Commandments, with all the 'nos' that it proposes to us, some have said that it closes the door to life."[12]

In *Principles of Catholic Theology*, Ratzinger provides more specificity in diagnosing the aetiology of this view in describing the two-pronged attack of Nietzsche on Christianity. On the one hand, Christianity is criticized as a capital crime against life in its denigration of worldly joy. On the other hand, Christianity stunts genuine autonomous human freedom with its slave morality. Ratzinger describes the distinct accusations thus:

---

[6] Cf. J. Ratzinger, "The Church and the New Pagans," *Homiletic and Pastoral Review*, January 30, 2017. Originally published as "Die neuen Heiden und die Kirche," *Hochland* 51/1 (1958), pp. 1–11.
[7] Id., *Principles of Catholic Theology: Building Stones for a Fundamental Theology* (San Francisco: Ignatius, 1987), p. 73.
[8] Cf. *ibid.*, p. 76.
[9] Cf. J. Murphy, *Christ Our Joy: The Theological Vision of Pope Benedict XVI* (San Francisco: Ignatius, 2008).
[10] Cf. F. Nietzsche, "Chapter IV. Apophthegms and Interlude," in *Beyond Good and Evil* (Cambridge: Cambridge University Press, 2002), §168. "Christianity gave Eros poison to drink:—he did not die from it, but degenerated into a vice."
[11] Benedict XVI, *Deus caritas est: Encyclical Letter on Christian Love* (Boston: Pauline Books and Media, 2006), §3.
[12] Id., *Meeting with the Clergy of the Rome Diocese*, March 2, 2006.

Two passages may make clear to us the change with which Nietzsche was concerned. "What has been until now the greatest sin here on earth? Was it not the word of him who said: 'Woe unto those who laugh here'?" The second passage reads: "'To be sure, unless you become like little children, you shall not enter the kingdom of heaven.' (And Zarathustra pointed upward with his hands.) But we do not want to enter the kingdom of heaven. We have become men—and so we want the kingdom of earth."[13]

This section will address the prior claim that Christianity is opposed to life and happiness. This view is commonplace today, especially with regards to the Catholic Church's teachings in the area of sexual ethics. Whilst Nietzsche actually urged that sexual instinct be subordinated to the will to power, nevertheless, Nietzsche's predilection for the "Dionysian principle" has proven prescient in relation to the contemporary exaltation of *eros* at the expense of morality.[14]

In 1869, Friedrich Nietzsche (1844–1900) was appointed Associate Professor of Philology at the University of Basel.[15] He took a leave of absence to volunteer as a medical orderly in the Franco-Prussian War (1870) and it was during this time that he began to write his first major published book, *Birth of Tragedy* (1872). There was much anticipation surrounding it; however, it was not well-received at the time.[16] It has since been reappraised as a classic in the field of aesthetics and was considered by De Lubac to be a work of genius.[17]

Nietzsche proposed that Greek tragedy was built upon the synthesis of two radically opposing principles, the Apollonian and the Dionysian. Its goal was to balance these principles.[18] The Apollonian principle is associated with dreams and order while the Dionysian principle is identified with intoxication and drunken ecstasy.[19] At this early stage of his career, despite his preference for Dionysus, Nietzsche will not propose which principle will

---

[13] J. Ratzinger, *Principles of Catholic Theology*, p. 76. Ratzinger is referencing, *Thus Spake Zarathustra* as it is quoted in the French edition of De Lubac's *Drama of Atheist Humanism*, pp. 313–14 (pp. 299–300 in the English edition).
[14] Cf. J. Merecki, "Has Christianity Poisoned *Eros*," in L. Melina and Carl A. Anderson (eds.), *The Way of Love: Reflections on Pope Benedict XVI's Encyclical* Deus caritas est (San Francisco: Ignatius, 2006), pp. 56–65, at p. 58.
[15] Cf. B. Magnus and K. M. Higgins, "Nietzsche's Works and Their Themes," in B. Magnus and K. M. Higgins (eds.), *The Cambridge Companion to Nietzsche* (Cambridge: Cambridge University Press, 1996), pp. 21–68, at p. 22.
[16] Cf. *ibid*.
[17] Cf. H. de Lubac, *The Drama of Atheist Humanism*, p. 74.
[18] Cf. B. Magnus and K. M. Higgins, "Nietzsche's Works and Their Themes," pp. 22–4.
[19] Cf. F. Nietzsche, "The Birth of Tragedy," in *The Birth of Tragedy and The Genealogy of Morals* (Garden City: Doubleday, 1956), p. 19. The original full title is *Die Geburt der Tragödie aus dem Geiste der Musik* (*The Birth of Tragedy from the Spirit of Music*).

emerge victorious.[20] Although, in the preface of *Ecce Homo* he refers to himself as a disciple of Dionysus.[21]

In his later writings, Nietzsche opposed the Dionysian principle to the crucified Christ.[22] In *The Will to Power* he contrasted the Dionysian affirmation of life with its antithesis, namely, "the 'Crucified as the innocent one'" whose suffering stands as an objection to life and as a "formula for its condemnation."[23] Regarding the opposition between the Crucified and Dionysius Nietzsche continues: "The god on the cross is a curse on life, a signpost to seek redemption from life; Dionysus cut to pieces is a *promise* of life: it will be eternally reborn and return again from destruction."[24]

The contrast escalates to its highpoint in *Ecce Homo*, his autobiography and last original work. He writes: "The concept 'God' was invented as the opposite of the concept life—everything detrimental, poisonous, and slanderous, and all deadly hostility to life."[25] His autobiography ends with a final, singular line: "Have you understood me? *Dionysus* versus *Christ*."[26]

Ratzinger's most sustained treatment of Nietzsche's critique is found in *Principles of Catholic Theology*. He frames the accusation thus: "We have now come to the heart of the problem: Did not Christianity forbid us the tree in the middle of the garden, and in doing so, really forbidden us everything?"[27] Ratzinger later notes that, ironically, contemporary society has eradicated moral taboos and therefore has no more "forbidden trees," yet people do not appear happier or more free. In fact, the newfound autonomy has resulted in enslavement and pervasive melancholy.[28] This leads him to seek the anthropological foundations of true joy.

In his analysis of the source of joy, Ratzinger draws upon the thought of Josef Pieper (1904–97). For Pieper, the "function" of love within existence is for the lover to express the goodness of the beloved's existence. The fruit of love is thus experienced on the side of the one who is affirmed and his identity awakens precisely within this encounter.[29] Employing Pieper's dialogical foundation of personal identity, Ratzinger describes the "self-acceptance" which is so essential in bringing one happiness. True inner-harmony, which is the fruit of self-acceptance, derives from the affirmation of one's *I* in relation

---

[20] Cf. H. de Lubac, *The Drama of Atheist Humanism*, p. 77.
[21] Cf. F. Nietzsche, "The Birth of Tragedy," pp. 76–9.
[22] Cf. R. Girard, "Dionysus versus the Crucified," *Modern Language Notes* 99/4 (1984), pp. 816–35.
[23] F. Nietzsche, *The Will to Power* (New York: Vintage Books, 1968), p. 543.
[24] *Ibid.*
[25] *Id., Ecce Homo* (Portland: Smith & Sale Printers, 1911), p. 59. Published in 1888, its full title is *Ecce Homo: Wie man wird, was man ist* (*Ecce Homo: How One Becomes What One Is*).
[26] *Ibid.*, p. 60.
[27] J. Ratzinger, *Principles of Catholic Theology*, p. 77.
[28] Cf. *ibid.*, p. 78.
[29] Cf. J. Pieper, *Faith, Hope and Love* (San Francisco: Ignatius, 2012), pp. 174–5. Original German edition: *Über die Liebe* (1972).

to another, from a *thou*. Ratzinger terms this "hospitalism"—the welcoming of the other and a rejoicing in his or her existence. Ratzinger states, "For it is the way of love to will the other's existence and, at the same time, to bring that forth again. The key to the *I* lies with the *thou*; the way to the *thou* leads through the *I*."[30] Ratzinger concludes that Christianity, far from negating personal value and thus joy, actually affirms the person. In fact, Christianity—precisely and paradoxically through the Cross—gives divine affirmation of the goodness of personal existence, and this is the source of Christianity's message of "glad tidings." Thus, rather than Christianity existing as the enemy of joy, it guarantees it. Ratzinger writes:

> The content of the Christian *evangelium* reads: God finds man so important that he himself has suffered for man. The Cross, which was for Nietzsche the most detestable expression of the negative character of the Christian religion, is in truth the center of the *evangelium*, the glad tidings: "It is good that you exist"—no, "It is necessary that you exist." The Cross is the approbation of our existence ... in an act so completely radical that it caused God to become flesh and pierced this flesh to the quick; that, to God, it was worth the death of his incarnate Son.[31]

Similar lines of argument emerge in *Deus caritas est* in response to Nietzsche's charge that Christianity poisoned *eros*. Benedict posits that biblical revelation sought to oppose the divinization of *eros*, especially as it was expressed in the ancient fertility cults. He maintains that undisciplined *eros* actually leads to the denigration of the person. This is because authentic *eros* requires purification and maturity without which the other will be objectified and therefore not affirmed in his or her personal value. The proof of this has been born out in the sexual revolution. When *eros* is reduced to pure physicality it necessarily diminishes the person who is commodified as something to be sold and exploited.[32] An unrestrained Dionysian frenzy, as he described elsewhere,[33] has not led to greater happiness and affirmation of the world and corporeality but rather to the denigration of human sexuality. Benedict quips: "This is hardly man's great 'yes' to the body."[34]

Christian ascesis, as it pertains to desire, in fact makes true *eros* possible. As it has been expressed above, authentic joy involves the affirmation of the other. This "yes" to the goodness of the other requires self-renunciation, not understood as a denial of love and desire, but rather for love to express genuine self-donation. Thus, we see the importance of *agape*, the love of

---

[30] J. Ratzinger, *Principles of Catholic Theology*, p. 80.
[31] *Ibid.*, p. 81.
[32] Cf. Benedict XVI, *Deus caritas est*, §5.
[33] Cf. J. Ratzinger, "Truth and Freedom," *Communio* 23/1 (1996), pp. 17–35, at p. 22.
[34] Benedict XVI, *Deus caritas est*, §5.

self-sacrifice, that enables *eros* to fulfill its inherent dynamism as desire.[35] Furthermore, Benedict argues that the person acts most fully as *himself* when he does so within his psychosomatic unity, i.e., when his body and soul are intimately united. Consequently, far from demeaning the value of the body (as it is often claimed) Christianity affirms it, for the body—precisely in its sexual differentiation—becomes the bearer and foundation for the expression of true desire.[36]

Has Christianity taken the joy out of life as Nietzsche claimed? Ratzinger would agree that the joyless Christian certainly presents a counter-Gospel that diminishes the credibility of the Christianity. Nevertheless, the fullness of the Christian Gospel—in its affirmation of the person (especially God's "yes" to humanity on the Cross), the body, and love—becomes the guarantor of *eros* and joy.

Freedom and Relativity toward the Other

As mentioned above, Ratzinger treats Nietzsche's charge that Christianity is a capital crime against life from another, although related, perspective in his writings. The Nietzschean description of Christianity as a "slave morality" and a religion of resentment presents an extremely insightful attack. In essence, the distinctiveness of Christianity has always resided in the Christian's love for one another (cf. John 13:35). Ratzinger refers to this critique in *Principles of Catholic Theology* in which he quotes Nietzsche: "The whole absurd residue of Christian fable, cobwebbery of concepts and theology matters little to us; if it were a thousand times more absurd, I wouldn't raise a finger against it."

> Until now, we have always attacked Christianity in a false, not just a timid, way. So long as we do not regard Christian morality as a capital crime against life, its defenders will have an easy time of it. The problem of the simple "truth" of Christianity ... is a quite secondary matter so long as we do not question the value of Christian morality.

"What has been until now the greatest sin here on earth? Was it not the word of him who said: 'Woe unto those who laugh here'?"[37]

In the nineteenth century, it was a commonplace understanding in philosophical circles that the mythology of Christianity was dead. Nevertheless, its vestigial remains continued, not in its truths *per se*, but rather in its morality and values.[38] Consequently, in targeting its morality Nietzsche had struck at the heart of Christianity's uniqueness.

---

[35] Cf. *ibid.*, §7.
[36] Cf. *ibid.*, §5.
[37] J. Ratzinger, *Principles of Catholic Theology*, p. 76.
[38] Cf. H. de Lubac, *The Drama of Atheist Humanism*, p. 118.

In his assessment of this charge De Lubac notes that in all the offensives launched against Christianity and its teachings, "never, before Nietzsche, had so mighty an adversary arisen, one who had so clear, broad and explicit a conception of his destiny and who pursued it in all domains with such systematic and deliberate zeal."[39] It was the remnants of Christian belief in its morality that became the one and only real problem for Nietzsche. De Lubac quotes Nietzsche on his solution to this problem: "War against the Christian ideal ... against the doctrine that makes beatitude and salvation the aim of life, against the supremacy of the poor in spirit, the pure in heart, the suffering, the failures .... "[40] It would appear that Ratzinger shared De Lubac's evaluation of the seriousness of Nietzsche's attack. This is implied as the Nietzschean quote from *Principles of Catholic Theology* is cited directly from De Lubac's *Drama of Atheistic Humanism*. Thus, Ratzinger would have been aware of De Lubac's assessment. Second, as it has already been noted, Ratzinger rarely engages Nietzsche at length yet does so here in addressing the claim that Christianity is a slave morality.

In his *Genealogy of Morals* (1887), Nietzsche traces the origins of what he terms the *"ressentiment"* inherent in Christian morality.[41] This drive for vengeance is located in a "slave morality" created by the weak-willed and those who are ill-suited to life. This was a reaction to a "master morality" of the strong and those who affirm life through their virtues of pride, power, and self-expression.[42] This disposition of *resentment*, or vengeance, toward the strong turns what is virtue into vice and vice into virtue. Hence, weakness becomes blessedness and pride becomes sin. For Nietzsche, this pattern is pervasive throughout the ethics of Christianity which represents the most historically important and toxic form of a slave morality.[43] In his later years, Nietzsche argued that the strong should despise Christianity in its indecency and seek to overthrow it.[44] Nietzsche will find his solution in his genealogical analysis, in which he concludes that the human person is ontologically "will to power."[45] Consequently, in displacing the slave morality of Christians, he will propose a master morality of self-expression and autonomy.[46]

Ratzinger's most significant treatment of the description of Christianity as a slave morality is found in *Principles of Catholic Theology* and *Jesus of*

---

[39] *Ibid.*
[40] *Ibid.*, p. 116.
[41] See the "First Essay," in F. Nietzsche, *The Birth of Tragedy and The Genealogy of Morals* (Garden City: Doubleday, 1956), pp. 158–88.
[42] Cf. W. R. Schroeder, *Continental Philosophy: A Critical Approach* (Malden: Blackwell, 2005), p. 126.
[43] Cf. J. Salaquarda, "Nietzsche and the Judaeo-Christian Tradition," in B. Magnus and K. M. Higgins (eds.), *The Cambridge Companion to Nietzsche* (Cambridge: Cambridge University Press, 1996), pp. 103–4.
[44] Cf. *ibid.*, p. 104.
[45] *Ibid.*
[46] Cf. *ibid.*, p. 107.

Nazareth (2007). In the former, he accepts the contrast between Nietzsche's Dionysus and his morality of the strongman with the Crucified and his virtues of the weak, although he concludes that such a world leads to violence and inhumanity.[47] In the latter, he indicates the seriousness of the challenge, describing it as influencing the manner in which the contemporary mindset approaches life.[48] In his discussion of the "Sermon on the Mount" in *Jesus of Nazareth*, Benedict asks whether the Christian view of morality as represented by the Beatitudes is indeed, a "capital crime against life"? After all, is it so bad to be rich, to eat one's fill, and to laugh? Benedict explains it thus: "Nietzsche sees the vision of the Sermon on the Mount as a religion of resentment, as the envy of the cowardly and incompetent, who are unequal to life's demands and try to avenge themselves by blessing their failure and cursing the strong, the successful, and the happy."[49]

In response, Benedict affirms that the words of the Sermon certainly ring true with the experience of the twentieth century. Totalitarian regimes and the abuse of economic power have proven the truth of Christ's warnings against riches and wealth. However, the real power of the Beatitudes lies in their demand of conversion, a turning away from self and a turning toward God and neighbor.

In *Principles of Catholic Theology*, as was seen above, Ratzinger locates the source of Christian joy in an *I-thou* interpersonal encounter. In *Jesus of Nazareth*, and in other places, he addresses Nietzsche from the related perspective of human freedom. The issue essentially distills into two competing notions of freedom. In essence, does the person become more free as a purely autonomous self or is it in conversion, a turning toward the other, that one paradoxically finds himself? We see the contrast between conversion and self-gift versus freedom as autonomy in a homily of Benedict: "Nietzsche scoffed at humility and obedience as the virtues of slaves, a source of repression. He replaced them with pride and man's absolute freedom."[50]

To this end, a major theme that is found in Ratzinger's work is the notion of egoism as a form of deceptive self-sufficiency.[51] In many passages, he utilizes Nietzsche as a dialogue partner who represents the view of freedom as autonomy. For example, in the context of Judas' rejection of Jesus in the Last Supper, Ratzinger references the autonomy that leads to a *no* to God. He does so by quoting Nietzsche: " ... [W]e want to make the world for

---

[47] Cf. J. Ratzinger, *Principles of Catholic Theology*, p. 77.
[48] Cf. *id.*, *Jesus of Nazareth: From the Baptism in the Jordan to the Transfiguration* (New York: Doublebay, 2007), p. 97.
[49] *Ibid.*
[50] Benedict XVI, *Homily at the Chrism Mass*, April 9, 2009.
[51] Cf. J. Ratzinger, *Eschatology: Death and Eternal Life* (Washington, DC: Catholic University of America Press, 1988), p. 205; Benedict XVI, *Spe salvi: Encyclical Letter on Christian Hope* (Boston: Pauline Books and Media, 2007), §47.

ourselves and are not ready to accept it as a gift from God. 'Sooner remain in debt than pay with a coin that does not bear our own portrait—that is what our sovereignty demands', as Nietzsche once said."[52]

In other writings, again using Nietzsche as a foil, he refers to the temptation to seek a freedom of independence. Ratzinger contrasts with the "way of the Cross" that dismantles false assurances and leads to one's true homecoming.[53] In another place Ratzinger traces the genealogy of freedom as autonomy—via Jean-Jacques Rousseau, Nietzsche, Karl Marx—with its promise of a godlike and independent freedom. In response, Ratzinger seeks to present an authentic vision of human freedom and fulfillment through love. A truly human freedom is properly constituted as a being "for," "from," and "with" another.[54]

In his writings Ratzinger locates the essence of personal being in relativity toward the other.[55] This has already been discussed above in the section on the awakening of self-identity through the other's affirmation. In his treatment of the anthropological and theological foundations of freedom, we see a complementary reading of relationality. In Ratzinger's contrasting of the freedom of autonomy with freedom as relationality, he grounds his vision in what he terms the "law of exodus." He references this philosophical analogue—namely, the law of spirit "being related beyond oneself"— of a theological truth. The law of exodus, central to biblical revelation, is expressed in Abraham's going forth and the Passover of Christ's own paschal mystery.[56] He describes this "law" in *Jesus of Nazareth*: "The true morality of Christianity is love. And love does admittedly run counter to self-seeking—it is an exodus out of oneself, and yet this is precisely the way in which man comes to himself."[57]

The theological *locus* of this view is found in the person's creation in the *imago Dei*. As such, the human person's creation to be for, from, and with another finds its archetype in Trinitarian relations. Ratzinger describes the Trinitarian processions in highly personalist terms although they express a Thomistic metaphysic. By his nature, God is entirely "being-for" (the Father is the relation of innascibility-paternity), "being-from" (the Son is the relation of filiation), and "being-with" (the Holy Spirit is the relation of spiration-communion). Because freedom is purely relational in God, any freedom that is conceived as non-relational, that is without a "for," a "from,"

---

[52] J. Ratzinger, *God Is Near Us: The Eucharist, The Heart of Life* (San Francisco: Ignatius, 2003), p. 31.
[53] Cf. *ibid.*, *Dogma and Preaching: Applying Christian Doctrine to Daily Life* (San Francisco: Ignatius, 2011), p. 161.
[54] Cf. *id.*, "Truth and Freedom," p. 28.
[55] Cf. *id.*, "Concerning the Notion of Person in Theology," *Communio* 17/3 (1990), pp. 439–54, at p. 452.
[56] Cf. *id.*, *Dogma and Preaching*, p. 161.
[57] J. Ratzinger, *Jesus of Nazareth*, p. 99.

and a "with," presupposes an anti-God—"because it harbors exactly the radical antithesis to the real God."[58]

For Ratzinger, Christian morality is not a slave morality, rather it is one of divine freedom and relativity. This is because it is a freedom directed toward another as it is expressed in the Gospel maxim that whoever loses his life for Christ will save it (cf. Luke 9:24). In the end, it is the ultimate meaning of the Cross—to give one's life for another.[59] Thus, the law of exodus, which is essentially the law of the Cross, does not represent the "crucifixion of man" but "rather the foundation of true humanity ..., " a true being *toward another*.[60] Of this freedom, grounded in love and relationality, Benedict writes:

> Compared with the tempting luster of Nietzsche's image of man, this way [of the cross] seems at first wretched, and thoroughly unreasonable. But it is the real high road of life; it is only on the way of love, whose paths are described in the Sermon on the Mount, that the richness of life and the greatness of man's calling are opened up.[61]

Baptism: Sacramental Participation in the Divine Other

The final Nietzschean theme to be discussed is the "death of God." One finds the declaration that God is dead in two significant passages in *Gay Science*[62] (1882) and several in *Thus Spake Zarathustra*[63] (1883–5). Many are familiar with the parable of the madman who yells in the marketplace, "Whither Is God?" When he is ridiculed by his listeners he responds, "I shall tell you. *We have killed him*—you and I. All of us are his murderers ... Is not the greatness of this deed too great for us? Must not we ourselves become gods simply to seem worthy of it?"[64] For Nietzsche, those who hear the rantings of the madman agree that the idea of God is no longer believable, and thus God is indeed dead.[65] Initially, the news that "the old god is dead" results in "amazement" and "anticipation" over the limitless potential of this new situation. However, and here we see Nietzsche's prescience, they

---

[58] *Id.*, "Truth and Freedom," p. 28.
[59] Cf. Benedict XVI, *Meeting with the Clergy of the Rome Diocese*, March 2, 2006.
[60] Cf. J. Ratzinger, *Dogma and Preaching*, p. 161.
[61] *Id.*, *Jesus of Nazareth*, p. 99.
[62] Cf. F. Nietzsche, *The Gay Science: With a Prelude in Rhymes and an Appendix of Songs* (New York: Vintage Books, 1974). Original German title, *Die fröhliche Wissenschaft*.
[63] Cf. *id.*, *Thus Spake Zarathustra* (Ware: Wordsworth Editions Ltd, 1997). Original German title, *Also sprach Zarathustra: Ein Buch für Alle und Keinen*.
[64] F. Nietzsche, *Gay Science*, p. 181.
[65] Cf. *ibid.*, p. 270.

do not understand the implications of the loss of God. In Europe especially, every aspect of culture and life has been shaped by belief in God. Later in *Gay Science*, Nietzsche will warn of the danger of nihilism that will follow the death of God. He describes the "breakdown, destruction, ruin, and cataclysm that is now impending."[66] His ultimate concern regarding nihilism is that it will produce a listless "Last Man," a people who lack passion. His solution is for humanity to become "godlike," in the form of the *Übermensch*.[67]

While there are several occasions in which Ratzinger references the death of God, the most significant engagement is found in *Introduction to Christianity* and his meditations on Holy Week published in *The Sabbath of History*. Ratzinger wrote both of these works in 1967 during the student revolutions in Europe.[68] In his treatment of the issue, Ratzinger addresses the death of God from two perspectives. First, he proposes that the lives of Christians, insofar as they are non-distinct from their secular counterparts, obscures God. When the Christian encloses God within the constraints of privatized and subjective religion, or concealing God with their lives, (living as if there were no God), the practical end result is that God has been killed.[69] Second, he describes the extreme suffering of the twentieth century, with its wars, gulags, and concentration camps as a century in which God is silent and, therefore, appears dead.[70] Furthermore, he situates the cause of the reduction of embryonic human life to "research material" or commodification of women through human trafficking within the eclipse of God in the west.[71] He writes: "But, as Nietzsche describes it, once the news really reaches people that 'God is dead' … then everything changes. This is demonstrated today … in the way that science treats human life: man is becoming a technological object while vanishing to an ever greater degree as a human subject …."[72]

Ratzinger connects the theme of the death of God, as the experience of the twentieth century, with Holy Saturday. In the Christian tradition, Holy Saturday is the liturgical commemoration between Good Friday and Easter Sunday in which Christ's body lies in the tomb while his soul descends into hell. Again, he follows the insights of De Lubac who made this connection prior. De Lubac depicts Fyodor Dostoevsky's profound experience while viewing Hans Holbein's painting of the crucified Christ in an art gallery in Basel. His wife recounts that Dostoevsky was shattered to the core. Later,

---

[66] *Ibid.*, p. 279.
[67] Cf. W. R. Schroeder, *Continental Philosophy*, p. 122.
[68] Cf. P. Seewald, *Benedict XVI: A Life Volume Two: Professor and Prefect to Pope and Pope Emeritus 1966–2021* (London: Bloomsbury Continuum, 2021), pp. 39–46.
[69] Cf. J. Ratzinger, *Introduction to Christianity* (San Francisco: Ignatius, 2000), p. 16.
[70] Cf. *ibid.*, p. 294.
[71] Cf. *ibid.*, pp. 17–18.
[72] *Ibid.*, p. 17.

Dostoevsky would express this encounter through the words of Prince Myshkin in *The Idiot*, when he said, "That picture! Do you know that to look at it might make a believer lose his faith?"[73] De Lubac notes that Dostoevsky linked the image of the dead Christ with the rising atheism of the nineteenth century and specifically Nietzsche's philosophy of the death of God.[74]

While indeed reliant on De Lubac for this insight, nevertheless, Ratzinger uniquely connects the death of God to the sacrament of Baptism. Ratzinger often relates that he was born and baptized on Holy Saturday, thus linking the sacrament and the descent in his own life.[75] He understands this to have been an act of divine providence, immersing his entire life in the Easter mystery. He adds: "To be sure, it was not Easter Sunday but Holy Saturday, but the more I reflect on it, the more this seems to be fitting for the nature of our human life: we are still awaiting Easter; we are not yet standing in the full light but walking toward it full of trust."[76]

In his theological exposition on Holy Saturday, Ratzinger recites an ancient homily to depict Christ's death. He quotes: "God has died in the flesh, and has gone down to rouse the realm of the dead."[77] For the living who exist on the other side of the grave, the death of God is experienced as silence and absence. It is this apparent silence of God that serves as a metaphor for the twentieth century which is one large Holy Saturday,[78] wherein "... God is simply absent, that the grave hides him, that he no longer awakes, no longer speaks ...."[79]

The Apostles' Creed articulates Holy Saturday as Christ's *descendit ad inferos*. Regarding this article of Christian faith, Ratzinger describes hell as the negation of relationality and affirmation referred to in the first sections of this chapter. Hell is thus framed as the inability for one's cry to reach another. He writes "[hell] denotes a loneliness that the word love can no longer penetrate."[80] In *The Sabbath of History* he delineates the fear of solitude that can only be overcome by the presence of another. Hell connotes an impenetrable and final solitude.[81] Thus, the affirmation of the other and relationality as freedom toward the other reaches their most radical expression in Christ's descent into hell. At the same time, the fact that God has entered into this final solitude, in a radical act of solidarity

---

[73] H. de Lubac, *The Drama of Atheist Humanism*, p. 288.
[74] Cf. J. Ratzinger and W. Congdon, *The Sabbath of History* (Washington, DC: The William G. Congdon Foundation, 2006), p. 20; H. de Lubac, *The Drama of Atheist Humanism*, pp. 289–92.
[75] Cf. J. Ratzinger, *Milestones*, p. 8.
[76] *Ibid*.
[77] J. Ratzinger and W. Congdon, *The Sabbath of History*, p. 20.
[78] Cf. *ibid*., p. 38.
[79] J. Ratzinger, *Introduction to Christianity*, p. 294.
[80] *Ibid*., p. 300.
[81] Cf. J. Ratzinger and W. Congdon, *The Sabbath of History*, p. 44.

with humanity, means that hell—and isolation—has been defeated once and for all. He expresses it thus:

> Christ strode through the gate of our final loneliness … [I]n his Passion he went down into the abyss of our abandonment. Where no voice can reach us any longer, there he is. Hell is thereby overcome, or, to be more accurate, death, which was previously hell, is hell no longer …. The door of death stands open since life—love—has dwelt in death.[82]

Furthermore, Christ's baptism in the Jordan at the beginning of his ministry anticipates his death and descent into hell. In *Jesus of Nazareth*, Benedict refers to the iconographic tradition which depicted Christ's baptism in the Jordan as a liquid tomb having the form of a dark cavern which is a symbol of hell.[83] Benedict quotes St. Cyril of Jerusalem's allegorical reading of Christ's baptism and its connection with his descent into the dead: "Jesus' descent into the watery tomb, into the inferno that envelops him from every side, is thus an anticipation of this act of descending into the underworld: 'When he went down into the waters, he bound the strong man'."[84]

The Gospel of Luke's account of Christ's baptism makes explicit that he is baptized along with all the people (cf. Luke 3:21). Benedict comments that Christ presented himself to be baptized in anticipation of his death and in his solidarity with the "gray mass of sinners waiting on the banks of the Jordan."[85] Thus, the unity of Christ with humanity in baptism foreshadows his complete solidarity in his descent into the hell of solitude. For Benedict, this descent into hell reveals that God is on the side of sinners.

Finally, due to God's sharing in humanity's death, the Christian can now participate in Christ's victory over death through baptism. Baptism therefore becomes the entry into Christ's death, his descent into hell, and his rising from the dead. For Nietzsche, we must kill God for humanity to be godlike. For Ratzinger the opposite is the case. God has shared in the death of humanity in order to divinize human nature. As such, God was never silent, rather through the Word taking flesh, and through this Word's death and descent into God-forsakenness, God has spoken the Word of total solidarity with humanity. This unity with God and the transformation of human nature are sacramentally effected through Baptism. Benedict states it in this manner:

> Baptism is more than a cleansing. It is death and resurrection. Paul himself, speaking in the Letter to the Galatians of the turning point in his life brought about by his encounter with the Risen Christ, describes

---

[82] J. Ratzinger, *Introduction to Christianity*, p. 301.
[83] Cf. *id.*, *Jesus of Nazareth*, p. 19.
[84] *Ibid.*
[85] *Ibid.*, p. 16.

it with the words: I am dead. At that moment a new life truly begins. Becoming Christian is more than a cosmetic operation that would add something beautiful to a more or less complete existence. It is a new beginning, it is rebirth: death and resurrection.[86]

Conclusion

Henri de Lubac lamented the "tragic misunderstanding" that constitutes modern atheism. Whereas in antiquity, the existence of God assured human dignity; with atheism, humanity must cast off God in order to grasp its greatness.[87] Nietzsche represents the most eloquent and forceful expression of this view. He contended that the fullness of life is affirmed by denying a crucified Christ, that true autonomy requires casting off Christian morality, and the divinization of humanity will be accomplished through killing God. Ultimately, Nietzsche views power and freedom dialectically and thus as a "zero-sum game" in which God must decrease so that humanity might increase. Ratzinger's response is to propose a view of God and humanity that is not dialectical but dialogical. Thus, the affirmation of the other, relativity toward the other, and sacramental union with the divine other are based upon an anthropology and metaphysics of participation. This is sacramentally effected through Christian baptism, in which the person is plunged into the death of God in order to share in his resurrection, and thus to attain joy, freedom, and abundance of life.

---

[86] Cf. Benedict XVI, *General Audience*, December 10, 2008.
[87] Cf. H. de Lubac, *The Drama of Atheist Humanism*, p. 24.

10

Martin Buber: Personalism and Relationality

Mariusz Biliniewicz

Introduction

Martin Buber (1878–1965) was arguably one of the most prolific and influential Jewish thinkers of the twentieth century.[1] Joseph Ratzinger (1927–2022), on the other hand, is one of the most well-known Catholic theologians of the late twentieth and early twenty-first centuries, especially since his election to the papacy in 2005. Ratzinger has stated that Buber's philosophy influenced his own thought, and he has referred to Buber and his ideas on a number of occasions. This chapter will explore some of the most evident ways in which Buber's philosophy impacted the theology of the man who went on to become a *peritus* at the Second Vatican Council (1962–5), Archbishop of Munich and Freising (1977–81), Prefect of the Congregation of the Doctrine of the Faith (1981–2005), Pope Benedict XVI (2005–13), and then Pope Emeritus (2013–22), the first Pope to have resigned from his office since the thirteenth century.

In his 1998 autobiography, Ratzinger discusses Buber's influence on his own thought as follows:

---

[1] Cf. T. Wright, "Self, Other, Text, God: The Dialogical Thought of Martin Buber," in M. L. Morgan and P. E. Gordon (eds.), *The Cambridge Companion to Modern Jewish Philosophy* (Cambridge: Cambridge University Press, 2007), pp. 102–21; see also M. Friedman, *Martin Buber: The Life of Dialogue. Fourth Edition Revised and Expanded* (London, New York: Routledge, 2002), especially pp. 319–26 on Buber's influence on Christian theologians.

After beginning his career with studies on Hegel and socialism, Steinbüchel [a scholar who taught moral theology in the seminary where the young Ratzinger studied] was now portraying in this book (under the influence above all of Ferdinand Ebner) his discovery of personalism, which had become a major turning point in his own intellectual development. We then found the philosophy of personalism reiterated with renewed conviction in the great Jewish thinker Martin Buber. This encounter with personalism was for me a spiritual experience that left an essential mark, especially since I spontaneously associated such personalism with the thought of St. Augustine, who in his *Confessions* had struck me with the power of all his human passion and depth.[2]

In *Last Testament: In His Own Words*, his final, book-length interview with Peter Seewald, the Pope Emeritus mentioned the importance of Buber's philosophy on his own work, saying:

I revered Martin Buber very much. For one thing he was the great representative of personalism, the I-Thou principle that permeates his entire philosophy. Of course I have also read his complete works. He was a bit fashionable at that time. He had newly translated the Holy Scriptures together with Rosenzweig. His personalistic viewpoint and his philosophy, which was nourished by the Bible, were made fully concrete in his Hasidic tales. This Jewish piety, completely uninhabited in faith and simultaneously always standing in the center of the concerns of this time, his mode of having faith in today's world, his whole person—all this fascinates me.[3]

Ratzinger recalls that it was Buber's personalism that left "an essential mark" in his own thought. This comes as no surprise given that Buber is probably best known, at least in Christian circles, precisely for this contribution to twentieth-century philosophy. This chapter will first focus on Buber's personalism and Ratzinger's appropriation of it. Then, in the second part, it will identify other possible commonalities between Buber and Ratzinger, without attempting to make an exhaustive list.

The Influence of Buber's Personalism and Philosophy of Dialogue on Ratzinger

Following Ratzinger's lead, scholars who analyze his thought recognize the existence of a clear link between Buber's personalism and Ratzinger's

---

[2] J. Ratzinger, *Milestones: Memoirs 1927–1977* (San Francisco: Ignatius, 1998), p. 44.
[3] Benedict XVI and P. Seewald, *Last Testament: In His Own Words* (London, New York: Bloomsbury, 2016), p. 99.

emphasis on relationality understood as a constitutive element of who we are as human beings. Christopher Collins, SJ, believes that Buber's "metaphysics of dialogue" helped the young Ratzinger to find "a contemporary philosophical grounding that would allow ... [him] to appropriate the Christian vision from the ancient biblical and patristic sources while enabling him to simultaneously engage contemporary culture in the sphere of its own concerns."[4] Buber's "I–Thou" paradigm made it possible for contemporary thinkers to tap into "the longing for relationship and overcoming the isolation so characteristic of the modern person."[5] Addressing this felt need helped them to bring theology back to "real life" in the contemporary world and to overcome the apparent gap that existed between academia's learned reflection and people's everyday existence.

Collins believes that Ratzinger's theology as a whole has a dialogical character, and that this character can be found in important areas of Ratzinger's interests like the theology of Divine Revelation, Christology, ecclesiology, the theology of creation, and eschatology.[6] Ratzinger's preference for dialogue and encounter allowed him to develop a theological style that revolves around the concept of communion. In Collins' view, Ratzinger primarily took on this style as a result of his reflections on Scripture and the Church Fathers; however, he also found confirmation of its value in his encounters with contemporary personalistic philosophers, among whom Martin Buber seems to be the most important figure.[7]

Emery de Gaál compares the importance of Buber's philosophy in the development of Ratzinger's theological mind with that of such influential figures as Romano Guardini, Henri de Lubac, St. Augustine, St. John Henry Newman, St. Bonaventure, and Josef Pieper. De Gaál argues that the young Ratzinger, who was not satisfied with the intellectualistic and propositional approaches in neo-Scholasticism, found in Guardini and Buber a relational God for whom he was longing, and for whom contemporary man was longing too.[8]

De Gaál reminds us that Ratzinger was led to the philosophy of Buber through the works of Theodore Steinbüchel.[9] In his view, Buber's philosophy made the most impact on Ratzinger in terms of the significant distinction between the I-It and the I-Thou relationships. The I-It relationship exists between a subject and an object—it is an instrumental

---

[4] C. S. Collins, *The Word Made Love: The Dialogical Theology of Joseph Ratzinger/Benedict XVI* (Collegeville: Liturgical Press, 2013), p. 13.
[5] *Ibid.*
[6] Cf. *ibid.*, p. 20. One could easily add to this list Ratzinger's theology of the liturgy, his Trinitarian theology and his reflections on certain aspects of moral theology.
[7] Cf. *ibid.*, pp. 17–20.
[8] Cf. E de Gaál, O. Lord, *I Seek Your Countenance: Explorations and Discoveries in Pope Benedict XVI's Theology* (Steubenville: Emmaus Academic, 2018), p. 88.
[9] He makes reference to T. Steinbuchel, "Die personalistische Grundhaltung des christlichen ethos," *Theologie und Glaube* 31 (1939), pp. 392–407.

and depersonalized relationship. Historically speaking, this may be the first way in which humans encounter realities that are other to themselves, but it does not exhaust their capacity for a truly human encounter. The I–Thou relationship, on the other hand, allows us to fully and authentically experience not only those whom we encounter, but also ourselves.[10] In de Gaál's judgment, Buber's philosophy "liberated the individual person from the cage of pathological individualism and constant monologues" and "informed Ratzinger, and numerous other readers, that human existence is intrinsically one of dialogue."[11]

Tracey Rowland traces Buber's influence on Ratzinger to Buber's critique of the anthropology of Martin Heidegger. In her estimation, Buber traced the contemporary cosmological and anthropological crises to authors like Baruch Spinoza, Immanuel Kant, Karl Marx, Georg Hegel, Ludwig Feuerbach, Friedrich Nietzsche, Arthur Schopenhauer, Soren Kierkegaard, Martin Heidegger, and Max Scheler. Buber concluded that, after Nietzsche, the human person is bound to seek communication only with him/herself.[12] This is why "Heidegger's existence is monological" and, in his world, "there is no true *Thou* spoken from being to being."[13] In contrast to this, Ratzinger's own approach has always been rooted in the personalistic vein represented by such authors like Peter Wust and Buber himself.[14]

The I–Thou Encounter and "Institutionalized Religion"

Rowland detects another area in which Buber's thought resonated with Ratzinger, namely the understanding of religion as more personalistic and dialogical than ritualistic and dogmatic.[15] Buber is well known for his aversion to "institutionalized religions" that, according to him, are not a help, but a hindrance to the human person's encounter with the living God.[16] "Religion is the great enemy of mankind," Buber used to say, and as Maurice Friedman explains:

> By "religion" Buber meant the tendency of every organized religion throughout history to promote and sanction a dualism that obscures the

---

[10] Cf. E. de Gaál, *The Theology of Pope Benedict XVI: The Christocentric Shift* (New York: Palgrave McMillan, 2010), p. 27.
[11] *Ibid.*, p. 27.
[12] Cf. T. Rowland, *Benedict XVI: A Guide for the Perplexed* (London, New York: T&T Clark, 2010), p. 95.
[13] *Ibid.*, p. 96, with reference to Buber's, *Between Man and Man* (London: Fontana, 1971), p. 203.
[14] Cf. *ibid.*, pp. 13–14, also p. 155.
[15] Cf. *ibid.*, p. 15.
[16] For more on this, see M. Friedman, *Martin Buber,* pp. xiii-xvi, 131–7.

face of God and leaves our ordinary lives unhallowed and unhallowable. Buber never attacked organized religion as such, but neither did he support it. It had to submit to the criterion of its place within the dialectic of the movement toward meeting with the eternal Thou and the movement away from it.[17]

As Markus Rutsche explains, Buber believed that, in the event of revelation, the human person receives something genuinely new, i.e., confirmation of the eternal presence of God that demands reciprocity and a relationship. However, from this relationship process, human nature demands the development of "a rhythm of temporal continuity, and a structure of steady cultic representation."[18] In other words, man's natural inclination stirs him toward structured religion. However, following this inclination relegates God again to becoming "a pure object of faith and cult … [where] the pure relationship of man to his eternal Thou is alienated again and again by objectification of God into the It-world."[19]

Some theologians, especially those working in the Reformed tradition, have accepted Buber's distinction between faith and "organized religion" and appropriated it, to a greater or lesser extent, in their own theologies. Karl Barth, for his part, criticized religion understood as a human attempt to grasp the ineffable mystery that can only be received through Revelation, and Dietrich Bonhoeffer openly talked of "religionless Christianity."[20]

In his own theology, Ratzinger obviously does not reject "organized religion" as such, even if he concurs with Buber's warning that mere membership in a religious organization, in and of itself, does not guarantee that one will live in authentic encounter with the divine Thou. Ratzinger is well known for his constant emphasis on the importance of a personal relationship with God in Christ, which cannot be replaced by any formal or institutionalized system. The often-quoted opening of his first encyclical as Benedict XVI is a good summary of this insight: "Being Christian is not the result of an ethical choice or a lofty idea, but the encounter with an event, a person, which gives life a new horizon and a decisive direction."[21]

---

[17] *Ibid.*, p. xiv.
[18] M. Rutsche, *Die Relationalität Gottes bei Martin Buber und Joseph Ratzinger* (Norderstedt: GRIN, 2007), p. 9.
[19] *Ibid.*, p. 9. For a detailed analysis of Buber's understanding of "religion," see I. Kajon, "*Religio* Today: The Concept of Religion in Martin Buber's Thought," in P. Mendes-Flohr (ed.), *Dialogue as a Trans-Disciplinary Concept: Martin Buber's Philosophy of Dialogue and Its Contemporary Reception* (Berlin, Boston: De Gruyter, 2015), pp. 101–11.
[20] Ratzinger talks about this in his *Truth and Tolerance: Christian Belief and World Religions* (San Francisco: Ignatius, 2003), pp. 49–54. There is a considerable amount of literature on Barth's understanding of religion and on the true meaning of his related teachings in Chapter 17 of his *Church Dogmatics*, but there is no need to get into this discussion here. The same applies to the extensive literature on Bonhoeffer's thoughts on this matter.
[21] Benedict XVI, *Encyclical letter* Deus caritas est, December 25, 2005.

Having said that, Ratzinger also stresses that personal faith and organized religion are not by definition mutually exclusive. He believes that an authentic I-Thou encounter with God does not take place in a vacuum, but it happens, at least in the Christian context, in a milieu that is both ecclesiological and sacramental. He agrees with Buber's concern about the danger of over-institutionalization of religion, but he also does not seem to think that a genuine encounter is possible in complete isolation from religion. For him, "the concept of Christianity without religion is contradictory and illusory. Faith has to express itself as a religion and through religion, though of course it cannot be reduced to religion."[22]

I–Thou Encounter and Impersonal Mysticism

Aidan Nichols, OP, draws attention to another prominent feature in Ratzinger's theology that can also be linked to Buber's I-Thou personalistic framework. This feature is the distinction that Ratzinger detects between the Western, Christian understanding of religious encounter with God, and the Eastern, Asiatic concepts of mysticism and salvation.[23]

Without denying the existence of some obvious similarities between the Judeo-Christian tradition and Eastern, Asiatic systems (such as their appreciation of the importance of spirituality, their eschatological horizon, their emphasis on the need for purification, etc.), Ratzinger has always been cautious about drawing close parallels between them. The main difference that he detects is their respective understandings of what salvation and unity with the divinity really are. While the expression "mysticism" is sometimes used to describe the religious experience of people immersed in spirituality in both the East and West, the Eastern-Asiatic tradition perceives the purpose of this mysticism differently. The East longs for the "totality of being," understood as a form of dissolution of the individual person into the overarching unity of the all-embracing divinity. On the other hand, the Christian tradition, following its Jewish origins, has always emphasized that unity with transcendence does not eliminate individuality, but rather brings it to another level through unity with the God who is, and remains, the Wholly Other.[24]

In *Truth and Tolerance*, Ratzinger refers to Josef Sudbrack's appropriation of Buber's rejection of his own early works in which he did not sufficiently account for the importance of a personal encounter between the I and the

---

[22] J. Ratzinger, *Truth and Tolerance*, p. 50.
[23] Cf. A. Nichols, *The Thought of Pope Benedict XVI. New Edition: An Introduction to the Theology of Joseph Ratzinger* (London, New York: Burns & Oats, 2007), pp. 208–9.
[24] *Ibid.*

Thou.²⁵ In his earlier writings, Buber's understanding of mysticism was quite de-personalized and vague, but, later on, upon development of the I–Thou framework, Buber became so repulsed by his early ideas that he refused to allow any reprint of the book in which he promoted his previous views.²⁶ The concept of an individual person—a person who is indeed relational with others, but also who never ceases to exist in his/her own individuality—became central to Buber's philosophy, and it remains central in Ratzinger's own thought. Referencing the works of Horst Bürkle,²⁷ as well as that of Emmanuel Levinas, Ratzinger insists that Christian mysticism and Eastern, Asiatic mysticisms are indeed different, and their main point of departure is found precisely in the I–Thou dynamics of the encounter. For Ratzinger, "unity of love is higher than formless identity."²⁸

Having said all that, Ratzinger does not reject the Eastern view as completely erroneous and without merit. In fact, it is precisely in dialogue with the Eastern view, and obviously with his own Catholic tradition, that Ratzinger offers a critique of Buber's I–Thou framework, pointing to areas that he thinks could be improved upon.

The Shortcomings of Buber's I–Thou Framework

While Ratzinger appreciates and welcomes Buber's I–Thou scheme as an important reminder of the significance of the communal nature of human persons, he does not think that it is completely without problems. It is in this context where, in his opinion, it is possible to "purify and accept the inheritance of Asia" in its refusal to "see individual identity as an encapsulated 'I' over against a similarly encapsulated 'Thou' of God." He is worried that an exclusive focus on the 'I' and 'Thou' can lead to "ignoring the existence of other 'I's which are themselves related individually and separately to this divine Thou."²⁹ He continues:

Here we see the limitation of the kind of personalism which was developed between the Wars by Ebner, Buber, Rosenzweig, E. Brunner,

---

²⁵ Cf. J. Ratzinger, *Truth and Tolerance*, pp. 46–7. He refers to J. Sudbrack, *Trunken vom helllichten Dunkel des Absoluten: Donysius der Areopagite und die Poesie der Gottesfahrung* (Ensiedeln: Johannes, 2001). See also M. Friedman, *Martin Buber*, pp. 29–30.
²⁶ The book in question is *Ekstatische Konfessionen*, originally published in 1909, now available as: M. Buber, *Werksusgabe. 2.2. Ekstatische Konfessionen. Heraugegeben, eingeleitet und kommentiert von David Groiser* (München: Gütterslohe, 2012).
²⁷ Cf. H. Bürkle, *Der Mensch and der Suche nach Gott—Die Frage der Religionem* (Paderborn: Bonifatius, 1996).
²⁸ J. Ratzinger, *Truth and Tolerance*, p. 47.
²⁹ *Id.*, *The Feast of Faith: Approaches to a Theology of the Liturgy* (San Francisco: Ignatius, 1986), p. 28.

Steinbüchel and others. Here God is portrayed in a way which conflicts with his nature as the ground of all being. Partnership between God and man is conceived in I–Thou terms in a way which deprives God of his infinity and excludes each individual "I" from the unity of being.[30]

In Andrew T. J. Kaethler's view, the first problem that Ratzinger detects in the personalism of Buber and others is that their system misconstrues God: God as pure Thou "conflicts with his nature as the ground of all being" and so "God becomes self-enclosed and is set too far away."[31] The second problem is of an ecclesiological nature: one cannot encounter God (in Christ) outside of the community (of the Church). We do not encounter God just as individualized 'I's, but also as "We": "by being myself I am in fellowship."[32] This means, according to Kaethler, that "Ratzinger's personalism is not an I–Thou dichotomy, but an I–Thou–We relationship in which the hyphens unite rather than separate."[33]

To these reflections one could also add the importance of Ratzinger's understanding of the divine "Thou" that is based on the Christian idea of the Triune God. Buber obviously does not share the Christian concept of God the Trinity, but it is precisely this Christian doctrine that makes it much easier to explain how it is that, on the one hand, God is personal and relational in his nature, but on the other, that he is ultimately transcendent toward the world he created. If an "I in itself" does not exist because every "I" involves a relationship to something else (I–It) or someone else (I–Thou),[34] and if a person is fully realized only when they are in relationship with others, then in what way could we say that God has always been personal, even prior to creation?

This is not an easy question to answer if one remains only within the I–Thou framework. Utilizing poetic language, Buber goes as far as to suggest that God somehow needs man "in the fullness of his eternity,"[35] presumably in order to be in relation with him. However, there are some obvious metaphysical difficulties with this view—if God is the supreme, perfect being that possesses existence in fullness, God does not "need" anything or anyone to be who he is. In order to avoid the risk of either de-personalizing God or denying the importance of relationality to being a person, the I–Thou framework may not be entirely sufficient.

---

[30] Ibid., p. 29.
[31] A. T. J. Kaethler, "The (Un)Bounded Peculiarity of Death: The Relational Implication of Temporality in the Theology of Alexander Schmemann and Joseph Ratzinger," *Modern Theology* 32/1 (2016), pp. 84–99, at p. 92.
[32] Ibid., p. 93.
[33] Ibid. See also his "'I Become a Thousand Men and yet Remain Myself': Self-Love in Joseph Ratzinger and Georges Bernanos," *Logos: A Journal of Catholic Thought and Culture* 19/2 (2016), pp. 150–67 (153–5).
[34] Cf. M. Rutsche, *Die Relationalität Gottes bei Martin Buber und Joseph Ratzinger*, pp. 4–5.
[35] M. Buber, *I and Thou* (Edinburgh: T&T Clark, 1937), p. 82.

In Christianity, God is indeed understood to be supreme, perfect, and one, but the Christian tradition also accounts for the existence of plurality within God's inner life. The one and indivisible God exists as three persons: Father, Son, and Holy Spirit. Understanding God as communion makes it easier to comprehend him as a relational being. This is where Ratzinger seemingly takes Buber's insights into the relationality of God further than Buber himself, and where he employs Buber's thought to explain the Christian understanding of God as Trinity.[36] God indeed is fully personal; that is, he exists in relation, but this does not mean that God needs man in the same way as man needs God. This is because God himself is a relation—the relationality of God is to be found in his very essence, the inter-trinitarian dynamics of the divine life.

In his essay *Concerning the Notion of Person in Theology*,[37] Ratzinger develops these insights in greater detail. Referring to St. Augustine, he states that "[r]elation ... is not something superadded to the [divine] person, but it *is* the person itself. In its nature, the person exists only *as* relation."[38] He illustrates this by stating that "the first person [the Father] does not generate in the sense that the act of generating a Son is added to the already complete person, but the person *is* the deed of generating, of giving itself, of streaming itself forth. The person is identical with this act of self-donation."[39] Therefore, in God, the notion of person is not located on the level of substance (the substance is one), but "on the level of dialogical reality, or relativity toward the other."[40] This allows for recognition of the notion of relation alongside the notions of substance and accident.

When Ratzinger transposes his Trinitarian insights into anthropology, it is hard not to hear some Buberian overtones when he says that "relativity toward the other constitutes the human person. The human person is the event or being of relativity. The more the person's relativity aims totally and directly as its final goal, at transcendence, the more the person is itself."[41]

---

[36] Cf. Ratzinger does not make explicit reference to Buber in this regard, but it is not difficult to see some very strong correlations with his thought here.

[37] Cf. J. Ratzinger, "Concerning the Notion of Person in Theology," *Communio* 17 (1990), pp. 439–54, originally published in German in 1973 as "Zum Personenversthädnis in der Theologie," in *Dogma und Verkündigung* (Munich: Erich Wewel, 1973), pp. 205–23; published in English as *Dogma and Preaching: Applying the Christian Doctrine to Daily Life. Unabridged Edition* (San Francisco: Ignatius, 2011).

[38] *Ibid.*, p. 444.

[39] *Ibid.*

[40] *Ibid.* In the original German, Ratzinger used the expression *relativität*, which was translated into English as "relativity." However, today, the word "relativity" would normally be used to describe something that Ratzinger did not have in mind here, and the word "relationality" (*relationalität*) would probably be a better term to convey his intended meaning. However, the original phrasing and its official translation are used in this work (see M. Rutsche's *Die Relationalität Gottes bei Martin Buber und Joseph Ratzinger*, p. 9, n. 52 for further comment on this).

[41] J. Ratzinger, *"Concerning the Notion of Person in Theology,"* p. 452.

On the other hand, a few paragraphs later, Ratzinger supplements the I–Thou framework with the Christian framework of I–Thou–*We*. In relation to both the human person and God, he states:

> In Christianity there is not simply a dialogical principle in the modern sense of a pure "I–thou" relationship, neither on the part of the human person that has its place in the historical "we" that bears it; nor is there such a mere dialogical principle on God's part who is, in turn, no simple "I," but the "we" of Father, Son, and Spirit. On *both* sides there is neither the pure "I," nor the pure "you," but on both sides the "I" is integrated into the greater "we." Precisely this final point, namely, that not even God can be seen as the pure and simple "I" toward which the human person tends, is a fundamental aspect of the theological concept of the person ... The Christian's relation to God is not simply, as Ferdinand Ebner claims somewhat one-sidedly, "I and Thou," but, as the liturgy prays for us every day, "*per Christum in Spiritu Sancto ad Patrem*" (Through Christ in the Holy Spirit to the Father). Christ, the one, is here the "we" into which Love, namely the Holy Spirit, gathers us and which means simultaneously being bound to each other and being directed toward the common "you" of the one Father.[42]

Therefore, according to Ratzinger, Buber's I–Thou framework works best when it is supplemented by the I–Thou–*We* framework, which Christianity contributes to the matter with its concept of God and the human person. Buber is correct in explicating the importance of the relational character of persons, but it is the Christian contribution that makes it easier to understand how exactly we, as relational beings, are made in the image and likeness of God.

Other Commonalities between Ratzinger and Buber

Apart from Ratzinger's self-professed and widely recognized engagement with Buber's I–Thou personalistic framework, there are other areas in which certain commonalities between these two thinkers stand out. One must be careful not to ascribe to these commonalities more than can be demonstrated, since the existence of similarities does not necessarily prove direct influence. It may well be that these similarities are coincidental, and that Ratzinger's inspiration in this regard originated elsewhere, e.g., from the richness of his own Catholic tradition. However, it may be a worthwhile

---

[42] Cf. *ibid.*, p. 453.

exercise to examine at least a few instances in which it is quite possible that Buber's philosophy may have had impact on Ratzinger's thought.

Augustine or Thomas?

Ratzinger's self-declared preference for the theological style of St. Augustine of Hippo over St. Thomas Aquinas is well known.[43] Of note, this preference, and the reasons that he gives for it, is quite in line with the preference expressed by Martin Buber, who, without denying the importance of the Angelic Doctor, nevertheless, like Ratzinger, found him to be too settled, too academic, and not sufficiently existential. Tracey Rowland quotes Buber's evaluation as follows, "Aquinas knows no special problem and no special problematic of human life, such as Augustine experienced and expressed with trembling heart. [With Aquinas] the anthropological question has here come to rest again; in man, housed and unproblematic, no impulse stirs to questioning self-confrontation, or it is soon appeased."[44] One cannot help but hear an echo of Ratzinger's assessment of Aquinas from as late as 1998, when he confessed that, during his seminary education, he had "difficulties in penetrating the thought of Thomas Aquinas, whose crystal-clear logic seemed to be too closed in on itself, too impersonal and ready-made."[45] Like Buber, Ratzinger gravitates toward Augustine in whom, again like Buber, he found a companion in the existential struggle of trying to grapple with life, faith, and the world.[46]

Revelation as Dialogue

The topic of divine revelation has always played an important role in Ratzinger's theology. He wrote his *Habilitationschrift* on this matter, and he played a role in drafting *Dei verbum*, the Dogmatic Constitution on Divine revelation from the Second Vatican Council.[47] His critiques of the first draft of the Constitution, *De Fontibus Revelationis*, expressed by Cardinal Josef Frings on the floor of the Council, played an important role not only in drafting the new text, but also in the way the Council progressed in general.

Ratzinger's understanding of revelation is dynamic, personalistic, and relational. A full description thereof goes beyond the constraints of this chapter but suffice it to refer to his 1969 commentary on *Dei verbum* in

---

[43] Cf. J. Ratzinger, *Milestones*, p. 44.
[44] T. Rowland, *Benedict XVI*, p. 14, quoting M. Buber, *Between Man and Man*, p. 101.
[45] J. Ratzinger, *Milestones*, p. 44.
[46] It is of course another matter how accurate, or realistic, Buber and Ratzinger's expectations and descriptions of Aquinas really are.
[47] For a detailed analysis of this, see J. L. Cong Quy, "Joseph Ratzinger's Contribution to the Preparatory Debate of the Dogmatic Constitution *Dei verbum*," *Gregorianum* 94/1 (2013), pp. 35–54.

which he makes explicit reference to Buber's influence during the lead up to the final version of the text as we know it now. Ratzinger stated that Catholic theology greatly benefits from encountering the theology of Karl Barth, which, in turn, was influenced by the personalistic thinking of Ebner and Buber.[48] According to Ratzinger, this influence is evident in

> the personal and theocentric starting-point when compared with Vatican I: it is God himself, the person of God, from whom revelation proceeds and to whom it returns, and this revelation necessarily reaches—also with the person who receives it—into the personal center of man, it touches him in the depth of his being, not only in his individual faculties, in his will and understanding.[49]

This emphasis on the dialogical and existential character of revelation, and on the need to receive it with the whole of one's being, rather than just with one's intellect, pairs well with Buber who believed that "revelation is neither experience nor knowledge. It is 'a presence as power' which transforms him into a different being from what he was when he entered the meeting."[50] In some ways, this understanding strongly resembles that of Bonaventure, and so Ratzinger's perception was certainly not influenced by Buber alone. However, Ratzinger also makes it clear that he found in Buber a contemporary ally who confirmed what he had already absorbed from the Christian tradition.[51]

Theology and Politics

Ratzinger is a well-known critic of certain forms of "political theology" that strongly emphasize the need to change societal structures and bring about the betterment of humankind. He is not critical of these projects because he disagrees with their intentions, but rather because he thinks that such theologies are often utopian due to their failure to sufficiently take into account the reality of sin and the fact that people embedded in those societal structures are still in need of personal conversion. In addition, he sometimes detects traces of Pelagianism in them due to their apparent emphasis on the need to bring about the Kingdom of God on earth through human effort,

---

[48] Cf. J. Ratzinger, "Dogmatic Constitution on Divine Revelation: Origin and Background," in H. Vorgrimler (ed.), *Commentary on the Documents of Vatican II* 3 (New York, London: Burns & Oats, Herder and Herder, 1969), pp. 155–272, at 170.
[49] *Ibid.*, p. 171.
[50] M. Friedman, *Martin Buber*, p. 86.
[51] Cf. For more on Buber's understanding of revelation, see M. Friedman, *Martin Buber*, pp. 86–7, pp. 289–332.

failing to devote sufficient attention to the divine grace without which we can do nothing.[52]

Buber also strongly emphasized the importance of personal conversion and responsibility as necessary aspects of any successful political or societal change. His lack of preference for either capitalism or communism certainly did not resonate well with Ratzinger. However, his distrust toward political utopia that remedies all evils by reforming structures[53] does find echo in Ratzinger's view of the true reform of the Church and, *mutatis mutandis*, true progress in the world.

Unity of the Bible

One of the instances in which Ratzinger explicitly references the works of Buber concerns Scripture. Ratzinger is a well-known critic of the way the historical-critical method has often been applied to Catholic exegesis in recent decades. He advocates a return to the understanding of the Bible as one book, and also as the Word of God. Without discarding the achievements of modern biblical scholarship, he thinks that, by focusing so much on the exegesis of individual books and passages, we frequently lose sight of Scripture's inherent unity as a whole.[54]

Buber of course does not read the Old Testament in the same way in which Ratzinger does, i.e., as a preparation for the coming of Jesus and the New Covenant. However, Ratzinger notes that, in their monumental translation of the Hebrew Bible, Buber and Rosenzweig managed to respect the inner coherence of the Bible as a whole. In Ratzinger's estimation, they "did not want to translate individual voices; what was ultimately decisive for them was the concrete entirety of the biblical text ... In its entirety, it expresses a purpose that goes beyond of what we may suppose were the intentions of the individual sources."[55]

Teaching Style

Ratzinger's similarity to Buber can be found not only in particular insights that have made their way into his thought, but also, to a certain extent, in

---

[52] Theologians associated with the movement of Liberation Theology have normally been subject to Ratzinger's criticisms of this kind. To what extent these criticisms are legitimate is of course a separate topic, and a considerable amount of literature exists on it.
[53] Cf. M. Friedman, *Martin Buber*, pp. 49–54.
[54] Cf. J. Ratzinger, *God's Word: Scripture, Tradition, Office* (San Francisco: Ignatius, 2008), last chapter "Biblical Interpretation in Conflict."
[55] *Ibid.*, pp. 123–4, including footnotes.

his teaching style. Apart from some dense academic writings, Buber was very well known for his Hasidic stories in which he was able to explain deep and difficult concepts using simple tales. Ratzinger himself is known for a certain ease of expression—during his papacy, pilgrims to Rome would sometimes say that, in the past, one would travel to the Eternal City to *see*, or experience, Pope John Paul II, but now one travels there to *listen* to Pope Benedict XVI. Recalling his experience as a catechist when he was a young priest, Ratzinger said that translating difficult and abstract concepts into language that school children could understand was a challenge, but one that he thoroughly enjoyed.[56]

Ratzinger is particularly fond of Buber's story of the encounter between an old Jewish rabbi and a young, unbelieving follower of Enlightenment thought who came to prove the old rabbi wrong with regard to faith and God. The rabbi had anticipated this, and before the young man said anything, the rabbi simply said to him—"But perhaps it *is* all true?" The young man was unable to collect himself to present his arguments against the rabbi's faith and, from that moment, he was forever haunted by the rabbi's "perhaps." Ratzinger never discusses in detail traditional, apologetic "proofs for the existence of God." On the contrary, he once stated that the best argument for the truth of Christianity is the beauty that it has brought about, and the lives of the saints.[57] Like Buber, he does not seem to be interested in trying to demonstrate God's existence in a rational way that would leave no room for doubt. Rather, he thinks that both faith and unbelief have to grapple with the problem of doubt, and that doubt cannot be removed from the lives of believers and unbelievers alike.[58]

Ratzinger makes other references to some of Buber's stories. In the context of service to the poor, he referred to Buber's tale about a rabbi who was asked to pass judgment on the idea that beggars should be banned from begging at the threshold of the house of prayer, and that a box for the poor should instead be set up there. The rabbi compared this idea to Sodom and Gomorrah where there may also have been such a custom that spared inhabitants of the city from looking their poor brethren in the eye.[59]

In the context of the intelligibility of the liturgy and the need to participate in it not only with intellect, but also with heart, Ratzinger refers to Buber's tale about Jewish merchants who, due to an insufficient number of phylacteries, had to rush through their morning prayers so quickly that it was impossible to understand the words that they were uttering. In

---

[56] Cf. *id.*, *Salt of the Earth: Christianity and the Catholic Church at the End of the Millennium. An Interview with Peter Seewald* (San Francisco: Ignatius, 1997), pp. 63–4.

[57] Cf. *id.*, "The Feeling of Things, the Contemplation of Beauty," *Message to the Communion and Liberation Meeting at Rimini*, August 24–30, 2002.

[58] Cf. *id.*, *Introduction to Christianity* (San Francisco: Ignatius, 2004), pp. 45–7.

[59] Cf. *id.*, *Dogma and Preaching*, p. 221, referring to M. Buber, *Werke* 3 (Munich, Heidelberg: Kösel, 1963), pp. 345–6.

response to a disconcerted rabbi who was not impressed by this rushed, garbled prayer, one of the merchants explained how a mother understands her child's babbling even if it is not comprehensible to anyone else. Use of this story is not meant to discourage the promotion of intelligibility in the liturgy, but rather to caution against approaching it in an overly rationalistic way that leaves no room for intimate communication with God, even if not all phrases or gestures used in worship are immediately understood by all the participants.[60]

Ratzinger also makes references to various expressions that Buber used. One of them is the "darkness of God," a phenomenon of inability, or unwillingness, to perceive God or to relate to him.[61] Another is Buber's insight that no other expression has been so misused in the history of mankind as the word "God."[62] The 2013 encyclical *Lumen fidei* contains a reference to Buber's definition of idolatry, namely "when a face addresses a face which is not a face."[63] While *Lumen fidei* was signed and published by Pope Francis, it is a well-known fact that it was primarily written by Benedict XVI before his resignation from the papacy, so it is reasonable to ascribe this reference to Benedict.[64]

Conclusion

As has been shown, it is possible to find many similarities between the thoughts of Martin Buber and Joseph Ratzinger. However, as said, not every similarity is necessarily a result of Buber's direct influence, so one must be careful not to ascribe to Buber more influence than he may have in fact exercised on Ratzinger.

Apart from instances of influence or engagement with Buber's individual ideas or insights, it is important to highlight the way in which Ratzinger engages in dialogue with Buber in general. While he accepts some of Buber's fundamental concepts, he does not do so in an unreflective or uncritical way. Rather, he carefully qualifies Buber's insights and develops them further, always in light of the Gospel and Christian tradition. The clearest example is of course Buber's personalism and the notion of encounter, both between God and man, and between human persons themselves. While Ratzinger welcomes and accepts Buber's main premises as refreshing and inviting

---

[60] Cf. *id.*, *God Is Near Us: The Eucharist, the Heart of Life* (San Francisco: Ignatius, 2003), pp. 72–3, referring to Buber's *Werke 3*, p. 334.
[61] Cf. *id.*, *God and the World: Believing and Living in Our Time. A Conversation with Peter Seewald* (San Francisco: Ignatius, 2002), p. 109.
[62] Cf. *ibid.*, pp. 169–70.
[63] Francis, *Encyclical Letter* Lumen fidei, June 28, 2013, §13, with reference to M. Buber, *Die Erzählungen der Chassidim* (Zürich: Manesse, 1949), p. 793.
[64] Cf. Francis, *Lumen fidei*, §7.

for contemporary human persons immersed in the spirit of individualism, he appropriates and enhances them with the Christian priority of grace, and with the Christological (and Christocentric) dimension of the God-man encounter. He also supplements Buber's personalistic framework with ecclesiological and sacramental insights: in Ratzinger, Buber's I–Thou becomes I–Thou–We, and the encounter between God and man finds its ultimate expression in the liturgy where the relational human person responds to the ever-relational God of the Trinity.

Therefore, in Ratzinger's theology, the philosophical, and even theological, insights from Buber do not really aid or supplement Christian revelation as such. Rather, they help to bring out what is already there, even if with time it may have been forgotten or overlooked. This is quite representative of the way that Ratzinger thinks Christian theology in general should engage with insights that originate from outside of Christianity—with appreciation and gratitude, but also with careful discernment and, if needed, with necessary qualifications. In other words, in a spirit of dialogue and encounter, an approach of which Martin Buber would surely have approved.

11

Hans Kelsen, Richard Rorty, and John Rawls: Philosophical Relativism and Religious Traditions of Wisdom

Rudy Albino de Assunção

Introduction

J. Ratzinger/Benedict XVI, attentive to social transformations and their impact on the life of the Church, has been accustomed to move through various spheres of knowledge and among them we clearly find *political philosophy*[1] and the *philosophy of law*.[2] For this reason, in this multifocal work, the task that fell to me was to expose the theoretical dialogue that Ratzinger established with three important authors from these fields: the Austrian jurist and philosopher Hans Kelsen (1881–1973) and the

---

[1] Cf. E. Eslava, *La filosofía de Ratzinger. Ciencia, poder, libertad, religión* (Chía: Universidad de La Sabana, 2014), pp. 21–47; T. Rourke, *The Social and Political Thought of Benedict XVI* (Plymouth: Lexington, 2010); G. Groppo, *Chiesa e politica nel pensiero di Joseph Ratzinger / Benedetto XVI* (Siena: Cantagalli, 2018); J. Schall, "The Political Philosophy of Joseph Ratzinger," *The Imaginative Conservative*, January 9, 2023.

[2] Cf. M. del Pozzo, "L'intelligenza del diritto di Benedetto XVI," *Ius Ecclesiae* 24/1 (2012), pp. 169–81, 2011; Id., *Magistero di Benedetto XVI ai giuristi* (Città del Vaticano: LEV, 2013); M. Cartabia and A. Simoncini (eds.), *Pope Benedict XVI's Legal Thought: A Dialogue on Foundation of Law* (New York: Cambridge University Press, 2015).

American philosophers John Rawls (1921–2002) and Richard Rorty (1931–2007). All of them read by Ratzinger/Benedict XVI from the same angle: the relationship between truth and politics, or better, between ethics, religion, law and politics. For this reason, the German theologian illustrates his discussion with them by using the question posed by a more distant but decisive character in the history of Christianity: the Roman governor Pontius Pilate.

Pilate's Question: "What Is Truth?" (John 8:38)—Democracy and Relativism

Before Pilate Jesus presented himself as king of a kingdom not of this world and as one who came into the world "to bear witness to the truth" (John 18:37). Beside this "negative" aspect of the concept (a kingdom without military power), Christ puts "a positive idea, in order to explain the nature and particular character of the power of this kingship: namely, truth."[3] For Pilate, the essence of a reign is power, authority (*exousía*); for Jesus, truth. In light of this, the "pragmatic Pilate asks him: 'What is truth'? (18:38)."[4] From this comes the question posed by Ratzinger himself that serves as the background for our investigation:

> Is truth a political category? [...] It is the question that is also asked by modern political theory: Can politics accept truth as a structural category? Or must truth, as something unattainable, be relegated to the subjective sphere, its place taken by an attempt to build peace and justice using whatever instruments are available to power? By relying on truth, does not politics, in view of the impossibility of attaining consensus on truth, make itself a tool of particular traditions that in reality are merely forms of holding on to power? And yet, on the other hand, what happens when truth counts for nothing? What kind of justice is then possible? Must there not be common criteria that guarantee real justice for all — criteria that are independent of the arbitrariness of changing opinions and powerful lobbies? Is it not true that the great dictatorships were fed by the power of the ideological lie and that only truth was capable of bringing freedom? What is truth? The pragmatist's question, tossed off with a degree of scepticism, is a very serious question, bound up with the fate of mankind.[5]

---

[3] J. Ratzinger, *Faith and Politics*. Selected Writings with a foreword by Pope Francis (San Francisco: Ignatius, 2018), p. 52.
[4] *Ibid.*
[5] *Ibid.*

In 1996, Cardinal Ratzinger spoke to the Latin American bishops' conferences (Guadalajara, Mexico) in view of the effects of the events of 1989 on faith and theology. Among other factors (such as liberation theology and the fall of communism), Ratzinger showed that at the time the main problem for faith was *relativism*: besides the incommensurability of truth, according to him, such concept is associated with tolerance and dialogue, because a single and universally valid truth would limit our freedom.[6] Relativism emerges as "the philosophical basis of democracy;"[7] no one can claim to have the right way, because democracy lives from the fragments of the common effort to find the best way and from competing knowledge that cannot be reduced to a common formula. "A free society is said to be a relativistic society; only on this condition can it remain free and open-ended."[8] But the cardinal weighs his position, without aprioristically and completely excluding political relativism: "In the realm of politics this view is to a great extent true. The one single correct political option does not exist. What is relative, the construction of a freely ordered common life for men, cannot be absolute—thinking that it could be was precisely the error of Marxism and of the political theologies."[9] In other words, the German cardinal's rejection of this phenomenon is not peremptory, as it might seem at first glance: "In the realm of politics and society, therefore, one cannot deny relativism a certain right. The problem is based on the fact that it sees itself as being unlimited."[10] So the problem for him is the absolutization of relativism or, in other terms, that it becomes a "new dogmatism,"[11] as he will say on another occasion.

Ratzinger establishes a critical and balanced confrontation both with theological relativism (with the Pluralist Theology of Religions, which he identifies mainly in the works of John Hick and Paul Knitter[12]) and with philosophical relativism. In general terms, our author will discuss the "necessary" relationship established between democracy and relativism: after all, modern liberal democracies are marked by the affirmation of the individual, free and autonomous, and that the pluralism of such societies comes from individual liberties and, therefore, there must be a separation between the public and private spheres.[13] Religion would remain in the latter. Pluralism is constitutive of liberal democracy.

---

[6] Cf. *id., Truth and Tolerance: Christian Belief and World Religions* (San Francisco: Ignatius Press, 2004), p. 117.
[7] *Ibid.*
[8] *Ibid.*
[9] *Ibid.*
[10] *Ibid.*, p. 118.
[11] J. Ratzinger and M. Pera, *Without Roots: The West, Relativism, Christianity, Islam* (New York: Basic Books, 2007), p. 127.
[12] Cf. J. Ratzinger, *Truth and Tolerance*, pp. 52 and 113–37.
[13] Cf. J. L. Martínez, "Religión en la democracia liberal: debate entre Rawls, Habermas y Ratzinger," *Estudios Eclesiásticos*, 86/337 (2011), p. 291.

Ratzinger then posits that our future lies between two basic orientations:

> relativism and faith. Relativism unites easily with positivism; it is indeed positivism's own philosophical basis. We do not wish to dispute the fact that in many situations a dash of relativism, a bit of skepticism, can be useful; but it certainly does not suffice as a common ground on which we can live. For where relativism is consistently thought through and lived (without clinging secretly to an ultimate trust that comes from faith), either it becomes nihilism or else it expands positivism into the power that dominates everything, thus ending once again in totalitarian conditions.[14]

As can be seen, Ratzinger unites relativism and positivism. This explains why he will treat Kelsen and Rorty as two exponents of the same position about law and morality he draws.

This analysis was echoed on April 18, 2005, when Cardinal Ratzinger, shortly before his election to the papal throne, made famous the expression "dictatorship of relativism:"[15] the Cardinal noted that believing clearly, according to the Church's Creed, is considered fundamentalism, and above all else, "that does not recognize anything as definitive and whose ultimate goal consists solely of one's own ego and desires."[16] In other words, relativism always has the danger of imposing itself in the political arena to the point of excluding those who reaffirm their own religious identity and want to expose it in the public square.

The Crisis of Morals and Law

It is necessary to make a brief nod to the crisis of morality and law exposed by Ratzinger. In modernity, according to him, humanity has lost its common moral patrimony, from which "the man's Being contains an imperative"[17] and "the conviction that he does not himself *invent* morality on the basis of calculations of expediency but rather *finds* it already present in the essence of things."[18]

Diverse worldviews share "the denial of the natural ethical law and the reduction of the world to 'mere' facts."[19] Ratzinger, on the contrary, wants

---

[14] J. Ratzinger, *A Turning Point for Europe? The Church in the Modern World* (San Francisco: Ignatius, 2010), pp. 108–9.
[15] *Id.*, *Homily at the Mass "Pro Eligendo Romano Pontifice,"* April 18, 2005. Toward a Critical Reception of the Papal Homily, cf. B. H. Smith, "Relativism, Today and Yesterday," *Common Knowledge* 13/2-3 (2007), pp. 227–49.
[16] J. Ratzinger, *Homily at the Mass "Pro Eligendo Romano Pontifice."*
[17] *Id.*, *A Turning Point for Europe?*, p. 34.
[18] *Ibid.*
[19] *Ibid.*, p. 40.

to defend that "practical reason too, on which genuinely ethical knowledge is based, is truly reason and not merely the expression of subjective feelings without any value as evidence."[20] Practical reason is reason in the highest sense because it penetrates the specific mystery of reality more than experimental reason.[21] And here the cardinal defends the contribution that the Christian faith can make in this field, an idea on which he will insist frequently: "The ethical vision of the Christian faith is not in fact something specific to Christianity but is the synthesis of the great ethical intuitions of mankind from a new center that holds them all together,"[22] because "in the ethical realm, essentially the moral message that lies in creation itself."[23] Christianity is presented here as a source of morality that goes beyond the specificity of the articles of faith because it is in tune with the law inscribed in hearts (cf. Rom 2:15).

This is why the moral problem leads to the juridical-legal one: "the heart of the modern crisis becomes clear—the loss of a common criterion of justice."[24] Therefore, Ratzinger reviews the essential ways in which modern law was founded and shaped: Hobbes' position, centered on *authoritas*, which becomes "the axiom of legal positivism, which has been able to establish itself widely since the nineteenth century."[25] In essence, law must collect and convert into norms the value judgments present in society. The majority opinion is the source of law.[26] Such a conception is connected to the notion of peace that comes from *utilitas*, which Ratzinger associates with Adam Smith and even with Immanuel Kant's notion of perpetual peace: the (spirit of) selfishness would be the peculiar instrument to maintain peace.[27]

According to Ratzinger the two above positions are characteristic of a post-metaphysical era, "in which the unknowability of the true and man's incapacity for the good seem to have become absolute certainties."[28] But Ratzinger casts a look at John Locke's triptych (life, liberty, property) described in the *Second Treatise on Government* (1690) against the backdrop of *Magna Charta*, the *Bill of Rights*, and the jusnaturalist tradition. Ratzinger points out that in Locke the doctrine of human rights is directed against state power. "But there is a sound core to the idea of human rights, and so it continues to be a guide to the truth and a protective barrier against positivism."[29]

---

[20] *Ibid.*, p. 41.
[21] Cf. *ibid.*
[22] *Ibid.*, p. 43.
[23] *Ibid.*, pp. 43–4.
[24] *Ibid.*, p. 50.
[25] *Ibid.*, p. 56.
[26] Cf. D. V. Twomey, *Pope Benedict XVI: The Conscience of Our Age. A Theological Portrait* (San Francisco: Ignatius, 2007), p. 114.
[27] Cf. J. Ratzinger, *A Turning Point for Europe?*, p. 57.
[28] *Ibid.*, p. 58.
[29] *Ibid.*, p. 59.

Kelsen is, precisely, the expression of the triumph of juridical positivism. Let's move on to Ratzinger's analysis of him.

Hans Kelsen and Richard Rorty: "Radical Relativism"

On March 21, 1992, Ratzinger delivered a conference in Bratislava, the capital of the future Slovakia, at the request of the bishops of the region, about the meaning of moral and religious values in a pluralistic society. The context of the exposition was still that of the fall of Marxist totalitarian systems, marked also by a multiculturalist tendency of a relativist type, which called on Christianity to express its universalist vocation in a different way from the one used until then.[30]

Three Theses on the Relationship between Truth and Politics

The cardinal showed that the conviction of the existence of the good, and consequently of truth, has been replaced by nihilism and relativism. He stressed the primacy that modernity gave to *freedom*:[31] individual autonomy is the main goal of the collectivity and the community loses value.[32] But he sees here a tension between freedom as the life *form* of democracy and right and good as its *content*.[33] With the rise of freedom as the supreme good, truth was shifted to the "zone of antidemocratic intolerance"[34] or as an expression of fundamentalism. This means that "the modern concept of democracy seems indissolubly linked to that of relativism. It is relativism that appears to be the real guarantee of freedom and especially of the very heart of human freedom, namely, freedom of religion and of conscience."[35]

In order to define his position, Ratzinger presents a tripartite vision of the most relevant intellectual positions for him in this field and, for this, he relies on a systematization carried out by the Italian philosopher Vittorio Possenti.[36] He establishes a division into two opposing positions and an intermediate one.

---

[30] Cf. G. Coccolini, *Alla ricerca di un ethos politico. La relazione tra teologia e politica in Joseph Ratzinger* (Trapani: Il Pozzo di Giacobbe, 2011), pp. 169–75.
[31] On the history of the concept of freedom since the Enlightenment and on the stance that the Christian must adopt in a pluralistic society, cf. J. Ratzinger, *Church, Ecumenism & Politics: New Endeavors in Ecclesiology* (San Francisco: Ignatius, 2008), pp. 175–92.
[32] Cf. id., *Values in a Time of Upheaval* (San Francisco: Ignatius, 2006), p. 54.
[33] Cf. ibid., pp. 54–5.
[34] *Ibid.*, p. 55.
[35] *Ibid.*
[36] Cf. V. Possenti, *Le società liberali al bivio. Lineamenti di filosofia della società* (Torino: Marietti, 1991).

The first, radical relativism, is represented precisely by Kelsen and Rorty. It is characterized by the effort to eradicate the idea of good from politics in order not to put freedom at risk; its advocates reject "natural law" for suspicion of metaphysics; and majority decision is the only political principle. In this way, democracy is not defined by the contents, but by the formal (procedural) question.

The essence of such a position is explained by Jesus' trial before Pilate, quoted at the very beginning. The question "What is truth?" (John 18:38) is put by Ratzinger here at the center of the discussion. That is why the theological cardinal begins with Kelsen's "*lectio*" on the biblical text and then moves on to his political philosophy. The text to which the Cardinal refers is Kelsen's short speech entitled *Democracy and Philosophy*,[37] in which the Austrian philosopher clearly states:

> The belief in absolute truth and absolute values furnishes the precondition for a metaphysical and, in particular, a religious-mystical worldview. The negation of this precondition, however, is the viewpoint that only relative truths and values are accessible to human cognition and that, consequently, every truth and every value must—just as the human individual who finds them—be prepared to abdicate its position and make room for others.[38]

This is the positivist position: "It thus rejects the assumption of an Absolute which transcends experience. This conflict of worldviews corresponds to a conflict between values and especially between basic political attitudes. The metaphysical-absolutistic worldview is linked to an autocratic, and the critical-relativistic to a democratic disposition."[39] In summary: "The idea of democracy thus presupposes relativism as its worldview."[40]

Further on, Kelsen asserts the importance of the majority for the formulation of law within a democratic society:

> The rule of the majority, which is so characteristic of democracy, distinguishes itself from all other forms of rule in that it not only by its very nature presupposes, but actually recognizes and protects—by way of basic rights and freedoms and the principle of proportionality—an opposition, i.e., the minority. The stronger the minority, however, the more the politics in a democracy become politics of compromise. Similarly, there is nothing more characteristic of the relativistic worldview than the

---

[37] Cf. H. Kelsen, *The Essence and Value of Democracy*, N. Urbinati and C. I. Accetti (eds.) (Lanham, Boulder, New York, Toronto, Plymouth: Rowan & Littlefield, INC, 2013), pp. 101–6.
[38] *Ibid.*, p. 103.
[39] *Ibid.*
[40] *Ibid.*

tendency to seek a balance between two opposing standpoints, neither of which can by itself be adopted fully, without reservation, and in complete negation of the other.[41]

Therefore, for Kelsen, the text in John 18:8 is a "tragic symbol for relativism and democracy."[42] And here the judge of Jesus appears: "And because he does not know what truth is and—as a Roman—is accustomed to think democratically, Pilate appeals to the People and conducts a vote."[43] The philosopher concludes by emphasizing that one's position on the outcome of the trial depends on one's personal conviction of possessing political truth: "Believers—political believers—may object that precisely this example argues against, rather than for, democracy. This objection must be granted, but only under one condition: that these believers are as certain about their political truth, which they will enforce with violence if necessary, as the Son of God was about his."[44]

Ratzinger's position confronts the Austrian jurist's view, precisely by focusing on the majority principle and the impact on the notion of truth:

> Kelsen sees Pilate's question as an expression of the skepticism that a politician must possess. In this sense, the question is already an answer: truth is unattainable. And we see that this is indeed how Pilate thinks from the fact that he does not even wait for an answer from Jesus but turns immediately to address the crowd. He leaves it to the people to decide the disputed question by means of their vote. Kelsen holds that Pilate acts here as a perfect democrat: since he himself does not know what is just, he leaves it to the majority to decide. In this way, the Austrian scholar portrays Pilate as the emblematic figure of a relativistic and skeptical democracy that is based not on values and truth but on correct procedures. Kelsen seems not to be disturbed by the fact that the outcome of Jesus' trial was the condemnation of an innocent and righteous man. After all, there is no other truth than that of the majority, and one cannot "get behind" this truth to ask further questions. At one point, Kelsen even goes so far as to say that this relativistic certainty must be imposed, if need be, at the cost of blood and tears. One must be as certain of it as Jesus was certain of his own truth.[45]

Ratzinger opposes to Kelsen's reading that of the theologian Heinrich Schlier, recalling that Jesus himself indicates that Pilate's sovereignty did not

---

[41] Ibid.
[42] Ibid., p. 104.
[43] Ibid., p. 105.
[44] Ibid.
[45] J. Ratzinger, *Values in a Time of Upheaval*, pp. 57-8.

come from him, but from on high (John 19:11).⁴⁶ Further on, the cardinal stresses that, in Kelsen, the relationship between religion and democracy can only be negative, particularly with Christianity, defender of absolute values, while politics requires skepticism to expose democratic relativism. "Kelsen understands religion as a heteronomy of the person, whereas democracy retains the autonomy of the person. This also means that the core of democracy is freedom, not the good, for that is something that puts freedom at risk."⁴⁷

For Ratzinger, alongside Kelsen

> the American legal philosopher Richard Rorty⁴⁸ is the best known representative of this view of democracy. His version of the connection between democracy and relativism expresses to a large extent the average awareness even of Christians today and therefore deserves close attention. Rorty argues that the only criterion for the formulation of law is the widespread conviction held by the majority of the citizens. Democracy does not have access to any other philosophy or any other source of law. Naturally, Rorty is aware that it is ultimately unsatisfactory to appeal to the majority principle as the only source of truth. We see this from his affirmation that pragmatic reason that is orientated to the majority will always include a number of intuitive ideas, such as the rejection of slavery.⁴⁹

Ratzinger shows that the historical experience of slavery belies Rorty's conviction. Where was the intuition that represented the rejection of freedom? Ratzinger reminds us that the majority that sees its will thwarted sees this as a denial of freedom and the essence of the democratic regime, as falling into dogmatism. But our theologian recalls the majority's capacity for error, referring to history near the twentieth century (alluding indirectly to the Nazi regime).

---

⁴⁶ Cf. *ibid.*, p. 58.
⁴⁷ *Ibid.*, p. 61.
⁴⁸ Jeffrey W. Robbins defines Rorty's approach as a "non-foundationalist thinking about democracy"; "Foreword. Richard Rorty: A philosophical guide for talking about religion," in R. Rorty, *An Ethics for Today: Finding Common Ground between Philosophy and Religion* (New York: Columbia University Press, 2011), p. xii. He argues that Rorty never intended his philosophy to be an "arbiter of truth" (p. viii). And more: "What should be discerned here is that Rorty's philosophical approach to the question of truth is part and parcel with his ethics. Just as he rejected all correspondence theories of truth, he also made clear his belief that there are no universally valid answers to moral questions. Rorty's approach here can be described as an ethics of decency and a politics of solidarity" (p. viii). Cf. also J. Stout, "Rorty on Religion and Politics" in R. E. Auxier and L. E. Hahn (eds.), *The Philosophy of Richard Rorty* (Chicago: Open Court, 2010), pp. 523–45.
⁴⁹ J. Ratzinger, *Values in a Time of Upheaval*, pp. 60–1.

We have also seen in our reflections on Kelsen that relativism contains a dogmatism of its own: this position is so sure of itself that it must be imposed even on those who disagree with it. In the last analysis, there is no way of avoiding here the cynicism which is so obvious in Kelsen and Rorty. If the majority, as in the case of Pilate, is always right, then what truly is right must be trampled upon. For then the only thing that counts is the power of the one who is stronger and knows how to win the majority over to his own views.[50]

The second thesis or position is the *metaphysical and Christian* one with roots in Plato, but clearly defended by Jacques Maritain[51], the one that holds that truth is not a product of politics, i.e., that precedence is of truth over praxis.[52]

Ratzinger will still cite intermediate positions that we can only allude to, those defended by N. Bobbio, K. Popper, and J. Schumpeter, but much earlier by Pierre Bayle (1647–1706), who separated metaphysical truth from moral truth, because for him practical truth is sufficient. For him Popper tries to save Bayle's relativistic position in a kind of moralistic faith that believes that the approach to truth comes in the process of scientific advancement, a rational kind of faith, for Popper knows that the majority principle has no absolute value.

But, after all, where does Ratzinger stand? A balance:

We must reject the absolute state that posits itself as the source of truth and law. We must also reject a strict relativism and functionalism, because the elevation of truth to the unique source of law threatens the moral dignity of man and tends toward totalitarianism. This means that the spectrum of acceptable theories would go from Maritain to Popper. Maritain has the greatest confidence in the rational evidential quality of the moral truth of Christianity and of the Christian image of man. Popper exemplifies the least measure of confidence, but this minimum is just enough to ward off a collapse into positivism.[53]

---

[50] *Ibid.*, p. 62.

[51] Cf. D. Madureira, *Maritain e Bento XVI. Sobre a modernidade e o relativismo* (Lisboa: Cáritas, 2014).

[52] Cf. J. Ratzinger, *Values in a Time of Upheaval*, pp. 56–7.

[53] *Ibid.*, p. 67. In Massimo Luciani's reading, ethical absolutism must be postulated, not rejected: "In essence, the Kelsenian objection to the union of ethical absolutism and democracy is not only repelled, but completely overturned: not only can democracy coexist with ethical absolutism, but it must propose it as the necessary prerequisite for itself to be a real possibility," "Concerning the Doctrine of Democracy in Benedict XVI," in M. Cartabia and A. Simoncini (eds.), *Pope Benedict XVI's Legal Thought*, p. 193. Luciani identifies some commonalities between Benedict XVI and Kelsen: the parliamentary, dialogical-discursive method, whose success can be a compromise decision; Kelsen believed that parliamentary procedure is the way to reach a middle way between opposing interests (p. 197). Moreover, in Benedict XVI the majority principle is not rejected *in toto*: "In essence, the majority principle gives way when two issues are in play: freedom of conscience and the right of active resistance" (p. 200).

The Utopia of Banality

Ratzinger returned to Rorty's thought on other occasions. On November 6, 1992, Ratzinger was received at the French Academy of Moral and Political Sciences, succeeding the Russian nuclear physicist Andreï D. Sakharov. On that occasion, he appropriated the reading of the German philosopher Robert Spaemann, who stated that after the "collapse of utopia, a banal nihilism is beginning to spread today, and that its results may be no less insidious,"[54] exemplified by "Richard Rorty, who has formulated the new utopia of banality. Rorty's ideal is a liberal society in which absolute values and criteria will no longer exist; a sense of well-being will be the only goal worth striving for."[55] It is on the concept of freedom that Ratzinger will focus, whose dignity lies in its relation to its foundation and its ethical task. A freedom that consists only in the satisfaction of one's own needs remains in the "animal realm" because "the individual's freedom can exist only in an order of freedoms."[56] It requires a "communal substance"[57] and needs to be completed "by two other concepts, those of law and of the good."[58] For, in the Ratzingerian reading, freedom, without a moral sense, without high goals, reduced to the possibility of doing everything, is empty. Morality is a public and collective responsibility and cannot be subject to the majority principle.

> For it is hard to see how democracy, which is based on the majority principle, can accord validity to moral values that are not sustained by the conviction of the majority unless it imports a dogmatism that is alien to its own nature. Rorty suggests here that a reason orientated to the majority will always include a number of intuitive ideas such as the rejection of slavery.[59]

And here he again quotes Pierre Bayle (seventeenth century), who believed that practical truth is sufficient while believing that there is a single moral, universal and necessary, accessible to all. But given that the unity of the faith had been broken, metaphysical truth was not a common good to be preserved. Ratzinger continued:

> The developments of the twentieth century have taught us that this evidential character—as the subsistent and reliable basis of all freedom—no longer exists. It is perfectly possible for reason to lose sight of essential

---

[54] J. Ratzinger, *Values in a Time of Upheaval*, p. 47.
[55] *Ibid.*
[56] *Ibid.*, p. 48.
[57] *Ibid.*
[58] *Ibid.*
[59] *Ibid.*, p. 49.

values. Nor is intuition, on which Rorty bases his system, absolutely reliable. For example, he adduces the insight that slavery is unacceptable; but for centuries, such an insight did not exist at all, and the history of the totalitarian states in the twentieth century demonstrates with sufficient clarity how easy it is to abandon this insight. Freedom can abolish itself. Freedom can weary of itself when it has become empty. The twentieth century has also offered examples of a majority decision that served to abrogate freedom.[60]

The formative experience of the United States is recurrently cited by Ratzinger as an example of building a society without denying the ethical-religious (Christian) values that were at its origin. That is why he refers to Alexis Tocqueville, *Democracy in America*, who was convinced that Protestant Christianity served as "a basic moral conviction"[61] for the consolidation of the American model of democracy. Therefore, he warns: "A culture and a nation that cuts itself off from the great ethical and religious forces of its own history commits suicide."[62]

On September 8, 2001, in Cernobbio (Italy), Cardinal Ratzinger gave a conference on the identity of Europe, in which he insisted that the founding fathers of European unification after the Second World War considered the Christian heritage and the great moral ideals of the Enlightenment compatible: the creator and revelator God was replaced by the god who gave the impulse of the universe, or even Baruch Spinoza's *Deus sive natura*, which still represented some faith in the human capacity to understand nature. But Marxism brought the radical break from such a background conception, for it says that the world is not the product of reason.[63] Allied to the view of Hegelian philosophy, the liberal dogma of progress, and its socioeconomic interpretation, the end product of the class struggle is the

---

[60] *Ibid.*, p. 50.
[61] *Ibid.*, p. 51. Ratzinger again refers to Tocqueville, reinforcing the Christian background in which American democracy was formed; cf. J. Ratzinger and M. Pera, *Without Roots: The West, Relativism, Christianity, Islam* (New York: Basic Books, 2007), pp. 108–9.
[62] J. Ratzinger, *Values in a Time of Upheaval*, p. 52. In his address to the UN on April 18, 2008, Benedict XVI recalled that the UN itself is born from the conviction that there are common values and that they are accessible to reason, inviolable and a condition for freedom, pointing out that the *Universal Declaration of Human Rights* is the fruit of a "convergence of different religious and cultural traditions," "based on the natural law inscribed on human hearts and present in different cultures and civilizations." Moreover, the common good is achieved not only by applying correct procedures or balancing competing interests, but with respect for justice: "When presented purely in terms of legality, rights risk becoming weak propositions divorced from the ethical and rational dimension which is their foundation and their goal," Benedict XVI, *Address at the Meeting with the Members of the General Assembly of the United Nations Organization*, Apostolic Journey to the United States of America and visit to the United Nations Organization Headquarters, April 18, 2008.
[63] Cf. J. Ratzinger, *Values in a Time of Upheaval*, p. 156.

"normative moral idea."⁶⁴ It is good or bad what favors or promotes it. A second Enlightenment excludes *Deus sive natura*, the evolutionist conception imposes the conviction that the world is the fruit of irrational chance.

> The attempt to deduce rules for human conduct from the rules of evolution is widespread, but scarcely convincing. An increasing number of philosophers, such as Singer, Rorty, and Sloterdijk, are raising their voices to tell us that man has the right and the duty to construct the world anew in a rational manner. Hardly anyone questions the need for a new world order, which must be a world order of rationality. So far, so good. But what is "rational"? The criterion of rationality is taken exclusively from the experience of technological production based on science. Rationality is oriented to functionality, to effectiveness, and to an increase in the quality of life for all.⁶⁵

A final nod to Rorty's thought by Ratzinger is in a direct dialogue with Vittorio Possenti, from 2002, in which the Cardinal Prefect showed the developments that have marked Europe since the beginning of the nineteenth century: the passage from liberalism, seen as a bourgeois ideology, to existentialism (and the philosophies of values, new emphases on metaphysics), following to Marxism. Ratzinger speaks of an insistence on a radical separation between rational and irrational worlds, the distancing of metaphysics and the sovereignty of positivism, although he identifies in E. Husserl's phenomenology a renewal for metaphysics and in personalism a new image for philosophy. Facing currents that unilaterally emphasize freedom as the supreme good, Ratzinger criticizes such a concept for its reduction to an individualistic conception, centered on freedom of choice. For him, freedom is always dependent on a system of mutual benefits, of mutual reciprocity. Freedom is not arbitrariness; that is why one must seek an ordering of freedom and the observation of its rules. It is in this context that he defines democracy as "a form of regulation of liberties."⁶⁶ After 1989 Marxism goes into a phase of hibernation, philosophies of rationalism like K. Popper's attune themselves to the contemporary sensibility, which is convinced that truth as such cannot be known. Truth is replaced by consensus; the distinction between good and evil is replaced by the majority principle:

> Of course, the evolution in this direction begins already in German Idealism, if one bears in mind that man could not know reality as such, but only the structure of his consciousness. In the meantime, philosophies

---

⁶⁴ *Ibid.*
⁶⁵ *Ibid.*, pp. 156–7.
⁶⁶ J. Ratzinger and V. Possenti, "La fe en el contexto de la filosofía actual," p. 379.

such as Singer's, Rorty's and Sloterdijk's show further radicalizations in the same direction: man plans and assembles the world without previously given measures, and in doing so, by necessity, also surpasses the concept of human dignity, thereby also calling human rights into question. In such a conception of reason and rationality there is no room left for the concept of God. But it turns out that, in the long run, it is not possible to defend human dignity without the idea of the Creator God.[67]

The Foundations of Law: Nature and Reason

Let us return exclusively to Kelsen. The most prominent reference to him by Benedict XVI is in his speech to the German Bundestag on September 22, 2011, "on the foundations of a free state of law,"[68] taking the biblical text 1 Kgs 3:9 as a starting point. Solomon "asks for a listening heart so that he may govern God's people, and discern between good and evil." Inspired by the Solomonic petition, right from the start the pope puts the ideal of political activity: "To serve right and to fight against the dominion of wrong is and remains the fundamental task of the politician."[69]

But how to distinguish the just from the unjust, the good from the evil, the true right from the apparent right?[70] Who decides on this?

The first highlight is Benedict XVI reminds us that "systems of law have almost always been based on religion: decisions regarding what was to be lawful among men were taken with reference to the divinity."[71] This, of course, does not mean that he appeals to a "divine," "revealed" right, because Christianity has always seen in *reason* and *nature* the authentic sources of law.

The second highlight is that Benedict XVI does not peremptorily reject the majority principle, so dear to juridical positivism, making a "realistic appreciation":[72]

---

[67] *Ibid.*, p. 380.
[68] Benedict XVI, *The Listening Heart: Reflections on the Foundations of Law*, Address at the Visit to the Bundestag, Apostolic Journey to Germany (September 22–5, 2011), Reichstag Building, Berlin, September 27, 2011.
[69] Benedict XVI, *Address at the Visit to the Bundestag*, September 27, 2011.
[70] Natalino Irti speaks of a "meta-positive criterion" in "Il diritto e il linguaggio della natura," *Vita e pensiero* 1 (2012), p. 62. Irti emphasizes that Benedict XVI holds that it is first of all up to the individual to search for the criteria of his own orientation—"criterio di giuridicità" (p. 62).
[71] Benedict XVI, *Address at the Visit to the Bundestag*, September 27, 2011.
[72] M. Cartabia and A. Simonicini, "A Journey with Benedict XVI Through the Spirit of Constitutionalism," in M. Cartabia and A. Simonicini (eds.), *Pope Benedict XVI's Legal Thought*, pp. 9–10. The authors situate Benedict XVI's position within the framework of contemporary European constitutionalism, distinct from that of the French eighteenth century, which predominated until the end of the Second World War, centered on the sovereignty of Parliament and the law as the expression of the general will of the people. The rights of the

For most of the matters that need to be regulated by law, the support of the majority can serve as a sufficient criterion. Yet it is evident that for the fundamental issues of law, in which the dignity of man and of humanity is at stake, the majority principle is not enough: everyone in a position of responsibility must personally seek out the criteria to be followed when framing laws.[73]

The Pope, here, will argue that *natural law*,[74] although it is too often taken as a very particular Catholic doctrine, must be rescued, because it allows to understand the "language of being."[75] It is clear that Kelsen appears as the main opponent of the jusnaturalism endorsed by the Pope, above all because of the dualism he establishes:

Fundamentally it is because of the idea that an unbridgeable gulf exists between "is" and "ought." An "ought" can never follow from an "is," because the two are situated on completely different planes. The reason for this is that in the meantime, the positivist understanding of nature has come to be almost universally accepted. If nature—in the words of Hans Kelsen—is viewed as "an aggregate of objective data linked together in terms of cause and effect," then indeed no ethical indication of any kind can be derived from it. A positivist conception of nature as purely functional, as the natural sciences consider it to be, is incapable of producing any bridge to ethics and law, but once again yields only functional answers. The same also applies to reason, according to the positivist understanding that is widely held to be the only genuinely scientific one. Anything that is not verifiable or falsifiable, according to this understanding, does not belong to the realm of reason strictly understood. Hence ethics and religion must be assigned to the subjective

---

people were codified in constitutional charters. But the catastrophe of the Second World War led to the revision of this legal positivism because of the racial laws in Germany during the war, the "*legal injustice*" (Gustav Radbruch) that was perpetrated. Thus, certain "inviolable rights" were safeguarded against the unpredictable will of the majority. But how is Benedict XVI different from continental European constitutionalism? First, constitutionalism tends to codify the limits that should be imposed on the majority in a text, a higher law, a superior law that obtains the criteria of validity of positive law. Benedict XVI evidently appreciates this stance, as made explicit in his speech to the UN, but it is not the final word. The pope opposes the positivist, closed, reduced, scientistic reason to an open reason. "This is clearly not an a priori attack on positivism, which he calls 'a most important dimension of human knowledge'. But Benedict rejects the idea that this vision of nature and reason can explain everything about the person. The positivist approach is not wrong, per se, but it is simply partial; therefore it falls into error whenever it is believed to be the only possibility, or is imposed as 'the only secular vision' or 'the only public reason' endowed with objectivity" (p. 19).
[73]*Ibid.*
[74]Cf. V. L. Strand and S. Z. Conedera, "Ratzinger's Republic: Pope Benedict XVI on Natural Law and Church and State," *Nova et Vetera* 18/2 (2020), pp. 669–94.
[75]Benedict XVI, *Address at the Visit to the Bundestag*, September 27, 2011.

field, and they remain extraneous to the realm of reason in the strict sense of the word. Where positivist reason dominates the field to the exclusion of all else—and that is broadly the case in our public mindset—then the classical sources of knowledge for ethics and law are excluded. This is a dramatic situation which affects everyone, and on which a public debate is necessary. Indeed, an essential goal of this address is to issue an urgent invitation to launch one.[76]

The big discussion, in fact, is in Pope's (re-)reading of the relationship between being (*Sein*) and ought-being (*Sollen*) in Kelsen. He adds:

Let us come back to the fundamental concepts of nature and reason, from which we set out. The great proponent of legal positivism, Kelsen, at the age of 84—in 1965—abandoned the dualism of "is" and "ought." (I find it comforting that rational thought is evidently still possible at the age of 84!) Previously he had said that norms can only come from the will. Nature therefore could only contain norms, he adds, if a will had put them there. But this, he says, would presuppose a Creator God, whose will had entered into nature. "Any attempt to discuss the truth of this belief is utterly futile," he observed. Is it really?—I find myself asking. Is it really pointless to wonder whether the objective reason that manifests itself in nature does not presuppose a creative reason, a *Creator Spiritus*?[77]

For some critics of the papal discourse, Kelsen did not abandon the difference between being and ought-being. The Austrian author would

---

[76] *Ibid.*

[77] *Ibid.* Also the philosopher who based Ratzinger's first readings on Kelsen also appreciated the Pope's speech in the Bundestag: "Kelsen's irredeemable error lies in taking a purely scientific meaning of the concept of nature and also applying it to that of human nature, which is neither merely nor primarily scientific but philosophical. In a certain way, Kelsen and numerous others with him are victims of an extremist application of Hume's so-called law that prohibits the shift from facts to values, from descriptive to prescriptive assertions. Which is true if precisely we refer to mere empirical facts: no one doubts that values can be deduced from the fact that it is raining today. But the argument is not as hopelessly trivial as a radical empiricist or positivist thinks it is. When we turn to human nature and the person we verify that they are not empirical facts and indeed harbor inclinations and finalisms that must be carefully examined and that go beyond mere fact. In other words, empiricists and positivists are blind to that which is beyond fact, for which alone the indeductibility of the prescriptive from the empirical descriptive applies. And of course for such schools natural law is dead, or is reduced to the law that the big fish eats the little one, which is 'natural' in physis. But the ontological notion of human nature belongs only partly to the realm of physis. It is for human nature that natural law as understood for long ages and even today by those who do not abandon the concept of human nature applies"; V. Possenti, "Umanesimo e antiumanesimo nelle società democratiche contemporanee. L'anima umanistica della democrazia," in F Monceri and M. S. Birtolo (eds.), *Autunno della democrazia?* Quaderno di Politica.eu, Università degli Studi di Molise, 2017, p. 20.

only have stated that norms come from the human will and if they are understood as products of nature—as the jusnaturalists would do in Kelsen's reading—it would lead to the assumption of a creator God, which he denies, maintaining his relativistic and skeptical assumptions. Horst Dreier,[78] for example, rejects the Pope's interpretation, which he classifies as a gross misunderstanding, that relied on the legal historian Wolfgang Waldstein.[79]

The latter believes that the validity of a norm lies in the specific form of its existence; it exists, therefore it belongs to being. And if a norm exists it has normative content, from which an ought-to-be can be derived. Rather, Dreier sees in Kelsen an "irrevocable dualism" ("unaufhebbarer Dualismus"[80]), even though he admits that in texts like *Derogation* (1962) and *Law and Logic* (1965)[81] there was a change in the way he expressed his ideas.[82]

Nadja El Beheiri, on the other hand, sought to clarify Benedict XVI's reading of Waldstein. Toward the end of his life, Kelsen criticized natural law on a different basis. He could only accept a natural law coming from the will of God, since every rule comes from the will. In *Law and Logic*, he proceeds to treat norms as *acts of will*. And the rules of logic only apply to *acts of thought* and only these can be true or not true. El Beheiri points out that Dreier accepts that Kelsen changed his theory about the application of the rules of logic and about basic norm theory. Therefore the author clarifies:

> The line of argumentation of Waldstein and Benedict XVI is now that Kelsen has left the schema of being and ought, just "renounced" [*aufgegeben*] it. In his later years, Kelsen argues in other categories. The dualism of being and ought, is replaced by the opposition between acts of thought and acts of will. The category of acts of thinking is exclusively used by Kelsen—as the examples about the distance of the sun to the earth and about gravitation show.[83]

Therefore, the change operated by Kelsen is categorical, conceptual, although the underlying reasoning remains the same. For this very reason

---

[78] H. Dreier, "Benedikt XVI. und Hans Kelsen," *Juristen Zeitung* 63/23 (2011), p. 1151–4.
[79] W. Waldstein, *Ins Herz geschrieben. Das Naturrecht als Fundament einer menschlichen Gesellschaft* (Augsburg: Paulinus, 2010).
[80] H. Dreier, "Benedikt XVI. und Hans Kelsen," p. 1153.
[81] Collected in *Essays in Legal and Moral Philosophy* (Dordrecht, Boston: D. Reidel, 1973), pp. 261–75 and 238–53, respectively.
[82] Cf. H. Dreier, "Benedikt XVI. und Hans Kelsen," p. 1152.
[83] N. El Beheiri, "'Natur und Vernunft als die Wahren Rechtsquellen' aus der Perspektive von Joseph Ratzinger/Benedikt XVI. und Wolfgang Waldstein," in N. El Beheiri and J. Edögy (eds.), "*Ins Herz Geschrieben.*" *Die Grundlagen des freiheitlichen Rechtsstaates. Aufsätze und Diskussionsbeiträge aus Anlass der Internationalen Tagung am 10* (Budapest: Pázmány, 2014), p. 34.

the pope emphasizes that Kelsen found it impossible to take the step of believing in the existence of a God whose will would give meaning and content to nature, from which a norm would be derived.

In Natalino Irti's words, in Kelsen, nature and norm are separate spheres; rather, there is an abyss between them. "The Kelsenian conception rests on the immanent subjectivity of the will, which knows nothing other than itself, and constructs itself from itself alone and for itself alone. [...] In opposition to this conception, the pontiff raises the *objectivity* of nature and 'reason open to the language of being': which is existentialist motion, not foreign to Benedict XVI's education and culture."[84]

Rorty's Response to Ratzinger: Relativism versus Fundamentalism

Rorty made nods in a few texts about Ratzinger's positions on his own thinking,[85] especially in a conference on the topic of "spirituality and secularism."[86] The philosopher criticizes the stance of Benedict XVI and the Catholic Church in general on homosexuality, moving right on to the central issue, the "nature of morality."[87] Rorty puts himself alongside J. S. Mill's utilitarianism as a stimulating moral ideal while saying that "there is no such thing as the structure of human existence."[88] He, in line with philosopher George Santayana, maintains that moral ideals are fruits of the imagination and that religion and poetry are identical in their essence (considered by Santayana as superstitions). Both should not even serve as instruments to tell us what is real. In short, we should renounce a moral, prior, transcendent ideal. "Most of Western philosophy is, like Christian

---

[84] N. Irti, "Il diritto e il linguaggio della natura," p. 62.
[85] A review of the English edition of the book with Rorty's essay as the main text is at B. Mesle, "*An Ethics for Today: Finding Common Ground between Philosophy and Religion*. Richard Rorty. NY: Columbia University Press, 2011 (Review)," *American Journal of Theology & Philosophy* 32/3 (2011), pp. 285–9. On Rorty's relevance for religious thought, cf. T. Shy, "Readind Rorty as Theology," *Harvard Divinity Bulletin*, Spring 2006.
[86] R. Rorty, *An Ethics for Today: Finding Common Ground between Philosophy and Religion* (New York: Columbia University Press, 2011), p. 8.
[87] *Ibid.*
[88] *Ibid.* For Rorty every vocabulary is "inherently perspectivist" (P. Jonkers, "'A Purifying Force for Reason'. Pope Benedict on the Role of Christianity in Advanced Modernity," in S. Hellemans and J. Wissink (eds.), *Towards a New Catholic Church in Advanced Modernity: Transformations, Visions, Tensions* (Zürich, Münster: LIT, 2012), p. 85), the "truth is a basically parochial matter, i.e., confined to the persons or local communities using or sharing these vocabularies" (p. 82) and, therefore, the impossibility of a "objective meta-vocabulary and, consequently, of a common ground for discussion" (p. 85). Toward a reading from the standpoint of the philosophy of language between Ratzinger and Rorty, cf. H. H. Klöger, "Beyond Dogma and Doxa: Truth and Dialogue in Rorty, Apel, and Ratzinger," *Dialogue and Universalism* 15/7–8 (2005), pp. 101–19.

theology, an attempt to get in touch with something larger than ourselves."[89] What he rejects is "ontotheology," as M. Heidegger called it, i.e., "ceasing to ask both metaphysical questions about the ground or the source of our ideals and epistemological questions about how one can be certain that one has chosen the correct ideal."[90]

And precisely Rorty will point out a way of thinking close to Plato in Ratzinger in his homily at the Mass *Pro Eligendo Pontifice*, quoted at the beginning: "What the pope disparagingly calls the relativists' habit of being carried about by every wind of doctrine is viewed by philosophers like myself as openness to new possibilities, willingness to consider all suggestions about what might increase human happiness. Being open to doctrinal change, we believe, is the only way to avoid the evils of the past."[91]

In a second moment he discusses the Pope's conceptualization of fundamentalism and relativism. He refuses to attribute to a theologian of the stature of Benedict XVI an absurdly uncritical reading of Scripture (the core of the original meaning of the concept), and also rejects the notion of relativism as the thesis that any moral conviction is as good as another. But he still qualifies as fundamentalism the thesis held by the Church that "ideals are valid only when grounded in reality."[92] Relativism would be the opposite of that: "Relativists on this definition are those who believe that we would be better off without such notions as unconditional moral obligations grounded in the structure of human existence."[93]

This is how Rorty reacts to Cardinal Ratzinger's 1996 conference. He said that Ratzinger's view of relativism (around the concepts of tolerance, dialectical epistemology, and freedom) is shared by him in the wake of Mill, Dewey, and alongside Habermas. Truth, under such an aspect, is what is imposed in the free market of ideas, not the correspondence to a previous reality. Nothing is sacred. Rorty claims that Ratzinger knows that relativism is endowed with intellectual resources and cannot be easily eliminated. And that his view is largely true; but what is relative, the construction of man's common and freely ordered life, cannot be. And here would be the error, according to the cardinal, of Marxism and political theology, which would believe that this is possible. The philosopher agrees with Ratzinger on this specific point, because he and other relativists deny that politics can try to be redemptive, but the reason for this denial is different from that of the Pope: for the American philosopher, redemption has always been a bad idea. Redemption presupposes, in his reading, making degraded men happier, immaterial souls in material bodies, once innocent but corrupted by original sin. Rorty sees man through the lens of Nietzsche, as "intelligent animals"

---

[89] R. Rorty, *An Ethics for Today*, p. 9.
[90] *Ibid.*
[91] *Ibid.*, pp. 10–11.
[92] *Ibid.*, p. 11.
[93] *Ibid.*

and denies the superiority of an immortal over a mortal part, of the former aspiring to eternity while the latter is content with finitude. He insists on papal Platonism, on the association of immortality with immateriality and infinitude. In addition, he shows that political idealism neither needs nor sees any use in the "idea that there is something over and above what Cardinal Ratzinger called 'the ego and its desires'. Not just my ego but the egos of all human beings."[94]

In line with William James and the other authors he has already mentioned, Rorty argues that there is no such thing as an intrinsically bad desire: "There are only desires that must be subordinated to other desires in the interests of fairness."[95] For him any wish has the right to be fulfilled as long as it does not interfere with the fulfillment of the wishes of others.

> In many of his writings, the pope has suggested that the need to conceive of moral obligations as imposed by an eternally fixed moral law has been shown by our historical experience with fascism and communism. But of course his opponents cite the horrors committed by the Catholic Church to argue for the opposite conclusion. Whereas the pope accuses relativism of leading to Auschwitz and the gulag, his opponents accuse fundamentalism of excusing the practice of burning homosexuals alive.[96]

He concluded:

> If one thinks of philosophy as an appeal to reason and of history as an appeal to experience, then I can sum up what I have said by saying that neither reason nor experience can do much to help us decide whether to agree with Benedict XVI or with Santayana, James, Mill, Dewey, and Habermas. There is no neutral court of appeal that will help us decide between these two accounts of the human situation, both of which have inspired many acts of moral heroism. In the pope's vision, humans must remain faithful to what he calls "the common human experience of contact with a truth that is greater than we are." In the relativist vision, there never was, and never will be, a truth that is greater than we are. The very idea of such a truth is a confusion of ideals with power. As relativists like myself see the matter, the struggle between relativism and fundamentalism is between two great products of the human imagination. It is not a contest between a view that corresponds to reality and one that does not. It is between two visionary poems. One offers a vision

---

[94] *Ibid.*, p. 15.
[95] *Ibid.*
[96] *Ibid.*, pp. 16–17.

of vertical ascent toward something greater than the merely human; the other offers a vision of horizontal progress toward a planetwide cooperative commonwealth.[97]

In a 2003 text on religion in the public sphere, Rorty compared religious belief to a ladder used by our ancestors, but which is now discarded and that, on balance, they have done more harm than good done: "we think that the occasional Gustavo Guttierez or Martin Luther King does not compensate for the ubiquitous Joseph Ratzingers and Jerry Falwells."[98] From the same, he in his last interview, with Danny Postel, referring to his and Habermas' thought in Iran in 2007, Rorty opposes Habermas' thought to that of Benedict XVI and the ayatollahs and suggests that enlightenment has made Christianity superfluous, one might say, in a way:

In recent decades, Habermas has been commending that culture to the Europeans. In opposition to religious leaders such as Benedict XVI and the ayatollahs, Habermas argues that the alternative to religious faith is not "relativism" or "rootlessness" but the new forms of solidarity made possible by the Enlightenment. The pope recently said: "A culture has developed in Europe that is the most radical contradiction not only of Christianity but of all the religious and moral traditions of humanity." Dewey and Habermas would reply that the culture that arose out of the Enlightenment has kept everything in Christianity that was worth keeping.[99]

John Rawls: Religion and "Public Reason"

We have already seen to some extent the widespread belief that modern societies, if they are to be fully secular, must exclude religious traditions[100] (Jonkers will call it the "ethnocentric view"[101]). And Ratzinger himself said that liberalism and Marxism "were in agreement in refusing religion both the right and the capacity to shape public affairs and the common future of mankind,"[102] but the second half of the twentieth century showed the power of religion in social life. For this very reason he is fully engaged in

---

[97] *Ibid.*, p. 17.
[98] R. Rorty, "Religion in the Public Square," *The Journal of Religious Ethics* 31/1 (2003), p. 142.
[99] D. Postel, "Last Words from Richard Rorty," *The Progressive Magazine*, June 11, 2007.
[100] A Piccinin recalls the rejection by many Christian thinkers of Rawls' political liberalism, which, with its notion of "public reason," tends to exclude *"religious reason,"* "Rawls and Catholicism: Towards Reconciliation?," *Cultural and Religious Studies* 7/1 (2019), p. 50.
[101] P. Jonkers, "A Purifying Force for Reason," p. 83.
[102] J. Ratzinger, *A Turning Point for Europe?*, p. 8.

rehabilitating the presence of religion in civil life and, for this to happen, in defending the requirement for religions to translate their doctrines into a universal language. On the first point, the German pope focuses on the thought of J. Rawls,[103] the most important liberal philosopher of the twentieth century, author especially of *A Theory of Justice* (1971) and *Political Liberalism* (1992).[104]

Liberal theory assumes that political decisions should be made independently of any conception of the good life. Liberal democracy is constitutively plural, in which no conception of the world can think itself superior to another. It is anti-liberal to believe that the human good is something homogeneous. Pluralism is the result of the activities of human reason and is therefore a normal condition of a culture of free institutions. Therefore, agreements and understandings cannot be reached if they rest on irreconcilable global doctrines of life. Public reason should not attack any global doctrine, except only if it is incompatible with public reason and democratic society. Reasonable doctrines must accept constitutional democracy and, consequently, legitimate law.[105]

The secularist culture saw the exclusion of "comprehensive theories of good" from public discourse as necessary—and Rawls was representative of this position, which eventually mitigated over time. But are democracy and comprehensive doctrines compatible?

Rorty was more hostile to the participation of the religious in the public sphere; he criticized the Church openly. Rawls, however, recognizes that it would be a contradiction to see Churches as forms of private life, but neither are they an expression of public life, "because its doctrines are particular and comprehensive and not the general doctrine of public reason with political values."[106]

Religion as Wisdom

Benedict XVI's confrontation with Rawls' thinking will appear explicitly in his speech written to La Sapienza University in Rome, dated January 17, 2008. Benedict XVI had a scheduled visit to the University, at the invitation

---

[103] For a further exploration of Rawls' view of religion and of the author's own religious background cf. *Brief Inquiry into the Meaning of Sin and Faith. With "On My Religion"* (Cambridge: Harvard University Press, 2009), particularly "On My Religion" (pp. 259–70), an essay in which he describes the Protestant (more specifically Episcopalian) context of his origin and the events that were decisive in shaping his view of religion, especially the Second World War.

[104] For the development of Rawls' view on religion cf. D. A. Dombrowski, *Rawls and Religion: The Case for Political Liberalism* (New York: State University of New York Press, 2001). For a first approximation between Ratzinger and Rawls, cf. A. Piccinin, "Rawls and Catholicism," pp. 50–6.

[105] Cf. J. L. Martínez, "Religión en la democracia liberal," p. 298.

[106] *Id.*, p. 324.

of the rector of the institution, to open the 2008 Academic Year, which was eventually cancelled due to protests. This "lamentable incident"[107] happened in the name of secular thinking: the pope, as a religious leader, should not speak at a university that purports to be the space for the free flow of ideas. That is why Benedict XVI will try to answer the question about what the pope, as the pastor of an ecclesial community, has to say to the university. He reminds us that, of course, his function is more focused on the interior of the believing community, but the Church is in the world and influences it: for the ethical reasoning of humanity.[108]

But the pope goes back to the even more fundamental, preliminary question, precisely the one that discusses the concept of reason before thinking about its public or private character:

> What is reason? How can one demonstrate that an assertion—especially a moral norm—is "reasonable"? At this point I would like to describe briefly how John Rawls, while denying that comprehensive religious doctrines have the character of "public" reason, nonetheless at least sees their "non-public" reason as one which cannot simply be dismissed by those who maintain a rigidly secularized rationality. Rawls perceives a criterion of this reasonableness among other things in the fact that such doctrines derive from a responsible and well thought-out tradition in which, over lengthy periods, satisfactory arguments have been developed in support of the doctrines concerned. The important thing in this assertion, it seems to me, is the acknowledgment that down through the centuries, experience and demonstration—the historical source of human wisdom—are also a sign of its reasonableness and enduring significance. Faced with an a-historical form of reason that seeks to establish itself exclusively in terms of a-historical rationality, humanity's wisdom—the wisdom of the great religious traditions—should be valued as a heritage that cannot be cast with impunity into the dustbin of the history of ideas.[109]

This allows us to answer the question of what role the Pope has before the university world and, by extension, in the public debate, as the authoritative and leading voice on the doctrines of the Church, but beyond this role:

---

[107] E. Guerriero, *Servitore di Dio e dell'umanità. La biografia di Benedetto XVI* (Milano: Mondadori, 2016), p. 390.
[108] Cf. Benedict XVI, *Lecture Prepared for the University of Rome "La Sapienza,"* January 17, 2008.
[109] *Ibid.* In fact, Rawls revisits his concept of public reason by showing more openness to the contribution of religion in public debate. For purposes of contrast, "The Idea of Public Reason," in J. Rawls (ed.), *Political Liberalism* (New York: Columbia University Press, 2005), pp. 212–54 and "The Idea of Public Reason Revisited," *The University of Chicago Law Review* 64/3 (1997), pp. 765–6.

The Pope speaks as the representative of a community of believers in which a particular wisdom about life has evolved in the course of the centuries of its existence. He speaks as the representative of a community that preserves within itself a treasury of ethical knowledge and experience important for all humanity: in this sense, he speaks as the representative of a form of ethical reasoning.[110]

That is, religion can provide "reserves of morality,"[111] especially as *wisdom*. In fact, the speech to La Sapienza was a "contribution of 'humanism' to collective life," in which "he put forward not Christianity's 'whole offering', but its humanistic core,"[112] to some extent an answer to the claims of Habermas and Rawls, extracting from Christian doctrine values in common with public reason.[113]

In this context we return to the question posed at the very beginning and which connects, for Ratzinger, the three authors in question:

At this point, though, Pilate's question becomes unavoidable: What is truth? And how can it be recognized? If in our search for an answer we have recourse to "public reason," as Rawls does, then further questions necessarily follow: What is reasonable? How is reason shown to be true? In any case, on this basis it becomes clear that in the search for a set of laws embodying freedom, in the search for the truth about a just polity, we must listen to claims other than those of parties and interest groups, without in any way wishing to deny the importance of the latter.[114]

---

[110] Benedict XVI, *Lecture Prepared for the University of Rome "La Sapienza,"* January 17, 2008.
[111] G. Bosetti, "When Habermas and Ratzinger Shared the Idea of a Post-Secular Age," *Reset Dialogues*, January 4, 2023.
[112] *Ibid.*
[113] Cf. *ibid.*
[114] Benedict XVI, *Lecture Prepared for the University of Rome "La Sapienza,"* January 17, 2008. For Peter Jonkers, Benedict XVI disagrees on at least two points with Rawls: he does not rely as much as the latter on human fundamental reasonableness as a guarantee of political legitimacy, for human beings are children of their time and culture and do not always correspond to the expectation of Rawls's liberalism, which believes that they can be reasonable to form principles and norms of just cooperation and may be willing to discuss them on the terms they propose; cf. "A Reasonable Faith. Pope Benedict's Response to Rawls," in T. Bailey and V. Gentile (eds.), *Rawls and Religion* (New York: Columbia University Press, 2015), p. 222. Second, Rawls excludes intrinsic views about truth and goodness because they introduce transcendent or metaphysical notions (pseudo-rational types of knowledge) that cannot be examined by reason. Rawls believes that comprehensive doctrines rest on authority. For Rawls comprehensive doctrines exclude others. Benedict advocates inclusivism. For example, metaphysics (Plato and Aristotle) sides with Christianity (Augustine and Thomas Aquinas) because both believe that there is only one rational conception of good. Jonkers claims that between Benedict and Rawls there is a little-noticed convergence on the "reasonableness of reason," not just the belief of reason in one's own capacities, but that reasonableness is inherent in reality (cf. p. 223). Benedict XVI's position is philosophical, but it is alien to the general framework of Rawls' thought, because for the latter, religious truth is authoritarian and intolerant. Therefore, "in fundamental opposition

According to Peter Jonkers, whom we follow here, the Pope appreciates Rawls' openness—the recognition of the reasonableness of comprehensive religious doctrines, though he does not accept them in the realm of public reason. "Rawls refuses to 'upgrade' their reasonableness to a (universal) truth."[115]

For the Pope, social stability is not necessarily the result of consensus and, for this very reason, he focuses on the fallibility of the democratic process of consensus building. For Rawls it is not an option to appeal to a transcendent truth in order to preserve the plural and democratic character of modern societies. Rawls, for example, trusts in the self-regulating capacities of reason, an optimism that Pope does not share.[116] But the pope also criticizes transcendent authoritarianism, and in this sense the pontiff agrees with Rawls in rejecting a transcendent normativity that is beyond rationality.

This is why Benedict XVI proposes the idea of wisdom as the common ground for interpreting the ethical role of religion.[117] Although the history of the Church shows the errors and contradictions of theologians and hierarchs, the history of the saints and Christian humanism is a true

> claim upon public reason. Of course, much of the content of theology and faith can only be appropriated within the context of faith, and therefore cannot be demanded of those to whom this faith remains inaccessible. Yet at the same time it is true that the message of the Christian faith is never solely a "comprehensive religious doctrine" in Rawls' sense, but is a purifying force for reason, helping it to be more fully itself.[118]

A "wisdom tradition"[119] is a type of life-guiding knowledge based on human experience or divine origin. This wisdom purifies reason because it stands over the partial rationality of group interests. Benedict does not say that Christianity is the only wisdom, nor that it possesses complete wisdom. But it contains what he called great ethical intuitions (human dignity, inviolability of life ...). A quick example is his reading of the Decalogue, for example:

---

to Rawls, he [Benedict XVI] states that reason and reasonable consensus should be subordinate to truth" (pp. 229–30). In others words, "one might say that the difference between Rawls and Pope Benedict comes down to that between a more 'horizontal' ideal of moral and political normativity, which eventually rests on a faith in reason, and a more 'vertical' one, which rests on a faith in God's *Logos* that is present in the world as a purifying force for reason" (p. 232). Rawls' view depends on his negative view of an authoritarian Church, an exclusivist religious truth, and a voluntarist God (p. 228). Benedict XVI does not accept the distinction between public reason and non-public reason (and proposes the history of the saints as public reason).
[115] P. Jonkers, "A Purifying Force for Reason," p. 97.
[116] Cf. *ibid.*, p. 98.
[117] Cf. *id.*, "A Reasonable Faith. Pope Benedict's Response to Rawls," p. 226.
[118] Benedict XVI, *Lecture Prepared for the University of Rome "La Sapienza,"* January 17, 2008.
[119] Cf. *id.*, "A Purifying Force for Reason," p. 99.

> [W]hat meaning do these Ten Commandments have for us, in the present cultural context in which secularism and relativism risk becoming the criteria of every choice and this society of ours that seems to live as if God does not exist? We answer that God gave us the Commandments to teach us true freedom and genuine love, so that we can be truly happy. They are a sign of the love of God the Father, of his desire to teach us how to distinguish between good and evil, truth and falsehood, right and wrong. They are comprehensible to all because they set fundamental values as concrete rules and regulations, by putting them into practice man can walk the path of true freedom, which set him firmly on the path that leads to life and happiness.[120]

The Foundation of Politics: Reason, Not Revelation

The general problem posed by Rawls (and by Rorty) appears when Benedict XVI goes to the British Parliament in 2010 precisely to address the problem of the "ethical foundations of civil discourse,"[121] which, for the Pope, is the great "challenge for democracy."[122] The Pope defends the affinity of many points of the English constitution with the social doctrine of the Church (safeguarding of human dignity, duty of the political authorities to seek the common good). And he does not fail to recall that pragmatic solutions are often inadequate and that precisely something important for English legislation such as the abolition of slavery (the subject of debate with Rorty, for example) was created on the basis of natural law. Relying on the mutual purifying and corrective role of reason and religion, on the dialogical character of this relationship, he will clearly defend the legitimacy of the role of religion in the public sphere, which does not jeopardize the distinction between the "world of secular rationality" and the "world of religious belief."[123] So the Pope asks:

> [W]here is the ethical foundation for political choices to be found? The Catholic tradition maintains that the objective norms governing right action are accessible to reason, prescinding from the content of revelation. According to this understanding, the role of religion in political debate is not so much to supply these norms, as if they could not be known

---

[120] Benedict XVI, *Video Message for Initiative "10 Squares for the 10 Commandments,"* September 8, 2012.
[121] Id., *Address at the Meeting with the Representatives of British Society, Including the Diplomatic Corps, Politicians, Academics and Business Leaders,* Apostolic Journey to the United Kingdom (September 16–19, 2010), City of Westminster, Westminster Hall, September 17, 2010.
[122] *Ibid.*
[123] *Ibid.*

by non-believers—still less to propose concrete political solutions, which would lie altogether outside the competence of religion—but rather to help purify and shed light upon the application of reason to the discovery of objective moral principles. This "corrective" role of religion vis-à-vis reason is not always welcomed, though, partly because distorted forms of religion, such as sectarianism and fundamentalism, can be seen to create serious social problems themselves.[124]

Finally, in *Caritas in veritate* (n. 56), the pope takes up the question about God's place in the political arena, claiming the "'citizenship status' for the Christian religion. [...]. Secularism and fundamentalism exclude the possibility of fruitful dialogue and effective cooperation between reason and religious faith."[125] That is why Benedict XVI, in his speech to the UN, already cited, argued that religious freedom cannot be reduced to freedom of worship. "The full guarantee of religious liberty cannot be limited to the free exercise of worship, but has to give due consideration to the public dimension of religion, and hence to the possibility of believers playing their part in building the social order."[126]

Conclusion

The objective of this study was to show on what ground and in what terms Ratzinger/Benedict XVI put the discussion with the three authors: with Kelsen we have the critique of positivist reason, of the exclusion of natural law and of the possibility of a should-be emerging from being; and more than that of moving from the notion that starting from the will (from which norms come) one takes the step to the understanding that nature itself contains a will inscribed by the creative *Logos*, God.

With Rorty the discussion is around truth, freedom, and, consequently, relativism. The big problem identified by our author is that relativism loses the notion of the moral substratum present in nature. For the relativist, morality cannot respond to superior and transcendent ideas, but only to a balance in the satisfaction of desires in view of the non-interference of the desires of one in those of others. Humanity has no ethical, transcendent standards that can give it guidance and prevent it from the assumption of power by a totalitarian majority.

With Rawls the discussion is around the idea of public reason. Benedict XVI has always been an ardent defender of the public role of Christianity;

---

[124] Ibid.
[125] Id., Encyclical Letter Caritas in veritate *on Integral Human Development in Charity and Truth*, June 29, 2009.
[126] Id., Address at the Meeting with the Members of the General Assembly of the United Nations Organization, April 18, 2008.

his defense has never been the imposition of the Christian creed on the collectivity (faith must be proposed, not imposed), but that the political body should benefit from the centuries-old wisdom that Christianity contains within itself, a synthesis of the great intuitions of humanity, some of which are precisely the dignity of the human person and the inviolability of life. Relegating religion to the private sphere represents a loss for society, because the practical and historical reason that religion contains serves as a discussion horizon for the formation of public life. And, of course, a loss for the individual himself, because the religious element (in the case of Christianity, God himself, Jesus Christ, the Gospel) is part of his citizen identity and cannot remain hidden in the exercise of citizenship.

I conclude with two statements by Benedict XVI that well summarize the spirit that the Pope asks from those who allow themselves to be questioned and guided by his reflections. The first is his defense of the notion of truth, well synthesized in the comment he makes on the motto of the flag of the president of the Czech Republic: *Veritas vincit*.

> In the end, truth does conquer, not by force, but by persuasion, by the heroic witness of men and women of firm principle, by sincere dialogue which looks beyond self-interest to the demands of the common good. [...] For in the end, what is more inhuman, and destructive, than the cynicism which would deny the grandeur of our quest for truth, and the relativism that corrodes the very values which inspire the building of a united and fraternal world? Instead, we must reappropriate a confidence in the nobility and breadth of the human spirit in its capacity to grasp the truth, and let that confidence guide us in the patient work of politics and diplomacy.[127]

Trust in the truth, in the rationality that reaches the moral message of nature, dignifies the human being, elevates him. Truth makes man greater and freer. This is what he did in his "spiritual quasi testament": "Man becomes smaller, not larger, when there is no longer room for an *ethos* that, based on its authentic nature, defers beyond pragmatism, when there is no longer room for looking to God. The proper place of positivist reason is in the great fields of action of technology and economics, and yet it does not exhaust the whole human."

---

[127] Benedict XVI, *Address by Holy Father, Meeting with the Civil and Political Authorities and with the Members of the Diplomatic Corps*, Apostolic Visit to the Czech Republic, Presidential Palace of Prague, September 26, 2009.

12

Romano Guardini: Liturgy, Christian Existence, Truth, and Ethics

Marcela Jiménez Unquiles

Introduction

In order to engage in a dialogue between Joseph Ratzinger and Romano Guardini, an apparently simple task, it is necessary to begin by highlighting some significant features of their lives. First of all, we find ourselves with the portrait of a theologian, a university professor who has been the successor of Peter.[1] In fact, Ratzinger acceded to "to the pontificate with the wisdom that accompanies many years of theological reflection, with wide experience regarding the Church's situation, with certain issues that he saw as poorly resolved and with full awareness of the limitations imposed by his age."[2] Ratzinger brought together a long academic career. We are referring to a life surrounded by books and study, marked from very early on by a clear objective: the discernment of the truth and the life of faith. He had inherited from his mother sensitivity and simplicity, and from his father, an interest in rationality. He had the gift of knowing how to express all his knowledge in very accessible terms for students

---

[1] Cf. Benedict XVI and P. Seewald, *Last Testament: In His Own Words* (London: Bloomsbury, 2016), p. xi.
[2] J. L. Lorda, "Benedicto XVI ha hecho un gran discernimiento del concilio," *Palabra* 597/3 (2013): p. 12, in P. Blanco Sarto, *Benedicto XVI. La Biografía* (Madrid: San Pablo, 2019), pp. 929–30.

uninitiated in the field of theology who, studying in other faculties such as Law or Philosophy, often came to listen to him.[3] In this regard, his long academic career was confined to some of the most prestigious universities in Germany. The first years of his teaching and research activity took place in Freising (1952–9), always surrounded by profound theological and philosophical debates between students and teachers. After the approval of his habilitation for free teaching, Ratzinger occupied chairs of fundamental theology and dogmatic theology at the universities of Bonn (1959–63), Münster (1963–6), Tübingen (1966–9), and, finally, at the University of Regensburg (1969–77), where he remained until his definitive transfer to Rome. This often allowed him to connect with the deepest and most human concerns of his students and disciples.[4] In González de Cardedal's opinion, the German theologian has taught what Christianity is in a personally valid and intellectually legitimate way.[5]

To speak of Ratzinger's theology means that we are referring to a very Guardinian theology, in which the great Augustinian and Franciscan theological tradition has never ceased to pulsate. A theology that has to deal with modern thought, atheism, secularism, scientism, and positivism, as well as religious pluralism and pseudo-humanism, but always from the perspective of Christianity's commitment to reason.[6] Thus, endowed with his own thought, Ratzinger has reflected intensely on the questions that affect man, showing a special interest in dogmatic theology. His theoretical knowledge and erudition have accompanied him in his long academic career and equally long ecclesiastical career; as such, many voices enrich his thought and work, in particular, his extensive Christological work developed in six decades[7] whose fundamental pillars have been the hermeneutics of faith and historical reason. In summary, it can be stated that within the matrix of ratzingerian though, there is a significant influence of Greek philosophy, along with Augustinian and Franciscan traditions, and Hebrew-personalist dialogue. They are all unmistakably present permeating his theology. And,

---

[3] At the University of Münster, enrollment in his courses reached 350 students, although between listeners and students from other faculties, the average per class was around 600. Cf. G. Valente, *El profesor Ratzinger 1946–1977: los años dedicados al estudio y a la docencia en el recuerdo de sus compañeros y alumnos* (Madrid: San Pablo, 2011), p. 145; J. L. Allen Jr., *Cardinal Ratzinger* (New York: Continuum, 2000), pp. 103, 145.
[4] Cf. J. Catalán Deus, *De Joseph Ratzinger a Benedicto XVI: Los enigmas del nuevo Papa* (Madrid: Espejo de Tinta, 2005), p. 338.
[5] Cf. O. Gonzázlez de Cardedal, "Retrato de un Papa intelectual," *El País* [Babelia] (2005) and in "Ratzinger en España," *El País* [Sección opinión] (2005) quoted by P. Blanco-Sarto, *Joseph Ratzinger. Una biografía* (Navarra: EUNSA, 2004), p. 104.
[6] Cf. the prologue to "El Solzhenitsyn del siglo XXI" from John Waters and G. Meotti, *¿El último Papa de Occidente?* (Madrid: Encuentro, 2021), pp. 11–12.
[7] Cf. the German edition: Joseph Ratzinger, G. S., *Jesus von Nazaret. Beiträge zur Christologie, Erster Teilband*, Band 6/1 (Freiburg: Herder, 2013).

in a very special way, the Guardinian work, which was never absent from his theological and philosophical formation, as can be seen from the allusions and references that Ratzinger always made to it.

When in 1978 the Catholic Academy of Bavaria awarded the Romano Guardini Prize to Doctor honoris causa Alfons Goppel, the then head of the Academy, Cardinal Ratzinger, in a more philosophical than religious context, called for the responsibility that Christians have in the world. But over and above this is theology and those responsible for it, i.e., the work of theologians who have an ultimate responsibility in vindicating the use of reason and showing the rational dimension of Christianity[8]. This is a constant throughout the history of thought and, therefore, a fundamental element of the Ratzingerian legacy. For as the Pope Emeritus says in his posthumous work: "The Christian faith was able to present itself in history as the true religion. Christianity's claim to universality is based on the openness of religion to philosophy."[9] In this aspect, it can be affirmed that the stimulating confrontation between fides and ratio has been the keystone of the work and the Magisterium of the Bavarian theologian.[10] It is true that the relationship between faith and reason is no longer even questioned by the current scientistic and technicist mentality, since the arrogance of the scientific praxis throws the sacred out of the life of man: God.[11] The voice of Romano Guardini and his prognosis then resounds: "Modernity is over: let's hope so!"[12] In Ratzinger's opinion, for Guardini, modernity would have been the main responsible for the disintegration of man and the world, and for his bet on a false and empty spirituality.[13] Today we must ask ourselves: is Guardini still a voice worth listening to? Does his lack of hope not reflect the seriousness of the times in today's society? Are not contempt for truth and the absence of values in some way the insignia of postmodern culture? Truth is the philosophical notion that

---

[8] Cf. J. Ratzinger, *Fundamental Speeches from Five Decades* (San Francisco: Ignatius, 2012), p. 218.

[9] Benedict XVI XVI, *Che cos'è il cristianesimo. Quasi un testamento spirituale* (Milano: Mondadori, 2023) p. 34.

[10] See relevant speeches that highlight the idea of broadening the horizons of reason: Benedict XVI, *Address at the Catholic University of the Sacred Heart*, November 25, 2005; *Faith, Reason and the University: Memories and Reflections*, Lecture in the Meeting with the Representatives of Science, Regensburg, September 12, 2006; *Address to the participants in the First European Meeting of University Lecturers*, June 23, 2007; *Address to Participants at the Sixth European Symposium for University Professors*, June 7, 2008; *Visit to the Federal Parliament in the Reichstag Building*, Berlin (Germany), September 22, 2011.

[11] Cf. J. Ratzinger, *The Nature and Mission of Theology: Essays to Orient Theology in Today's Debates* (San Francisco: Ignatius, 1995), pp. 7–9.

[12] Ratzinger perceives the shock that Guardini experienced with the arrival of a new ideology hand in hand with technology, an ideological power that, as Pope, he spoke of both in his works and in his magisterial texts, cf. *JROC* VI/2, pp. 692–5.

[13] Cf. R. Guardini, *El ocaso de la Edad Moderna*, vol. 1 (Madrid: Cristiandad, 1981), p. 67.

no longer finds an answer in the adequacy of the intellect to reality (the old metaphysical formula), but in the certainties originated by *the dogma of transformation and feasibility*, or even more, by the unjust or blind agreements reached by the majorities. Truth is accompanied by demands and obligations, because it is often uncomfortable. Perhaps for this reason, as Ratzinger points out, truth is cornered in the region of intolerance and anti-democracy.[14] Certainly, with its power and strength, truth is one of the essential categories for both theologians. We will return to it later.[15] Having said that, secondly, let us get to know some of the most relevant aspects of the man who has been a convinced defender of truth in the university environment.

Similarities in Some Biographical Notes

Romano Guardini was born in Verona in 1885, although a year later his family moved to Mainz. From that moment on, his life—including studies, academic activity, and the search for his vocation—took place in some of the main cities of Germany (Berlin, Freiburg, and Munich).[16] For Ratzinger, too, the first years of his life were marked by the continuous moves from his family home[17] because of the profession of his father, who had publicly criticized the government of terror imposed by National Socialism, which, with a rationally designed program, unleashed cruelty, violence, and contempt for the human being. In this historical context, Guardini refers to how the systematic use of technology served to imprison and exterminate people.[18] Certainly, Guardini showed his courage and effort by coming into conflict with certain Berlin authorities of the time. But against all difficulties, he always knew how to defend "the truth [...] in the midst of the reign of lies."[19] Hence his interest in some of the figures of the history of the human spirit, such as the heroes of Dostoevsky's works, who, from a psychological

---

[14]Cf. J. Ratzinger, *Values in a Time of Upheaval* (San Francisco: Ignatius, 2006), pp. 55–8.
[15]Cf. id., *Satz der Erde. Christentum und katholische Kirche an der Jahrtausenwende. Eis Gespräch mit Peter Seewald* (Stuttgart: Deutsche Veroag-Anstalt, 1997), pp. 53–4.
[16]For more on the life and work of Romano Guardini, see the work of A. L. Quintás, *Romano Guardini, maestro de vida* (Madrid: Palabra, 1998).
[17]The Ratzinger family's different homes, as well as the German theologian's different places of residence before his definitive transfer to Rome are listed out in what follows: Marktl am Inn (1925–9), Tittmoning (1929–32), Aschau (1932–7), Hofschlag (Traunstein 1937–46), Freising Seminary until his priestly ordination (1946–51), first service as vicar in Munich (1951), professor of theology in Freising (1952–9), University of Bonn (1959–63), University of Münster (1963–6), University of Tübingen (1966–9), University of Regensburg, his last teaching position (1969–77) before leaving for Rome.
[18]Cf. R. Guardini, *La cuestión judía* (Buenos Aires: Sur, 1963), pp. 13, 16.
[19]*JRCW* 11, p. 177.

and metaphysical perspective, have been part of the religious experience itself.[20]

Although they were born in different eras and experienced the horrors of Nazism in different ways, there is no lack of similarities in the lives of Ratzinger and Guardini. As for the teaching work they carried out, it was not always easy and was not always free of moments of frustration and bitterness. Let us recall that on February 21, 1957, the Bavarian theologian gave the public lesson of qualification for access to the professorship, after having experienced the drama of free teaching as he himself indicated years later in his autobiography.[21] In fact, both Guardini and Ratzinger chose for the defense of their theses the study of a man of government, St. Bonaventure, a medieval mystic and intellectual. This was the way they both began their academic activity at the University of Bonn.[22] They also shared a rather reserved character and delicate health.[23] Moreover, they wrote their autobiographies at the height of their intellectual maturity. In the case of Guardini, in the style of the Augustinian confession, the memories are limited to the period between 1943 and 1945, after his chair at the University of Berlin was suppressed by the Nazis in 1939. A chair created expressly for him under the name of *Catholic philosophy of religion and Catholic vision (Weltanschauung) of the world*.[24] Thanks to the advice of Max Scheler, this chair was accepted by Guardini in 1923, although, once it was eliminated during the National Socialist era, Guardini was forced to take a forced retirement. This fact allowed him to develop an important desk job. Thus, the fruitful literary activity of those years resulted in such important publications as *The Death of Socrates* and *The Spirit of the Liturgy*. In Ratzinger's opinion, the Berlin chair had rejected Guardini's methodological project, based on the defense of a new idea of a university that seeks above all the truth, which had been annihilated by the *Dritte Reich*. The German university had to distance itself from any politicization

---

[20] Spanish and Italian editions can be consulted: R. Guardini, *El universo religioso de Dostoyevski* (Buenos Aires: Emecé, 1954, ²1958); id., *Il mondo religioso di Dostoevskij* (Brescia: Morcelliana, 1995).

[21] Cf. J. Ratzinger, *Milestones: Memoirs 1927–1977* (San Francisco: Ignatius, 1998), pp. 103ss.

[22] Cf. R. Guardini, *Apuntes para una autobiografía* (Madrid: Encuentro, 1992), pp. 35–7. See J. Ratzinger, *Die Geschichtstheologie des heiligen Bonaventura* (München: Schnell & Steiner, 1959; St. Ottilien, 1992).

[23] As Alfonso López Quintás (1928–) indicates in his study of Guardini's ethics treatise, his physical and mental health was extremely delicate. Starting in 1955, Guardini began suffering from trigeminal neuralgia and asthma, and later heart problems, with painful consequences for his health. Cf. R. Guardini, *Ética. Lecciones en la Universidad de Múnich* (Madrid: BAC, 1999), p. xxi. Cited from *id.*, *Wahrheit des Denkens und Wahrheit des Tuns* (Paderborn: Schöningh, 1980), p. 33.

[24] For Guardini, perhaps it would have been better if it were called the Chair of Philosophy of Religion and nothing more. He questioned the meaning of the adjective *catholic*. In his view, there is no Catholic, Protestant, or Buddhist philosophy of religion, but simply a true philosophy of religion. Cf. R. Guardini, *Apuntes para una autobiografía*, p. 51.

and instrumentalization, otherwise its own greatness and the future of future generations would be compromised. However, the time of rehabilitation had come for the German university, which remained after the shame of National Socialism, as a place open to any great and serious search for truth.[25] Of that time Ratzinger says: "Romano Guardini, in the letters he wrote to parish priest Weiger [...], describes in a fascinating way how in Berlin the power of profane culture and the poverty of Catholicism in the face of it brought him down and shook him, even physically."[26] After rejecting all the offers received by Guardini to hold professorships at the universities of Tübingen, Munich, Göttingen, and Freiburg, in 1948 he finally accepted the proposal made to him by the University of Munich and later in 1962 he was appointed professor emeritus. In 1965, Pope Paul VI offered him the dignity of cardinal, although due to his serious health problems Guardini declined the proposal. In this regard, we can recall that the nuncio Guido del Mestri, visiting the city of Regensburg, had to hold a conversation on the divine and the human with Ratzinger in order to be able to give him a letter with the episcopal appointment.

For his part in 1977, Ratzinger became Archbishop of Munich and Freising, despite his critical view of the offices within the Church.[27] Once some doubts were dissolved, Ratzinger accepted the appointment. A month after his episcopal consecration, he also received the cardinal's capelet with the title of the Church of Santa Maria Consolatrice, located in the Roman district of Tiburtino.[28] The appointments did not stop there, for in 1981 he assumed the custody of Catholic orthodoxy, as well as the presidency of the International Theological Commission and the Pontifical Biblical Commission. Finally, after the long Wojtylian pontificate, in less than twenty-four hours and in only four ballots, on April 19, 2005, Ratzinger became the 265th successor of Peter, the first German pope to be elected after Hadrian VI (1522–3).

Life Orientation

Both theologians carried out important teaching and academic work, committed to the truth until the end of their lives. In their academic activity,

---

[25] Cf. Ratzinger, *Fundamental Speeches from Five Decades*, pp. 256–8.
[26] This relates to correspondence between Guardini and his dear friend Josef Weiger; the two spent some time together at Father Weiger's country home to avoid bombings during the war. Cf. Benedict XVI and P. Seewald, *Last Testament: In His Own Words* (London: Bloomsbury, 2016), p. 213.
[27] Cf. G. B. Brunori, *Benedicto XVI. Fe y profecía del primer Papa emérito de la historia* (Madrid: Paulinas, 2018), p. 146; cf. J. Ratzinger, *Milestones: Memoirs 1927–1977*, pp. 152 ss.
[28] Upon his return to the city of Munich, Ratzinger recalled the words of Paul VI on the importance of the color red for cardinals vestment, a symbol of their willingness to become martyrs for the faith. Cf. J. Ratzinger, *Co-Workers of the Truth: Meditations for Every Day of the Year* (San Francisco: Ignatius, 1992), p. 207.

both Guardini and Ratzinger brought together in their classes listeners from a wide variety of backgrounds. Students from different faculties and also professionals from different sectors often attended their classes. With his personalized teaching method and distinctive pedagogical approach to problem solving, Guardini achieved great success. His lively and captivating style, accompanied by a fine intuition, remained in both his teaching and literary work. In addition, the limited teaching load of three hours of class per week and two hours of seminar allowed Guardini to develop his own original and highly artistic pedagogical method.[29] Guardini confessed that speaking made him very excited, even spending the whole hour of the class on tiptoe, something that left him physically exhausted. Thus, the attention of the audience made him participate in an authentic and true spiritual experience. Nevertheless, and in spite of having more than three hundred students in some of his classes, Guardini often felt the rejection of the University. In his autobiographical writings, the theologian from Verona describes how his years before teaching were the hardest moments of his life, the years filled with insecurity, anguish, and deep melancholy. It was a period in which he tried to carry out an authentic work of introspection regarding the decisions made about his studies, which logically had to give meaning to a vocation full of doubts. This process was always in struggle with a rather nostalgic temperament, inherited from his mother. After abandoning his studies in chemistry and political science, he found his true vocation in theology in Tübingen. Finally, he managed to achieve balance and, in a way, what he had always longed for: emotional stability. According to him, melancholy allowed him to develop his creativity and to delve into the true meaning of life in a more skillful way. However, for his father, the crisis suffered by his son Romano were only the cause of a "fickle and unstable character."[30] On the contrary, Ratzinger discovered his vocation as a teacher and his passion for writing at an early age. When he learned something new, he felt the need to share it with others. While scientific theology was his passion, the decision to become a priest was accompanied by some hesitation, although Ratzinger's final answer was a resounding, categorical, and definitive *fiat*.[31]

The Italian-German philosopher and theologian, one of the great humanists of the twentieth century, died in 1968 pronouncing the beautiful words of the master Augustine that best capture, with extraordinary force, the double movement between God and the creature: "You have made us for yourself O Lord & our heart is restless until it rests in you."[32] On the other hand the last day of the year 2022, Joseph Ratzinger-Benedict XVI passed away confessing his love for the Lord. For both theologians, God

---

[29] Cf. R. Guardini, *Apuntes para una autobiografía*, pp. 55–66.
[30] During the summer of 1905, after debating with a pro-Kantian colleague about the existence of God, Guardini suffered a serious crisis of faith. Cf. *ibid.*, pp., 94–105.
[31] Cf. J. Ratzinger, *Salz der Erde*, p. 42.
[32] Augustine of Hippo, *The Confessions of Saint Augustine* (Grand Rapids, MI: Christian Classics Ethereal Library, 1999), p. 17.

and the creature, two fundamental poles of the existential space, act as a hermeneutical key in the knowledge of the truth about man. This is one of the central themes in Guardini's anthropological and theological work, as can be seen in one of his well-known publications, entitled *Only Those Who Know God Know Man*.[33] This idea reached its greatest notoriety at the Second Vatican Council, because during the Council debates the doctrine of divine revelation and its transmission were discussed.[34] The way of interpreting Scripture, of applying the historical method, and the role of theological hermeneutics acquired great importance in the Council sessions, to the point of becoming fundamental keys to know and deepen the Christian event. Essential themes such as Revelation, Scripture, Tradition, and the Magisterium, together with liturgical renewal and ecumenism, condensed the high points of the Council, in which the young professor Joseph Ratzinger, as expert and advisor to Cardinal Frings, made his voice heard.

The Liturgical Movement

As a theologian, cardinal, and pope, Ratzinger often confessed the desire to follow in the footsteps of the great master Guardini and, in many aspects of his life, he did so. Formed in the orbit of Guardinian work, for him the genesis of the Liturgical Movement was to be found in the midst of a wealth of literature, namely, in the early works of Guardini.[35] It follows that the lighthouse responsible for illuminating the liturgical movement of the twentieth century was the work published in 1918 under the title *The Spirit of the Liturgy*. Three quarters of a century later and due to the situation prompted by the conciliar reform, without losing sight of the perspective of his teacher Guardini, Pope Ratzinger wrote in 2000 *The Spirit of the Liturgy: An Introduction*—a book that contains the nuclear keys to animate the liturgy and the life of the Church. It is a systematic study of the essence,

---

[33] Buber and Ebner's dialogical abundance lies here. According to López Quintás, Guardini was inspired by and expanded on Ebner's idea of truly knowing man only when truly knowing God. Cf. The Introduction to R. Guardini, *Experiencia religiosa y fe* (Madrid: BAC, 2016), pp. xii–xiii; F. Ebner, *Das Wort ist der Weg* (Viena: Herder, 1949), pp. 99, 114, 145, 219. In another publication, Guardini points out the correct way to know and experience God, i.e., as a living reality starting from one's condition as creature and based on a filial relationship that transforms the limits of human existence with the close and overflowing experience of love. Cf. R. Guardini, *El espíritu del Dios viviente* (Barcelona: Belacqva, 2005), pp. 98–100.
[34] See Vatican Council II, *Dogmatic Constitution* Dei verbum *on Divine Revelation*, November 18, 1965, §2–4. The Pastoral Constitution on the Church in the Modern World also teaches us that, "The truth is that only in the mystery of the incarnate Word does the mystery of man take on light ... " Vatican Council II, *Pastoral Constitution on the Church in the Modern World* Gaudium et spes, §22, December 7, 1965.
[35] Cf. *JROC* VIII/2, p. 1238; *JRGS* 8/1, 8/2.

space, and time of the liturgy, including the most relevant aspects of sacred art and music. For Ratzinger, as it was for Guardini, the fundamental objective of the work is none other than the understanding of the Christian faith.[36]

Probably, being aware of the risks that any comparison could entail, Ratzinger tries to recover in his *Theology of the Liturgy* the rites that could avoid the dangers to which the liturgy was exposed as a result of the renewal and the conciliar reforms.[37] The Bavarian theologian even speaks of "a kind of liturgical anarchy in which the celebrants tried to anticipate the new, as yet unpublished books through their own creativity."[38] What is certain is that, after the Council, Guardini's popularity declined notably and with it the interest in his thought and work. He himself confessed in his autobiography: "En lo que respecta a mi trabajo literario, el mundo laico lo ha acogido con simpatía, pero la teología lo ha ignorado en su conjunto hasta el momento. El profesor Schmaus fue el primero en reconocerlo y utilizarlo en su Dogmática."[39] It was only after his death in 1968 that Guardini's thought regained prominence with the publication of his *Collected Works*.[40]

Dialogical and Personalist Philosophy

Having said this, let us now consider the influence of the personalist current, cultivated by contemporary authors of Guardini, on Ratzinger's philosophical and theological thought.[41] Undoubtedly, dialogical philosophy in a Christian key appears everywhere in Ratzinger's work, whether through the thought of Romano Guardini or through Martin Buber's own personalist philosophy. The latter, nourished by a powerful dialogical anthropology, seeks to bring human existence to its fullness through man's relations with others like himself and with the divine Other. Underlying this is the Buberian idea that "the fundamental fact of human existence is man with man."[42] This is a good part of the heritage received by Guardini, as well as the dialectical philosophy of Hegelian inspiration. From the unity of differences, the philosophy of contrast (*der Gegensatz*), between obedience and freedom, personal prayer and liturgy, modernity and Church, is presented in a very

---

[36] Cf. O. de Cardedal, "Introducción a la edición española," in J. Ratzinger, *El espíritu de la liturgia: una introducción* (Madrid: Cristiandad, 2001) pp. 27–48.
[37] Cf. *JRCW* 11, pp. 99, 132, 245.
[38] Prologue March 19, 2014, in *JROC* IV, p. xviii; *JRGS* 4.
[39] R. Guardini, *Apuntes para una autobiografía*, pp. 171–2.
[40] The initiative taken by the Catholic Academy of Bavaria even made it possible to publish some of the author's posthumous works: *Cartas a un amigo teólogo. Pensamientos en la frontera de la vida* (edición alemana de 1976); *La existencia del cristiano* (Madrid: BAC, 1977) and *El contraste. Ensayo de una filosofía de lo viviente concreto* (Madrid: BAC, 1996).
[41] Cf. Benedict XVI, *Last Testament*, p. 76.
[42] M. Buber, *¿Qué es el hombre?* (México: Fondo de Cultura Económica, 2014), pp. 146–7.

logical and suggestive language to the reader of Guardini's work, helping him to grasp the essence of reality and to penetrate the mysterious universe of human existence. As Ratzinger sums up, using one of Guardini's favorite expressions, the aim is to "become essential, to get out of the multiple distractions of our existence, of our Christian condition, and to find access to the essential."[43] Guardini refers, as is natural, to the very essence of Christianity.[44] In other words, becoming essential means knowing Christ and taking him as the model of our existence. In this sense, the essence of Christianity, far from finding its foundation in an idea or system of thought, or in a program of morality—as the Veronese theologian says—is found in a person who is essential: Jesus Christ. It should not be forgotten that for Ratzinger the book *Der Herr* has never lost its relevance, and even today it still has an important theological mission ahead of it in order to reach a correct understanding of the figure of Jesus. At the beginning of his pontificate, Benedict XVI spoke to us of the proclamation and encounter with a Person, with a fact or, in other words, with a historical event. This is what his first encyclical affirms: "Being Christian is not the result of an ethical choice or a lofty idea, but the encounter with an event, a person, which gives life a new horizon and a decisive direction." [45] In short, and varying a Nietzschean idea, one can say the same as Guardini:

> The unprepared look at reality says: God exists. The human desire for autonomy replies: He cannot exist, for then I cannot become what I want to be. And the gaze towards reality eventually gives way. The greatest, and at any rate the most constant, force of influence does not correspond to the conscious, but to the unconscious positions taken: therefore, very little is achieved here by intellectual indoctrination and correction of the conscious attitude. It remains the task of inner conversion.[46]

The Truth of Christianity in the Origin of Europe

Guardini emphasizes the substance of Christianity: Christ.[47] This is how his Christological theology expands through an intimate contemplative meditation on "the *Logos*, the flesh, the entrance into the world, the eternal

---

[43] J. Ratzinger, "Introduction," in R. Guardini, *The Lord* (Washington, DC: Regnery, 2001), pp. xiii–xiv.
[44] Cf. R. Guardini, *La esencia del cristianismo* (Madrid: Ediciones Nueva Época, 1945), pp. 10–13.
[45] Benedict XVI, *Encyclical Letter* Deus caritas est *on Christian Love*, December 25, 2005, §1.
[46] R. Guardini, *Religión y Revelación* (Madrid: Ediciones Guadarrama, 1961, ²1964), pp. 258–9.
[47] Cf. *JROC* VII/1, p. 547; *JRGS* 7/1.

origin, the palpable earthly reality, the mystery of unity."[48] We refer to Guardini's reflections on Jesus of Nazareth in his work *The Lord*. With Jesus, truth takes on such importance that, for the German theologian of Italian origin—a restless observer of his time who lived through and suffered the disasters of two world wars—if the "source of authentic strength is not recognized: the truth; the truth that man does not create on his own, but receives,"[49] then man is lost, aimless, and fearful In Ratzinger's opinion, truth becomes the most pressing task in Romano Guardini's life. There comes "the hour of truth, that moment when a man is struck by the truth"[50] and has to defend it with courage and effort, against all difficulties, as Guardini did when defending it *in the midst of the reign of lies*, he came into conflict with the Berlin authorities of the time.[51] Truth is sought in the origin of history; of economic, political, cultural phenomena; and, of course, in the very origin of human existence. But after the disasters of the twentieth century historicism becomes a problem, so that the scientific method, based on repeatable experience and mathematics, gives way to a new program: "*verum quia faciendum.*"[52] For this reason he points out that "the religion of the incarnate *Logos* can hardly fail to appear profoundly reasonable to anyone who sincerely seeks the truth and the ultimate meaning of his or her own life and history."[53] With an Augustinian philosophical background, the theologian Ratzinger devoted much of his reflections to the Greco-Christian encounter, the heritage of the West, and the roots of Europe.[54] In short, to the not at all coincidental encounter between Greek reason, Roman heritage, and biblical faith, which gave rise to Europe. But at this historic moment, we must ask ourselves: what does the future hold for the old continent? To forget that it has been a beacon of civilization and a stimulus of progress for the world? Who will have a place in a Europe that forgets and does not respect its history and its roots? Europe is trying to disrobe itself of its own history, but as Marcello Pera points out in dialogue with the Bavarian Cardinal: "The only thing worse than living without roots is struggling to get by without a future."[55] The truth is that the cultured and Christian Europe, defender of moral values, the person and his dignity, seems to be in agony.

---

[48] R. Guardini, *The Lord*, p. 5.
[49] *Id., Experiencia religiosa y fe*, p. 145.
[50] J. Ratzinger, *Fundamental Speeches from Five Decades*, p. 242.
[51] Cf. *JRCW* 11, p. 177.
[52] Mathematical and conceptual thought are not mutually exclusive, quite the contrary. Therefore, both are totally legitimate and necessary, although an answer to the question of meaning is difficult to obtain through demonstrable knowledge. Cf. J. Ratzinger, *Introduction to Christianity (Revised Edition)* (San Francisco: Ignatius, 2004), pp. 70–2.
[53] Benedict XVI, Post-Synodal Apostolic Exhortation Verbum domini on the Word of God in the Life and Mission of the Church, September 30, 2010, §36.
[54] See his doctoral thesis (*Doktorarbeit*) on the ecclesiology of Saint Augustine in *JRGS* 1.
[55] J. Ratzinger and M. Pera, *Without Roots: The West, Relativism, Christianity, Islam* (New York: Basic Books, 2006), p. xii.

If Europe wishes to maintain its identity and not endanger the democracies based on it, it must place itself at the service of the common good and build an integral humanism that respects the most elementary anthropological questions. In this aspect, Guardini stands out for presenting a personalist approach in his anthropology and an integrating perspective of the person, which earned him the Erasmus Prize for the best European humanist (1962). His concern for the dignity of man and the uncertain future of humanity led him to make some rather surprising and, above all, very accurate predictions about the postmodern era. His work *The End of Modernity* emerges as an authentic and disturbing portrait. In this regard, Guardini continually warns of the dangers that will be brought about by the spiritual attrition to which Europe has been plunged, having become immersed in an intellectualism based on growing technical virtuosity.[56] As for science, it should be noted that it is not an all-embracing but a limited knowledge, hence it cannot respond to all the problems of man. For this there are other ways of knowing. If scientific rationality does not have a monopoly on human knowledge, it is simply because reality is something more vast than the region delimited by empirical experience. There are realities, as Benedict XVI suggests in the *lectio magistralis* of Regensburg, that science does not and cannot contemplate.[57] On the other hand, ethics and moral development have not advanced at the same pace as technology. This issue presents us with an important challenge. In his third encyclical, *Caritas in veritate*, the Pope calls for the promotion of moral responsibility and an ethical and moral use of technology for the common good of humanity. Technology is never just technology. It manifests who man is and which:

> For this reason, technology is never merely technology. It reveals man and his aspirations towards development, it expresses the inner tension that impels him gradually to overcome material limitations. [... But] For this reason technology can appear ambivalent [when] has come to be seen as coinciding with the possible. [...] The process of globalization could replace ideologies with technology, allowing the latter to become an ideological power that threatens to confine us within an a priori that holds us back from encountering being and truth. Were that to happen, we would all know, evaluate and make decisions about our life situations

---

[56] Cf. R. Guardini, *El fin de la modernidad. Quien sabe de Dios conoce al hombre* (Madrid: PPC, 1995), p. 17.
[57] In L. J. Prieto López, "La crítica del cientificismo en el Discurso de Ratisbona de Benedicto XVI," *Revista Agustiniana* 157 (2011): pp. 203–12.

from within a technocratic cultural perspective to which we would belong structurally, without ever being able to discover a meaning that is not of our own making.[58]

Ethics, Reason, and Science in the University Environment

Following these reflections we come across one of Guardini's most important works, his *Ethics*. A compilation of writings produced during his stay at the Universities of Bonn (1920–2), Berlin (1923–43), Tübingen (1945–8), and Munich (1950–62). For him, the correct interpretation of ethics rests "on the understanding of what the human being is, and how he is what he is."[59] In this respect, Guardinian ethics is a perfect synthesis of the work and thought of the Veronese theologian. It is a natural ethic based on the light of revelation and the Christian *ethos*, but which at this moment in history has lost its luster, due to the profane vision of the world and man's lack of religious capacity. Indeed, the cultural and intellectual crisis with which modernity is coming to an end has given way to a new form of technological totalitarianism and digital servitude, exposing the globalization of a skepticism that scorns all questions of ultimacy. Hence the Ratzingerian proposal to broaden reason and its use, specifically in the university space, since *University*—from *Universitas studiorum*—means the *universality of the studies* that the institution represents and promotes. We must not forget that the university is a privileged space for fostering interdisciplinary dialogue among the sciences, or, in other words, open and respectful dialogue among the different scientific disciplines. It is necessary to promote a more integral vision of reality, although this must avoid the excessive fragmentation of knowledge and the absolutization of scientific knowledge (scientism). Only from the service of truth and the humble recognition of "the self-limitation of reason which, paradoxically, is based on its successes"[60] will reason and research be able to shed light on humanity. At a time of strong divisions,

---

[58] Benedict XVI, *Encylical Letter* Caritas in veritate *on Integral Human Development in Charity and Truth*, June 29, 2009, §§68–71.
[59] The attendance at his Ethics lessons was crowed, according to the number of listeners, that each class reached about 650. Cf. R. Guardini, *Ética. Lecciones en la Universidad de Múnich* (Madrid: BAC, 1999), p. xxxv.
[60] J. Ratzinger, "La fe, entre la razón y el asentimiento," *Archivo Teologico Torinese* vol. 5/1 (1999/1), pp. 7–19, in *id.*, *Fe y ciencia. Un diálogo necesario* (Santander: Sal Terrae, 2011), pp. 131–52. The quote on p. 145.

Ratzinger addresses a plea to the German university: today as well as tomorrow, do not allow "political passion to stifle the free ord of the search for truth. Do not allow it! Guardini remains a yardstick of our university."[61] In this sense, it can be said that the young Ratzinger learned from Guardini how to resolve the opposition between science and faith thanks to Christ.[62] So when he was shown in 2017 a magazine commemorating his ninetieth birthday with "photos of the thinkers who had influenced him—Romano Guardini, John Henry Newman, Henri de Lubac, Hans Urs von Balthasar—Benedict pointed to the first photo and said to Archbishop Gänswein: 'Guardini ….'"[63]

---

[61] Id., *Fundamental Speeches from Five Decades*, pp. 256–8.
[62] Cf. P. Seewald, *Benedicto XVI. Una vida* (Bilbao: Mensajero, 2020), p. 202. In German: P. Seewald, *Benedikt XVI. Ein Leben* (München: Broemer, 2020).
[63] P. Blanco-Sarto, *Benedicto XVI. La Biografía*, p. 971.

13

Ludwig Wittgenstein: The Scope of Reason

Tracey Rowland

Introduction

Ludwig Wittgenstein (1889–1951) was born a generation ahead of Joseph Ratzinger into a wealthy Viennese family of Jewish origins. Members of his family had adopted Catholicism as the official family religion, though precisely where Wittgenstein stood, theologically speaking, could be said to be something known to God alone. A line from the *Internet Encyclopaedia of Philosophy* began a discussion of this subject with the statement: "Wittgenstein himself was baptized in a Catholic church and was given a Catholic burial, although between baptism and burial he was neither a practicing nor a believing Catholic."[1] Certainly his theological orientations are a subject of interpretation, and it is clear that they changed over time, as did his philosophy.

Stages and Receptions

Most commentators divide Wittgenstein's philosophy into two periods: that of the *Tractatus Logico-Philosophicus* and that of the *Philosophical Investigations*, though some commentators add a third period, described as

---

[1] D. J. Richter, "Ludwig Wittgenstein," *Internet Encyclopedia of Philosophy*, https://iep.utm.edu/wittgens/.

the middle period, between the late 1920s and the early or mid-1930s and a fourth period from 1946 until his death in 1951.

The *Tractatus*, from the time of its publication in 1922 up until the early 1930s, influenced the Viennese circle of logical positivists; while the *Philosophical Investigations* had a much greater impact in the UK, especially in the universities of Oxford and Cambridge, where it contributed to the rise of a school of thought known as "ordinary language philosophy." In the final decade of the twentieth century it could also be described as an influence on the development of analytical Thomism. The most illustrious of the British interpreters of Wittgenstein was G. E. M. Anscombe who was the English translator of his *Philosophical Investigations*. Anscombe was a devout Catholic and a convert who maintained a close association with the Order of Preachers. She held posts in philosophy at the Universities of Oxford and Cambridge where so-called analytical philosophy dominated philosophical discourse in the twentieth century. In part, through her mediation, the work of Wittgenstein has heavily influenced British Catholic philosophy and theology, manifest in such works as Fergus Kerr's *Theology after Wittgenstein*[2] and the more recent *Nature as Guide: Wittgenstein and the Renewal of Moral Theology* by David Goodill, both of whom are Dominicans.[3] The Australian philosopher Eric D'Arcy who became the archbishop of Hobart and who was a collaborator with Joseph Ratzinger on the compilation of the *Catechism of the Catholic Church* even thought that Wittgenstein's philosophy might be valuably applied to the field of Christology.[4] Somewhat paradoxically a man whose theological convictions might best be described as enigmatic and whose sexual orientations were ambivalent has been posthumously pressed into the service of the defense of Catholic moral teaching. Significantly, this is made possible by the fact that Anscombe and those Catholic scholars who followed in her trajectory do not read the *Tractatus* as an affirmation of logical positivism.

In contrast to the British Thomists, Joseph Ratzinger has never been enthusiastic about the philosophy of Wittgenstein. Indeed, as Bruce D. Marshall has noted, "the world of French and German-speaking Thomas interpretation remains virtually untouched by analytic philosophy, and *a fortiori* by 'analytical Thomism'."[5] Ratzinger is not alone among German theologians in having little, if anything, to do with the tradition of analytical philosophy.

---

[2] Cf. F. Kerr, *Theology after Wittgenstein* (London: SPCK, 1997).
[3] Cf. D. Goodill, *Nature as Guide: Wittgenstein and the Renewal of Moral Theology* (Washington, DC: Catholic University of America Press, 2022).
[4] Cf. E. D'Arcy, "Towards the First Golden Age?," *The Australasian Catholic Record* 74/3 (1997), pp. 294–306.
[5] B. D. Marshall, "In Search of an Analytic Aquinas," in J. Stout and R. MacSwain (eds.), *Grammar and Grace: Reformulations of Aquinas and Wittgenstein* (London: SCM, 2004), pp. 55–74 at 56.

A Variety of Interpretations

The primary reason for Ratzinger's lack of enthusiasm for Wittgenstein would seem to be that Wittgenstein's publications leave themselves open to a diverse array of interpretations and appropriations, and Ratzinger's interpretations could best be located in the early stream of Wittgenstein interpretation when Wittgenstein was still based in Europe, not in the Cam River stream of the older Wittgenstein. Ratzinger's Wittgenstein is more the Wittgenstein of logical positivist readings of the *Tractatus* than the Wittgenstein of Anscombe and others influenced by Anscombe's translation of Wittgenstein's *Philosophical Investigations*. Indeed, in his essay "Faith and Knowledge," Ratzinger not only classified Wittgenstein as a positivist but declared that positivism has "now very largely taken possession of philosophy—thanks to the impact made by Wittgenstein."[6] Auguste Comte may have been the father of positivism but Ratzinger regards the contribution of Wittgenstein as a kind of accelerant for the positivist movement. In an address to accept an honorary doctorate at the University of Wrocław Ratzinger remarked that "without the anticipation of faith, thought would be groping around in emptiness; it would be able to say nothing further about the things that are really essential to man. It would have to conclude, with Wittgenstein, that we must be silent about what is ineffable."[7] In this context Ratzinger implies that without the theological virtue of faith, positivism may be the only option open to the person searching for truth.

Joost Hengstmengel, author of "Philosophy to the Glory of God: Wittgenstein on God, Religion and Theology," noted that "the number of books and articles on religious remarks and topics in Wittgenstein's work is countless," but nonetheless he has marshalled the interpretations of Wittgenstein's thought in these subject areas into the following three subgroups:

1   In an early reading, Wittgenstein's religious thoughts have been labelled "Wittgensteinian fideism"... Nowadays it stands for the view that religious truths can only be known by means of faith and not by reason, and are therefore independent of it or even hostile to it. Religious truths are in other words pre-rational or over-rational. The Wittgensteinian variant of fideism is variously characterized by subscribing to one or more of the following theses: 1) that religion is logically cut off from other aspects of life, 2) that religious discourse is essentially self-referential and does not allow us to talk about reality, 3) that religious beliefs can be understood only by religious believers, and 4) that religion cannot be criticized.

---

[6] J. Ratzinger, *Faith and the Future* (San Francisco: Ignatius, 2009), p. 27.
[7] *Id.*, *Pilgrim Fellowship of Faith: The Church as Communion* (San Francisco: Ignatius, 2005), p. 27.

2   In a second interpretation, Wittgenstein is depicted as a religious anti-realist or relativist. In contrast to realists, anti-realists do not believe in a reality independent of our conceptions of it … Religion is not a matter of scientific knowledge or evidence, but an attempt to speak about God, who does not reveal himself in our reality. Moreover, what counts is what religions mean for our practical life. Since the religious discourse is interwoven with religious language, there is no possibility of standing outside it and to criticize or to support religion on the basis of, for example, external facts.

3   Finally, Wittgenstein's ideas have been summarized as a "theology for atheists," an understanding of religion from the outside. It is said Wittgenstein conceived religion as an anthropological phenomenon and studied it almost phenomenologically from a third-person viewpoint.[8]

Narrowing the Scope of Reason

In his most extensive reference to the thought of Wittgenstein, Ratzinger appears to fall within the first class of interpreters. In the essay "Faith and Philosophy" (first published in German in 1970) he was critical of Wittgenstein for narrowing the scope of philosophy and implied, though did not say explicitly, that this narrowing forecloses the possibility of a symbiotic relationship between faith and philosophy. He wrote:

> The name Wittgenstein stands for the program whose aim is to turn philosophy once and for all into an exact science by causing it to renounce completely all attempts to solve unanswerable questions about reality and to confine itself to the analysis of human language. Even the attempt to elucidate consciousness seems, according to this program, to be too ambitious; that which is immediately accessible is merely the expression of consciousness in language, and it is the structures of language that are elucidated. This is a feasible task and one that yields much valuable knowledge. But it does not fulfill the function of philosophy, for man has to go on living and fill his life with a meaning that extends beyond the bounds of arbitrary theorizing and is to be found in responsibility toward reality.[9]

---

[8] Cf. J. Hengstmengel, *Philosophy to the Glory of God: Wittgenstein on God, Religion and Theology*, February 22, 2010.
[9] J. Ratzinger, *Faith and the Future*, pp. 78–9. The German version of *Faith and Philosophy* which appears as the third essay in the book *Faith and the Future* was published as a chapter in *Glaube und Zukunft* (Münich: Kösel, 1970) and is also found in volume 3/1 of the German *Collected Works* or *JRGS* at pp. 238–51.

Ratzinger goes on to say that "something of very great import is revealed by all of this: the moment that philosophy finally submits to the canon of the exact sciences and tries to fit into the last available space in the system of modern thought, this completion of the system leads to absurdity."[10] He further declared that "a man who can no longer transcend the limits either of his consciousness or of his speech, fundamentally can no longer speak of anything at all."[11]

Ratzinger therefore regards Wittgenstein's philosophy as an example of what he calls "narrowing the range of reason" or "amputating reason." He cites "the triumphantly sober sentence" with which Wittgenstein concludes his *Tractatus logico-philosophicus*: "What we cannot speak about we must consign to silence" and he argues that this statement is only "apparently logical." Rather, he asserts, "the *logos*, the intellect of man reaches farther than formal logic. Man simply has to speak about the inexpressible if he would speak about himself. He must reflect precisely on the incalculable if his thinking is to reach the sphere of the truly human."[12] So unimpressed was Ratzinger by the *Tractatus* that he remarked that Ludwig von Ficker "showed good taste by declining to print the *Tractatus* in 'Der Brenner', the newspaper of which Ficker was editor and which purported to be an organ serving the cause for progressive thinking that was concerned about the humanity of man."[13] In his footnote to these remarks Ratzinger referenced three works: one by Ludwig von Ficker, one by Ulrich Steinvorth, and one by Joseph Möller. He described Ficker's essay as "one of the best comprehensive appraisals there is of Wittgenstein's aims and work."[14]

Ficker on Wittgenstein

Ficker began his discussion by noting that "the not very extensive work [what became known as the *Tractatus*], which also used formulas from higher mathematics to clarify his [Wittgenstein's] thoughts and contained an excursus on the basics of arithmetic," presented a lay mind like Ficker's "with difficulties that could hardly be resolved."[15] Moreover the work was of such a form that it put "the logician in a straitjacket from the outset"

---

[10] J. Ratzinger, *Faith and the Future*, p. 79.
[11] *Ibid.*, p. 80.
[12] *Ibid.*, p. 81.
[13] *Ibid.*, pp. 82–3. For an account of Ficker's rejection of the manuscript see A. Janik, "Wittgenstein, Ficker, and Der Brenner," in C. G. Luckhardt (ed.), *Wittgenstein: Sources and Perspectives* (Hassocks, Sussex: Harvester, 1979), pp. 161–89. For translations of Wittgenstein's letters to Ludwig von Ficker see A. Janik, "Letters to Ludwig von Ficker," in C. G. Luckhardt (ed.), *Wittgenstein: Sources and Perspectives* (Hassocks, Sussex: Harvester, 1979), pp. 82–99.
[14] J. Ratzinger, *Faith and the Future*, pp. 82, n. 8.
[15] L. von Ficker, *Denkzettel und Danksagungen. Aufsätze* (München: Kösel, 1967), p. 209.

and assumed the "physiognomy of an unusual intellectual achievement."[16] Nonetheless, while acknowledging that this form "made demands on the comprehension of the reader," Ficker concluded:

> The view of all eminent logicians that the clarification of true philosophical insight can only be served by disregarding all transcendence and by sealing off any kind of metaphysics probably encountered in Wittgenstein's person and intellectual disposition a latent counter-current of doubts and reservations, which for him had their origin in an uncontrollable reality beyond anything imaginable, calculable, discussable and thus [such things] already belonged to the zone of absolutely silent being.[17]

According to this reading Wittgenstein is no common garden-variety positivist but someone suffering a high level of existential angst about what to make, philosophically speaking, of the ineffable.

Steinvorth on Wittgenstein

Steinvorth's article, published in the journal *Hochland* in 1969, takes the form of a long review of George Pitcher's *The Philosophy of Wittgenstein*.[18] Steinvorth praises Pitcher for offering a user-friendly introduction to the thought of Wittgenstein but is critical of his account of Wittgenstein's notion of a language game. Steinvorth emphasizes that for Wittgenstein, "the meaning of the words is not determined by objects that are assigned to the words" but rather, "the behaviour that connects speaking and other activities or occurrences, namely the language game, determines the meaning of the words."[19] Perhaps of greater significance, however, is the fact that Steinvorth noted that Pitcher "agrees with Miss Anscombe" when he "makes it clear that the *Tractatus* does not offer an epistemology and therefore does not commit itself to elementary propositions being empirical [as the logical positivists thought]."[20] Nonetheless, Steinvorth noted that "Pitcher argues very convincingly that the facts represented by elementary propositions must be observable according to the main claims of the *Tractatus*, and this gives the logical positivists the right to invoke the *Tractatus*."[21] Steinvorth also argues that the prefaces to the *Tractatus* and the *Philosophical Investigations*, while "extremely interesting, obscure rather than reveal the specific aim of these works," and that it is only be "presenting the nature,

---

[16] *Ibid.*
[17] *Ibid.*, p. 215.
[18] Cf. G. Pitcher, *The Philosophy of Wittgenstein* (Englewood Cliffs: Prentice-Hall, 1964).
[19] U. Steinvorth, "Georg Pitcher, Die Philosophie Wittgensteins," *Hochland* (1969), p. 571.
[20] *Ibid.*, p. 570.
[21] *Ibid.*

context and development of the questions and problems that occupied Wittgenstein even before the writing of the *Tractatus* and the *Philosophical Investigations*" that it is possible to explain the "perplexity of Wittgenstein's indefatigable arguments."[22]

Möller on Wittgenstein

Of the three authors cited by Ratzinger, it is, however, Joseph Möller who offers the most passionately critical account of where Wittgenstein stands on the relationship between philosophy and theology. Möller begins his discussion by quoting from the *Tractatus*: "Everything that can be thought at all can be thought clearly. Anything that can be said can be said clearly" and "What we cannot talk about [clearly] we must pass over in silence." Möller responds to these statements with a series of rhetorical questions:

> Can only what is categorically unambiguously determined be expressed? What about language and its meaning in poetry, such as Hölderlin and Rilke? Are the statements of physics clear in what they want to tell us, i.e., completely unambiguous statements? In the realm of microphysics, cannot a question of 'reality' and 'structure' be asked beyond the physical formula? And what about the human being himself, the human being whom art, literature, mu–ic and also—among—ther things—philosophy strive for, without ever being able to say 'clearly' what he actually is?.[23]

Möller further argues that in Wittgenstein's later work theological questions are reduced to "language games" with the result that theology becomes a "strange intertwining of sociological-historical statements and meaningless questions."[24] In a statement that sounds as if it could have been written by Ratzinger himself, Möller concludes that "the attempt to tear believing away from thinking fails. It fails because existence is determined by reason."[25]

Intrinsic Relationship between the True and the Good

A second Ratzinger criticism of Wittgenstein can be found in the work published as *Truth and Tolerance*. Here Ratzinger argues that the question

---

[22] *Ibid.*, p. 572.
[23] J. Möller, *Glauben und Denken im Widerspruch? Philosophische Fragen an die Theologie der Gegenwart* (München, Freiburg: Erich Wewel, 1969), p. 40.
[24] *Ibid.*, p. 41.
[25] *Ibid.*, p. 42.

of the true and the good cannot be separated from each other: "If we can no longer recognise what is true and can no longer distinguish it from what is false, then it becomes impossible to recognise what is good; the distinction between good and evil loses its basis."[26] Having made this point Ratzinger remarks that he wished to indicate "one more variant of the renunciation of truth in religion, which arises, this time, not from history, but from philosophical thought—the theses Wittgenstein posed concerning our subject" (the relationship between truth and freedom).[27] He then cited two theses that according to Elizabeth M Anscombe represented the positions of Wittgenstein:

1. There is no such thing as being true for a religion. This is perhaps suggested when someone says: "This religious statement is not the same as a statement of natural science."
2. Religious faith may be compared rather to a person's being in love than to his being persuaded that something is true or false.[28]

Ratzinger concluded: "In accordance with this logic, Wittgenstein noted, in one of his many notebooks, that it would make no difference to the Christian religion whether or not Christ had actually done some of the things recounted concerning him or whether indeed he had existed at all."[29] In Ratzinger's judgment this sounded like Bultmann's position whereby "believing in a God who is the Creator of heaven and earth does not mean that we believe that God really created heaven and earth but only that we understand ourselves as being his creatures and thereby live a more meaningful life."[30] Ratzinger has no patience for such a view of Christianity that is no longer the truth, merely what he called a "make-believe" world. In his footnotes to these remarks Ratzinger cited Wittgenstein's essays "Culture and Value" and "On Certainty" as well as comments about Wittgenstein made by Josef Seifert. Seifert declared:

For Wittgenstein, the religious person and the nonreligious live, as it were, in two make-believe worlds and move upon different planes without contradicting one another. According to Wittgenstein, in religious statements nothing is basically being said... just as little as would be said in a game of chess or of checkers about the people represented by the pieces outside of these games. Religion must there be interpreted, he said,

---

[26] J. Ratzinger, *Truth and Tolerance: Christian Belief and World Religions* (San Francisco: Ignatius, 2004), p. 214.
[27] *Ibid.*, p. 215.
[28] Cf. *ibid.*
[29] *Ibid.*
[30] *Ibid.*, p. 216.

not in the same way as meaningful sentences with some claim to truth, but in a purely anthropological and entirely subjective sense, like a game that is simply someone's personal preference.[31]

Love, Reason, and Faith

Discussions about the true and the good are never far away from the subject of love. It is therefore not surprising that Ratzinger/Benedict turned to Wittgenstein's comparison of the experience of belief and the experience of falling in love when he drafted the encyclical *Lumen fidei* that was promulgated under the name of Francis. In §27 he remarked:

The explanation of the connection between faith and certainty put forward by the philosopher Ludwig Wittgenstein is well known. For Wittgenstein, believing can be compared to the experience of falling in love: it is something subjective which cannot be proposed as a truth valid for everyone. Indeed, most people nowadays would not consider love as related in any way to truth. Love is seen as an experience associated with the world of fleeting emotions, no longer with truth.

In *Lumen fidei* at §27 he accepts that love "engages our affectivity" but he further argues that "only to the extent that love is grounded in truth can it endure over time, can it transcend the passing moment and be sufficiently solid to sustain a shared journey." There is, in other words, a logic within love, a *veritas amoris*, in order for love to be genuine love and not mere sentimentality.

The same principle was underscored in his encyclical *Caritas in veritate*. At §30 we find the statement that "Intelligence and love are not in separate compartments: love is rich in intelligence and intelligence is full of love." In the work *Truth and Tolerance* he further declared that "Love and reason should converge with one another as the essential foundation pillars of reality: real reason is love and love is real reason. In their unity, they are the real basis and goal of all reality."[32]

Just as love and reason "should converge with one another as the essential foundation pillars of reality," Ratzinger strongly emphasizes the symbiotic relationship between faith and reason. Here he follows Robert Spaemann in regarding the relationship between these disciplines as a relationship of mutual purification. As Spaemann wrote: "every speculative concept becomes internally dialectical the moment it is removed from its natural

---

[31] J. Seifert, quoted in J. Ratzinger, *Truth and Tolerance*, p. 216, n. 11.
[32] J. Ratzinger, *Truth and Tolerance*, p. 183.

context, the moment it loses its relationship to its contrary concept."[33] Reason without faith or faith without reason both generate social pathologies. Their symbiotic relationship began to unwind in the period of late medieval scholasticism. It then came under heavy fire from Martin Luther and was finally "blown up" by Immanual Kant. Ratzinger follows the trajectory of Spaemann, Ratzinger's *Doktor Vater* Gottlieb Söhngen, Romano Guardini, Hans Urs von Balthasar, and Josef Pieper, among other German-speaking scholars of the twentieth century, in attending to the work of re-building the bridge that Kant thought he had destroyed. In particular, Ratzinger follows Josef Pieper's position that all philosophy that is worthy of the name is influenced by a sacred tradition. Pieper wrote:

> The very moment someone engaged in philosophizing ceased to take his bearing from sacred tradition, two things happen to him. First, he loses sight of his true subject, the real world and its structure of meaning, and instead talks about something entirely different, namely, philosophy and philosophers. Second, having forfeited his legitimate hold on the only authoritative tradition, he must illegitimately and (by the way) vainly seek support in the mere facts handed down, in randomly chosen historical "material."[34]

Ratzinger echoes Pieper when he argues that "there is no great philosophy that does not draw its life from listening to and accepting religious tradition. Wherever this relationship is cut off, then philosophical thinking withers and becomes a mere game of concepts."[35]

Conclusion

A doctoral dissertation is begging to be written on the reception of Wittgenstein's later work by British Catholic scholars and more specifically on the influence of the British tradition of analytical philosophy on British theology. For Ratzinger however, it may be said, in the Bavarian idiom, that philosophy as a mere game of concepts was "not his beer," and it is precisely a notion of philosophy as a game of concepts that would seem to be Ratzinger's understanding of where the philosophy of Wittgenstein leads. Although it is clear that Ratzinger is at least aware of some of Wittgenstein's later works, and of Anscombe's judgments on Wittgenstein, Ratzinger's

---

[33] R. Spaemann, "Nature," in D. C. Schindler and J. H. Schindler (ed. and trans.), *A Robert Spaemann Reader: Philosophical Essays on Nature, God and the Human Person* (Oxford: Oxford University Press, 2015), p. 30.
[34] J. Pieper, *Scholasticism: Personalities and Problems of Medieval Philosophy* (New York: McGraw-Hill, 1960), p. 126.
[35] J. Ratzinger, *Truth and Tolerance*, p. 252.

"Wittgenstein" is more the Wittgenstein of the Danube, of Positivist Vienna, rather than the Wittgenstein of the Cam and what his British Dominican friends made of Wittgenstein's later publications. However, Ratzinger would no doubt approve of the fact that Wittgenstein's friends in the British Dominican circle saw to it that their Austrian friend received the Last Rites from a Catholic priest and was buried according to Catholic Rites. This fact exemplifies Ratzinger's judgment that friendship is needed for the pursuit of truth. As St. John Paul II declared in §33 of his encyclical *Fides et ratio*: "It must not be forgotten that reason too needs to be sustained in all its searching by trusting dialogue and sincere friendship."

14

Martin Heidegger: Being and Time

Conor Sweeney

Introduction

In 1927, Martin Heidegger published words that would shape a generation. "The question of Being," he wrote in *Being and Time*, "has today been forgotten."[1] These words mark the beginning of Heidegger's ambitious project of rethinking Being as *Dasein* under the primacy of the dimension of time, transcending the classical tradition of metaphysics he calls "onto-theological." By 1962 the complete lineaments of his thinking of *Dasein* were in place, where questioning now realizes itself in "the place of stillness from which alone the possibility of the belonging together of Being and thinking, that is, presence and perceiving, can arise at all."[2] Arguably, this perspective finds its terminus in his famous *Der Spiegel* interview in 1966 a decade before his death where, in referring to the impotence of philosophy in face of the totalizing achievements of scientific rationality, he remarked cryptically that "Only a god can save us. The only possibility available to us," he continued, "is that by thinking and poetizing we prepare a readiness for the appearance of a god, or for the absence of a god in [our] decline, insofar as in view of the absent god we are in a state of decline."[3]

In 1974, two years prior to Heidegger's death, Joseph Ratzinger, then occupying a chair of dogma at the University of Regensburg, identified the

---

[1] M. Heidegger, *Being and Time* (New York: Harper & Row, 1962), p. 2.
[2] *Id.*, "The End of Philosophy and the Task of Thinking," in *On Time and Being* (New York: Harper & Row, 1972), pp. 55–73, at p. 58.
[3] *Id.*, "Only a God Can Save Us," in T. Sheehan (ed.), *Heidegger: The Man and the Thinker* (London: Routledge, 2017), p. 57.

relationship of Being and time as a central question of the age, referring to "the problem of the relationship of history and ontology, of the mediation of history in the realm of ontology...."[4] This "problem," which he does not hesitate to call the "fundamental crisis of our age,"[5] touches contemporary man in his existential roots in a particularly urgent way, forcing him to confront himself anew in his essential truth. "Is there," asked Ratzinger, "in the course of historical time, a recognizable identity of man with himself? Is there a human 'nature'? Is there a truth that *remains* true in every historical time because it *is* true?"[6] His response during his Regensburg years to our consciousness "of the distance—or indeed, the contradiction—... between our historical and our ontological nature"[7] took the form of a meticulous anthropological reconstruction of the grounds of Christian identity and universality by reference to the mediation of truth in time via tradition, in which the Church as *communio*, sacrament, and memory emerges as the source of the abiding truth of Christian faith.[8] But more fundamental than all of this in terms of a meaning that subsists in and across time has been Ratzinger's Chalcedonian belief in the realism of the Incarnation. Unlike Heidegger, whose "God" remains at best a perennial question mark, Ratzinger's is the God of Abraham, Isaac, and Jacob *who has truly and definitively given himself to man in history* in his Son Jesus Christ. History, then, for Ratzinger has become the place of salvation in the definitive self-disclosure of meaning in the Son who reveals and gives himself to be known in experience, encounter, and dialogue (cf. *Deus caritas est*, 1); above all, in the experience, encounter, and dialogue made possible by faith. God has appeared, not as *gnosis*, but as living historical presence, first through the embodied historical signs and types of the Old Covenant and then *definitively* in the incarnate and hypostatic *Logos*, so that to encounter and know God means the necessity of existing and experiencing the other *in* time. With Heidegger, then, Ratzinger agrees that time *is* of the essence, but precisely because God has given himself to be known in time through the incarnate Son. Being, therefore, has a necessarily "event"-like quality. The difference is that unlike Heidegger, Ratzinger believes that this event

---

[4] J. Ratzinger, *Principles of Catholic Theology* (San Francisco: Ignatius, 1987), p. 158. Tracey Rowland is one of very few Catholic scholars in the Anglosphere who have engaged with Ratzinger's interest in the relationship between history and ontology. Cf. T. Rowland, *Benedict XVI: A Guide for the Perplexed* (London: T&T Clark, 2010), pp. 93–113. An exception to this, at least in relation to Ratzinger's early writings, is J. L. Cong Quy, "Athens and Jerusalem: Christian Philosophy According to Ratzinger," *The Heythrop Journal* 56/6 (2015), pp. 948–57.
[5] J. Ratzinger, *Principles of Catholic Theology*, p. 160.
[6] *Ibid.*, p. 17.
[7] *Ibid.*, p. 153.
[8] Cf. *ibid.*, pp. 151–2. See C. Sweeney, "Sacraments-Sacramentality," in R. A. de Assunção, P. Blanco-Sarto, T. Rowland, and C. Schaller (eds.), *Joseph Ratzinger Dictionary* (San Francisco: Ignatius, forthcoming), for this theme.

has truly happened. "The Incarnation of the *Logos* brings eternity into time and time into eternity."[9]

The goal of this chapter is to expose the essential aspects of Ratzinger's engagement with the thought of Heidegger. It will trace the central references to Heidegger in Ratzinger's *oeuvre* which, as it happens, will take us on a tour of some of the central themes in Ratzinger's writing. Even if an honest assessment of the influence of Heidegger on Ratzinger must admit that not once (at least to my knowledge), does Ratzinger in his published works directly reference a *text* from Heidegger, a compelling case can nevertheless be made that the fundamental themes thrown up by the Marburg philosopher have preoccupied Ratzinger for his entire theological career, shaping his theological vision in distinctive ways. A remarkably unified vision emerges from Ratzinger's engagement with Heidegger: an existential approach to meaning that engages questions of belief, knowledge, conversion, and their conditions, and a multi-faceted engagement with the relationship between faith and reason set within the primacy of the mystery of a saving event that elevates reason to the end its questioning seeks after and that sets the individual on a pilgrim path of discipleship and communion wherein the highest truths of being are mediated via an experience, encounter, dialogue, and relation to the risen Lord in his divine and human countenance.

Belief, Conversion, and Decision

It appears that early on Ratzinger took some interest in the "existential" character of the approach embodied, not just in Heidegger, but also in Karl Jaspers. Ratzinger recalls how "Heidegger and Jaspers interested me a great deal, along with personalism as a whole"[10] while at the seminary in Freising between 1945 and 1947. By the time Ratzinger published *Introduction to Christianity* in 1968 perceptible, if subtle influences of an existential and phenomenological flavor from Heidegger are easily detected. For example, Joseph L. Cong Quy identifies a number of terms and phrases used by Ratzinger that can be said to be of generally Heideggerian provenance: *Daseinsort* (place of being), *Kehre* (Turn), *Wende des Seins* (Turn of being), and *Da-Sein* (Being-There).[11] The existential and phenomenological character of Ratzinger's thinking indicated here is particularly evident in how he treats belief and its essential conditions. Belief as a capacity to entrust oneself to something beyond the perceptible order can begin anew only via a "fundamental mode of behaviour toward being, toward existence, toward

---

[9] J. Ratzinger, *Principles of Catholic Theology*, p. 26.
[10] Id., *Salt of the Earth: Christianity and the Church at the End of the Millennium. An Interview with Peter Seewald* (San Francisco: Ignatius, 1997), p. 60.
[11] Cf. J. L. Cong Quy, "Athens and Jerusalem," p. 950.

one's sector of reality, and toward reality as a whole."[12] In other words, what Ratzinger seems to have been doing here in terms of illuminating the possibility of *faith* in an age that has forgotten and obscured the things of divinity is to cleave closely to a kind of phenomenological mode reminiscent of Heidegger as a preliminary to solving this problem. Heidegger's notion of "care" (*Sorge*) is perhaps implicit here, as is something analogous to Heidegger's notion of "releasement" (*Gelassenheit*), i.e., a deeper, reflexive mode of attunement and availability to Being by which something beyond the temporal order is able to manifest. Concerned with explaining the *credo* of Christian faith, it is precisely this initial stance of availability toward being in its givenness that then provokes what Ratzinger calls a "change of direction" without which "there can be no belief."[13] This Ratzinger describes with the Scriptural language of "turning back" and "con-version" as the necessary condition for man to open himself to the possibility of something beyond the visible. Belief in this sense is for Ratzinger always "a decision," a kind *existential stand in favour of mystery*, we could say, a "calling on the depths of existence, a decision that in every age demanded a turnabout by man that can only be achieved by the effort of will."[14] Significantly, Heidegger reappears some pages later when Ratzinger gives an account of the transition from the anthropological to the *theological* decision for belief. Ratzinger explains that the *credo* of faith "could here be literally translated by 'I hand myself over to' 'I assent to'." This "signifies an all-encompassing movement of human existence...."[15] And he again channels Heidegger to explain this process: "to use Heidegger's language, one could say that it signifies an 'about-turn' by the whole person that from then on constantly structures one's existence."[16]

Belief and Faith

Somewhat more critical perspectives begin to emerge in the context of Ratzinger's indication that belief requires the religious horizon of faith if it is to discover its true grandeur—although this should be interpreted not as *undermining* the approach just delineated but *expanding* it. However more significant divergences emerge here simply on the basis that Ratzinger believes strongly in the Incarnation and becomes critical of Heidegger only insofar as he could not take this path. In *Principles of Catholic Theology* he notes the limitations of remaining within the horizon of Being alone, taking

---

[12] J. Ratzinger, *Introduction to Christianity* (San Francisco: Ignatius, 2004), p. 50.
[13] *Ibid.*, p. 51.
[14] *Ibid.*, p. 52.
[15] *Ibid.*, p. 88.
[16] *Ibid.*

it as axiomatic that the dimension of faith corresponds to a mystery *outside* of man that compels him to respond in "obedience and faith" to the absolute: "It is not just the turning to oneself that saves," says Ratzinger, perhaps alluding to the Heideggerian idea of "authenticity" (*Eigentlichkeit*).[17] "Salvation comes not just from inwardness, for this inwardness can be rigid, tyrannical, egoistical, evil."[18] Rather, *authentic* authenticity involves entrusting oneself to an absolute Other. Therefore, it is the "turning away from oneself and toward the God who calls" that is most essential. "Man is oriented," Ratzinger explains, "not to the innermost depths of his own being, but to the God who comes to him from without, to the Thou who reveals himself to him and, in doing so, redeems him." It follows, then, that because Ratzinger believes in the event of Christ, he can also believe in a specific kind of "certainty" that comes with the gift of faith in Christ "working through love" (Gal 5:6), a certainty whose essential character consists, not in man's possession of the truth but in *truth's possession of man*, vitally grounded in the love of Christ given to man. Consequently, man can no longer adequately define his existence simply by waiting, thinking, or questioning, even within the aforementioned hermeneutics of "decision" for belief at an existential level. Engaging critically with Heidegger's notion of "thrownness" (*Geworfenheit*),[19] Ratzinger refers to how existence illuminated by Christ exposes an idea and a love that precedes and envelops me:

> He loved me first, before I myself could love at all. It was only because he knew me and loved me that I was made. So I was not thrown into the world by some operation of chance, as Heidegger says, and now have to do my best to swim around in this ocean of life, but I am preceded by a perception of me, an idea and a love of me. They are present in the ground of my being.[20]

If this is present as an ontological truth of my being, it can only be evoked and perceived in its fullness in the light of faith, which for Ratzinger cannot

---

[17] Cf. J. Ratzinger, *Principles of Catholic Theology*, p. 60. On other occasions, Ratzinger explicitly references Heidegger's idea of authenticity. "Modern philosophers have described this historical state of mankind in various ways, as for example when Martin Heidegger speaks of being reduced to the impersonal, of existing in 'inauthenticity'," *Id., Jesus of Nazareth: Holy Week: From the Entrance into Jerusalem to the Resurrection* (San Francisco: Ignatius, 2011), p. 101. See *Id., Relativism: The Central Problem for Faith Today. Address to the Presidents of the Doctrinal Commissions of the Bishops Conferences of Latin America*, Guadalajara, May 1996.

[18] *Id., Principles of Catholic Theology*, p. 60.

[19] "As something thrown," says Heidegger, "Dasein has been thrown *into existence*. It exists as an entity which has to be as it is and as it can be," *Being and Time*, p. 321.

[20] J. Ratzinger, *God and the World: Believing and Living in Our Time: A Conversation with Peter Seewald* (San Francisco: Ignatius, 2002), p. 26.

be partitioned off from what constitutes man's essential knowledge of himself. The belief that comes from faith "is certainty that God has shown himself and has opened up for us the view of truth itself."[21]

Faith as Tradition and Communion

If it is true that in the incarnate Son the triune God has truly given himself to man, then it is from here that belief must strike off on a distinctively *Christological* path well beyond Heidegger. The primacy of a Christological measure of belief—faith—is indicated in Ratzinger's claim that the path to God "does not lead by way of pure reflection but, rather, through encounter... is a way; it means discipleship ...."[22] Note again the emphasis that salvation cannot come through the mere fact of thinking and questioning or by means of a purely meditative stance in relation to Being. Correlative to the primacy of encounter and event in his thought, then, is his meticulous reconstruction of Christian identity vis-à-vis the baptismal *symbolon* as the answer to the problem of history and ontology. In baptism are the essential coordinates of a love that grounds and structures man's being across time, freeing him from the prison of an endless questioning that always risks slippage into rationalism and narcissism.[23] The sacrament of baptism capacitates a genuine act of belief (the *credo* of faith) in the triune God who in Jesus Christ has acted definitively for man in history. Baptism locates its recipient in the communion that is the *Church*, "the seat of all faith," the "*memoria Ecclesiae*,"[24] the "locus that gives unity to the content of faith" and that therefore mediates this faith across time.[25] This is that form of faith as a "way" and "discipleship" that immerses the disciple into the mystery of God as sons in the Son through baptism. What is being mediated above all in the faith guarded and treasured in the Church, then, is an embodied encounter with a person within real history and communion, an exchange and "fusion" of existences that finds its source and unity in the eucharistic liturgy.[26] In an essential way, then, faith as "tradition" and "communion" (and therefore, faith as Christocentric encounter, dialogue, and relation[27])

---

[21] *Id.*, "Faith and Theology," in *Pilgrim Fellowship of Faith: The Church as Communion* (San Francisco: Ignatius, 2005), p. 20.
[22] *Id.*, "Contemporary Man Facing the Question of God," in *Dogma and Preaching: Applying Christian Doctrine to Daily Life* (San Francisco: Ignatius, 2011), p. 87.
[23] Cf. Francis, *Encyclical Letter* Lumen fidei, paragraphs §§40–5 for a much later crystallization of Ratzinger's thinking here.
[24] Cf. J. Ratzinger, *Principles of Catholic Theology*, p. 23.
[25] Cf. *ibid.*, p. 24.
[26] Cf. Joseph Ratzinger, *Called to Communion: Understanding the Church Today* (San Francisco: Ignatius, 1996), pp. 36–40.
[27] Ratzinger's emphasis on faith's embodied and personal nature leads him to reject the "short formulas" of faith proposal of Karl Rahner who thought they could make Christian faith relevant again, cf. *Principles of Catholic Theology*, pp. 25–7, 122–30.

emerges as Ratzinger's response to the problem of history[28]; not just *any* tradition and community, of course, but the ecclesial and scriptural tradition and community that finds its life in the mystery of the Incarnate and hypostatic Son.

Pilgrimage as Answer to Onto-theology

Now, it is these strong claims in relation to faith that next need to be confronted, specifically, as regards their implications for any remaining validity of reason, whether on its own or within the hermeneutics of faith. For does not faith, a Heideggerian might ask, with its clear pretensions to totality indicated above, do violence to questioning as an act of entrusting oneself to mystery? Is not faith but a continuation of the drive to mastery that Heidegger identifies in the Greek spirit of metaphysics? Ratzinger is by no means dismissive of such questions. In a 2001 address Ratzinger attributes the following to both Heidegger and Jaspers: "They say: *Faith excludes philosophy, real research into and seeking for ultimate realities. For faith supposes it knows all that already.*"[29] Heidegger, in a kind of reversal of Kant's famous words, denies faith to make room for questioning. It is clear by any conventional measure that for Heidegger faith and reason must remain categorically separate, with absolute priority afforded to the latter: "The unconditional character of faith, and the problematic character of thinking, are two spheres separated by an abyss"[30]; "theology is a positive science, and as such, it absolutely different from philosophy."[31] Faith is properly itself for Heidegger only when it prescinds from purporting to answer the questioning that belongs to philosophy. For its part, philosophy is properly itself, as we have seen, as questioning—a kind of primary questioning that faith cannot purport to answer.

Ratzinger's response to this question begins with further clarification of the nature of faith. As he did in *Introduction to Christianity*, he reiterates faith now some thirty-three years later as "assent," "decision," and "taking one's stand, and standing firm, on what is hoped for" as a condition necessary to avoid being "eternally open, and keeping oneself open in all directions …."[32] But, drawing on St. Thomas' Augustinian approach to faith, as he sees it,

---

[28] Cf. *id.*, "Christocentrism in Preaching," in *Dogma and Preaching*, p. 53. The reader is encouraged to carefully follow the argument Ratzinger sustains in *Principles of Catholic Theology*, especially through chapters 1 and 2. I argue that fundamental structural conditions of his thinking as a whole can be found here.
[29] *Id.*, "Faith and Theology," p. 20.
[30] M. Heidegger, *What Is Called Thinking?* (New York: Harper & Row, 1968), p. 177.
[31] *Id.*, "Phenomenology and Theology," in W. McNeill (ed.), *Pathmarks* (Cambridge: Cambridge University Press, 1998), p. 44.
[32] J. Ratzinger, "Faith and Theology," p. 22.

he also critically distinguishes between the knowledge gained by faith and the knowledge gained by "science." In the latter, the "obviousness of the business forces us, by inner necessity, into assent." That is, the truth that belongs to science arrives at its conclusion by the logical self-evidence of premises.[33] By contrast, thinks Ratzinger, the act of assent that comes from *faith* is of a different nature. Here, knowledge is generated "not through the degree of evidence bringing the process of thought to its conclusion, but by an act of the will, in connection with which the thought process remains open and still under way." The "will," Ratzinger specifies, echoing Pascal, ought to be understood as something more akin to "the heart,"[34] a kind of affective organ of comprehension by which man is capacitated to consent to a different order of knowledge. What is different is that the knowledge generated by the will/heart belongs more to an inner order of intuition and dialogue, an *affective* appropriation of the real by a "sym-pathy with what is perceived." And this, thinks Ratzinger, terminates in something different than the stasis and instrumentality produced by scientific knowledge. Its effect is to draw the subject into a dialogue *with* rather than possession *of* the mystery encountered. It is to set man upon a "way" of knowing, a "pilgrimage of thought, which is still following the way."[35] Thus, the knowing proper to faith does not purport to *close* the questioning of reason, but rather to place it in a new context where the journey can continue anew. "Struggling and questioning thought remains present," he affirms, "which ever and again has to seek its light from that essential light which shines into the heart from the Word of God."[36]

Ratzinger seems to want to assure Heidegger that faith need not necessitate an *absolute* closure or inhibiting of questioning, that faith, in its inmost core, does not belong to a monolithic or a-historical mode of truth. The novelty of faith is not that it closes questioning, but that it sets the interlocutor into a condition of belief by which a *deeper* form of questioning can begin. It is at this point that Ratzinger highlights the historical character of God's speech to man, and here aspects of his theology of revelation are pertinent.[37] God's speech to man whereby he reveals himself through the light of faith does not consist only of doctrinal propositions or ecclesiastical structures—as if

---

[33] Like Heidegger, Ratzinger is keenly attuned to the dangers of instrumental-calculative thinking. Not surprisingly, then, he is sympathetic to Heidegger's distinction between "calculating and reflective thought," J. Ratzinger, *Introduction to Christianity*, p. 71. He notes that "the Freiburg philosopher has a good deal of justification for expressing the fear that in an age in which calculating thought is celebrating the most amazing triumphs man is nevertheless threatened, perhaps more than ever before, by thoughtlessness, by the flight from thought" (*Ibid.*).
[34] J. Ratzinger, "Faith and Theology," p. 23.
[35] *Ibid.*, p. 25. For this theme of faith as path see *id.*, "The Truth of Christianity?," in *Truth and Tolerance: Christian Belief and World Religions* (San Francisco: Ignatius, 2004), p. 145.
[36] *Ibid.*, p. 25.
[37] See *id.*, *The Theology of History in Bonaventure* (Chicago: Franciscan Herald, 1971); *id.*, *Milestones: Memoirs 1927–1977* (San Francisco: Ignatius, 1998), pp. 108–9.

they are not themselves the product of history and subject to the judgments of tradition. Rather, within the mystery of faith as pilgrimage, what is given to be known takes place within history and is thus always dialogical in character; a dialogue between the infinite and absolute God who speaks and the finite and limited creature who listens and responds, whether with or without faithfulness. Within *this* perspective, Ratzinger stresses the "never finished pilgrimage of faith towards Christ"—"the Word of God is always in advance of us and our thinking."[38] Faith opens a horizon of truth that is never finished, an exchange between God and man that no single era of faith can hope to complete. "History shows us that thinking along with the Word of God always has something new in store and never becomes boring, never pointless," thus: "Anyone who encounters the history of theology sees that the suspicions of Heidegger and Jaspers are unfounded. The preknowledge of faith does not oppress thought," rather, it "really challenges thought and sets it in a restless motion that produces results."[39]

Christian Philosophy

However, a slightly different emphasis can be observed in the reply to Heidegger and Jaspers formulated in the context of Ratzinger's related discussion in *The Nature and Mission of Theology*, first published in 1993. Here, Ratzinger attributes the following to Heidegger: "philosophy is by its very nature questioning. Whoever believes that he has the answer is no longer capable of philosophizing. Since the philosophical question is folly in the eyes of theology, Christian philosophy is a sham."[40] Quite possibly Ratzinger has in mind here (but does not cite!) Heidegger's well-known statement that "Christian philosophy" is a contradiction in terms: "Will Christian theology make up its mind one day to take seriously the word of the apostles and thus also the conception of philosophy as foolishness?"[41] Where in the preceding section we saw his assurance that faith need not foreclose mystery absolutely, here Ratzinger's rejoinder to Heidegger is twofold: first, reason is capable of more than just questioning, i.e., it has a genuine metaphysical capacity, but second, reason needs the stimulus and clarification supplied by faith if it is to discover the true depth of its metaphysical range. Regarding the latter, he begins by pointing out that the greatest expressions of philosophical thinking have always been vitally connected to a religious consciousness. "Since Plato," he argues, "philosophy has always thrived on critical dialogue with some great religious tradition."[42]

---

[38] Id., "Faith and Theology," p. 26.
[39] Ibid.
[40] Id., *The Nature and Mission of Theology* (San Francisco: Ignatius, 1995), p. 17.
[41] M. Heidegger, "The Way Back into the Ground of Metaphysics," in W. Kaufman (ed.), *Existentialism from Dostoevsky to Sartre* (New York: Meridian, 1975), p. 276.
[42] J. Ratzinger, *Nature and Mission of Theology*, p. 20.

In other words, as he puts it elsewhere, there is no such thing as pure reason. "In practice ... a pure rational evidential quality independent of history does not exist. Metaphysical and moral reason comes into action only in a historical context."[43] Philosophy's "own standing has always been bound to the status of the traditions which lie at the starting point of its struggle for truth. Whenever it discontinues such dialogue, it quickly dies out even as pure philosophy."[44] These are statements that belong to the social and cultural dynamics of tradition per se; but for Ratzinger it is above all else one that relates to the way *religion* shapes thinking. It is here that faith makes its return as that which is understood by Ratzinger to be the animating feature of the best kind of philosophical questioning. "Faith, as an historical instrument," as he puts it, "can set reason itself free again—reason can once more see properly for itself."[45] By contrast, an "autonomous reason that refuses to know about faith, to pull ourselves out of the slough of uncertainties by our own hair, so to speak, can hardly succeed in the end. For human reason is not autonomous at all."[46]

Salvation History and the Problem of Metaphysics

Next, however, Heidegger and Jaspers also spark Ratzinger's further specification that reason qua reason, when not held to artificial positivistic standards of purity and autonomy divorced from faith, remains capable of great things. Here his commitment to reason's *metaphysical* depth comes into view. In this mode, his answer is to claim that reason possesses a fullness and potential which cannot be foreclosed from the perspective of limitations necessarily imposed by its historical mediation. The context of this question, it should be made clear at the outset, has specifically theological implications beyond Heidegger, and Ratzinger's reference to his compatriot's reduction of reason to questioning is but a microcosm of his much larger project of addressing the twentieth-century theological debate surrounding the question of salvation vis-à-vis history, metaphysics, and eschatology. And so in *Nature and Mission* his reply to Heidegger builds gradually from an account of the specific anti-Hellenistic trajectory already to be found in the history of theology from Luther to Barth where reason

---

[43] *Id.*, "Truth, Values, Power: Touchstones of a Pluralistic Society," in *Faith and Politics: Selected Writings* (San Francisco: Ignatius, 2018), p. 147; "human reason is not autonomous at all. It is always living in one historical context or other," *id.*, "The New Questions that Arose in the Nineties," in *Truth and Tolerance: Christian Belief and World Religions* (San Francisco: Ignatius, 2004), p. 136.
[44] *Id.*, *Nature and Mission of Theology*, p. 20.
[45] *Id.*, "New Questions," p. 136.
[46] *Ibid.*

came to be conceived as "the self-expression of man who in ignorance of grace attempts to construct for himself his own wisdom and righteousness."[47] As he explains it elsewhere, by the twentieth century anti-Hellenism had become the problem of the age in the form of a fundamental questioning of Christianity's adoption of Greek philosophy.[48] In terms specific to debates within theology about questions of revelation and how God speaks to man in history Ratzinger describes the first (Protestant) phase of this debate in this way: "salvation-historical theology was introduced as the opposite of metaphysics or of theology from a metaphysical standpoint; salvation history and metaphysics were regarded as contradictory and their relationship as something to be studied."[49] One effect of this sharp contemporary turn against metaphysics in favor of a pure actualism of the event, recounts Ratzinger, was the reaction of Rudolph Bultmann who ended up transcending *both* event and ontology in favor of an emphasis on the word understood in existential and eschatological terms thus leading to a new "antithesis between salvation history and eschatology."[50] In various places, Ratzinger observes the influence on Bultmann by Heidegger in this regard.[51] Regarding Catholic approaches to the problem, Heidegger crops up very briefly in Ratzinger's characterization of early attempts by Catholic thinkers to affect a rapprochement between the more ontological theology approach of St. Thomas and the new emphasis on salvation history as an essential mode of theological truth. "The philosophical Thomistic interpretation," he writes in passing, "had very early sought to build a bridge from Thomas to Heidegger" by way of a Bultmannian eschatological-existential reduction.[52] In *Principles*, Ratzinger's response to both ontological and existential-eschatological approaches to God's creative action in history begins with his contention that *both* the Greek concept of God "as a pure and changeless being of whom, consequently, no action could be predicated" *and* the "purely existential version of the gospel message" where everything becomes narrowed down to a "for me" mentality are ultimately inadequate.[53] Instead, drawing on the Chalcedonian affirmation of the statement that Jesus is God, Ratzinger argues that the "is" is not just an "ontological statement" such that core of Christianity must then revolve around metaphysics, but rather that "the 'is' of Chalcedon includes an event: the Incarnation of God ...."

---

[47] Id., *Nature and Mission of Theology*, p. 19.
[48] Cf. id., *Principles of Catholic Theology*, p. 158.
[49] Ibid., pp. 172–3.
[50] Ibid., p. 179.
[51] See id., "Biblical Interpretation in Crisis," in R. J. Neuhaus (ed.), *Biblical Interpretation in Crisis: The Ratzinger Conference on Bible and Church* (Grand Rapids: Eerdmans, 1989).
[52] Cf. id., *Principles of Catholic Theology*, pp. 178–9.
[53] Cf. ibid., p. 185. See id., *Introduction to Christianity*, pp. 143–8 for the same theme.

The Greatness of Reason

Nevertheless, Ratzinger's clear theological decision in favor of a "preeminence of history over metaphysics" in that God "is not just one who is timeless but also one who is above time, whose existence is known to us only through his action"[54] should not be taken in the sense that it would for a Heideggerian. A footnote evidently added some time later in *Principles* indicates Ratzinger's desire to clarify that his emphasis on the historical "*prae* of God's action"[55] does not imply the "overcoming" of metaphysics, to employ language often used by those favorable to Heidegger's *destruktion* of metaphysics. Against this, Ratzinger alludes to the "irreplaceability and preeminence of the ontological aspect and, therefore, of metaphysics as the basis of any history."[56] Flagging the first article of the Creed, he adds that "Christian belief includes, theologically, the basic character of the ontological statements and the indispensability of the metaphysical, that is, of the Creator God who *is* before all becoming." With this, the final piece of the puzzle of Ratzinger's long-term engagement with Heideggerian themes comes fully into view with his strong affirmation of the essential contribution of the "Greek spirit" to both faith and reason. In certain respects this peaked in his Regensburg address in 2006, a kind of scholarly last will and testament in terms of his vision of faith and reason where, against all forms of nominalism, voluntarism, rationalism, and scientific reductions of reason, he affirmed that "biblical faith, in the Hellenistic period, encountered the best of Greek thought at a deep level, resulting in a mutual enrichment evident especially in the later wisdom literature."[57] Ratzinger unequivocally rejects anti-Hellenist attitudes that regard Greek philosophy as a merely relative historical inculturation, calling this interpretation "false," "coarse," and "lacking in precision." Against it, pointing out that the "New Testament was written in Greek and bears the imprint of the Greek spirit, which had already come to maturity as the Old Testament developed," he contends that "the fundamental decisions made about the relationship between faith and the use of human reason are part of the faith itself; they are developments consonant with the nature of faith itself." More concretely, writing three years prior to the Regensburg address, Ratzinger indicated how essential Greek philosophy is in terms of historical clarification of Christological and trinitarian doctrine. "The great fundamental decisions of the early councils," he says, "which were expressed in the creeds, do not bend the faith into a philosophical theory; rather, they give verbal expression to two essential,

---

[54] *Id., Principles of Catholic Theology*, p. 185.
[55] *Ibid.*, p. 186.
[56] *Ibid.*, p. 190, n. 172.
[57] Benedict XVI, *Faith, Reason and the University: Memories and Reflections. Lecture in the Meeting with the Representatives of Science*, Apostolic Journey to München, Altötting and Regensburg (September 9–14, 2006), Regensburg, September 12, 2006.

unchanging elements of the biblical faith."[58] They "assure the realism of the biblical faith" and so prevent a "merely symbolic or mythological interpretation" and they "assure the rational character of biblical faith which in fact goes beyond reason itself and any possible 'experiences' it may have yet nonetheless appeals to the reason and comes forward with the claim to be telling the truth—to be opening up access for man to the very heart of the truth." To illustrate this claim Ratzinger uses the example of the Nicene description of the Son as *homoousios* with the Father, which clarified that the "word 'Son' is not meant poetically or allegorically (or mythologically, symbolically), but quite realistically. That is what Jesus *is* in reality; that is not just what he is being called. The realism of biblical faith is being defended, that is all; the reality and seriousness of the event, of what happens, of what comes in from outside."[59] What remains so important about Greek philosophy for Ratzinger, then, is that it sought a truth that is more than appearance, opinion, or myth; it refers us, rather, to the possibility of an order of reality that transcends a mere temporality of Being and time.

To return finally to the claim in the text that began this conversation, we see his specific answer to Heidegger (and Jaspers) expressed in this way: "no one can exclude the question of metaphysics from philosophical inquiry, degrading it to a holdover from Hellenism. To cease asking about the origin and goal of the whole of reality is to leave out the characteristic element of philosophical questioning itself."[60] His reply accents the way philosophical questioning impels us to seek the truth of things; its grandeur lies not so much in its ability to *answer* the profound questions that it raises but in a questioning that awakens us urgently to the mystery of existence. And so questioning cannot dispense with this orientation to the absolute without narrowing its scope as in the example of the "exact" sciences.[61] A philosopher "can never rid himself of the goad of the question of God, which is the question regarding the origin and goal and being itself."[62] We cannot, continues Ratzinger, "begin to be silent about what we cannot speak of, for we thereby silence the characteristic dimension of our being."[63] Bringing his reflections to a close, he returns to the relationship of reason with faith, again holding up faith as the possibility of the true greatness of reason, that which prevents it from becoming mere "gnosis," but also affirming faith's need for philosophy: "faith needs philosophy because it needs man who questions and seeks. It is not questioning, in fact, which places obstacles to faith but that closure which no longer wants to question and holds truth to be unreachable or not worth striving for. Faith does not destroy philosophy, it champions it."[64]

---

[58] J. Ratzinger, "Variations on the Theme of Faith, Religion, and Culture," in *Truth and Tolerance*, pp. 92–3.
[59] *Ibid.*, p. 94.
[60] *Id.*, *Nature and Mission of Theology*, p. 21.
[61] Cf. *ibid.*, p. 28.
[62] *Ibid.*, p. 22.
[63] *Ibid.*, p. 28.
[64] *Ibid.*, p. 29.

Conclusion

In the end, Ratzinger's engagement with Heidegger is perhaps best framed by what remains for the former the definitive measure of the ontological and historical truth of man. For Ratzinger, "phenomenology and existential analysis, helpful as they are, cannot suffice for Christology. They do not reach deep enough, because they leave the realm of real 'being' untouched."[65] The same can be said for metaphysics qua metaphysics. "Real being," for Ratzinger—man who has come "to himself by moving out beyond himself"[66] in the path of belief, conversion, and reason through faith—is to be found in nothing else but the definitive historical "coinciding of man and God"[67] in Jesus Christ who, without "confusion, change, division, or separation," as Chalcedon expressed it, "is the one who has moved right out beyond himself and, *thus*, the man who has truly come to himself."[68] In *this* man is held all the tensions of Being and time, faith and reason, belief and conversion within the unmixed reciprocity of divine and human being united in the mystery of the Word made Flesh. This is why Ratzinger has said that "Chalcedon, the definitive ecclesial formulation of Jesus' Divine Sonship, is still, for preaching and piety as well, the pivotal truth that decides everything."[69] But, anxious to avoid a "certain parallelism of the two natures in Christ"[70] that he thinks remains if Chalcedon is not interpreted in a more "spiritual" way according to terms evoked by the Third Council of Constantinople, Ratzinger spoke in 1981 of the union of natures in Christ in terms of a "mutual indwelling" made possible in the conformity of Christ's *human* will with the will of the Father. In this definitive Scriptural moment—"Not what I will, but what though wilt" (Mk 14:36)—says Ratzinger, "Jesus' human will assimilates itself to the will of the Son. In doing this, he receives the Son's identity, i.e., the complete subordination of the I to the Thou, the self-giving and self-expropriation of the I to the Thou."[71] Expressed "from the other side," Ratzinger formulates it thus:

> the *Logos* so humbles himself that he adopts a man's will as his own and addresses the Father with the I of this human being; he transfers his own I to this man and thus transforms human speech into the eternal Word,

---

[65] Id., *Introduction to Christianity*, p. 228.
[66] *Ibid.*, p. 235.
[67] *Ibid.*, p. 226.
[68] *Ibid.*, p. 235.
[69] Id., "Christocentrism in Preaching?," p. 42. Cf. *id.*, "What Does Jesus Christ Mean to Me?," in *Dogma and Preaching*, p. 123.
[70] Id., *Behold the Pierced One: An Approach to a Spiritual Christology* (San Francisco: Ignatius, 1986), p. 37.
[71] Cf. *ibid.*, p. 41.

into his blessed 'Yes Father'. By imparting his own I, his own identity, to this human being, he liberates him, redeems him, makes him God.[72]

It is therefore in the mystery of this prayer, of the *Logos'* assuming of our human response, that *our* being and *our* time, *our* faith and *our* reason, *our* belief and *our* conversion, can find their resolution in the mystery of Christ's sublation of Being into divinity. Accusations of "onto-theology" ring remarkably hollow here, at least for the one who discovers prayer as the answer to existence.

What matters, then, for Ratzinger, is whether the temporality of Being, concretized anew in every act of human freedom, can hear and respond to the prayer of Christ. In 1977 Ratzinger very briefly referenced Heidegger's claim that "only a god can save us." Calling to mind Heidegger's statement that the only possibility left for humanity is "to prepare the way for the readiness to receive the appearing of the god," Ratzinger affirms what he calls this "genuine insight."[73] This "readiness to expect," he says, "is itself transforming. The world is different, depending on whether it awakens to this readiness or refuses it." However, indicating the terms of his departure from Heidegger's alertness to the question of being, Ratzinger continues: "Readiness, in its turn, is different, depending on whether it waits before a void or goes forth to meet the One whom it encounters in his signs such that, precisely amid the ruin of its own possibilities, it becomes certain of his closeness."[74] In the mystery of the Word made Flesh, in the taking up of humanity into divinity via the prayer of Jesus Christ, all questions of Being and time find their *denouement*: "The Incarnation of the *Logos* brings eternity into time and time into eternity."[75]

---

[72] *Ibid.*
[73] *Id., Eschatology: Death and Eternal Life* (Washington, DC: Catholic University of America Press, 1988), p. 201.
[74] *Ibid.*
[75] *Id., Feast of Faith*, p. 26.

15

Edith Stein: The Reasonableness of Faith

Mary Frances McKenna

Introduction

Faith is something reasonable in relation to something real, and it has been Benedict's life goal to defend the faith of the Church from whatever quarter, philosophical, theological, religious, ideological, or cultural, and to share that faith, that precious gift, with the world: ever renewing it among the faithful, explicating it for atheists and agnostics and offering it to those searching for meaning and truth. At the beginning of his work as a theologian this task is most readily seen in his effort to release Catholic theology from the suffocating grip of neo-Scholasticism. He wanted to open the path to an encounter, and a subsequent relationship with, the living person of Jesus Christ, two natures in one person. He was, as a result, labelled and indeed self-identified as a progressive.[1] In an official capacity that task commenced at Vatican II through his contributions as peritus, or advisor, to Cardinal Frings, a leader of the German delegation to the Council, at a time when the Rhine flowed into the Tiber. Specifically, this is seen in his work on *Dei verbum*.[2] At the close of his pontificate Benedict XVI initiated the Year of Faith (October 2012–November 2013) the purpose of which was to facilitate the rediscovery of the faith and the renewal of its transmission. Benedict XVI's statements during the Year of Faith are a summation of

---

[1] Cf. P. Seewald, *Benedict XVI: A Life. Volume One: Youth in Nazi Germany to the Second Vatican Council 1927–1965* (London: Bloomsbury, 2020), pp. 143, 162–3, 280, 286, 290, 310.
[2] Cf. *ibid.*, pp. 307–463.

what at times remained assumed in his theological and pastoral work. The implicit is made explicit in a non-exhaustive manner.

In an attempt to elucidate important aspects of Benedict's clarification on the nature of faith during the Year of Faith, I will consider them in relation to Edith Stein's work on faith. Given the importance Ratzinger saw in Stein's own work on faith and reason, it seems appropriate to consider Benedict XVI's work on faith in light of Stein's, particularly given the points of intersection of their lives. Both produced German translations of Aquinas' work at a time when they were only available in Latin. Ratzinger was prefect of the Congregation for the Doctrine of the Faith when Edith Stein was canonized in 1998 and then made a co-patron of Europe in 1999, and when *Fides et ratio* (1998) was promulgated by John Paul II which included her in a list modern thinker whose "courageous research" demonstrates the "fruitful relationship between philosophy and the word of God."[3]

In what follows I consider Benedict's statements and writings during the Year of Faith in conjunction with two articles of Stein's included in the volume *Faith and Knowledge*.[4] In particular I will draw on Benedict's apostolic letter initiating the Year of Faith, his catechesis on faith offered during the Wednesday audience talks of that year, and the encyclical, *Lumen fidei*, which was promulgated by Francis on the solemnity of St. Peter and St. Paul, June 29, 2013, the 62nd anniversary of Ratzinger's ordination to the priesthood. Francis acknowledged in the introduction that the encyclical was essentially the work of his predecessor Benedict XVI, stating that the encyclical is "meant to supplement what Benedict XVI had written in his encyclical letters on charity and hope" and that he, Francis, took up the near completed first draft and "added a few contributions of my own."[5] This corpus of statements on faith is systematic in that it is a single coherent body of work on the topic of faith, not that it is in any way exhaustive of his own thought on faith nor of the Church's.[6] The first of two articles

---

[3] John Paul II, *Encyclical Letter* Fides et ratio *on the Relationship between Faith and Reason*, §74.
[4] Cf. E. Stein, *Knowledge and Faith* (Washington, DC: ICS, 2000).
[5] Francis, *Encyclical Letter* Lumen fidei, June 29, 2013, §7. The encyclical was originally to be issued in October 2012 but Benedict felt it was not ready. "It did not yet have the feeling of an encyclical." January was considered for the publication of the revised encyclical, but Benedict again deferred it, feeling it was inappropriate to issue an encyclical shortly before a new pope was installed, cf. P. Seewald, *Benedict XVI: A Life. Volume Two: Professor and Prefect to Pope and Pope Emeritus 1966—The Present* (London: Bloomsbury, 2021), p. 508.
[6] Benedict XVI's thought on reason is outlined in a series of five addresses commencing with the 2006 Regensburg Address and concluding with his address to the Reichstag in 2011. In this series of addresses he challenges modernity to undertake two tasks. First to re-assess its assumptions on reason and to answer questions on rationality. Second to establish rational criteria for the reasonableness of reason, the ethical foundations of political decisions, and the legality of the law. For a consideration of this series of addresses see M. F. McKenna, "In Search of Justice and Peace: Benedict XVI's Questions to the Cultures and Religions of the World," *Religions* 13/10:910 (1990), pp. 1–18.

by Stein to be considered discusses the theme of faith in relation to the philosophy of Thomas Aquinas and Edmund Husserl. The second discusses the way of knowing God in relation to the symbolic theology of Dionysius the Areopagite. I will then highlight aspects of faith that emerge from their very different if parallel considerations of the subject. These principles both recommend themselves as a basis for a Theological Historical Method and point to how Benedict's and Stein's work on faith can continue to be further developed together to achieve their original goals.

By placing their biblical, philosophical, and theological perspectives on faith side by side, over layering them as it were, a kaleidoscope effect emerges illuminating the multiple dimensions of faith. In taking up Benedict's and Stein's work, one from a pope-theologian who regularly engaged the modern world, the other from a philosopher of modern philosophy (phenomenology) who latterly converted to Catholicism and entered religious life as a Carmelite nun, a plethora of avenues surface for further exploration of the nature of faith and the "inexhaustible riches of this mystery."[7] What we will find is complementary considerations in which Stein provides explicit philosophical foundations for Benedict's theological claims which bolster those claims vis-à-vis modern philosophies where God is largely absent. While Benedict provides biblical and theological foundations for Stein's marriage of medieval and modern philosophy which personalize the encounter that faith speaks to and concretize its expression in the witness and testimony of the figures of salvation history and the Church's Tradition.

Benedict XVI on Faith as the Door to Communion with God

The immediate context of Benedict's declaration of a Year of Faith is twofold. In his consideration of Christianity in relation to other cultures and religions, Ratzinger noted that the broadening of the concept religion to refer to humanity's relationship with the transcendent that has occurred in the latter half of modernity has caused confusion not least for Christianity itself.[8] Moreover, Christian faith while expressing itself via religion is not interchangeable with the concept of religion. In light of the changes that have occurred, arising from the dialogues between cultures and religions and the

---

[7] Francis, *Lumen fidei*, §36.
[8] See, for example, the articles included in *Habermas on Religion* which when discussing religion have Christianity in mind but generally fail to differentiate among the wide spectrum of understandings of God, truth, and religion itself and that some religions are based on revelation while others on mystical experience. Cf. C. Calhoun, E. Mendieta, and J. Vanantwerpen (eds.), *Habermas on Religion* (Cambridge: Polity, 2013).

developments within the philosophy of religions, Ratzinger argues that the concepts of faith and separately religion require renewed consideration to clarify the meaning of both identifying how each specifically relates to the other. Not all religions have faith and even where they do faith means different things to different religions. Ratzinger notes that Thomas Aquinas designated religion as a subdivision of the virtue of righteousness which is something other than the "infused virtue of faith." To facilitate a more thorough understanding of the theology of religions, and to avoid confusion arising from the interchangeable usage of these two concepts in dialogue among the cultures and religions of the world, Ratzinger called for the "precise clarification of the concepts of faith and religions."[9]

Those observations dovetailed with the crises he saw within Christianity itself, and biblical interpretation in particular. He argued that the historical critical method, central to modern approaches to biblical interpretation, mistook philosophy, a philosophy that a priori determined that the Gospel witness was not or could not be what happened, for history.[10] Such a philosophy sundered the historical Jesus from the Jesus of the Gospels, that of faith. But he asked in *Jesus of Nazareth* what could faith mean if it did not relate directly to the real historical Jesus. In contrast, based on his faith, Ratzinger trusts that the Gospels present us with the real historic Jesus.[11] What he saw was that the crisis in biblical interpretation was neither a crisis of philosophy nor of history but ultimately a crisis of faith, notwithstanding the real crisis that stalked those disciplines. Hence, the burning necessity felt by Benedict to address the crisis of faith through the Year of Faith.

Before considering Benedict's thought on faith, the question of how to understand Benedict's magisterial documents as against his own personal theological contribution must be considered. There are clear lines of continuity between Ratzinger the theology and the content of Benedict XVI's statements on faith as pope for the Year of Faith. In other publications during his pontificate, he clearly delineates them from the Church's teaching magisterium, specifically stating of his trilogy on *Jesus of Nazareth* that it is his own personal work and should be critiqued by scholars as such.[12] There is no such delineation here. A central thesis of Lieven Boeve and Gerard Mannion critique of Ratzinger is that the dividing lines are blurred between the theologian Joseph Ratzinger and the teaching charisms and authority of the Church in his role as perfect of the Congregation of the Doctrine of Faith, or indeed pope. Their implication is that Ratzinger's own theological perspective became inappropriately enmeshed in official statements of the

---

[9] J. Ratzinger, *Truth and Tolerance: Christian Belief and World Religions* (San Francisco: Ignatius, 2004), pp. 50–1.
[10] Cf. *id.*, *Biblical Interpretation in Crisis: On the Question of the Foundations and Approach of Exegesis Today* (Paper presented at New York, USA: St. Peter's Church, January 1988).
[11] Cf. J. Ratzinger, *Jesus of Nazareth* (London: Bloomsbury, 2007), pp. xi–xxiv.
[12] Cf. *ibid.*, pp. xxiii–xxiv.

magisterium.¹³ While this issue is not specific to Ratzinger as perfect of the Congregation of the Doctrine of Faith or as pope, as it relates directly to the papacy and the Church's teaching magisterium, it is entirely reasonable to ask whether Benedict's statements appropriately express what the Catholic Church means by the term "faith." And whether, while offering the clarity evidently required on faith, Benedict XVI did so without creating distortions in the Church's teachings from personal lines of thought misaligned to the Church's Tradition.

Ratzinger made clear statements on the role of the pope and the teaching authority of the magisterium both as a theologian and subsequently in his various official capacities. Those roles are first and foremost responsible for protecting the memory of the Church. The pope is not a political figure who can change aspects of the faith that the party who installed him want amended.¹⁴ On the other hand, while Revelation is definitively closed, the Church continually deepens its understanding of it through the Tradition of the Church: developments can occur such that they build upon what Tradition has already perceived.¹⁵ I have described this elsewhere as innovation within the Tradition.¹⁶ This brief reflection does not respond directly to Boeve and Mannion's criticism; however, it does set parameters for how an established theologian should operate when holding official Church positions.¹⁷ With regards to the topic at hand I will say a few words on that question at the end of this section.

The Year of Faith 2012–13

Benedict XVI's remedy for the crisis of faith he diagnosed is credible witnesses to the Lord who act as windows into the divine for those who seek for what is true and meaningful. To that end, he pronounced a Year of Faith, from October 11, 2012, to November 24, 2013, when the Church would dedicate itself to the rediscovery of faith and a renewal of its transmission. In what he referred to as the spiritual desertification of today's world, he sought to offer all people the *Porta Fidei*, the door of faith, through which one passes for communion with God. That communion is possible, "when the word of

---

¹³Cf. L. Boeve and G. Mannion, *The Ratzinger Reader* (London: T&T Clark, 2010), pp. 96, 147, 179–80, 187.
¹⁴Cf. J. Ratzinger, "The Primacy of the Pope and the Unity of the People of God," in *Church Ecumenism and Politics: New Endeavours in Ecclesiology* (San Francisco: Ignatius, 2008), pp. 36–50. Originally published in 1978 in German.
¹⁵Cf. *id.*, God and the World: Believing and Living in Our Time: A Conversation with Peter Seewald (San Francisco: Ignatius, 2000), p. 38; Id., *God's Word: Scripture, Tradition, Office* (San Francisco: Ignatius, 2008).
¹⁶Cf. M. F. McKenna, *Innovation within Tradition: Joseph Ratzinger and Reading of the Women of Scripture* (Minneapolis: Fortress Press, 2015).
¹⁷Cf. I address this issue in an upcoming article that discusses the topic of the Hermeneutic of Reform, specifically taking up Boeve's challenge on "which hermeneutics of reform?".

God is proclaimed and the heart allows itself to be shaped by transforming grace."[18] Benedict very consciously linked the Year of Faith to the 50th anniversary of the opening of Vatican II and the 20th anniversary of the Catechism of the Catholic Church, drawing extensively from both during the Year of Faith.[19] Describing Vatican II as "the great grace bestowed" on the Church in the twentieth century which he insists, when guided by the right hermeneutic, is a "sure compass" for the Church in the new century. Benedict positioned the Catechism as "an indispensable tool" for systematic knowledge of the content of the faith that is an essential resource for those who discover or rediscover the faith.

The Year of Faith was not in any way to be an abstract esoteric discussion on the theme of faith. To facilitate real engagement with faith, and in that way open real encounters with the Lord, the Congregation for the Doctrine of Faith, at Benedict's invitation, issued pastoral recommendations for the Year of Faith. Forty specific recommendations were outlined for living the grace of the Year of Faith with ten recommendations given to four specific groups: the Universal Church; the Episcopal Conferences; Dioceses; Parishes, Communities, and Movements. These initiatives centered upon engagement with the content of faith via the documents of Vatican II and the Catechism as well as through pilgrimages, conferences and ecumenical dialogues and intensification of the celebration of the Eucharist.[20]

Benedict's own specific pastoral initiatives, in addition to initiating the Year of Faith, were a catechesis on faith and the encyclical *Lumen fidei* which offers a broad and deep exhortation on faith, which at times directly responded to objections of philosophers such as Jean Jacques Rousseau, Frederick Nietzsche, Ludwig Wittgenstein.[21] These exhortations are based on the Catechism, which itself is based on the Creed, and the documents of Vatican II supported by references from the Old Testament, the Gospels, Acts, Letters, and Revelation, with a strong accent on Pauline texts and the Letter to the Hebrews. In the Year of Faith Benedict set out to explain what Christian faith is and what it means to say I believe, thereby outlining the concrete content of the essence of Christianity. In describing what faith is, Benedict sought to demystify it, demonstrating its reasonableness and pointing others toward that path so they may have the opportunity to journey along the way that transforms the whole of existence through

---

[18] Benedict XVI, *Apostolic letter* Porta fidei, October 11, 2011, §§5, 11. Also, see the full index for the year of faith: http://www.vatican.va/special/annus_fidei/index.
[19] Cf. *Lumen fidei* states it is in continuity with the Church's magisterium's pronouncements on faith specifically linking it to *Dei verbum* as Vatican II's statement on the theological virtue of faith, the Catechism and Vatican I's *Dei filius*. *Lumen fidei*, §7.
[20] Cf. W. Levada, *Note with Pastoral Recommendations for the Year of Faith*, January 6, 2012.
[21] Cf. Benedict XVI, *Homily for the Holy Mass opening the Year of Faith*, October 11, 2012; *Id.*, *Catechesis of the Holy Father During the Year of Faith*, October 17, 24, 31, 2012; November 7, 14, 21, 28, 2012; December 5, 12, 19, 2012; January 2, 9, 16, 23, 30, 2013; February 6, 13, 27, 2013.

communion with the God who is love. What Benedict bestowed is a rich elucidation of the content and practice of faith that builds upon and expresses in a manner understandable by contemporary society what the Church has already spoken on the nature of faith.

Faith as a Relational Act of Communion with the God Who Is Love

Immediately evident is the relational nature of faith, the relationship between the human being and God in conjunction with the wider relationship with all believers and God the Father, Son, and Holy Spirit. Those relationships, which form a communion, are historical, existing in the lives of people down through the ages. A number of key themes on faith emerge from Benedict's teaching on faith: faith is faith in a God who exists, who entered history and is present to us now. Faith is relational and the Person of Jesus Christ draws us into the communion of the we of the triune God, Father, Son, and Holy Spirit. The path of faith leads to knowing God who is a superabundance of sense, meaning, truth, and being. Faith has two dimensions, the historical and the visible which leads to the invisible. We are able to perceive the true nature of reality because being touched by God's love we are transformed into a new creature. Faith, through Scripture, provides the authentic grammar of the truth of the human being. I will detail these now.

Faith is an act of the person emanating from the heart in response to an encounter with God who reaches out to us. The act of faith is a Yes from the wholeness of the human being to the God who has self-revealed through the face of Jesus Christ. While faith is a supernatural gift, it is also a profoundly free act in which a person abandons themselves to the love of God who gives trust, hope, and certitude to life. In the person's Yes to God, which is an exodus from the enclosed I, the I entrusts itself to the You who loves me and whose love is indestructible and offers eternity. In entrusting oneself to God the gift of "profound meaning that sustains the world" is received, something that we cannot give to ourselves. Faith is the fruit of a relationship and dialogue. In listening, receiving, and responding to the Lord, the Lord draws me out of myself into communion with those who have walked the path of faith. Faith is not extraneous to life, nor is faith a private affair. Faith entails public testimony in which one publicly stands with the Lord. "Faith commits every one of us to become a living sign of the presence of the Risen Lord in the World." Moreover, faith without charity is fruitless. It is through faith that we can see in the marginalized a reflection of the face of the Lord.

The act of faith transforms existence and that conversion is an act of mind and heart. Faith in Jesus Christ, and the communion with God that it offers, in shaping one's entire existence renews human relationships. In being fully human, revealing who the human being truly is, Jesus shows the logic of love through which solidarity and brotherhood emerge. True humanity, Benedict states, is motivated by the love that comes from God.[22] Through the conversion of faith we come to know and meet God and, in that way, enter into the profound dynamics of the human being. The desire for God is innate in all human beings and the signs of that desire are everywhere, even if only implicit and expressed negatively. In experiencing love human beings are drawn out of themselves toward "the mystery that encompasses the whole of existence." Human beings, however, do need a pedagogy of desire, as Benedict puts it, to free desire so it can reach its "true height" through love.[23] Divine power is the force of love that cleanses evil by responding to evil with good. God, the Father Almighty, is the origin and creator of all things which means that reason, freedom, and love sustain the universe. There was no clash with evil forces at creation, neither did existence emerge from irrationality. It is sin that distorts and does so through the destruction of humanity's relationship with God through which all other relationships are likewise distorted. Only the Creator can heal that chain of broken relationships by becoming human.[24] The "unfathomable mystery" of the interweaving of holiness and sin should, Benedict insists, produce an ongoing conversion in the hearts of people of faith so as to continually experience the Father's mercy.

The Church is the subject of faith and faith is received from the Church through the sacraments.[25] One believes through the grace of the Holy Spirit in communion of the faithful. The "I believe" of the faith is both a personal profession and the profession of the Church, our mother. The "We believe" is the faith of the Church confessed by both bishops in council and by the liturgical assembly of believers. In faith our I is connected to the we of the Church that stretches through all the generations of the faithful. While faith is a theological virtue given by God, it is nonetheless the Church who transmits faith throughout history to enlighten every culture.[26] This interplay of I and we is a crucial aspect of the Church. The act of faith engages the whole person. Faith is not the result of reflection or thought. It is, however, an intellectual act that rejects fideism, the desire to believe against reason, on the one hand, and, on the other, a culture of feasibility that only accepts what can be verified. God is mystery not absurdity. God is light not darkness: we are blinded by the light of the divine and it is faith in God's self-Revelation that allows us to see God through the face of Jesus Christ.[27]

We can speak of God, according to Benedict, because God has first spoken to us in the history of salvation and in Scripture, and that means we

---

[22] Cf. *id.*, *General Audience*, October 17 and 24, 2012.
[23] Cf. *id.*, *General Audience*, November 7, 2012.
[24] Cf. *id.*, *General Audience*, January 30 and February 6, 2013.
[25] Cf. Francis, *Lumen fidei*, §§37–45.
[26] Cf. Benedict XVI *General Audience*, October 31, 2012.
[27] Cf. *id.*, *General Audience*, November 21, 2012.

must first listen. We can then enter dialogue with God and speak of God to others.[28] God's Revelation in history gradually unfolded in the history of a specific people, of Israel, and did so through God's deeds and promises which were fulfilled in Jesus Christ who gives meaning to the whole of human history.[29] Faith is to be understood through those "illuminous figures" of salvation history who have lived a life of faith.[30] Abraham and Mary, as well as Moses, are pre-eminent among them. Abraham and Mary's journey of faith, Benedict tells us, is the same journey as ours. In responding to God's call, they trusted even when that word was difficult to accept or misaligned to their wishes. God's choice of these illuminous figures is not to exclude; rather, they act as a bridge to all.

Abraham is the father of faith because he trusted in God's promise and presence. In hearing but not seeing God, Abraham's faith renounces the immediate possession that sight appears to offer and an embrace of that which reveals itself over time. Abraham's faith is an act of remembrance of God's promise for the future which places hope in God.[31] For her part, Mary became model and Mother of all believers because she placed her trust in the word of the messenger.[32] With Mary's Yes at the Annunciation she opened herself to God without reserve so that she lived from and in her relationship with God. Listening, pondering, and holding together what she hears, Mary enters a deep conversation with the Word of God. In mediating on and in holding together all the events she gives herself the opportunity to understand what God wants of her. In relation to Moses, God speaks to Moses and Moses acts as God's mediator telling others of the Lord's will. The role of mediator opened to Israel shared knowledge via the vision of another.[33] Faith is revealed through and linked to the concrete life-stories of particular people reflecting faith's essential relational nature: God is the God of persons, of Abraham, Isaac, Jacob, and Jesus Christ.

Knowledge of the Truth through Faith and Love

The encyclical *Lumen fidei* promulgated by Francis shortly after his election as pope, but in effect written by Benedict, speaks of faith as providing a trustworthy and sound foundation to stand upon against the vagaries of life. Recognizing that modernity views faith as an "illusionary light" distorting knowledge the encyclical, in contrast, states that faith is, in fact, a unique light capable of illuminating human existence and the depth of being. It

---

[28] Cf. *id.*, *General Audience*, November 28, 2012.
[29] Cf. *id.*, *General Audience*, December 5 and 12, 2012.
[30] Cf. *id.*, *General Audience*, January 16 and 23, 2013.
[31] Cf. Francis, *Lumen fidei*, §§8–11.
[32] Cf. Benedict XVI *General Audience*, December 19, 2012 and January 2, 2013; Francis, *Lumen fidei*, §§58–60.
[33] Cf. Francis, *Lumen fidei*, §14.

does so because that light comes not from us but from God. *Lumen fidei* considers Christian faith in relation to a wide gamut of themes explicating the meaning of faith. I will now briefly touch on two critical aspects highlighted. First, the intrinsic interconnection of Faith, Love, and Truth and second faith knowledge from hearing and seeing. Faith relates to truth because God as the Truth is history's origin and destination and explains the purpose and meaning of life for both individuals and society. Truth is "memory of something prior to ourselves."[34] Faith relates to Love because God has self-revealed God's self as love. Love needs truth to transcend the momentariness of life, giving it firm foundations over time, while love is a relational way of seeing and offering shared knowledge of the truth. Faith then is faith in the God who is Love and who is the Truth meaning faith, love, and truth are intrinsically linked. It is love of God who is the Truth that sets us free.

In being touched by the love of God the human being is transformed into a new creature with new vision who can see more dimensions of reality than sight alone offers. By conforming to Jesus Christ we "receive the eyes needed to see him."[35] In that way, faith offers new criteria for understanding which transcends knowing in favor of seeing from the heart "which is the authentic sacred space."[36] In the Bible it is the heart where "all dimensions intersect." Faith then provides knowledge because love is a way of seeing in the way Jesus sees which illuminates what is true and real. Faith's understanding emerges from love which gives certainty and which unifies. Importantly, faith knowledge is not simply an inward knowledge but is a knowledge arising from the contemplation of Jesus' life and his continuing presence. "For the light of love is born when our hearts are touched and we open ourselves to the interior presence of the beloved, who enables us to recognise his mystery."[37] That faith knowledge relates to the "entire history of the created world" and is open to all.[38] Those who seek the true and the good draw near to God like the Magi whose journey toward the star is directed by God.[39]

Faith knowledge arises from a combination of hearing God's words and Word and seeing God's signs as most manifestly shown in John's Gospel. In hearing and seeing the believer follows Jesus Christ and that leads to deeper vision. In Greek philosophy seeing or sight, the encyclical notes, was associated with ascertaining a comprehensive understanding of reality. Sight provides a view of the whole arising from its parts. In Scripture hearing the words and Word of God occurs over time and the encyclical notes that

---

[34] *Ibid.*, §24.
[35] *Ibid.*, §31.
[36] *Ibid.*, §§7, 10.
[37] *Ibid.*, §31.
[38] Cf. *ibid.*, §28, 30.
[39] Cf. *ibid.*, §35.

the assimilation of those words is a journey of discipleship. Faith does not impart knowledge and understanding that is immediately apprehended. That discipleship is a personal vocation necessitating obedience. The Old Testament, the encyclical states, combines both hearing and seeing which prepared for the dialogue with Greek culture with its desire for truth: "God's words are accompanied by a desire to see God's face." In Jesus Christ a synthesis of the two occurs such that faith knowledge emerges from contemplating and gazing at Jesus Christ.[40] Faith opens dimensions otherwise closed and is required by theology if it is to truly consider what God has spoken about God's self. "Right faith orientates reason to open itself to the light which comes from God so that reason, guided by love of the truth, can come to a deeper knowledge of God."[41] Notwithstanding the very specific nature of faith, faith is for all, for in speaking of the truth faith is a common good. In "immersing themselves in the circle of Christ's light" the more capable one becomes "of understanding and accompanying the path of every man and woman."[42]

There is a strong Augustinian assent to *Lumen fidei* reflective of the influence of Augustine on Ratzinger/Benedict. He consigned his first encyclical *Caritas Deus Est* to the Church and the world before Augustine's tomb in Pavia and stated that his second encyclical *Spe salvi* (in hope we are saved Rom 8:24) was largely indebted to him and his encounter with the God of Jesus Christ who is truth and love.[43] *Lumen fidei* again underscores the Pauline-Augustinian nature of that influence rather than the neo-Platonic-Augustinianism that others have claimed and critiqued.[44] *Lumen fidei* notes that Augustine was aware of neo-Platonism's symbolism of God's light descending from above illuminating all reality. It was this symbolism, the encyclical notes, that "liberated" him from Manichaeism enabling him to acknowledge sin and so turn to good. This path prepared the way for his "hearing" the words in the garden of Milan telling him to "take up and read" that was the decisive moment of his conversion. From reading Romans chapter 13 Augustine was to integrate the sight of Greek philosophy with the hearing of the God who speaks and makes himself known to us personally.[45] Benedict, as student Ratzinger in early 1946, was assigned the translation of Thomas Aquinas' work on Love, which to that point had only been available in Latin. It was through this work that he first came into contact with Stein's work, a translation of Aquinas' *On Truth*.

---

[40] Cf. *ibid.*, §§29–31, 57.
[41] *Ibid.*, §36.
[42] *Ibid.*, §§35, 50–7.
[43] Cf. Benedict XVI, *General Audience*, February 27, 2008.
[44] Cf. J. Corkery, *Joseph Ratzinger's Theological Ideas* (Dublin: Dominican Press, 2009); T. P. Rausch, *Pope Benedict XVI: An Introduction to His Theological Vision* (New York: Paulist Press, 2009). Also see McKenna, *Innovation within Tradition*, pp. 12–29, 50–5.
[45] Cf. Francis, *Lumen fidei*, §33.

The outcome was a hundred page translation through which Benedict the student experienced Aquinas' thought with its "crystal logic" to be "too tightly closed in upon itself, too impersonal, somewhat lifeless, static—too ready made and lacking in dynamism." We see here the theologian as against a philosopher and he quickly gravitated to Augustine and Bonaventure and the theme of the person of Jesus Christ, God's self-Revelation to humanity.[46] Nonetheless, whether as a theologian or Church leader, he regularly drew on Thomas' resources when explicating the faith and tradition of the Church. *Lumen fidei* explicating its theme refers to Thomas' description of the apostles' faith as "a faith which sees."[47]

Person: Relationship without Reserve

Underpinning Benedict's description of faith is the theological notion of person, relationship without reserve, he articulated in an article published in German in 1973.[48] The article was published in English in 1990 with a cluster of other papers which mutually inform each other and describe the theological understanding of the human being: the human being is a creature under the gaze of the Creator and the human being fulfils their potential when they actualize their person by transcending their human nature and living in relatedness without reserve with God. Mary exemplifies this notion of person.[49] In that article Benedict, as a professor in Regensburg, argues that Jesus lacks nothing in having one divine person. There is nothing missing in his humanity and person, as understood through the triune God, is fully applicable to the human being through Christ.[50] It is in faith that we not only see the divine person of Jesus Christ, but also, through our relationship without reserve with God, that we actualize in our lives, and in that way, reach toward the full potential of the human being. Ratzinger's description points towards that state as being two natures in one person. We participate in the divine, in the body of Christ through our relationship with Jesus in faith, being gathered up into the we of the Church and, hence, the we of the Father, Son, and Holy Spirit. Benedict, as professor Ratzinger, noted that this notion of person

---

[46] Cf. P. Seewald, *Benedict XVI: A Life. Volume One*, pp. 164–6.
[47] Francis, *Lumen fidei*, §31.
[48] Cf. J. Ratzinger, "Concerning the Notion of Person in Theology," *Communio* 17/3 (1990), pp. 439–54. Originally published in German as "Zum Personenversthdnis in der Theologie," in *Dogma und Verkündigung* (Munich: Erich Wewel, 1973), pp. 205–23.
[49] Cf. J. Ratzinger, "Man between Reproduction and Creation: Theological Questions on the Origin of Human Life," *Communio* 16 (1989), pp. 197–211; *Id.*, "'You are full of grace': Elements of Biblical Devotion to Mary," *Communio* 16 /1 (1989), pp. 54–68.
[50] Cf. *id.*, "Notion of Person in Theology," p. 445. Ratzinger made it clear that this phenomenon of complete relativity "is realised in its entirety only in the one who is God" but through Christ that phenomenon denoted by person is fully applicable to the human being through Christ. "There is a transition from the doctrine of God into Christology and into anthropology."

that denotes relation transitioned antiquity from Platonism to faith and identified a third fundamental category to the Greek categories of substance and accident, that of the personal phenomenon of complete relativity.[51] This third category of relation supplements existing philosophical thought offering additional avenues for humanity to access and perceive reality.

This returns us to the open question of blurring lines between Ratzinger the theologian and Ratzinger as consequential Church leader. Here we see the relational emphasis of Ratzinger's theological perspective informing his articulation of the nature of faith as Benedict XVI. That notion of person takes up and develops the Church's Tradition on person in God and humanity by adding important insights setting the trajectory of considerations on the humanity of Jesus, and hence humanity itself. Indeed, to truly understand Ratzinger the theologian one should start with his understanding of person and its infusion into every aspect of his theology and wider thinking. What Benedict did through his articulation of faith was to open a window into the divine. This is not the window into the divine but a window, and just as the Father has many rooms in His house there must be many more windows. So long as we are united to the Father through the Son in the Holy Spirit the unity that enables true diversity to exist is provided firm foundations and is anchored in the truth of the God who is love.

Edith Stein on Faith and Knowledge

Stein's philosophical thinking was formed and matured under Edmund Husserl. First as a doctoral student who was to undertake a work on the critical theme for phenomenology of empathy, and then as his research assistant, playing an important role in editing his papers in preparation for the publication of *Ideas* II and III.[52] Even though Stein was to eventually resign that position in frustration at Husserl's lack of engagement on critical issues she raised in relation to that work, her influence on the final manuscript was latterly seen to have been significant.[53] Unable to find a supervisor, Stein never completed her habilitation. Her philosophical thought was subsequently developed through the attention she paid to Thomas Aquinas. These two ways of thinking, the modern and medieval, were the tools with which Stein explored the "great questions of being," even though from her own perspective "an inner clash" between them was "inevitable."[54] Mette Lebech argues that Stein understood phenomenology, the description and discussion of experience

---

[51] Cf. *id.*, *Introduction to Christianity* (San Francisco: Ignatius, 2004), p. 160, 180–4; *Id.*, "Notion of Person in Theology," pp. 444–5.
[52] Cf. E. Stein, *On the Problem of Empathy* (Washington, DC: ICS, 1989).
[53] Cf. *id.*, *Life in a Jewish Family 1891–1916* (Washington, DC: ICS, 1986).
[54] Cf. *id.*, "Sketch of a Forward to Finite and Eternal Being," in *Knowledge and Faith* (Washington, DC: ICS, 2000), p. 81. Sketch date dated 1935.

as it is experienced, as the center of philosophy. Metaphysics was integral to that approach from the beginning "since it is the meaning of being that is the theme of Stein's metaphysics."[55] Importantly, Stein retained her phenomenological approach to philosophy throughout her life with the reconciliation of phenomenological and metaphysical thought being the core concern of her later thought. In addition, Stein was to come to understand that Christian faith was required if phenomenology was to attain its goal, "a view of the existing world in its entirety."[56]

Alasdair MacIntyre, in *Edith Stein: A Philosophical Prologue 1913–1922*, maintains that Stein's overall body of work is a single philosophical and theological enterprise which sought to answer two questions: "How is the finitude, the temporality and the particularity of human existence to be understood? And can it be understood except by its contrast with and its relationship to infinite and eternal being?"[57] This juxta positioning of the finite with the infinite and eternal in Stein's work reflects her encounter with an "otherworldly power." Stein's post-doctoral dissertation, "Individual and Community" (1919), a work produced prior to her 1922 conversion to Catholicism from post-Judaic atheism, concludes with a reflection on the inner sphere of the soul. Stein asserts that the soul is beyond our powers to affect and that when it is affected it is not by our own actions. "If a change enters into this sphere, then it's not the occurrence of a 'development', but rather is to be regarded as a transformation through an 'otherworldly' power, that is, a power situated outside of the person and outside of all of the natural connections in which she is entangled."[58]

Stein's family were observant Jews living in Breslau, East Germany, who ran a lumber business. Edith, the youngest of eleven children, was born in 1891 on Yom Kipper, the Day of Atonement, the holiest day of the Hebrew calendar. Her father died when she was a young child forcing her mother, with a large young family, to manage, and manage successfully, the family business. Auguste Stein was devout but did not force that observance upon her children and the young children, at that time, were not personally committed to it. By age fifteen, Edith had lost her childhood faith making a deliberate and conscious decision to stop praying. At that time, she also withdrew from the guidance of her family becoming "an independent person," as she described it, concerned with ideological questions not considered at school. Stein, however, does note that her mother's faith had

---

[55] M. Lebech, *The Philosophy of Edith Stein from Philosophy to Metaphysics* (Bern: Peter Lang, 2015), pp. xiii, 179.
[56] *Ibid.*, pp. 1, 12, 1–26.
[57] A. MacIntyre, *Edith Stein: A Philosophical Prologue 1913–1922* (New York: Rowman & Littlefield, 2006), p. 185. This work is part of MacIntyre's overall contribution to the development of the Catholic Philosophical tradition in response to *Fides et ratio* (1988).
[58] E. Stein, "Individual and Community," in *Philosophy of Psychology and the Humanities* (Washington, DC: ICS, 2000), p. 233.

subconsciously become deeply engrained within her, recalling the influence of her mother's maxims which were infused with her strong faith when writing about her struggle, at the commencement of her PhD studies, to attain clarity on the "question at hand" for phenomenology. That question she determined to be the question of empathy: "As one strives, so will God help."[59]

The reflection above on the "otherworldly power" indicates the deep waters running through her life even when she had consciously separated herself from God and is to be understood as a prelude that provides some explanation for her conversion to Catholicism. It also reflects the open questions and dissatisfaction with the answers offered by modern philosophy that were a prelude to reading St. Teresa of Ávila's autobiography in the summer of 1921 which was the immediate tangible spark of her conversion. Stein's later work, including the two articles to be considered presently, sought to incorporate and describe that fullness of reality into philosophical, both modern and medieval, and theological discourse. The first of the two articles considered is a philosophical text entitled, "Husserl and Aquinas: A Comparison."[60] It was written in the late 1920s, after her conversion to Catholicism but before entering the Carmelite convent in Cologne, being published in the 1929 Festschrift, edited by Martin Heidegger, for Edmund Husserl's seventieth birthday. The second article is a theological text entitled, "Ways to Know God: The 'Symbolic Theology' of Dionysius the Areopagite and Its Objective Presuppositions."[61] It was written between 1940 and 1941 when Stein was a professed Carmelite nun and published after her death in *The Thomist*, July 1946. Over ten years separate the two articles, and, while they tackle different aspects of faith, faith vis-à-vis natural reason and knowledge, and faith vis-a-vis knowledge of God, there is continuity within her thought.

The Extent of Natural and Supernatural Reason and Philosophy

In her comparison of Husserl's and Thomas' thought on reason, Stein's aim was to achieve a Thomist (Scholastic) "rapprochement with moderns."[62] She finds both significant points of confluence and critical points of divergence which reflect those between Medieval Scholasticism and modern philosophy. This comparison is, in part, Stein's response to the limitations

---

[59] *Id., Life in a Jewish Family 1891–1916*, pp. 138, 148, 277, 441.

[60] Cf. *id.*, "Husserl and Aquinas: A Comparison," in *Knowledge and Faith* (Washington, DC: ICS, 2000), pp. 1–38.

[61] Cf. *id.*, "Ways to Know God: The 'Symbolic Theology' of Dionysius the Areopagite and Its Objective Presuppositions," in *Knowledge and Faith* (Washington, DC: ICS, 2000), pp. 86–9.

[62] E. Stein, "Husserl and Aquinas: A Comparison," p. 20.

she found in Husserl and phenomenology. In Thomas, whom Stein refers to as the Master, she found a teacher who showed her important additional layers of philosophy that could be taken up without the need to jettison phenomenology.[63] The spirit of *philosophia perennis* is, for Stein, the inner need to search out the *logos*, mind, reason of this world, its *ratio* as Thomas termed it. While both Thomas and Husserl followed in this tradition they differed as to the extent that human reason can achieve the goal of *ratio*. For Thomas, *ratio* had two components, natural and supernatural reason. For Husserl reason lay beyond such empirical distinctions and was reason as such. Stein expressed Husserl's understanding of reason as "what must be the case—notwithstanding any empirical distinctions—wherever reason is meaningfully discussed."[64] In this undifferentiated reason Stein sees problems in that phenomenology proceeds as if human natural reason has no limits in principle. Its goal and regulative idea are full truth, even if it acknowledges that its task is endless and knowledge is an unending process.

Husserl's approach, for Stein, fails to adequately deal with the need for reason to set its own limits and to acknowledge the process for doing so. Thomas, Stein noted, understood Husserl's approach to be that of natural reason. Full truth for Thomas is divine knowledge which is endless, infinite, and fullness at rest. This means there are two ways to knowledge, the way of natural reason and separately the way of faith. For Thomas, faith, Stein states, is not as it is for Husserl, a "specific philosophical issue" that is reflected upon and critiqued. Faith marks the boundaries of natural reason. Faith is the Archimedean fulcrum that allows us to get outside of natural reason to see its limits.[65] In that way, there is a body of truths accessible through natural reason, and supernatural reason assesses these truths to keep it from error, while also supplementing natural reason. Equally, natural reason has the task of analyzing the truths of faith, and, of implementing, or utilizing, those truths.

Faith, for Stein, is a way to truth and truths, and, on this earthly journey faith provides a certainty to knowledge that is unsurpassed, even if Stein acknowledged that certainty "lacks the obviousness of insight." As a result, Stein argues philosophy has two dependences upon faith. These dependencies arise because philosophy aspires to truths to the greatest possible extent and to the greatest possible certainty. If faith makes truth and truths accessible which otherwise would be unavailable, philosophy, with its universal claim to truth, cannot disregard that truth. If it does it risks falsehoods entering into the body of knowledge given the organic interconnectivity of all truth; anything cut off from the whole of truth could "appear in a false light." As a consequence, Stein asserted the material dependence of philosophy on faith. She also asserts a formal dependence of philosophy on faith arising from philosophy's claim to "bestow the highest certainty." Faith bestows

---

[63] MacIntyre questions the accuracy of Stein's interpretation of Aquinas here. If this is the case then it makes Stein's discussion all the more her own.
[64] *Ibid.*, p. 10.
[65] Cf. *ibid.*, p. 16.

that highest certainty and therefore philosophy must "make the certainty of faith its own." It does so by absorbing the truths of faith and using them as a final criterion to gauge truth. The criterion of faith, according to Stein, is faith itself. Faith is a gift of grace which relativizes all other certainty such that "supposed knowledge which contradicts faith" can be "given up." The consequence of these dependencies, from Stein's perspective, is the construction of philosophy based on faith.[66]

Stein readily admits that faith as a starting point for philosophy is radically different to that of much modern philosophy which excludes faith and utilizes natural reason alone. As against that Stein draws attention to the fact that a philosopher who starts out upon the ground of faith, unlike the modern philosopher, "*has* from the outset the absolute certainty he needs to build a sound edifice; others must first search for some such starting point."[67] The result of such searching for a solid starting point, Stein contends, is that in the modern era the critique of knowledge has become the fundamental area of consideration. This is seen in Husserl's effort to identify an absolute reliable method, to find a "knowledge that would be absolutely one with its object and hence safe from all doubt."[68] The issue here again, for Stein, is that such a goal from the Thomist perspective is unattainable. It is so because such an idea of knowledge is God's knowledge where being and knowing are one; knowledge for human beings is fragmentary where being and knowing are separate.

Thomas and Husserl start from the premise that objective existence is separate to the human being seeking or knowing; however, they depart from each other Stein notes on first truth and first philosophy. God, for Thomas, is first Truth and hence the principal criterion of all truth. From God proceeds any truth we hold, as a result, philosophy "must make God as its object" and establish not only the relationship between God and all that exists, but also the relationship of divine knowledge to the knowledge of other knowing beings. The theory of knowledge, which modern philosophy places as the outset to justify its approach, is for Thomas part of the general theory of being and all questions ultimately are questions of being and hence philosophy is part of a great ontology or metaphysics. As Stein puts it,

> God imparts to every being what it is and the manner of its being {*Wesen*}, its essence and existence, but he also imparts to it, in accordance with its essence and existence, the extent and manner of its knowing and striving, the truth and perfection which it can attain. In this way logic, knowledge theory, and ethics, as far as their material content is concerned, are contained within ontology.[69]

---

[66] Cf. *ibid.*, pp. 17–22.
[67] *Ibid.*, p. 22.
[68] *Ibid.*, pp. 23–4.
[69] *Ibid.*, p. 30. Stein does note that logic, knowledge theory, and ethics "may also be constructed in another way, given a normative turn, as disciplines in their own right."

Stein maintains that it is this ontological difference that delineates Thomas' and Husserl's basic positions. Husserl's positing of the subject as the starting point and center of all philosophical inquiry in his attempt to address the problems of phenomenology meant, as Stein saw it, that reality is subject related, even though, Husserl had commenced his considerations looking for a "truth and reality free from any relatedness to the subject."[70] The intellectual search for truth, where existence is self-identifying for consciousness, as Stein puts it, will never be at rest. Such an approach relativizes God and contradicts faith. Consequently, she diagnoses that the orientation of Catholic philosophy is theocentric while that of phenomenology is egocentric.

In considering Stein's comparison of Thomas and Husserl four observations can be made. First is that Scholasticism continued in two forms. It continued as a strand within modern philosophy with one important omission, that of God, while also continuing in its Catholic form where God is included. Reason in the first paradigm relates to or encompasses what had previously been separated between natural reason and supernatural reason, while Scholasticism reserved full knowledge, knowing and being as one, to God alone. The first paradigm no longer acknowledges this distinction yet still that fullness of knowledge is sought and claimed for reason. Second, and in reference to the first observation, is that the fragmentary nature of human knowledge, whether that knowledge is philosophical, scientific, or theological, sits in contrast to the fullness of knowledge that is God's in whom knowing and being are one. Third is that the interlinked nature of faith, truth, and certainty means that faith holds a place in the discussion of truth and certainty at the very least within theology, but also in philosophy where truth and certainty are sought. Where truth and certainty have been abandoned by philosophy, there is no place for God or faith. Yet where truth has been abandoned the question can be asked as to what exactly is the purpose, goal, and meaning of that philosophy? Fourth, reason is *rational* and not blind sequence and that rationality of reason emanates from the God of faith.

Fides as Acceptance and Retention of Revealed Truth: Dionysius the Areopagite's Symbolic Theology

We turn now from a philosophical consideration of faith to a theological consideration of faith vis-à-vis knowledge of God and the knowledge of God Scripture imparts. In her consideration of Dionysius the Areopagite's thought on knowing God and "symbolic theology," Stein identifies a hierarchy in the Areopagite's thought regarding the order of being and order of knowing in relation to the "dazzling brilliance" and the "unapproachable

---

[70] *Ibid.*, p. 32.

light veiling Primal Be-ing." Creatures closest to God can grasp a ray of this light and these pure spirits who are enlightened by this light pass knowledge of it to the lower orders, including created spirits, angels, and human beings so that knowing God and witnessing to God go together. Theology, for the Areopagite, is Holy Scripture, not systematics or doctrine, while theologians are the sacred authors of Holy Scripture, not scholars, and the various theologies are different ways or manners of knowing, or not knowing, God.

The higher the knowledge of God the darker and more mysterious it is impacting our ability to express it such that this higher knowledge leads to silence. Lower levels of knowledge of God are more suited to words. The two ways human beings can speak of God are negative and positive theology.[71] The first is a negation procedure in which God is described through what God is not. The second, positive theology, God is described by what is closest to him, such as life and goodness. Negative and positive theology are not opposed to each other but complement each other's ascent: The parallelisms of being between Creator and creature sit beside the greater dissimilarities. The ascent through negative and positive theology leads to the summit which is mystical theology where God reveals both his mysteries and the sense of their inscrutability. At this point one "in utter stillness enters into union with the Ineffable."[72]

The lowest level of positive theology is symbolic theology. Symbolic theology relates to sense perception and is the use of "image language" as the Areopagite terms it. The image points to God as its figure. Symbolic theology uses image language to communicate what is unknown and unfamiliar through known and familiar images of the natural world. God's symbolic theology is the whole of creation. Names of sensible things are transferred to the divine to make God's self accessible to human beings. Images come in two categories. The first is "as revealed" through which God directly self-Reveals God's self and second, as inspired, through which God moves the sacred authors, or theologians as the Areopagite refers to them, to take up an image.[73] The meaning imparted in Scripture by image language is not something that is immediately beheld. Rather, "God's revealing light" is found by those striving for holiness and with spiritual sensitivity. Image language points to a higher spiritual level through the initial sense perception. A journey that commences with sense perception of image language ends at a point beyond the realm of sense perception. Critical for our consideration is that in the Areopagite's symbolic theology God as Primal theologian when speaking of his Divine Word speaks of the primal symbol. The Primal Theologian reveals God's

---

[71] Cf. *id.*, "Ways to Know God: The 'Symbolic Theology' of Dionysius the Areopagite and Its Objective Presuppositions."
[72] *Ibid.*, p. 89.
[73] Cf. *ibid.*, p. 90.

self in the Primal symbol, Jesus Christ.[74] So what can be said is that Jesus Christ is the image language through which God Self-reveals to human sense perception and like all image language it points to a higher spiritual level. In Stein's consideration of the Areopagite's symbolic theology, she places it in the context of Thomas' three ways of knowing God: 1) natural knowledge of God; 2) faith—the ordinary way of supernatural knowledge of God; 3) supernatural experience—the extraordinary way of supernatural knowledge of God. Natural knowledge of God is acquired through natural experience and natural reason's knowledge of the created world. It is intuitive and based on conceptual thinking and scientific procedure including what is sensed in terms of inner structure and conformity to law, for example, causality. The natural world points beyond itself offering natural knowledge of God. Faith, the ordinary way of supernatural knowledge of God is something radically different. Stein speaks of faith as *fides* in terms of God's self-communication through the Word, and not as some general belief. Faith as *fides* is an accepting and retaining of supernatural revelation such that for the Old Testament sacred authors God is the God of Abraham, Isaac and Jacob whose actions they have heard about. The knowledge provided in that supernatural revelation is specifically "the communication of God's mysteries hidden in himself."[75]

There is a critical link between *fides* and symbolic theology in that symbolic theology, through image language which human sense perception can grasp, is God's method of communicating revealed truth to humanity reaching its zenith in the Word made flesh. God's Word and words reveal supernatural truth and require faith as *fides* if it is to be accepted and retained. Faith, Stein maintains, is knowledge in that faith "confers the possession of truth."[76] It is knowledge not available through natural reason. Stein distinguishes faith knowledge from natural knowledge in that faith knowledge lacks the evidence of insight. Faith knowledge is dark knowledge which yearns for revealed clarity. Supernatural experience of God is something different to faith as *fides* even if experiential knowledge of God is the goal of all theology. Natural knowledge of God and faith do not necessarily precede supernatural experience of God, they stand in themselves even if they point beyond themselves. Through supernatural experience of God, being "touched inwardly by God without word and image," the person knows God personally. What is evident here is that it is open to the person of faith to blend the three various knowledges of God, enriching their image of God.

A critical aspect here is that faith as *fides* is the key to knowing God through Scripture. Stein notes that academics who study Scripture only to learn how God is conceived in a particular instance do not come to know

---

[74] Cf. *ibid.*, p. 117.
[75] *Ibid.*, 101.
[76] *Ibid.*

God, unless in the course of the study of Scripture faith is awakened. In such an event Stein sees a transition from one outlook to another. Even where faith exists there are different levels of understanding and knowing. Words may be accepted in faith as revealed truth without grasping the meaning in a deep way in a manner which would affect the life of the reader. This does not preclude or negatively impact biblical scholarship; rather, Stein wanted to highlight that when reading Scripture *something* can occur that radically changes our view of a passage in Scripture which impacts greatly on our life. As she put it, "we feel the difference clearly when all of a sudden we see a passage we have often read 'in a new light'." Yet, for Stein this still does not bring us before God to the point where "*God himself is speaking*, and he is speaking to *me*." In such an *experience* of God faith as *fides* remains even if at that time "I am raised above it."[77] The difference between the experience of God and faith as *fides* is important to Stein. Her own journey of experience of the "otherworldly" power prior to accepting and retaining revealed truth (*fides*) informs her clarity on the three ways she identifies for knowing God, and that each of the ways of knowing is not necessarily sequential, but each stands alone while also pointing to one another.

Stein on the Knowledge from Faith

To conclude our consideration of Stein's thought, we can posit that faith, as articulated by Stein, has two facets. The first is faith's relationship with philosophy and the specific nature of the limits of natural reason and knowledge vis-à-vis supernatural reason and knowledge. The second, the supernatural experience of God, of the "otherworldly power" that acts in our soul, is different to faith as *fides*. Such a distinction illustrates forcefully the very specific nature of the acceptance and retention of revealed truth as against an experience of God whether we know of that revealed truth or not. The clear distinction Stein identified in relation to knowledge of God does not explicitly call out the human being's *faith response* to an experience of God where "*God himself is speaking*, and he is speaking to *me*." That response, epitomized in Mary's Yes, "Be it done unto me according to your will" (Luke 1:26), is a critical aspect of salvation history and Christian faith. God simply acts in the world so that we may have knowledge of God and to do that God reaches out to humanity through human beings. God seeks a positive response to his call, a relationship of love. The experience of God, in Steinian terms, by Abraham, Isaac, and Jacob led to a collection of deeds which subsequently Israel held in faith as God's words and actions. It is from this faith that Mary's Yes emerges. Here we see the philosopher as against the theologian.

---

[77] *Ibid.*, p. 110.

Benedict XVI and Edith Stein on Faith: Discerned Principles and Next Steps

The foregoing discussion, limited as it is to a small selection of their work, is only a first step in exploring the rich expansiveness of Benedict's and Steins's work on faith. The complementary nature of their considerations on faith mutually reinforces the theological exposition of Benedict and the philosophical investigations of Stein. The points of convergence center upon the distinct knowledge available from faith as against natural reason alone and the role God as the Truth plays in philosophical enterprise. A next step would be to extend that consideration to the wider context of their work. For Benedict XVI, that means his explication of reason, the Creative Reason of the *Logos*, specifically in the five papal addresses he gave to representatives of modern European society, as well as his thought before his elevation to the papacy in 2005.[78] For Stein, that means her work on *Finite and Eternal Being*, as well as her other thoughts pre and post her conversion in 1922, specifically on empathy in phenomenology.

Notwithstanding the limitedness of this consideration, its inability to do justice to the depth and breadth of Benedict's and Stein's theological and philosophical thought on faith and the need to place this work in the context of each thinker's wider corpus, a set of principles on faith can be discerned. The non-exhaustive set of principles of faith outlined below is a basis for a Theological Historical Method that informs scholarly work, including biblical interpretation, which either presupposes faith or attempts to build upon it. Seven such aspects are outlined below and would be significantly enhanced through the integration of and refinement from additional complementary perspectives.[79] In addition, the set of principles also point to how Benedict and Stein's work can be further developed in response to open questions in modern thought.

---

[78] Benedict XVI, *Faith, Reason and the University: Memories and Reflections. Lecture in the Meeting with the Representatives of Science*, Apostolic Journey to München, Altötting and Regensburg (September 9–14, 2006), Regensburg, September 12, 2006.; *id.*, *Lecture Prepared for the University of Rome "La Sapienza,"* January 17, 2008 (due to protests this address was not able to be given); *id.*, *Address in the Meeting with Representatives from the World of Culture*, Apostolic Journey to France on the occasion of the anniversary of the apparitions of the Blessed Virgin Mary at Lourdes (September 12–15, 2008), September 12, 2008; *id.*, *Address at the Meeting with the Representatives of British Society, Including the Diplomatic Corps, Politicians, Academics and Business Leaders*, Apostolic Journey to the United Kingdom (September 16–19, 2010), City of Westminster, Westminster Hall, September 17, 2010; *Address at the Visit to the Bundestag*, Apostolic Journey to Germany (September 22–5, 2011), September 27, 2011.

[79] See for just one example: A. MacIntyre, "On Being a Theistic Philosopher in a Secularized Culture," *Proceedings of the American Catholic Philosophical Association* 84 (2010), pp. 23–32.

1. Faith is a free act of the person in response to God's initiative from which a personal relationship with the divine emerges. In hearing God's call the person expresses their Yes to Jesus who draws us into the we of the triune God. The relational nature of faith and the human being's response, their Yes to God's call, repeats the exemplar Yeses of Abraham and Mary. Faith is an active not passive act requiring the courage and patience demonstrated by Abraham and Mary. Faith is a conversion of the believer in as much as they open themselves interiorly to God's love which transforms them into a new creature who can see reality anew. That transformation infuses every aspect of the believer.

2. We know of the God of Abraham, Isaac, Jacob, and Jesus Christ from testimony and witness to happenings that occurred in the past. History and faith are rightly paired as they both speak of the particular, the relational, and the historical. History and faith are distinct from philosophy and such distinction reflects the Aristotelian approach to history, which, taken up by Leopold van Ranke, critiqued the philosophy of history of Hegel and Fichte.[80]

3. Faith is light not darkness. Nonetheless, the light of the Primal Being is dazzling brilliance and unapproachable light which blinds us. When we no longer have the light of faith we are left to search in darkness for truth and certainty, having to determine a starting point that must be justified. We see reality anew through the luminosity of the face of Jesus that enables us to see the Father. In seeing reality through the eyes of love we see reality as it truly is because we see with the eyes of God's love.

4. Faith is about the truth because God, as origin and destiny of all things, who imparts meaning to the whole of life and the entire history of the world, is the truth. That God has self-revealed as Love and *Logos*. The God of Christian faith is the God who is Love and *Logos*. This is the truth of reality. God is then the object of faith and the Church, the community of all believers in heaven and earth, is the subject of faith. All persons who respond to God's initiative with the act of faith join that community.

5. Faith knowledge emanates from the God who is truth, love and *logos* who is perceivable through a combination of hearing God's words and Word and seeing God's signs which is synthesized in the person of Jesus Christ. By conforming to Jesus Christ we can perceive and begin to comprehend faith knowledge. Faith knowledge, which seen

---

[80] Cf. Aristotle, *Poetics*, 1451a22–3, 1451a36–51b12, and 1459a24–32. L. von Ranke, *The Theory and Practice of History* (London: Routledge, 2011), pp. 4–25. Articles in this volume were written between 1820 and 1869. Also see E. H. Carr, *What Is History* (London: Penguin, 1987).

through the eyes of love, is a knowledge that we assimilate over time and cannot be immediately apprehended. The person of faith, like Mary, ponders what they have heard and the signs they have seen holding them together, remembering and contemplating them trustingly. In this discipleship the relational nature and the meaning of the things of faith knowledge, which reflect the love and *logos* of God, reveal what is real and true.

6   Human reason has limits that faith transcends which offers knowledge of the Truth and provides certainty. God as the object of faith means God is first Truth. Faith then provides philosophy with a sound foundation to build upon through the God who is Truth. Faith ensures that knowledge is included in ontology releasing the philosopher from the subjectivity trap ensnarling modern philosophy with the ensuing centrality of the critique of knowledge. In faith's access to truth and certainty, philosophy which aspires to truth and certain must integrate these so that philosophy is not distorted by the loss of essential knowledge.

7   There are three ways of knowing God corresponding to the dissimilarity between God, in whom knowing and being are one, and humanity, in whom knowledge remains fragmentary: natural reason, faith as fides, and supernatural experience of God. The lowest level of knowledge of God is suitable for words, higher knowledge leads to silence and stillness in light of the inscrutable mystery of God. God uses familiar things to communicate what is unfamiliar (God) through symbolic theology and image language. Sense perception can grasp these symbols and images which point beyond themselves to the higher spiritual levels. Jesus Christ is the Primal Symbol of the Primal Being who communicates who and what God is in a manner human sense perception is capable of consuming.

   a. Natural reason is distinguished from supernatural reason and each plays a role in the elucidation of the other. Faith gives access to supernatural reason which offers truth and certainty while natural reason analyzes these truths and utilizes them. Faith, in the Creator, guarantees the priority of rationality over against irrationality; however, faith can become pathological without the guardianship of reason and vice versa.

   b. Faith as *fides* is specific knowledge of God that God has self-revealed to humanity and believers accept and retain, which is different to a supernatural experience of God. Nonetheless, faith as *fides* can open the door to a new dimension of Scripture enabling the reader to see what previously could not be perceived. With faith as *fides* Scripture offers knowledge of God, Father, Son, and Holy Spirit and can be a catalyst for supernatural experience.

c. Supernatural experience of God occurs when "*God himself is speaking*, and he is speaking to *me*."

Scholars, whether philosophers, theologians, or of any other disciple, seek firm ground to stand upon. The above principles of faith demonstrate that the perspective of *hearing God's voice speak* must once again be brought to bear on the knowledge and understanding arising from sight so that the solid ground sought becomes more widely available. The encounter and hearing from which faith arises and in which our relationship with God commences is truly personal and is not repeatable at our will nor at our disposal. Only an individual human being can experience these things and act in response, doing so as part of a community of faith. I encounter, I hear, I follow because we encounter, we hear, we follow. The relational, the particular, and the historical aspects of faith require appropriate integration with modern thought. The philosophical integration of the third fundamental category that Benedict, as professor Ratzinger, highlighted faith discovered, which stands in addition to the Greek categories of substance and accident, that of the personal phenomenon of complete relativity, i.e., person, must be integrated into modern thought if the love and *logos* of the divine and the truth and certainty of faith is to be release for the contemporary world. Stein's work provides essential philosophical foundations from which to commence that task. Questions which present themselves for such an undertaking are: If our sense perception is supplemented by relatedness, relationship ultimately with God, how does that transform our access to reality? In such a transformation, what insights are available from Stein's work on empathy in phenomenology, the description and discussion of experience as experience, and on bridging the metaphysical and post metaphysical worlds, to explore the application of the category of relation and the shared knowledge it offers to philosophy?[81]

---

[81] See: M. F. McKenna, "Ratzinger and the Truly Human: Person Transcending their Human Nature to Participate in Divinity," *Oxford Handbook on Joseph Ratzinger*, Francesca Aran Murphy and Tracey Rowland (eds.) (Oxford: Oxford University Press, forthcoming 2024).

16

Karl Popper: Fideism, Rationalism, and Rationality

Eduardo Echeverría

Introduction

This chapter discusses Popperian fideism, on the one hand, its roots in the theory of rationality of Karl R. Popper (1902–94), which leaves us with a way to justify all sorts of ultimate commitments, indeed, a rational excuse for an irrational commitment and, on the other, Ratzingerian rationality that is not guilty of fideism and its irrational implications.[1] Popper's student, William W. Bartley, III (1934–90), correctly formulates the problem that stems from Popper's theory of rationality, which is the problem that will hold my attention in this article, namely:

> [W]hether some form of relativism is inescapable because rationality is so limited, logically as well as practically, that the choice between ultimately competing religious, moral, and philosophical positions is, in the last resort, *arbitrary*. For example, is an individual's decision to become a *rationalist*—even from a rational point of view—any less subjective, relative, arbitrary, irrational than an individual's decision to become a Christian?[2]

---

[1] This article is a much shorter and revised version of my article, "The Views of Karl Popper and Joseph Ratzinger/Benedict XVI on a Theory of Rationality," *Sapientia* LXIX (2013), pp. 31–72.
[2] W. W. Bartley III, *The Retreat to Commitment*, 2nd ed. (LaSalle/London: Open Court Publishing Co., 1984), p. xxv.

Joseph Ratzinger (1927–2002) develops an account of rationality in which an intellectual commitment to the Logos renders faith an advocate of reason's truth-attaining capacity, and hence "faith is the 'yes' to the truth."[3] This is so because we know that the truth-attaining capacity of reason, indeed, our very orientation as truth-seekers, is underwritten by the truthfulness of the *Logos*, of creative Reason, who grounds not only the existence of truth, but also that man's own mind, his own *logos*, his own reason, has been made to attain truth itself. Ratzinger/Benedict XVI explains:

> I believe that here we can see the profound harmony between what is Greek in the best sense of the word and the biblical understanding of faith in God. Modifying the first verse of the Book of Genesis, the first verse of the whole Bible, John began the prologue of his Gospel with the words: "In the beginning was the λόγος" ... Logos means both reason and word—a reason which is creative and capable of self-communication, precisely as reason. John thus spoke the final word on the biblical concept of God, and in this word all the often toilsome and tortuous threads of biblical faith find their culmination and synthesis. In the beginning was the *logos*, and the *logos* is God, says the Evangelist.[4]

Ratzinger's view in the above passage raises the question: what *must* reality, including I, as a knower, be like in order that human knowledge be intelligible at all? Ratzinger's answer to this basic question is a philosophical elaboration of the biblical teaching of the presence of God as Creator, as the *Logos*, conferring and sustaining the existence of both knower and known. Given the *Logos*, man's *logos* has an intrinsic affinity for truth, the apprehension of objective truth being its purpose—the *logos* can attain truth, keep it, recognize it, and preserve the recognition. It is the same *Logos* who guarantees a correspondence between being and knowing, subject and object, the reality outside of us and the laws of thought within us. All of this makes sense if the truth-attaining capacities of the human mind are underwritten by a metaphysical framework—the *Logos* gives us that framework for trusting our rational faculties.

Comprehensive vs. Critical Rationalism

What is the principle of immanence that is central to rationalism? John Paul II argues that the principle of immanence has to do with the self-sufficiency or autonomy of human reason; in other words, with the idea

---

[3] Benedict XVI, *Lecture Prepared for the University of Rome "La Sapienza,"* January 17, 2008.
[4] Benedict XVI, *Faith, Reason and the University: Memories and Reflections. Lecture in the Meeting with the Representatives of Science*, Apostolic Journey to München, Altötting and Regensburg (September 9–14, 2006), Regensburg, September 12, 2006.

that human reason is self-grounded. This is the view that Karl Popper called "comprehensive rationalism," and he argues for the baselessness of its demands. Popper rejects the excessive rationalism of the so-called "comprehensive rationalist" who claims, "I am not prepared to accept anything that cannot be defended by means of argument or experience." Comprehensive rationalism holds that any assumption that cannot be supported either by argument or by experience is rationally unacceptable. Popper argues that comprehensive rationalism can be critically demonstrated to be baseless by virtue of its inconsistency, i.e., self-referentially inconsistent, failing its own test for rationality. He argues,

> it cannot, in its turn, be supported by argument or by experience' without involving itself in some kind of circularity. And thus, it is self-referentially incoherent, failing to measure up to its own standards of rationality, namely, argument and experience. Put differently, 'The rationalist attitude is characterized by the importance it attaches to argument and experience. But neither logical argument nor experience can establish the rationalist attitude; for only those who are ready to consider argument or experience, and who have therefore adopted this attitude already will be impressed by them ... We have to conclude from this that no rational argument will have a rational effect on a man who does not want to adopt a rational attitude. Thus a comprehensive rationalism is untenable.[5]

Furthermore, Popper shows not only the baselessness of comprehensive rationalism by its being self-referentially inconsistent, but also uncritical. One might say that comprehensive rationalism is dogmatic, adds Popper, because the comprehensive rationalist has not made rationalism a *critical* problem. He lacks self-criticism. By contrast, Popper is self-critical about rationalism, and thus he regards his brand of rationalism to be *critical rationalism*. Moreover, John Paul II is right about currents of irrationalism. Popper claims that rationalism cannot be justified, which means that reason has limits,[6] or is without foundations, and hence Popper opts for an "irrational *faith in reason.*" Hence, he drifts into a current of irrationalism. "Irrationalism is logically superior to uncritical rationalism." Critical rationalism "frankly admits its origin in an irrational decision and which, to that extent, admits a certain priority of irrationalism."[7]

---

[5] K. R. Popper, "Chapter 24," in *The Open Society and Its Enemies* 2 (New York: Harper & Row, 1963), pp. 224–58, and for this quote, pp. 230–1.
[6] Since the critical rationalist holds the principle that "*nothing is exempt from criticism,*" critical reason has limits in the sense that the total explicit justification of belief, once and for all, is ruled out by Popper, as I understand him.
[7] K. R. Popper, *The Open Society and Its Enemies* 2, p. 231.

Still, adds Popper, "rationalism is necessarily far from comprehensive or self-contained."[8] Elsewhere he explains: "My rationalism is not dogmatic. I fully admit that I cannot rationally prove it ... [M]y rationalism is not self-contained, but rests on an irrational faith in the attitude of reasonableness. I do not see that we can go beyond this. One could say, perhaps, that my irrational faith in equal and reciprocal rights to convince others and be convinced by them is a faith in human reason; or simply, that I believe in man."[9]

But this is no reason for adopting comprehensive irrationalism—to escape from reason. Indeed, Popper rejects comprehensive irrationalism and opts for faith in reason.

Moreover, the position of critical rationalism is logically tenable whereas comprehensive rationalism is not. But it is clearly not logically superior to comprehensive rationalism. One act of faith is logically no better than another—on this level they are equally arbitrary. And adopting this option is a moral matter because our view of reason implies how we should treat others. "But I believe that the only attitude which I can consider to be morally right is one which recognizes that we owe it to other men to treat them and ourselves as rational."[10] Given Popper's critical rationalism, his faith in reason, even this choice of moral principle is subjective, arbitrary. Indeed, according to Popper, the choice is not between knowledge and faith, "but only between two kinds of faith. The new problem is: which is the right faith and which is the wrong faith."[11] But Bartley correctly states: "Now, if any adequate theory of rationality aims to escape fideism, Popper's discussion of rationality is inadequate. For it is itself obviously fideistic."[12]

Rationalism as a Confession of Faith

Jürgen Habermas provocatively stated that Popper saved rationalism at least as a "confession of faith."[13] Indeed, Popper's critical rationalism came under fire for embracing fideism.[14] His own student, Bartley, charged Popper with providing "a *rational excuse* for irrational commitment."[15] Popper

---

[8] Ibid.
[9] K. R. Popper, "Utopia and Violence," in *Conjectures and Refutations* (New York: Harper & Row, 1963), pp. 355–63, at p. 357.
[10] K. R. Popper, *The Open Society and Its Enemies* 2, p. 240.
[11] Ibid., p. 431.
[12] W. W. Bartley III, *The Retreat to Commitment*, p. 104.
[13] On this, see J. Habermas, *Erkenntnis und Interesse* (Frankfurt: Suhrkamp, 1968), p. 22.
[14] See W. W. Bartley III, *The Retreat to Commitment*. Fideism (the Latin word for faith is *fides*) in Popper's case meant that his decision for reason is not determined by argument and hence is not rational. This suggested that his faith in reason was invulnerable to any questioning, criticism, or revision. This point was generalized by some into the *tu quoque* argument.
[15] Ibid., p. 72.

argued that rationality is limited. "Since all argument must proceed from assumptions, it is plainly impossible to demand that all assumptions should be based on argument."[16] This argument was generalized by some into the *tu quoque* argument. "Just what is the powerful *tu quoque* argument? It argues that (1) for certain logical reasons, rationality is so limited that *everyone* must make a dogmatic irrational commitment; (2) therefore, [everyone] has a right to make whatever commitment he pleases; and (3) therefore, no one has a right to criticize him (or anyone else) for making such a commitment."[17] Since one's assumptions are held independently of argument, they are immune to criticism. But this implies that everyone else's assumptions are also immune to criticism. The upshot of Bartley's criticism is that generalizing Popper's argument "one gains the right to be irrational at the expense of losing the right to criticize." Bartley adds, "One gains immunity from criticism for one's own commitment by making any criticism of commitment impossible."[18] In sum:

> The limits of rational argument within any particular way of life seem, then, to be defined by reference to that object or belief in respect to which commitment is made or imposed, in respect to which an argument is brought to a close. Thus reason is relativized to one's halting place or standards, and cannot arbitrate among different standards. Different halting places—i.e., standards, criteria, presuppositions, conventions, dogmas, articles of faith—are taken by different individuals and define irreconcilable communities. Whatever may explain how such difference arises, reason can never dissipate them.[19]

One contributing factor to Popper's opting for an irrational faith in reason is his presupposition that the world itself is at root *not* rational. Accordingly, Popper stresses the importance of the "demand *that we submit or subject it [this non-rational world] to reason*, as far as possible."[20] Reason, then, has its origin in the irrational, being as such without ground. But Popper's claim leaves unanswered the question about the relation between reason and reality. In this connection, Joseph Ratzinger puts the following fundamental question to views like Popper's:

> The question is whether reason, or rationality, stands at the beginning of all things and is grounded in the basis of all things or not. The question is whether reality originated on the basis of chance and necessity (or,

---

[16] K. R. Popper, *The Open Society and Its Enemies* 2, p. 230.
[17] W. W. Bartley III, *The Retreat to Commitment*, p. 72.
[18] *Ibid.*, p. 82. For a similar critique, see W. Pannenberg, *Theology and the Philosophy of Science* (Philadelphia: The Westminster Press, 1976), pp. 43–5.
[19] W. W. Bartley III, *The Retreat to Commitment*, p. 74.
[20] K. R. Popper, *The Open Society and Its Enemies* 2, p. 357, n. 19.

as Popper says, in agreement with [Samuel] Butler, on the basis of luck and cunning) and, thus, from what is irrational; that is, whether reason, being a chance by-product of irrationality and floating in an ocean of irrationality, is ultimately just as meaningless; or whether the principle that represents the fundamental conviction of Christian faith and of its philosophy remains true: "*In principio erat Verbum*"—at the beginning of all things stands the creative power of reason. Now as then, Christian faith represents the choice in favor of the priority of reason and of rationality.[21]

Ratzinger states that the rationality of faith "is not a blind surrender to the irrational."[22] This statement is opposed to views, such as Popper's, in which reason has its origin in the irrational, being as such without ground. Recall that Popper's critique of comprehensive rationalism clearly showed the emptiness—the self-referential inconsistency—of the demand that reason be self-sufficient. In response, he opts for a critical rationalism that cannot be justified, but rather "rests on an irrational faith in the attitude of reasonableness,"[23] in short, an "irrational *faith in reason*."[24] In contrast to this position, Ratzinger claims that the rationality of faith involves "a movement toward the *Logos*, the *ratio*, toward meaning and so toward truth itself, for in the final analysis the ground on which man takes his stand cannot possibly be anything else but the truth revealing itself."[25] The main point here is that not only does truth exist but also that man's own mind, his own *logos*, his own reason, has been made to attain truth itself. "Thus the Christian act of faith intrinsically includes the conviction that the meaningful ground, the *Logos*, on which we take our stand, precisely because it is meaning, is also truth. Meaning or sense that was not truth would be nonsense."[26] The question that must be asked here of Ratzinger is about his account of the correspondence between the knower and the known, of the subject and the object, of thought and being, of *logos* of the one *Logos*. Ratzinger provides a theological-metaphysical grounding to this correspondence by going back to an infinite intellect, the divine mind. There exists an indissoluble relation between reality, truth and knowability, not in the human mind, but rather in God's divine mind, with his knowledge being alone the foundation of how things really are. He explains:

---

[21] J. Ratzinger, *Truth and Tolerance: Christian Belief and World Religions* (San Francisco: Ignatius, 2004), p. 181. Ratzinger refers to K. Popper, *Unended Quest: An Intellectual Autobiography* (La Salle: Open Court, 1976), p. 180.
[22] *Ibid.*, *Einführung in das Christentum: Das Glaubensbekenntnis* (München: Kösel, 2000), p. 68; *Id.*, *Introduction to Christianity* (San Francisco: Ignatius, 2004), p. 75.
[23] K. R. Popper, "Utopia and Violence," p. 357.
[24] *Id.*, *The Open Society and Its Enemies* 2, p. 231.
[25] J. Ratzinger, *Einführung in das Christentum*, p. 68 [75].
[26] *Ibid.*, p. 69 [76].

Being itself is true, in other words, apprehensible, because God, pure intellect, made it, and he made it by thinking it. To the creative original spirit, the *Creator Spiritus*, thinking and making are one and the same thing. His thinking is a creative process. Things are, because they are thought. In the ancient and medieval view, all being is, therefore, what has been thought, the thought of the absolute spirit. Conversely, this means that since all being is thought, all being is meaningful, *Logos*, truth. It follows from this traditional view that human thinking is rethinking of being itself, rethinking of the thought that is being itself. Man can rethink the *Logos*, the meaning of being, because his own *logos*, his own reason, is *logos* of the one *Logos*, thought of the original thought,of the creative spirit that permeates and governs his being.[27]

To say that man's own *logos* is *logos* of the *one divine Logos* is to say that our own intellect, although not itself the divine *Logos*, nevertheless participates in it. Furthermore, to say that being is truth (*verum est ens*) is to say that the thing is created true, is meaning, and hence has the potentiality of being known, apprehended. What makes knowledge of the truth possible is that thought and being have a preexistent correspondence—a theological correspondence—with each other in the mind of the Creator. Therefore, to confess, "'I believe that God exists' also implies opting for the view that the [divine] *Logos* ... is the originating and encompassing power of all being. In other words, faith means deciding for the view that thought and meaning do not just form a chance by-product of being; that, on the contrary, all being is a product of [divine] thought and, indeed, in its innermost structure is itself thought."[28] Put differently, says Ratzinger, the Christian faith means deciding for the truth, and this kind of truth called ontological truth appears to be demanded by the very idea of "*Credo in Deum*—I believe in God," namely, that "being itself is truth, comprehensibility, [and] meaning."[29] Ratzinger adds,

> This means nothing else than the conviction that the objective mind we find present in all things, indeed, as which we learn increasingly to understand things, is the impression and expression of subjective [divine]

---

[27] Ibid., p. 53 [59]. The German text capitalizes *Logos*, not distinguishing between the human *logos* and the divine *logos*. The English translation never capitalizes *Logos*. In order to distinguish between human thinking and divine thinking, which Ratzinger naturally affirms, I only capitalize the divine *Logos*. Ratzinger adds in a note (p. 346, n. 9 [59, n. 9]): "This statement is of course only fully true of Christian thinking, which with the idea of the *creation ex nihilo* attributes to God the material, too; for the ancient world, this remained the a-logical element, the universal matter alien to the divine, thus also marking the limit to which reality could be comprehended."

[28] Ibid., p. 140 [152].

[29] Ibid.

mind and that the intellectual structure that being possesses and that we can *re*-think is the expression of a creative *pre*-meditation, to which they owe their existence.[30]

So God has made the world to be the embodiment of his thoughts and the human mind engages in *re*-producing and *re*-flecting on those embodied thoughts. Elsewhere Ratzinger writes, "This surely means that all our thinking is, indeed, only a rethinking of what in reality has already been thought out beforehand. It can only try in a paltry way to trace over that being-thought which things are and to find truth in it."[31] When we know the truth about the world we are, in effect, thinking God's thoughts after him. Naturally Ratzinger does consider the difference between divine thought and human thought. Indeed, Benedict stresses this point in his Regensburg Lecture, "The Church has always insisted that between God and us, between his eternal Creator Spirit and our created reason there exists a real analogy, in which—as the Fourth Lateran Council in 1215 stated—unlikeness remains infinitely greater than likeness, yet not to the point of abolishing analogy and its language."[32] Still, "The world is objective mind; it meets us in an intellectual structure, that is, it offers itself to our mind as something that can be reflected upon and understood."[33] Still, this rethinking is possible because there is a correspondence between the *Logos*, subjective rationality, and the objective rationality of the world; the latter two stem from the same *Logos*.

Now, before going on with Ratzinger's view, we need to deter any misconstruing of his view that "Being is being-thought" as a version of theistic (Berkelian) idealism, i.e., that things must exist because God thinks them, meaning thereby that they must be ideas in the divine mind.[34] Ratzinger explains, contrasting his own Christian view from materialism and idealism:

> The idealistic solution to the problem of being accordingly signifies the idea that all being is the being-thought by one single consciousness. The

---

[30] *Ibid.*
[31] *Ibid.*, p. 141 [153].
[32] Benedict XVI, *Faith, Reason and the University: Memories and Reflections.* The pope is referring here to the *de fide catholica* of Lateran IV: "Inter creatorem et creaturam non potest similitudo notari, quin inter eos maior sit dissimilitudo notanda" ["For between creator and creature there can be noted not similarity so great that a greater dissimilarity cannot be seen between them"], p. 2. H. Denzinger, *Compendium of Creeds, Definitions, and Declarations on Matters of Faith and Morals*, P. Hünermann (Latin-English ed.), R. Fastiggi and A. Englund Nash [English eds.]; (San Francisco: Ignatius, 2012), §806.
[33] J. Ratzinger, *Einführung in das Christentum*, p. 143 [155].
[34] Cf. G. Berkeley, *Principles of Human Knowledge and Three Dialogues* (Oxford, New York: Oxford University Press, 1996), pp. 1710, 1713. See also, S. J. F. Copleston, *A History of Philosophy 5* (Westminster, Maryland: The Newman Press, 1959), p. 246; and C. Taliaferro, *Contemporary Philosophy of Religion* (Oxford: Blackwell, 1998), p. 352.

unity of being consists in the identity of the one consciousness, whose impulses constitute the many things that are. The Christian belief in God is not completely identical with either of these two solutions. To be sure, it, too, will say, being is being-thought. Matter itself points beyond itself to thinking as the earlier and more original factor.[35]

Let us pause for a moment to see why, even if only briefly, Ratzinger rejects the materialist solution. The materialist solution to the question of the one and the many—"what is the one being behind the many 'things' which nevertheless all 'exist'?"[36]—is that ultimate reality is matter. "*This* is the only thing that always remains as demonstrable reality and, consequently, represents the real being of all that exists." Ratzinger rejects the materialistic solution because the

> reduction of all being to matter as the primary form of reality consequently implies that the beginning and ground of all being is constituted by a form of being that does not itself understand being; this also means that the understanding of being only arises as a secondary, chance product during the course of development. This at the same time also gives us the definition of "mind": it can be described as being that understands itself, as being that is present to itself.[37]

In other words, the reduction of everything that exists to one single, ultimate materiality means that there is no personal choice or will, and also no mind, behind matter. This point brings us back to the claim that materialism prioritizes the irrational over the rational (understanding), and that view raises Ratzinger's critical remark that "the attempt to distill rationality out of what is in itself irrational quite visibly fails."[38] Continuing now with Ratzinger's rejection of theistic idealism, he argues:

> But in opposition to idealism, which makes all being into moments of an all-embracing consciousness, the Christian belief in God will say: Being is being-thought—yet not in such a way that it remains only thought and the appearance of independence proves to be mere appearance to anyone who looks more closely. On the contrary, Christian belief in God means that things are the being-thought of a creative consciousness, of a creative freedom, and that the creative consciousness that bears up all things has released what has been thought into the freedom of its own, independent existence. In this it goes beyond any mere idealism. While the latter, as we

---

[35] J. Ratzinger, *Einführung in das Christentum*, pp. 144–5 [157].
[36] Ibid., p. 144 [156].
[37] Ibid.
[38] Id., *Truth and Tolerance*, p. 182.

have just established, explains everything real as the contents of a single consciousness, in the Christian view what supports it all is a creative freedom that sets what has been thought in the freedom of its own being, so that, on the one hand, it is the being-thought of a consciousness and yet, on the other hand, is true being itself.[39]

We are, therefore, according to Ratzinger, not mere moments of God's all-embracing consciousness. Furthermore, we are also not substantial entities held in existence by God's enduring thoughts—as if to suggest that those entities have no independent existence. Yes, God's all-embracing consciousness "bears up all things," but "what has been thought" has been released "into the freedom of its own, independent existence." Moreover, Ratzinger affirms the primacy of the *logos* as opposed to mere matter, or one single, ultimate materiality, but "the belief that the original thought, whose being-thought is represented by the world [that is, its objective mind], is not an anonymous, neutral consciousness but rather freedom, creative love, a person."[40] What, then, prevents Ratzinger's option for the primacy of the *logos* from remaining mere idealism is that the "Christian option for the *logos* means an option for a personal, creative meaning" as well an "option for the primacy of the particular as against the universal."[41] He elaborates:

Let us content ourselves with the indispensable elucidations by first asking what it really means to say that this *Logos*, whose thought is the world, is a person and that therefore faith is the option in favor of the primacy of the particular over the universal [such as cosmic necessity or natural law]. In the last analysis, the answer can be put quite simply: It means nothing else than that [1] the creative thinking we found to be the precondition and ground of all being is truly conscious thinking and that it knows not only itself but also its whole thought. It means [2] further that this thinking not only knows but [also] loves; it is creative because it is love; and that, because it can love as well as think, it has given its thought the freedom of its own existence, objectivized it, [and] released it into distinct being. So the whole thing means that this thinking knows its thought in its distinct being, loves it and, loving, upholds it ... But if the *logos* of all being, the being that upholds and encompasses everything is consciousness, freedom, and love, then it follows automatically that the supreme factor in the world is not cosmic necessity but freedom [and love].[42]

---

[39] Id., *Einführung in das Christentum*, p. 145 [157].
[40] Ibid., p. 146 [158].
[41] Ibid.
[42] Ibid., p. 147 [159]; see also, p. 136 [148]: "The *Logos* of the whole world, the creative original thought, is at the same time love; in fact, this thought is creative because, as thought, it is love, and, as love, is thought."

Now, because God is love, He can only be love if, in effect, His Being includes the dimension of relationship. Although I cannot argue the point here, Ratzinger holds that it becomes possible to glimpse love as the starting point of the confession of faith in the revealed truth that God is triune. Thus, says Ratzinger, "the profession of faith in God as a person necessarily includes the acknowledgment of God as relatedness, as communicability, as fruitfulness. The unrelated, unrelatable, absolutely One could not be person. There is no such thing as person in the categorical singular."[43] Furthermore, if God were not consciousness, freedom, creative love, then, he could not be personal, either.[44] God, then, is supremely personal. Although much more could be said regarding Ratzinger's doctrine of God, for example, on his account of the relation between the God of faith and the God of the philosophers, it must suffice for now to say that I have shown why affirming the primacy of the *Logos* in Christian faith is something different from mere idealism.

Rationality of Faith

In this light, we can proceed to consider Ratzinger's account of the rationality of faith. What, then, is faith? Ratzinger understands faith to cover not only the entirety of man's stance toward od and to reality as a whole—*fides qua creditor*, which is the faith *with which* one believes—but also, inseparably including, belief, meaning thereby a propositional content, a *fides quae creditur*, the faith *which* one believes.[45] How does one come to faith? "'Faith comes from what is heard', says St. Paul (Rom 10:17)," and, he adds, "what is heard comes by the preaching of Christ."[46] Ratzinger's epistemology of faith elevates testimony and proclaiming the Word to a position of priority in coming to faith. He says, "believing does not come from seeing, from perceiving, but from hearing."[47] Thus, the realities of faith come to man from outside, with testimony and proclamation proposing them outwardly. Thus, his epistemology of faith subordinates reflection—faith is not a mere product of reflection, a quasi-Cartesian private search for truth, where man pulls himself up to God by his own intellectual boot-straps—to hearing, receiving, and answering the Word of God by way of the testimony of

---

[43] *Ibid.*, p. 167 [180].
[44] Cf. R. Letham, *The Holy Trinity* (Phillipsburg: Presbyterian & Reformed Publishing Co., 2004), p. 444.
[45] The German language uses only one word both for faith and belief—*Glauben*—and so the context determines when Ratzinger means beliefs and when he means faith as man's total stance.
[46] J. Ratzinger, *Einführung in das Christentum*, p. 82 [91].
[47] *Id.*, "Faith and Theology," in S. O. Horn and V. Pfnür (eds.), *Pilgrim Fellowship of Faith: The Church as Communion* (San Francisco: Igantius, 2005), pp. 17–28, and at p. 25.

Scripture, the revealed Word of God.[48] Put differently, Ratzinger is making reference here to a *principium cognoscendi externum*, namely, the economy of God's self-revelation in word and deed.[49]

> [Faith's] nature lies in the fact that it is not the thinking out of something that can be thought out and that at the end of the process is then at my disposal as the result of my thought. On the contrary, it is characteristic of faith that it comes from hearing, that it is the reception of something that I have not thought out, so that in the last analysis thinking in the context of faith is always a thinking over of something previously heard and received.[50]

In other words, starting with myself I would never discover the realities of faith; rather, they have been communicated to me through the testimony of others, through the instrument of the creeds, the source of the testimony being revelation, the revealed Word of God. He continues:

> Faith ... comes to man from outside, and this very fact is fundamental to it. It is—let me repeat—not something thought up by myself; it is something said to me, which hits me as something that has not been thought out and could not be thought out and lays an obligation on me. This double structure of "Do you believe?—I do believe?," this form of the call from outside and the reply to it, is fundamental to it.[51]

Moreover, there is also an *ecclesiological a priori* that refers to ecclesial faith, the faith of the Church, carried forward by the Church's tradition, meaning thereby the "social character of belief" that binds us together.[52] But what actually binds us together? Is that bond the Word as true? Ratzinger explains:

> The primary factor for belief is, as we have seen, the proclaimed Word. While a thought is interior, purely intellectual, the Word represents the element that unites us with others. It is the form in which the mind is, as it were, human, that is, corporeal and social. This primacy of the Word means that faith is focused on community of mind ... Faith [then] is

---

[48] T. Aquinas states, "Other things being equal, sight is more certain than hearing; but if (the authority) of the persons from whom we hear greatly surpasses that of the seer's sight, hearing is more certain than sight ... and much more is a man certain about what he hears from God who cannot be deceived, than about what he sees with his own reason which can be mistaken" (*Summa Theologiae* [IIa, IIae, q. iv, a.8. ad.2]).
[49] Cf. Vatican Council II, *Dogmatic Constitution* Dei verbum *on Divine Revelation*, November 18, 1965, §2.
[50] J. Ratzinger, *Einführung in das Christentum*, p. 83 [91].
[51] *Ibid.*, p. 83 [91–2].
[52] Cf. *ibid.*, p. 84 [92].

first of all a call to community, to unity of mind through the unity of the Word. Indeed, its significance is, a priori, an essentially social one: it aims at establishing unity of mind through the unity of the word.[53]

Unity of mind through the unity of the word? Does that statement bring us any closer to answering the question regarding what binds us together?

I presume the unity of mind does not refer to states of mind but rather to propositional truth that comes into perspective when we attend to the Word of God as true. One must not separate the word from the truth, namely, its propositional content. And what I mean by a proposition is simply whatever can be believed to be true or affirmed as true. What, then, binds us together is the Word as true. Bernard Lonergan, SJ, rightly holds that this makes sense because "the word of God contains a realism, both because it is to be believed [affirmed as true] and not contradicted, and also because it is a true word, telling of things as in fact they are."[54] Ratzinger is, then, a realist about truth. Lonergan continues: "For realism consists in this, that the truth that is acknowledged in the mind corresponds to reality. But whoever believes the true word of God certainly acknowledges truth in his mind."[55] In this light, we can understand why Ratzinger states that dogma unites people in a common profession of faith in the community of those who confess the Word of God. This brief reflection on propositional truth brings us back to Ratzinger's understanding of faith.

Naturally faith, then, includes belief, its propositional content, but faith is not identical with belief. Rather, says Ratzinger, the organizing center of faith is trust: "Faith is thereby defined as taking up a position, as taking a stand trustfully on the ground of the Word of God."[56] In other words, "The Christian attitude of faith is expressed in the little word 'Amen', in which the meanings trust, entrust, fidelity, firmness, firm ground, stand, truth all interpenetrate each other; this means that the thing on which man can finally take his stand and that can give him meaning can only be truth itself. Truth is the only ground suitable for man to stand upon." Faith, then, is the entirety of the stance of man in the totality of reality, entrusting himself to the meaning that upholds him and the world. Ratzinger adds that this meaning is indissolubly connected to ground and truth and hence faith means "understanding our existence as response to the word, the *logos*, that upholds and maintains all things."[57] Two things remain to be said.

First, understanding the meaning that man has received as the ground and truth of his own existence and the world's presupposes standing in the truth, the truth of being itself. Standing in the truth is an indispensable prerequisite

---

[53] *Ibid.*, pp. 84–5 [93].
[54] B. J. F. Lonergan, S.J., *The Way to Nicea* (Philadelphia: The Westminster Press, 1976), p. 128.
[55] *Ibid.*
[56] J. Ratzinger, *Einführung in das Christentum*, p. 62 [69].
[57] *Ibid.*, p. 66 [73].

for understanding "to grasp the ground on which we have taken our stand as meaning and truth; that we learn to perceive that *ground* represents *meaning*." In other words, "'Understanding' only reveals itself in 'standing', not apart from it. One cannot occur without the other, for understanding means seizing and grasping as *meaning* the meaning that man has received as *ground*."[58] This standing requires the illumination of man through the Holy Spirit—a *principium cognoscendi internum*—because faith may only be attained, adds Ratzinger, "by what the language of the Bible calls 'turning back', 'con-version'."[59] This is the interior light that leads to assent, says Aquinas. *Credo ut intelligam*: I believe in order that I may understand. Faith is the condition of understanding and understanding, conversely, is the end of faith. In Ratzinger's own words, "Understanding grows only out of faith. That is why theology as the understanding, *logos-like* (=rational, understanding through reason) discussion of God is a fundamental task of Christian faith. This context is also the basis of the inalienable right of Greek thought to a place in Christianity." In sum, he adds, "Believing and understanding belong together no less than believing and 'standing', simply because standing and understanding are inseparable. To this extent the Greek translation of the sentence in Isaiah [7:9] about believing and abiding reveals a dimension that is implicit in the biblical attitude itself if it is not degraded into fanaticism, sectarianism."[60] *Fides quarens intellectum*: faith seeking understanding of the content of revelation, stirring reason into motion so as to understand the inner coherence and intelligibility of that revelation. And in this disciplined exploration of the content of revelation, the Christian faith does not "cut off the path of thought," indeed; it not only draws upon philosophical resources but also stimulates philosophical inquiry.

Second, the rationality of Christian faith is not merely about taking a stance with respect to the firm ground, the *Logos*, of the world. Rather, Christian faith involves faith's personal knowledge, not an impersonal knowledge, that Jesus Christ "is the presence of the eternal itself in this world."[61] More concretely, "The belief that Christ *is* the only Son of God, that God really dwells among us as man in him, that the man Jesus is eternally in God, is God himself, and therefore is, not a figure in which God appears, but rather the sole and irreplaceable God."[62] As Ratzinger also puts this point about faith's personal knowledge, faith "is not 'I believe in something', but 'I believe in Thou'. It is the encounter with the man Jesus, and in this encounter it experiences the meaning of the world as a person."

---

[58] *Ibid.*, p. 70 [77].
[59] *Ibid.*, p. 45 [51].
[60] *Ibid.*, p. 70 [78].
[61] *Ibid.*, p. 72 [80].
[62] *Ibid.*, p. 18 [21].

Faith's personal knowledge is a relational knowing because in knowing Jesus Christ we ourselves are known, are transformed. He elaborates:

> Thus faith is the finding of a "Thou" that upholds me and amid all the unfulfilled—and in the last resort unfulfillable—hope of human encounters gives me the promise of an indestructible love that not only longs for eternity but also guarantees it. Christian faith lives on the discovery that not only is there such a thing as objective meaning but that this meaning knows me and loves me, that I can entrust myself to it like the child who knows that everything he may be wondering about is safe in the "Thou" of his mother. Thus in the last analysis believing, trusting, and loving are one, and all the theses around which belief revolves are only concrete expressions of the all-embracing about-turn, of the assertion "I believe in Thou"—of the discovery of God in the countenance of the man Jesus of Nazareth ... "I believe in Thou, Jesus of Nazareth, as the meaning (*logos*) of the world and of my life."[63]

Alternatively put, although propositional truth is an indispensable dimension of truth itself, how truth is authenticated—that is, lived out, practiced, carried out—cannot be reduced to it—to being merely believed, asserted, and claimed because faith's personal knowledge of God involves believing, trusting, and loving, a relational knowing of Jesus Christ, the *Logos*, in which we ourselves are known, and hence transformed.

---

[63] *Ibid.*, pp. 72–3 [80–1].

17

Josef Pieper: Philosophy, Philology, and Theology

Hanna-Barbara Gerl-Falkovitz

Personal Encounters

The personal contact between the philosopher Josef Pieper and the then young Dogmatics professor Joseph Ratzinger covers three close years at the University of Münster from 1963 to 1966. Apart from moments at the university, both met regularly on Saturday afternoons throughout the semester with two other university philologists[1] in Pieper's house to exchange ideas. "In the 1960s we were allowed to sit together by your fireplace every Saturday for a while and search for knowledge together in a small groups of friends."[2] The contact between philosophy, philology, and theology was the inexhaustible theme, also in view of the already crisis-ridden period after the Second Vatican Council. The inaugural lecture of the 32-year-old fundamental theologian Ratzinger in Bonn in 1959 had developed the necessary, repeatedly blurred distinction, between the "God of faith and the

---

[1] This paper is dedicated to Professor Dr. Berthold Wald, the renowned Pieper scholar, on his seventieth birthday.
　Heinrich Lausberg (1912 Aachen–1992 Münster) Romanist, Linguist and scholar of Rhetoric; Franz Beckmann (1895. Fürstenau-1966 Münster), classical philology, especially in Roman literature and cultural history—see in the years 1963–6: M. Schlögl, *Joseph Ratzinger in Münster* (Münster: Dialog-Medien, 2012).
[2] Letter from Cardinal Ratzinger in Rome on May 3, 1974, for Pieper's seventieth birthday. The transcript of Ratzinger's letters (created by P. Albert Kühlem OP) was given to me by Prof. Dr. Berthold Wald, to whom I am very grateful. The originals are in the German Literature Archive in Marbach. Pieper's letters in the Ratzinger Archiv in Regensburg will not be available until thirty years after the death of Benedict XVI.

God of philosophers."³ With that, the *Cantus firmus* was intoned, which was to be found in the writings of Pope Benedict XVI about *Fides et ratio*: about the (super) reasonableness of faith, which fertilizes the reason of the world and at the same time, surpassing it, challenges, stimulates and attracts.

Even after Ratzinger's appointment to Tübingen in 1966—which, as is well known, was on the recommendation of Hans Küng—Ratzinger and Pieper remained in constant contact until Pieper's death in November 1997. This is reflected in numerous letters. Ratzinger's fundamental theological writings repeatedly show clear influences from Pieper's philosophy. Manuel Schlögl has already emphasized a number of these topics in approaches to a biography of Ratzinger: the view of liturgy (*"Praeambula sacramenti"*), the "rehabilitation of Plato and the immortality of the soul"; "Faith Hope Love"; ultimately the common critical judgment of modern times and the high regard for the interaction of faith and reason.⁴

In the present essay, the (so far unevaluated) letters—especially with the controversies about identity theology and priesthood—as well as the first encyclical of Pope Benedict *Deus caritas est* are presented in their latent relation to Pieper.

What was the philosophical focus of Josef Pieper?

Thinking within the Horizon of Contemporary Philosophy

Josef Pieper (May 4, 1904, Elte/Westphalia–November 6, 1997, Münster) represents an exceptional phenomenon in German-speaking philosophy. As a contemporary of almost the entire twentieth century, he was familiar with the changing philosophical currents, but belonged neither to neo-Kantianism nor to phenomenology, neither to neo-Thomism nor to existential philosophy or later to analytic philosophy. Rather, Pieper developed a "philosophical anthropology"—the title of his professorship in Münster (1959–72)—in which he made Plato, Aristotle, Augustine, and Thomas Aquinas fruitful for the present due to his profound knowledge of ancient and medieval philosophy. What is less known is that Pieper also critically processed the Enlightenment (Kant) and German idealism (Schelling) and constructively set his theses apart from contemporary and also sociological concepts (Heidegger, Sartre, Gadamer, Gehlen). In addition to Romano Guardini, Erich Przywara SJ and Stanislaus von Dunin-Borkowski SJ (who has been

---

³J. Ratzinger, *Der Gott des Glaubens und der Gott der Philosophen. Ein Beitrag zum Problem der Theologia naturalis* (München, Zürich: Schnell & Steiner, 1960).
⁴Cf. M. Schlögl, "Der Glaube braucht den Mut der Vernunft zu sich selbst," in T. Möllenbeck and B. Wald (eds.), *Die Wahrheit bekennen. Josef Pieper im Dialog* (München: Pneuma, 2017), pp. 275–93.

forgotten today), can also be considered theological stimuli for his thinking. Pieper described Dunin-Borkowski as "one of the very few people I have known to whom I would not hesitate to ascribe the attribute of 'wisdom'."[5]

Pieper's thinking is characterized by a clear relocation of philosophizing in "reality" since the turn of the century in 1900. With his methodical doubts about the direct correspondence between the world of things and knowledge, Kant had created an unavoidable insight that knowledge does not simply describe the world of things, but that reason for its part prescribes the conditions of cognition, such as the visual forms of space and time that accompany all of our cognition. The thought is plausible: Reason as the "vessel" of knowledge also gives content and form. This idea had already been formulated by Thomas Aquinas. But Kant's "Copernican turn" became a threatening loss of the world in neo-Kantianism: the "thing in itself" differs not only from the "thing for us," but remains insurmountably unknowable. Consequently, the recognition of the subject, which is tied to transcendental presuppositions, does not provide any possibility of the final verification of what has been seen.

In this way, neo-Kantianism of the nineteenth century brought about a psychologization and subjectification not only of thought but also of ethics, reinforced by the historicization of "truth." Truth could no longer simply be translated into a universally valid hermeneutics of existence, nor simply into doing the right thing (in the sense of meaningful correspondence between being and ought).

However, Husserl's and Scheler's phenomenology introduced a major turning point. With Kant and beyond Kant, it was possible to prove that the appearance of phenomena not only conveys an impression to the subject, but that something primarily appears. "So that what is presented is not a mere appearance, but something real becoming clear."[6] Husserl's cognitive question was not only: *How* does something appear, but with a different emphasis: How does *something* appear?

With this "Copernican turn against Kant" and beyond Kant, it was possible to go beyond the skeptical epistemology developed in modern times. Husserl's demonstration that self-transcendence to the world of things is already inherently and intentionally inscribed in man was decisive here. Scheler argued similarly in the theory of value. Thus, a renewed connection between metaphysics and theology appeared to be possible—phenomenology was even suspected of being a "crypto-Catholic philosophy."[7]

In this way, phenomenology had initiated a new ontology and value-oriented thinking. However, this reconnection is not to declare Pieper

---

[5] J. Pieper, *Noch wusste es niemand. Autobiographische Aufzeichnungen 1904–1945* (München: Kösel 1976), p. 73.
[6] R. Guardini, *Ethik. Vorlesungen an der Universität München.* 2 (Mainz, Paderborn: Grünewald, 1993), p. 290.
[7] E. Peterson, "Machruf auf Scheler," *Theologische Blätter* 7 (1928), pp. 165–7.

a phenomenologist in the sense of the school of Husserl. Moreover, this prevents a problem that Husserl did not solve: when demonstrating the intentionality of consciousness (*noesis*), he did indeed look at the matter as a correlate of consciousness (*noema*), but only as something immanent to consciousness, i.e., already enclosed by consciousness. "Perception grasps the essence as essence and in no way posits existence."[8] So the question remains: How does one mentally return from essence to the existence of things, to the "relationship with the world?"

Shortly before the completion of Pieper's dissertation in 1929 on the ontic basis of morality according to Thomas Aquinas, Heidegger's *Being and Time* appeared in 1927 as a beacon of a new memory of being against an assumed forgetting of being. Pieper also explores man's relationship to the world, by no means in a naive recourse to Aristotle and Thomas, but sharpened by the reflections of the twentieth century.

"Everything That Is, Is Good": The Reality of the Good

"The good is the realistic" ("Das Gute ist das Wirklichkeitsgemäße") was the formulation of Romano Guardini (1885–1968) in the early 1920s at Rothenfels Castle, the center of the then Catholic youth movement "Quickborn," to which Pieper belonged.[9] The dissertation by the twenty-five-year-old philosophy student Pieper will thoroughly spell out this thesis. In 1935, the title of the book was reworded to be less academic and more catchy: "Reality and the Good." Aware of the challenge, the principle reads:

> Everything should be based on being (...) The good is what is realistic. Whoever wants to know and do the good must direct his attention to the objective world of being. Not on one's own 'attitude', not on 'conscience', not on 'values', not on 'ideals' and 'role models' set by one's own authority. He must disregard his own act and look at reality.[10]

Therefore: *omne ens est bonum*. This also and especially applies to human nature: it is inherently good. Apart from the Judeo-Christian revelation,

---

[8] E. Husserl, *Philosophie als strenge Wissenschaft* (Frankfurt: Vittorio Klostermann 1971), p. 40.
[9] Cf. J. Pieper, "Bedeutende Fördernis durch ein einziges Wort. Romano Guardini zum 70. Geburtstag" (1955), *Werke in act Bänden* 8/2 (Hamburg: Felix Meiner, 1995–2008), pp. 658–60. See: *id*. "Guardininis gewaltlose Revolution" (1981), pp. 664–9. See: "Die Beziehung zu Ihnen him habe ich immer empfunden ..., " in H. B. Gerl-Falkovitz, *Geheimnis des Lebendigen. Versuche zu Romano Guardini* (Heiligenkreuz: Be&Be, 2019), pp. 131–43.
[10] J. Pieper, *Die Wirklichkeit und das Gute* (München: Kösel, 1949), p. 11. See: *Id.*, "Wirklichkeit und Wahrheit," in *Interpretationen zu Thomas von Aquin: Quaestiones Disputatae de Veritate* 2 (Hamburg: Meiner, 1950–1), pp. 58–111.

Pieper can show that the exploration of the "good" in the entire classical, i.e., pre-biblical, philosophy proceeds from the goodness of beings. For this reason, too, Pieper sees theology and philosophy as essentially siblings, as the "original intertwining of the philosophical and theological world statement."[11]

For Plato and Aristotle, the good is the measure of reality that gives man the space to work. "To be open to the truth of real things and to live the truth that has been grasped: that is what constitutes the essence of the moral human being."[12] Or, in the words of Thomas Aquinas: "Every movement of the will that is in accordance with true insight is good in itself; but every movement of the will that corresponds to a wrong judgment is in itself evil and a sin."[13]

How logically Pieper applies his discoveries of the "good" can be seen in his passage through the entire classical doctrine of virtue. In addition to the quartet[14] of the cardinal virtues of prudence, justice, fortitude, and temperance, Pieper also undertook the interpretation of the trinity of faith, hope, and love, which in the classical tradition are called the theological virtues because they lead man to the deity in order to make him "divine." Virtue, arete, is Greek for the ethos of human attitudes and powers (*hexeis*) as an answering echo of reality. Ethos literally means "pasture fence," as many Greek terms come from the language of farmers and fishermen. The herd remains protected within the fence; outside there are confusion and threats. The ethos thus creates the space for a life-serving reality; it marks the border to the insurmountable, protects against being dissolved by the lie that leads to the unreal. Extremes also lead to such destruction, and they even exist, yes, precisely there, in the area of love, namely a misunderstood commitment to selflessness. With the investigation *About Love* from 1972, it was again the case that Pieper spoke critically and clarifyingly into a time that changed language and behavior from *eros* to a forced sexuality—a revolution that continues to this day. After half a century of sexual revolution, the analysis seems fresh, comprehensive, realistic. All of these exposures are devoid of any pious undertone, just as Pieper's language is both sober and at the same time surprisingly moved by the "wing beat of the spirit."

All in all, Pieper's "reality" gains a knowledge-driven, but also knowledge-resistant depth that shifts back to its justifications in being, the true, and the good. Being, truth, and goodness undergird the cognitive faculty and trigger

---

[11] *Id.*, "Theologie—philosophisch betrachtet," in *Werke* 7 (Hamburg: Meiner, 1974) pp. 129–41, at p. 41. See: H. Holm, *Die Unergründlichkeit der kreatürlichen Wirklichkeit. Eine Untersuchung zum Verhäaltnis von Philosohie und Wirklichkeit bei Josef Pieper* (Dresden: Thelem 2011), pp. 87–97.

[12] J. Pieper, "Zucht und Maß," in *Werke* 4 (Hamburg: Meiner, 1996), p. 155.

[13] STh II-IIae, q. 20, a. 1, c.

[14] Cf. J. Pieper, *Das Viergespann* (München: Kösel 1964). This book gathers the volumes published individually from the mid-1930s on the four cardinal virtues.

an interminable movement of knowledge. This unfathomable element that pervades creation in a challenging manner puts Pieper's arguments in a fruitful openness that is compatible with Ratzinger's thinking.

The Influence on Joseph Ratzinger: Issues and Consensus

Many of the topics mentioned are directly related to Ratzinger, who is twenty-five years Pieper's junior. Pieper became his guarantor for the methodical question of truth; he called him "teacher" and "master" and finally "friend."[15] As Pope, Ratzinger was visibly happy about the establishment of the Josef Pieper position at the Paderborn Faculty of Theology in 2009 and emphasized his connection to the internationally renowned philosopher. "I have learned that the great thinkers of bygone times are very present in their struggle for truth, and that philosophy does not become obsolete when it walks honestly and humbly toward truth."[16]

However, this late and repeated judgment somewhat obscures the initial issues. They were even significant and sometimes lasted for years.

Pieper was quite stubborn about some of the younger colleague's theses and was unyielding in his own way, while Ratzinger tended more toward a reconciliation of the theories—more on that in the following. Of course there were also agreements and confirmations, and what was fought out in written statements continued to have an effect—even Pope Benedict XVI took up the decisive clarifications gained in such disputes.

A first controversial issue in 1965/6 was the keyword "identity theology." Ratzinger had taken up the question concerning his own discipline, how dogmatics had to be interpreted in a contemporary way, i.e., how it itself had a historical characteristic.[17] Pieper, on the other hand, saw in the "tradition"[18] the identity of what is revealed as having an indispensable effect, which does not change historically, although the mode of language is changeable, but not changeable at its core. Later, on April 1, 1979, Ratzinger, as archbishop of Munich, wrote about Pieper's treatise on

---

[15] Cf. M. Schlögl, "Der Glaube braucht den Mut der Vernunft zu sich selbst," p. 275, n. 4.

[16] Benedict XVI, *Brief Papst Benedikts XVI, an Erzbischof Hans-Josef Becker aus Anlass der Errichtung der Josef-Pieper-Arbeitsstelle [Letter of Pope Benedict XVI to Archbishop Hans-Josef Becker on the Occasion of the Establishment of the Josef Pieper Workplace]*, July 4, 2009; cited by M. Schlögl, "Der Glaube braucht den Mut der Vernunft zu sich selbst," p. 283, n. 4.

[17] Cf. J. Ratzinger, "Das Problem der Dogmengeschichte in der Sicht der katholischen Theologie" (1966), in *JRGS* 9/1, pp. 553–80; "Diskussion," pp. 580–95. Cf. J. Pieper, "Identitätstheologie" (1966), in *Werke* 8 (Hamburg: Meiner, 2005), pp. 167–70. See: M. Schlögl, "Der Glaube braucht den Mut der Vernunft zu sich selbst," pp. 279–82.

[18] Cf. J. Pieper, "Überlieferung. Begriff und Anspruch," in *Werke* 3 (Hamburg: Felix Meiner, 2004), pp. 236–99.

interpretation: "Two things particularly pleased me: your confrontation with the problem of historicism, its broken relationship to tradition and its rejection of the question of truth, which is already justified in the method."[19] Similarly on April 27, 1989: "(...) the retreat into historicism and into formal forms of philosophizing seems to largely paralyze the true philosophical impulse. But I am sure that a work like yours has such great vitality that sooner or later it will ignite again and set new philosophical thinking in motion from the spirit of the great tradition." The second issue, "priesthood," became more heated; Pieper wrote a kind of *Philippika* to Ratzinger on December 18, 1968:

> However, your essay on the priesthood (Spirit and Life) tempts me to engage in a friendly argument.[20] Even the ironic treatment of the image of the priest in the first sermons, although it is certainly justified by the milieu of your audience, makes me uncomfortable; even if the illustration is a thousand times too crude and the terminology too sentimental—what is meant should not be ironized. I have no difficulty, as an old man and as an intellectual, in calling the little chaplain "Reverend" and even "Father"—though not in relation to his preaching and pastoral function, which seems to depend largely on his personal maturity and education, but with regard to what is specifically priestly about him, which he received in ordination. However, this aspect is simply neglected in your presentation, unless it is ignored and suppressed outright. I find the conclusions that young theology students and chaplains are drawing from this extremely disturbing (because it seems to me that what is specifically Catholic is going to hell here). Instead of Saturday afternoons[21] there is now a group of young theologians in my house (deacons, chaplains, ex-theologians); and we discussed your essay last night; I was really shocked. (...) However, I dispute that an interpretation of the priestly ministry in which the *sacerdotium* simply disappears in the magisterium ("kerygma") corresponds to what the Catholic Church has actually said on this subject and also says in Vatican II. You hardly say a word about the "offering of the sacrifice," about the consecration, about the connection between Eucharistic Real Presence and priestly execution! And after reading your essay, one is absolutely not prepared for it (the young theologians were almost incredulously surprised when I read them the relevant passages) to find what is said in the documents of Vaticanum II (...) I do not say, of course, that you deny what is said in these sentences; but based on your description, no one will think that there is such a thing in the documents

---

[19] J. Ratzinger, Letter, April 1, 1979 (Cf. *supra*. n. 2).
[20] Cf. J. Ratzinger, "Zur Frage nach dem Sinn des priesterlichen Dienstes," in *Geist und Leben* 41/10 (1968), pp. 347–76. The article summarizes two lectures given by Ratzinger on 2.8.1967 at a conference of German-speaking regents in Brixen/South Tyrol.
[21] Cf. *supra*, n. 2.

of Vatican II (...) I am indeed very engaged and deeply concerned here. Indeed, I fear that what is most sacramental will be made to disappear in such a way, and that the "Word" and the "Preacher" will remain. (...) I also do not deny that the word spoken in the performance of the sacrament (e.g. *Ego te absolvo* ...) has the character of proclamation; but: that I, the recipient, by hearing such words and letting them be said to me, may be granted an insight that may transform me (...)—this is something different from the actual redemption of my sins that takes place in the sacrament.[22]

The sharply pointed criticism is of Ratzinger's failure to address the significance of the Eucharistic sacrifice that the priest has to offer and his overemphasis on the preaching word in which Pieper sees an approximation to Protestantism. Pieper made this objection public again in the equally clearly critical essay entitled "Astonished Remarks by a Layman on the Subject of Priesthood" (1969).[23] Without mentioning Ratzinger's name, but partly using the same formulations as in the letter, Pieper takes a sharp stance. He goes even further in the essay "What Distinguishes the Priest? A Forced Attempt at Clarification" (1971).[24]

Ratzinger's answer in a letter dated February 13, 1969, reads:

First of all, I must emphasize that I did not use the "Word" as the actual guiding concept for determining the priestly office, but rather "pastoral care" (mission) and "Gospel." Both have a much wider radius than the Word in the Protestant sense. Both point to the authority of the incarnated *Logos* and to the empowering mission that he gives through his church. So I have by no means simply described the Eucharistic event as a cultic proclamation, but expressly as "authorized proclamation" (...), which quite expressly differs from that other form of proclamation (...) The authority of this proclamation, which is assigned to the spiritual office to which it is bound is shown in the sacramental reality that sets it (...).

As can be seen, despite various clarifications, Ratzinger generally tends to agree [that Pieper has a point] and ultimately allows himself to be corrected. This is also the case with Pieper's thematically related small essay "Not Words, but Reality. The Sacrament of Bread" from 1974.[25] Ratzinger replied

---

[22] J. Pieper, *Letter*, December 18, 1968; cf. *supra*, n. 2. Ida Friederike Görres (1901–74) also wrote about Ratzinger's contribution, not only approvingly but also critically: "Fragen eines Laien zur theologischen Diskussion über das priesterliche Amt," *Geist und Leben* 42 (1969), pp. 220–3. Ratzinger's answer can be read in *ibid.*, 223–4.
[23] J. Pieper, *Werke* 7, pp. 448–53.
[24] *Ibid.*, pp. 454–74.
[25] Cf. *ibid.*, pp. 420–7.

on July 16, 1973, from Regensburg that "I read it immediately and knew I was gratefully enriched by it." In any case, Pieper's criticism of 1969 ran deep and was taken seriously by Ratzinger.

Apparently the gratitude of the younger to the master deepens more and more. On May 5, 1979, on the occasion of Pieper's 75th birthday, a *summa* of appreciation read:

> Now I would like to do it in writing and to you for the service that you have rendered in our confused epoch with no other purpose than that of your conscience and your beliefs thank you from the bottom of my heart—officially as a bishop, so to speak, but at the same time personally as one who has become your student through your books and knows that you have given and taught him many things. During the past few weeks I have been able to finish reading the second volume of your memoirs,[26] and in doing so have mentally followed the vast space of your thoughts and work, which stretched out over a time that spanned from the hopeful dawn of the post-war period to the resigned or revolutionary materialism of the present (...). They have kept the program that philosophy is considering the whole and the search for the whole, in a world of specializations that has become, almost by definition, a rejection of the whole and thus a rejection of philosophy, thereby paralyzing itself.

And in an echo of his early years, in which Ratzinger also knew he was being corrected, it says on May 3, 1994:

> When the great confusion of thinking arose in the seventies, you once again proved yourself as a spiritual leader in a magnanimous way to a generation shaken by buzzwords. With your calm objectivity and the superior breadth of your education, you sought to return to the humility of hearing and looking. So, as a philosopher of theology, you have done an irreplaceable service and, thank God, you are still doing it.

Pieper's Doctrine of Virtue and Pope Benedict's Encyclical *Deus caritas est*

An immediate, deep agreement between the student Ratzinger and Pieper was found in Pieper's famous doctrine of virtue, the "four-horse chariot." On May 3, 1994, the cardinal wrote on Pieper's 90th birthday: "When I

---

[26] Cf. J. Pieper, *Noch nicht aller Tage Abend. Autobiographische Aufzeichnungern 1945–1964* (München: Kösel, 1979), p. 277. Pieper writes that Pope John XXIII based his Spiritual Exercises on his "quartet."

began my theological studies in January 1946, your four little books on the cardinal virtues were one of the first readings I came across; so you became my guide to philosophy early on and thus also a signpost in my theological thinking."

The quartet was followed by the trio of the divine virtues of faith, hope and love and these left deep traces in Ratzinger and were even fruitful for the universal church. Many of the thoughts in the two, actually three, papal encyclicals: *Deus caritas est* (on love), *Spe salvi* (on hope), and the draft of *Lumen fidei* (on faith) are shaped subliminally by Pieper's previous thinking. The younger one had already dedicated a corresponding three-part "exercise"[27] to the older one and wrote to him on March 7, 1989, from Rome: "I had just read your book 'Love-Hope-Faith' and then held the retreat on Faith-Hope-Love and took the guide more or less from your book, which was still fresh in my mind. So I thought it would be a meaningful birthday present to dedicate this *opusculum* to you, which would not have been born without your opus."

Let's stay with the most exciting keyword. Pope Benedict XVI signed his first encyclical *Deus caritas est* on December 25, 2005. It was received with great excitement. Surprisingly, in his account of love he combined *eros* and *agape*. *Eros*, which comes from below and can go astray or come to an end, is, within the sacrament of marriage, held, guided, and sanctified by *agape*, the love from above. Already here the Pope sketches what later became known as a comprehensive ecology of man, in which a powerfully blossoming love can unfold, sanctified and healed in God.

Pieper, too, had opened up a leeway between *eros* and *agape*, that excludes neither side nor drives it into exaggeration.[28] Against the long-standing assertion that *agape* is purely unselfish, associated with the work of Erich Fromm and Andres Nygren, Pieper develops a wonderfully expansive counter-statement, with good reason, from antiquity to Thomas Aquinas to Goethe and classical modernity: the happiness of the lover consists not only in selflessly releasing, but primarily in winning and enjoying the loved one. Love is also hunger and thirst—even if it wants to make the other happy. She is not simply selfless, but needy, needing; she is giving, appreciative, but precisely because of this she demands an echo.

This does not mean that love is purposeful; it is rather something else: meaningful. Focusing your whole self on the loved one leads to the highest form of love: "being smitten" or "living and dying for," in any case: letting yourself be deeply moved by someone else. Ultimately, it is the "event

---

[27] J. Ratzinger, *Auf Christus schauen. Einübung in Glaube, Hoffnung, Liebe* (Freiburg: Herder, 1989).
[28] Cf. J. Pieper, *Über die Liebe* (München: Kösel, 1972). See: H. B. Gerl-Falkovitz, *Vorwort zur Neuausgabe* (München: Kösel, 2012), pp. 11–26.

character" that moves the lover away. Pieper translates the affection and passion as Plato's "God-given *mania*."[29] But this being torn away is not selfless in the sense described, since it corresponds to the deepest self of the lover. Pieper thus opens up a space between *eros* and *agape* that does not exclude either side or take it to extremes. The self-evident and natural, namely self-love, is preserved in the scope, it is even assumed and cultivated through the relationship. There is no ethical duty to overexploitation, to self-loss—just as little as selfish self-preservation and disinterested coolness lead to the heart of loving.

This does not mean self-interest and badly hidden self-enjoyment. Rather it means that in the happiness of the other, one finds one's own happiness reflected. There is no isolated, one-sided happiness, that would be a direct contradiction in itself—the uplifting is precisely the mutually wonderfully increasing echo. This leeway between being carried away and self-discovery decides on the success or failure of *Eros*, which escalates into *agape*. Powerfully condensed: "All happiness is love happiness."[30]

Pope Benedict adopts Pieper's basic idea in the encyclical *Deus caritas est*:

> Yet *eros* and *agape*—ascending love and descending love—can never be completely separated. The more the two, in their different aspects, find a proper unity in the one reality of love, the more the true nature of love in general is realized. Even if *eros* is at first mainly covetous and ascending, a fascination for the great promise of happiness, in drawing near to the other, it is less and less concerned with itself, increasingly seeks the happiness of the other, is concerned more and more with the beloved, bestows itself and wants to "be there for" the other. The element of *agape* thus enters into this love, for otherwise *eros* is impoverished and even loses its own nature. On the other hand, man cannot live by oblative, descending love alone. He cannot always give, he must also receive. Anyone who wishes to give love must also receive love as a gift.[31]

The fact that a papal encyclical for the first time so naturally appreciatively leads *Eros* to *Agape* is inconceivable without Pieper's forethought in his book *About Love*. In fact, he is the *spiritus rector* of this comprehensive interpretation. On March 15, 1996, already looking back on Pieper's words about the "God-given mania," the cardinal wrote:

---

[29] J. Pieper, "Gottgeschenkte mania. Eine Platon-Interpretation," *Internationale Katholische Zeitschrift Communio* 3 (1994), pp. 260–70.
[30] *Id.*, *Alles Glück ist Liebesglück* (Hamburg: Katholische Akademie, 1992).
[31] Benedict XVI, *Encyclical Letter* Deus caritas est *on Christian Love*, December 25, 2005, §7.

Your speech of thanks at the symposium in Münster in 1994 reminded me of your book about the "divine madness" according to Plato[32], which has become for me a key lecture. You considered what was said there and placed it in the diverse contexts of encounters with poets and philosophers. It seems to me that you are impressively reconciling the exclusivity of our culture of making with the need to receive and the need of suffering, which alone is the way in which purification is granted to us, how contact with the mystery of God can become real.

The encyclical emphasizes again: "Yes, love is 'ecstasy', but ecstasy not in the sense of an intoxicating moment, but ecstasy as a constant path out of the self-contained ego to the release of the ego, to devotion and thus to self-discovery, yes, to the discovery of God."

The theologian sums up the constant dialogue with the philosopher in the great encomium: Pieper creates as *"verus doctor vetera et nova ex thesauro sapientiae."*[33] "By becoming a friend of the truth, you have become a friend of Christ, who himself is the truth and the life. May he one day receive you with open arms and lead you into the unveiled vision of eternal truth."[34]

Translation from German by Tracey Rowland

---

[32] Cf. J. Pieper, *Begeisterung und göttlicher Wahnsnn. Über den platonischen Dialog, "Phaidros"* (München: Kösel, 1962).
[33] J. Ratzinger, *Letter*, January, 1997. Cf. *supra*, n. 2.
[34] *Id.*, *Letter on the Occasion of Pieper's 90th Birthday*, May 3, 1994. Cf. *supra*, n. 2.

18

Jean-Paul Sartre: Truth, Freedom, and Responsibility

Alejandro Sada

Introduction

Jean-Paul Sartre is unquestionably one of the giants of the existentialist movement that marked the history of twentieth-century thought.[1] Offering a precise definition of existentialism is not a simple matter. It is generally understood, as Thomas R. Flynn notes, as a way of thinking about that which is individual and concrete, as opposed to abstract and timeless philosophy. Its typical themes are 1) the precedence of existence over essence, 2) temporality as part of essence, 3) humanism, 4) freedom and responsibility, and 5) the priority of ethical issues.[2] If Flynn is right, this cultural movement as a whole has clearly left a deep imprint on Joseph Ratzinger's way of thinking. For the German theologian, all five themes are highly relevant and are discussed repeatedly throughout his work. Particularly important is his insistence that philosophy carries at its core the question of the *humanun* in its concrete existence as its fundamental

---

[1] Sartre, however, would not be altogether comfortable with this title, as R. C. Solomon points out in his book *Dark Feelings, Grim Thoughts: Experience and Reflections in Camus and Sartre* (Oxford, New York: Oxford University Press, 2006), p. 5.
[2] Cf. T. R. Flynn, *Existentialism: A Very Short Introduction* (New York: Oxford University Press, 2006), p. 8. See also the *Preface*.

and ultimate question.³ In this regard, there is a methodological affinity that brings Ratzinger close to existentialism; as Esther Gómez de Pedro points out, the German theologian always confronts theory with the experience of concrete human existence, "The type of experience known as 'experiential or *Existentialerfahrung*'."⁴

Peter Seewald says that Joseph Ratzinger avidly read Jean-Paul Sartre as a young man.⁵ Benedict XVI himself explains that Sartre was someone to be read at that time because he translated Heidegger's existentialism into concrete terms. According to him, the fact that Sartre wrote his philosophy in French cafés made it more penetrating and realistic.⁶ Ratzinger considers him—along with Albert Camus and Simone de Beauvoir—to be a thinker who represents a whole generation.⁷ In this chapter, I will examine how Ratzinger dialogues with a well-known theme in Sartre's philosophy, namely, freedom and responsibility, which is, as noted, one of the issues to which existentialist philosophy continually returns.⁸

Radical Responsibility

Sartre's philosophy of freedom is perhaps the most radical approach that the twentieth century saw on this issue. According to Sartre, man is pure freedom, capable of defining himself and, therefore, lacks *a priori* criteria that guide his actions. This makes him radically responsible for his own reality. From this abysmal freedom follows an experience of terrible anguish, for it is unbearable to discover that we are responsible for everything that motivates our actions. When we discover that we are entirely dependent on ourselves,

---

³In my doctoral dissertation, I devoted considerable space to explain the centrality of human existence in Ratzinger's idea of philosophy. Cf. A. Sada, *Naturaleza y misión de la filosofía en el pensamiento de Joseph Ratzinger* (Doctoral thesis, Pamplona: Universidad de Navarra, 2020), pp. 147–59. I show that, for Ratzinger, "the search for truth springs from the structure of human existence, which is experienced as an enigma." Cf. *id.*, *Sentido y verdad. Hacia una nueva comprensión de la filosofía desde el pensamiento de Joseph Ratzinger* (Madrid: BAC, 2023).
⁴M. E. Gómez de Pedro, *Libertad en Ratzinger: riesgo y tarea* (Madrid: Encuentro, 2014), p. 19.
⁵Cf. P. Seewald, *Benedict XVI. Una vida* (Bilbao: Mensajero, 2020); in English: *Benedict XVI. A Life* 2 (London: Bloomsbury, 2020–1), p. 208.
⁶Cf. Benedict XVI and P. Seewald, *Last Testament: In His Own Words* (London: Bloomsbury, 2016), p. 153. It is necessary to acknowledge that this affirmation of Benedict XVI is quite debatable. Heidegger himself took distance from Sartre's thought. In particular, in his *Letter on Humanism*, the German philosopher wants to make clear his differences with Sartre, who, in *Existentialism Is a Humanism*, had identified Heidegger's thought as belonging to his own existentialist tradition. I thank my friend Vicente de Haro for this observation.
⁷Cf. *JROC* XI, p. 291.
⁸For a detailed study of Sartre's existentialism, see: J. Webber, *The Existentialism of Jean-Paul Sartre* (New York, London: Routledge, 2009).

that we have no excuse, that we are radically responsible, we experience a sort of unpleasant vertigo.[9] We then try to run away from it by reducing the burden of our responsibility.[10] This is what Sartre generally refers to when he speaks of *bad faith (mauvaise foi)*. According to Jonathan Webber, bad faith in its general usage, amounts to what Sartre calls "psychological determinism," which the French philosopher describes as an "attitude of excuse," a "reflective conduct with respect to anguish" that "provides us with a nature productive of our acts."[11] This attitude of bad faith, originally common to the whole human condition, resists recognizing the radicality of freedom and attempts to see human beings as limited by some fixed nature. It seems, then, that all men are condemned to live in this false escape from reality.

Faced with this situation, Sartre anticipates a possible way out in *Being and Nothingness*, which he calls *authenticity*. This project implies a radical escape from *bad faith* through a "self-recovery of being which was previously corrupted,"[12] for which a "radical conversion"[13] is necessary. However, in that same work, he refuses to give more details, but promises a study of ethics to properly address the issue. That study, however, never reached the public. Although some related notes were published in a posthumous notebook, we will not pay heed to them—following Webber—since they

---

[9] In his philosophical *magnum opus*, *Being and Nothingness*, Sartre opposes any form of determinism. He attempts to show that human action cannot be causally explained on the basis of its motives, but rather that the subject has control over his motives, which are constitutive elements of action itself. Now, these motives are manifestations of our character, which is constituted by the set of individual projects that the subject pursues, which have been freely chosen and can eventually be reversed or replaced by new projects. In this regard, Sartre speaks of the radical nature of our freedom, as we can always modify our projects—our character—and act upon new motives. Cf. J.-P. Sartre, *Being and Nothingness: An Essay on Phenomenological Ontology* (New York: Washington Square Press, 1978), pp. 438, 464.

[10] This escape from anguish denies our condition of free beings without fixed natures. Thus, our fundamental project is established, our project of projects, which consists of pretending to have a human nature. In fact, Sartre says that, "the fundamental project of human reality" is "to reach toward being God"; in this way, human beings are "the desire to be God." The idea of God expresses both a fixed nature and a personal reality, realities that for Sartre are contradictory. Thus, as Webber explains, when Sartre says that we want to be God, he is not referring to a desire to be omniscient and all-powerful, but rather that we want to possess a solid nature at the same time while also not wanting to lose our condition as conscious beings, which, as mentioned, is a contradictory idea for Sartre, as consciousness is itself a dynamic reality. Thus, we desire a nature that frees us from the abysmal freedom of our human condition, that excuses us and lightens the burden of responsibility. In one way or another, all our projects express this tendency in multiple ways. Cf. J.-P. Sartre, *Being and Nothingness*, p. 566; J. Webber, *The Existentialism of Jean-Paul Sartre*, p. 107.

[11] J.-P. Sartre, *Being and Nothingness*, p. 40; cf. J. Webber, *The Existentialism of Jean-Paul Sartre*, p. 74.

[12] J.-P. Sartre, *Being and Nothingness*, p. 70, n. 9.

[13] *Ibid.*, p. 412, n. 14.

are often confusing and misleading.[14] Instead, we will try to reconstruct an answer from his published texts.

In his lecture, *Existentialism Is a Humanism*, Sartre offers a response and an alternative project to that of *bad faith*. In it, he explicitly states that *bad faith* is "an error," "a lie," "because it is a dissimulation of man's full freedom of commitment."[15] He also speaks of the true universal condition of human existence, in which "there is no human nature," and therefore, "man is nothing other than what he makes of himself,"[16] so he alone is "responsible for what he is;"[17] "man is freedom."[18] If *bad faith* is an escape from the radical freedom in which we find ourselves, the project of authenticity must consist of accepting the truth of the human condition without attempting to hide the fact that we do not have a nature or values on which to base ourselves. But how does one accept having radical freedom without a foundation and how does one express this freedom in the concrete tasks of our lives without a desire to have a determined nature? Sartre's answer is very enigmatic. For authentic choices to be so, they must be truly free in a radical sense; in other words, that ought to be creators of value and do not pretend to be sustained by *a priori* values. The authentic man has to take on a commitment to invent his values so that anything is permissible as long as our freedom over our nature is recognized. The only condition of free action is that it be truly free, so "freedom, under any concrete circumstance, can have no other aim than itself."[19] Otherwise, it would be claiming to act according to *a priori* values. This, according to Sartre, is the source of man's responsibility, for there is nothing outside man himself that establishes the pattern of his own existence. He alone defines himself, and therefore, he alone is responsible for his being.

Atheism and Rebellion against the Truth

In a magnificent article on Jean-Paul Sartre's philosophical method, German philosopher Josef Pieper identifies three definitions that Sartre offers for explaining what existentialism is,[20] namely: 1) an attempt to extract all the

---

[14] Cf. J. Webber, *The Existentialism of Jean-Paul Sartre*, p. xiii.
[15] J.-P. Sartre, *Existentialism Is a Humanism* (New Haven, London; Yale University Press, 2007), pp. 47–8.
[16] *Ibid.*, p. 22.
[17] *Ibid.*, p. 23.
[18] *Ibid.*, p. 29.
[19] *Ibid.*, p. 48.
[20] Cf. J. Pieper, *For the Love of Wisdom: Essays on the Nature of Philosophy* (San Francisco: Ignatius, 2006), pp. 173–84. This article is very important because Joseph Ratzinger thoroughly read and appreciated it. In fact, he refers to it more than once. See, for example, J. Ratzinger, *Truth and Tolerance: Christian Belief and World Religions* (San Francisco: Ignatius, 2004), p. 244, n. 7; *Church, Ecumenism, and Politics: New Endeavors in Ecclesiology* (San Francisco: Ignatius, 2008), p. 182, n. 4.

consequences of a coherent atheistic position, 2) a philosophy whose first principle is that there is no human nature whatsoever, and 3) a philosophy that affirms that existence precedes essence.[21] Pieper suggests that these three definitions are interdependent from each other.[22] Nevertheless, if one had to identify a root that triggers all of Sartre's existentialist philosophy, perhaps one would have to point to his position in favor of the non-existence of God. It is not by chance that he himself calls his own philosophy an "atheistic existentialism."[23]

Ratzinger is well acquainted with Sartre's line of thought. In 1975, he relied on Josef Pieper's thought to develop his ideas.[24] Ratzinger explains that, for the French philosopher, "human beings and things cannot have a nature. If they did [...] there would have to be a God,"[25] which Sartre would not be willing to accept. What is reality then? What is man? "If reality itself does not proceed from a creative consciousness, if it is not the realization of a design, of an idea, then it will always be a structure without firm contours, to be used as one will."[26] It is precisely from here that Sartre draws his conviction that man is an indefinite existence that is self-fulfilled through an abysmal freedom: "if God does not exist, there is at least one being in whom existence precedes essence—a being whose existence comes before its essence, a being who exists before he can be defined by any concept of it."[27] "If I have eliminated God the Father—so says the Existentialist—, there has to be someone to invent values. [...] To say that we invent values means neither more nor less than this: life has no meaning *a priori*. Life itself is nothing until it is lived, it is we who give it meaning, and value is nothing more that the meaning that we give it."[28] But what values should we invent? We already know how Sartre would answer: Choose what you want, as long as you choose it in the name of freedom. When he faces the issue of morality, he also relies on his fundamental atheism. That is why he takes the words that Dostoevsky puts into Kirillov's mouth as his starting point: "If God does not exist, everything is permissible." This is, according to Sartre, "the starting point of existentialism."[29] He tells us that, when a student approached him for advice on how to solve a delicate moral question, his answer was, "you are free to choose; in other words, invent."[30] His conception of morality

---

[21] Cf. J. Pieper, *For the Love of Wisdom*, pp. 173–4. Cf. J. P. Sartre, *Existentialism Is a Humanism*, pp. 22, 53, 55.
[22] Cf. J. Pieper, *For the Love of Wisdom*, p. 173.
[23] J.-P. Sartre, *Existentialism Is a Humanism*, p. 22.
[24] Cf. J. Ratzinger, *Principles of Catholic Theology: Building Stones for a Fundamental Theology* (San Francisco: Ignatius, 1985), p. 72.
[25] *Ibid.*
[26] *Ibid.*
[27] J.-P. Sartre, *Existentialism Is a Humanism*, p. 22.
[28] *Ibid.*, p. 51.
[29] *Ibid.*, pp. 28–9.
[30] *Ibid.*, p. 33.

resembles, according to his own explanation, a work of art, because we are in the same creative situation as an artist who does not have *a priori* aesthetic criteria to produce his work.[31] In this, Sartre finds the greatness of the human being. Once liberated from God, he becomes his own god.

For Ratzinger, at the heart of philosophies such as that of Sartre, we find precisely a radical rebellion against God and, therefore, against the understanding of human existence as a reality created with a nature. Contrary to what the Frenchman thinks, namely, that we flee from radical freedom in order to wrap ourselves in *bad faith* with the protection of a nature, Ratzinger sees in Sartre's proposal a rejection of our fundamental creaturely condition in order to be "free" from any kind of limit. What Sartre would call *authenticity*—understood now as rebellion against our creaturely condition—for Ratzinger is true rebellion against what we really are, and this would be the true *bad faith*. In a penetrating homily, he explains that the story of the temptation experienced by Adam and Eve stands for the proposal to rebel against "the limitations of their existence," to choose "not to be bound by the limitations imposed by good and evil, or by morality in general."[32] They are invited to abandon any boundaries that define their existence.

Perhaps with a nod to Sartre, Ratzinger makes a comparison with an artist. In art, there seem to be no limits; artists "may do what they can do," "they have no limitations."[33] In this context, "the measure of human beings is what they can do and not what they are, not what is good or bad. What they can do they may do."[34] But what happens if we extend this context to the totality of human existence? What happens, for example, if instead of asking ourselves what can be done in art, we question what human beings are allowed to do in the realm of technique? Should we be allowed to do everything that can be done? Ratzinger offers a couple of examples to make us aware of the dire consequences of this approach. First, he recalls how Robert Oppenheimer described how physicists were fascinated by the possibilities offered by the atomic bomb to the point of considering it to be the *technically sweet*, the fascinating thing. In an equally appalling way, Rudolf Höss, the last commandant of Auschwitz, claimed in his diary that the extermination camp had been an impressive technical masterpiece. He found the program so perfect and captivating that it justified itself.[35] Human beings, Ratzinger concludes, always have their very being as their standard, and "when they reject this standard they deceive themselves in opposition

---

[31] Cf. *ibid.*, pp. 45–6.
[32] J. Ratzinger, "*In the Beginning ...*" *A Catholic Understanding of the Story of Creation and the Fall* (Grand Rapids: Eerdmans, 1995), p. 67.
[33] *Ibid.*, p. 68.
[34] *Ibid.*
[35] Cf. *ibid.*, pp. 68–9. Ratzinger takes both examples from Josef Pieper's study, *Über den Begriff der Sünde*.

to the truth." When this happens, "they are destroying themselves and the world."[36] Attempting to divinize man by eliminating God is the most profound form of what the Christian tradition calls *sin*:

> At the very heart of sin lies human beings' denial of their creatureliness, inasmuch as they refuse to accept the standard and the limitations that are implicit in it. They do not want to be creatures, do not want to be subject to a standard, do not want to be dependent. They consider their dependence on God's creative love to be an imposition from without. But that is what slavery is and from slavery one must free oneself. Thus human beings themselves want to be God.[37]

Sin is, therefore, the opposition to the truth of our being, to that truth that we call nature.

In an anthropology such as the one proposed by Sartre, the existence of God is interpreted as a reality that is antagonistic to human beings in such a way that if God exists, human freedom is annulled or reduced. The existence of God, therefore, is uncomfortable. Sartre, of course, would not accept this assertion. On the contrary, according to him, "existentialists [...] find it extremely disturbing that God no longer exists, for along with his disappearance goes the possibility of finding values in an intelligible heaven."[38] Gradually, however, his true understanding of the matter comes to the surface. Once God has been eliminated and man has been placed in the radicality of a freedom without natures, it seems to him that justice has finally been done for human beings: "this is the only theory that endows man with any dignity, and the only one that does not turn him into an object."[39] Having nature is, for Sartre, the same as being "a set of predetermined reactions," so that, rather than being free, we would be like "a table, a chair, or a stone."[40] Nature and freedom are opposed in that they seem to exclude one another.

The inevitable love we all have for freedom undergoes a dizzying crisis when we understand that it is incompatible with the limits set by the boundaries of nature. Thus, rejecting the truth seems more attractive, if we comprehend truth as an idea derived from the concept of nature. If we eliminate all nature from man, we are saying that man's truth is that he has no definite truth, his truth is indeterminate existence. When freedom is looked upon as a reality opposed to nature, the result can become a frightful hatred of truth, for it can only be seen as enslaving. Nowhere have I found a better representation of this rebellion against the self as the one

---

[36] J. Ratzinger, *"In the Beginning ...,"* p. 69.
[37] *Ibid.*, p. 70.
[38] J.-P. Sartre, *Existentialism Is a Humanism*, p. 28.
[39] *Ibid.*, p. 41.
[40] *Ibid.*

that Camus offers in his Caligula character. After the emperor expresses his schizophrenic desire for a voracious and limitless freedom, his wife Caesonia presents him with the limits of the world's harsh reality. "You will not be able to make heaven not heaven, or a beautiful face ugly, or a human heart insensitive." Caligula retorts stubbornly, "I want to mix heaven with the sea, to confound ugliness and beauty, to make laughter spring forth from suffering." But Caesonia insists, "There is the good and the bad, the high and the low, the just and the unjust. I assure you that none of this will change." "My will is to change it," rages Caligula, "I shall give this century the gift of equality." The emperor wants for nothing to matter, for nothing to have any boundaries, for everything to be the same. And so he concludes, "To live, Caesonia, is the opposite of loving." This amounts to "freely" and hatefully rejecting all that is true, because truth is understood as enslaving. While strangling Caesonia, the emperor shouts vehemently,

> I live, I kill, I exercise the delirious power of the destructor, compared to which the power of the creator seems like a parody. This is what it means to be happy. This is happiness, this unbearable liberation, this universal contempt, the blood, the hatred around me, this unparalleled isolation of the man who holds his whole life under his haze, the boundless joy of the unpunished murder, this implacable logic that crushes human lives (he laughs), that crushes you, Caesonia, finally achieving the eternal solitude that I desire.[41]

Truth as the Foundation of Freedom

For Ratzinger, truth is not an obstacle to freedom; on the contrary, it is freedom's very foundation. Only in truth can we be truly free. The truth of being human is not in conflict with the freedom we desire. Rather, truth itself is the only space in which that freedom can flourish. "Against Sartre," Pablo Blanco-Sarto explains, "[for Ratzinger] man is not just 'terrifying freedom,' but being and freedom at the same time; in other words, a being-in-freedom."[42] But what does properly human freedom look like, one that unfolds in harmony with the creaturely limits of our nature? Ratzinger's best answer to this question is presented in a 1995 text published in *Truth and Tolerance*.[43] Before offering a possible solution, he suggests looking at the thought of Jean-Paul Sartre, "where the whole seriousness and stature of the question become clear."[44] It is, says Ratzinger, "the most radical philosophy

---

[41] A. Camus, *Caligula* (Paris: Gallimard, 1993), pp. 63–4, 170.
[42] P. Blanco-Sarto, *La teología de Joseph Ratzinger. Una introducción* (Madrid, Palabra, 2011), p. 326.
[43] Cf. J. Ratzinger, *Truth and Tolerance*, pp. 231–58.
[44] *Ibid.*, p. 244.

of freedom in this past century."[45] In just a few lines, he offers us his analysis of the French philosopher's thought:

> Sartre regards the freedom of man as being his damnation. In contrast to animals, man has no "nature." An animal lives its life according to the pattern of law that it has inbuilt within it; it does not need to consider what to do with its life. But the being of man is undetermined. It is an open question. I have to decide for myself what I understand by "being a man," what I can do about it, what shape I can give it. Man has no nature but is simply freedom. He has to live his life in some direction or other, yet it runs out into nothingness even so. His meaningless freedom is man's hell. What is exciting about this proposition is that the separation of freedom and truth is carried through quite radically here: there is no truth. Freedom is without direction or measure.[46]

For Ratzinger, man is certainly free, but his freedom is not pure freedom. Rather, it is measured by the way in which he exists in the context of a coexistence of freedoms. In the modern world, "people have narrowed down the concept of freedom to individual rights and freedoms and have thus robbed it of its human verity."[47] However, when freedom is viewed only from an individual point of view, the concept is robbed of its human reality, which is not a solitary, isolated existence but a coexistence of freedoms in a relationship of mutual dependence and responsibility. To clarify this idea, Ratzinger uses the paradigmatic case of abortion. A woman who wishes to have an abortion appeals to the freedom she has to decide regarding her body, in the same way she has the right to self-determination. However, if she actually carries within her a person different from herself, she is also deciding about someone else. By annulling the life of that other-person, she deprives it of life, which is the space of freedom. The child's freedom, therefore, is in competition with the woman's freedom. Faced with this situation, Ratzinger asks: "what kind of a freedom is this that numbers among its rights that of abolishing someone else's freedom right from the start?"[48]

The case of abortion aptly illustrates a structure of radical dependency. One being is so intertwined with another that it can only exist in coexistence with the other. Although the baby exists in physical unity with the mother, it is nevertheless a person with its own self. We are dealing with a being that, for the moment, is completely and very concretely a being-from-another. The mother's existence is involved in the existence-for-the-other that contradicts her own will and, therefore, is experienced as contrary to her own freedom.

---

[45] *Ibid.*
[46] *Ibid.*
[47] *Ibid.*, p. 245.
[48] *Ibid.*, p. 246.

It seems to Ratzinger that, in this case, "the basic shape of human freedom, its typically human character, becomes clear,"[49] as it exemplifies how people are embedded in a web of mutual dependence. When the child is born, although it is no longer as radically dependent on the mother as a being-for—since someone else could take care of him—nevertheless, its being is still in complete need of the being-for of someone: "it remains the derived being, demanding someone be there for it."[50] The child would perish if no one were to offer him their being-for. This, according to Ratzinger, also applies to the totality of human existence, as the adult is also a being-with-another and a being-from-another. No person is self-sufficient, so every human being radically presupposes the being-for of others, as can be clearly seen in the network of services.

We are thus faced with a paradox. When we only focus on individual freedom, we fail to consider that this freedom exists in a network of mutual dependence and that this structure of intertwined freedoms is a source of obligations and responsibilities, upon the fulfillment of which depends the existence not only of individual freedom, but of all the freedoms that are intertwined in this network. When this being-for is not accepted as a responsibility, the reality of human existence, which presupposes the being-for of all the members of the community, is denied. Humanity and freedom, then, are seen as conflicting realities.

This being-for-from-with the other, i.e., the relational dimension of human existence, is perhaps the most characteristic aspect of what it means to be a person. For this reason, it cannot be renounced if true freedom for all is to be achieved. Sartre goes so far as to affirm that in willing freedom, "we discover that it depends entirely on the freedom of others, and that the freedom of others depends on our own," thus "I am obliged to will the freedom of others at the same time as I will my own."[51] This good intuition is quite close to Ratzinger's position. However, it is difficult to justify from the whole of Sartrean philosophy. The relationship between the Sartre's project of authenticity and the need to respect the freedom of others is not clear. If I look at others as instruments that I can use and subdue to achieve the goals I have freely set for myself, what stops me from doing so? Why should I respect them? What stops me from growing in power and subduing everything around me if that is what I want and can do?[52]

To answer this question from Ratzinger's point of view, one can resort to the conviction that each person is the bearer of an absolute and inviolable dignity, which is untenable if one does not accept the idea that human beings have been created in the image and likeness of God himself. Every person is special because, as the theologian says in one of his interviews with Peter

---

[49] *Ibid.*
[50] *Ibid.*
[51] J.-P. Sartre, *Existentialism Is a Humanism*, pp. 48–9.
[52] It is not clear to Webber himself that the need to respect the freedoms of others follows from Sartre's philosophy. Cf. J. Webber, *The Existentialism of Jean-Paul Sartre*, pp. 144–5.

Seewald, "God's breath is within him." "He is not just a combination of biological building blocks, but a personal conception of God."[53] This is precisely what Benedict XVI reminded the Church of at the enthronement Mass: "We are not some casual and meaningless product of evolution. Each of us is the result of a thought of God. Each of us is willed, each of us is loved, each of us is necessary."[54] The fact of having been created in a particular way by the love of God is most important "to perceive the uniqueness and value of man and, thereby, the basis of all human rights."[55] In this sense, the idea that we have human rights is a metaphysical idea. It means that "inherent in being itself there is an ethical and legal claim."[56] To say that man is worthy and, for the same reason, a bearer of rights, means that his reality is ontologically good and radically valuable in such a way that he must be guarded and protected and, therefore, is a source of responsibilities for himself and for others.

It is evident that, for Ratzinger, the idea of freedom is different from the Sartrean idea of indeterminacy. It has to do, rather, with a way of being that is contrary to that of a slave. Freedom is "the possession of full rights, full membership, being at home ... Freedom is identical with the possession of rights and with a certain ontological dignity."[57] This means that one is in possession of being and not only a subject to being. In this regard, we can say that God is freedom personified, because "he is the possession of being in its totality."[58] Within this positive formulation, freedom is an idea associated with ontological height, with the possibility of being in contact, like at home, with the source of being, with the wellspring of all good, truth, and love. If we understand that freedom is an idea associated with the stature of a dignified and valuable being, a bearer of rights that produces moral duties for all, we can also understand that moral duty is not man's prison from which he must free himself, but that, on the contrary, bonding morality constitutes his very dignity in such a way that, if it were to disappear, we would no longer be free and would take a step backward, "to the level of a machine, of a mere thing." Therefore, according to Ratzinger, "if there is no longer any obligation to which he can and must respond in freedom, then there is no longer any realm of freedom at all."[59] Therefore, recognizing the sphere of morality is nothing more than recognizing our own dignity, our true ontological stature.

---

[53] J. Ratzinger, *God and the World: Believing and Living in Our Time: A Conversation with Peter Seewald* (San Francisco: Ignatius, 2002), p. 77.
[54] Benedict XVI, *Mass, Imposition of the Pallium and Conferral of the Fisherman's Ring for the Beginning of the Petrine Ministry of the Bishop of Rome*, April 24, 2005.
[55] J. Ratzinger, *God and the World*, p. 77.
[56] *Id., Truth and Tolerance*, p. 238.
[57] *Id., Church, Ecumenism, and Politics*, pp. 186–7.
[58] *Ibid.*, p. 188.
[59] *Id., A Turning Point for Europe? The Church in the Modern World: Assessment and Forecast* (San Francisco: Ignatius, 1994), p. 41.

Solitary Freedom or Freedom in Communion?

According to Sartre's philosophy, there is no worthy human nature to which one can appeal in order to derive human rights that are morally binding for all. In fact, as we have already seen, nothing is ontologically valuable for him. Human relations, far from being understood as interpersonal relationships among dignified beings who support one another, are always relationships of domination in which each person moves solely toward the fulfillment of their own projects. Human beings are understood as an isolated individual reality on the horizon of an abyss of possibilities that are all directed toward final nothingness and mean nothing more than what the subject wants them to mean. In that tiresome confinement, people try to overcome loneliness through love.[60] But love, says Sartre, comes from the project of *bad faith* and is alienating because, as Webber explains, view of it is always filtered by what human beings judge to be useful or by what represents an obstacle to their own projects in such a way that others are always something that serves them or something that hinders them. Therefore, the way that others see me expresses what they are, not what I am.[61] The result is that all attempts at love end in catastrophe because when two freedoms fail to reach each other in true communion, the lovers are plunged into a deeper and more desolate abyss of loneliness.[62]

From this philosophy of individual freedoms seeking the fulfillment of solitary projects, I do not see how we can overcome a vision of human relationships beyond a struggle by all individuals to extend the dominion of that which facilitates the fulfillment of their respective projects. I do not see how to stop someone who finds in the immoral subjugation of others a way to facilitate the fulfillment of their chosen goals in total freedom. How is a solid morality that overcomes pure conflict of interests and power struggles possible when no *a priori* value is recognized? What can limit the capricious will when "the brute mass of being in-itself does not contain positive or negative values of any kind," when "nothing that we value possesses any value in and of itself"?[63]

---

[60] Cf. J. G. McGraw, "Loneliness, its nature and forms: an existential perspective," *Man and World* 28 (1995), p. 49.

[61] Cf. J. Webber, *The Existentialism of Jean-Paul Sartre*, p. 140; Sartre, *Being and Nothingness*, p. 380.

[62] Cf. J. G. McGraw, "Loneliness, its nature and forms," pp. 49–50. Ratzinger considers philosophers such as Sartre and Camus to be representative of an entire generation when they describe man's feeling of isolation and radical loneliness. He refers to this issue repeatedly. For example, *JROC* XI, pp. 255, 291; *Images of Hope: Meditations on Major Feasts* (San Francisco: Ignatius, 2006), p. 67; *Co-Workers of the Truth: Meditations for Every Day of the Year* (San Francisco: Ignatius, 1992), pp. 83–4.

[63] J. Webber, *The Existentialism of Jean-Paul Sartre*, p. 68.

Perhaps Sartre is right in discovering how harsh the gaze of others can be and the fact that, all too often, we look at one another as objects from which we can draw some advantage. But we must ask ourselves, is this situation really inevitable? Is a genuinely loving gaze in any way possible? This is a question of tremendous importance because, for Ratzinger, the gift of love is the ultimate reason for our free existence.[64] If love were not possible, human existence would be meaningless. Ratzinger is not unaware that, all too easily, we reduce others to mere things in order to use them or even destroy them.[65] However, he thinks that the way we view others depends on a secret decision that "passes through the *heart* of each one of us, in that hidden interior room where our freedom decides for good or evil."[66] All by itself, a person's face reflects the full radicality of his dignity. Therefore, it always appears with an appeal to my liberty to welcome and care for him, "asking me to affirm his value *per se*, not merely to the extent to which he may happen to coincide with my own interests."[67] The experience of the dignified face, in which a person's unique and unrepeatable value is revealed, demands a response on my part. However, I must freely want to view him according to the dignity he manifests. In that case, "I am deciding on conversion, I am resolving to let the other address his appeal to me, to go beyond the confines of my own self and to make space for him,"[68] or, in Sartrean terminology, to make the other my own project. Therefore, the perception of moral values depends on a profound, free decision. However, Sartre's reflections remain a serious challenge: Can man really love the other on his own sake? Can he make the other his own project? Ratzinger believes that the humanity of our gaze ultimately depends on our being able to experience how God looks at us: as a child can "open himself confidently to love if he knows he is loved, and he can develop and grow if he knows that he is followed everywhere by his parents' look of love," similarly, "we too succeed in looking at others in a manner that respects their personal dignity if we experience how God looks at us in love. It is this look that reveals to us how precious is our person."[69] Therefore, it seems to Ratzinger that Christianity is the memory of God's loving gaze that allows us, in turn, to look lovingly at one another.

Freedom, which makes us capable of loving, is a consequence of being created in the image of God. An unlimited ontological stature has been

---

[64] Cf. For example: J. Ratzinger, "*In the Beginning …,*" pp. 98–9; *God and the World*, pp. 190–1; *id.*, *Church, Ecumenism, and Politics*, p. 188.
[65] Cf. *id.*, *Christianity and the Crisis of Cultures* (San Francisco: Ignatius, 2006), pp. 65–73; Also: *id.*, *El elogio de la conciencia. La Verdad interroga al corazón* (Madrid: Palabra, 2010), pp. 39–51.
[66] *Id.*, *Christianity and the Crisis of Cultures*, p. 65. The quoted passage is part of a text on the right to life and the problem of abortion. However, Ratzinger's reflection on how we look at one another can be extended to any case of recognition or rejection of human dignity.
[67] *Ibid.*, p. 66.
[68] *Ibid.*
[69] *Ibid.*, p. 71.

bestowed upon us. Therefore, what Ratzinger detects behind many modern philosophies of freedom, namely, man's desire to be like God, is not entirely mistaken. The error does not consist in the desire itself, which comes from our infinite dignity, as, indeed, man is called to be like God. Rather, the problem arises when we base ourselves on an idolatrous image of divinity, when we think of God as a being who does not depend on anything or anyone, whose freedom is not limited by any external freedom.[70] We can trace this idea at least as far back as Feuerbach, who suggests, in Ratzinger's words, to retrieve "the 'projection' of God that man has released from himself," so to actualize the divinity of man, "thus allowing man to become as free as the God he has imagined."[71] In this way, man intends to be entirely free, "without the competition of any other freedom, without any 'from' and 'for'."[72] But that idea of a solitary radical freedom imagines God in a purely egoistical sense. "The god thus conceived of is, not God, but an idol, indeed, the image of what the Christian tradition would call the devil, the anti-god, because therein lies the radical opposite of the true God: the true God is, of his own nature, being-for (Father), being-from (Son), and being-with (Holy Spirit)."[73] Again and again, Ratzinger insists that man is the image of God, and therefore being-for, being-from, and being-with constitute his fundamental anthropology. When someone moves toward total autonomy, disconnected from any responsibility toward others, he does not move toward the divine, but quite the opposite: he moves "toward dehumanizing, toward the destruction of being itself through the destruction of truth."[74]

Directing ourselves toward a truly free existence means steering toward an authentic divinization. The actions that can truly free us are those that lead us to live according to our ontological dignity, those that cause us to live up to our vocation to love because being like God means being like the triune God, who is love. This is, in short, a responsible existence. Contrary to Sartre's idea of responsibility, which holds that we are responsible because we define ourselves out of nothing, Ratzinger understands responsibility as a response to man's vocation. To be responsible is to live in response to what we truly are. Freedom, therefore, is not man's creation from a total lack of definition, but the capacity to respond to what we have been called to be. In other words, the fundamental project—in Sartre's terms—has been given to us as a vocation, which we can freely respond to or reject.

When rejection occurs, far from freeing the human being, his reality is rebelliously destroyed. A few pages ago, we said that, for Ratzinger, *Logos*, a

---

[70] Cf. *id.*, *Truth and Tolerance*, pp. 247–8.
[71] *Id.*, *Church, Ecumenism, and Politics*, p. 247.
[72] *Id.*, *Truth and Tolerance*, p. 248.
[73] *Ibid.*
[74] *Ibid.*

creating Word, is at the origin of existence. Therefore, freedom is the capacity to respond to that Word and thus remain in a relationship of dialogue with it. If there is no Word at the origin, human existence cannot be thought of as a response. If man has no vocation, his abysmal freedom responds to nothing, so that, according to Ratzinger, Sartre's worldview does not make man responsible, but, on the contrary, it strips him of all responsibility and all meaning.

For Ratzinger, the tragedy of Sartre's approach is that it leaves the decision of what it means to be man up to the human being, a task he does not know and cannot do. He has to live life with some orientation, but he sees nothing but emptiness in any direction. Such a freedom, without any limits, can only be experienced as a damnation. This is how Sartre himself expressed it.[75] On the contrary, Ratzinger sees a marked path toward a genuinely human and responsible existence in the Decalogue, in which "God presents himself, depicts himself, and at the same time interprets human existence, so that truth is made manifest, as it becomes visible in the mirror of God's nature, because man can only rightly be understood from the viewpoint of God."[76] Living out the Decalogue means, therefore, living according to the divine likeness in us as the path of our divinization and of true freedom. If Sartre's path leaves us trapped in the prison of unbearable solitude, the Decalogue shows us how to direct ourselves toward the dynamism of being for-from-with others, which leads to "the fusing of our being with the Divine Being and the resulting harmony of all with all."[77] Having a human nature, therefore, is not equivalent to having "a set of predetermined reactions," like "a table, a chair, or a stone," as Sartre would like to think.[78] Rather, it means that God has an idea of what it means to be human, and this idea is presented to us so that our existence can respond to it faithfully. In other words, having human nature does not imply losing the capacity to choose, but having the capacity to be responsible before the Creator, who expects our free participation in the universal project of love.

Ratzinger believes that an existence such as the one Sartre suggests—without essence, meaningless, thrown into a dreadful kind of freedom, condemned to solitude—would indeed be a condemnation, a hellish existence. In fact, *hell* is "the expression of enclosure in one's own being alone," it is "what happens when man barricades himself up in himself."[79] On the contrary, true human nature is not one of isolated individual existences,

---

[75] Cf. *ibid.*, p. 244; J.-P. Sartre, *Existentialism Is a Humanism*, p. 29; id., *Being and Nothingness*, p. 439.
[76] J. Ratzinger, *Truth and Tolerance*, p. 254.
[77] *Ibid.*
[78] Cf. J.-P. Sartre, *Existentialism Is a Humanism*, p. 41.
[79] J. Ratzinger, *Introduction to Christianity* (San Francisco: Ignatius, 2004), pp. 312–13.

but one of persons who are in a relationship of mutual dependence, responsible for one another. This dependence, however, is not degrading when it maintains the form of love, for love sees others neither as useful nor as a hindrance, but rather takes the form of "I want you to be." Love is the creative power that can affirm that which is different as different, without alienation or envy. Therefore, it "transforms dependence into freedom."[80]

Translation from Spanish by Christa Byker

---

[80] Id., "In the Beginning ...," pp. 98–9. Cf. M. E. Gómez de Pedro, *Libertad en Ratzinger*, pp. 65–6.

19

Albert Camus: The Meaning of Life

Alejandro Sada

Introduction

Albert Camus is, along with Jean-Paul Sartre[1], among the first names that come to mind when thinking of the existentialist movement that marked the history of twentieth-century thought.[2] Despite their political differences, these controversial thinkers are kindred spirits who, to a great extent, share the same philosophy, as Robert C. Solomon shows in his book *Dark Feelings, Grim Thoughts*.[3] Their common recurring themes are typical of existentialist philosophy in general and include 1) the precedence of existence over essence, 2) temporality as part of essence, 3) humanism, 4) freedom and responsibility, and 5) the priority of ethical issues.[4] As this book's chapter on Jean-Paul Sartre notes, existentialist questions are also quite frequent in the writings of Joseph Ratzinger. Therefore, we can speak of a certain methodological proximity between the German theologian and the existentialist movement, since, as María Esther Gómez de Pedro

---

[1] It is advisable to read this chapter in continuity with the previous one, dedicated to Jean-Paul Sartre. Originally, the two texts were a single chapter dedicated to existentialism. Subsequently, for various editorial reasons, it was decided to split them into separate studies.
[2] Neither of them, however, would be entirely comfortable with that title, as R. C. Solomon points out in his book *Dark Feelings, Grim Thoughts: Experience and Reflections in Camus and Sartre* (Oxford, New York: Oxford University Press, 2006), p. 5.
[3] Cf. *ibid*.
[4] Cf. T. R. Flynn, *Existentialism: A Very Short Introduction* (Oxford, New York: Oxford University Press, 2006), p. 8. See also the preface.

argues, Ratzinger always confronts theory with the experience of concrete human existence, i.e., "the type of experience known as 'experiential o *Existentialerfahrung*'."[5]

Peter Seewald recalls that Albert Camus was among the writers that Ratzinger avidly read in his youth.[6] It is clear that Ratzinger considered him an important author; we can confirm this in the fact that the Algerian was among the thinkers that the young professor recommended to his students for their class work and doctoral dissertations.[7] He came to regard him—together with Jean-Paul Sartre and Simone de Beauvoir—as an author who represented an entire generation.[8] The number of times the theologian mentions him in his texts reveals how familiar he is with his work. He is fascinated by the strength of Camus' narrative, and constantly resorts to his rich imagery to express his own ideas. He especially and often uses it to show how difficult the path of unbelief is—for, while faith is difficult, life without faith is much harder[9]—and he repeatedly draws on Camus' descriptions of a meaningless and hopeless world, reduced to an irrelevant existence.[10] In Camus, he finds unparalleled texts that reveal the full tragic density of the absence of God. Naturally, we cannot stop to examine Ratzinger's every mention of the author, nor can we reconstruct an exhaustive dialogue on all the classic themes of existentialism. Instead, we will offer a dialogical reconstruction of how both authors understand the topic of the meaning of life.[11]

The Absurd Man

Twentieth-century existentialist thinkers most often refer back to the theme that human reality is absurd. With their own respective nuances, they believe that the universe itself is empty of meaning, and therefore "whatever meaning our world may harbour is created by individuals either alone or in

---

[5] M. E. Gómez de Pedro, *Libertad en Ratzinger: riesgo y tarea* (Madrid: Encuentro, 2014), p. 19.
[6] Cf. P. Seewald, *Benedicto XVI. Una vida* (Bilbao: Mensajero, 2020), p. 208.
[7] Cf. *ibid.*, p. 542.
[8] Cf. *JRCW* 11, p. 262.
[9] Cf. J. Ratzinger, *Salz der Erde. Christentum und katholische Kirche an der Jahrtausendwende* (Stuttgart: Deutsche Verlags-Anstalt, 1996), p. 23.
[10] See, for example, *JRCW* 11, pp. 238, 262, 303, *Salz der Erde*, p. 31, *Introduction to Christianity* (San Francisco: Ignatius, 2004), p. 259, *Principles of Catholic Theology: Building Stones for a Fundamental Theology* (San Francisco: Ignatius, 1987), pp. 76–80, *Images of Hope: Meditations on Major Feasts* (San Francisco: Ignatius, 2006), p. 67, *Faith and the Future* (San Francisco: Ignatius, 2009), pp. 57–8, *Co-Workers of the Truth: Meditations for Every Day of the Year* (San Francisco: Ignatius, 1992), pp. 83–4, *Called to Communion: Understanding the Church Today* (San Francisco: Ignatius, 1996), p. 144.
[11] For a more extensive study on the question of the meaning of life according to Joseph Ratzinger, see A. Sada, "Cristianismo y sentido de la vida: una reflexión a partir del pensamiento de Joseph Ratzinger," *Scripta Theologica* 53/3 (2021), pp. 595–624.

social relations."[12] Particularly interesting is the case of Camus, who, shortly before the outbreak of the Second World War, was working on an "Essay on the Absurd," later entitled *The Myth of Sisyphus*.[13] It is clear there that, like Jean-Paul Sartre, the Algerian thinker also assumes the non-existence of God as a starting point.[14] His case, however, is more disguised than that of the Frenchman. While Sartre explicitly and unequivocally declares that his intention is to show all the consequences of a coherent atheistic position, Camus' atheism is camouflaged.[15] He states that his starting point is not the non-existence of God but what he calls "the absurd."[16] However, when we look closely at the text, it becomes clear that his approach is also fundamentally atheistic, for the absurd presupposes a world in which God does not exist.

When speaking of the absurd, Camus normally appeals to everyday experience and offers a phenomenological analysis that at first sight does not appear to be based on the absence of God. In fact, Robert Solomon argues that the general narrative that life is absurd "does not depend on the premise that there is no God [...]. Camus, rather, tries to impress on us, with image after image, that our lives, from various perspectives, don't seem to make sense."[17] However, when the author attempts to move on from mere phenomenology and offer a metaphysical argument for the reality of the absurd, he explains that the absurd depends on two opposing elements: *man* and the *world*. On the one hand, "[man] feels within him his longing for happiness and for reason,"[18] experiences a deep *appetite for understanding*, and suffers from intense *nostalgia for the absolute*.[19] On the other hand, the world remains silent in the face of all human cries. We find ourselves in an "indescribable universe where contradiction, antinomy, anguish or impotence reigns."[20] "The absurd is born of this confrontation between the human need and the unreasonable silence of the world,"[21] Camus claims.

Although the Algerian thinker does not seem to start with atheism as clearly as Sartre does, it is nevertheless clear that the world can only be as he

---

[12] T. R. Flynn, *Existentialism*, p. 47.
[13] Cf. R. Zaretsky, *A Life Worth Living: Albert Camus and the Quest for Meaning* (Cambridge, Massachusetts; London, England: The Belknap Press of Harvard University Press, 2013), pp. 16, 27–8.
[14] Cf. chapter on Jean-Paul Sartre.
[15] Cf. J.-P. Sartre, *Existentialism Is a Humanism* (New Haven, London: Yale University Press, 1999), p. 53.
[16] Cf. A. Camus, *The Myth of Sisyphus* (Middlesex, England: Penguin, 1979), p. 10, "the absurd, hitherto taken as a conclusion, is considered in this essay as a starting point"; in addition, *The Rebel: An Essay on Man in Revolt* (New York: Vintage International, 2010), p. 8: the absurd is "a point of departure, the equivalent, in existence, of Descartes's methodical doubt."
[17] R. C. Solomon, *Dark Feelings, Grim Thoughts*, p. 46.
[18] A. Camus, *The Myth of Sisyphus*, p. 31.
[19] Cf. *ibid.*, p. 38.
[20] *Ibid.*
[21] *Ibid.*, pp. 31–2.

describes if there truly is no God like the one found in Christianity, or even in philosophy. The absurdity that Camus identifies as evident and fundamental in *The Myth of Sisyphus* can only subsist if the world is indeed irrational. The author himself comes to recognize that the most radical aspect of his approach cannot be the absurd, but rather, precisely, his conviction of the worlds' irrationality: "I said that the world is absurd but I was too hasty," the author writes. "This world in itself is not reasonable, that is all that can be said."[22] However, we must ask ourselves, is it true that the world is not reasonable?

The Universality of Faith as a Stance in Front of the Whole of Reality

Joseph Ratzinger does not hold a direct dialogue with Albert Camus when dealing with this question. However, in his writing, the theme is present enough that an indirect dialogue can be reconstructed. In *The Myth of Sisyphus*, Camus is quite sure that the world is irrational. It is immediately evident to him that chance and anarchy reign.[23] What he sees is meaninglessness, and he finds everything else inaccessible, "I don't know whether this world has a meaning that transcends it. But I know that I do not know that meaning and that it is impossible for me just now to know it."[24] He sees himself as quite rational when limiting himself to immediate evidence and not making any kind of Kierkegaardian leap of faith. In his article on Camus' atheism, Angel Ramirez Medina describes this attitude well:

> The atheist adheres exclusively to reason—lacking the faith that the believer himself holds as indispensable to belief—, and his reason sees no convincing arguments to sustain the existence of a being that is radically other, that is, of a nature different from everything else that is known. Faced with this situation, the non-believer affirms the existence of that which is perceptible and nothing else, and although he may recognize the usefulness of believing in this other consoling reality, he prefers not to nourish himself with the roses of illusion.[25]

Camus viscerally refers to this *preference of not to be nourished by illusions* as a dogged persistence:

---

[22] *Ibid.*, p. 26.
[23] Cf. *ibid.*, p. 51.
[24] *Ibid.*
[25] A. Ramírez Medina, "Anti-teodicea y ateísmo en Albert Camus," *Pensamiento* 64/241 (2008), pp. 487–98.

Let us insist again on the method: it is a matter of persisting. At a certain point on his path the absurd man is tempted. History is lacking neither in religions nor prophets, even without gods. He is asked to leap. All he can reply is that he doesn't fully understand, that it is not obvious. Indeed, he does not want to do anything but what he fully understands ... Hence what he demands of himself is to live *solely* with what he knows, to accommodate himself to what is and to bring in nothing that is not certain.[26]

Is this really the safest, most rational and realistic option? Of course, it would be tremendously naive to rely on illusions. But are we sure that God is just that, an illusion and nothing more?

In the first part of his famous book *Introduction to Christianity*, Ratzinger deals precisely with the theme of man in the face of the question of God.[27] He believes it a mistake to think, without further ado, that there are believers on one side and non-believers on the other, since we all have a certain form of faith in the sense that we are all continually threatened by doubt and uncertainty. Just as the believer "is always threatened with an uncertainty,"[28] the non-believer—someone like Camus—"can never be absolutely certain of the autonomy of what he has seen and interpreted as a whole; he remains threatened by the question of whether belief is not after all the reality it claims to be."[29] Camus' supposed confidence in maintaining that the world is irrational is part of the typical attitude found in people who only rely on that which is "evident" or "certain." In the face of this position, Ratzinger unmasks "the secret uncertainty," which is unable to stop considering the possibility that there may be something more than the observable, something that escapes our field of vision: "Anyone who makes up his mind to evade the uncertainty of belief will have to experience the uncertainty of unbelief."[30] So, Ratzinger concludes, "neither can quite escape either doubt or belief."[31]

For Joseph Ratzinger, the question of God is not a distant hypothesis outside of concrete experience. On the contrary, it is an inescapable question in which each person adopts an existential position regarding the totality of reality. In other words, when we say, "I believe in God," we are not adding one more object to our universe of beliefs—as if to say "I believe in the North Pole"—but rather, we are making a declaration about the way in which we understand all things; it is equivalent to manifesting our deepest existential orientation. The same is true if we say, "I believe that God does

---

[26] A. Camus, *The Myth of Sisyphus*, pp. 52–3.
[27] Cf. J. Ratzinger, *Introduction to Christianity*, pp. 39–47.
[28] *Ibid.*, p. 42.
[29] *Ibid.*, p. 45.
[30] *Ibid.*
[31] *Ibid.*, p. 47.

not exist." In this case, we also express a fundamental orientation that specifically interprets the totality of reality. This is the true realm of faith, which inevitably concerns all of us because "every man must adopt some kind of attitude toward the realm of basic decisions, decisions that, by their very nature, can only be made by entertaining belief."[32]

The Fundamental Positions before the Mystery of Being

When Ratzinger reflects on the radical decisions that we can make in the face of the mystery of being, he suggests that an ultimate position regarding the totality of reality is formulated in two basic ways: By understanding original reality—the ultimate *Stoff* of things—as pure matter, or as mind:

> The first and most obvious would run something like this: Everything we encounter is in the last analysis stuff, matter; *this* is the only thing that always remains as demonstrable reality and, consequently, represents the real being of all that exists—the materialistic solution. The other possibility points in the opposite direction. It says: Whoever looks thoroughly at matter will discover that it is being-thought, objectivized thought. So it cannot be the ultimate. On the contrary, before it comes thinking, the idea; all being is ultimately being-thought and can be traced back to mind as the original reality; this is the 'idealistic' solution.[33]

The Primacy of Matter

The materialist solution—that of Camus—suggests that the primary form of reality is pure matter, i.e., a certain type of being that does not understand itself. The appearance of spiritual realities—those that have an understanding of themselves—is a coincidental and secondary accident on the path of development. For Ratzinger, this means that thought and meaning are "by-products" of being and have no structure or regulatory meaning for reality as a whole.[34] They are only the result of chance occurrence, not foundational realities. This is precisely why, for Camus, rationality cannot be understood as something that belongs to the totality of reality, but rather is always reduced to the human realm. For him, understanding the world cannot mean—as Ratzinger would say—reflecting on the intellectual structure of reality, for Camus does not accept that things are rational in

---

[32] *Ibid.*, p. 71.
[33] *Ibid.*, p. 156.
[34] Cf. *ibid.*, p. 152.

their origin. He is left to claim that "understanding the world for a man is reducing it to the human, stamping it with his seal."[35] In other words, for him, thinking signifies snatching the being thought of from his reality and clothing him with human categories. However, this would be tantamount to saying that to "understand" the world is to not understand it, since it would be an attempt to reduce into the human realm what is not in itself human. We would be asking the universe to offer something that it is unable to give. And it is here that the absurd appears, since there is a tremendous "confrontation of the irrational and the wild longing for clarity whose call echoes in the human."[36] We find ourselves "in a universe suddenly divested of illusions and lights"[37] feeling like strangers, reduced to despair, immersed in a path of indifferent experiences, incapable of forming value judgments.[38]

In 1977, Ratzinger wrote a text in which he evokes the feeling of mortal strangeness that a young Albert Camus recalled from his visit to the city of Prague:

> [I was afraid] of being alone in my hotel room, without money and without zeal, reduced just to myself and my miserable thoughts. I got lost in sumptuous baroque churches, trying to find a homeland in them. But I left them emptier and more desperate because of the disappointing conversation I carried on with myself [...]. I tried to calm my anguish in all the works of art. Classic trick: I wanted to dissolve my inner uprising in melancholy. But it was in vain. As soon as I came out [of those places], I was again a stranger [...]. Churches, gold and incense, everything rejects me in a daily routine in which my anguish assigns its value to everything.[39]

According to Ratzinger, for the Algerian writer, Prague represents a dark prison that aptly symbolizes the situation in which thousands of people find themselves—cloistered in a city whose language they do not know, confined to deathly solitude. In the end, beauty becomes a mockery and "the prisoner drowns in the abyss of the absurd."[40] However, the German theologian wonders if Camus is right, asking whether we are an absurd creature after all whose only hope is to accept the absurd and "to roll the rock of Sisyphus uphill again and again, knowing full well that it will roll back down again."[41]

---

[35] A. Camus, *The Myth of Sisyphus*, p. 23.
[36] *Ibid.*, p. 26.
[37] *Ibid.*, p. 13.
[38] Cf. *ibid.*, p. 59.
[39] *Id.*, *L'Envers et l'endroit* (Paris: Gallimard, 1958), pp. 86–7. Ratzinger refers to this passage in *Principles of Catholic Theology*, p. 77.
[40] J. Ratzinger, *Principles of Catholic Theology*, p. 77.
[41] *Ibid.*, p. 78.

The Primacy of the *Logos*

Ratzinger's alternative favors the primacy of the *Logos*. The most primordial and radical being is not matter, but rather, reality that knows itself and communicates through love in an act that we call *creation*: "the *logos*—that is, the idea, freedom, love—stands not merely at the end but also at the beginning."[42] For the same reason, the world is truly rational, and existence is good in itself. Being does not remain silent and indifferent in the face of human beings' deepest cries. Every man is truly loved and sustained by the creator *Logos*. "If man realized that the universe like him can love and suffer, he would be reconciled,"[43] wrote Camus. If this is so, perhaps a reconciliation is truly possible since, as it turns out, the Absolute itself, the *Logos* of all that exists, has shown us that it is indeed capable of loving and suffering. That which Camus did not dare to dream is the same truth that fills our life with meaning. If human existence has been absolutely loved and affirmed, it is truly good and joyful. This is precisely what the cross of Jesus Christ reveals us:

> God finds man so important that he himself has suffered for man. The Cross, which was for Nietzsche the most detestable expression of the negative character of the Christian religion, is in truth the center of the evangelium, the glad tidings: "It is good that you exist"—no, "It is necessary that you exist." The Cross is the approbation of our existence, not in words, but in an act so completely radical that it caused God to become flesh and pierced this flesh to the quick; that, to God, it was worth the death of his incarnate Son. One who is so loved that the other identifies his life with this love and no longer desires to live if he is deprived of it; one who is loved even unto death—such a one knows that he is truly loved. But if God so loves us, then we are loved in truth. Then love is truth, and truth is love. Then life is worth living.[44]

In the face of this ministry of the absurd, Ratzinger invites us to be missionaries of joy.[45] We do not have to give meaning to our lives because they already have meaning. When we discover that the origin of our being is a love that precedes us and awaits us, we experience life as a joyful vocation. Regarding the issue of suicide that Camus posed, Ratzinger suggests that existence is good and, therefore, should not only not be annihilated, but should be celebrated. In discovering that I am so radically loved by someone truly significant for the totality of existence, I become capable of loving

---

[42] *Id.*, *Introduction to Christianity*, p. 152.
[43] A. Camus, *The Myth of Sisyphus*, p. 23.
[44] J. Ratzinger, *Principles of Catholic Theology*, p. 81.
[45] Benedict XVI invited young people to take up this assurance in his *Message for the XXVII World Youth Day*, March 15, 2012.

myself. I discover that my existence is truly good news. I can own the words Benedict XVI used when addressing young people in 2012—and not to console myself with illusions or farces, but because they reflect reality: "I am loved; I have a place in the world and in history; I am personally loved by God. If God accepts me and loves me and I am sure of this, then I know clearly and with certainty that it is a good thing that I am alive."[46]

A Ratzingerian *reductio ad absurdum*

The indirect dialogue reconstructed here between Camus and Ratzinger on the meaning of life allows us to visualize one of the German theologian's fundamental methodological presuppositions. For Ratzinger, the search for truth and the meaning of existence do not run independent of one another, but rather, are related and exist in deep communion. Thus, the question of the *humanum* even functions as a criterion of truth. In other words, for Ratzinger, an explanation of reality is true to the extent that it can account for the meaning of human existence.[47]

The primary purpose of philosophy is to lead human beings to the truth and, in it, to the discovery of the meaning of their existence. Therefore, when a philosophy like that of Camus or Sartre concludes that human existence is absurd, far from fulfilling the fundamental task of philosophy, philosophical thought ends up betraying itself. Ratzinger uses some of Camus' heart-wrenching images to ask himself, "What is wrong with man [...] Was Camus right? Have we no recourse but to admit that, seen in the light, man is an absurd creature whose only hope is to accept the absurd; to roll the rock of Sisyphus uphill again and again, knowing full well that it will roll back down again?"[48] We can already anticipate his answer. Any philosophy that abandons human beings to meaninglessness is unacceptable and must be rejected as false, "we can surely not accept the premise that man is absurd; we are so constructed that we must find meaning if we are to live at."[49] We could call this a Ratzingerian *reductio ad absurdum*. Just as the rules of thought force us to deny an assumption that has resulted in an absurd conclusion, so life demands that we abandon a system of thought that affirms the absurdity of human existence. Life cannot stop there, for life is, above all, a search for meaning.[50]

---

[46] *Ibid.* Regarding the joy of faith in the magisterium of Benedict XVI, see J. García-Valiño Abós, "'Gaudete semper in Domino (Fil 4:4)'. La alegría de la fe a la luz del magisterio de Benedicto XVI," *Scripta Fulgentina* 22/43-4 (2012), pp. 131-8.

[47] Cf. A. Sada, *Naturaleza y misión de la filosofía en el pensamiento de Joseph Ratzinger* (Doctoral Thesis, Pamplona: Universidad de Navarra, 2020), pp. 159–64. For a published versión, cf. *Sentido y verdad. Hacia una nueva comprensión de la filosofía desde el pensamiento de Joseph Ratzinger* (Madrid: BAC, 2023).

[48] J. Ratzinger, *Principles of Catholic Theology*, p. 78.

[49] *Ibid.*

[50] Cf. *id.*, *La Eucaristía centro de la vida. Dios está cerca de Nosotros*, p. 136.

Conclusion

As noted, Ratzinger has a methodological affinity with existentialist philosophy, in the sense that he always tests theory by confronting it with the experience of concrete human existence, the *Existentialerfahrung*.[51] However, the distance between his intellectual world and that of Camus is vast. The underlying reason for this divergence lies in the fundamental position that each of them adopts in the face of reality as a whole, in that positioning to which Ratzinger refers when he says that "every man must adopt some kind of attitude toward the realm of basic decisions, decisions that, by their very nature, can only be made by entertaining belief."[52]

Faith is what separates these authors. One stands for the primacy of *Logos* and the other for the primacy of matter. Opting for *Logos* allows Ratzinger to understand the world as a created reality, with meaning, truth, significance, and vocation. The primacy of Matter, on the other hand, leaves no room for thinking of a creation. Things are reduced to mere existence without meaning, while freedom is experienced without purpose and human reality seems unintelligible. The idea of creation is the starting point from which Ratzinger's worldview develops.[53] His option, therefore, is the option for truth in a strong sense. Camus, on the other hand, finds himself in a world that lacks truth or, in other words, a world in which the truth is that there is no meaning and, therefore, no hope. When philosophy cannot engage in the search for meaning, it will instead try to construct meaning on its own accord or develop therapies to withstand the absurd. This is what Ratzinger calls ideology. Ideological thought arises when man confronts absurdity either by inventing a hope or by enduring despair. Existentialists chose the latter option with philosophies that, without the truth and meaning that can only come from faith understood in the Christian sense, have been transformed into ideologies of despair.

Translation from Spanish by Christa Byker

---

[51] Cf. M. E. Gómez de Pedro, *Libertad en Ratzinger*, p. 19.
[52] J. Ratzinger, *Introduction to Christianity*, p. 71.
[53] Mention should also be made of the mystery of the Incarnation, for through it, man attains his highest dignity and the path is cleared for the complete fulfillment of his vocation.

20

Robert Spaemann: Person, Ethics, and Politics

Christian Schaller

Introduction

Joseph Ratzinger had already documented contact with the philosopher, historian, theologian, and Romanicist Robert Spaemann (1927–2018) in 1967, when he was a professor of dogmatics and history of dogma in Tübingen.[1] Due to Spaemann's engagement with the theses of Karl Marx, he was known in conservative circles after the war as a "leftist Catholic," who was only able to perceive the scope of the Communist regime through extensive engagement with the political reality in the USSR. He completed his studies at the universities of Münster, Munich, Fribourg, and Paris. In his dissertation, he dedicated himself to the French statesman and philosopher Louis-Gabriel-Ambroise de Bonald, an influential thinker in the eighteenth century, who emerged in a particular way with essays on state and religion.[2] Spaemann's habilitation (1962) on François Fénelon[3] began his academic career, which led him to the University of Stuttgart until 1968, when he

---

[1] There are two letters in the archive of the Pope Benedict XVI Institute in connection with a television broadcast: a first missive from Spaemann to Ratzinger dated November 20, 1967, with thanks for the good collaboration and a short estimation of the impact of the TV show on the audience; the second letter, dated December 1, 1967, is Ratzinger's answer with corroboration of the positive response. Unfortunately, the content and time slot of the broadcast as well as the broadcasting station could not be more precisely determined to date.
[2] Cf. R. Spaemann, *Der Ursprung der Soziologie aus dem Geist der Restauration. Studien über L. G. A. de Bonald* (Stuttgart: Klett-Cotta, 1998).
[3] Cf. *id.*, *Reflexion und Spontanität. Studien über Fénelon* (Kohlhammer: Stuttgart, 1963).

moved to Heidelberg, where he stayed until moving to Munich in 1972. He was in Munich until his retirement in 1992. He died in 2018 in Stuttgart at the age of ninety-one.

Included in Spaemann's extensive works are texts on philosophy of law, euthanasia, animal ethics, environmental ethics, philosophy of nature, philosophy of religion, and pedagogy.[4] This plethora of material and the variety of subject areas make his writings an outstanding discussion partner, particularly with an eye to Joseph Ratzinger's statements on the concept of God, on the understanding of truth, on fundamental moral concepts, on political utopias, on structures of democracy and civilization, and on Europe as not only an economic entity, but as a common space for culture and religion. But Ratzinger also draws on Spaemann on the topics of personal responsibility in the formation of conscience and the protection of the dignity of human beings from their beginning to their death.

Fundamental Moral Concepts: The Conscience

In Ratzinger's article "Der Streit um die Moral"[5] Spaemann's work serves as a support for his argument regarding a notion of morality and values that defies the attempts of human beings to construct them. It is a matter of the binding character of moral laws that defy the subjective; a binding character, i.e., that does not rest only on the convention of respective situations.[6] On this topic, Spaemann says that "the conscience is not an oracle"[7] that privileges mere individualization but denies the application of concrete, binding value judgments. Ratzinger adopts the conceptual explanation of the conscience in this text wholesale from Spaemann and extensively paraphrases a passage from his book *Grundbegriffe*: "The conscience is an organ, not an oracle. It is an organ, that is, it is something given to us that belongs to our being, not something made externally. ... it needs growth, education, and training." The human being—Ratzinger continues, following Spaemann—is "an entity that needs the help of others in order to become what he actually is of himself."[8] Ratzinger picks up

---

[4] In 2019, Klett-Cotta Verlag published Spaemann's collected works under the title: Robert Spaemann, *Gesammelte Werke in Einzelbänden*.
[5] Cf. J. Ratzinger, "Der Streit um die Moral. Fragen der Grundlegung ethischer Werte" (1984), in *JRGS* 4 (Freiburg: Herder, 2014), pp. 718–31.
[6] Ratzinger refers to Spaemann's work published in 1982 in Munich: R. Spaemann, *Grundbegriffe* (München: Beck, 1982).
[7] Cf. R. Spaemann, *Grundbegriffe*, pp. 73–84. Ratzinger alludes to this text in *JRGS* 4, 723–5, nn. 3–6.
[8] *JRGS* 4, p. 724. The quote is from R. Spaemann, *Grundbegriffe*, p. 79.

on the fundamental notion of conscience formation, which is composed of many elements. Parents, family, friends, living conditions, crises ... all these factors in conjunction give rise to the human being in his actual existence. The "obligation of conscience formation"[9] is therefore a profoundly human demand, which deepens and strengthens the person's disposition to the good. That this ability exists clearly shows that there is, in addition to a technical-analytical rationality, also a moral rationality which supports the human being's ability to develop his or her perceptiveness of the good and the values in us.

Pre-political Foundations, Europe, Democracy

In his reflections on the hopes and dangers encompassed by the European idea,[10] Ratzinger integrates Spaemann's unconditional advocacy of human dignity. If human dignity is no longer the object of inviolable certainty, the consequences at which Spaemann arrives are, for Ratzinger, "inescapable."[11] If, as Spaemann says in the citation by Ratzinger, human dignity is relativized because it can only be derived from Christian metaphysics—whose acceptance is on the wane—then one denies the "evident postulate" of the oppressed and suffering. If God is no longer communicated, then unbelief is passed on: "that is, the conviction that there is no truth, no right, that the good does not exist."[12] Ratzinger and Spaemann agree that a world without God would mean the complete relativization of human dignity. (Spaemann even invokes Friedrich Nietzsche in saying that the belief that "God is truth, that truth is divine"). Any communalization of people would be placed under the "survival of the fittest" to decide freely and arbitrarily about the lives of others. Moreover, there would be no moral and ethical anchorage which could escape the subjective appropriation of the human being. Without a normativity that installs that stated norms, the weak, the sick, the suffering, the poor would remain without any protective argument for their own dignity. Ultimately—and here Ratzinger and Spaemann meet again—the future of humanity will be decided by this question: Do we surrender to the freedom of creatureliness, or do we remain in inner-worldly conditioning, which reduces the human being to a one-dimensional level? But if we opt for the latter, Ratzinger continues, we will lose the chance to

---

[9] *JRGS* 4, p. 725.
[10] Cf. *id.*, "Europa—Hoffnungen und Gefahren," in *JRGS* 3/2, pp. 645–66.
[11] Ibid., p. 664.
[12] R. Spaemann, "Universalismus oder Eurozentrismus?," in K. Michalski (ed.), *Europa und die Folgen* (Stuttgart: Klett-Cotta, 1988), p. 319. Spaemann's remarks and the quotes are found in J. Ratzinger, "Europa—Hoffnungen und Gefahren," p. 664.

bring together the traditions of humanity in a reciprocal giving and receiving that endows all with the same dignity and the same chances.[13]

In connection with the endangerment of democracy in the present, Ratzinger draws on Spaemann's contribution to political utopia, published in 1977.[14] At the beginning the question is asked what endangers democracy in the twentieth century: Man has become unable to accept his own imperfection. This manifests itself in the unconditional turn to an innerworldly idea of redemption, which fulfills itself, so to speak, of its own accord as history progresses. "The new society" has become the standard of morality—but without in any way stating values necessarily connected with it—and is praised as the beginning of a better and more just world. Here a bare structuralism shines forth, which sees ethics as the ordering object of structure. Ultimately, it is the compulsion, the lack of freedom of the one who wants to see the human being as perfect and who therefore wants to abolish the imperfect human being. Behind this stands a deficient modern concept of reason with its reduction of the mind to quantitative reason: only the measurable, the countable appears as reason.

An increasingly emerging nihilism proves to be a further threat to democracy. Here, too, Ratzinger seeks to integrate Spaemann's remarks into his discourse.[15] In nihilism we find the attempt to make society completely liberal, a society without absolute values and without regulations. The goal sought in the shaping of one's life is supposed to be merely a kind of "wellbeing." Here an "emptying of the human" takes place, which results from the "banal nihilism" cited by Spaemann in the same place.[16]

Another reference to Spaemann's work is found in the article "Christliche Orientierung in der pluralistischen Demokratie?"[17], which deals with the prescribed retreat of Christianity (and every other religion) into the private sphere: No binding value system is "allowed" within society because it contradicts a pluralistic social order. However, such a conception is not compatible with the truth claim of faith. At this point, Ratzinger quotes Spaemann, who wants the Church to be understood as "locus of an absolute public sphere, surpassing the state, under the legitimizing claim of God."[18] The tension expressed in this remains: How can the Church influence the state without the state losing its claim to pluralism? For Ratzinger and Spaemann, the urgency of resolving this question becomes clear in the fact

---

[13] Cf. *ibid.*, p. 665.
[14] Cf. R. Spaemann, *Zur Kritik der politischen Utopie. 10 Kapitel politischer Philosophie* (Stuttgart: Klett-Cotta, 1977).
[15] J. Ratzinger, "Die Freiheit, das Recht und das Gute. Moralische Prinzipien in demokratischen Gesellschaften," in *JRGS* 3/1, pp. 561–7; the text of Spaemann which is referenced is: "La perle préciuese et le nihilisme banal," *Catholica* 33 (1992), pp. 43–50.
[16] J. Ratzinger, "Die Freiheit, das Recht und das Gute," p. 563; Spaemann, "La perle," p. 45.
[17] *JRGS* 3/1, pp. 527–44.
[18] R. Spaemann, "Einführung," in *Gesellschaft und Staat* XV-XVIII (Stuttgart: Klett-Cotta, 1982).

that the Church alone, as moral advocate, can secure fundamental rights, dignity, freedom ... for human beings. A purely inner-worldly regulation merits all skepticism since it remains humanly indifferent and exposed to the danger of arbitrariness.

The Concept of God, the Church as a Segment of Society

In the context of Ratzinger's reflections on the ecclesial setting of theology, Spaemann's remarks are used to provide supporting argumentation for the nature of proclamation in the homily.[19] Ratzinger says, "Proclamation in the homily teaches in a binding way; that is its essence."[20] Proclamation is not a content-less pursuit, mere "religious entertainment," but rather a means of imparting to human beings the ability to recognize who they are and how they must act. Ultimately, proclamation seeks to bind the hearer to the truth par excellence and to the truth of himself. With Spaemann, Ratzinger compares this obligatory character of proclamation to myths or to mere hypotheses whose content is interchangeable or outdated. Truth, in contrast, stands for a reality that is binding; it is the matter of reflection, just as proclamation itself is the matter of reflection in theology. Ratzinger invokes Spaemann's analysis in order to make the case for a proclamation that, following an anthropological order, grants the "prae" to perception: "The great things of being human," Ratzinger says, "are grasped in a simple perception that is fundamentally accessible to everyone and that is never fully captured in reflection."[21] In this respect, proclamation belongs to the magisterium of the Church, and thus the office of proclamation is the magisterium for theology as well.

Another multi-layered spectrum is indicated in the context of the ecumenical question. Ratzinger situates the way to the unity of the church among the conceptual pairs "authority and tradition," "history and story" and wants to show with this that there is a vitality in that which has historically developed which can be of service under the guidelines of the constant purification and spiritual penetration of the content of the tradition. To explain this, he uses Spaemann's idea of the aforementioned hypothesis, whose "certainty is the certainty of thought, but not the certainty of life."[22]

---

[19] Cf. *id.*, "Die christliche Religion und das Ende des modernen Bewußtseins," *Internationale katholische Zeitschrift Communio* 8 (1979), pp. 251–70.
[20] J. Ratzinger, "Vom geistlichen Grund und vom kirchlichen Ort der Theologie," *JRGS* 9/1, pp. 135–58, at p. 150.
[21] *Ibid.*, p. 151.
[22] *Id.* "Probleme und Hoffnungen des anglikanisch-katholischen Dialogs," *JRGS* 8/2, pp. 984–1018, at p. 1004. Cf. "Die christliche Religion und das Ende des modernen Bewußtseins," pp. 264–8.

For ecumenical work, this means an ongoing commitment to reflect on the univocalities and clarifications that emerge in history, which in turn are a measure of the search for beginnings and commonalities.

Faith and Reason

In the context of his reflections on the nature of theology, Ratzinger also takes up the topic of the relation between faith and reason.[23] In Christian faith, reason emerges precisely because faith strives for reason. And in reason, Christian faith emerges because faith is the specific locus of reason and reasonableness. In the literary discourse with Spaemann, the necessity of a predetermined absoluteness as a condition for the recognition of truth is deduced from this relation between faith and reason. The denial of the presupposed absoluteness of truth leads with inner logic to the justification of the irrational and makes reason an accident.[24] In the faith-reason thematic complex one of the most important points of intersection between theology and philosophy can be seen. In the description of the essence of theology, one of the basic principles is that what is believed is reasonable, is reason itself. In this respect, it is part of the mission of theology to understand and penetrate the foundation and content that determine what is believed. With a clear, generally accepted method and by means of recourse to the fundamental questions of the philosophy of the Greeks, which placed the question of truth and being themselves at the center,[25] theology is presented as the guarantor of a search for truth on the basis of a truth-capable human being. In the course of critical discussion with Marxism (here seen as a philosophical question), Spaemann is quoted again as a support for the argument with his remarks in the "Einsprüche"[26] published in 1977. Marxism, established in pure materialism, sees no predetermined truth. It can only be determined by human beings, whereby the motives can hardly be objective, but rather are biased or subjective. Spaemann speaks of the "completion of that functional system of technical rationality," a definition which Ratzinger takes up and puts into the context of his own thoughts.[27]

---

[23] Cf. J. Ratzinger, "Theologie und Kirchenpolitik," *JRGS* 9/1, pp. 340–53.
[24] Cf. J. Ratzinger, "Theologie und Kirchenpolitik," p. 341. As support for the argument, R. Spaemann, "Die christliche Religion und das Ende des modernen Bewußtseins," is used.
[25] Cf. J. Ratzinger, "Theologie und Kirchenpolitik," p. 342.
[26] R. Spaemann, *Einsprüche. Christliche Reden* (Einsiedeln: Johannes, 1977).
[27] Cf. J. Ratzinger, "Theologie und Kirchenpolitik," *JRGS* 9/1), p. 344, especially n. 5 with the exhaustive quote from Spaemann, *Einsprüche. Christliche Reden*, p. 8.

Conclusion

Robert Spaemann is considered one of the outstanding thinkers of the twentieth and twenty-first centuries in German-speaking philosophy. His search for knowledge by means of rational arguments, which moved within the coordinates of philosophical lines of tradition, but—taking up modernity and its contemporary issues—always endeavored to offer solutions that have become an integral part of scholarly dispute, nationally and internationally. His reflections on political theories and fundamental theological questions bear witness to the diversity of the topics he discussed, the relevance of which has been preserved to this day. Joseph Ratzinger was inspired in his scholarly dialogue with Spaemann and referred to his arguments in the discussions outlined only briefly above.

21

Jürgen Habermas: Democracy and Religion in Pluralistic Societies

Mary Frances McKenna

Introduction

Ratzinger has long engaged in public debate on Christianity in the world, starting with an article in the German Catholic magazine *Hochland* in October 1958 entitled "The New Pagans and the Church."[1] His dialogue with Habermas is a continuation of this engagement and is to be situated in a series of engagements Ratzinger undertook at that time with philosophers, including Paolo Flores D'Arcais (Italian Social Democrat) in 2000 and Marcello Pera (Italian Senate President) May 2004.[2] The dialogues with Habermas and Pera might have been Ratzinger's swan song. At seventy-seven, past the age of retirement for bishops and perfects of the Vatican congregations, and with an ailing pope John Paul II, Ratzinger no doubt thought that in his immediate future lay either elevation to the papacy or swift departure to pastures new. Given how many have entered the conclave

---

[1] J. Ratzinger, "The New Pagans and the Church," *Hochland* (1958). For more recent contributions see, *Values in a Time of Upheaval* (San Francisco: Ignatius, 2006); *Christianity and the Crisis of Cultures* (San Francisco: Ignatius, 2006); *A Turning Point for Europe* (San Francisco: Ignatius, 2010); and "'The Spiritual Roots of Europe Yesterday, Today, and Tomorrow' and 'Letter of Marcello Pera'," in *Without Roots: The West, Relativism, Christianity, Islam* (New York: Basic Books, 2006).
[2] See my consideration of Marcello Pera's contribution in "A Consideration of Christianity's Role in a Pluralistic Society," *The Way* 55/4 (2016), pp. 31–47.

as papabili and left as cardinals, Ratzinger could reasonably have expected that his official work was coming to its close, and that the Habermas and Pera dialogues would be some of the last opportunities to have an impact upon Christianity's dialogue with the secular world and philosophy. Yet as we know, Ratzinger left the conclave as Pope Benedict XVI and the high point of his life's work was to come, and that his dialogue with Habermas, like so much of his work to that point, came to have an added significance.

The Habermas–Ratzinger dialogue in January 2004, at the invitation of the Catholic Academy of Bavaria, brought together two intellectual leaders who were not afraid to defy their public caricatures to speak on the topic of reason and religion in the post secular sphere.[3] The purpose of the debate, according to the Academy's director, Dr. Florian Schuller, was to hold a conversation in Germany in a manner that was taken for granted elsewhere (Italy and France): parties with a plurality of positions on similar themes which impact on society and its institutions coming together to reflect on their differing views.[4] In addition, Habermas' call shortly after the September 11 terrorist attacks for secular societies to gain a renewed understanding of religion, a key theme of Ratzinger's consideration of secular society, gave an added impetus for this dialogue. The theme of the encounter was "The Pre-Political Foundations of the State" through which the Academy sought a consideration of basic questions of human existence in which each speaker was to outline the "basic assumptions and axioms and ultimate religious and secular justifications" for their arguments.[5] For Habermas that meant "practical reason of a post metaphysical secular thinking." For Ratzinger it meant "the reality, antecedent to every rational secular decision that may be taken, of man as a creature who receives his life from his Creator."[6]

In this paper I consider whether the 2004 dialogue between Habermas and Ratzinger was just a polite conversation that generated surprise, applause, shock, and curiosity but nothing more, or are there points of contact that can truly be built upon? Is it a basis for real encounter? Furthermore, did the encounter spark a subsequent response in the work of each speaker? To attempt answers to these questions the paper is structured in three sections. I will first explore the context from which each thinker entered the 2004 dialogue to establish the trajectory of their thought on reason and religion. I will then consider each contribution to that dialogue and what impact,

---

[3] For a broader consideration of Ratzinger and Habermas' thought see J. Carr, *Catholicism and Liberal Democracy: Forgotten Roots and Future Prospects* (Washington, DC: Catholic University of America Press, 2022). For two other perspectives on the 2004 dialogue see M. Welker, "Habermas and Ratzinger on the Future of Religion," *Scottish Journal of Theology* 64/4 (2010), pp. 456–73; and E. Echeverría, "A Decade Later: Lessons from the Habermas and Ratzinger Debate," March 4, 2015, University of Cambridge.
[4] Cf. F. Schuller, "Forward," in J. Habermas and J. Ratzinger, *The Dialectics of Secularization: On Reason and Religion* (San Francisco: Ignatius, 2006), p. 11.
[5] *Ibid.*, p. 13.
[6] *Ibid.*, p. 15.

if any, emerged in their subsequent thought that could be attributed to their encounter. To conclude I will suggest a response to the role Habermas latterly posits for religion in a secular democratic constitutional state.[7]

Ratzinger on the Uniqueness of Christianity within World Cultures and Religions

Ratzinger's dialogue with Habermas specifically builds upon his twofold consideration of Christianity's place within the history of world religions and cultures, and its engagement with secular modernity. These contributions were in part a response to criticisms of *Fidei et Ratio* (1998) and *Dominus Iesus* (2000) and his response to Liberation theology.[8] The premise of Ratzinger's thinking is that "from its very origin, and in its essential nature, it [Christian faith] claims to know and to proclaim the one true God and the one Saviour of all mankind ... (Acts 4:12)."[9] As per the tradition of the Church, he understands Christianity as unique because Christ is the only real and final salvation of humanity. Christianity is about truth because Jesus reveals who God truly is. In that way, Christianity tells the human being who they are, and so how to live. Christ is the fullness of salvation, which means the various religions of the world are not equal parallel roads to God and salvation. Nonetheless, it is truth, Ratzinger insists, which all religions and all enlightenment point to and move toward, such that all religions, in fact, are on their way to Jesus Christ. In that way, Ratzinger contends that other religions have an adventual character for Christianity. People today can still be living in the "before Christ" era.[10] Underpinning Ratzinger's thought is the conviction that Christian faith is for everyone, that it is a gift of saving knowledge, redeeming love, and liberating truth,

---

[7] This paper builds on a number of other papers I have published including: "Moral Values and Social Consensus in Democratic Secular Societies: Challenges and Responsibilities," *The Heythrop Journal* 56/4 (2015), pp. 663–76; "The Idea of Europe as the Point of Encounter between Power and Freedom, Interests and Universal Values: A Consideration of Kissinger's and Ratzinger's Visions of Europe," *European Review* 25/4 (2017), pp. 655–69; "On the Future of Europe: Philosophical and Theological Perspectives on Pre-Political Foundations of Europe and the State from Ratzinger, Habermas, and MacIntyre," *The Heythrop Journal* 60 (2019), pp. 910–25; "The Promise of Enlightenment and the Incalculability of Freedom: A Consideration of Horkheimer and Adorno's Critique of Enlightenment in Relation to Ratzinger's Notion of Freedom," *Logos* 21 (2018), pp. 114–39.

[8] In what follows I draw on a series of articles published in *Truth and Tolerance* (2002 [2004]), the first of which was written in 1963 with the remainder being presented in the 1990s and very early 2000s, Ratzinger details how Christianity relates to the cultures and religions of the world.

[9] J. Ratzinger, *Truth and Tolerance: Christian Belief and World Religions* (San Francisco: Ignatius, 2004), pp. 9–11, 79–94, 193.

[10] Cf. *ibid.*, pp. 18–22, 25–7, 44, 53–4, 66–7, 72, 78–9, 82–4, 92–9, 103–5, 108–9, 169–74.

something for which all people yearn. Jesus of Nazareth is the meaning of history, the *Logos* who became a human being. As such, Christianity concerns all of humanity at all times.[11]

Gerard Mannion has argued that Ratzinger's statements position Christianity as superior to other religions, that other religions fall short of full salvation, and as a result that in statements on this topic Ratzinger has caused needless confusion, anger, hurt, and offense.[12] Ratzinger rejects the claim that these statements are in anyway arrogant or intolerant, instead insisting that what is at issue is the question about truth and the positive meaning of religion.[13] While a deepening of understanding, whether that of his own or of the wider Church, of the riches of other cultures and religions is always possible, dialogue is not collaborative theologizing where all religions would ultimately integrate into one religion. This, for Ratzinger, would not move humanity closer to God, but quite the reverse, it would move away from God as it moves away from Jesus Christ. Consequently, Ratzinger contends that Christianity has a positive and a negative relationship with other cultures and religions reflective of two attitudes to other religions evident in Scripture: the first is a partial recognition as preparation for Christ; the second a firm rejection. The first Ratzinger notes was Christ's own view of the faith of Israel and argues is an approach that has latterly been shown can be taken with other religions. The second was the approach of the Old Testament prophets.[14]

Ratzinger categorizes the cultures and religions of the world in three distinct groups which include those who see themselves apart from religion: eastern mysticism of Asia, monotheism (or religions of revelation), and enlightenment.[15] In Enlightenment, which first occurred in Ancient Greece, myth is rejected in favor of rational knowledge which itself becomes an absolute value, and religions and religious values are deemed meaningless.[16] Mysticism and monotheism are radically different.[17] In mysticism, defined by the imageless unmetaphorical religious experience of the undifferentiated all, the oneness of ultimate reality shows that all distinctions are only provisional: "inwardness holds first place; spiritual experience is posited as absolute."[18] Ratzinger contrasts this situation to the God who acts and to the Thou and I distinction characteristic of Christian monotheism, stating: "The last word about being is, no longer the unnamable absolute, but love,

---

[11] Cf. *ibid.*, pp. 18–22, 25–7, 44, 53–5, 72, 78–9, 82–4, 92–9, 103–5, 108–9, 169–74, 181–3.
[12] Cf. L. Boeve and G. Mannion, *The Ratzinger Reader* (London: T&T Clark, 2010), pp. 139–49, 154, 172–4.
[13] Cf. J. Ratzinger, *Truth and Tolerance*, pp. 9–11.
[14] Cf. *ibid.*, pp. 20–1.
[15] Cf. *ibid.*, pp. 28–32.
[16] Cf. *ibid.*, p. 28.
[17] Cf. *ibid.*, pp. 32–9, 45.
[18] *Ibid.*, p. 36.

which makes itself visible in the God who himself became a creature and thus unites the creature with the Creator."[19] This relationship reflects God as a person and hence the human being as a person, which for Ratzinger has important consequences: the value and dignity of each person rests on the foundation of God as person.[20] In terms of monotheistic faiths which are characterized by revelation, Ratzinger notes that Christianity sees itself as the fulfillment of Israel's messianic hopes, in the prophets continual struggle against idolatry and in belief in creation and God as Creator.[21] In Islam, while Ratzinger sees a great monotheistic religious culture, he also notes Islam's different understanding of God.[22] Islam's rejection of God as *Logos*, because of the limits that would place upon an unlimited God, has radical and far-reaching consequences.[23]

While Ratzinger insists that Christianity has more in common with the great religions of ancient cultures than rationalistic modernity, he also notes that Christianity's pre-history is in Greek philosophy's critique of religions with its rejection of myth and custom, and its yearning for and its incessant questioning that sought truth. In that way, Christianity's precedents and inner groundwork lie in philosophical enlightenment, notwithstanding the fact that modern enlightenment's self-understanding is that it has moved beyond the domain of religion.[24] Ratzinger argues in that regard how religions, in particular Christianity, establish a relationship with rational knowledge is decisive for the future of religion, and hence humanity.[25] This is different to how Christianity establishes a relationship with other religions, both eastern mysticism and other monotheistic religions, in particular Islam. Ratzinger seeks for Christianity to engage with all cultures and religions because the dialogue on truth, on what is right and just, is, he insists, an essential task for Christianity in every era.[26]

---

[19] *Ibid.*, p. 84.
[20] Cf. *ibid.*, pp. 47, 102–5.
[21] Cf. *ibid.*, pp. 36–44, 144–56, 198–9.
[22] Cf. *ibid.*, pp. 202–4. Also see, *id., Church Ecumenism, and Politics: New Endeavours in Ecclesiology* (San Francisco: Ignatius, 2008), p. 211.
[23] See Benedict XVI's Regensburg address which discusses the theme of the intrinsic rationality of God: *Faith, Reason and the University: Memories and Reflections. Lecture in the Meeting with the Representatives of Science,* Apostolic Journey to München, Altötting and Regensburg (September 9–14, 2006), Regensburg, September 12, 2006. For an Islamic outline of how reason relates to God in Islam see R. Aslan, *No God But God: The Origins, Evolution and Future of Islam* (London: Arrow Books, 2011), pp. 153–64. For a consideration of the difficulties that arise from Islam's view of God and reason from a (critical) Catholic perspective see J. V. Schall, *On Islam: A Chronological Record, 2002–2018* (San Francisco: Ignatius, 2018), pp. 66–85, 89–112, 135–44, 183–91, 204–6, 230–9.
[24] Cf. J. Ratzinger, *Truth and Tolerance*, pp. 169–74.
[25] Cf. *ibid.*, pp. 29, 28–42, 142–4, 156–9, 223–7.
[26] Cf. *ibid.*, pp. 66–7, 95–8, 208–9; J. Ratzinger and J. Habermas, *The Dialectics of Secularization: On Reason and Religion* (San Francisco: Ignatius, 2006), pp. 77–80.

In parallel to situating Christianity within world cultures and religions, Ratzinger has been a forthright critic of modern philosophy, particularly the Kantian line taken up by Habermas.[27] First, he identified major problems with limits Kant placed on human reason and perception. Second, he views Marxism, in its various forms, as misguided in attempting to actualize hope in divine things in the here and now, seeking as it does to achieve liberation by restructuring societal structures to eliminate poverty, oppression, and injustice. Ratzinger's view is that when politics attempts to be redemptive it promises something it cannot deliver. But more than that, in trying to do the work of God it becomes demonic. Liberation and freedom are not ultimately political outcomes actualized through political or revolutionary activity. It is the truth, the truth of Jesus Christ that God is unity in multiplicity, that God is both love and reason and hence person in freedom, that makes us free and liberates us. Although the collapse of the Soviet Union discredited Marxism, Ratzinger believes the attraction of Marxism remains potent and he sought to dissuade others from repeating its mistakes in new contexts.[28] The priority given to practice over knowledge, orthopraxy over orthodoxy, arising out of the renunciation of metaphysics, for him, leads to action in the absence of knowing. The question that arises for Ratzinger is, when we do not know what is right and hence how to act rightly, how can we act rightly? Action, or praxis, he contends provides no light.[29] More than that, he argues the rejection of metaphysics has a direct impact on Christian faith: "If the doors to metaphysical knowledge remain barred, if we cannot pass beyond the limits of human perception set by Kant, then faith will necessarily atrophy, simply for lack of breathing space."[30] Ratzinger here sees parallels with the neo-Scholastic attempt to reconstruct Christian faith "with pure rational certainty, by means of rational argument that was strictly independent of any faith." Ratzinger insists that only with faith, and with it an encounter with Jesus Christ, can reason be healed.[31]

Underpinning Ratzinger's dialogue with Habermas and modernity is the challenge to modernity's faith in reason, in its belief that reason is rational, something he maintains is not determinable solely by science nor philosophy. The challenge Ratzinger puts to modern reason is, how and why does rationality have primacy over irrationality?

---

[27] Cf. *ibid.*, pp. 130–6, 203–9, 240–5.
[28] Cf. *ibid.*, pp. 115–17.
[29] Cf. *ibid.*, pp. 123–4. For critical critiques of Ratzinger's theological approach to religious pluralism and Liberation theology see: J. Corkery, *Joseph Ratzinger's Theological Ideas* (Dublin: Dominican Press, 2009); T. P. Rausch, *Pope Benedict XVI: An Introduction to His Theological Vision* (New York: Paulist Press, 2009); and also J. Allen Jr., *Cardinal Ratzinger, Enforcer of the Faith* (New York: Continuum, 2002).
[30] *Ibid.*, p. 135.
[31] Cf. *ibid.*, p. 136.

The question is whether reason, or rationality, stands at the beginning of all things and is grounded in the basis of all things or not. The question is whether reality originated on the basis of chance and necessity ... or ... luck and cunning ... from what is irrational; that is whether reason, being a chance by product of irrationality and floating in an ocean of irrationality, is ultimately just as meaningless; or whether the principle that represents the fundamental conviction of Christian faith and of its philosophy remains true: "In principio erat Verbum"—at the beginning of all things stands the creative power of reason ... a choice in favour of the priority of reason and of rationality.[32]

This question goes to the heart of modernity and the enlightenment project itself. It is not one Ratzinger is alone in addressing. Jacques Derrida in his 1983 article "The Principle of Reason: The University in the Eyes of Its Pupils" discusses this issue, albeit from a radically different perspective.[33] Derrida notes that the university's reason for being has always been reason itself, wryly noting that no university has been established to be or to argue against reason. Yet, while Derrida insists that reason rationally explains effects through their causes, reason must nonetheless also give an account of its own roots. Cautioning that the principle of reason cannot ground itself, reason cannot be the origin or grounds of reason, Derrida notes here that the necessary origin, or ground of reason, has yet to be established by enlightenment thought. Derrida goes as far as stating that by not accounting for the origin of reason, the grounds upon which the principle of reason stands, the contemporary university itself stands over an abyss, an empty gorge. Reason then, like the university, "would have to hold itself suspended above a most peculiar void."[34] It is this void, and the implications and meaning it points to, that Ratzinger has sought to bring to the fore through his engagement with representatives of modern Western culture.

Creation answers this question definitively for Ratzinger. Not only does God as Creator guarantee the reasonableness of nature and of rationality. God, having created humanity from the dust of the earth in God's own image, after the Fall both heals and elevates humanity through the second Adam, Jesus Christ. More than that, what the biblical creation accounts tells us is that in contradistinction to contemporaneous creation accounts such as that

---

[32] *Ibid.*, p. 181.
[33] J. Derrida, "The Principle of Reason: The University in the Eyes of Its Pupils," *Diacritics* 13 (1983), pp. 2–20.
[34] *Ibid.*, pp. 7–9. The history of reason, Derrida maintains, is one in which the concept of reason has shifted from *logos*, to ratio, *raison*, and so forth, and that enlightenment understands reason in terms of "the principle of reason." Derrida explains the principle of reason based on Leibniz's first two principles of all reasoning: 1) that of non-contradiction, and 2) that of rendering reason, or in other words, that a reasoned account is possible of any truth or true proposition.

of Babylonia's account of Enuma Elish, in which the world and the human being is fashioned from a dragon's body and blood, human beings are not from negative forces nor are demons or evil spirits. The human being is not just good but very good and it is God's breadth, breathed into the nostrils of the body, through which the human being receives life. Here heaven and earth meet.[35] Ratzinger does acknowledges that in light of extreme poverty and injustice and the desperate isolation, loneliness and brokenness experienced by so many the fullness of Christianity can seem too little, too ineffective.[36] The practice of theology and its perennial task to explicate and protect the faith of the Church can appear disconnected or abstracted from that reality. Ratzinger would definitively be in tune with Tracey Rowland's assessment that: "In the final analysis, the most significant achievement of the Liberation Theology movement is that it has drawn attention to what Gutierrez and Muller have described as the twin errors of the 'vericalism of a disembodied spiritual union with God' (which recognizes God's transcendence but not His immanence) and a 'socioeconomic-political horizontalism' (focused on the immanence and neglectful of the transcendence)."[37] Avoiding these two errors while also engaging the world in the fullness of Christian faith and actively working to address the real immediate needs of so many, is the ever present challenge for those engaged in theology.

Habermas' Contribution: Religions as a Source of Solidarity for Egalitarian Universalism

While it is wrong to see Habermas making a break with his past thought on religion in early 2000s, it would be right to see a pivot that responds to the unexpected fact of pluralism in Western societies. So, like Ratzinger, the framework and principles of this thought have remained essentially consistent. It is the world around him that has changed, and he has applied his framework and principles to that new situation. What seems new is something that has been repurposed in response to unexpected outcomes. More than that, Eduardo Mendieta argues that Habermas remains in continuity with the critique of religion informed by the Frankfurt School's Critical Theory albeit through his own critique of Horkheimer's and Adorno's theory of negative theology.[38] Based on the claim that "the absolute

---

[35] Cf. J. Ratzinger, *"In the Beginning ..." A Catholic Understanding of Creation and the Fall* (London: T&T Clark, 1995), pp. 8–18.
[36] Cf. *id.*, "Vorfragen zu einer Theologie der Edosung," in L. Scheffczyk, *Edosung und Emanzipation* (Freiburg: Herder, 1973), pp. 141–55. An English version can be found in in L. Boeve and G. Mannion (eds.), *The Ratzinger Reader* (London: T&T Clark, 2010), p. 57.
[37] T. Rowland, *Catholic Theology* (London: T&T Clark, 2017), p. 203.
[38] Cf. E. Mendieta, "Introduction," in J. Habermas, *Religion and Rationality: Essays on Reason, God, and Modern   ity* (Cambridge: Polity, 2002), pp. 12–4.

is unrepresentable" and that the yearning for "the wholly other is a figure of thought that seeks to preserve" hope in justice in an unjust world, religion is to be rescued by translation of religious concepts into language accessible by modernity. Horkheimer and Adorno's critique of religion, which Habermas takes up by critiquing, is encapsulated in five theses: First, enlightenment is catalysed by religion because religion is the critique of myth; Second, in that process religion is assimilated and secularized becoming divested of its social and philosophical role; Third, nonetheless religion remains a source of humanity's deepest hopes for justice and reconciliation; Fourth, Critical Theory's use of reason against reason guides a methodological skepticism to religion which guards against "facile and glib dismissals of certain social phenomena"; Fifth and foremost, religion is reappropriated not rejected: reason and remembrance require each other "memory remains ineffective if it were not married to universality."[39]

Mendieta describes Habermas as a social theorist and a philosopher who works to reconstruct historical materialism. He understands secularization as arising from a learning process or capacity for critique inherent in enlightened world views. Having acted as the mechanism through which individuals integrated into society and cognitively engage the natural world, religion and metaphysics enable their own de- and re-legitimzsation. In this way the concept of God is reformulated into the rationality of communicative structures of society that gives coherence and unity of meaning. Through the appropriation and translation of religious concepts and symbols via the learning process of rationalization and secularization, society becomes the locus of moral norms which exercise their power via non-coercive coercion.[40] Mendieta identifies four phases to Habermas work stretching over five decades, and these phases each demonstrate a continual intensification of Habermas' engagement with religion.

In the first phase from 1952–71, which is dominated by Habermas' thought on the emergence of consciousness through historical and material conditions reflective of social learning, religion is understood to prefigure philosophical concepts and categories. The second phase from 1971 to 82 in which Habermas sought to rescue and transform Marxism via systems theory, development psychology and social theory, religion is engaged with from a sociological lens where questions of religion are assimilated into questions on the rationalization of worldviews and social practices. The third phase from 1982 to 2000 he considered the consequences for philosophy of the linguistification of reason as describe by his theory of communicative rationality. In this period Habermas's interest in religion increased due to the importance played by moral norms and normative content in those considerations. Habermas concludes that the unconditional is present in

---

[39] *Ibid.*, pp. 2–11, at 11.
[40] Cf. *ibid.*, pp. 16–24.

language and hence there is no need for an indispensable transcendent Other as a guarantor of moral norms. However, Habermas insists that while "post-metaphysical philosophy dispenses with God as an onto-metaphysical referent, it retains the insight of a normative claim that constrains as it frees, for, as created creatures, we nonetheless remain utterly free." Morality is implicit in language; therefore, philosophy salvages religion without the need for God. In the fourth and last phase identified from 2000 to present (2013), Habermas sought to avoid a clash of civilizations through the learning processes of secularization. And it is to this phase that we turn to now.[41]

The immediate context to Habermas' dialogue with Ratzinger was three lectures he gave in 2000 and 2001 and an interview in 2002 with Mendieta on God and the World. In the first paper Habermas considers post-metaphysic's restraint regarding ethics in terms of "binding positions on substantive questions of the good life or the un-misspent life." In light of advances in bio and genetic technology he argues that moral questions have been generated that "are of an *altogether different kind*." Habermas, while agreeing with Rawls that the just society is one where individuals develop their ethical self-understanding in equal freedom according to one's abilities and choices, argues that these technical advances place questions over the ethical self-understanding of humanity and that successfully being able to be oneself is now only one options among many. As a result, he maintains that the question of the good life has "taken on new life" and philosophers must engage in public discourse on the "right understanding of cultural forms of life." Where moral insights effectively bind the will, ethical self-understanding of one's own well-being is joined to interest in justice.[42]

In the second paper given in 2001, which includes a postscript from 2002 that responds to objections raised to the original presentation, Habermas considers the impact of liberal eugenics practices. From the perspective of the second person, he considers the interventions into the genome of an embryo that can occur at the discretion of the parent of a future person who will then, he claims, be genetically programmed.[43] Habermas insists that the consent of the second person for such interventions is only justifiably assumed in the face of future extreme suffering which he views as an evil. Bio and genetic technologies, in Habermas' view, will alter the relations between generations because by intervening in the prenatal genetic resources of a person redefines "those naturally fixed ranges of opportunities and scopes of possible decision" unique to that person. The designer (parent) "changes

---

[41] Cf. E. Mendieta, "Appendix Religion in Habermas' Work," in C. Calhoun, E. Mendieta, and J. Vanantwerpen (eds.), *Habermas and Religions* (Cambridge: Polity, 2013), pp. 391–407, at 402.
[42] Cf. J. Habermas, "Are There Postmetaphysical Answers to the Question: What Is the 'Good Life'?," in *The Future of Human Nature* (London: Polity, 2003), pp. 1–15; at pp. 2, 4, 14–15.
[43] Ratzinger responded to this same concern in "Man between Reproduction and Creation: Theological Questions on the Origin of Human Life," *Communio* 16 (1989), pp. 197–211.

the initial conditions for the identity formation of another person in an asymmetrical and irrevocable manner." In this process, Habermas argues, the designer (parent) "makes himself the co-author of the life of the another" and intrudes "into the other's consciousness of their own autonomy." Such interventions do not impact the freedom of the "genetically programmed" person, rather, they potentially negatively impact on their self-understanding as an autonomous, responsible moral agent. A self-devaluation of their moral self-understanding may result that negates their cognitive ability to be "sole authors" and take "sole responsibility for her own life." Habermas maintains that in such a situation "of alienating dilution or fracturing of one's own identity is a sign that an important boundary has become permeable—the deontological shell which assures the inviolability of the person, the uniqueness of the individual, and the irreplaceability of one's own subjectivity."[44]

It is not just the risk to the future programmed person that Habermas is concerned about. He argues that liberal eugenics raises questions about the value of morality itself the effects of which are, for him, horrifying. If the naturalistic futurism that strives for the self-optimization of human beings via bio and genetic technologies changes the moral language game so that the arguments of that game will no longer be effective, "the aggregated preferences of consumers in the genetic supermarket ... might change the moral status of future persons." The morality of egalitarian universalism that Habermas advocates, embedded as it is in a species-ethical self-understanding and justified via rational reasons bequeathing modernity with an autonomous morality, human rights, equal respect, and solidarity for all, is not in his view threatened by other moralities. Egalitarian universalism, he argues, is an advance gifted by modernity offering the only rationally acceptable approach for managing cultural differences in pluralistic societies. A reversion to metaphysics would for Habermas be a retrograde step returning to treacherous uncertainties, intolerance, and cultural conflict. However, it is possible that through the normalization in society of practices that instrumentalize prepersonal life that egalitarian universalistic morality will be overtaken, toppled as he puts it.[45]

The third lecture is entitled "Faith and Knowledge," and it is the themes from this last lecture, given weeks after the 911 terrorist attacks at his acceptance of the Peace Prize of the German Book Trade, that are taken up in his dialogue with Ratzinger. Here Habermas considers the process of secularization in a post secular society and the burden that the learning process places upon citizens of faith and those of no faith in a democratic constitutional state. His aim is threefold: 1) protect the process

---

[44] J. Habermas, "The Debate on the Ethical Self-Understanding of the Species," in *The Future of Human Nature*, pp. 75–82, at 79, 82.
[45] Cf. *ibid.*, pp. 91–7.

of secularization in the West and globally; 2) prevent secular modern reason from blindly succumbing to the latent power of religion; 3) prevent the lose of resources of meaning available from religion.[46] Insisting that secularization is not a zero-sum game of winners and losers, Habermas contends that religions be considered reasonable only if they refrain from violence and take a threefold view of pluralistic society. First, they overcome the cognitive dissonance of the existence of other denominations and religions. Second, they accept the monopoly of authority held by science over the sources of secular knowledge. Third, they accept the constitutional state is grounded in profane morality. In addition, Habermas here rejects any science that does not completely account for the intentionality of human consciousness and normative action, and that seeks to replace it with objectivating self-description. All that is, Habermas contends, is bad philosophy not science. This threefold approach to secular society is necessary from religion for without it he claims, "monothesisms in relentlessly modernised societies unleash a destructive potential." In Habermas' worldview the state in secular societies remains neutral to political decisions while remaining open to both science and religion. However, the outcomes of those political decisions must avoid strong traditions and comprehensive worldviews.[47]

Habermas acknowledges two difficulties to his approach. The first is that it places a burden on religious citizens to split their identity between private and public. Second, unless non-religious citizens remain sensitive to the language of religion, the views of religious citizens will be excluded from decision-making, something he clearly views as detrimental for secular society. Moreover, Habermas contends that the "boundaries between secular and religious reason are fluid" and that it is up to both the religious and the secular citizens to collaborate on identifying where the boundary lines. To do that they must all take the perspective of the other. As a result, the secular state should not regulate secularization vis-à-vis religious communities alone. The democratic constitutional state should examine the arguments of these communities to understand what can be learnt from them. In particular, he sees that religions offer valuable resources, such as the social bonds that arise from mutual recognition, for dealing with aggressive globalization and market deregulation with its egocentric orientation.[48]

Habermas also notes Enlightenment has at times asked too much of reason with the result that essential tasks have remained incomplete such as adequate concepts to express the difference between a moral wrong and something that is profoundly evil. In the light of those shortcomings, Habermas seeks to engender a profane reason which respects the "glowing embers" of religion while maintaining its distance. In a nod to Horkheimer

---

[46] Cf. *id*., "Forward," in *The Future of Human Nature* (London: Polity, 2003), pp. vii–viii.
[47] Cf. *id*., "Faith and Knowledge," in *The Future of Human Nature*, pp. 104–5, 106–7.
[48] Cf. *ibid*., pp. 109–10.

and Adorno's Dialectic of Enlightenment, he states: "It knows that the profanation of the sacred begins with those world religions which disenchanted magic, overcame myth, sublimated sacrifice, and disclosed the secret."[49] At the heart of such a profanation of the sacred is not, he claims, a hostile takeover but a translation. What he is seeking is to salvage the moral intuitions of religions so that they can again find universal resonance in the secular sphere, and in that way enable the West to act as a non-destructive secularizing force in the world.[50]

In the 2002 interview with Mendieta on God and the World—a striking title given that Ratzinger had published a book interview on the same topic in 2000—Habermas acknowledges the importance of the Judeo Christian heritage of enlightenment thought. Making it clear that when he speaks of religion he is referring to this tradition, he credits the organizational forms of "Hellenised Christianity" and the educational forms of the Catholic Church (universities, monasteries, and cathedrals) as the precursor to modern forms of consciousness and mental structures. It is from here that the ideals of universalistic egalitarianism of freedom and collective life in society, the autonomous conduct of life and emancipation, the individual morality of conscience, human rights and democracy, emerged. He argues that the reformation produced a transformation of religious consciousness and the modernization of faith, which in his view secularized society. Arising from those dynamics, society now demands both a "restructuring of faith and Church praxis" to occur so that it accommodates itself to truth claims of other faiths and to the scientific claims of secular society. For Habermas the modernization of faith is required for religious tolerance and the construction of a neutral state power, insisting that only strict Kantian universalism is compatible with modern conditions. For while he claims to admire Thomas Aquinas he also contends that colonialism and eurocentrism are intrinsically linked to Christianity in an "unholy alliance."[51] Ultimately, Habermas contends that philosophy has not yet done justice to the intuitions captured by religions when translating religious concepts into philosophical ethics. In particularly he has in mind the "indispensable potential for meaning" in the Bible's description of the individual person.[52]

In light of the all too brief survey above, what is evident is that Habermas' pivot to religion draws on his existing framework: religious moral intuitions are to be translated into language generally accessible by all. That language is the "natural reason" of post-metaphysics. Those translations are necessary to harness sources of social solidarity and meaning that democratic

---

[49] *Ibid.*, pp. 110–12 at 112.
[50] Cf. *ibid.*, pp. 114–15.
[51] E. Mendieta and J. Habermas, "A Conversation about God and the World," in J. Habermas (ed.), *Religion and Rationality: Essays on Reason, God, and Modernity* (Cambridge: Polity, 2002), pp. 147–67, 147–52.
[52] *Ibid.*, p. 162.

constitutional secular societies are unable to reproduce. While religious citizens must accept the profane morality of modernity, secular citizens must likewise a priori accept that religions can be sources of meaning. Developments in bio and genetic technologies and the potential threats he sees arising from them for the autonomous self-understanding of individual persons concretize this need. At no point does Habermas yield the primacy and self-sufficiency of post-metaphysical philosophy nor does he see religion as in any way an equal partner to reason. His aim as a philosopher is to protect the gains achieved by modernity from multiple threats. These threats include religious fundamentalism and metaphysical world views, that he sees as intolerant, but which, in fact, mainly emerge from those within the liberal enlightenment tradition who have radicalized the critique of reason such that it has become self-destructive. Committed to modernity as understood in the line of post-metaphysical thought running through Kant, Hegel, and Marx with its aim of a more just and rational society, Habermas rejects secularism, positivism, deconstructionism, scientism, and any form of thought skeptical of reason's capability to respond to the challenges of modernity. In his defense of modernity Habermas sees in the Judeo-Christian tradition sources that post-metaphysics needs and can leverage to its benefit. However, what he offers in return is an inhospitable process where the principles of modernity envisioned by post-metaphysics create the framework of engagement that all others must accept and pre-modern religion becomes essentially a source of things that are missing in modernity.

Catholic Academy of Munich, January 2004: A Dialogue or Two Monologues?

At the time of his dialogue with Ratzinger, Habermas was developing his thought on religion in the public sphere in response to John Rawl's political theory, in particular his concept of the "public use of reason" and critiques of it by Nicholas Wolterstorff and Paul J Weithmann, who reject the requirement for religious citizens to translate their faith based public contributions into generally accessible arguments that outline good reasons for their political statements.[53] At the core of his response Habermas argues that public arguments must be accessible to all citizens and as such must be based on the shared standards of common natural reason. Only then can legitimate law be generated in a democracy. This for Habermas distinguishes a community integrated by constitutional values and those marked by

---

[53] Cf. J. Habermas, "Religion in the Public Sphere," *European Journal of Philosophy* 14/1 (2006), pp. 1–25, at 1. First published in English as chapter 5 of *Between Naturalism and Religion* (Cambridge: Polity, 2006). Originally published in *Zurischen Naturalismus und Religion* (Frankfurt: Suhrkamp, 2005).

competing worldviews vying among each other for power.[54] This forms the backdrop of his contribution to the dialogue and Habermas may have used the opportunity of the dialogue with Ratzinger to gauge the reaction to his arguments with those who are subjects of it. In that Habermas outlines three core elements of his political theory. First, the modern democratic secular society is self-sufficiently legitimate based upon arguments from the political liberalism of Kantian republicanism and the philosophy of the seventeenth- and eighteent-century Enlightenment. Such states require no resources outside itself, whether religious or metaphysical, to justify its political rule. Law is legitimate if it is based on "legal procedures born of democratic procedures." Such argument is based upon two premises. First, democracy is a process of legitimate legislations so long as it is based on "an inclusive and discursive formation of opinion and will' for then the output can be assumed to be 'rationally acceptable." Second, and following from the first, is that human rights in terms of basic liberal and political rights are interconnected with democracy and as a result are granted simultaneously. The legitimacy of law arises from its legality such that the constitution in a democratic constitutional state has an autonomous justification that is rationally acceptable.[55]

Second, the demands placed upon citizens in democratic constitutional states where they are (co)-legislators are significantly greater than in states where citizens are subjects of the law. They must be willing to engage on behalf of others and accept sacrifices for the common good. Political virtues are "the practices and modes of thought of a free political culture" of which social solidarity is a core practice. Habermas describes social solidarity as "a coordination of action based on values, norms and a vocabulary intended to promote mutual understanding."[56] That solidarity is "nourished by springs that well forth spontaneously—springs that one may term 'pre-political.'" The uniting bond, Habermas claims, "is the democratic process itself—a communicative praxis that can be exercised only in common and that has its ultimate theme the correct understanding of the constitution."[57] Threats to this solidarity, a solidarity in which the "principles of justice have penetrated more deeply into the complex of ethical orientations of a culture," arise when the ability of citizens to participate in the formation of opinion and will is negated. This happens when the political formation of a democratic constitutional states is negatively impacted by the influence of the Markets and bureaucracies.[58]

Third, secularization occurs via a double learning process in which enlightenment and religion listen and learn from each other. Habermas

---

[54] Cf. *id.*, "Religion in the Public Sphere," pp. 8–11, 13.
[55] Cf. *id.*, in J. Ratzinger and J. Habermas, *Dialectics of Secularization*, pp. 25–8.
[56] *Ibid.*, pp. 45–6.
[57] *Ibid.*, pp. 30–4.
[58] Cf. *ibid.*, pp. 5–36, 43–7.

insists that the process of secularization "compels both the traditions of Enlightenment and religious doctrines to reflect on their own respective limits."[59] Through these reflections the moral intuitions kept alive by religious communities can be translated by philosophy into accessible language which removes religious dogmatism and coercion while not emptying the intuitions of meaning. The exemplar here is the translation of the biblical concept of man in the image of God into the philosophical statement of the identical dignity of all men that deserves unconditional respect.[60] This complementary learning process, for Habermas has implications for both religious and non-religious citizens placing specific demands on both alike in a democratic secular state. First, religious citizens must integrate into the state and that integration must be more than simply an accommodation of a worldview. In doing so they have the possibility to influence society. Second, non-religious citizens must acknowledge that religious convictions are not simply irrational. In doing so they have access to the sources of meaning and solidarity it otherwise would not have. Third, the ethical freedom of each citizen is guaranteed by the state's maintenance of a neutrality toward questions of worldviews.[61]

Ultimately, Habermas' political theory and its place for religion in the public sphere rest on the assumption that the sacred is capable of being translatable into the profane such that profane language is capable of retaining the meaning of sacred concepts. Or as Cristina Lafont puts it, translation "presupposes that it is possible to arrive at the same results by different [secular and religious] epistemic means."[62] It is far from clear that this is the case. Indeed, a cursory look at the Christian understanding of creation and the typological interpretation of Jesus Christ as the final Adam, as touched upon above, would indicate that the sacred and profane understanding of the individual person are radically different, one relational the other autonomous, raising serious and fundamental questions as to the tenability of Habermas' approach.[63]

---

[59] Ibid., p. 23.
[60] For a critique of the notion of human dignity, that is central to Habermas' thought, see Alasdair MacIntyre's presentation "Human Dignity: A Puzzling and Possibly Dangerous Idea?" presented at the University of Notre Dame de Nicola Centre for Ethics and Culture 2021 Fall Conference, on November 12, 2021, entitled "I Have Called You by Name: Human Dignity in a Secular World."
[61] J. Ratzinger and J. Habermas, *Dialectics of Secularization*, pp. 48–52.
[62] C. Lafont, "Religion in the Public Sphere: Remarks on Habermas's Conception of Public Deliberation in Postsecular Societies," *Constellations* 14/2 (2007), pp. 239–59, at 245.
[63] See a detailed consideration of creation, the human being and the theological notion of person in the following articles by J. Ratzinger, "*In the Beginning ...*," "Man between Reproduction and Creation: Theological Questions on the Origin of Human Life," *Communio* 16 (1989), pp. 197–211; "Concerning the Notion of Person in Theology," *Communio* 17 (1990), pp. 439–54; See also: M. F. McKenna, "Ratzinger and the Truly Human: Person Transcending their Human Nature to Participate in Divinity," in Francesca Aran Murphy and Tracey Rowland (eds.), *Oxford Handbook on Joseph Ratzinger* (Oxford: Oxford University Press, forthcoming 2024).

Ratzinger's Contribution: A Socratic Pauline Encounter

Ratzinger saw in Habermas a representative of philosophers, reflective of wider society, who reject metaphysic, religion, or the symbioses of these, but strive for a moral order of right living and a just society. Somewhat like in the manner *Lumen gentium* speaks of aspects of the People of God or in the manner of an Augustinian ecclesiology where some in the Church are only apparently so, being, in fact, against it, while, others outside it unknowingly belong to it.[64] In their dialogue, Ratzinger plays the role of the Socratic–Pauline figure who reaches out to those who seek truth, who seek the right way to live and the unknown God. Having considered Habermas' then most recent statements concerning religion and society, and finding concerns very similar to his own, Ratzinger proceeds to ask questions of Habermas' position. Ratzinger's hope, if I am right, is that in asking the right questions those who seek what is right and just cannot but pursue answers to those questions. Ratzinger is not seeking to convince by means of the force of argument, but to bring about intellectual turning points emanating from questions about truth. In response to Habermas' vision of a continued process of complementary learning between post-metaphysics and religions, Ratzinger raises queries as to the nature of law, power, and justice, and how reason and religion relate to these.

How does law come into being? How is law the instrument of justice rather than the instrument of arbitrary power? If, as is the case, religion can be a source of terror, is religion a source of good that saves and heals, or is it a source of intolerant false universals? If, as is the case, reason produces technologies of awesome destructive potential, now with the power to make human beings into a product and thereby change the very relationship humanity has with itself, is reason reliable and a source of good? Based on an affirmative answer to both these latter questions, should then both reason and religion be put under some type of guardianship to protect humanity? And who would that guardian be? While acknowledging that democracy provides for a shared collaboration in creation of law which guarantees that it is everyone's law and so should be respected, he also notes that majorities can be blind and unjust. Under these circumstances can law still be spoken of as law and justice? Moreover, Ratzinger asks whether there can be things that can never be law and are always unjust. Are there self-subsistent values related to the essence of humanity that are antecedent to every majority and every law? Even if the West's two cultures, the secular and the Christian, answer in the affirmative to the foregoing question, Ratzinger wonders

---

[64] Cf. Vatican Council II, *Lumen gentium*, November 24, 1964, §§9, 16. Also see J. Ratzinger, *Church, Ecumenism and Politics*, and P. Seewald, *Benedict XVI: A Life. Volume Two: Professor and Prefect to Pope and Pope Emeritus 1966–Present* (London: Bloomsbury 2021), p. 539.

whether that yes is sustainable in the face of Islam's own list of human rights and China's question as to whether human rights are a Western invention? Ultimately the question Ratzinger asks is whether in a global community characterized by power and with differing views of law and morality, is it possible to establish an "effective ethical conviction ... with sufficient motivation and vigour to answer the challenges" the world faces today?[65]

Ratzinger notes that Ancient Greece faced a comparable situation as the world does today when divine law no longer was persuasive and a counterbalance to positive law was sought in the nature of humanity itself. Likewise at the discovery of America and at the disintegration of Europe into multiple Christian denominations, a law not dependent on dogma but nonetheless a law binding on all nations was sought based on nature, humanity's mutual relations, and human reason. Yet today Ratzinger notes Natural Law is a blunt instrument which as a result he does not utilize. The theory of evolution in the eyes of secular society has overturned the view that nature and reason overlapped and that nature itself is rational. Only the notion of Human Rights remains from the legacy of Natural Law. In response to this situation, Ratzinger proposes that these rights should be supplemented with a list of human obligations and limitation, which might then enable others to see the rationality of nature and the rationality of humanity's existence in the world. This proposal is not directed solely at Western secular society, but to all the cultures and religions of the world. However, he notes that secular rationality arose in a specific cultural context and that the non-Western cultures place question marks over the West's claim to rationality and Christianity's claim of universal revelation.

While Ratzinger's work on Luther would raise questions about Habermas' understanding of the Reformation with Ratzinger elsewhere ironically noting that it was not Luther's intend that an absolute reason would displace an absolute faith,[66] he is in agreement with Habermas' insistence on reason and religions learning from each other and the need for reason and religions to accept their own self-limitation. In Ratzinger's proposal philosophy and religion are co-equal partners in a collaboration in which religion must allow the divine light of reason to act on it as a controlling organ and reason must listen to the great religious traditions of mankind.[67] This collaboration is to occur in an intercultural context in which, due to the reach of their influence, Christian faith and Western secular rationality will be the main partners in this engagement. Nonetheless, they must learn to listen to other cultures. By doing so, "a polyphonic relatedness, in which they themselves are receptive to the essential complementarity of reason and faith," can occur such that "a universal process of purifications (in the plural!) can proceed."[68] In that way

---

[65] J. Ratzinger and J. Habermas, *Dialectics of Secularization*, p. 66.
[66] Id., *Church, Ecumenism and Politics*, pp. 100–38.
[67] Cf. J. Ratzinger and J. Habermas, *The Dialectics of Secularization*, p. 78.
[68] *Ibid.*, 79.

Ratzinger contends that the essential values and norms that are known to humanity will be perceived afresh.

Ratzinger's hope is that his dialogue with Habermas will be replicated across the great cultures and religions of world history. In that way Christianity has the opportunity not only to be both purified and to purify those other cultures and religions but also to open new perspectives on God's self-revelation through a potential repeat of Christianity's engagement with Greek Philosophy with the philosophies of India and China. In those encounters the insights on biblical faith garnered through Greek philosophy are retained and those of other cultures both build upon and refine them while in no way contradicting them. Christianity is, Ratzinger insists, first and foremost an encounter with the person of Jesus Christ, and it is upon faith in Jesus Christ that all of Ratzinger's thought stands or falls. The equation of the God who is revealed to be love in Jesus Christ with the expansive reason of *Logos* creates the enterprise that Ratzinger advocates and which he seeks to bring into dialogue with the other great religions and cultures of the world. Ultimately, Ratzinger's position depends on faith in Jesus Christ, and such faith arises from an encounter with the whole Other. A thorough and robust description of faith falls outside of engagements with the secular and philosophical world. Yet the absence of an understanding of the nature of faith Ratzinger is referring to leaves a significant gap into which irrational ideas are read by many. To truly appreciate Ratzinger's engagement with the modern world his understanding of the rational nature of faith and its reasonableness is essential.

Lasting Impacts from the Habermas and Ratzinger 2004 Encounter

The 2004 dialogue was a polite engagement which belied the raging currents of the battle between two worldviews. As is evident from the above discussion, the outcome of the Munich dialogue was significant agreement between Habermas and Ratzinger at a surface level on how democracy should operate in the pursuit of a just and moral society which sat in parallel to deep differences as to why that is so and what process should be applied to pursue a just and moral society. These differing approaches reflect radically different concepts of reality which lead to fundamentally different understandings of the human being. The trajectory of Habermas' and Ratzinger's thought post Munich 2004 reflects the lines evident long before their dialogue which in themselves reflective of their commitment to post-metaphysics and Christian tradition and thought respectively. Notwithstanding these clear trajectories, the question I now briefly turn to is whether there is evidence of an impact on the thought of either Ratzinger's or Habermas' from their 2004 engagement. What is evident is that their dialogue did continue in the immediate aftermath of their encounter but with new audiences and each remained within the bounds of their original 2004 contribution.

Ratzinger, as Pope Benedict XVI, continued to engage with representatives of modernity, and these are in continuity with his dialogue with Habermas. There are five addresses of particularly note:[69] that with academia at the University of Regensburg 2006 and the talk he had intended to give at La Sapienza University in Rome in 2008 (this talk did not proceed due to protests at the university), the meeting with representatives of culture at the College des Bernardins, Paris in 2008, the meeting with representatives of British society at Westminster Hall London in 2010, and the meeting with lawmakers at the Reichstag Berlin in 2011. In these engagements Ratzinger, as Benedict XVI, vigorously advocates for the Catholic understanding of a broad and creative reason and with it its consequent ethical philosophy and vision of the human being. Equally, in his forthright rejection of modernity's acceptance of the limits Kant placed upon reason he notes that it nonetheless "still covertly [is] drawing upon God's raw materials, which we refashion into our own product."[70] In his Regensburg address, Benedict XVI insisted on the grandeur of reason, stating that "*Logos* means both reason and word—a reason which is creative and capable of self-communication, precisely as reason' and that truth is not equated with knowledge, rather, 'the purpose of knowing the truth is to know the good."[71] His La Sapienza talk can be seen in part as a response to Habermas' 2007 address to the Jesuits in Munich which itself can be understood as a critical critique of Benedict's Regensburg address. There he took up points of agreement with both John Rawls and Habermas while also critically critiquing the main thrusts of their arguments. He highlighted open issues with their respective approaches by asking decidedly simple questions of their central theses: how is reasonableness in an argument demonstrated? What is truth? And how can it be recognized?

These addresses lay the groundwork for his engagement with that of culture. In that address he outlines the cultural dynamic created by monasticism from its search for the ultimate and the true, for the *Logos*, which gave rise to Western civilization. An aspect of this description is a critique of modernity's replacement of God with language that Habermas advocated. In the two engagements with Westminster and Berlin he takes up again the questions

---

[69] See my discussion of these five papal addresses in M. F. McKenna, "In Search of Justice and Peace."
[70] Benedict XVI, *Address during the Visit to the Federal Parliament in the Reichstag Building*, Apostolic Journey to Germany (September 22–5, 2011), Berlin, September 22, 2011.
[71] *Id.*, *Faith, Reason and the University: Memories and Reflections. Lecture in the Meeting with the Representatives of Science*, Apostolic Journey to München, Altötting and Regensburg (September 9–14, 2006), Regensburg, September 12, 2006; and *id.*, *Lecture Prepared for the University of Rome "La Sapienza,"* January 17, 2008, respectively.

as to what is law and what is justice. He raises problems with consensus as the sole basis for law insisting upon the legitimate role of religions which is not a problem to be solved but a vital contributor to "the national conversation."[72] Ratzinger argues that what lawmakers require is a listening heart, and like Solomon (1 Kg 3:9) should ask God for the gift to be able to discern what is good and what is evil, and, in that way, "establish true law to serve justice and peace."[73]

In addition to those engagements with representatives of the modern world, in two of Benedict XVI's encyclicals addressed to the faithful, *Deus caritas est* (2006) and *Spe salvi* (2008), there are important critiques of post-metaphysical thought. These were some of the first papal encyclicals to refer to philosophy, and Benedict specifically rejects the philosophical line of historical materialism that Habermas embraces. *Deus caritas est* critiques Marxism in light of Christian charity and *Spe salvi* critiques Marxism's faith in progress in light of Christian hope. There he sought to demonstrate for Christians the true meaning of charity and hope that emanates from God which eschews power and material gain for love and divine things. Not only is God love but "faith is the substance of hope."[74] What he means by faith was latterly answered in his final works as pope in the Wednesday audience talks for the Year of Faith (2012–13) and what is essentially his fourth encyclical, *Lumen fidei* (2013): faith is an encounter that subsequently develops into a relationship of trust with the Word become flesh, Jesus Christ. This encyclical along with Benedict's Wednesday audience catechesis on faith during the Year of Faith (2012–13) offers a missing link in his engagement with the world. It is faith that is presupposed in those engagements and, as noted, they can only truly be understood when considered in light of his description of the nature of faith.

The five engagements and his encyclicals have the same character and purpose as his dialogue with Habermas. Namely, to engage his audience with precisely chosen questions that go to the very heart of the world views he sought to critique, and to demonstrate in parallel the reasonableness of the Catholic Christian option. In the Socratic manner, he takes aim at both the expressed positions and the unexpressed presuppositions via questions to expose what he sees as deep incoherence. In those engagements are contained the whole gamut of questions he poses to modernity in its reject of Christian faith and metaphysics. They are in fact a treasure trove of questions to be taken up by those who seek to continue his engagement

---

[72] *Id.*, *Address at the Meeting with the Representatives of British Society, Including the Diplomatic Corps, Politicians, Academics and Business Leaders*, Apostolic Journey to the United Kingdom (September 16–19, 2010), City of Westminster, Westminster Hall, September 17, 2010.
[73] *Id.*, *Address at the Visit to the Bundestag*, Apostolic Journey to Germany (September 22–5, 2011), September 27, 2011.
[74] *Id.*, *Encyclical Letter* Spe salvi *on Christian Hope*, November 30, 2007, §10.

with the modern world offering avenues for robust dialogue in the service and pursuit of the truth, and hence justice.

Habermas like Benedict produced a substantive body of work during this period and again it follows the line of thought well established at the time of their dialogue. On the face of it the impact of Ratzinger's contribution to the dialogue on Habermas' thought would appear to be minimal. In his subsequent published works there is hardly a footnote referencing Ratzinger's contribution, although Habermas published his contribution in a 2008 collection of essays entitled *Between Naturalism and Religion*. Shortly after Habermas' important 2005 article "Religion in the Public Sphere" was published that formed the backdrop of his 2004 talk, Habermas returned to Munich in 2007 this time at the invitation of the Jesuits. In these later two papers the inhospitable nature of the double learning process proposed becomes increasingly evident. Habermas maintains that religious and metaphysical worldviews were shattered by modern science and that those world views in a modern context must now accept the authority of "natural" reasons, which remains nonetheless fallible, and must recognize the legitimacy of the neutral state based on postmetaphysical terms. In the double learning process modernity transforms the moral intuitions of religions and metaphysics by redirecting them via secularism. Habermas insists that the modern world, and with it secular reason, has turned its back on religion and metaphysics and appears surprised that Benedict "resists" the power of its arguments including, what he describes as, the three staged process of de-Hellenization commenced by Dun Scotus that ran through nominalism and then Kant. This is the very line of thought Ratzinger as Benedict XVI rejected in his Regensburg address. Habermas takes postmetaphyscial reason as a fact of modernity while refraining to take up the legitimate questions Ratzinger/Benedict poses to that worldview, not least the question as to how arguments are established as reasonable and what is truth.[75]

In 2008 Habermas published a substantive collection of papers in *Between Naturalism and Religion*, in which his dialogue with Ratzinger is included. In these papers Habermas again advocates for the postmetaphyical position of "the normative meaning of a detranscendentalised reason" against both a faith in science and a faith in religion. His aim is the defense of civic cohesion in a democratic constitutional state marked by religious and ideological pluralism.[76] Specifically in the paper "The Boundary between Faith and Knowledge: On the Reception and Contemporary Importance of Kant's Philosophy of Religion," Habermas can be interpreted to continue to respond to Ratzinger's, now Benedict's, advocacy of a broad concept of

---

[75] Cf. J. Habermas, "An Awareness of What Is Missing," in *An Awareness of What Is Missing. Faith and Reason in a Post Secular Age* (Polity, Cambridge, 2010), pp. 15–23.
[76] Cf. *id.*, "Introduction," in *Between Naturalism and Religion* (Cambridge: Polity, 2008), pp. 1–7, at 7.

reason. There he contends that Kant initiated the philosophy of religion by bringing religion "before the bar of reason."[77] In their introduction to *The Power of Religion in the Public Sphere* (2011), Eduardo Mendieta and Jonathan Vanantwerpen describe the Munich debate alongside Habermas' engagement with John Rawls as of "particular note" since Habermas' increasing turn to questions of religion.[78] In Habermas' paper included in that volume, originally presented in 2009, he essentially restates his early position of religion in the public sphere, which in themselves are a restatement of the core tenets of his philosophy in response to the fact of pluralism. In a 2013 collection of papers presented at a conference in 2011 on the theme of Habermas and Religion, there is only one reference to Ratzinger outside that of noting the dialogue's occurrence. That reference is made by John Milbank when he argues against Habermas based on Ratzinger Regensburg address.[79]

Habermas characterized his thought on religion in his 2013 response to those collection of papers that his thought on religions is "not yet sufficiently developed" and sought to provide clarity on a number of points.[80] Even after five decades of work in which as we saw earlier religion has been a growing aspect of consideration, it is striking that the place of religion in society defied a satisfactory resolution for Habermas. What is also noteworthy, given the urgency of the dangers he perceived from the potential of bio and genetic technologies evident in his 2000 and 2001 lectures, is that it is a theme that does not later resurface as a substantial consideration. What again appears is the pejorative view of religion which justifies its limited and controlled access to the democratic process. Based on the dubious premise that prior to secular reason political communities had no shared basis to resolve pressing problems in a manner satisfactory to all, he positions pre-secular (religious and metaphysical) reason as the "militant" power of belief liking its validity claims to those of ancient empires who sought political and cultural domination. In contradistinction, he restates his claim that the secularization of political power ushered in rational reason and rational law formed in the process of discursive will formation whose outcome could be accepted as legitimate by all.[81] It will be up to those who follow in Habermas' footsteps to understand the lacuna noted above in relation to the potential of bio and genetic technologies and to craft a more apt place for religion in the democratic constitutional liberal state of a post-metaphysical world.

---

[77] *Id.*, "The Boundary between Faith and Knowledge: On the Reception and Contemporary Importance of Kant's Philosophy of Religion," in *Between Naturalism and Religion* (Cambridge: Polity, 2008), pp. 209–47, at 209.
[78] E. Mendieta and J. Vanantwerpen, "Introduction," in *id.* (eds.), *The Power of Religion in the Public Sphere* (New York: Columbia University Press, 2011), pp. 3, 13.
[79] Cf. J. Millbank, "What Lacks Is Feeling: Hume verus Kant and Habermas," in C. Calhoun, E. Mendieta and J. Vanantwerpen (eds.), *Habermas and Religion* (Cambridge: Polity, 2013), pp. 322–46.
[80] J. Habermas, "Reply to My Critics," in *ibid.*, p. 347.
[81] *Ibid.*, pp. 372–5.

Conscience as the Shared Language of Humanity

In response to the unexpected fact of pluralism Habermas pivoted his thought to consider religion but offered only a restatement of his already existing framework and principles. Ratzinger, in acknowledging that Natural Law had become a blunt instrument in dialogue with modernity, offers a set of questions about truth and the nature of law and justice in light of the pathologies of both reason and religion. There is a logical unfolding to their arguments arising from their starting points: the development of humanity must in some way be explained or rationalized by historic materialism with progress replacing truth, while, the synthesis of biblical faith and Greek rationality fuses God's creative act with the *Logos* so that God is the ultimate point of consideration with truth determined by and equating the Good. So, it is not surprising that while Ratzinger and Habermas both call for reason and religion to learn from each other, their visions of this learning process are strikingly different. Ratzinger seeks in that learning process for reason and faith to act as co-equal partners who purify each other of pathologies. The pathologies of religion that Ratzinger refers to are at the forefront of Habermas' thinking on religion. However, the pathologies of reason would appear for Habermas to be anomalies. The corollary of the partnership of reason and faith Ratzinger seeks is for Habermas a transactional exchange between unequal players, self-sufficient reason and that which is inextinguishable.

To answer the original question as to how Habermas' double learning process should be understood, the answer is twofold. On the one hand, it offers an opportunity for dialogue. In such dialogues Christians should enter with a clear understanding of the framework that is being offered. Retaining open the possibility of a deeper understanding of a dialogue partners positions goes hand in hand with an awareness of what should not be conceded. In this regard, the separation of things that are Caesar's and the things that are God's always remains acknowledged, which of course is not something that came about at the reformation. Those dialogues must allow for mutual critiques. Christianity should welcome such critiques as they offer the opportunity to purify as well as to clarify Christianity's self-understanding both to ourselves and to others. On the other hand, the framework within which Habermas offers dialogue on reason and religion and on religion's place within the political and public spheres must be acknowledged for what it is. It is not simply as Nicholas Adams determined with regard to Habermas vis-à-vis theology that he is not a serious partner for theology.[82] Rather, Habermas offers a framework that recognizes post-metaphyscial

---

[82] Cf. N. Adams, *Habermas and Theology* (Cambridge: Cambridge University Press, 2006), p. 13.

philosophy, and its determination of modernity, as the legitimate worldview for modernity that other worldviews must accommodate themselves to. As a result, that worldview is not only insulated from appropriate scrutiny, thereby releasing it from having to offer good or reasonable arguments for its positions and worldview in response to legitimate questions from other worldviews (religions and the metaphysical worldview). The "musts" and "allowed to" that then arise for religions entrench a limited understanding of reason's capability and truncate the vision of reality, and hence of the human being.

Notwithstanding Habermas' and Ratzinger's advocacy of fundamentally opposing worldviews in response to a set of shared concerns, and the inhospitable nature of the double learning process Habermas offers, there is potential for real encounter if Habermas' notion of religion's moral intuition is considered in light of Ratzinger's understanding of conscience. Central to Ratzinger notion of conscience is that it is an integral aspect of anthropology as per Paul's statement in Romans 2:14-15. "When gentiles who have not the law do by nature what the law requires, they are a law to themselves, even though they do not have the law. They show that what the law requires is written on their hearts, while their conscience also bears witness." Ratzinger takes up the Medieval tradition where there are two distinct but interrelated concepts *synderesis* and *conscientia*. Preferring the Platonic terms anamnesis to synderesis, Ratzinger describes the first level as "an abiding existential quality" of the person, as the primal remembrance of the good and the true which is the anamnesis of our origin as created in the image of God.[83] This transcending of the subject to hear the voice of truth can be linked to his theological notion of person as relatedness without reserve that Christ fully realized and through Christ is fully applicable to human beings.[84] The second level is an action performed. It is this level that Thomas Aquinas termed *conscientia* and Ratzinger argued was the aspect of conscience taken up by modernity. In the Medieval tradition anamnesis provides the orientation to the Good which is presupposed in the second level which then "applies this knowledge to specific situations." Conscience

---

[83] J. Ratzinger, "If You Want Peace ... Conscience and Truth," in *Values in a Time of Upheaval* (San Francisco: Ignatius, 2006), pp. 75–99, at 90–7. This paper was originally published in full in *Wahrheit, Werte, Macht: Prufsteine der pluralistischen* Gesellschaft (Freiburg: Herder, 1995), pp. 11–24. See for a discussion of Ratzinger on conscience: D. V. Twomey, *Pope Benedict XVI: The Conscience of Our Age. A Theological Portrait* (San Francisco: Ignatius, 2007).

[84] Cf. J. Ratzinger, "Concerning the Notion of Person in Theology," *Communio* 17/3 (1990), pp. 439–54. Originally published in German as "Zum Personenversthdnis in der Theologie," in *Dogma und Verkündigung* (Munich: Erich Wewel, 1973), pp. 205–23.

(*anamnesis* and *conscientia*) as a constitutive aspect of anthropology is the point of convergence for all humanity, and this is the point of a shared language for mutual understanding across worldviews, cultures, and religions. Through the shared language of conscience (*anamnesis* and *conscientia*) answers which place the true, the good, and the just at their core can be sought in a mutual effort to address the common challenges of humanity.

22

Gianni Vattimo: Nihilism and Truth

Thomas G. Guarino

Introduction

Speaking of a philosophical dialogue between Joseph Ratzinger/Benedict XVI and Gianteresio (Gianni) Vattimo, the well-known Italian philosopher, may seem a bit strained. After all, there is no record of any dialogue between them as, for example, the explicit one that took place between Ratzinger and the German philosopher, Jürgen Habermas.

Nonetheless, it is difficult to believe that interchange between the two thinkers has not taken place. Ratzinger has lived in Rome since 1981. During that time, Vattimo has been one of the leading philosophers in Italy and in Europe generally. Is it possible that the cardinal and later pope, a man with intense intellectual interests, would have ignored the Torinese's thought? Not likely. Indeed, it would be virtually impossible for any European intellectual to ignore the prodigious writings of Gianni Vattimo.

On the other hand, Vattimo's writings make crystal clear that Ratzinger's ideas have never been far from his mind. In fact, I will argue that Vattimo and Ratzinger have engaged in a lively philosophical exchange, even if, on the surface, the dialogue can appear to be a bit one-sided.

"Dictatorship of Relativism"

A good place to start the examination of this exchange is with Cardinal Ratzinger's famous homily, delivered at the Mass *Pro Eligendo Romano*

Pontifice on April 18, 2005. Commenting on the reading from St. Paul's letter to the Ephesians, Ratzinger states that if we listen carefully to this epistle, we realize that we can no longer be children, "tossed here and there, carried about by every wind of doctrine."[1]

The cardinal insists that St. Paul's description is timely. How many winds of doctrine—ideological currents—have sought to overturn the ship of Christian faith? Ratzinger enumerates them: Marxism, liberalism, libertinism, collectivism, radical individualism, atheism, agnosticism, syncretism, and so the list continues. Indeed, every day new sects spring up, enticing people into error. But this relativism, Ratzinger argues, this tossing about by every wind of doctrine, serves only to establish "a dictatorship of relativism that does not recognize anything as definitive and whose ultimate goal consists solely of one's own ego and desires." Ratzinger's phrase, *dictatorship of relativism* soon became both renowned and notorious, cited worldwide as his diagnosis of contemporary society's pathologies.

Counterposed to this dictatorship, Ratzinger claimed, is the Church's faith in Jesus Christ, the man who is the measure of "true humanism." A mature Christian faith does not follow changing trends and novelties. Rather, this faith is rooted in friendship with Christ, a friendship which allows us to distinguish truth from falsehood and deceitfulness. Truth and love, Ratzinger continued, coincide in Jesus. To the extent that we draw close to Christ, truth and love are blended in our own lives—in contrast to those who are continually tossed about by the surging waves of error.

Cardinal Ratzinger's accusation of a "dictatorship of relativism" drew theoretical responses from several intellectuals, Gianni Vattimo among them. For the moment, however, let us continue with Ratzinger's understanding of truth, a central issue in his dialogue with the Torinese philosopher.

One place where Ratzinger's understanding of truth is on full display is his famous Regensburg Lecture of 2006.[2] Many commentators on that address focused on Pope Benedict's controversial remarks about Islam. In fact, the most important insights to emerge from the pope's challenging speech are those pertaining to the faith-reason relationship, an issue at the heart of Ratzinger's papacy.[3] In the course of his lecture, Benedict refers to the rapprochement that took place in the early church between biblical faith and Greek thought. This confluence was (and remains) legitimate, the

---

[1] All quotes in this section are taken from J. Ratzinger, *Homily at the Mass "Pro Eligendo Romano Pontifice,"* April 18, 2005.
[2] Cf. Benedict XVI, *Faith, Reason and the University: Memories and Reflections. Lecture in the Meeting with the Representatives of Science*, Apostolic Journey to München, Altötting and Regensburg (September 9–14, 2006), Regensburg, September 12, 2006.
[3] Benedict XVI devoted years of catechetical speeches to major Christian thinkers, focusing on their understanding of the faith-reason rapport. See *Great Christian Thinkers: From the Early Church through the Middle Ages* (Minneapolis: Fortress Press, 2011) and *Doctors of the Church* (Huntington, Indiana: Our Sunday Visitor, 2011).

pope argues, because both the bible and the best of Hellenistic philosophy are interested in the truth of being, in the *ontos on*. In Exodus 3:14, for example, God reveals his name as "I am"—as the fullness of being and existence. And the "I am" of Exodus is convergent with the "I am" of Jesus found in St. John's Gospel (John 8:24; 8:58). These biblical affirmations, Ratzinger insists, stand in a close relationship to the attempt by Socrates to overcome the myths of Greek religion in his desire for unvarnished truth. In the bible and Greek philosophy, one may discern a concurrence between faith and reason—for it is the truth of being, of reality in its profoundest depths—that is always at stake.

This marriage between biblical faith and the best of philosophical thinking Benedict describes as a "mutual enrichment." And it is precisely this mutuality that has long been a feature of his thought. For example, in his early work, *Introduction to Christianity* (explicitly cited in the Regensburg Lecture), Ratzinger states that "belief is wedded to ontology."[4] But understanding this marriage properly requires theological attentiveness. It is certainly not the subservience of the Christian faith to an alien philosophical position, a viewpoint rightly derided as "ontotheology" in the worst possible sense. It is the claim, rather, that both biblical faith and serious philosophical thinking are interested in the primacy of truth, of being, of the real.

This collaboration between Hellenistic thought and the bible, Ratzinger argues, was providential. As he points out, the Acts of the Apostles (16: 6-10) testify that St. Paul's path to Asia was blocked while a Macedonian pleaded for his aid, crying out, "Come over to Macedonia and help us!" This Pauline vision can be interpreted, Benedict insists, as indicating the necessity of a rapprochement between Christian faith and Greek inquiry.

Crucial here, of course, is the positive valuation of philosophy that has virtually always characterized the Catholic tradition. As a faculty of human nature, reason maintains independence and *relative* autonomy. Of course, to assert the relative autonomy of philosophical thinking is not to contend that philosophy guarantees the truth of revelation—as if some secular criterion or benchmark was needed to justify God's word. It *is* to recognize, however, that philosophy has its own legitimate independence, even if it must always learn from the light of faith.[5]

Ratzinger lauds the philosophical thirst for the truth of the existing realm as a decisive turning point in history. Similarly, he hails the comment made by Tertullian, even calling it one of the "great assertions" of the early

---

[4] J. Ratzinger, *Introduction to Christianity* (San Francisco: Ignatius, 2004), p. 119.
[5] The proper relationship between philosophy and theology is carefully developed in John Paul II, *Encyclical Letter* Fides et ratio *on the Relationship between Faith and Reason*. I have examined the encyclical's central assertions in T. G. Guarino, *The Unchanging Truth of God? Crucial Philosophical Issues for Theology* (Washington, DC: Catholic University of America Press, 2022), pp. 65–95.

Church: "Our Lord Christ called himself truth, not custom."[6] It is Tertullian's accent on truth that is crucial—since his comment reveals the profound collaboration that must take place between theology and philosophy. This collaboration leads Benedict to conclude: "This inner rapprochement between Biblical faith and Greek philosophical inquiry was an event of decisive importance not only from the standpoint of the history of religions, but also from that of world history—it is an event which concerns us even today."[7]

It is this concern for the stability and solidity of truth that led Benedict to decry the voluntarism of Duns Scotus—a voluntarism that gives rise, ultimately, to the "image of a capricious God, who is not even bound to truth and goodness." On the contrary, God has revealed himself as the one who is the truth, the one who acts with reason, not with a profligate freedom unrelated to human rationality. This is the great wisdom of the well-known teaching of Lateran IV: There exists an analogical similitude between God and humanity, even if God's transcendence always demands a greater dissimilitude.

Of grave concern for Ratzinger, then, are the attempts of those who wish to "de-hellenize" the Christian faith. He recounts various attempts at de-hellenizing Christianity—starting with the Reformation and increasingly radicalized by Kant and von Harnack. Why, Ratzinger asks, would one seek such uncoupling since the best of philosophy and the Christian faith are united in their insistence on knowing the truth of being? Benedict rebukes those who view the confluence of philosophy and biblical truth as a pernicious invasion of the Greek spirit on the purity of the Gospel. Rather, he insists, "The fundamental decisions made about the relationship between faith and the use of human reason are part of the faith itself; they are developments consonant with the nature of faith itself."

It is precisely this close relationship between the Christian faith and philosophy—united in their search for truth—that leads Ratzinger to condemn the "dictatorship of relativism"—a tyranny which appears to lack all belief in truth—and to relegate the fundamental questions about nature and meaning merely to humanity's sovereign will.

Truth and Tolerance

In a volume entitled *Truth and Tolerance* Ratzinger once again centralizes the issue of truth. The crucial questions, he states, are easily identifiable: Given that our age celebrates tolerance and diversity, are truth-claims by necessity

---

[6] See Tertullian, *De virginibus velandis*, I, 1. Cited in *Introduction to Christianity*, p. 141.
[7] Benedict XVI, *Faith, Reason and the University: Memories and Reflections*. The quotations in the following two paragraphs are drawn from this speech.

arrogant and intolerant? And are truth-claims particularly inappropriate when speaking about non-empirical realities such as religion? Ratzinger goes to the heart of the matter: "Thus it becomes apparent that, beyond all particular questions, the real problem lies in the question about truth."[8]

The idea that there is universal and binding truth—which in the religious sphere is centered on Jesus Christ—is today regarded as a "real assault upon the spirit of the modern age and ... as the fundamental threat to the highest good of that age, freedom and tolerance."[9] Nonetheless, Ratzinger insists, making truth-claims has been a distinguishing characteristic of the Christian faith from the beginning. Indeed, Christianity saw itself as embodying the fullness of knowledge and truth—and so its mission was, necessarily, universal. It was not simply one religion among many others; rather, the Christian faith had a message that needed to be carried to all peoples and cultures.[10]

Today, however, claims to truth and certainty are regarded as aggressive assaults upon freedom and upon liberal broad-mindedness. Not that this attitude is entirely new; one can find it in the early days of the Church. In 384, the Roman senator Symmachus implored the emperor Valentinian II to restore the Altar of Victory in the Senate. Symmachus pleaded his case in tones that sound contemporary: no one can attain to the great mystery of the divine by one path alone. What difference does it make if various paths are traveled? Ratzinger concludes, "This is exactly what the enlightenment is saying today: We do not know truth as such .... So great a mystery as the Divinity cannot be fixed in *one* image which would exclude all others—to *one* path obligatory for all."[11] Ratzinger firmly resists this emphasis on philosophical and theological nescience, insisting, "It is the peculiarity of Christianity ... that it claims to tell us the truth about God, the world, and man and lays claim to being the *religio vera*, the religion of truth."[12] In fact, the entire missionary thrust of Christianity—the guiding light of its institutions—is that it concerns all human beings and is not simply the product of one culture or intended only for one people.

Insofar as the Christian faith makes strong and definitive truth-claims, Ratzinger continues, it necessarily involves philosophy. It is for this reason that John Paul II, in his 1998 encyclical, *Fides et ratio*, focuses at length on both the nature of philosophy and the nature of truth. The pope's intention was to defend the traditional notion of truth at a time when various forms

---

[8] J. Ratzinger, *Truth and Tolerance: Christian Belief and World Religions* (San Francisco: Ignatius, 2004), p. 10.
[9] *Ibid.*, p. 120.
[10] Cf. *ibid.*, p. 170.
[11] *Ibid.*, p. 176.
[12] *Ibid.*, p. 184.

of philosophical relativism dominate.[13] Why this papal preoccupation with philosophy? One reason is that theology needs a dialogue partner that is able, in its own order, to defend the intelligibility of Christianity's truth claims. As the encyclical states, "theology needs philosophy as a partner in dialogue in order to confirm the intelligibility and universal truth of its claims."[14] In other words, Catholic doctrinal teachings—the Creed of Nicaea for example—are intended to be universally, transculturally, and transgenerationally true, as true in twenty-first century Nairobi and New York as in fourth-century Nicaea. But if this claim to universal and perpetual truth is to be intelligible, then one must be able to philosophically defend the *very possibility* of universal and transcultural truth and the *very possibility* of meaning-invariance over time. In short, the robust affirmations of the Christian doctrinal tradition need philosophies capable of reinforcing their claims to universality, perpetuity, and meaning-invariance, claims that are essential to the Catholic understanding of truth.

Today, however, much philosophy, particularly hermeneutical and postmodern thought, is more at home speaking about contextualized and circumscribed rationality—about "truths" rooted in cultural embeddedness, ideological determination, and socio-linguistic paradigms. Precisely because of this, Ratzinger states, "the encyclical is quite simply attempting to give us the courage for the adventure of truth."[15] Of course, he means truth as traditionally understood, i.e., as universal, transcultural, and transgenerational—and as reflecting states of affairs.

For Ratzinger, the question of truth is *the one crucial question for the Christian faith*. No doubt he would firmly agree with the statement of the American Lutheran theologian, Robert Jenson, who asserted that theology "knows the one decisive fact about all things, so that theology must be either a universal and founding discipline or a delusion."[16] Because truth is the foundational issue, Ratzinger expresses profound concern about contemporary hermeneutical philosophies which shy away from the question of truth putting the accent, rather, on continuing interpretation.[17] In opposition to these approaches, Ratzinger counterpoises the statement from *Fides et ratio*: "The interpretation of this word [i.e., the Word of God]

---

[13] Cf. *ibid.*
[14] John Paul II, *Fides et ratio*, §77.
[15] J. Ratzinger, *Truth and Tolerance*, p. 184.
[16] R. Jenson, *Systematic Theology* I (New York: Oxford University Press, 1997), p. 20.
[17] In fact, hermeneutical philosophers such as Hans-Georg Gadamer *are* concerned with the issue of truth. But not with truth as traditionally understood and as defended by Ratzinger. Gadamer rejects the idea of perduring and universal theoretical truth, invoking instead *phronēsis*, the truth of practical reason. Only this kind of truth is legitimate given the socio-cultural-linguistic strictures that encircle all thought. For Gadamer, "truth" arises within a contingent, finite, socially conditioned situation (and not only arises within, but is totally delimited by these factors). Consequently, only the truth of practical reason is available to us. For an extended discussion of these issues, see *The Unchanging Truth of God?*, pp. 139–53.

cannot merely keep referring us to one interpretation after another, without ever leading us to a statement that is simply true."[18] To give up on truth is to allow humanity to be "dominated by what is accidental and arbitrary." Truth protects man from the "dictatorship of what is accidental," restoring his dignity "which consists precisely in the fact that no human institution can ultimately dominate him, because he is open to the truth."[19] Ratzinger points to the trial of Jesus, wherein Christ tells the Roman governor, Pilate, that he has come into the world to "bear witness to the truth" (John 18:37). Reflecting on this passage, Ratzinger notes that Pilate's skeptical rejoinder, "What is truth?" is entirely understandable given his pragmatism. However, the question of truth "is a very serious question, bound up with the fate of mankind."

The question of truth is clearly at the forefront of Ratzinger's/Benedict's thought.[20] But how does his integration of philosophy and theology, in service to the truth, compare with another contemporary European thinker, Gianni Vattimo?

Vattimo in Dialogue with Ratzinger

Some readers may not be familiar with the name Gianni Vattimo, yet he is a highly influential thinker in Italy and throughout Europe. His philosophical output has been prodigious, and his major works have been translated into many languages.[21]

Vattimo was born in Turin, Italy, in 1936. After graduating from the university there, he went to Heidelberg to study with Karl Löwith and Hans-Georg Gadamer. From the early 1960s until 2008 he was a professor at the University of Turin, with specialties in hermeneutics, Heidegger, and Nietzsche. Vattimo has amassed an extraordinary array of publications, with scores of books and hundreds of articles in both professional journals as well as in newspapers and general interest magazines. He is the Italian translator of Gadamer's magnum opus on hermeneutics, *Truth and Method,* and delivered the prestigious Gifford Lectures at the University of Glasgow in 2010. Throughout his career, he has written on the points of convergence between postmodern thought and the Christian faith.

---

[18] John Paul II, *Fides et ratio*, §84.
[19] J. Ratzinger, *Truth and Tolerance*, p. 191.
[20] For other examples, see Benedict's carefully wrought addresses at Westminster Hall in London (2010) and at the Reichstag in Berlin (2011), where he insists that even in democracies, *it is the truth of objective moral principles that is ultimately at stake.* I have discussed these addresses in "Vattimo, Diversity and Catholicism," in *Justice through Diversity? A Philosophical and Theological Debate*, M. J. Sweeney (ed.) (Lanham: Rowman and Littlefield, 2016), pp. 533–50.
[21] For an introduction to the major themes in Vattimo's philosophy, see T. G. Guarino, *Vattimo and Theology* (London: T&T Clark, 2009). Also, *id.*, "The Return of Religion in Europe? The Postmodern Christianity of Gianni Vattimo," *Logos: A Journal of Catholic Thought and Culture* 14/2 (2011), pp. 15–36.

The "Dictatorship of Relativism" Revisited

The most explicit dialogue between Ratzinger and Vattimo may be found in Vattimo's pointed response to Ratzinger's "dictatorship of relativism" homily of April 2005. In that essay, one finds displayed several of Vattimo's axial philosophical themes, particularly his understanding of truth. As we have already seen, Ratzinger regards "truth" as the crucial and fundamental issue at the heart of both the Christian faith and human rationality. Vattimo agrees that the truth-question is decisive, but his conclusions about the nature of truth—and so his understanding of the relationship between theology and philosophy—move in a completely different direction.

Central to understanding Vattimo's thought is the work of Friedrich Nietzsche and Martin Heidegger, the Torinese's two "patron saints." While there is no space here to explain their impact on Vattimo's philosophy, it is enough to say that both thinkers insist that reason must abandon its claims to finality and certitude.[22] Heidegger's announcement of the "end of metaphysics" and Nietzsche's insistence on the profoundly interpretative nature of life and thought have had a marked effect on Vattimo's philosophy. Echoing Nietzsche, the Torinese states, "there exists no order, truth or stability outside the will itself."[23] In other words, reality is not objectively "given"; it is constructed and constituted by the play of endless interpretations.

Given these influences, how does Vattimo respond to Ratzinger's famous homily, with its indictment of an imperious relativism? *Common Knowledge,* a scholarly journal based at Duke University (USA), sponsored a symposium of scholars replying to Ratzinger's notorious diagnosis of contemporary culture. The journal rightly understood the cardinal's comments as a direct challenge to the contemporary academic community—and sought responses to it.

Vattimo offered the first rejoinder, opening his essay with a famous citation from Talleyrand, "*Surtout pas de zéle.*"[24] This adage offers an immediate clue to the Torinese's point: Zeal for the truth, zeal for certitude, becomes a barrier to dialogue and, especially, to the broad-minded tolerance of other viewpoints. Vattimo concedes that Ratzinger did not intend to offer a precise, philosophical description of relativism. Nonetheless, the cardinal was expressing grave concerns about the idea of liberal tolerance, the idea that there exist no ultimate standards but that "everything's relative."

In response, Vattimo asks, is this kind of relativism really as bad as Ratzinger implies? Is permissive tolerance—just about anything goes—truly dangerous for civilization? Or, on the contrary, is the real danger to

---

[22] For Nietzsche's and Heidegger's influence on Vattimo's notion of truth, see *Vattimo and Theology,* pp. 42–50.
[23] G. Vattimo, *Dialogue with Nietzsche* (New York: Columbia University Press, 2006), p. 19.
[24] Cf. *id.*, "A 'Dictatorship of Relativism,'" *Common Knowledge* 13 (2007), pp. 214–18, at 214. The following paragraphs will draw upon this essay.

society the kind of ardor and passion that too much certainty inspires? Adducing historical examples, Vattimo warns against the religious fervor of the Crusaders (*Deus lo vult*) or the "scientific certainty with which Hitler organized the extermination of 'inferior' races ...."[25] The danger posed in these situations was not a vague relativism. On the contrary, it was absolute certainty about bedrock "truth."

These examples illustrate themes that have long characterized Vattimo's work. His signature philosophical idea is known as *il pensiero debole* or "weak thought." What is meant by this term? With this idea, Vattimo intends to overcome modern construals of rationality with their assertive pronouncements about the "*ontos on*," the "really real," and "scientific objectivity." The philosopher wishes to show that the world is not simply "given" to us as an uninterpreted reality. On the contrary, we are constantly dealing with interpretations—and interpretations of interpretations.

Contemporary hermeneutical philosophy—thinking here primarily of Heidegger and Gadamer—has taught us that men and women are observers who are deeply embedded within socio-cultural-linguistic contexts. Interpreting agents, then, exist only within a determined subjectivity, an enveloping historicity, and an ideologically saturated perspective. Taking account of these delimiting horizons, weak thought concludes that, because the world is an interpreted reality, all claims to truth, to certainty, and to objectivity overlook and bury the significant dimensions of provisionality and contingency that inexorably cling to all understanding. This is what Heidegger meant in his jeremiad against those ignoring our enmeshment in the "worldhood of the world," the profound embeddedness that *Dasein* is tempted to conceal in the unremitting search for unencumbered certitude and absolute first principles.

This is why Vattimo frequently cites Nietzsche's claim: there are no facts, only interpretations. And this too, is an interpretation![26] This aphorism is meant to remind us that we are deeply conditioned, circumscribed interpreters. And this, in turn, helps us to understand what Vattimo's "weak thought" is: All warrants for truth are located within specific forms of life and contingent cultural circumstances. There exists a multiplicity of interpretations, none of which is self-justifying by appeals to universally available first principles. To claim, then, as "strong" thought does—to have objectivity, or the "really real," or bedrock truth, is philosophically naïve and unjustified.

For precisely these reasons, Vattimo is also attracted to Nietzsche's parable "How the World Became a Fable" from *The Twilight of the Idols*.[27] In this tale, Nietzsche tells us that the "true world," the *ontos on*,

---

[25] *Ibid.*, p. 216.
[26] Cf. F. Nietzsche, *The Will to Power* (New York: Random House, 1967). For Vattimo's citations of this text, see *Nihilism and Emancipation: Ethics, Politics and Law*, S. Zabala (ed.) (New York: Columbia University Press, 2004), p. 155 and *Dialogue with Nietzsche*, p. 74.
[27] Cf. F. Nietzsche, *The Twilight of the Idols* (London: Penguin, 1990), pp. 50–1.

was first available to the wise and virtuous disciple of Plato. Gradually, however, the true world, the truth, became progressively more elusive. It was *promised* to the Christian who committed himself to a life of holiness. With Kant, the *ontos on* became unknowable and unattainable because the noumenal world (reality itself) was beyond humanity's cognitive grasp. Finally, Nietzsche concludes, the very idea of the "true world" no longer serves a purpose; it is an idea best abolished! Vattimo interprets Nietzsche's parable to mean that reality is not "given" to us as a pre-existing entity—and then gradually discovered; reality, rather, is constituted by our ongoing interpretations. In fact, the "world," the *ontos on*, is simply the continuing play of interpretations.[28]

Unsurprisingly, weak thought has profound doubts about claims to "the truth" as traditionally understood. Indeed, assertions about finality and certitude lend themselves to violence. As Vattimo says, "The pretense of authority by those who possess, or believe they possess, or claim to have discovered the truth ... is merely a violence to which we are accustomed in a certain way within a certain cultural and political tradition."[29] Moreover, claims about reality and unchanging human nature (such as one finds in natural law thinking) suppress creativity and freedom; on the other hand, envisioning the world as the continuing play of interpretations allows human beings to shape their own lives and their own meanings apart from pre-determined ideas imposed, allegedly, by the *logos* structure of reality. Weak thought offers to human beings not a preordained straitjacket about life, nature and eternally valid moral norms, but emancipatory freedom—the right of the sovereign will to self-creation.

Given this understanding of *il pensiero debole,* we can see why Vattimo is at pains to attack Ratzinger's pejorative description of a "dictatorship of relativism." The Torinese philosopher finds it extraordinary that in a world where so many ardently believed "truths" have turned out to be dangerous falsehoods, "there remains, undiminished, the desire for a true truth—one that can be trusted without doubts and hesitations ...." For Vattimo, on the contrary, we must be freed of our last idolatry, "the adoration of Truth as our god."[30]

Conclusion

In this dialogue between Ratzinger and Vattimo, we have a clear clash of ideas concerning the nature of truth and, consequently, the role of philosophy and theology. For Ratzinger, truth is given, preeminently, in

---

[28] Cf. G. Vattimo, *Beyond Interpretation: The Meaning of Hermeneutics for Philosophy* (Stanford: Stanford University Press, 1997), p. 7.
[29] *Id., Of Reality: The Purposes of Philosophy* (New York: Columbia University, 2016), p. 169.
[30] *Id.,* "A 'Dictatorship of Relativism'," pp. 217–18.

and by Jesus Christ, who speaks of himself as "the way, the truth and the life" (John 14:6). Christ is the standard for truth—the ultimate criterion by which all other truth-claims are judged. As Ratzinger says, "the world is 'true' to the extent that it reflects God: the creative logic, the eternal reason that brought it to birth."[31]

For Vattimo, on the other hand, God plays no part in his understanding either of truth or of the world. When Vattimo does cite a biblical text—which is rare—he usually invokes the well-known "kenotic" passage of St. Paul's letter to the Philippians, interpreting this to mean that God has renounced all power—and, therefore, all claims to truth (Phil 2:6-7). Indeed, Vattimo does not hesitate to speak of a "farewell" to truth understood as a stable and objective correspondence with the world.[32] In Vattimo's view, Christianity's most significant contribution to humanity is not to be found in some alleged "objective truth" about God and man. Rather than *veritas*, the Christian faith's foundational contribution to civilization is *caritas*, its universal call to charity (which, for Vattimo, means tolerance for all non-violent points of view). As he says, "The Christian inheritance that 'returns' in weak thought is primarily the Christian precept of charity and its rejection of violence."[33] Even more ardently, he writes, "In comparison with charity, there is no truth worth affirming."[34]

Given these sentiments, it is unsurprising that Vattimo is deeply critical of Catholic truth-claims: "Adherents of the religion revealed and transmitted authoritatively by the Universal Church, with the aid of the Holy Spirit, have no doubts about where, and where only, such truth is to be found."[35] But is this sentence, written in direct response to Ratzinger's 2005 homily, accurate? There is no doubt that Pope Benedict, along with all Christians, would say that the truth about God and humanity is uniquely centered in Jesus Christ. But many theologians, Ratzinger included, would hesitate before Vattimo's claim that truth is found *only* in Jesus and the Church. On the contrary, one of the greatest achievements of Vatican II was its recognition, based on the principles of participation and analogy, that truth—partial and imperfect, to be sure—is certainly found in other Christian churches, in other religions (Judaism pre-eminently) and even in those striving for just societies.[36]

While Ratzinger and Christianity at large stand at a significant remove from Vattimo's understanding of truth, in one sense, it can be legitimately

---

[31] J. Ratzinger, *Faith and Politics: Selected Writings* (San Francisco: Ignatius, 2018), p. 53.
[32] Cf. G. Vattimo, *A Farewell to Truth* (New York: Columbia University Press, 2011).
[33] *Id.*, *Belief* (Stanford: Stanford University Press, 1999), p. 44.
[34] *Id.*, "A 'Dictatorship of Relativism'," p. 218.
[35] *Ibid.*, p. 217
[36] On the significant role played by participatory and analogical thinking—two metaphysical themes developed by St. Thomas Aquinas—at Vatican II, see T. G. Guarino, *The Disputed Teachings of Vatican II: Continuity and Reversal in Catholic Doctrine* (Grand Rapids: Eerdmans, 2018).

claimed that Catholicism became a little "weaker" (to use Vattimo's term) at Vatican II, not in the sense of diminishing or abandoning its own truth-claims, but in its evaluation of others. Like Vattimo, the bishops and theologians at the great council were concerned about violence. They had lived through the Second World War. They had seen the European continent (the homeland for many of them) destroyed by war. They had seen the Holocaust take place in the heart of Christian Europe. They had seen atomic weapons dropped on Japan. And, as the council unfolded, they were living through a tense nuclear standoff between the United States and the Soviet Union.

Thus, violence was indeed on the minds of the thousands of bishops and theologians gathered in Rome. Is it any surprise that Vatican II contained no anathemas (condemnations) of other positions? Or that the council did not stress what Catholicism perceives as the theological errors of others? On the contrary, Vatican II placed a marked accent on those dimensions of truth that it *shares* with others. The council notes the real (if imperfect) relationship Catholicism has with other Christians, with other religions (particularly Judaism) and with the world. Indeed, one may say that *the entire philosophical style of Vatican II is analogical in nature*. This analogical emphasis in no way entailed an abandonment of Catholic truth-claims, but it did involve a willingness to see and appreciate the significant dimensions of truth found in other positions.

Ultimately, the difference between Ratzinger and Vattimo is rooted in their divergent understandings of the relationship between faith and reason. The Torinese philosopher remains in thrall to Nietzsche and Heidegger, two thinkers who influence his thought much more profoundly than does the biblical Christ. As Vattimo often says, Christianity expresses (or transcribes) theologically what is true philosophically. By this he means that the story of Jesus Christ is little more than a concrete expression of *il pensiero debole*. This is why the actual life of Jesus figures so little in Vattimo's thought—even his thought on Christianity. What we see in the Torinese thinker is the classical Hegelian *Aufhebung* of religion—the annulment, erasure, and sublation of the concrete, historical Christian singular by philosophical speculation.

For Ratzinger, on the other hand, Christ is the center of history and Christianity is the story of the world. While Christianity may learn from other thinkers—and certainly has learned from philosophy, both ancient and modern—it is the biblical narrative that is always decisive, disciplining and measuring other forms of thought. In the third century, Origen spoke of taking "spoils from Egypt"—that is, of Christianity utilizing other forms of thought but always *integrating* them into the Christian narrative. That, in fact, is Ratzinger's approach.

Is there, then, any room for a rapprochement between Vattimo and Ratzinger? Or are the two thinkers worlds apart, with one a postmodern relativist and the other a traditional Christian denouncing the "dictatorship of relativism"? While it is true that Vattimo's philosophy represents little more than a subsumption of the Christian faith by philosophy, a sublation that eviscerates it of its fundamental meaning, it is also true that the Torinese thinker continually struggles with the presence and absence of God, with the meaning of kenosis, and with the Christian notion of *caritas*. Perhaps in all of this, one may see something of St. Augustine's *cor inquietum*, the restless heart always in search of transcendence. This, we suspect, Ratzinger the Augustinian would fully understand

BIBLIOGRAPHY

Introductory Study: Gottlieb Söhngen's Understanding of Theology and Philosophy

Benedict XVI, *Address on the Conferral of the First "Ratzinger Prize,"* June 20, 2022.
Bonaventure, *Opera Omnia*, Collegium S. Bonaventurae (ed.) (Florence: Quaracchi, 1882–1902).
Kant, I., *Kritik der reinen Vernunft* 2, W. Weischedel (ed.) (Frankfurt, Main: Suhrkamp, 1974).
Pfister, P. (ed.), *Joseph Ratzinger und das Erzbistum München und Freising* (Regensburg: Schnell und Steiner, 2006).
Poncelet, C., *Dreifacher Gebrach der Vernunft* (Regensburg: Friedrich Pustet, 2017).
Röd, W., *Der Weg der Philosophie von den Anfängen bis ins 20. Jahrhundert* 2 (München: Beck, 1996).
Söhngen, G., "Die Weisheit der Theologie durch den Weg der Wissenschaft," in J. Feiner and M. Löher (eds.), *Mysterium Salutis: Grundriss heilsgeschichtlicher Dogmatik* 1 (Einsiedeln, Zürich, Köln: Benziger, 1978), pp. 907–80.
Söhngen, G., *Analogie und Metaphor: Kleine Philosophie und Theologie der Sprache* (Freiburg im Breisgau: Karl Alber, 1962).
Söhngen, G., *Grundfragen einer Rechtstheologie* (München: Anton Pustet, 1962).
Söhngen, G., "Gesetz und Evangelium," in J. Hofer and K. Rahner, *Lexikon für Theologie und Kirche* 4 (Freiburg: Herder, 1960), pp. 831–5.
Söhngen, G., *Der Weg der abendländischen Theologie: Grundgedanken zu einer Theologie der Weges* (München: Anton Pustet, 1959).
Söhngen, G., *Gesetz und Evangelium: Ihre analoge Einheit. Theologisch, philosophisch, staatsbürgerlich* (Freiburg, München: Karl Alber, 1957).
Söhngen, G., *Philosophische Einübung in die Theologie: Erkennen, Wissen, Glauben* (Freiburg, München: Karl Alber, 1955).
Söhngen, G., "Zur Frage eines christlichen Sozialismus. Soziale Struktur und soziales Ethos," *Politische Studien* 5/54 (1954), pp. 6–20.
Söhngen, G., "Vorwort," in *Die Einheit in der Theologie* (München: Zink, 1952).
Söhngen, G., *Humanität und Christentum* (Essen: Augustin Wibbelt, 1946).
Söhngen, G., *Symbol und Wirklichkeit im Kultmysterium* (Bonn: Hanstein, 1940).
Söhngen, G., *Der Wesensaufbau des Mysteriums* (Bonn: Hanstein, 1938).
Söhngen, G., "Philosophie," in M. Buchberger (ed.), *Lexikon für Theologie und Kirche* 8 (Freiburg: Herder, 1936), pp. 244–7.
Söhngen, G., "Bonaventura als Klassiker der analogie fidei," *Wissenschaft und Weisheit* 2 (1935), pp. 97–111.

Söhngen, G., "Analogia Fidei, II: Die Einheit in der Glaubenswissenschaft," *Catholica* 3 (1934), pp. 176–208.
Söhngen, G., "Irrational," in *Lexikon für Theologie und Kirche* 5 (Freiburg: Herder, 1933), pp. 603ff.
Söhngen, G., *Sein und Gegenstand: Das scholastische Axiom ens et unum convertuntur als Fundament metaphysischer und theologischer Spekulation* (Münster: Aschendorff, 1930).
Speer, A., *Triplex veritas: Wahrheitsverständnis und philosophische Denkform Bonaventuras* (Werl, Westfalen: Coelde, 1987), pp. 48–52.
Wendte, M., "Von Göttern, Engeln und Idealisten: Philosophie und Theologie in neuem Gespräch über alte Fragen," *Philosophische Rundschau* 57 (2010), pp. 228–53.
Wenzel, K., "Theologische Implikationen säkularer Philosophie? Vom 'Kampf um Anerkennung' zur Anerkennung unbedingten Anerkanntseins," *Theologie und Philosophie* 86 (2011), pp. 182–200.

Chapter 1. Plato: God, Conscience, and Truth

Bugiel, D., *Diktatur des Relativismus? Fundamentaltheologische Auseinandersetzung mit einem kulturpessimistischem Deutungsschema* (Münster: LIT, 2021).
Gnilka, C., "Der Begriff des rechten Gebrauchs," in *Chresis I* (Basel: Schwabe, 2012).
Gnilka, C., "Kultur und Conversion," in *Chresis II* (Basel: Schwabe, 1993).
Gruber, M. (ed.), *Diktatur des Relativismus: Der Kampf um die absolute Wahrheit für die Zukunft Europas* (Heiligenkreuz: Be&Be, 2014).
Hastetter, M. C., *Vergegenwärtigung der Vätertheologie. Joseph Ratzingers/Papst Benedikts XVI: Beitrag in der patristisch-ökumenischen Theologie im Nachgang zu Georg Florowskis Neo-Patritischer Synthese* (St. Ottilien: EOS, 2019).
von Ivánka, E., *Plato christianus: Übernahme und Umgestaltung des Platonismus durch die Väter* (Einsiedeln: Johannes, 1990).
Jall, A., *Erfahrung von Offenbarung: Grundlagen, Quellen und Anwendungen der Erkenntnislehre Joseph Ratzingers* (Regensburg: Anton Pustet, 2019).
Kasper, W., "Das Wesen des Christlichen: Rezension zu Joseph Ratzinger, 'Einführung in das Christentum'," *Theologische Revue* 65 (1969), pp. 182–8.
Marschler, T., "'Seele'—Joseph Ratzingers Stellungnahmen zu einem eschatologischen Zentralbegriff und ihre Relevanz für die aktuelle Diskussion," in G. Nachtwei (ed.), *Hoffnung auf Vollendung: Zur Eschatologie von Joseph Ratzinger* (Regensburg: Pustet, 2015), pp. 97–124.
Nichols, A., *The Thought of Pope Benedict XVI: An Introduction to the Theology of Joseph Ratzinger* (London: Burns&Oates, 2007).
Nüllmann, H., *Logos Gottes und Logos des Menschen: Der Vernunftbegriff Joseph Ratzingers und seine Implikationen für Glaubensverantwortung, Moralbegründung und Interreligiösen Dialog* (Würzburg: Echter, 2012).
Ratzinger, J., *Aus meinem Leben: Erinnerungen (1927–1977)* (München: Deutsche Verlags-Anstalt, 1998).
Ratzinger, J., "Das Christentum—die wahre Religion?," *JRGS* 3/1, pp. 439–56.

Ratzinger, J., "Der Dialog der Religionen und das jüdisch-christliche Verhältnis," *JRGS* 8/2, pp. 1120–36.
Ratzinger, J., "Der Geist der Liturgie," *JRGS* 11, pp. 29–194.
Ratzinger, J., "Die Bedeutung der Väter im Aufbau des Glaubens," *JRGS* 9/1, pp. 498–521.
Ratzinger, J., "Die christliche Brüderichkeit," *JRGS* 8/1, pp. 37–101.
Ratzinger, J., "Die Gabe der Weisheit," *JRGS* 5, pp. 257–69.
Ratzinger, J., "Die Geschichtstheologie des heiligen Bonaventura," *JRGS* 2, pp. 419–659.
Ratzinger, J., "Einführung in das Christentum," *JRGS* 4, pp. 54–322.
Ratzinger, J., "Eschatologie," *JRGS* 10, pp. 29–276.
Ratzinger, J., "Europa—Hoffnungen und Gefahren," *JRGS* 3/2, pp. 646–66.
Ratzinger, J., "Europa—verpflichtendes Erbe für die Christen," *JRGS* 3/2, pp. 701–16.
Ratzinger, J., "Gewissen und Wahrheit," *JRGS* 4, pp. 696–717.
Ratzinger, J., "Glaube, Geschichte und Philosophie: Zum Echo auf meine 'Einführung in das Christentum,'" *JRGS* 4, pp. 323–39.
Ratzinger, J., "Glaube und Bildung," *JRGS* 9/2, pp. 916–28.
Ratzinger, J., "Glaube-Wahrheit-Toleranz," *JRGS* 3/1, pp. 483–500.
Ratzinger, J., "Salz der Erde," *JRGS* 13/1, pp. 205–458.
Ratzinger, J., "Theologie der Liturgie," *JRGS* 11, pp. 639–56.
Ratzinger, J., "Theologische Probleme der Kirchenmusik," *JRGS* 11, pp. 571–85.
Ratzinger, J., "Variationen zum Thema Glaube, Religion und Kultur," *JRGS* 3/1, pp. 365–89.
Ratzinger, J., "Volk und Haus Gottes in Augustins Lehre von der Kirche," *JRGS* 1, pp. 41–418.
Ratzinger, J., "Vom Verstehen des Glaubens: Anmerkungen zu Karl Rahner, 'Grundkurs des Glaubens'," *JRGS* 9/1, pp. 296–312.
Schlögl, M., "'Um möglichst viele zu gewinnen' (1 Kor 9, 19): Zur Transformation der jüdisch-hellenistischen Antike durch das Christentum," *Internationale Katholische Zeitschrift Communio* 4 (2021), pp. 422–30.
Schlögl, M., "Der Glaube braucht den Mut der Vernunft zu sich selbst," in T. Möllenbeck and B. Wald (eds.), *"Die Wahrheit bekennen": Josef Pieper im Dialog* (München: Pneuma, 2017), pp. 275–93.
Schlögl, M. "Chresis: Zum Verhältnis von Glaube und Kultur in der Religionstheologie Joseph Ratzingers," in R. Voderholzer, C. Schaller und Franz-Xaver Heibl (eds.), *Mitteilungen des Instituts Papst Benedikt XVI 8* (Regensburg: Schnell & Steiner, 2015), pp. 82–9.
Schneider, M., *Einführung in die Theologie Joseph Ratzingers* (Köln: Patristisches Zentrum Koinonia-Oriens, 2008).
Sottopietra, P., *Wissen aus der Taufe: Die Aporien der neuzeitlichen Vernunft und der christliche Weg im Werk von Joseph Ratzinger* (Regensburg: Anton Pustet, 2003).
Weimann, R., *Kontinuität: Ein Zugang zum Dogmenverständnis in der Theologie Joseph Ratzingers* (Doctoral Thesis, Pontifical Athenaeum Regina Apostolorum, 2010).

Chapter 2. Augustine of Hippo: The Reciprocal Dependence of Faith and World

Andreotti, G., *30 Giorni* ([interview]; 5/2005), http://www.30giorni.it/articoli_id_8926_l3.htm.
Augustine, *Confessions*, https://ccel.org/ccel/augustine/confessions/confessions.xiii.html.
Burns, D. E., "Ratzinger on the Augustinian Understanding of Religious Freedom," *Communio* 44 (2017), pp. 296–328.
Cong Quy, J. L., "Der Einfluss des Augustinus auf die Theologie des Papstes Benedikt XVI," *Augustiniana* 56 3/4 (2006), pp. 411–32.
Daniélou, J. and H. Vorgrimler, *Sentire Ecclesiam—Das Bewußtsein von der Kirche als gestaltende Kraft der Frömmigkeit. Festschrift zum 60. Geburtstag von H. Rahner* (Freiburg, Basel, Wien: Herder, 1961).
Fletcher, P., *Resurrection Realism: Ratzinger the Augustinian* (Eugene: Cascade, 2014).
George, T., "Benedict XVI, the Great Augustinian," *First Things*, February 19, 2013, https://www.firstthings.com/web-exclusives/2013/02/benedict-xvi-the-great-augustinian.
van Ittersum, M., *Baptism in the Tradition of Augustine? The Theology of Joseph Ratzinger with Respect to Baptism* (Enschede: Ipskamp Printing, 2018).
Koster, M. D., *Ekklesiologie im Werden* (Paderborn: Bonifacius, 1940).
Müller, L. G., "'Augustinus ist mir immer ein großer Freund und Lehrer geblieben' Präsentation von *JRGS* 1 an der Deutschen Botschaft am Heiligen Stuhl am 14. März 2012," in *Mitteilungen Institut Papst Benedikt XVI* 5/2012 (Regensburg: Steiner & Schnell, 2013).
Rahner, H., *Mary and the Church* (London: Darton, Longman and Todd, 1961).
Rahner, H., *Mater Ecclesia: Lobpreis aus dem ersten Jahrtausend christlicher Literatur* (Köln: Benzinger, 1944).
Ratzinger, J., *The Unity of the Nations: A Vision of the Church Fathers* (Washington, DC: Catholic University of America Press, 2015).
Ratzinger, J., "Einführung in das Christentum," in *JRGS* 4 (Freiburg: Herder, 2014).
Ratzinger, J., *Great Christian Thinkers, From the Early Church through the Middle Ages* (Minneapolis: Fortress, 2011).
Ratzinger, J., "Volk und Haus Gottes in Augustins Lehre von der Kirche: Die Dissertation und weitere Studien zu Augustinus und zur Theologie der Kirchenväter," in *JRGS* 1 (Freiburg: Herder, 2010).
Ratzinger, J., "'Unruhig ist unser Herz, bis es ruhet, o Gott, in dir': Augustinus der erste moderne Mensch. Am Fest des heiligen Augustinus," in *JRGS* 1 (Freiburg: Herder, 2010), pp. 697–703.
Ratzinger, J., "Originalität und Überlieferung in Augustins Begriff der *confessio*," in *JRGS* 1 (Freiburg: Herder, 2010), pp. 457–79.
Ratzinger, J., *Leidenschaft für die Wahrheit: Augustinus* (Augsburg: Sankt Ulrich, 2009).
Ratzinger, J., *General Audience*, January 9, 2008.
Ratzinger, J., *Introduction to Christianity* (San Francisco: Ignatius, 2004).

Ratzinger, J., "The Holy Spirit as *Communio*: Concerning the Relationship of Pneumatology and Spirituality in Augustine," *Communio* 25 (1998), pp. 325–37.
Ratzinger, J., *Eschatology: Death and Eternal Life* (Washington, DC: Catholic University of America, 1988).
Ratzinger, J., *Das neue Volk Gottes: Entwürfe zur Ekklesiologie* (Düsseldorf: Patmos, 1969, reprint 1970).
Ratzinger, J., "Fraternité," in M. Viller et al (ed.), *Dictionnaire de Spiritualité ascétique et mystique* 5 (Paris: Beauchesne, 1964), pp. 1141–67.
Ratzinger, J., "Die Kirche in der Frömmigkeit des heiligen Augustinus," in J. Daniélou and H. Vorgrimler (eds.), *Sentire cum ecclesiam: Das Bewusstsein der Kirche als gestaltende Kraft der Frömmigkeit. Festschrift für Hugo Rahner zum 60. Geburtstag* (Freiburg: Herder, 1961), pp. 152–75.
Ratzinger, J., "Herkunft und Sinn der Civitas Dei-Lehre Augustins. Begegnung und Auseinandersetzung mit Wilhelm Kamlah," in *Augustinus Magister II* (Paris: Beauchesne, 1954), pp. 965–79.
Tertullian, *Adversus Marcionem libri quinque*, Patrologiae Cursus Completus, Series Latina 2, J. P. Migne (ed.) (Paris: Ares, 1844).
Vatican Council II, *Dogmatic Constitution on the Church* Lumen gentium, November 21, 1964.

Chapter 3. Bonaventure of Bagnoregio: The Metaphysics of History

Aristotle, *Nicomachean Ethics*, C. Rowe (ed.) (Oxford: Oxford University Press, 2002).
Aristotle, *Poetics*, D. W. Lucas (ed.) (Oxford: Clarendon Press, 1968).
Aquinas, T., *On the Eternity of the World* (1997), Medieval Sourcebook of Fordham University, https://sourcebooks.fordham.edu/basis/aquinas-eternity.asp.
Augustine, *On the Catechising of the Uninstructed*, P. Schaff (ed.) (Buffalo: Christian Literature Publishing Co., 1887). New Advent, K. Kinght (ed.), http://www.newadvent.org/fathers/1303.htm.
Bonaventure, *Opera omnia* 9, The Fathers of the Collegii S. Bonaventura (ed.) (Florence: Quaracchi, 1882–1902).
Bonaventure, *Collationes de septem donis* 8 (1891), pp. 455–505.
Bonaventure, *Collationes in Hexaëmeron* 5 (1891), pp. 327–455.
Bonaventure, *Commentaria in Quatuor Libros Sententiarum Magistri Petri Lombardi* 1 (1882).
Bougerol, J. G., *Introduction to the Works of St. Bonaventure* (Paterson: St. Anthony Guild Press, 1964).
Boulter, M., *Repetition and Mythos: Ratzinger's Bonaventure and the Meaning of History* (Eugene: Pickwick, 2022; the doctoral thesis is available at https://mural.maynoothuniversity.ie/13540/1/Boulter%20Thesis%2C%20final%20%28post-viva%29%20A4.pdf.
Callus, D. A., "Introduction of Aristotelian Learning to Oxford," *Proceedings of the British Academy* 29 (1943), pp. 229–81.

Castillo, G., "Dominio y uso en la noción de pobreza de San Buenaventura en la Apología pauperum," *Cauriensia* 11 (2016), pp. 141–55.
Corkery, J., "Reflection on the Theology of Joseph Ratzinger (Pope Benedict XVI)," *Acta Theologica* 32 (2012), pp. 17–34.
Cullen, C. M., *Bonaventure* (Oxford: Oxford University Press, 2006).
Ebbesen, S., 'Averroism', *The Routledge Encyclopedia of Philosophy* (Taylor and Francis, 1998), https://www.rep.routledge.com/articles/thematic/averroism/v-1.
Habermas, J. and J. Ratzinger, *Dialectics of Secularization: On Reason and Religion* (San Francisco: Ignatius, 2006).
Heidegger, M., *Supplements: From the Earliest Essays to* Being and Time *and Beyond*, J. van Buren (ed.) (Albany: State University of New York Press, 2002).
Heidegger, M., *The Question Concerning Technology and Other Essays* (New York; London: Garland, 1977).
Kovach, F. J., "The Question of the Eternity of the World in St. Bonaventure and St. Thomas—A Critical Analysis," *The Southwestern Journal of Philosophy* 5/2 (1974), pp. 141–72.
Leitane, I., "Transcendence and Immanence," in A. L. C. Runehov and L. Oviedo (eds.), *Encyclopedia of Sciences and Religions* (Dordrecht: Springer, 2013), pp. 2275–85.
McGinn, B., "The Significance of Bonaventure's Theology of History," *The Journal of Religion* 58 Supplement (1978), pp. 64–81.
McKeon, R., "Philosophy and Theology, History and Science in the Thought of Bonaventura and Thomas Aquinas," *The Journal of Religion* 58 Supplement (1978), pp. 24–51.
Nichols, A., *The Theology of Joseph Ratzinger* (Edinburgh: T&T Clark, 1988).
Pasnau, R., "The Latin Aristotle," in C. Shields (ed.), *The Oxford Handbook of Aristotle* (Oxford: Oxford University Press, 2012), pp. 665–90.
Patenaude, W. L., *Loving in the Present: The Theological and Pastoral Influences of St. Bonaventure's Critical Retrieval of Joachim of Fiore on Joseph Ratzinger/ Benedict XVI* (Theology Graduate Thesis, Providence College, 2013), https://digitalcommons.providence.edu/cgi/viewcontent.cgi?article=1005&context=theology_graduate_theses.
Ratzinger, J., *Faith and the Future* (San Francisco: Ignatius, 2009).
Ratzinger, J., *Values in a Time of Upheaval* (San Francisco: Ignatius, 2006).
Ratzinger, J., *Introduction to Christianity* (San Francisco: Ignatius, 2004).
Ratzinger, J., *Introduction to Christianity (Revised Edition)* (San Francisco: Ignatius, 2004).
Ratzinger, J., *Milestones: Memoirs, 1927–1977* (San Francisco: Ignatius, 1998).
Ratzinger, J., *The Theology of History in St. Bonaventure* (Chicago: Franciscan Herald Press, 1989).
Ratzinger, J., *Principles of Catholic Theology* (San Francisco: Ignatius, 1987).
Ratzinger, J., *"In the Beginning …" A Catholic Understanding of the Story of Creation and the Fall* (Grand Rapids: William B. Eerdmans Publishing Co., 1985).
Reeves, M., *The Influence of Prophecy in the Later Middle Ages: A Study in Joachimism* (Notre Dame: University of Notre Dame Press, 1994).
Reeves, M., "'The Originality and Influence of Joachim of Fiore," *Traditio* 36 (1980), pp. 269–316.

Riedl, M., "Longing for the Third Age: Revolutionary Joachism, Communism, and National Socialism," in M. Riedl (ed.), *A Companion to Joachim of Fiore* (Leiden: Brill, 2017), pp. 267–318.
Rowland, T., *Ratzinger's Faith: The Theology of Pope Benedict XVI* (Oxford: Oxford University Press, 2008).
Şenocak, N., "The Making of Franciscan Poverty," *Revue Mabillon* 24 (2013), pp. 5–26.
Warner, K. D., "Bonaventure in Benedict: Franciscan Wisdom for Human Ecology," in J. Schaefer and T. Winright (eds.), *Environmental Justice and Climate Change: Assessing Pope Benedict XVI's Ecological Vision for the Catholic Church in the United States* (Lanham: Lexington, 2013), pp. 3–18.

Chapter 4. Thomas Aquinas: How We Know God

Aquinas, T., *De veritate*, https://www.corpusthomisticum.org.
Bachanek, G., "Šv. Tomas Akvinietis Josepho Ratzingerio (Benedikto XVI) apmąstymuose," *Logos* 65 (2010), pp. 29–40.
Bellandi, A., *Fede cristiana come stare e comprendere: La giustificazione dei fondamenti della fede in Joseph Ratzinger* (Roma: Pontificia Università Gregoriana, 1996).
Benedicto XVI and P. Seewald, *Luz del mundo. El papa, la Iglesia y el signo de los tiempos* (Barcelona: Herder, 2010).
Blanco-Sarto, P., "Analogia entis, analogia fidei. Karl Barth dialoga con teólogos católicos," *Scripta theologica* 51/1 (2019), pp. 67–95.
Blanco-Sarto, P., 'Logos. Joseph Ratzinger y la historia de una palabra', *Límite* 14 (2006/1), pp. 57–86.
Blanco-Sarto, P., *Joseph Ratzinger: razón y cristianismo. La victoria de la inteligencia en el mundo de las religiones* (Madrid: Rialp, 2005).
Correas Mazuecos, M. Á., "Los 'pensadores de la fe' de Joseph Ratzinger. Tradición y diálogos teológicos," *Excerpta e dissertationibus in sacra theologia: Cuadernos doctorales de la facultad de teología* 67 (2018), pp. 159–217.
Gaál, E., *The Theology of Benedict XVI: The Christocentric Shift* (New York: Palgrave McMillan, 2010).
Guardini, R., *Christliches Bewusstsein: Versuche über Pascal* (München: Kösel, 1950 [1935]).
Hofmann, P., "Offenbarung und Geschichte: Joseph Ratzingers Kommentar zu Gaudium et spes als angewandte Bonaventura-Rezeption," in M. Schlosser and F. X. Heibl (eds.), *Gegenwart der Offenbarung* (Regensburg: Friedrich Pustet, 2011), pp. 74–103.
Kaes, D., *Theologie im Anspruch von Geschichte und Wahrheit* (St. Ottilien: Dissertationen Theologishe Reihe, 1997).
Krieg, R. A., "Kardinal Ratzinger, Max Scheler und eine Grundfrage der Christhologie," *Theologische Quartalschrift* 160 (1980), pp. 111–24.
Läpple, A., *Benedikt XVI. und seine Wurzeln: Was sein Leben und seinen Glauben prägte* (Augsburg: Sankt Ulricht, 2006).

Le Redaction, "Le futur Benoît XVI et Henri de Lubac," *Bulletin de la Association Internationale Cardenal Henri de Lubac* 7 (2005), pp. 4–9.

Martuccelli, P., *Origine e natura della chiesa: la prospettiva storico-dogmatica di Joseph Ratzinger* (Frankfurt am Main: Peter Lang, 2001).

Nichols, A., *The Theology of Joseph Ratzinger: An Introductory Study* (Edimburgh: T&T Clark, 1988).

Prestige, G. L., *Dios en el pensamiento de los Padres* (Salamanca: Sígueme, 1975).

Ratzinger, J., "Offenbarungsverständnis und Geschichtstheologie. Bonaventuras Habilitationsschrift und Bonaventura-Studien," in *JRGS* 2 (Freiburg: Herder, 2012).

Ratzinger, J., *Convocados en el camino de la fe: La Iglesia como comunión* (Madrid: Cristiandad, 2004).

Ratzinger, J., *Milestones: Memoirs (1927–1977)* (San Francisco: Ignatius, 1998).

Ratzinger, J., *Cristianismo e Iglesia católica ante el nuevo milenio* (Madrid: Palabra, 1997).

Ratzinger, J., "Der Gott des Glaubens und der Gott der Philosophen: Ein Beitrag zum Problem der Theologia Naturalis," in S. Otto Horn (ed.), *id.*, *Vom Wiederauffinden der Mitte: Grundorientierungen: Texte aus vier Jahrzehnten* (Freiburg, Basel, Wien: Herder, 1997), pp. 40–59.

Ratzinger, J., "Messaggio inaugurale," in M. Belda et al (eds.), *Santitá e mondo: Atti del Convegno teológico di studio sugli insegnamenti del beato Josemaría Escrivá (Roma, 12–14 ottobre 1993)* (Roma: Editrice Vaticana, 1994), pp. 19–28.

Ratzinger, J., *Teoría de los principios teológicos: Materiales para una teología fundamental* (Barcelona: Herder, 1985).

Ratzinger, J., *El nuevo pueblo de Dios: Esquemas para una eclesiología* (Barcelona: Herder, 1972).

Ratzinger, J., *El Dios de la fe y el Dios de los filósofos* (Madrid: Taurus, 1962).

Ratzinger, J., "Die christliche Lehre von Gott," in E. Brunner, *Dogmatik I*, Erster Band: Die Lehre vom Wort Gottes (Evangelischer, Zollikon-Zürich, 1953).

Rausch, T. P., *Pope Benedict XVI: An Introduction to his Theological Vision* (New York, Mahwah: Paulist Press, 2009).

Rossi, M., T. Rossi and T. F. Rossi, *L'anima tomista di Benedetto XVI: L'impronta di san Tommaso nei temi chiave di Papa Ratzinger: un'eredità per la chiesa del futuro* (Roma: Angelicum University Press, 2013).

Rowland, T., *La fe de Ratzinger: La teología del papa Benedicto XVI* (Granada: Nuevo Inicio, 2008).

Schenk, R., "Bonaventura als Klassiker der analogia fidei: Zur Rezeption der theologischen Programmatik Gottlieb Söhngens im Frühwerk Joseph Ratzingers," in M. Schlosser and F. X. Heibl (eds.), *Gegenwart der Offenbarung*, Ratzinger Studien 2 (Regensburg: Friedrich Pustet, 2011), pp. 37–44.

Sicouly, P. C., "Fe y razón en la lectura del pensamiento patrístico y medieval de Joseph Ratzinger-Benedicto XVI: una mirada a sus primeras obras (1951–1962)," *Ciencia Tomista* 138 (2011), pp. 107–32.

Söhngen, G., *Die Einheit in der Theologie* (München: Zink, 1952).

Tura, R., "La teologia di J. Ratzinger: Saggio introduttivo," *Studia Patavina* 21 (1974), pp. 154–61.

Valente, G., *El profesor Ratzinger (1946–1977): Los años dedicados al estudio y a la docencia en el recuerdo de sus compañeros y alumnos* (Madrid: San Pablo, 2011).

Verweyen, H., *Ein unbekannter Ratzinger: Die Habilitationsschrift von 1955 als Schlüssel zu seiner Theologie* (Regensburg: Friedrich Pustet, 2010).

Voderholzer, R., "Offenbarung und Kirche: Ein Grundegedanke von Joseph Ratzingers Habilitationsprojekt (1955/2009) und seine theologische Tragweite," in M. Schlosser and F. X. Heibl (eds.), *Gegenwart der Offenbarung* (Regensburg: Friedrich Pustet, 2011), pp. 50–73.

Chapter 5. Immanuel Kant: Distinguishing *Verum* and *Ens*

Agbaw-Ebai, M. A., *Light of Reason, Light of Faith—Joseph Ratzinger and the German Enlightenment* (South Bend, Indiana: St Augustine's Press, 2021).

Benedict XVI, *Faith, Reason and the University: Memories and Reflections. Lecture in the Meeting with the Representatives of Science*, Apostolic Journey to München, Altötting and Regensburg (September 9–14, 2006), Regensburg, September 12, 2006.

De Gaál, E., *O Lord I Seek Your Countenance: Explorations and Discoveries in Pope Benedict XVI's Theology* (Steubenville: Emmaus Academic, 2018).

Fisher, S., *Revelatory Positivism?* (Oxford: Oxford University Press, 1988).

Grotius, H., *De iure belli ac pacis libri tres* (Indianapolis: Liberty Fund, 2005).

Guyer, P., "Introduction," in P. Guyer (ed.), *The Cambridge Companion to Kant's Critique of Pure Reason* (Cambridge: Cambridge University Press, 2010).

Guyer, P., *Kant* (London: Routledge, 2006).

Hume, D., *A Treatise of Human Nature* (Oxford: Clarendon Press, 2007).

Janz, P. D., *God the Mind's Desire* (Cambridge: Cambridge University Press, 2004).

John Paul II, *Encyclical Letter* Fides et ratio *on the Relationship between Faith and Reason*, September 14, 1998.

Kant, I., *The Critique of Pure Reason*, P. Guyer and A. W. Wood (eds.) (Cambridge: Cambridge University Press, 1999).

Kant, I., *Kants Gesammelte Schriften*, Königlichen Preußischen (later Deutschen) Akademie der Wissenschaften (ed.) (Berlin: Georg Reimer [later Walter De Gruyter], 1900–).

Matteo, A. M., "Marechal's Dialogue with Kant: The Roots of Transcendental Thomism and the Search for Ultimate Reality and Meaning," *Ultimate Reality and Meaning* 22/4 (1999), pp. 264–75.

Pasternack, L. and C. Fugate, "Kant's Philosophy of Religion," in E. N. Zalta (ed.), *The Stanford Encyclopedia of Philosophy*, Summer 2022 Edition, https://plato.stanford.edu/archives/sum2022/entries/kant-religion/.

Phillips, J., "After *etsi veluti si Deus daretur*: Joseph Ratzinger and Robert Cardinal Sarah," in M. A. Agbaw-Ebai and M. Levering (eds.), *Joseph Ratzinger and the Future of African Theology* (Eugene: Pickwick, 2022).

Phillips, J., *Human Subjectivity in Christ in Dietrich Bonhoeffer's Theology: Integrating Simplicity and Wisdom* (London: T&T Clark, 2019).

Ratzinger, J., *Christianity and the Crisis of Cultures* (San Francisco: Ignatius, 2006).

Ratzinger, J., *Values in a Time of Upheaval* (San Francisco: Ignatius, 2006).

Ratzinger, J., *Introduction to Christianity* (San Francisco: Ignatius, 2005).
Ratzinger, J., *Milestones: Memoirs 1927–1977* (San Francisco: Ignatius, 1998).
Ratzinger, J., *The Nature and Mission of Theology* (San Francisco: Ignatius, 1995).
Rowland, T., *Ratzinger's Faith: The Theology of Pope Benedict XVI* (London: Bloomsbury, 2008).
Seung, T. K., *Kant: A Guide for the Perplexed* (London: Continuum, 2007).
Vatican Council I, *Dogmatic Constitution* Dei Filius, April 24, 1870.

Chapter 6. Georg Wilhelm Friedrich Hegel: Reason, Historicity, and Community

Benedict XVI, *Faith, Reason and the University: Memories and Reflections*. Lecture in the Meeting with the Representatives of Science, Apostolic Journey to München, Altötting and Regensburg (September 9–14, 2006), Regensburg, September 12, 2006.
Hegel, G. W. F., *The Phenomenology of Spirit* (Cambridge: Cambridge University Press, 2018).
Hegel, G. W. F., *Lectures on the Philosophy of World History, Volume I: Manuscripts of the Introduction and the Lectures of 1822–3* (Oxford: Oxford University Press, 2011).
Hegel, G. W. F., *Philosophy of Mind* (Oxford: Oxford University Press, 2010).
Hegel, G. W. F., *Lectures on the History of Philosophy: Medieval and Modern Philosophy* (Lincoln: University of Nebraska Press, 1995).
Hegel, G. W. F., *Lectures on the History of Philosophy: The Lectures of 1825–1826, Volume III: Medieval and Modern Philosophy* (Berkeley: University of California Press, 1990).
Hodgson, P. C., "Introduction," in G. W. F. Hegel, *Lectures on the Philosophy of Religion, Volume III: The Consumate Religion* (Oxford: Oxford University Press, 2007), pp. 1–60.
Küng, H., *The Incarnation of God: An Introduction to Hegel's Theological Thought as Prolegomena to a Future Christology* (New York: Crossroad, 1989).
Ratzinger, J., "Belief in Creation and the Theory of Evolution," in *Dogma and Preaching* (San Francisco: Ignatius, 2011).
Ratzinger, J., *Der Gott des Glaubens und der Gott der Philosophen* (Leutesdorf: Johannes, 2005).
Ratzinger, J., *Introduction to Christianity* (San Francisco: Ignatius, 2004).
Ratzinger, J., *Truth and Tolerance: Christian Belief and World Religions* (San Francisco: Ignatius, 2004).
Ratzinger, J., *The Spirit of the Liturgy* (San Francisco: Ignatius, 2000).
Ratzinger, J., *Principles of Catholic Theology: Building Stones for a Fundamental Theology* (San Francisco: Ignatius, 1987).
Ratzinger, J., "Sources and Transmission of the Faith," *Communio* 10/1 (1983), pp. 17–34.
Sada, A. "Reason," in R. A. Assunção, P. Blanco-Sarto, T. Rowland and C. Schaller (eds.), *Joseph Ratzinger Dictionary* (San Francisco: Ignatius, upcoming).
Schulz, M., "Grenzgänge des Denkens: Ratzinger im Disput mit Hegel," *Internationale katholische Zeitschrift Communio* 38 (2009), pp. 261–74.

Stern, R., "'This Is the Very Essence of Reformation: Man in His Very Nature Is Destined to Be Free': Hegel, Luther and Freedom," in D. Moyar, K. P. Walsh and S. Rand (eds.), *Hegel's Philosophy of Right: Critical Perspectives on Freedom and History* (New York: Routledge, 2022), pp. 45–65.
von Stosch, K., *Trinität* (Tübingen: UTB, 2017).
Trawny, P., *Die Zeit der Dreinigkeit* (Würzburg: Königshausen & Neumann, 2002).

Chapter 7. Auguste Comte: Science, Reason, and Religion

Benedict XVI, *Address to the Participants at the 20th International Conference Organized by the Pontifical Council for Health Pastoral Care on the Theme of The Human Genome*, November 19, 2005.
Benedict XVI, *Address to the Members of the Pontifical Academy of Sciences and the Pontifical Academy of Social Sciences*, November 21, 2005.
Benedict XVI, *Address to the Roman Curia Offering Them His Christmas Greetings*, December 22, 2005.
Benedict XVI, *Faith, Reason and the University: Memories and Reflections. Lecture in the Meeting with the Representatives of Science*, Apostolic Journey to München, Altötting and Regensburg (September 9–14, 2006), Regensburg, September 12, 2006.
Benedict XVI, *Address to the Members of the Pontifical Academy of Sciences*, November 6, 2006.
Benedict XVI, *Lecture Prepared for the University of Rome "La Sapienza,"* January 17, 2008.
Benedict XVI, *Address to Participants in an Interacademic Conference on "The Changing Identity of the Individual" Organized by the "Académie des Sciences" of Paris and by the Pontifical Academy of Sciences*, January 28, 2008.
Benedict XVI, *Address to Participants in the Plenary Assembly of the Pontifical Council for Culture*, March 8, 2008.
Benedict XVI, *Address to Participants in a Congress Held on the Occasion of the 10th Anniversary of the Publication of Pope John Paul II's Encyclical* Fides et ratio, October 16, 2008.
Benedict XVI, *Address to Participants in the Colloquium Sponsored by the Vatican Observatory on the Occasion of the International Year of Astronomy*, October 30, 2009.
Benedict XVI, *Address to Participants in the Plenary Session of the Pontifical Academy of Sciences*, October 28, 2010.
Bourdeau, M., "Auguste Comte," in Edward Zalta (ed.), *The Stanford Encyclopedia of Philosophy*, Spring 2022 Edition, https://plato.stanford.edu/archives/spr2022/entries/comte/.
Comte, A., *The Positive Philosophy of Auguste Comte*, vol. III, H. Martineau (ed.) (Kitchener: Batoche Books, 2000).
Comte, A., *Oeuvres d'Auguste Comte* (Paris: Anthropos, 1968–70).
Comte, A., *System of Positive Polity* (London: Longmans, Green and Co., 1875–7).
De Lubac, H., *The Drama of Atheist Humanism* (San Francisco: Ignatius, 1995).

Eslava, E., "La razón mutilada: Ciencia, razón y fe en el pensamiento de Joseph Ratzinger," *Scripta Theologica* 39 (2007), pp. 829–51.
Ratzinger, J., *Faith and the Future* (San Francisco: Ignatius, 2009).
Ratzinger, J., *Church, Ecumenism, and Politics* (San Francisco: Ignatius, 2008).
Ratzinger, J., *Europe Today and Tomorrow: Addressing the Fundamental Issues* (San Francisco: Ignatius, 2007).
Ratzinger, J., *Christianity and the Crisis of Cultures* (San Francisco: Ignatius, 2006).
Ratzinger, J., *Values in a Time of Upheaval* (New York, San Francisco: Ignatius, Crossroad, 2006).
Ratzinger, J., "That Which Holds the World Together: The Pre-Political Moral Foundations of a Free State," in J. Ratzinger and J. Habermas, *Dialectics of Secularization: On Reason and Religion* (San Francisco: Ignatius, 2006), pp. 53–80.
Ratzinger, J., *Europa: raíces, identidad y misión (1927–1977)* (Madrid: Ciudad Nueva, 2004).
Ratzinger, J., *Introduction to Christianity (Revised Edition)* (San Francisco: Ignatius, 2004).
Ratzinger, J., *Truth and Tolerance: Christian Belief and World Religions* (San Francisco: Ignatius, 2004).
Ratzinger, J., *Milestones: Memoirs 1927–1977* (San Francisco: Ignatius, 1998).
Ratzinger, J., *Salt of the Earth* (San Francisco: Ignatius, 1997).
Ratzinger, J., *The Nature and Mission of Theology: Essays to Orient Theology in Today's Debates* (San Francisco: Ignatius, 1995).
Ratzinger, J., *Verdad, Valores, Poder* (Madrid: Rialp, 1995).
Ratzinger, J., *A Turning Point for Europe? The Church in the Modern World* (San Francisco: Ignatius, 1994).
Sanguineti, J., *La filosofía de la ciencia según Santo Tomás* (Pamplona: Eunsa, 1977).
Vitoria, M., "Auguste Comte," in Francisco Fernández and Juan Mercado (eds.), *Philosophica: Enciclopedia filosófica online*, http://www.philosophica.info/archivo/2009/voces/comte/Comte.html.

Chapter 8. Karl Marx and Marxism: The Problem of the Priority of Praxis

Arendt, H., "Introduction," in W. Benjamin, *Illuminations: Essays and Reflections*, H. Arendt (ed.) (New York: Schocken Books, 1968), pp. 1–51.
Benedict XVI, *Spe salvi* (Rome: Editrice Vaticana, 2007).
Congregation for the Doctrine of the Faith, *Instruction on Certain Aspects of the Theology of Liberation* (Rome: Editrice Vaticane 1984).
Daniélou, J., *The Lord of History* (London: Longmans, 1958).
Guardini, R., *The End of the Modern World* (Wilmington: Intercollegiate Studies Institute, 2001).
Guardini, R., *Bericht über mein Leben: Autobiographische Aufzeichnungen* (Düsseldorf, 1984).

Kołakowski, L., *Main Currents of Marxism: Volume III* (Oxford: Clarendon Press, 1978).
Löwith, K., *Meaning in History: The Theological Implications of the Philosophy of History* (Chicago: University of Chicago Press, 1957).
Marx, K. and F. Engels, *The German Ideology* (Eastford: Martino Fine Books, 2011).
Ratzinger, J., "The Undefeated Light: Joseph Ratzinger on the True Meaning of Christmas," *London Catholic Herald* (December 19, 2019), pp. 97–100.
Ratzinger, J., *Fundamental Speeches from Five Decades* (San Francisco: Ignatius, 2012).
Ratzinger, J., *A Turning Point for Europe* (San Francisco: Ignatius, 2010).
Ratzinger, J., *Church, Ecumenism and Politics. New Endeavours in Ecclesiology* (San Francisco: Ignatius, 2008).
Ratzinger, J., "On Hope," *Communio* 35/2 (2008), pp. 301–15.
Ratzinger, J., *Europe: Today and Tomorrow* (San Francisco: Ignatius, 2007).
Ratzinger, J., *Christianity and the Crisis of Cultures* (San Francisco: Ignatius, 2006).
Ratzinger, J., *Introduction to Christianity* (San Francisco: Ignatius, 2004).
Ratzinger, J., "The End of Time," in T. R. Peters and C. Urban (eds.); M. Ashely (trans. and ed.), *The End of Time? The Provocation of Talking about God* (New York: Paulist Press, 2004).
Ratzinger, J., *Truth and Tolerance: Christian Belief and World Religions* (San Francisco: Ignatius, 2003).
Ratzinger, J., *Eschatology: Death and Eternal Life* (Washington, DC: Catholic University of America Press, 1988).
Ratzinger, J., *Principles of Catholic Theology: Building Stones for a Fundamental Theology* (San Francisco: Ignatius, 1987).
Ratzinger, J., *Faith and the Future* (Chicago: Franciscan Herald Press, 1971).
Ratzinger, J., *Christian Brotherhood* (London: Sheed & Ward, 1966).
Ratzinger, J. and J. Habermas, *The Dialectics of Secularization: On Reason and Religion* (San Francisco: Ignatius, 2006).
Schütz, D., *The Messianic Shape of History and the Critique of the Ideology of Progress in the Eschatologies of Walter Benjamin and Joseph Ratzinger* (Masters' Thesis, Melbourne: University of Divinity, 2021).

Chapter 9. Friedrich Nietzsche: Eros, Morality, and the Death of God

Benedict XVI, *Homily at the Chrism Mass*, April 9, 2009.
Benedict XVI, *General Audience*, December 10, 2008.
Benedict XVI, *Spe salvi: Encyclical Letter on Christian Hope* (Boston: Pauline Books and Media, 2007).
Benedict XVI, *Deus caritas est: Encyclical Letter on Christian Love* (Boston: Pauline Books and Media, 2006).
Benedict XVI, *Meeting with the Clergy of the Rome Diocese*, March 2, 2006.
De Lubac, H., *The Drama of Atheist Humanism* (San Francisco: Ignatius, 1995).

Girard, R., "Dionysus versus the Crucified," *Modern Language Notes* 99/4 (1984), pp. 816–35.
Magnus, B. and K. M. Higgins, "Nietzsche's Works and Their Themes," in B. Magnus and Higgins (ed.), *The Cambridge Companion to Nietzsche* (Cambridge: Cambridge University Press, 1996), pp. 21–68.
Merecki, J., "Has Christianity Poisoned *Eros*," in L. Melina and C. A. Anderson (eds.), *The Way of Love: Reflections on Pope Benedict XVI's Encyclical*, Deus caritas est (San Francisco: Ignatius, 2006), pp. 56–65.
Murphy, J., *Christ Our Joy: The Theological Vision of Pope Benedict XVI* (San Francisco: Ignatius, 2008).
Nietzsche, F., *Beyond Good and Evil* (Cambridge: Cambridge University Press, 2002).
Nietzsche, F., *Thus Spake Zarathustra* (Ware: Wordsworth, 1997).
Nietzsche, F., *The Gay Science; With a Prelude in Rhymes and an Appendix of Songs* (New York: Vintage Books, 1974).
Nietzsche, F., *The Will to Power* (New York: Vintage Books, 1968).
Nietzsche, F., "The Birth of Tragedy," in *The Birth of Tragedy and The Genealogy of Morals* (Garden City: Doubleday, 1956).
Nietzsche, F., "The Genealogy of Morals," in *The Birth of Tragedy and The Genealogy of Morals* (Garden City: Doubleday, 1956), pp. 158–88.
Nietzsche, F., *Ecce Homo* (Portland: Smith & Sale Printers, 1911).
Pieper, J., *Faith, Hope and Love* (San Francisco: Ignatius, 2012).
Ramage, M. J., *The Experiment of Faith: Pope Benedict XVI on Living the Theological Virtues in a Secular Age* (Washington, DC: Catholic University of American Press, 2020).
Ratzinger, J., "The Church and the New Pagans," *Homiletic and Pastoral Review* (January 30, 2017).
Ratzinger, J., *Dogma and Preaching: Applying Christian Doctrine to Daily Life* (San Francisco: Ignatius, 2011).
Ratzinger, J., *Jesus of Nazareth: From the Baptism in the Jordan to the Transfiguration* (New York: Double Day, 2007).
Ratzinger, J., *Homily at the Mass "Pro Eligendo Romano Pontifice,"* April 18, 2005.
Ratzinger, J., *God Is Near Us: The Eucharist, The Heart of Life* (San Francisco: Ignatius, 2003).
Ratzinger, J., *Introduction to Christianity* (San Francisco: Ignatius, 2000).
Ratzinger, J., *Milestones: Memoirs 1927–1977* (San Francisco: Ignatius, 1998).
Ratzinger, J., "Truth and Freedom," *Communio* 23/1(1996), pp. 17–35.
Ratzinger, J., "Concerning the Notion of Person in Theology," *Communio* 17/3 (1990), pp. 439–54.
Ratzinger, J., *Eschatology: Death and Eternal Life* (Washington, DC: Catholic University of America Press, 1988).
Ratzinger, J., *Principles of Catholic Theology: Building Stones for a Fundamental Theology* (San Francisco: Ignatius, 1987).
Ratzinger, J. and W. Congdon, *The Sabbath of History* (Washington, DC: The William G. Congdon Foundation, 2006).
Salaquarda, J., "Nietzsche and the Judaeo-Christian Tradition," in B. Magnus and K. M. Higgins (eds.), *The Cambridge Companion to Nietzsche* (Cambridge: Cambridge University Press, 1996), pp. 103–4.

Schroeder, W. R., *Continental Philosophy: A Critical Approach* (Malden: Blackwell, 2005).
Seewald, P., *Benedict XVI: A Life Volume Two: Professor and Prefect to Pope and Pope Emeritus 1966–2021* (London: Bloomsbury Continuum 2021).

Chapter 10. Martin Buber: Personalism and Relationality

Benedict XVI, *Encyclical Letter* Deus caritas est, December 25, 2005.
Benedict XVI and P. Seewald, *Last Testament: In His Own Words* (London, New York: Bloomsbury, 2016).
Buber, M., *Werksusgabe. 2.2. Ekstatische Konfessionen: Heraugegeben, eingeleitet und kommentiert von David Groiser* (München: Gütersloher Verlanghaus, 2012).
Buber, M., *Between Man and Man* (London: Fontana, 1971).
Buber, M., *Werke 3* (Munich, Heidelberg: Kösel, 1963).
Buber, M., *Die Erzählungen der Chassidim* (Zürich: Manesse, 1949).
Buber, M., *I and Thou* (Edinburgh: T&T Clark, 1937).
Bürkle, H., *Der Mensch and der Suche nach Gott—Die Frage der Religionem* (Paderborn: Bonifatius, 1996).
Collins, C. S., *The Word Made Love: The Dialogical Theology of Joseph Ratzinger/Benedict XVI* (Collegeville: Liturgical Press, 2013).
Cong Quy, J. L., "Joseph Ratzinger's Contribution to the Preparatory Debate of the Dogmatic Constitution *Dei verbum*," *Gregorianum* 94/1 (2013), pp. 35–54.
de Gaál, E., *O Lord, I Seek Your Countenance: Explorations and Discoveries in Pope Benedict XVI's Theology* (Steubenville: Emmaus Academic, 2018).
de Gaál, E., *The Theology of Pope Benedict XVI: The Christocentric Shift* (New York: Palgrave McMillan, 2010).
Francis, *Encyclical Letter* Lumen fidei *on Faith*, June 23, 2013.
Friedman, M., *Martin Buber: The Life of Dialogue. Fourth Edition Revised and Expanded* (London, New York: Routledge, 2002).
Kaethler, A. T. J., "'I Become a Thousand Men and yet Remain Myself': Self-Love in Joseph Ratzinger and Georges Bernanos," *Logos: A Journal of Catholic Thought and Culture* 19/2 (2016), pp. 150–67.
Kaethler, A. T. J., "The (Un)Bounded Peculiarity of Death: The Relational Implication of Temporality in the Theology of Alexander Schmemann and Joseph Ratzinger," *Modern Theology* 32/1 (2016), pp. 84–99.
Kajon, I., "*Religio* Today: The Concept of Religion in Martin Buber's Thought," in P. Mendes-Flohr (ed.), *Dialogue as a Trans-disciplinary Concept: Martin Buber's Philosophy of Dialogue and Its Contemporary Reception* (Berlin, Boston: De Gruyter, 2015), pp. 101–11.
Nichols, A. *The Thought of Pope Benedict XVI. New Edition: An Introduction to the Theology of Joseph Ratzinger* (London, New York: Burns & Oats, 2007).
Ratzinger, J., *Dogma and Preaching: Applying the Christian Doctrine to Daily Life. Unabridged Edition* (San Francisco: Ignatius, 2011).
Ratzinger, J., *God's Word: Scripture, Tradition, Office* (San Francisco: Ignatius, 2008).

Ratzinger, J., *Introduction to Christianity* (San Francisco: Ignatius, 2004).
Ratzinger, J., *God Is Near Us: The Eucharist, the Heart of Life* (San Francisco: Ignatius, 2003).
Ratzinger, J., *Truth and Tolerance: Christian Belief and World Religions* (San Francisco: Ignatius, 2003).
Ratzinger, J., *God and the World: Believing and Living in Our Time. A Conversation with Peter Seewald* (San Francisco: Ignatius, 2002).
Ratzinger, J., "The Feeling of Things, the Contemplation of Beauty," *Message to the Communion and Liberation Meeting at Rimini*, August 24–30, 2002.
Ratzinger, J., *Milestones: Memoirs 1927–1977* (San Francisco: Ignatius, 1998).
Ratzinger, J., *Salt of the Earth: Christianity and the Catholic Church at the End of the Millennium. An Interview with Peter Seewald* (San Francisco: Ignatius, 1997).
Ratzinger, J., "Concerning the Notion of Person in Theology," *Communio* 17/3 (1990), pp. 439–54.
Ratzinger, J., *The Feast of Faith: Approaches to a Theology of the Liturgy* (San Francisco: Ignatius, 1986).
Ratzinger, J., "Dogmatic Constitution on Divine Revelation: Origin and Background," in H. Vorgrimler (ed.), *Commentary on the Documents of Vatican II* 3 (New York, London: Burns & Oats, Herder and Herder, 1969), pp. 155–272.
Rowland, T., *Benedict XVI: A Guide for the Perplexed* (London, New York: T&T Clark, 2010).
Rutsche, M., *Die Relationalität Gottes bei Martin Buber und Joseph Ratzinger* (Norderstedt: GRIN, 2007).
Steinbuchel, T., "Die personalistische Grundhaltung des christlichen ethos," *Theologie und Glaube* 31 (1939), pp. 392–407.
Sudbrack, J., *Trunken vom hell-lichten Dunkel des Absoluten: Donysius der Areopagite und die Poesie der Gottesfahrung* (Ensiedeln: Johannes, 2001).
Wright, T., "Self, Other, Text, God: The Dialogical Thought of Martin Buber," in M. L. Morgan and P. E. Gordon (eds.), *The Cambridge Companion to Modern Jewish Philosophy* (Cambridge: Cambridge University Press, 2007), pp. 102–21.

Chapter 11. Hans Kelsen, Richard Rorty, and John Rawls: Philosophical Relativism and Religious Traditions of Wisdom

Benedict XVI, *Che cos'è il cristianesimo: Quasi un testamento spirituale* (Milano: Mondadori, 2023)
Benedict XVI, *Video message for initiative "10 squares for the 10 Commandments,"* September 8, 2012.
Benedict XVI, *Address at the Visit to the Bundestag,* Apostolic Journey to Germany (September 22–5, 2011), Reichstag Building, Berlin, September 27, 2011.
Benedict XVI, *Address at the Meeting with the Representatives of British Society, Including the Diplomatic Corps, Politicians, Academics and Business Leaders,*

Apostolic Journey to the United Kingdom (September 16–19, 2010), September 17, 2010.

Benedict XVI, *Address at the Meeting with the Civil and Political Authorities and with the Members of the Diplomatic Corps, Apostolic Visit to the Czech Republic*, Presidential Palace of Prague, September 26, 2009.

Benedict XVI, *Encyclical Letter* Caritas in veritate *on Integral Human Development in Charity and Truth*, June 29, 2009.

Benedict XVI, *Address in the Meeting with the Members of the General Assembly of the United Nations Organization*, Apostolic Journey to the United States of America and visit to the United Nations Organization Headquarters, April 18, 2008.

Benedict XVI, *Lecture at the University of Rome 'La Sapienza'*, January 17, 2008.

Bosetti, G. 'When Habermas and Ratzinger Shared the Idea of a Post-Secular Age', January 4, 2023, *Reset Dialogues*, https://www.resetdoc.org/story/habermas-ratzinger-postsecular-age/.

Cartabia, M. and A. Simoncini, "A Journey with Benedict XVI Through the Spirit of Constitutionalism," in M. Cartabia and A. Simoncini (eds.), *Pope Benedict XVI's Legal Thought: A Dialogue on Foundation of Law* (New York: Cambridge University Press, 2015), pp. 1–30.

Coccolini, G., *Alla ricerca di un ethos politico: La relazione tra teologia e politica in Joseph Ratzinger* (Trapani: Il Pozzo di Giacobbe, 2011), pp. 169–75.

Dombrowski, D., *Rawls and Religion: The Case for Political Liberalism* (New York: State University of New York Press, 2001).

Dreier, H., "Benedikt XVI. und Hans Kelsen," *Juristen Zeitung* 63/23 (2011), pp. 1151–4.

El Beheiri, N., "'Natur und Vernunft als die Wahren Rechtsquellen' aus der Perspektive von Joseph Ratzinger/Benedikt XVI. und Wolfgang Waldstein," in N. El Beheiri and J. Edögy (eds.), *"Ins Herz Geschrieben:" Die Grundlagen des freiheitlichen Rechtsstaates. Aufsätze und Diskussionsbeiträge aus Anlass der Internationalen Tagung am 10* (Budapest: Pázmány, 2014), pp. 27–45.

Eslava, E., *La filosofía de Ratzinger: Ciencia, Poder, Libertad, Religión* (Chía: Universidad de La Sabana, 2014).

Groppo, G., *Chiesa e politica nel pensiero di Joseph Ratzinger/Benedetto XVI* (Siena: Cantagalli, 2018).

Guerriero, E., *Servitore di Dio e dell'umanità: La biografia di Benedetto XVI* (Milano: Mondadori, 2016).

Irti, N., "Il diritto e il linguaggio della natura," *Vita e pensiero* 1 (2012), pp. 61–6.

Jonkers, P., "A Reasonable Faith: Pope Benedict's Response to Rawls," in T. Bailey and V. Gentile (eds.), *Rawls and Religion* (New York: Columbia University Press, 2015), pp. 221–41.

Jonkers, P., "'A Purifying Force for Reason'. Pope Benedict on the Role of Christianity in Advanced Modernity," in S. Hellemans and J. Wissink (eds.), *Towards a New Catholic Church in Advanced Modernity: Transformations, Visions, Tensions* (Zürich, Münster: LIT, 2012), pp. 79–102.

Kelsen, H., *The Essence and Value of Democracy*, N. Urbinati and C. I. Accetti (eds.) (Lanham, Boulder, New York, Toronto, Plymouth: Rowan & Littlefield, INC, 2013).

Kelsen, H., *Essays in Legal and Moral Philosophy* (Dordrecht-Boston: D. Reidel Publishing Co., 1973).

Klöger, H. H., "Beyond Dogma and Doxa: Truth and Dialogue in Rorty, Apel, and Ratzinger," *Dialogue and Universalism* 15/7–8 (2005), pp. 101–19.
Luciani, M., "Concerning the Doctrine of Democracy in Benedict XVI," in M. Cartabia and A. Simoncini (eds.), *Pope Benedict XVI's Legal Thought: A Dialogue on Foundation of Law* (New York: Cambridge University Press, 2015), pp. 187–204.
Madureira, D., *Maritain e Bento XVI: Sobre a modernidade e o relativismo* (Lisboa: Cáritas, 2014).
Martínez, J. L., "Religión en la democracia liberal: debate entre Rawls, Habermas y Ratzinger," *Estudios Eclesiástico* 86/337 (2011), pp. 291–327.
Mesle, B., "*An Ethics for Today*: Finding Common Ground Between Philosophy and Religion. Richard Rorty. NY: Columbia University Press, 2011," *American Journal of Theology & Philosophy* 32/3 (2011), pp. 285–9.
Piccinin, A., "Rawls and Catholicism: Towards Reconciliation?," *Cultural and Religious Studies* 7/1 (2019), pp. 50–6.
Possenti, V., "Umanesimo e antiumanesimo nelle società democratiche contemporanee: L'anima umanistica della democrazia," in F. Monceri and M. S. Birtolo (eds.), *Autunno della democrazia?*. Quaderno di Politica.eu, Università degli Studi di Molise, 2017, pp. 14–30.
Possenti, V., *Le società liberali al bivio: Lineamenti di filosofia della società* (Bologna: Marietti, 2005).
Postel, D., "Last Words from Richard Rorty," *The Progressive Magazine*, June 11, 2007, https://progressive.org/magazine/last-words-richard-rorty/.
Del Pozzo, M., *Magistero di Benedetto XVI ai giuristi* (Città del Vaticano: LEV, 2013).
Del Pozzo, M., "L'intelligenza del diritto di Benedetto XVI," *Ius Ecclesiae* 24/1 (2012), pp. 169–81.
Ratzinger, J., *A Turning Point for Europe? The Church in the Modern World* (San Francisco: Ignatius, 2010).
Ratzinger, J., *Church, Ecumenism & Politics: New Endeavors in Ecclesiology* (San Francisco: Ignatius, 2008).
Ratzinger, J., *Values in a Time of Upheaval* (San Francisco: Ignatius, 2006).
Ratzinger, J., *Homily at the Mass "Pro Eligendo Romano Pontifice,"* April 18, 2005.
Ratzinger, J., *Truth and Tolerance: Christian Belief and World Religions* (San Francisco: Ignatius Press, 2004).
Ratzinger, J., *Faith and Politics* (San Francisco: Ignatius, 2018).
Ratzinger, J. and M. Pera, *Without Roots: The West, Relativism, Christianity, Islam* (New York: Basic Books, 2007).
Ratzinger, J. and V. Possenti, "La fe en el contexto de la filosofía actual. Un diálogo en el filósofo Vittorio Possenti," *Communio* 24 (2002), pp. 375–82.
Rawls, J., *A Brief Inquiry into the Meaning of Sin and Faith: With "On My Religion"* (Cambridge: Harvard University Press, 2009).
Rawls, J., "The Idea of Public Reason Revisited," *The University of Chicago Law Review* 64/3 (1997), pp. 765–6.
Rawls, J. (ed.), *Political Liberalism* (New York: Columbia University Press, 2005).
Robbins, J. W., "Foreword. Richard Rorty. A Philosophical Guide for Talking About Religion," in R. Rorty, *An Ethics for Today: Finding Common Ground*

between Philosophy and Religion (New York: Columbia University Press, 2011), pp. vii–xxii.

Rorty, R., *An Ethics for Today: Finding Common Ground between Philosophy and Religion* (New York: Columbia University Press, 2011).

Rorty, R., "Religion in the Public Square," *The Journal of Religious Ethics* 31/1 (2003), pp. 141–9.

Rourke, T., *The Social and Political Thought of Benedict XVI* (Plymouth: Lexington, 2010).

Schall, J. V., "The Political Philosophy of Joseph Ratzinger," *The Imaginative Conservative*, January 9, 2023, https://theimaginativeconservative.org/2023/01/political-philosophy-joseph-ratzinger-james-v-schall.html.

Shy, T., "Readind Rorty as Theology," *Harvard Divinity Bulletin* (Spring 2006), https://bulletin.hds.harvard.edu/reading-rorty-as-theology/.

Smith, B. H. S., "Relativism, Today and Yesterday," *Common Knowledge* 13/2–3 (2007), pp. 227–49.

Stout, J., "Rorty on Religion and Politics," in R. E. Auxier and L. E. Hahn, *The Philosophy of Richard Rorty* (Chicago: Open Court, 2010), pp. 523–45.

Strand, V. L. and S. Z. Conedera, "Ratzinger's Republic: Pope Benedict XVI on Natural Law and Church and State," *Nova et Vetera* 18/2 (2020), pp. 669–94.

Twomey, D. V., *Pope Benedict XVI: The Conscience of Our Age. A Theological Portrait* (San Francisco: Ignatius, 2007).

Waldstein, W., *Ins Herz geschrieben: Das Naturrecht als Fundament einer menschlichen Gesellschaft* (Augsburg: Paulinus, 2010).

Chapter 12. Romano Guardini: Liturgy, Christian Existence, Truth, and Ethics

Augustine of Hippo, *The Confessions of Saint Augustine* (Grand Rapids, MI: Christian Classics Ethereal Library, 1999).

Allen Jr., J. L. *Cardinal Ratzinger* (New York: Continuum, 2000).

Battista Brunori, G., *Benedicto XVI: Fe y profecía del primer Papa emérito de la historia* (Madrid: Paulinas, 2018).

Benedict XVI, *Che cos'è il cristianesimo: Quasi un testamento spirituale* (Milano: Mondadori, 2023).

Benedict XVI, *Post-Synodal Apostolic Exhortation* Verbum domini *on the Word of God in the Life and Mission of the Church*, September 30, 2009.

Benedict XVI, *Encyclical Letter Caritas in veritate on Integral Human Development in Charity and Truth*, June 29, 2009.

Benedict XVI, *Encyclical Letter* Deus caritas est *on Christian Love*, December 25, 2005.

Benedict XVI and P. Seewald, *Last Testament: In His Own Words* (London: Bloomsbury, 2016).

Blanco-Sarto, P., *Benedicto XVI: La Biografía* (Madrid: San Pablo, 2019).

Blanco-Sarto, P., *Joseph Ratzinger: Una biografía* (Navarra: EUNSA, 2004).

Buber, M. *¿Qué es el hombre?* (México: Fondo de Cultura Económica, 2014).

Catalán Deus, J. *De Joseph Ratzinger a Benedicto XVI: Los enigmas del nuevo Papa* (Madrid: Espejo de Tinta, 2005).

de Cardedal, O. G., "Introducción a la edición española," in J. Ratzinger, *El espíritu de la liturgia: una introducción* (Madrid: Cristiandad, 2001, reprinted ⁷2014), pp. 27–48.
Ebner, F., *Das Wort ist der Weg* (Viena: Herder, 1949).
Guardini, R., *Experiencia religiosa y fe* (Madrid: BAC, 2016).
Guardini, R., *El espíritu del Dios viviente* (Barcelona: Belacqva, 2005).
Guardini, R., *The Lord* (Washington, DC: Regnery, 2001).
Guardini, R., *Ética: Lecciones en la Universidad de Múnich* (Madrid: BAC, 1999).
Guardini, R., *Apuntes para una autobiografía* (Madrid: Encuentro, 1992).
Guardini, R., *El ocaso de la Edad Moderna*, vol. 1 (Madrid: Cristiandad, 1981).
Guardini, R., *Wahrheit des Denkens und Wahrheit des Tuns* (Paderborn: Schöningh, 1980).
Guardini, R., *La cuestión judía* (Buenos Aires: Sur, 1963).
Guardini, R., *Religión y Revelación* (Madrid: Ediciones Guadarrama, 1961).
Guardini, R., *La esencia del cristianismo* (Madrid: Ediciones Nueva Época, 1945).
Meotti, G., *¿El último Papa de Occidente?* (Madrid: Encuentro, 2021).
Ratzinger, J., *Jesús de Nazaret: Escritos de cristología*. Obras completas VI/2 (Madrid: Biblioteca de Autores Cristianos, 2021); in German: *Jesus von Nazareth: Beiträge zur Christologie*, Band 6/2 (Freiburg: Herder, 2014).
Ratzinger, J., *Iglesia: Signo entre los pueblos*. Obras completas VIII/2 (Madrid: Biblioteca de Autores Cristianos, 2020); in German: *Kirche—Zeichen unter den Völkern. Schriften zur Ekklesiologie und Ökumene*, Band 8/2 (Freiburg: Herder, 2010).
Ratzinger, J., *Introducción al cristianismo*. Obras completas IV (Madrid: Biblioteca de Autores Cristianos, 2018); in German: *Einführung in das Christentum: Bekenntnis—Taufe—Nachfolge*, Band 4 (Freiburg: Herder, 2014).
Ratzinger, J., *Sobre la enseñanza del concilio Vaticano II*. Obras completas VII/1 (Madrid: Biblioteca de Autores Cristianos, 2014); in German: *Zur Lehre des Zweiten Vatikanischen Konzils: Formulierung—Vermittlung—Deutung*, Band 7/1 (Freiburg: Herder, 2012).
Ratzinger, J., *Fundamental Speeches from Five Decades* (San Francisco: Ignatius, 2012).
Ratzinger, J., *Fe y ciencia: Un diálogo necesario* (Santander: Sal Terrae, 2011).
Ratzinger, J., *Values in a Time of Upheaval* (San Francisco: Ignatius, 2006).
Ratzinger, J., *Introduction to Christianity (Revised Edition)* (San Francisco: Ignatius, 2004).
Ratzinger, J., *El espíritu de la liturgia: una introducción* (Madrid: Cristiandad, 2001).
Ratzinger, J., *Satz der Erde: Christentum und katholische Kirche an der Jahrtausenwende. Eis Gespräch mit Peter Seewald* (Stuttgart: Deutsche Verlag-Anstalt, 1997).
Ratzinger, J., *The Nature and Mission of Theology: Essays to Orient Theology in Today's Debates* (San Francisco: Ignatius, 1995).
Ratzinger, J., *Milestones: Memoirs 1927–1977* (San Francisco: Ignatius, 1998).
Ratzinger, J., *Co-Workers of the Truth: Meditations for Every Day of the Year* (San Francisco: Ignatius, 1992).
Ratzinger, J. and M. Pera, *Without Roots: The West, Relativism, Christianity, Islam* (New York: Basic Books, 2006).
Seewald, P., *Benedicto XVI: Una vida* (Bilbao: Mensajero, 2020).

Valente, G., *El profesor Ratzinger 1946–1977: los años dedicados al estudio y a la docencia en el recuerdo de sus compañeros y alumnos* (Madrid: San Pablo, 2011).
Vatican Council II, *Pastoral Constitution on the Church in the Modern World* Gaudium et spes, December 7, 1965.
Vatican Council II, *Dogmatic Constitution* Dei verbum *on Divine Revelation*, November 18, 1965.

Chapter 13. Ludwig Wittgenstein: The Scope of Reason

D'Arcy, E., "Towards the First Golden Age?," *The Australasian Catholic Record* 74/3 (1997), pp. 294–306.
von Ficker, L., *Denkzettel und Danksagungen: Aufsätze* (München: Kösel, 1967).
Goodill, D., *Nature as Guide: Wittgenstein and the Renewal of Moral Theology* (Washington, DC: Catholic University of America Press, 2022).
Hengstmengel, J., *Philosophy to the Glory of God: Wittgenstein on God, Religion and Theology*, February 22, 2010, https://hengstmengel.wordpress.com/2010/02/22/philosophy-to-the-glory-of-god-wittgenstein-on-god-religion-and-theology/.
Janik, A., "Letters to Ludwig von Ficker," in C. G. Luckhardt (ed.), *Wittgenstein: Sources and Perspectives* (Hassocks, Sussex: Harvester, 1979), pp. 82–99.
Janik, A., "Wittgenstein, Ficker, and Der Brenner," in C. G. Luckhardt (ed.), *Wittgenstein: Sources and Perspectives* (Hassocks, Sussex: Harvester, 1979), pp. 161–89.
Kerr, F., *Theology after Wittgenstein* (London: SPCK, 1997).
Marshall, B. D., "In Search of an Analytic Aquinas," in J. Stout and R. MacSwain (eds.), *Grammar and Grace: Reformulations of Aquinas and Wittgenstein* (London: SCM, 2004), pp. 55–74.
Möller, J., *Glauben und Denken im Widerspruch? Philosophische Fragen an die Theologie der Gegenwart* (Munich: Erich Wewel, 1969).
Pieper, J., *Scholasticism: Personalities and Problems of Medieval Philosophy* (New York: McGraw-Hill, 1960).
Pitcher, G., *The Philosophy of Wittgenstein* (Englewood Cliffs: Prentice-Hall, 1964).
Ratzinger, J., *Faith and the Future* (San Francisco: Ignatius, 2009).
Ratzinger, J., *Pilgrim Fellowship of Faith: The Church as Communion* (San Francisco: Ignatius, 2005).
Ratzinger, J., *Truth and Tolerance: Christian Belief and World Religions* (San Francisco: Ignatius, 2004).
Richter, D. J., "Ludwig Wittgenstein (1889–1951)," *Internet Encyclopedia of Philosophy*, https://iep.utm.edu/wittgens/.
Spaemann, R., "Nature," in D. C. Schindler and J. H. Schindler (eds.), *A Robert Spaemann Reader: Philosophical Essays on Nature, God and the Human Person* (Oxford: Oxford University Press, 2015).
Steinvorth, U., "Georg Pitcher, Die Philosophie Wittgensteins," *Hochland* 61 (1969), pp. 569–72.

Chapter 14. Martin Heidegger: Being and Time

Benedict XVI, *Encyclical Letter* Deus caritas est *on Christian Love*, December 25, 2005.
Benedict XVI, *Faith, Reason and the University: Memories and Reflections. Lecture in the Meeting with the Representatives of Science*, Apostolic Journey to München, Altötting and Regensburg (September 9–14, 2006), Regensburg, September 12, 2006.
Cong Quy, J. L., "Athens and Jerusalem: Christian Philosophy According to Ratzinger," *The Heythrop Journal* 56/6 (2015), pp. 948–57.
Cong Quy, J. L., "Truth, Values, Power: Touchstones of a Pluralistic Society," in *Faith and Politics* (San Francisco: Ignatius, 2018), pp. 95–150.
Francis, *Encyclical Letter* Lumen fidei, June 29, 2013.
Heidegger, M., "Only a God Can Save Us," in T. Sheehan (ed.), *Heidegger: The Man and the Thinker* (London: Routledge, 2017), pp. 45–69.
Heidegger, M., "Phenomenology and Theology," in W. McNeill (ed.), *Pathmarks* (Cambridge: Cambridge University Press, 1998), pp. 39–62.
Heidegger, M., "The Way Back into the Ground of Metaphysics," in W. Kaufman (ed.), *Existentialism from Dostoevsky to Sartre* (New York: Meridian, 1975), pp. 265–79.
Heidegger, M., "The End of Philosophy and the Task of Thinking," in *On Time and Being* (New York: Harper & Row, 1972), pp. 55–73.
Heidegger, M., *What Is Called Thinking?* (New York: Harper & Row, 1968).
Heidegger, M., *Being and Time* (New York: Harper & Row, 1962).
Ratzinger, J., *Behold the Pierced One: An Approach to a Spiritual Christology* (San Francisco: Ignatius Press, 1986).
Ratzinger, J., "Christocentrism in Preaching?," in M. J. Miller (ed.), *Dogma and Preaching: Applying Christian Doctrine to Daily Life* (San Francisco: Ignatius, 2011), pp. 40–58.
Ratzinger, J., "Contemporary Man Facing the Question of God," in M. J. Miller (ed.), *Dogma and Preaching: Applying Christian Doctrine to Daily Life* (San Francisco: Ignatius, 2011), pp. 77–87.
Ratzinger, J., *Eschatology: Death and Eternal Life* (Washington, DC: Catholic University of America Press, 1988).
Ratzinger, J., *Jesus of Nazareth: Holy Week: From the Entrance into Jerusalem to the Resurrection* (San Francisco: Ignatius, 2011).
Ratzinger, J., "Faith and Theology," in *Pilgrim Fellowship of Faith: The Church as Communion* (San Francisco: Ignatius, 2005), pp. 17–28.
Ratzinger, J., *Introduction to Christianity* (San Francisco: Ignatius, 2004).
Ratzinger, J., "The New Questions That Arose in the Nineties," in *Truth and Tolerance: Christian Belief and World Religions* (San Francisco: Ignatius, 2004), pp. 80–109.
Ratzinger, J., "The Truth of Christianity?," in *Truth and Tolerance: Christian Belief and World Religions* (San Francisco: Ignatius, 2004), pp. 138–209.
Ratzinger, J., "Variations on the Theme of Faith, Religion, and Culture', in *Truth and Tolerance: Christian Belief and World Religions* (San Francisco: Ignatius, 2004), pp. 80–106.
Ratzinger, J., *God and the World: Believing and Living in Our Time: A Conversation with Peter Seewald* (San Francisco: Ignatius, 2002).
Ratzinger, J., *Milestones: Memoirs 1927–1977* (San Francisco: Ignatius, 1998).

Ratzinger, J., *Salt of the Earth: Christianity and the Church at the End of the Millennium. An Interview with Peter Seewald* (San Francisco: Ignatius, 1997).
Ratzinger, J., *Called to Communion: Understanding the Church Today* (San Francisco: Ignatius, 1996).
Ratzinger, J., *Relativism: The Central Problem for Faith Today*, Address to the Presidents of the Doctrinal Commissions of the Bishops Conferences of Latin America, Guadalajara, May 1996, https://www.ewtn.com/catholicism/library/relativism-the-central-problem-for-faith-today-2470.
Ratzinger, J., *The Nature and Mission of Theology* (San Francisco: Ignatius, 1995).
Ratzinger, J., "Biblical Interpretation in Crisis," in R. J. Neuhaus (ed.), *Biblical Interpretation in Crisis: The Ratzinger Conference on Bible and Church* (Grand Rapids: Eerdmans, 1989), pp. 1–23.
Ratzinger, J., *Principles of Catholic Theology* (San Francisco: Ignatius, 1987).
Ratzinger, J., *The Feast of Faith: Approaches to the Theology of the Liturgy* (San Francisco: Ignatius, 1986).
Ratzinger, J., *The Theology of History in Bonaventure* (Chicago: Franciscan Herald, 1971).
Rowland, T. *Benedict XVI: A Guide for the Perplexed* (London: T&T Clark, 2010), pp. 80–109.
Sweeney, C. "Sacraments-Sacramentality," in R. A. Assunção, P. Blanco-Sarto, T. Rowland and C. Schaller (eds.), *Joseph Ratzinger Dictionary* (San Francisco: Ignatius, forthcoming).

Chapter 15. Edith Stein: The Reasonableness of Faith

Aristotle, *Poetics* (London: Penguin, 1996).
Benedict XVI, *Catechesis of the Holy Father during the Year of Faith*, October 17, 24, 31 2012; November 7, 14, 21, 28 2012; December 5, 12, 19 2012; January 2, 9, 16, 23, 30 2013; February 6, 13, 27 2013.
Benedict XVI, *Homily for the Holy Mass Opening the Year of Faith*, October 11, 2012.
Benedict XVI, *Apostolic letter* Porta fidei, October 11, 2011.
Benedict XVI, *Address at the Visit to the Bundestag*, Apostolic Journey to Germany (September 22–5, 2011), September 27, 2011.
Benedict XVI, *Address at the Meeting with the Representatives of British Society, Including the Diplomatic Corps, Politicians, Academics and Business Leaders*, Apostolic Journey to the United Kingdom (September 16–19, 2010), City of Westminster, Westminster Hall, September 17, 2010.
Benedict XVI, *Address in the Meeting with Representatives from the World of Culture*, Apostolic Journey to France on the occasion of the anniversary of the apparitions of the Blessed Virgin Mary at Lourdes (September 12–15, 2008), September 12, 2008.
Benedict XVI, *Lecture Prepared for the University of Rome "La Sapienza,"* January 17, 2008.
Benedict XVI, *Faith, Reason and the University: Memories and Reflections. Lecture in the Meeting with the Representatives of Science*, Apostolic Journey to München, Altötting and Regensburg (September 9–14, 2006), Regensburg, September 12, 2006.

Boeve, L. and G. Mannion, *The Ratzinger Reader* (London: T&T Clark, 2010).
Calhoun, C., E. Mendieta and J. Vanantwerpen (eds.), *Habermas on Religion* (Cambridge: Polity, 2013).
Carr, E. H., *What Is History* (London: Penguin, 1987).
Corkery, J., *Joseph Ratzinger's Theological Ideas* (Dublin: Dominican Press, 2009).
Francis, *Encyclical Letter* Lumen fidei, June 29, 2013.
John Paul II, *Encyclical Letter* Fides et ratio *on the Relationship between Faith and Reason*, September 14, 1998.
Lebech, M., *The Philosophy of Edith Stein from Philosophy to Metaphysics* (Bern: Peter Lang, 2015).
Levada, W., *Note with Pastoral Recommendations for the Year of Faith*, January 6, 2012, www.vatican.va/roman_curia/congregations/cfaith/documents/rc_con_cfaith_doc_20120106_nota-anno-fede.
MacIntyre, A., "On Being a Theistic Philosopher in a Secularized Culture," *Proceedings of the American Catholic Philosophical Association Philosophy and Language* 84 (2010), pp. 23–32.
MacIntyre, A., *Edith Stein: A Philosophical Prologue 1913–1922* (Lanham: Rowman & Littlefield, 2006).
McKenna, M. F., *Innovation within Tradition: Joseph Ratzinger and Reading of the Women of Scripture* (Minneapolis: Fortress, 2015).
McKenna, M. F., "In Search of Justice and Peace: Benedict XVI's Questions to the Cultures and Religions of the World," *Religions* 13/10:910 (1990).
Ratzinger, J., *God's Word Scripture, Tradition, Office* (San Francisco: Ignatius, 2008).
Ratzinger, J., "The Primacy of the Pope and the Unity of the People of God," in *Church Ecumenism and Politics: New Endeavours in Ecclesiology* (San Francisco: Ignatius, 2008), pp. 36–50.
Ratzinger, J., *Jesus of Nazareth* (London: Bloomsbury, 2007).
Ratzinger, J., *Introduction to Christianity* (San Francisco: Ignatius, 2004).
Ratzinger, J., *Truth and Tolerance: Christian Belief and World Religions* (San Francisco: Ignatius, 2004).
Ratzinger, J., *God and the World: Believing and Living in Our Time: A Conversation with Peter Seewald* (San Francisco: Ignatius, 2000).
Ratzinger, J., "Concerning the Notion of Person in Theology," *Communio* 17/3 (1990), pp. 439–54.
Ratzinger, J., "Man between Reproduction and Creation: Theological Questions on the Origin of Human Life," *Communio* 16 (1989), pp. 197–211.
Ratzinger, J., "'You are Full of Grace': Elements of Biblical Devotion to Mary," *Communio* 16/1 (1989), pp. 54–68.
Ratzinger, J., *Biblical Interpretation in Crisis: On the Question of the Foundations and Approach of Exegesis Today*, January 1988, https://www.ewtn.com/catholicism/library/biblical-interpretation-in-crisis-on-the-question-of-the-foundations-and-approaches-of-exegesis-today-10146.
Ratzinger, J., "Zum Personenversthdnis in der Theologie," in *Dogma und Verkundigung* (Munich: Erich Wewel, 1973), pp. 205–23.
von Ranke, L., *The Theory and Practice of History* (London: Routledge, 2011).
Rausch, T. P., *Pope Benedict XVI: An Introduction to His Theological Vision* (New York: Paulist Press, 2009).
Seewald, P., *Benedict XVI: A Life. Volume Two: Professor and Prefect to Pope and Pope Emeritus 1966–The Present* (London: Bloomsbury, 2021).

Seewald, P., *Benedict XVI: A Life. Volume One: Youth in Nazi Germany to the Second Vatican Council 1927–1965* (London: Bloomsbury, 2020).
Stein, E., "Husserl and Aquinas: A Comparison," in *Knowledge and Faith* (Washington, DC: ICS, 2000), pp. 1–38.
Stein, E., "Individual and Community," in *Philosophy of Psychology and the Humanities* (Washington, DC: ICS, 2000), pp. 261–94.
Stein, E., *Knowledge and Faith* (Washington, DC: ICS, 2000).
Stein, E., "Sketch of a Forward to Finite and Eternal Being," in *Knowledge and Faith* (Washington, DC: ICS, 2000).
Stein, E., "Ways to Know God. The 'Symbolic Theology' of Dionysius the Areopagite and Its Objective Presuppositions," in *Knowledge and Faith* (Washington, DC: ICS, 2000).
Stein, E., *On the Problem of Empathy* (Washington, DC: ICS, 1989).
Stein, E., *Life in a Jewish Family 1891–1916* (Washington, DC: ICS, 1986).

Chapter 16. Karl Popper: Fideism, Rationalism, and Rationality

Aquinas, T., *Summa Theologiae*, https://www.corpusthomisticum.org.
Bartley III, W.W., *The Retreat to Commitment* (LaSalle, London: Open Court, 1984).
Benedict XVI, *Lecture Prepared for the University of Rome "La Sapienza,"* January 17, 2008.
Benedict XVI, *Faith, Reason and the University: Memories and Reflections. Lecture in the Meeting with the Representatives of Science*, Apostolic Journey to München, Altötting and Regensburg (September 9–14, 2006), Regensburg, September 12, 2006.
Berkeley, G., *Principles of Human Knowledge and Three Dialogues*, H. Robinson (ed.) (Oxford/New York: Oxford University Press, 1996).
Copleston, S. J. F., *A History of Philosophy 5* (Westminster, Maryland: The Newman Press, 1959).
Denzinger, H., *Compendium of Creeds, Definitions, and Declarations on Matters of Faith and Morals*, Hünermann, P. (Latin-English ed.); Fastiggi, R. and Nash, A. E. (English ed.) (San Francisco: Ignatius, 2012).
Echeverría, E., "The Views of Karl Popper and Joseph Ratzinger/Benedict XVI on a Theory of Rationality," *Sapientia* LXIX, (2013), pp. 31–72.
Habermas, J., *Erkenntnis und Interesse* (Frankfurt: Suhrkamp, 1968).
John Paul II, *Encyclical Letter* Fides et ratio *on the Relationship between Faith and Reason*, September 14, 1998.
Letham, R., *The Holy Trinity* (Phillipsburg: Presbyterian & Reformed Publishing Co., 2004).
Lonergan, B. J. F., *The Way to Nicea* (Philadelphia: The Westminster Press, 1976).
Pannenberg, W., *Theology and the Philosophy of Science* (Philadelphia: The Westminster Press, 1976).
Popper, K. R., *Unended Quest: An Intellectual Autobiography* (La Salle, Ill.: Open Court, 1976).

Popper, K. R., "Chapter 24," in *The Open Society and Its Enemies* 2 (New York: Harper & Row; 1963), pp. 224–58.
Popper, K. R., "Utopia and Violence," in *Conjectures and Refutations* (New York: Harper & Row, 1963), pp. 355–63.
Ratzinger, J., "Theology and Church Politics," in *Church, Ecumenism and Politics: New Endeavors in Ecclesiology* (San Francisco: Ignatius, 2008).
Ratzinger, J., "Faith and Theology," in S. O. Horn and V. Pfnür (eds.), *Pilgrim Fellowship of Faith: The Church as Communion* (San Francisco: Ignatius, 2005), pp. 17–28.
Ratzinger, J., *Introduction to Christianity* (San Francisco: Ignatius, 2004).
Ratzinger, J., *Truth and Tolerance: Christian Belief and World Religions* (San Francisco: Ignatius, 2004).
Ratzinger, J., *Einführung in das Christentum: Das Glaubensbekenntnis* (München: Kösel, 2000).
Taliaferro, C., *Contemporary Philosophy of Religion* (Oxford: Blackwell, 1998).
Vatican Council II, *Dogmatic Constitution* Dei verbum *on Divine Revelation*, November 18, 1965.

Chapter 17. Josef Pieper: Philosophy, Philology, and Theology

Aquinas, T., *Summa Theologica*; Aquinas, T., *De veritate*, https://www.corpusthomisticum.org.
Benedict XVI, *Encyclical Letter* Deus caritas est *on Christian Love*, December 25, 2005.
Gerl-Falkovitz, H. B., *Vorwort zur Neuausgabe* (München: Kösel, 2012).
Guardini, R., *Ethik: Vorlesungen an der Universität München* 2 (Mainz, Paderborn: Grünewald, 1993).
Holm, H., *Die Unergründlichkeit der kreatürlichen Wirklichkeit: Eine Untersuchung zum Verhäaltnis von Philosohie und Wirklichkeit bei Josef Pieper* (Dresden: Thelem, 2011).
Husserl, E., *Philosophie als strenge Wissenschaft* (Frankfurt: Vittorio Klostermann, 1971).
Peterson, E., "Machruf auf Scheler," *Theologische Blätter* 7 (1928), pp. 165–7.
Pieper, J., "Identitätstheologie" (1966), in *Miszellen: Register und Gesamtbibliographie, Werke* 8 (Hamburg: Meiner, 2005), pp. 167–70.
Pieper, J., "Gottgeschenkte mania: Eine Platon-Interpretation," *Communio* 3 (1994), pp. 260–70.
Pieper, J., *Noch nicht aller Tage Abend: Autobiographische Aufzeichnungern 1945–1964* (München: Kösel, 1979).
Pieper, J., *Noch wusste es niemand: Autobiographische Aufzeichnungen 1904–1945* (München: Kösel 1976).
Pieper, J., "Theologie—philosophisch betrachtet," in *Religionsphilosophische Schriften, Werke* 7 (Hamburg: Meiner, 1974), pp. 129–41.
Pieper, J., *Über die Liebe* (München: Kösel, 1972).
Pieper, J., "Überlieferung. Begriff und Anspruch," in *Schriften zum Philosophiebegriff, Werke* 3 (Hamburg: Meiner, 1970), pp. 236–99.

Pieper, J., *Das Viergespann* (München: Kösel 1964).
Pieper, J., *Begeisterung und göttlicher Wahnsnn: Über den platonischen Dialog, "Phaidros"* (München: Kösel, 1962).
Pieper, J., "Wirklichkeit und Wahrheit," in *Interpretationen zu Thomas von Aquin: Quaestiones disputatae de veritate* 2 (1950–1), pp. 58–111.
Pieper, J., *Die Wirklichkeit und das Gute* (München: Kösel, 1949).
Ratzinger, J., *Auf Christus schauen: Einübung in Glaube, Hoffnung, Liebe* (Freiburg: Herder, 1989).
Ratzinger, J., "Verehrte Frau Görres!," in Görres, I. F., "Fragen eines Laien zur theologischen Diskussion über das priesterliche Amt," *Geist und Leben* 42 (1969), pp. 223–4.
Ratzinger, J., "Zur Frage nach dem Sinn des priesterlichen Dienstes," *Geist und Leben* 41/10 (1968), pp. 347–76.
Ratzinger, J., "Das Problem der Dogmengeschichte in der Sicht der katholischen Theologie" (1966), *JRGS* 9/1, pp. 533–95.
Ratzinger, J., *Der Gott des Glaubens und der Gott der Philosophen: Ein Beitrag zum Problem der Theologia naturalis* (München/Zürich: Schnell & Steiner, 1960).
Schlögl, M., "Der Glaube braucht den Mut der Vernunft zu sich selbst," in T. Möllenbeck and B. Wald (eds.), *Die Wahrheit bekennen: Josef Pieper im Dialog* (München: Pneuma, 2017), pp. 275–93.
Schlögl, M., *Joseph Ratzinger in Münster* (Münster: Dialog-Medien, 2012).

Chapter 18. Jean-Paul Sartre: Truth, Freedom, and Responsibility

Benedict XVI, *Mass, Imposition of the Pallium and Conferral of the Fisherman's Ring for the Beginning of the Petrine Ministry of the Bishop of Rome*, April 24, 2005.
Benedict XVI and P. Seewald, *Last Testament: In His Own Words* (London: Bloomsbury, 2016).
Blanco-Sarto, P., *La teología de Joseph Ratzinger: Una introducción* (Madrid: Palabra, 2011).
Camus, A., *Caligula* (Paris: Gallimard, 1993).
Flynn, T. R., *Existentialism: A Very Short Introduction* (New York: Oxford University Press, 2006).
Gómez de Pedro, M. E., *Libertad en Ratzinger: riesgo y tarea* (Madrid: Encuentro, 2014).
McGraw, J. G., "Loneliness, Its Nature and Forms: An Existential Perspective," *Man and World* 28 (1995), pp. 43–64.
Pieper, J., *For the Love of Wisdom: Essays on the Nature of Philosophy* (San Francisco: Ignatius, 2006).
Ratzinger, J., *El elogio de la conciencia: La Verdad interroga al corazón* (Madrid: Palabra, 2010).
Ratzinger, J., *Church, Ecumenism, and Politics: New Endeavors in Ecclesiology* (San Francisco: Ignatius, 2008).

Ratzinger, J., *Christianity and the Crisis of Cultures* (San Francisco: Ignatius, 2006).
Ratzinger, J., *Images of Hope: Meditations on Major Feasts* (San Francisco: Ignatius, 2006).
Ratzinger, J., *Introduction to Christianity* (San Francisco: Ignatius, 2004).
Ratzinger, J., *Truth and Tolerance: Christian Belief and World Religions* (San Francisco: Ignatius, 2004).
Ratzinger, J., *God and the World: Believing and Living in Our Time: A Conversation with Peter Seewald* (San Francisco: Ignatius, 2002).
Ratzinger, J., *"In the Beginning ..." A Catholic Understanding of the Story of Creation and the Fall* (Grand Rapids: Eerdmans, 1995).
Ratzinger, J., *A Turning Point for Europe? The Church in the Modern World: Assessment and Forecast* (San Francisco: Ignatius, 1994).
Ratzinger, J., *Co-Workers of the Truth: Meditations for Every Day of the Year* (San Francisco: Ignatius, 1992).
Ratzinger, J., *Principles of Catholic Theology: Building Stones for a Fundamental Theology* (San Francisco: Ignatius, 1985).
Sada, A., *Sentido y verdad: Hacia una nueva comprensión de la filosofía desde el pensamiento de Joseph Ratzinger* (Madrid: BAC, 2023).
Sada, A., *Naturaleza y misión de la filosofía en el pensamiento de Joseph Ratzinger* (Doctoral Thesis, Pamplona: Universidad de Navarra, 2020).
Sartre, J. P., *Existentialism Is a Humanism* (New Haven, London: Yale University Press, 2007).
Sartre, J. P., *Being and Nothingness: An Essay on Phenomenological Ontology* (New York: Washington Square Press, 1978).
Seewald, P., *Benedict XVI: Una vida* (Bilbao: Mensajero, 2020); in English: *Benedict XVI: A Life* 2 (London: Bloomsbury, 2020–1).
Solomon, R. C., *Dark Feelings, Grim Thoughts: Experience and Reflections in Camus and Sartre* (Oxford, New York: Oxford University Press, 2006).
Webber, J., *The Existentialism of Jean-Paul Sartre* (New York, London: Routledge, 2009).

Chapter 19. Albert Camus: The Meaning of Life

Benedict XVI, *Message for the XXVII World Youth Day*, March 15, 2012.
Camus, A., *The Rebel: An Essay on Man in Revolt* (New York: Vintage International, 2010).
Camus, A., *The Myth of Sisyphus* (Middlesex: Penguin, 1979).
Camus, A., *L'Envers et l'endroit* (Paris: Gallimard, 1958).
Flynn, T. R., *Existentialism: A Very Short Introduction* (Oxford, New York: Oxford University Press, 2006).
García-Valiño Abós, J., "'Gaudete semper in Domino (Fil 4:4)'. La alegría de la fe a la luz del magisterio de Benedicto XVI," *Scripta Fulgentina* 22/43–4 (2012), pp. 131–8.
Gómez de Pedro, M. E., *Libertad en Ratzinger: riesgo y tarea* (Madrid: Encuentro, 2014).

Ramírez Medina, A., "Anti-teodicea y ateísmo en Albert Camus," *Pensamiento* 64/241 (2008), pp. 487–98.

Ratzinger, J., "Theology of the Liturgy: The Sacramental Foundation of Christian Existence," in *JRCW*, 11 (San Francisco: Ignatius, 2014).

Ratzinger, J., *Salz der Erde: Christentum und katholische Kirche an der Jahrtausendwende* (Stuttgart: Deutsche Verlags-Anstalt, 1996); in English: *Salt of the Earth* (San Francisco: Ignatius, 2013).

Ratzinger, J., *Faith and the Future* (San Francisco: Ignatius, 2009).

Ratzinger, J., *Images of Hope: Meditations on Major Feasts* (San Francisco: Ignatius, 2006).

Ratzinger, J., *Introduction to Christianity* (San Francisco: Ignatius, 2004).

Ratzinger, J., *Called to Communion: Understanding the Church Today* (San Francisco: Ignatius, 1996).

Ratzinger, J., *Co-Workers of the Truth: Meditations for Every Day of the Year* (San Francisco: Ignatius, 1992).

Ratzinger, J., *Principles of Catholic Theology: Building Stones for a Fundamental Theology* (San Francisco: Ignatius, 1987).

Sada, A., *Sentido y verdad: Hacia una nueva comprensión de la filosofía desde el pensamiento de Joseph Ratzinger* (Madrid: BAC, 2023).

Sada, A., "Cristianismo y sentido de la vida: una reflexión a partir del pensamiento de Joseph Ratzinger," *Scripta Theologica* 53/3 (2021), pp. 595–624.

Sada, A., *Naturaleza y misión de la filosofía en el pensamiento de Joseph Ratzinger* (Doctoral Thesis, Pamplona: Universidad de Navarra, 2020).

Sartre, J. P., *Existentialism Is a Humanism* (New Haven, London: Yale University Press, 1999).

Seewald, P., *Benedicto XVI: una vida* (Bilbao: Mensajero, 2020); in English: *Benedict XVI: A Life. Volume Two: Professor and Prefect to Pope and Pope Emeritus 1966–Present* (London: Bloomsbury, 2023).

Solomon, R. C., *Dark Feelings, Grim Thoughts: Experience and Reflections in Camus and Sartre* (Oxford, New York: Oxford University Press, 2006).

Zaretsky, R., *A Life Worth Living: Albert Camus and the Quest for Meaning* (Cambridge, London: Harvard University Press, 2013).

Chapter 20. Robert Spaemann: Person, Ethics, and Politics

Böckendorfe, E. W. and R. Spaemann, *Menschenrechte und Menschenwürde: Historische Voraussetzungen—säkulare Gestalt—christliches Verständnis* (Stuttgart: Klett-Cotta, 1987).

Geach, P., F. Inciarte and Spaemann, *Persönliche Verantwortung* (Köln: Lidenthal-Institut Colloquium, 1982).

Löw, R. and R. Spaemann, *Die Frage Wozu? Geschichte und Wiederentdeckung des teleologischen Denkens* (München: Piper, 1981, 3. Auflage 1991). New edition titled: *Natürliche Ziele: Geschichte und Wiederentdeckung des teleologischen Denkens* (Stuttgart: Klett-Cotta, 2005).

Ratzinger, J., "Der Streit um die Moral: Fragen der Grundlegung ethischer Werte" (1984), *JRGS* 4, pp. 718–31.

Ratzinger, J., "Die Freiheit, das Recht und das Gute: Moralische Prinzipien in demokratischen Gesellschaften," in *JRGS* 3/1, pp. 561-7.
Ratzinger, J., "Europa—Hoffnungen und Gefahren," *JRGS* 3, pp. 645-66.
Ratzinger, J., "Probleme und Hoffnungen des anglikanisch-katholischen Dialogs," *JRGS* 8/2, pp. 984-1018.
Ratzinger, J., "Theologie und Kirchenpolitik," *JRGS* 9/1, pp. 340-53.
Ratzinger, J., "Vom geistlichen Grund und vom kirchlichen Ort der Theologie," *JRGS* 9/1, pp. 135-58.
Spaemann, R., *Der Ursprung der Soziologie aus dem Geist der Restauration: Studien über L. G. A. de Bonald* (Stuttgart: Klett-Cotta, 1998).
Spaemann, R., "Die christliche Religion und das Ende des modernen Bewußtseins," *Internationale katholische Zeitschrift Communio* 8 (1979), pp. 251-70.
Spaemann, R., "Einführung," in Koslowski, P., *Gesellschaft und Staat: ein unvermeidlicher Dualismus* (Stuttgart: Klett-Cotta, 1982), pp. xv-xviii.
Spaemann, R., *Einsprüche: Christliche Reden* (Einsiedeln: Johannes, 1977).
Spaemann, R., *Grundbegriffe* (München: Beck, 1982).
Spaemann, R., "La perle préciuese et le nihilisme banal," *Catholica* 33 (1992), pp. 43-50.
Spaemann, R., *Reflexion und Spontanität: Studien über Fénelon* (Kohlhammer: Stuttgart, 1963).
Spaemann, R., "Universalismus oder Eurozentrismus?," in K. Michalski (ed.), *Europa und die Folgen* (Stuttgart: Denoël, 1988).
Spaemann, R., *Zur Kritik der politischen Utopie: 10 Kapitel politischer Philosophie* (Stuttgart: Klett-Cotta, 1977).
Spaemann, R., *Moralische Grundbegriffe* (München: Beck, 1982; 5 Auflage 1994); in English: *Basic Moral Concepts* (Abingdon: Routledge 1990).

Chapter 21. Jürgen Habermas: Democracy and Religion in Pluralistic Societies

Adams, N., *Habermas and Theology* (Cambridge: Cambridge University Press, 2006).
Allen Jr., J., *Cardinal Ratzinger, Enforcer of the Faith* (New York: Continuum, 2002).
Aslan, R., *No God But God: The Origins, Evolution and Future of Islam* (London: Arro, 2011).
Benedict XVI, *Encyclical letter* Spe salvi *on Christian Hope,* November 30, 2007.
Boeve, L. and G. Mannion (eds.), *The Ratzinger Reader* (London: T&T Clark, 2010).
Carr, J., *Catholicism and Liberal Democracy: Forgotten Roots and Future Prospects* (Washington, DC: Catholic University of America Press, 2022).
Corkery, J., *Joseph Ratzinger's Theological Ideas* (Dublin: Dominican Press, 2009).
Derrida, J., "The Principle of Reason: The University in the Eyes of Its Pupils," *Diacritics* 13 (1983), pp. 2-20.
Echeverría, E. J., "A Decade Later: Lessons from the Habermas and Ratzinger Debate," University of Cambridge, March 2015, www.vhi.st-edmunds.cam.ac.uk/system/files/documents/Revision%20Lessons_from_the_Habermas_Ratzinger_Debate.pdf.

Habermas, J., "Reply to My Critics," in *Habermas and Religion* (Cambridge: Polity, 2013), pp. 347–90.

Habermas, J., "An Awareness of What Is Missing," in *An Awareness of What Is Missing: Faith and Reason in a Post Secular Age* (Cambridge: Polity, 2010), pp. 15–23.

Habermas, J., "Introduction," in *Between Naturalism and Religion* (Cambridge: Polity Press, 2008), pp. 1–7.

Habermas, J., "The Boundary Between Faith and Knowledge: On the Reception and Contemporary Importance of Kant's Philosophy of Religion," in *Between Naturalism and Religion* (Cambridge: Polity Press, 2008), pp. 209–47.

Habermas, J., "Religion in the Public Sphere," *European Journal of Philosophy* 14/1 (2006), pp. 1–25.

Habermas, J., "Are There Postmetaphysical Answers to the Question: What Is the 'Good Life'?," in *The Future of Human Nature* (London: Polity, 2003), pp. 1–15.

Habermas, J., "Faith and Knowledge," in *The Future of Human Nature* (London: Polity, 2003), pp. 101–15.

Habermas, J., "Forward," in *The Future of Human Nature* (London: Polity, 2003), pp. vii–viii.

Habermas, J., "The Debate on the Ethical Self-Understanding of the Species," in *The Future of Human Nature* (London: Polity, 2003), pp. 75–82.

Lafont, C., "Religion in the Public Sphere: Remarks on Habermas's Conception of Public Deliberation in Postsecular Societies," *Constellations* 14/2 (2007), pp. 239–59.

MacIntyre, A., "Human Dignity: A Puzzling and Possibly Dangerous Idea?," presented at the University of Notre Dame de Nicola Centre for Ethics and Culture 2021 Fall Conference, entitled *I Have Called You By Name: Human Dignity in a Secular World* (November 12, 2021), FC21 Plenary.

McKenna, M. F., "On the Future of Europe: Philosophical and Theological Perspectives on Pre-Political Foundations of Europe and the State from Ratzinger, Habermas, and MacIntyre," *The Heythrop Journal* 60 (2019), pp. 910–25.

McKenna, M. F., "The Promise of Enlightenment and the Incalculability of Freedom: A Consideration of Horkheimer and Adorno's Critique of Enlightenment in Relation to Ratzinger's Notion of Freedom," *Logos* 21 (2018), pp. 114–39.

McKenna, M. F., "The Idea of Europe as the Point of Encounter between Power and Freedom, Interests and Universal Values: A Consideration of Kissinger's and Ratzinger's Visions of Europe," *European Review* 25/4 (2017), pp. 655–69.

McKenna, M. F., "Moral Values and Social Consensus in Democratic Secular Societies: Challenges and Responsibilities," *The Heythrop Journal* 56/4 (2015), pp. 663–76.

McKenna, M. F., "In Search of Justice and Peace: Benedict XVI's Questions to the Cultures and Religions of the World," *Religions* 13/10:910 (1990), pp. 1–18.

Mendieta, E., "Appendix Religion in Habermas' Work," in *Habermas and Religions* (Cambridge: Polity, 2013), pp. 391–407.

Mendieta, E., "Introduction," in *Religion and Rationality: Essays on Reason, God, and Modernity* (Cambridge: Polity, 2002), pp. 12–14.

Mendieta, E. and J. Habermas, "A Conversation About God and the World," in *Religion and Rationality Essays on Reason, God, and Modernity* (Cambridge: Polity, 2002), pp. 147–67.

Mendieta, E. and J. Vanantwerpen, "Introduction," in *The Power of Religion in the Public Sphere* (New York: Columbia University Press, 2011), pp. 3–13.

Millbank, J., "What Lacks Is Feeling: Hume versus Kant and Habermas," in *Habermas on Religion* (Cambridge: Polity, 2013), pp. 322–46.

Pera, M., "A Consideration of Christianity's Role in a Pluralistic Society," *The Way* 55/4 (2016), pp. 31–47.

Ratzinger, J., *A Turning Point for Europe* (San Francisco: Ignatius, 2010).

Ratzinger, J., *Church Ecumenism, and Politics: New Endeavours in Ecclesiology* (San Francisco: Ignatius, 2008).

Ratzinger, J., *Christianity and the Crisis of Cultures* (San Francisco: Ignatius, 2006).

Ratzinger, J., "If You Want Peace ... Conscience and Truth," in *Values in a Time of Upheaval* (San Francisco: Ignatius, 2006), pp. 75–99.

Ratzinger, J., "The Spiritual Roots of Europe: Yesterday, Today, and Tomorrow" and "Letter of Marcello Pera," in J. Ratzinger and M. Pera, *Without Roots: The West, Relativism, Christianity, Islam* (New York: Basic Books, 2006), pp. 51–80 and 107–36.

Ratzinger, J., *Values in a Time of Upheaval* (San Francisco: Ignatius, 2006).

Ratzinger, J., *Truth and Tolerance: Christian Belief and World Religions* (San Francisco: Ignatius, 2004).

Ratzinger, J., *"In the Beginning ..." A Catholic Understanding of Creation and the Fall* (London: T&T Clark, 1995).

Ratzinger, J., *Wahrheit, Werte, Macht: Prufsteine der pluralistischen* Gesellschaft, 3rd edition (Freiburg: Herder, 1995), pp. 11–24.

Ratzinger, J., "Concerning the Notion of Person in Theology," *Communio* 17/3 (1990), pp. 439–54.

Ratzinger, J., "Man between Reproduction and Creation: Theological Questions on the Origin of Human Life," *Communio* 16 (1989), pp. 197–211.

Ratzinger, J., "Vorfragen zu einer Theologie der Edosung," in *Edosung und Emanzipation* (Freiburg: Herder, 1973), pp. 141–55.

Ratzinger, J., "Zum Personenversthdnis in der Theologie," in *Dogma und Verkiindigung* (Munich: Erich Wewel, 1973), pp. 205–23.

Ratzinger, J., "The New Pagans and the Church," *Hochland* (1958), www.hprweb.com/2017/01/the-new-pagans-and-the-church/.

Rausch, T. P., *Pope Benedict XVI: An Introduction to His Theological Vision* (New York: Paulist Press, 2009).

Rowland, T., *Catholic Theology* (London: T&T Clark, 2017).

Schall, J. V., *On Islam: a Chronological Record, 2002–2018* (San Francisco: Ignatius, 2018).

Schuller, F., "Forward," in J. Ratzinger and J. Habermas, *The Dialectics of Secularisation: On Reason and Religion*. San Francisco: Ignatius, 2006), pp. 7–18.

Seewald, P., *Benedict XVI: A Life. Volume Two: Professor and Prefect to Pope and Pope Emeritus 1966–Present* (London: Bloomsbury, 2021).

Twomey, D. V., *Pope Benedict XVI: The Conscience of Our Age. A Theological Portrait* (San Francisco: Ignatius, 2007).

Vatican Council II, *Dogmatic Constitution on the Church* Lumen Gentium, November 21, 1964.
Welker, M., "Habermas and Ratzinger on the Future of Religion," *Scottish Journal of Theology* 64/4 (2010), pp. 456–73.

Chapter 22. Gianni Vattimo: Nihilism and Truth

Benedict XVI, *Faith and Politics: Selected Writings* (San Francisco: Ignatius, 2018).
Benedict XVI, *Doctors of the Church* (Huntington, Indiana: Our Sunday Visitor, 2011).
Benedict XVI, *Great Christian Thinkers: From the Early Church through the Middle Ages* (Minneapolis: Fortress Press, 2011).
Benedict XVI, *Faith, Reason and the University: Memories and Reflections. Lecture in the Meeting with the Representatives of Science*, Apostolic Journey to München, Altötting and Regensburg (September 9–14, 2006), Regensburg, September 12, 2006.
Guarino, T. G., *The Unchanging Truth of God? Crucial Philosophical Issues for Theology* (Washington, DC: Catholic University of America Press, 2022).
Guarino, T. G., *The Disputed Teachings of Vatican II: Continuity and Reversal in Catholic Doctrine* (Grand Rapids: Eerdmans, 2018).
Guarino, T. G., "Vattimo, Diversity and Catholicism," in M. J. Sweeney (ed.), *Justice Through Diversity? A Philosophical and Theological Debate* (Lanham: Rowman and Littlefield, 2016), pp. 533–50.
Guarino, T. G., "The Return of Religion in Europe? The Postmodern Christianity of Gianni Vattimo," *Logos: A Journal of Catholic Thought and Culture* 14/2 (2011), pp. 15–36.
Guarino, T. G., *Vattimo and Theology* (London: T&T Clark, 2009).
Jenson, R., *Systematic Theology* I (New York: Oxford University Press, 1997).
John Paul II, *Encyclical Letter* Fides et ratio *on the Relationship between Faith and Reason*, September 14, 1998.
Nietzsche, F., *The Twilight of the Idols* (London: Penguin, 1990).
Nietzsche, F., *The Will to Power* (New York: Random House, 1967).
Ratzinger, J., *Homily at the Mass "Pro Eligendo Romano Pontifice,"* April 18, 2005.
Ratzinger, J., *Introduction to Christianity* (San Francisco: Ignatius, 2004).
Ratzinger, J., *Truth and Tolerance: Christian Belief and World Religions* (San Francisco: Ignatius, 2004).
Vattimo, G., *Of Reality: The Purposes of Philosophy* (New York: Columbia University, 2016).
Vattimo, G., *A Farewell to Truth* (New York: Columbia University Press, 2011).
Vattimo, G., "A 'Dictatorship of Relativism'," *Common Knowledge* 13 (2007), pp. 214–18.
Vattimo, G., *Dialogue with Nietzsche* (New York: Columbia University Press, 2006).
Vattimo, G., *Nihilism and Emancipation: Ethics, Politics and Law* (New York: Columbia University Press, 2004).
Vattimo, G., *Belief* (Stanford: Stanford University Press, 1999).
Vattimo, G., *Beyond Interpretation: The Meaning of Hermeneutics for Philosophy* (Stanford: Stanford University Press, 1997).

CONTRIBUTORS

ALBINO DE ASSUNÇÃO, Rudy: Doctor of Political Sociology from the Universidade Federal de Santa Catarina (Brazil); Professor at the Universidad Internacional de La Rioja (Spain).

BILINIEWICZ, Mariusz: Doctor of Philosophy from the National University of Ireland; Professor at the School of Philosophy and Theology of the University of Notre Dame and Director of the Liturgy Office of the Archdiocese of Sydney (Australia).

BLANCO-SARTO, Pablo: Doctor of Philosophy from the Pontificia Università della Santa Croce (Italy) and of Theology from the Universidad de Navarra (Spain); Professor at the Universidad de Navarra (Spain).

CHARPENEL, Eduardo: Doctor of Philosophy from the Universität Bonn (Germany); Professor at the School of Philosophy of the Universidad Panamericana (Mexico).

DE GAÁL, Emery: Doctor of Philosophy from the Duquesne University; Professor at the University of Saint Mary of the Lake/Mundelein Seminary (USA).

ECHEVERRÍA, Eduardo: Doctor of Philosophy from the Vrije Universiteit (Holland); Professor at Sacred Heart Major Seminary (USA).

ESLAVA, Euclides: Doctor of Philosophy from the Universidad de Navarra (Spain), professor and Director of the Master of Theology Program at the Universidad de La Sabana (Colombia).

GERL-FALKOVITZ, Hanna-Barbara: Doctor of Philosophy from the Ludwig-Maximilians-Universität München (Germany); Director of the Europäisches Institut für Philosophie und Religion, Heiligenkreuz (Austria).

GONZÁLEZ GINOCCHIO, David: Doctor of Philosophy from the Universidad de Navarra (Spain); Professor of Aesthetics and Medieval Philosophy, Universidad Internacional de La Rioja (Spain).

GUARINO, Thomas G.: Doctor of Theology, Catholic University of America (USA); Professor at Seton Hall University (USA).

JIMÉNEZ UNQUILES, Marcela: Doctor of Law and Society/Philosophical Theological System from the Universidad a Distancia de Madrid (Spain); Professor at Universidad a Distancia de Madrid and the Universidad Católica de Ávila (Spain).

McKENNA, Mary Frances: Doctor of Humanities in Theology from All Hallows College/Dublin City University (Ireland); Fellow of the Centre for Marian Studies (UK).

PHILLIPS, Jacob: Doctor of Theology from King's College London (UK); Director of the Institute of Theology and Liberal Arts and Associate Professor at St Mary's University (UK).

PONCELET, Christian: Doctor of Theology from the Theologische Fakultät Trier (Germany); Professor of French and Religious Education at the Cusanus-Gymnasium Wittlich (Germany).

ROWLAND, Tracey: Doctor of Theology from the Pontificia Università Lateranens (Italy), Doctor of Divinity from Cambridge University (UK); Professor of the St. John Paul II Chair of Theology at the University of Notre Dame (Australia).

SADA, Alejandro: Doctor of Philosophy from the Universidad de Navarra (Spain); Professor of Philosophy and Theology at Universidad Panamericana (Mexico).

SCHALLER, Christian: Doctor of Theology from the Ludwig-Maximilians-Universität München (Germany); Assistant Director of the Institut Papst Benedikt XVI (Germany).

SCHLÖGL, Manuel: Doctor of Theology from the Universität Münster (Germany); Professor at the Kölner Hochschule für Katholische Theologie (Germany).

SWEENEY, Conor: Doctor of Theology from the Roman Session of the John Paul II Institute for Marriage and the Family; Professor at Christendom College (USA).

VYNER, Owen: Doctor of Philosophy from the John Paul II Institute for Marriage and the Family (Australia); Professor and Chair of the Department of Theology at Christendom College (USA).

NAME INDEX

Adams, Nicholas 355
Adorno, Theodor 143–4, 339–40
Agbaw-Ebai, Maurice 79
Alexander of Hales 42
Andreotti, Giulio 23
Anscombe, G. E. M. 222, 226, 228, 230
Arendt, Hannah 145
Aristotle 18, 49, 51, 53, 56, 63, 70, 89, 138, 288, 291
Augustine 14, 22–42, 57, 67–9, 77, 122, 164, 165, 171, 173, 257, 370
Aquinas, Thomas 8, 24, 67, 69–76, 89, 138, 173, 238, 248–50, 257, 262–3, 288–90, 296
Averroës 55

Bacon, Francis 135
Balthasar, Hans Urs von 220, 230
Barth, Karl 72, 87, 167, 174
Bartley, William W. III 272, 276
Bayle, Pierre 189
Beauvoir, Simone de 300, 316
Benjamin, Walter 145–6
Bergson, Henri 67
Bernanos, Georges 66
Bloch, Ernest 136–7
Bobbio, Norbert 188
Bonald de, Louis-Gabriel-Ambroise 325
Brunner, Emil 73–4, 88–9, 169
Buber, Martin 66, 163–79, 215
Bultmann, Rudolf 39

Camus, Albert 300, 306, 315–25
Cardedal, González de 208
Cicero, Marcus Tullius 30
Claudel, Paul 66
Collins, Christopher 165
Comte, Auguste 118–33
Corkery, James 59

Daniélou, Jean 146
D'Arcais, Paolo Flores 332
D'Arcy, Eric 222
Derrida, Jacques 338
Descartes, René 72, 123
Dewey, John 198
Dionysius the Areopagite 261, 264
Dostoevsky, Fyodor 66, 159, 210, 303
Dreier, Horst 195
Dunin-Borkowski, Stanislaus von 289
Duns Scotus 42, 353, 361

Ebner, Ferdinand 66, 164, 169
Einstein, Albert 66
El Beheiri, Nadja 195
Engels, Friedrich 94

Fénelon, François 325
Feuerbach, Ludwig 94, 166
Ficker, Ludwig von 225
Frederick Wilhelm II 84
Friedman, Maurice 166
Fromm, Erich 296

Gaál, Emery de 79, 165–6
Gadamer, Hans-Georg 288, 364, 366
Galilei, Galileo 108
Gänswein, George 220
Girard, René 95
Goethe, Johann Wolfgang von 296
Goodhill, David 222
Gregory the Great, Pope 38
Guardini, Romano 20, 66, 142, 207–21, 288, 290
Guttierez, Gustavo 199

Habermas, Jürgen 145, 197–9, 202, 332–58, 275
Haecker, Theodor 66
Harnack, Adolf von 87, 361

Hartmann, Nicolai 8
Hegel, Friedrich 94–118, 345
Heidegger, Martin 66, 166, 232–47, 261, 288, 290, 365, 366
Heisenberg, Werner 66, 119
Hengstmengel, Joost 223
Hilary of Poitiers 28
Hitler, Adolf 366
Horkheimer, Max 143–4, 339–40
Hugh of St. Victor 45
Hume, David 82–3
Husserl, Edmund 249, 261–4, 289

Isidore of Seville 38

James, William 198
Jamros, Daniel 95
Jaspers, Karl 66, 234, 238, 240, 244
Jenson, Robert 363
Joachim of Fiore 46, 49
John Paul II/Karol Wojtyła, Pope and Saint 139, 141, 143, 176, 231, 248, 273–4, 332, 362
Jonkers, Peta 203

Kaes, Dorothea 68
Kaethler, Andrew, T. J. 170
Kamlah, Wilhelm 39–40
Kant, Immanuel 7, 78–94, 166, 183, 230, 238, 288, 337, 345, 351, 353–4, 361, 367
Karl Jaspers 234, 238, 240, 244
Kelsen, Hans 179–207
Kerr, Fergus 222
Kierkegaard, Søren 40, 94, 111, 166
King, Martin Luther 199
Knitter, Paul 181
Kołakowski, Leszek 136, 145
Kuhn, Helmut 20
Küng, Hans 288

Lauren, Quentin 95
Lebech, Mette 259
Le Fort, Gertrude von 66
Leibniz, Gottfried Wilhelm 81
Levinas, Emmanuel 169
Livy 30
Locke, John 183
Lombard, Peter 45

Lonergan, Bernard 284
Löwith, Karl 145, 364
Lubac, Henri de 1, 24, 38, 149, 155, 159, 160, 162, 220
Luther, Martin 86, 230, 349

Mill, John Stuart 196, 198
MacIntyre, Alasdair 260
Magnus, Donatus 27
Maritain, Jacques 188
Marshall, Bruce, D. 222
Marx, Karl 94, 124, 133–48, 166, 325, 345
Mendieta, Eduardo 339–41, 344
Mestri, Guido de 212
Metz, Johann-Baptist 137, 138, 146
Möller, Joseph 225–7
Möltmann, Jürgen 137

Newman, John Henry 19, 220, 165
Nichols, Aidan 20, 168
Nietzsche, Friedrich 67, 148–63, 197, 252, 327, 322, 365, 367
Nüllmann, Heiko 13
Nygren, Andres 296

Optatus of Milevis 27
Origen 37, 39

Pascal, Blaise 85, 89
Pedis, Esther Gómez de 300, 315
Pera, Marcello 92, 217
Pieper, Josef 20, 66, 137, 152, 165, 230, 287–99, 302, 303
Pitcher, George 226
Planck, Max 119
Plato 13–22, 240, 291, 297
Pontius Pilate 180, 185, 188, 364
Popper, Karl 188, 191, 272–87
Possenti, Vittorio 184, 191
Prosper of Aquitaine 31
Przywara, Erich 288

Quintilian, Marcus Fabius 30

Rahner, Hugo 38
Rahner, Karl 16
Rawls, John 200–5, 341, 345
Rochelle, Jean de la 42

Rorty, Richard 180, 196–7, 200, 205
Rosenzweig, Franz 169
Rousseau, Jean-Jacques 157, 252
Rowland, Tracey 69, 79, 166, 173, 339
Rutsche, Markus 167

Sakharov, Andrei 189
Santayana, George 196–8
Sartre, Jean-Paul 288, 299–315
Seneca, Lucius Annaeus 30
Scheler, Max 69, 166, 289
Schelling, Friedrich Wilhelm Joseph 97, 288
Schenk, Richard 70
Schleiermacher, Friedrich 78, 111
Schlier, Heinrich 185
Schlosser, Marianne 43
Schmaus, Michael 215
Schlögl, Manuel 288
Schneider, Michael 14
Schopenhauer, Arthur 166
Schumpeter, Joseph 188
Schuller, Florian 333
Schütz, David 145–6
Seewald, Peter 164, 300, 309, 316
Seifert, Josef 228
Singer, Peter 191–2
Sixtus V, Pope 42
Sloterdijk, Peter 191–2
Söhngen, Gottlieb 4–13, 67–8
Socrates 18, 19
Söhngen, Gottlieb 4–13
Smith, Adam 183
Spaemann, Robert 20, 229, 325–6
Spinoza, Baruch 81, 166, 190
Stein, Edith 247–72
Steinbüchel, Theodor 66, 165, 170
Steinvorth, Ulrich 225–6
St. Albert 89
St. Ambrose of Milan
St. Athanasius 28
St. Augustine, *see* Augustine
St. Bonaventure 5, 42–70, 165
St. Cyprian 26–7
St. Cyril of Jerusalem 161
St. Eucherius of Lyon 31

St. Gregory the Great, *see* Gregory the Great, Pope
St. Hilary of Poitiers, *see* Hilary of Poitiers
St. Isidore of Seville, *see* Isidore of Seville
St. Jerome 31, 37
St. John Chrysostom 28
St. John Henry Newman, *see* Newman, John Henry
St. Josemaría Escrivá 75
St. John Paul II, *see* John Paul II/Karol Wojtyła
St. Justin Martyr 101, 120
St. Luke 161
St. Matthew 63
St. Optatus of MIlevis, *see* Optatus of Milevis
St. Paul 121–2, 134, 356, 359–60
St. Prosper of Aquitaine, *see* Prosper of Aquitaine
St. Teresa of Ávila 261
St. Thomas Aquinas, *see* Aquinas
Symmachus 362

Talleyrand 365
Taylor, Charles 95
Tertulllian 26, 28, 39
Tocqueville, Alexis de 190

Valentinian II 362
Varro, Marcus Terentius 122
Vattimo, Gianteresio (Gianni) 358–71
Vico, Giambattista 86, 123
Voderholzer, Rudolf xi

Waldstein, Wolfgang 195
Warner, Keith Douglass 42
Webber, Jonathan 301
Weimann, Ralph 14
Weithmann, Paul J. 345
Wilmsen, Arnold 68
Wittgenstein, Ludwig 221–32, 252
Wolterstorff, Nicholas 345
Wust, Peter 66, 166

SUBJECT INDEX

analogia creaturae 9
analogia fidei 9
analogia e naturali cognitione 9
analogia entis 9, 73
analytical philosophy 222
analytical Thomism 222
Apollonian principle 151
Aristotelianism 14, 52
atheism 134, 359
Averroism 49, 52–3, 56

bad faith 301
baptism 113, 161, 162, 237

caritas 28, 34
Caritas in veritate 205, 218, 229
communio 25, 35, 112
comprehensive rationalism 274
conscience 326, 327, 356–7
critical rationalism 274
Critical Theory 339, 340

Dei verbum 247
democracy 180–1, 184, 186–7, 190–1, 200, 204, 327, 328, 345, 348, 350
Der Brenner 225
determinism 126
Deus caritas est 257, 288, 295, 296, 297, 352
dictatorship of relativism/relativism 127, 180–2, 187–8, 197, 359, 365–6, 369
Dionysian principle 151–2
Dominus Iesus 334

eros and *agape* 153–4, 296–7
evolutionism 124, 191
existentialism 300, 303, 316

Fides et ratio 10, 248, 288, 334, 362
Fourth Lateran Council 279

German Idealism 143, 288, 191
Gospel of St. John 256

Hellenization/de-Hellenization 98–9, 134, 352–3, 361
Hinduism 97
historicism 123, 217, 293
Hochland 226, 332
human rights 115, 349
humanism 202, 218, 302, 359
humanitas 10
humanitas christiana 10

Joachimism 46, 57

kerygma 9

liberalism 191
liberation theology 56–7, 61, 138, 334
Liturgical Movement 214
logos 205, 217, 234–46, 268, 273, 277–9, 282, 286, 322, 335, 351
Lumen fidei 177, 229, 252, 256–8, 296, 352
Lutheranism 103

Manicheanism 14
Marxism 133, 139–40, 142, 145–6, 148, 184, 190–1, 197, 199, 300, 337, 340, 352, 359
materialism 144
modernity 182, 209, 218, 345, 355, 356
Mysterium Salutis 5, 7

natural law 193–5, 349, 355–6
neo-Kantianism 8, 67, 80, 95, 289
neo-Platonism 14, 33, 46, 97, 102
neo-Scholasticism 8, 68, 90, 93, 164, 165, 247, 337
New World Order 142
nomos 6, 7

People of God 25, 29, 113
personalism 164, 191, 215
phenomenology 8, 44, 95, 245, 259
phronesis 6
Platonism 13, 14, 20, 197–8
political liberalism 346
political moralism 144
positivism 125–7, 183–5, 191–2, 194, 222–3, 226
praxis 63, 138, 144, 337

Reformation 103–4

Regensburg Address 78, 87, 243, 279, 351, 354, 360

scholasticism 67–8, 261, 264
Second Vatican Council 24–5, 163, 247, 252, 287, 368–9
Soviet Union/Soviet Communism 136, 337
Spe salvi 257, 296, 352

Thomism 68–9, 71, 77
triplex usus legis 6
triplex usus philosophiae 5

usus cosmicus 5, 9, 11
usus philosophicus 5, 8
usus theologicus 5, 11

Westminster Address 204, 350, 351

Zoroastrianism 97